T0223738

Lecture Notes in Computer Science

Vol. 245: H.F. de Groote, Lectures on the Complexity of Bilinear Problems. V, 135 pages. 1987.

Vol. 246: Graph-Theoretic Concepts in Computer Science. Proceedings, 1986. Edited by G. Tinhofer and G. Schmidt. VII, 307 pages. 1987.

Vol. 247: STACS 87. Proceedings, 1987. Edited by F.J. Brandenburg, G. Vidal-Naquet and M. Wirsing. X, 484 pages. 1987.

Vol. 248: Networking in Open Systems. Proceedings, 1986. Edited by G. Müller and R.P. Blanc. VI, 441 pages. 1987.

Vol. 249: TAPSOFT '87. Volume 1. Proceedings, 1987. Edited by H. Ehrig, R. Kowalski, G. Levi and U. Montanari. XIV, 289 pages. 1987.

Vol. 250: TAPSOFT '87. Volume 2. Proceedings, 1987. Edited by H. Ehrig, R. Kowalski, G. Levi and U. Montanari. XIV, 336 pages. 1987.

Vol. 251: V. Akman, Unobstructed Shortest Paths in Polyhedral Environments. VII, 103 pages. 1987.

Vol. 252: VDM '87. VDM – A Formal Method at Work. Proceedings, 1987. Edited by D. Bjørner, C.B. Jones, M. Mac an Airchinnigh and E.J. Neuhold. IX, 422 pages. 1987.

Vol. 253: J.D. Becker, I. Eisele (Eds.), WOPPLOT 86. Parallel Processing: Logic, Organization, and Technology. Proceedings, 1986. V, 226 pages. 1987.

Vol. 254: Petri Nets: Central Models and Their Properties. Advances in Petri Nets 1986, Part I. Proceedings, 1986. Edited by W. Brauer, W. Reisig and G. Rozenberg. X, 480 pages. 1987.

Vol. 255: Petri Nets: Applications and Relationships to Other Models of Concurrency. Advances in Petri Nets 1986, Part II. Proceedings, 1986. Edited by W. Brauer, W. Reisig and G. Rozenberg. X, 516 pages. 1987.

Vol. 256: Rewriting Techniques and Applications. Proceedings, 1987. Edited by P. Lescanne. VI, 285 pages. 1987.

Vol. 257: Database Machine Performance: Modeling Methodologies and Evaluation Strategies. Edited by F. Cesarini and S. Salza. X, 250 pages. 1987.

Vol. 258: PARLE, Parallel Architectures and Languages Europe. Volume I. Proceedings, 1987. Edited by J.W. de Bakker, A.J. Nijman and P.C. Treleaven. XII, 480 pages. 1987.

Vol. 259: PARLE, Parallel Architectures and Languages Europe. Volume II. Proceedings, 1987. Edited by J.W. de Bakker, A.J. Nijman and P.C. Treleaven. XII, 464 pages. 1987.

Vol. 260: D.C. Luckham, F.W. von Henke, B. Krieg-Brückner, O. Owe, ANNA, A Language for Annotating Ada Programs. V, 143 pages. 1987.

Vol. 261: J. Ch. Freytag, Translating Relational Queries into Iterative Programs. XI, 131 pages. 1987.

Vol. 262: A. Burns, A.M. Lister, A.J. Wellings, A Review of Ada Tasking. VIII, 141 pages. 1987.

Vol. 263: A.M. Odlyzko (Ed.), Advances in Cryptology – CRYPTO '86. Proceedings. XI, 489 pages. 1987.

Vol. 264: E. Wada (Ed.), Logic Programming '86. Proceedings, 1986. VI, 179 pages. 1987.

Vol. 265: K.P. Jantke (Ed.), Analogical and Inductive Inference. Proceedings, 1986. VI, 227 pages. 1987.

Vol. 266: G. Rozenberg (Ed.), Advances in Petri Nets 1987. VI, 451 pages. 1987.

Vol. 267: Th. Ottmann (Ed.), Automata, Languages and Programming. Proceedings, 1987. X, 565 pages. 1987.

Vol. 268: P.M. Pardalos, J.B. Rosen, Constrained Global Optimization: Algorithms and Applications. VII, 143 pages. 1987.

Vol. 269: A. Albrecht, H. Jung, K. Mehlhorn (Eds.), Parallel Algorithms and Architectures. Proceedings, 1987. Approx. 205 pages. 1987.

Vol. 270: E. Börger (Ed.), Computation Theory and Logic. IX, 442 pages. 1987.

Vol. 271: D. Snyers, A. Thayse, From Logic Design to Logic Programming. IV, 125 pages. 1987.

Vol. 272: P. Treleaven, M. Vanneschi (Eds.), Future Parallel Computers. Proceedings, 1986. V, 492 pages. 1987.

Vol. 273: J.S. Royer, A Connotational Theory of Program Structure. V, 186 pages. 1987.

Vol. 274: G. Kahn (Ed.), Functional Programming Languages and Computer Architecture. Proceedings. VI, 470 pages. 1987.

Vol. 275: A.N. Habermann, U. Montanari (Eds.), System Development and Ada. Proceedings, 1986. V, 305 pages. 1987.

Vol. 276: J. Bézivin, J.-M. Hullot, P. Cointe, H. Lieberman (Eds.), ECOOP '87. European Conference on Object-Oriented Programming. Proceedings. VI, 273 pages. 1987.

Vol. 277: B. Benninghofen, S. Kemmerich, M.M. Richter, Systems of Reductions. X, 265 pages. 1987.

Vol. 278: L. Budach, R.G. Bukharajev, O.B. Lupanov (Eds.), Fundamentals of Computation Theory. Proceedings, 1987. XIV, 505 pages. 1987.

Vol. 279: J.H. Fasel, R.M. Keller (Eds.), Graph Reduction. Proceedings, 1986. XVI, 450 pages. 1987.

Vol. 280: M. Venturini Zilli (Ed.), Mathematical Models for the Semantics of Parallelism. Proceedings, 1986. V, 231 pages. 1987.

Vol. 281: A. Kelemenová, J. Kelemen (Eds.), Trends, Techniques, and Problems in Theoretical Computer Science. Proceedings, 1986. VI, 213 pages. 1987.

Vol. 282: P. Gorny, M.J. Tauber (Eds.), Visualization in Programming. Proceedings, 1986. VII, 210 pages. 1987.

Vol. 283: D.H. Pitt, A. Poigné, D.E. Rydeheard (Eds.), Category Theory and Computer Science. Proceedings, 1987. V, 300 pages. 1987.

Vol. 284: A. Kündig, R.E. Bührer, J. Dähler (Eds.), Embedded Systems. Proceedings, 1986. V, 207 pages. 1987.

Vol. 285: C. Delgado Kloos, Semantics of Digital Circuits. IX, 124 pages. 1987.

Vol. 286: B. Bouchon, R.R. Yager (Eds.), Uncertainty in Knowledge-Based Systems. Proceedings, 1986. VII, 405 pages. 1987.

Vol. 287: K.V. Nori (Ed.), Foundations of Software Technology and Theoretical Computer Science. Proceedings, 1987. IX, 540 pages. 1987.

Vol. 288: A. Blikle, MetaSoft Primer. XIII, 140 pages. 1987.

Vol. 289: H.K. Nichols, D. Simpson (Eds.), ESEC '87. 1st European Software Engineering Conference. Proceedings, 1987. XII, 404 pages. 1987.

Vol. 290: T.X. Bui, Co-oP A Group Decision Support System for Cooperative Multiple Criteria Group Decision Making. XIII, 250 pages. 1987.

Vol. 291: H. Ehrig, M. Nagl, G. Rozenberg, A. Rosenfeld (Eds.), Graph-Grammars and Their Application to Computer Science. VIII, 609 pages. 1987.

Vol. 292: The Munich Project CIP. Volume II: The Program Transformation System CIP-S. By the CIP System Group. VIII, 522 pages. 1987.

Vol. 293: C. Pomerance (Ed.), Advances in Cryptology — CRYPTO '87. Proceedings. X, 463 pages. 1988.

Vol. 294: R. Cori, M. Wirsing (Eds.), STACS 88. Proceedings, 1988. IX, 404 pages. 1988.

Vol. 295: R. Dierstein, D. Müller-Wichards, H.-M. Wacker (Eds.) Parallel Computing in Science and Engineering. Proceedings, 1987. V, 185 pages. 1988.

Lecture Notes in Computer Science

Edited by G. Goos and J. Hartmanis

334

K.R. Dittrich (Ed.)

Advances in Object-Oriented Database Systems

2nd International Workshop on Object-Oriented Database Systems
Bad Münster am Stein-Ebernburg, FRG
September 27–30, 1988
Proceedings

Springer-Verlag
Berlin Heidelberg New York London Paris Tokyo

Editor

Klaus R. Dittrich
Forschungszentrum Informatik (FZI)
Haid-und-Neu-Str. 10–14, D-7500 Karlsruhe, FRG

Workshop Committee:

Antonio Albano (University of Udine, Italy)
Horst Biller (Siemens, Germany)
Alex Buchmann (CCA, USA)
Umesh Dayal (CCA, USA)
Klaus Dittrich (FZI, Germany)
Roger King (University of Colorado, USA)
Peter Lyngbaek (Hewlett Packard, USA)
Stan Zdonik (Brown University, USA)

Local Arrangements: Angelika Kotz (FZI, Germany)

Treasurer: Gisela Schlimm (FZI, Germany)

Sponsors:

Gesellschaft für Informatik (GI)
Forschungszentrum Informatik an der Universität Karlsruhe (FZI)
in cooperation with IEEE Computer Society, TC on Data Engineering

CR Subject Classification (1987): H.2, D.3

ISBN 3-540-50345-5 Springer-Verlag Berlin Heidelberg New York
ISBN 0-387-50345-5 Springer-Verlag New York Berlin Heidelberg

Printing and binding: Druckhaus Beltz, Hemsbach/Bergstr.
2145/3140-54321

Preface

Object-orientation is currently within the mainstream of computer science research and development in general. It is therefore little wonder that a substantial part of the database community has turned its interest towards exploiting the ideas behind this concept during the past couple of years.

Object-oriented database systems have been approached with mainly two major intentions in mind:

- to better support new application areas including CAD/CAM, office automation, knowledge engineering, and the like where units of interest in the real world tend to be composed out of other such units in more or less arbitrary ways and where a broad variety of application-specific unit types (including of course appropriate ways of operating on them) has to be dealt with,

- to overcome the ´impedance mismatch´ between data models and programming languages that has always been a severe problem with relational, network, and similar models.

Accordingly, the notion of object-orientation in database systems is a broader one than e.g. in the area of programming languages. **Structural object-orientation** provides for data model mechanisms that allow the direct representation and manipulation of highly-structured entities; **behavioral object-orientation** cares for facilities to associate arbitrary user-defined type-specific operations with data entities; finally, **full object-orientation** tries to combine the advantages of both categories.

Though data model concepts are the decisive feature of object-oriented database systems, numerous other system aspects have to be reconsidered or allow better solutions, respectively, in this light. They include e.g. transactions, implementation techniques, optimization, formalization, the inclusion of rules, and the integration with other systems. A number of research prototypes and even some commercial systems are meanwhile available. Both, approaches to extend databases with object-oriented capabilities and approaches to extend object-oriented programming languages with database features have been and are being investigated. As the table of contents shows, object-oriented database systems are a good meeting ground for specialists from both areas.

This volume contains the accepted submissions for the 2nd International Workshop on Object-Oriented Database Systems that was held at the Ebernburg, a 13th century castle located near Bad Münster am Stein in the southwest of Germany. No need to mention that the relaxing atmosphere within the historic walls of the ´shelter of justice´ and, of course, the tempting products coming from the surrounding vineyards create a stimulating environment for good work, and thus a large number of people from many countries responded to the call for participation.

As attendance had to be limited, every applicant was required to submit either a full paper or a position statement. All committee members undertook to read all sumissions; less than half of them have been accepted for presentation and publication in these proceedings, among them 13 full and 25 short (i.e. up to six pages) papers. A small number of additional applicants have been invited for participation in the extensive workshop discussions.

The idea for the ooDBS-workshop was first phrased at an early (1984) informal meeting on this subject organized by Alex Buchmann in Mexico City and including only a handful of people. A first open (but also limited attendance) workshop has been held at Asilomar/California in 1986 (proceedings have been published by IEEE Computer Society Press). The 1988 workshop shows how fast progress has been made since then. Meanwhile, the topic has been integrated into all major database conferences and some others (e.g. OOPSLA). Thus our mission to provide a forum for exchanging ideas in a young area is fulfilled, and as we never intended to add another regular event to an already ever increasing calendar of conferences and workshops, what might be ´ooDBS-III´ will probably be on some different topic.

I would like to thank all colleagues for preparing such a large number of good submissions, in particular those who finally had to live with being turned down for one reason or another. Though some of them have not been satisfied with the committee´s decision, I sincerely hope they will forgive us and nevertheless find some interesting reading in this volume. Next time, it will be your turn for being accepted, folks! Many thanks also to my fellow committee members for their hard work in reading that many submissions and making a decision, especially to Umesh Dayal and Alex Buchmann from the original Mexico crew who from the first day contributed so much of their time to make it all happen. Angelika Kotz and Gisela Schlimm have to be commented for their cheerful and expert engagement in local arrangements and finances. The sponsorship of Gesellschaft für Informatik (GI) and Forschungszentrum Informatik an der Universität Karlsruhe (FZI) and the cooperation of the IEEE Computer Society, TC on Data Engineering, is greatly acknowledged.

Klaus R. Dittrich

Contents

Implementation, Existing systems, and Transactions

Formalization and Inclusion of Rules

Integration of Existing Systems

Models

Data Manipulation and Persistent Languages

Optimization and Performance

The Design and Implementation of O_2, an Object-Oriented Database System

Francois Bancilhon, Gilles Barbedette, Véronique Benzaken, Claude Delobel, Sophie Gamerman, Christophe Lécluse, Patrick Pfeffer, Philippe Richard and Fernando Velez

Altaïr[1]
BP 105
78153 Le Chesnay Cedex
France

Abstract

This paper describes the design and implementation of the first version of the O_2 object-oriented database system. The Altaïr project is currently designing and implementing a complete environment for developing data intensive applications. As a first step, we have implemented a quick prototype of an object-oriented DBMS. We report here on this implementation. The first part of the paper describes the system interface as seen by the application programmer, the second part describes the architecture of the system.

1 Objectives and assumptions

One of the major objectives of Altaïr is to prototype the DBMS of the 1990's. More precisely, we want to build a complete development environment for data intensive applications. Thus, the functionalities of the system should include those of a DBMS, those of a programming language and those of a programming environment. In this paper, we specifically report on the merge of programming language technology and database technology. Other reports [Cazalens et al 88] cover the user interface part of our effort.

The target applications for our system are (i) traditional applications such as business and transactional (excluding however very high performance transaction processing systems), (ii) office automation applications and (iii) spatial data management (such as geographic data management). Note that, at this stage of the game, no specific emphasis is given to CAD/CAM, CASE or knowledge base applications (whatever these may be),

---

[1] Altaïr is a consortium funded by IN2 (the computer subsidiary of the Intertechnique group), INRIA (the French National Institute of Research in Computer and Control) and LRI (the Computer Science Laboratory of the University of Paris XI). The consortium started in September of 86 and is created for 5 years.

but we believe that, in a later stage, the system could be enhanced to serve also these applications.

The target customers of our system are (i) application programmers and (ii) end users. Our main interest is in application programmers, since we consider the major problem is to increase programmer productivity. We are not interested in the so-called naïve user and we assume that both end users and application programmers have a reasonable training with the system and use it on a regular basis.

The hardware configuration we are targeting at, consists of a single server connected to a set of workstations. Three facts are important: (i) computing power is more and more in the workstation rather than in the server, thus the ultimate workload left on the server will be archiving and data sharing (ii) workstations are chosen by the customer and thus the set of workstations will be heterogeneous and (iii) we believe that restricting ourselves to the single server case makes sense. This does not preclude the server from talking to another server to get its data, it justs imposes that, in the context of one application, each workstation sees only one server which is in charge of archiving and sharing data.

From a software point of view, our objective was to use, as much as possible existing products. The project was started with the idea of developing the server software around the Pick operating system and Pick file management system. We also had planned on using Score, a transaction management software developed by IN2 on top on Pick. The first prototype was built with these ideas in mind; emphasis has now been shifted differently and we are examining alternate solutions based on Unix [2] for the next prototype.

We made the decision, to meet all these requirements, to build an object-oriented database system, named O_2 and its programming environment. Our motivations for this choice are the following:

- We do believe that the main bottleneck to the productivity of the application programmer is the impedance mismatch between the programming language and the query language. This impedance mismatch cannot be solved by redefining the database box (i.e. by changing the frontier between the programming language and the database system) but by mixing database technology and programming language technology to build a complete system which will have the functionalities of a DBMS and of a programming language.
- We do believe that, among the available technologies produced by programming language people and among the possible approaches, the object-oriented approach is the best one to mix with database technology. This is due both to the intrinsic characteristics of the approach and to the appeal this paradigm has to programmers.

The next choice concerned the programming language of the system. Among the possible solutions (extend an existing language, design a new language or try to be language independent), we have chosen the last one mainly for marketing reasons (from a pure technical point of view the second was probably the best). Thus the system is viewed by the user as consisting of a Data Definition Language by which the user can declare the type structure and hierarchy. The user can attach methods to types and to objects by

[2]Unix is a trademark of AT&T Bell laboratories

writing these methods in a set of languages. Our target set of languages consists of C, Basic and Lisp. This set was chosen for market reasons and for technical reasons.

2 The V0 prototype

Before we started the design and implementation of the system, we decided to implement a throw-away prototype. The idea was to do a quick implementation of the system, without being bothered by code reliability or performance. This paper reports on this specific experiment.

This first prototype has a large subset of the functionalities of the final prototype. It has the features of a database system: persistence, disk management, concurrency and recovery. It is an object-oriented system: it has static type checking, encapsulation, object identity, complex objects management, simple inheritance, overloading and late binding.

We limited ourselves, with respect to our final goal, in the following way: the system is mono-language (using C), it runs between an IN-8000 server on top of Pick and Score and a set of Sun workstations running Unix. Connection between the stations and the server was insured by a serial line (!) between a Sun server and the IN-8000. Concurrency control and recovery was done on the database (by the Score transaction manager) but not on the schema. Only an *ad hoc* interface was implemented for the purpose of a flashy demo. The server was only used to store the object base and methods were exclusively run on the workstations. No index mechanism was used and the system did not have a query language.

3 The O_2 Programming Environment

In this section, we give an overview of the O_2 programming language. We do not give a formal description of the language, or of the O_2 data model, these are described respectively in [Barbedette et al 87] and [Lécluse et al 88]. We present the main features of the programming environment through examples. The O_2 system allows the user to define, access and update complex objects. These objects are built using atomic objects (such as integers and strings) and the *set* and *tuple* constructors. Moreover, every object has an *identity* which is independent from the actual value of the object. Object identity allows object sharing and updating. It makes our object definition more powerful than the nested relation approach. O_2 is an object-oriented layer running on top of C. This layer is in charge of the definition and the manipulation of objects whereas C deals with all computational aspects. In this section, we show the features of the resulting CO_2 language. Programming in CO_2 consists in writing C programs which contain special primitives for object manipulation. We have followed the standard syntax of object-oriented languages such as Smalltalk 80. Thus, the basic construct of the O_2 layer is the *message passing*. A message is an expression of the form "<receiver> <message> (<arguments>)" where <receiver> is the object to which the message is sent, <message> is the name of the method to be applied and <arguments> are the arguments. A method returns a result, to which another message can be sent. This allows us to write compact expressions such as "myCar getMotor display" which first extracts the motor of the object "myCar" and then display this motor object. In a CO_2 program, message to the O_2 layer are separated from the C code by square brackets. The only reason for doing this, is that we designed a precompiler for the first CO_2 prototype and wished to isolate O_2 messages without scanning the C code. The O_2 layer is in charge of the transaction management. For the V0 prototype, we design a very simple transaction mechanism. Every CO_2 program is a transaction and is enclosed between the keywords *begin* and *end*, but transactions can not be interleaved.

3.1 Types

CO_2 is a strongly typed language: every object is an instance of a type and all message expressions are statically type-checked. On the other hand, we keep the dynamicity of object-oriented languages where the actual code, associated to a message passing, is determined only at run time. When a user wants to program in CO_2, he/she first defines types and methods and then creates instances of these types. In contrast with standard object-oriented languages such as Smalltalk [Goldberg and Robson 83], types and methods creation is not done through message passing but through special commands in the header of the program, as in standard imperative programming languages. This restriction is necessary in order to have a static type checking and safe programs.
A type has a structure which is either *basic*, *tuple* or *set*. This defines the common structure of all instances of the type. Consider the following type definition:

```
new_type propeller is
{ structure tupleof (fuel: string;
                     power: int;
                     nominal_consumption: float;
                     identifier: string)
}
```

The type "propeller" is tuple structured and has four fields which are strings, integer or float. The **int** and **float** types are mapped on the corresponding C types, and the **string** type is a shorthand for the "char*" C type. This propeller type is a simple type, obviously equivalent to a classical record structure.

3.1.1 Type inheritance

Type inheritance is an important modeling tool. It allows the programmer to specialize a type. In [Lécluse et al 88], we give a set-inclusion semantics for type inheritance. That is, the set of all instances of a subtype is included in the sets of instances of its supertypes. In CO_2, we restrict ourselves to simple inheritance, that is a type inherits from only one type, which is referred to as its *supertype*. This restriction was mainly motivated by ease of implementation. We define below two subtypes of the type propeller. Inheritance is expressed by the **supertype** clause.

```
new_type motor is
{ supertype propeller
structure tupleof (cubic_capacity: int; turbo_compressor: boolean; injector: boolean)
};

new_type jet_engine is
{ supertype propeller
  structure tupleof (category: string; thrust: int)
};
```

The type "motor" is a tuple-structured type having all fields of the propeller type plus its three own fields described in the **tuple of** clause. The user cannot define arbitrary inheritance relationships between types. The O_2 data model defines a subtyping relationship which must be satisfied by the user defined inheritance relationship. For example the following type definition is incorrect:

```
new_type motor is
{ supertype propeller
  structure setof int
};
```

because a set structured type cannot inherit from a tuple structured type. At the top of the hierarchy, we find a special predefined type named **Object**. The structure of this type is the special basic structure **Any** and every type of the system inherits from it. So, the definition of the type propeller above would be equivalent, if we add the clause **supertype Object** to it.

Types can be more sophisticated than the "propeller" type. In the next example, we define two types "part" and "setofpart" which reference each other. Indeed, "setofpart" is defined as a set of "part" whereas "part" is a tuple having "setofpart" as one of its components.

```
new_type part is
{ structure tupleof (name: string; specific_weight: float; components: setofpart )
};

new_type setofpart is
{ structure setof part
};
```

These two types allow the programmer to build parts and subparts hierarchies in O_2.

3.1.2 Persistency of Types

Persistency is the ability of types (or methods, or objects) to "survive" the execution of the module (the program or method in our system) in which these types (or instances) are defined and created. This persistency mechanism is one of the characteristics of database programming languages. The claim that independent persistence for types and objects is necessary [Atkinson and Buneman 85] is widely accepted. Persistency has two distinct aspects:

- the type is not destroyed when the program (or method) in which it is defined terminates, and
- the type is associated to a global name by which it can be referenced throughout the system.

These two aspects of persistency must not be confused, because the first one deals with the internal garbage collection of types, while the second one deals with the scope of the type definition. In the first version of CO_2, there is a unique global space of names for persistent types. The user can declare a type to be persistent using the **persist as** clause in the type definition as follows:

```
new_type propeller is
{ structure tupleof (fuel: string;
                     power: int;
                     nominal_consumption: float;
                     identifier: string)
  persist_as Propeller;
}
```

Inside the program (or method) which created it, this persistent type can be accessed by two distinct names: "propeller" and "Propeller". When this program terminates, and outside this program, this type can only be referred through the name "Propeller". There is an alternate way to make a type persistent. The user can write the following command, anywhere in the program:

persist propeller as Propeller

Instances of persistent types may be persistent or not. However they are not given names and it will be impossible to reference them directly outside the program which creates them. The user will only access them by the special command **apply on_type** as we shall see later. Thus the only persistent names are type names and the only handle we have on the persistent space is through the type names.

3.2 Methods

In the previous subsection, we have shown how types are defined in CO_2. We now turn our attention to methods. Methods are associated to types and define the behaviour of the instances of the type. One important feature of the object-oriented approach followed here, is encapsulation. The instances of a type can *only* be manipulated using the methods associated to this type. This encapsulation allows information hidding and provides an abstraction mechanism. The methods associated to a type can be written directly in the type definition using the "methods" clause as follows:

```
new_type propeller is
{ structure tupleof (fuel: string;
                     power: int;
                     nominal_consumption: float;
                     identifier: string)
  methods
     consumption return float
     begin
        return(⟨self.nominal_consumption ⟩);
     end;
  persist_as Propeller
}
```

```
new_type vehicle is
{ structure tupleof (name: string;
                     wheels_nb: int;
                     propeller: propeller ;
                     designer: string;
                     components: setofpart)
  methods
     consumption return float
     begin
        return(⟨self.propeller consumption ⟩);
     end;
  persist_as Vehicle
};
```

The type vehicle is created with an associated method consumption which returns a float. The CO_2 code associated to it only extracts the propeller field of the receiver (self.propeller) and applies the method "consumption" to this propeller. The consumption of the vehicle is thus defined as the consumption of its propeller. Because writing methods to read and write tuple fields can be tedious, these will be automatically generated by the system upon user demand. The tags **r** and **w** are implicit methods definitions. If the tag **r** (resp **w**) is associated to a field "fname: Tname" appearing in the structure of a type T, the system automatically generates a method of name "fname" (resp "w_fname") defined by:

```
new_type T is
{ structure tupleof (fname: Tname)
  methods
   fname return Tname
   begin
      return(⟨self.fname ⟩);
   end;
```

```
    w_fname (Tname : x) return T
    begin
        ⟨self.fname ← x ⟩;
        return(⟨self⟩);
    end;
}
```

Methods can of course define local types and/or methods. The following example illustrates a possible use of a local type defined in a method. It is also an example of the way we can add new methods to existing types.

```
new_method show_consumption return float in Vehicle is
    begin
        ⟨ new_type consumption is
            { structure tupleof(name: string w; consumption: float w)} ⟩;
        float x;
        x = ⟨ self.consumption⟩;
        ⟨new(consumption) w_name(self.name) w_consumption(x) display⟩;
        return(x);
    end;
```

The type "consumption" is local to the method "show_consumption". Type "consumption" is created at compile time when the method "show_consumption" is compiled. It is activated when the method is run and deactivated at the end of the execution of the method. The method "show_consumption" creates an instance of the type "consumption" (using the command **new**), writes the name of the vehicle and its consumption into the corresponding fields and applies the display method on this new object. We can see the local type "consumption" as a display mask. The following two methods are example of more complex computational methods. They are associated to the types "part" and "setofpart" and recursively compute the weight of a part and of a set of parts

```
new_method weight return float in part is
    begin
        return(⟨self.specific_weight⟩ + ⟨self.components weight⟩);
    end;

new_method weight return float in setofpart is
    begin
        ⟨part aPart⟩;
        if (⟨self count⟩ == 0) return(0.0);
        ⟨aPart ← self element⟩;
        return(⟨aPart weight⟩ + ⟨self copy drop(aPart) weight⟩);
    end;
```

The method "weight" in type part returns the sum of the specific weight of the part and the weight of its component set of parts. The weight of a set of parts is computed by applying the method weight to all the elements of the set. We can see in this example the use of some standard set manipulation methods. These methods are automatically associated with all set structured types. They implement standard set operations. The method "count" returns an integer which is the cardinality of the set. The method "drop(x)" removes the element x from the receiver set. The method "element" chooses an element in the receiver set. We also used the method "copy" which is a predefined method of the type Object. This method returns a new object, copy of the receiver. We used a copy in the method above because we did not want to remove aPart from the original set of parts.

The following example uses these two weight computation methods in order to define a more sophisticated consumption method for a special kind of vehicles. We assume that the nominal consumption is that of an one ton vehicle.

```
new_type car is
{   supertype Vehicle
    structure tupleof ( redefine propeller: Motor rw;
                        nb_seats: int rw;
                        category: string rw)
    methods
      consumption return float
      begin
        return(⟨self.propeller consumption⟩ * ⟨self weight⟩/ 1000.0);
      end;
    persist_as Car
};
```

The type "Car" is a refinement of the type "Vehicle". So it is a tuple structured type having all fields of the Vehicle type plus the "nb_seat" and "category" fields. Moreover, we can see that Car *redefines* the field propeller inherited from Vehicle. The propeller field is refined from Propeller (in Vehicle) to Motor. Such a redefinition is possible since Motor is a subtype of Propeller. Notice that this new consumption method for Car overrides the consumption method inherited from Vehicle.

3.3 Object Creation and Manipulation

Instances of types are created by the "new" command. However, such instances have "crude" default values and must be initialized. If the object is a tuple with all the corresponding w tags, the user can initialize a newly created object by writing an O_2 expression like:

```
⟨new(Propeller) w_fuel('water') w_identifier('water12/5')⟩
```

If the user wants to encapsulate the structure of its type, then he has to write an initialization method. Following the same example as above, in order to initialize water-powered propellers, one can implement the following method;

```
new_method init return Propeller in Propeller is
   begin
   return (⟨self w_fuel('water')w_identifier('water12/5')⟩);
   end;
```

In the examples of the previous subsection, we have seen some object manipulations as the standard method "copy" defined in Object. The list of methods defined for Object is the following:

- "display" calls the graphical interface and displays the receiver object.
- "is_same(x)" returns a boolean which is true iff the receiver and x are the same object.
- "is_equal(x)" returns a boolean which is true iff the receiver and x have the same value.
- "is_value_equal(x)" returns a boolean which is true iff the receiver and x have the same span-tree (the span-tree of an object is obtained by recursively replacing each identifier in the value by the value of the object it identifies).
- "deep_copy", (resp "shallow_copy") returns a copy value_equal, (resp equal) of the receiver object.
- "kill" destroys the receiver object.
- "error(x)" is the standard way to stop a CO_2 program with an error condition where x is an error message.

To each set structured type, the following list of set manipulation methods is associated:

- "element" returns an element of the receiver.
- "count" returns the cardinality of the receiver.
- "is_empty" returns a boolean which is true if the receiver set is empty.
- "intersection(x)" (resp "union(x)" and "difference(x)") returns a new set which is the intersection (resp union and difference) of the receiver and x.
- "contains(x)" returns a boolean which is true iff x is an element of the receiver set.
- "add(x)" adds the element x to the receiver.
- "drop(x)" removes the element x from the receiver.

Set structured objects rely upon object identity. Objects in a set are all distinct for the "is_same" method but may be equal or value_equal. However, predefined methods can be overriden by user defined methods. One can thus override the "is_same" method in order to test value equality rather than object identity. This allows the user to implement sets where the elements are distinct for the "is_equal" or "is_value_equal" methods. Finally, we provide two commands allowing the user to dispatch a message to all instances of a type, or to all elements of a set. In O_2 type extensions are automatically maintained. To each type is associated the set of all its instances (the *extension*). Each time an instance of a type is created, the system puts it in a set containing all other instances of this type. This set is accessible to the user through the command **apply** ... **on_type**. For example, if we want to display all the cars which are in the system, we can write:

⟨**apply**(display) **on_type** Car⟩

On the other hand, if we want to destroy all parts which are in the set of parts x, we can write:

⟨**apply**(kill) **on_set** x⟩

where x is the O_2 variable referencing the set of parts. Notice that such a "strange" manipulation does not lead to system inconsistencies because the destroyed objects will be considered as the **nil** object.

4 Architecture of the O_2 System

We now describe the design and implementation of the architecture of the system.

4.1 Logical Architecture

As described in Figure 1, the system consists of four modules: the *Data Manager*, the *Method Manager*, the *Type Manager* and the *Precompiler*. The Data Manager creates, stores and maintains objects. The Type Manager creates, stores and maintains type structure descriptions, it corresponds to the notion of a schema manager in a classical database system, but it also manages the description of application programs (methods). The Method Manager creates, stores and maintains source and object code of methods. Its data corresponds to the application programs in a classical database system. Descriptions of existing methods and types will be referred to as the *catalog* in the sequel. The Precompiler takes as input CO_2 programs, calls the type and method manager to perform type checking, and generates C programs with calls to the data and method managers.

A complete functional specification of the data, method and type manager is given in [Bancilhon et al 87], where a simplified version of the interface of each of the four modules is described .

The Precompiler is called when a new type is introduced in the system, or when an existing type is being modified. It monitors compiling, dynamic linking and loading of object code corresponding to methods. The Precompiler also translates every name into an internal representation: method names are replaced by an internal code, type names are

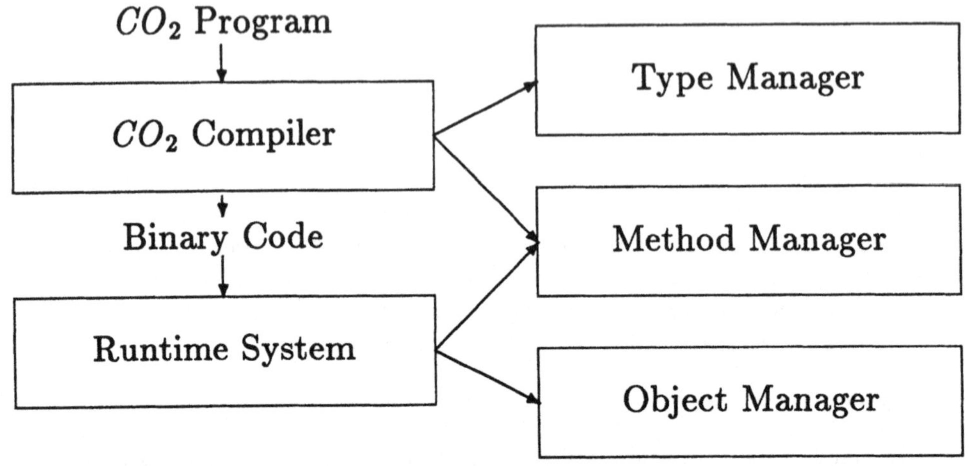

Figure 1: Logical Architecture

replaced by type identifiers (tid), and attribute names are replaced by an attribute number. Thus the Data, Type and Method Managers only deal with fixed length representations and never see the actual names.

At run time, the Data Manager is activated by message passing: it receives a message name and an object identifier. It first fetch the object to retrieve its actual type which is used to determine the actual method code to be applied. This binding is delayed until runtime as we allow method redefinition in subtypes of a given type (this is called "late binding"). Finally, the selected method code is executed.

4.2 Physical Architecture

The server is an IN-8000 machine. It is a 68020-based multi-processor machine supporting the Pick operating system and the Pick File System (PFS). It provides support for managing record structured files with varying size attributes, virtual memory management, transaction management and concurrency control and recovery management. The server manages the disk and we consider the workstations as diskless, either because they really are or because we leave the management of the disk to the local operating system: we do not manage any part of the database on the local disk.

On top of the Pick file system, we run Score, a transaction manager insuring concurrency control and recovery.

On the workstation, we run the Object Manager, the Method and Type Manager and the CO_2Compiler. The Object Manager stores the objects in Pick files and uses the primitives supplied by Score. Figure 2 above illustrates this Physical Architecture.

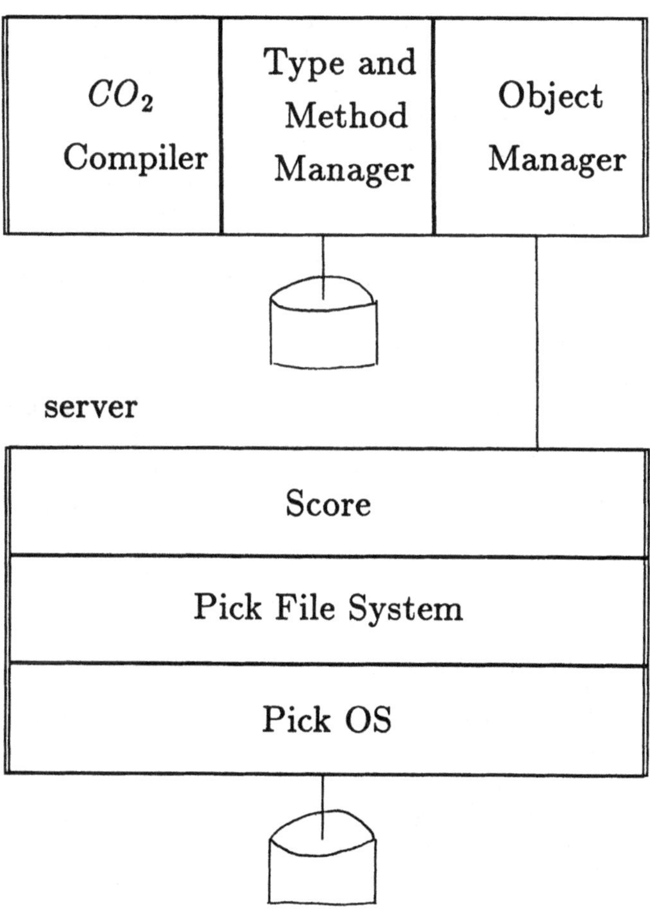

Figure 2: Physical Architecture

4.3 Architecture of the CO_2 compiler

The CO_2 compiler is in charge of transforming a CO_2 source program into an object code dynamically loaded into the running process and executed. CO_2 programs can include types and methods definitions. An important feature of the CO_2 system is that all types and methods are compiled and loaded into the system *when the program is compiled.* In order to preserve the consistency of the system (the user must not see a method until the program is executed), a hiding mechanism is used. So, the actual creation of the types and methods, at run time, consists in a flag setting in the system.

Another important feature of the compiler is that each method is compiled separately from the others, and the CO_2 source code for each method is extracted from the CO_2 program source code. This feature is important, since the computational unit, in an object-oriented system, is the method. So we must be able to deal individually with each method in the system (to recompile it, for example) without any reference to the program which defined it. The CO_2 compiler uses C as an intermediate language, transforming the CO_2 code into C code and invoking a C compiler. The split of the CO_2 program into several parts (one for each method and one for the main program) is done at the C level. The compiler generates a C function for each method. When all these C functions have been generated without compile-time errors, the C compiler is invoked on each part, each resulting object code is dynamically loaded and the object source corresponding to the main program is executed. In the following, we detail these compilation steps.

4.3.1 The Precompilation Phase

The precompilation phase takes a CO_2 program source, performs syntactic and semantic analysis of the O_2 part of the program and generates a C function for each method defined in the program plus a C function corresponding to the main program. The precompiler checks that all referenced types and objects are valid, and typechecks every O_2 expression. In particular, when a new type or method is defined, the precompiler verifies that the subtyping relationship [Lécluse et al 88] is preserved by this schema modification. However, the precompiler does not analyze the C part of the CO_2 program and syntactic or semantic errors into the C part of the program will be detected only during the C compilation phase. The results of the precompilation phase are the following:

- All types and methods defined in the program are appended to the type and method manager. However, they will become "active" (visible to the user) only after the execution of the program. The object code associated to the method will of course be introduced only at the end of the compilation process.

- The CO_2 source code for each defined method is extracted from the original CO_2 program and stored in the system.

- A pure C function is generated for each method and for the main program.

- In case of syntactic or semantic error during the precompilation phase, a message is displayed and the whole compilation is aborted.

4.3.2 The C Compilation Phase

The C compilation phase is invoked only if the precompiler finds no error in the CO_2 source. In this case several C functions have been generated. The C compilation phase only consists of invoking the C compiler on each function separately. The result of this C compilation phase is a collection of object code files corresponding to the methods and to the main program.

4.3.3 The Linking Phase

The linking phase is invoked when the C compiler has generated all the object code files. The linking phase consists in a dynamic linking of all these object files into the running process. In order to realize this dynamic linking, we used a special option of the standard Unix linker (UNIX BSD 4.3) allowing incremental linking together with a special hacking tool to load the linked code into the running process (this is only specific to this particular version of UNIX). Dynamic linking is a central point for all object-oriented systems implemented over static environments such as UNIX.

4.3.4 The Execution Phase

In the execution phase, all the references to the loaded object code of all the defined methods are given to the method manager, the defined types and methods are activated (the activation flag is switched) and the code corresponding to the main program is executed. After execution, temporary types and methods are deactivated. The persistent types and methods remain active.

4.3.5 The O_2 Interpreter

Most transactions are simple programs which only retrieve and display objects. These programs are structurally very simple and it can be very cumbersome to do all the above processing (generating, compiling, linking and loading a C function) to execute them. A user asking for the display of some objects will not accept to wait the time of a program compilation. In order to avoid such an overhead, we developed an O_2 interpreter which recognizes only a simple subset of the CO_2 language, namely O_2 message passing. This interpreter is invoked automatically when a compilation is run. If the CO_2 program is recognized by the interpreter then it is interpreted and no compilation is done. If the interpreter fails in recognizing the program then it is passed to the compiler. This mechanism is fully transparent for the user. However, it can save a lot of time for simple programs corresponding to elementary queries to the system. Of course, programs which create, update or delete types and/or methods will be compiled. This is not a penalty, since these programs are mainly schema manipulations and are scarce. Figure 3 gives a graphical representation of the overall compiler architecture.

4.4 Architecture of the Type and Method Managers

These modules have been implemented in an *ad hoc* manner, that is, without any kind of support from the Data Manager nor the Transactional Manager of Pick file system. The

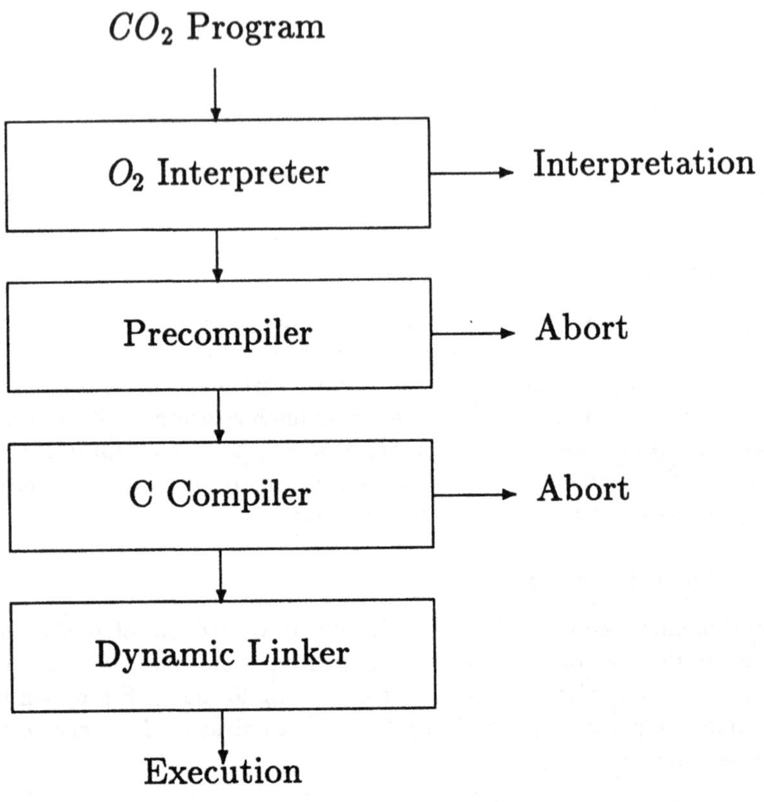

Figure 3: Architecture of the O_2 compiler

main advantage of implementing the Type and Method Managers in an *ad-hoc* manner is that we can have a custom concurrency control mechanism for the catalog. This could be faster and take into account semantic information about schema updates to allow for increased parallelism, as the catalog is *the* hot spot of the system. The drawbacks are development time and the need for a reasonable connection to PFS anyway for recovery purposes.

Before running an application, all the data for the Method Manager and the Type Manager are loaded on the workstation main memory (and of course similarly on the server). Here is the rationale behind this choice:

(i) The situation we want to compare ourselves against is that of an application running in main memory: this application has all its necessary information: types and subroutines. This means that all this can fit in memory and that, if we want to be as good as this case, we have to put ourselves in the same situation.

(ii) We assume that, before starting an application, the system loads in the workstation all the necessary schema information.

As the body of a method can be redefined at any moment in any of its subtypes (yet keeping the same name), the system has to bind a method name to binary code at run time. This late binding operation is critical since it is involved in message passing, and therefore, we provide special support for it:

(i) While solving a method m for a type T, we avoid visiting the ancestors of T (it could be the case that m is inherited from one of its ancestors). Otherwise, solving m for T can take a time proportional to the depth of T in the inheritance hierarchy. This is accomplished by generating the "transitive closure" of methods through the inheritance hierarchy.

(ii) A hash-based storage structure for storing method information is used. If there are no collisions, one table lookup plus one field fetch is enough for solving a method, once the object has been fetched and its type has been retrieved.

4.5 Architecture of the Data Manager

The Data Manager is composed of three layers. The innermost layer is responsible for communicating with the server machine. The intermediate layer deals with the memory hierarchy. It implements an object virtual memory mechanism. Objects are uniformly referred to by their identifier (see below) and the mechanism establishes the correspondence with main memory addresses.

The outermost layer is composed of primitives providing the following support:

(i) Message passing to an object, to all instances of a type and to all instances of a set. These primitives rely on the late binding operation provided by the Method Manager.

(ii) Predefined method implementation. This includes the predefined methods of type Object, the predefined methods for sets and the primitives to read and write an attribute value of a tuple structured object.

(iii) Object creation and deletion.

(iv) Transaction management primitives connecting to those provided by PFS.

In the following, we present our design choices: object access, object representation, storage management and connection to PFS transactions.

4.5.1 Object Access

We are concerned here with accessing objects both in secondary storage and in main memory. Objects are accessed in the same way whether they are persistent or not. Objects are persistent only if they belong to the extensions of persistent types, and they continue to exist until they are explicitly deleted by a *kill* operation.

Objects are transferred to the workstation on demand and stored in the server either at the end of the session or when they are purged because there is no more space in memory. Pure object identity is maintained and objects are uniformly accessed by an identifier. The identifier of an object o gives its location in secondary memory[3]: it is a pair (f, r) to be interpreted by PFS, where f is the file name in which the object is to be stored, and r is the identifier for the record of f containing o. The mapping from record identifiers to disk addresses is handled by PFS, so we don't have to maintain ourselves a location table for all objects as in other object managers (for example, [Hornick and Zdonik 87]).

The address space is potentially infinite as there is no restriction in PFS on the number of records of a file, but our implementation encodes object identifiers in 4-byte integers. The high-weight 11 bits encode file numbers and the remaining 21 low-weight bits encode record numbers (this gives a maximum of 2048 different files and more than 2 million records per file). We do not reuse identifiers of deleted objects. However, the number of objects in the system has been reduced by not considering atomic objects as "real" objects, i.e., with identifiers. Only their values are stored within composite objects.

The object virtual memory is implemented by a hash table of resident objects: an object in memory will correspond to an entry of this table obtained by applying a hashing function to its identifier. The memory address, a 4-byte pointer, is stored in this entry. Collisions are dealt with coalesced lists pointing to entries of the table, which performs better than open addressing schemes when the occupancy rate of the table is high. Objects must be purged from main memory when the table is full and/or when the memory space reserved for objects is full. LRU has been used as the replacement algorithm (as in OOZE [Kaehler 81] and its successor LOOM [Kaehler 86]).

Clean objects, that is objects which have not been altered while they were cached in main memory, are not rewritten to disk at purge time. A clean bit is associated with each object, and it is overwritten whenever the contents of the object changes. An object may be made unswappable. This has shown useful when dispatching a method to all instances of a type (or to all elements of a set): an artificial set object representing the type extension is constructed, it contains old (i.e., not newly created) instances of the type. Making this object unswappable greatly simplifies the code and enhances performance.

---

[3]this is true even for temporary objects, as they can be purged at any moment. See the section on storage management below for a discussion on the choice of this kind of identifiers.

4.5.2 Object Representation

Types and Files
Each type extension is represented by a unique file. A file is shared by several types, namely, all descendants of a direct subtype of the predefined type "Object". Lets consider, for instance, type "Propeller", a direct subtype of "Object", and subtypes "Motor" and "Jet_engine". All instances of these three types will be stored on the same PICK file. As the semantics given to subtyping is set containment on type extensions (see [Lécluse et al 88]), an instance of type "Motor" will be an instance of type "Propeller". It will be stored only once in the file. The fact that PICK files can have records with different number of attributes makes our life easier, as nulls don't have to be handled.

Objects and Records
Each object has a header containing information about the (most specialized) type of the object, a reference count of the number of owners of the object in the composition hierarchy, and a deletion bit indicating if the object has been explicitly deleted or not. The latter is a consequence of maintaining type extensions. Referential integrity is supported: an already deleted object will not be physically deleted from the database until its reference count decreases to zero. This prevents dangling references from objects owning a deleted object.
Attribute values of tuple objects or components of set objects can be either identifiers of composite objects or atomic values. The former are stored as attributes in the corresponding PICK record. Sets are stored using the fact that attributes in a PICK record may be non-atomic, that is, composed of "fields": each field contains one element. The size of the set is also stored. The number of fields in an attribute and the number of attributes in a record is limited by the size of a record, which can grow up to 32K bytes. As PFS handles varying size attributes and records, we don't have to worry about secondary space management when a set grows or shrinks within this limit.

Main Memory Representation
We have decided to represent objects in the workstation as they are represented in disk. The main advantage is to avoid translations from one addressing space to the other. When an object arrives at the workstation, space is found for him and some conversions are performed, as an attribute value of a PICK file is a string of ASCII characters. Attribute values representing integers and floats will be converted to their corresponding representations (this includes object identifiers). In order to avoid rewriting an object when a variable length field is modified in main memory, strings have a fixed length. Also, we have not attempted to manage large objects.

4.5.3 Connection to PFS Transactions

We have established a simple connection with transactions: any CO_2 program will be a transaction and will be delimited by calling the ***begin-transaction*** and ***end-transaction*** primitives of the PFS.

Objects are neither written nor deleted from the object table until the end of a transaction unless they are swapped to disk. This allows to "batch" multiple commands to the server, thereby minimizing the transmission delays between the server and the workstation.

4.5.4 Storage Management

In Main Memory
Space for objects in main memory is managed in a simple way. As mentioned before, as we deal only with fixed length data, we only have to worry about updates on sets and with creation and deletion of objects. A large memory buffer is allocated when the system is initialized, and allocation of space for objects is dealt by updating a pointer in this buffer. When objects are deleted (at the end of a transaction), the space occupied is put into a free list. When the buffer fills up, the free space is recovered by compacting the occupied space to the beginning of the buffer. If there is still not enough place to allocate an object, the system proceeds to purge old objects.

Space management for sets in main memory is handled as follows: when a set is created, space for a default number of elements is reserved. When a set is loaded from secondary memory, enough space is allocated to contain all its elements. When the set overflows by adding elements, another chunk of the same size as the previous one is allocated and linked to it. If the set shrinks subsequently, chunks may become empty. This space is recovered when the memory buffer is full.

Clustering Objects in Disk
It is recognized that, for complex object management, clustering is an important issue. Take for instance an implementation where each component of a complex object is stored in a different PICK record, then, when we want to retrieve a complex object consisting of 50 components, we have to make 50 disk accesses.

Because PICK uses a hash-based scheme, we have no control over physical placement of records on the disk. We cluster objects within a single Pick record, so a record can be used to store many objects (as a file is used to store many type extensions).

Objects are shared by reference and they are never duplicated. This means, for instance, that if an object o is a component of two other objects o1 and o2 and if we want to cluster o with its owner, we have to make a choice of storing o with o1 or with o2: we reject the solution where we would make two copies of o and store one with o1 and the other one with o2 and ask the system to maintain the two copies identical. The choice to cluster an object with one among many owners is not trivial. A crude solution has been implemented which clusters an object with the first object owning it. We are currently looking for more sophisticated solutions for this problem.

Object identifiers become then a triple (f, r, o) where f and r are as before and o is an offset from the beginning of the owning object (an attribute number, for example).

5 Current status and conclusions

The quick prototype consists of 35000 lines of C code. Design started in February of 87, coding started in August of 87 and the prototype was demoed end of December. We also designed a portable Sun version of this prototype for demo purposes. We built an ad hoc interface for the purpose of the demo.

This prototype is not intended for re-use and none of the code developed will be used for the next versions of the system. We found the exercise extremely profitable, since it allowed us to face most of the problems we will have to solve in the final prototype. For most of these problems, we have chosen a simple and easy solution, but have envisaged the alternatives. In the process, we have of course identified a series of technical problems which we had not foreseen in the initial phase.

We are currently redesigning the data model and the language and designing programming environment tools. The next version of the system is scheduled for January of 89 with the final prototype due September of 89.

6 Authorship and acknowledgements

The main designers of the data model and the language were Christophe Lécluse, Philippe Richard and Fernando Velez. The system was designed by Francois Bancilhon, Véronique Benzaken, Claude Delobel and Fernando Velez. The implementation was done by Gilles Barbedette, Véronique Benzaken, Vineeta Darnis, Sophie Gamerman, Christophe Lécluse, Sabine Letellier, Patrick Pfeffer Jean-Claude Mamou, Philippe Richard and Fernando Velez.

The design of this version of the system benefited from comments, corrections and suggestions of Alex Borgida, Peter Buneman, David DeWitt and David Maier.

References

[Atkinson and Buneman 85] M. Atkinson and P. Buneman, "Database Programming Language Design", *to appear in ACM Computing Surveys.*

[Bancilhon et al 87] François Bancilhon, Véronique Benzaken, Claude Delobel and Fernando Velez, "Interface to the Object Manager", *Altaïr internal Report.*

[Barbedette et al 87] G. Barbedette, C. Lécluse, P. Richard and F. Velez, "Connecting the O_2 Data Model to Programming Languages, Version V0", *Technical Report, 13-87, GIP Altaïr, 1987.*

[Bloom and Zdonik] T. Bloom and S. Zdonik, "Issues in the Design of Object-Oriented Database Programming Languages", *Proceedings on the OOPSLA'87 Conference, October 1987.*

[Cardelli 84] L. Cardelli, "A Semantics of Multiple Inheritance", Semantics of Data Types, *Lecture Notes in Computer Science, 1984.*

[Cardelli and Wegner 85] L. Cardelli and P. Wegner, "On Understanding Types, Data Abstraction, and Polymorphism", *ACM Computing Surveys, Vol 17:4, 1985.*

[Cazalens et al 88] R. Cazalens, A. Doucet, C. Lepenant, D. Plateau and B. Poyet, "Benchmarking some User Interface Toolkits", *Technical Report, 17-88, GIP Altaïr*, March 88.

[Goldberg and Robson 83] A. Goldberg and D. Robson, "Smalltalk 80, the Language and its Implementation", *Addison Wesley, 1983.*

[Hornick and Zdonik 87] M. Hornick and S. B. Zdonik, "A shared, Segmented Memory for an Object-Oriented Database", *ACM TOOIS, Vol 5, No. 1, January 1987.*

[Kaehler 81] Ted Kaehler, "Virtual Memory for an Object-Oriented language", *BYTE, August 1981.*

[Kaehler 86] Ted Kaehler, "Virtual Memory on a Narrow Machine for an Object-Oriented language",*Proceedings of the OOPSLA'86 Conference, Portland, September 1986.*

[Lécluse et al 88] C. Lécluse , P. Richard and F. Velez, "O_2, an Object-Oriented Data Model", *Technical Report, 10-87, GIP Altaïr, 1987, to appear in Proc of the ACM-SIGMOD Conference, Chicago, 1988.*

[Maier et al. 85] D. Maier, A. Otis and A. Purdy, "Development of an Object-Oriented DBMS", in *a Quaterly Bulletin of the IEEE Computer Society Technical Committee on Database Engeneering, Special issue on Object-Oriented Systems, Vol 8:4, 1985.*

ZEITGEIST:
Database Support for Object-Oriented Programming

Steve Ford, John Joseph, David E. Langworthy, David F. Lively, Girish Pathak, Edward R. Perez, Robert W. Peterson, Diana M. Sparacin, Satish M. Thatte, David L. Wells, and Sanjive Agarwala[1]

Texas Instruments Incorporated
P.O Box 655474, M/S 238
Dallas, Texas 75265

Abstract

The Zeitgeist Object-Oriented Database System under development in the Information Tech-ologies Laboratory of Texas Instruments is designed to support design applications and large scale rogramming projects by providing a nearly seamless interface to Common Lisp. Zeitgeist is cur-ently being used within Texas Instruments by a VLSI CAD system and a hypermedia system. This aper describes the architecture of Zeitgeist, and the design and implementation of its base layer (the ersistent Object Store). Particular emphasis is given to our development experiences, including the ationale for certain data model and implementation decisions, our interactions with users of the ystem, and system performance.

Introduction

nheritance and encapsulation of code and data in the *object-oriented programming* paradigm allow efinition of the behavior (rather than just the structure) of data, and provide an elegant model or representing and reasoning about the world being modeled. The result is that a programmer no onger needs to understand an object's implementation in order to use it. In addition, object-oriented rogramming appears to provide significant improvements in programmer productivity by facilitating oftware reuse[Ueb87][Tes86].

It is our contention that the bulk of future large scale programming efforts will follow the object-riented approach, provided that the underlying system supports appropriate development and main-enance tools such as object-oriented databases, configuration managers for object-oriented software ystems, change management tools to allow the orderly evolution of object interfaces and implemen-ations, and debuggers for object-oriented programs. The field is now sufficiently mature that we are eeing a standardization effort for object-oriented programming in the Common Lisp Object System CLOS)[2].

This paper describes the goals, development, and status of the Zeitgeist[3] Object-Oriented Database

[1]Sanjive Agarwala is a member of Texas Instruments' VLSI Design Laboratory, where Zeitgeist is being used to support VLSI CAD system. All other authors are members of Texas Instruments' Information Technologies Laboratory, where eitgeist is being developed.

[2]the Common Lisp Object System is part of the ANSI X3J13 effort.

[3]The name *Zeitgeist* is a German word meaning "spirit of the age," and is intended to reflect the leading edge aracteristic of the project, as well as the elements of time included in the project architecture.

(OODB) System being built by the Information Technologies Laboratory of Texas Instruments in support of an object-oriented programming environment. Section 2 describes our goals for Zeitgeist and discusses how these goals differ from the goals of OODBs being developed elsewhere. Section 3 presents an overview of our software architecture, discusses how our goals drive this architecture, and why our goals lead to an architecture different from other OODBs. The bulk of the paper, Section 4, concentrates on the lowest level of our architecture: the Persistent Object Store (POS). In Section 4, we present the data model supported at the POS level, outline the architecture of the POS, discuss the individual components in some depth, and conclude with a summary of the major lessons we learned from developing and using the POS. Section 5 presents the experiences of one application development team with the currently available capabilities of Zeitgeist. Section 6 summarizes our progress to date and presents some unresolved issues.

2 Zeitgeist Goals

The traditional goals of databases have been to provide long-term storage and to facilitate sharing of information in a controlled way. This has generally been achieved by database management systems that support a data model which is different from other parts of the programming environment, e.g., a relational or CODASYL model, and that interact with the rest of the environment in a limited way, that is, by means of a specialized query or data manipulation language, rather than through a general purpose programming language.

These characteristics are impediments to productivity, since programmers and applications must use different languages and modeling paradigms in the two environments, and since a great deal of explicit data retrieval and translation must be done to get data from one environment to the other. It is our opinion that a database should be integrated with the rest of the programming environment as seamlessly as possible. Since the application environment consists of programs, data, and objects created and manipulated in a real-world object-oriented language, our database must support the same collection of programs, data, and objects as that supported by the language.

Our belief in a seamless interface to a real programming language arose from interviews with the application developers who are potential users of the OODB, as well as programmers responsible for maintaining existing code. From these interviews, five important user demands emerged:

1. Application developers and maintainers were not interested in an OODB that would require them to write their applications in a different programming language, or use a data model different from the one offered by their programming language.

2. Application developers and maintainers would not use an OODB that restricted their use of language constructs for objects stored in the data base or required them to explicitly translate their objects into a form the database could handle.

3. Application developers and maintainers strongly preferred that operations involving persistent objects[4] be indistinguishable from operations on non-persistent objects.

4. When presented with the option, application developers and maintainers preferred a data base interaction model that did not require explicit fetches of objects before they could be manipulated.

[4]Persistent objects are objects that normally reside in the database.

5. Application developers, maintainers, and their managers preferred a database able to operate in a world of distributed computers using a variety of architectures.

If these demands were not met, no production applications would use our OODB, and without production applications our OODB would have languished in the research laboratory. We believe these demands are not unique to Texas Instruments, but are typical of industry.

A truly seamless integration of computational and data storage environments requires that both use the same language and data model. This means that the same data types should be allowed to exist in both environments, and that they should be manipulated by the same operators. The lifetime of objects should be immaterial to programs manipulating them. If a programming language supports both encapsulated and unencapsulated data, the database should not restrict programs to using only encapsulated objects. It is also important that the same model of sharing and object identity be supported in both environments. This goal is consistent with the notion of "orthogonal persistence" as articulated by Atkinson and others[AB87].

The goal of a seamless integration of database and programming environments is ambitious and probably unattainable with current programming languages. For example, there are concepts critical to the database domain, such as concurrency control and transaction atomicity, that are supported poorly, if at all, in programming languages. In addition, because programming languages essentially recognize only the present tense, i.e., all objects and operations refer to current machine state, there is no natural way to handle the many past states that are the primary purpose of a database.

Because the gulf between current computational environments and conventional databases is such a serious impediment to their effective use, we are committed to reducing the "impedance mismatch" as much as possible. This will probably require us to augment the programming language or data model in cases where a relevant construct does not exist, and to require the programmer or user to perform operations to use the database that would not be required if all data were transient. Our success will be measured by how the databases enhances and supports good application design and programming style, and by how closely the resulting combination resembles the original language paradigm and practice. It is important to note that we propose to have minimal impact on good programming style; programmers who violate the stylistic conventions of the language, or designers who execute a poor design, probably will have difficulty using the language itself.

Our approach is somewhat like that being used in the E language[RC87], a C++ with extensions for persistent data. Other OODB developers have either created a new object-oriented data model (e.g., Hewlett Packard's IRIS[FBC*87] data model), rely on proprietary extensions to languages (e.g., Ontologic's C extensions[Ont86]), require explicit retrieval of objects through a query language (e.g., POSTGRES[SR86]). Finally, there are data models different enough from the programming language that the application developer must mentally shift perspective when moving from one to the other (e.g., MCC's ORION[BCG*87], or ServioLogic's SmallTalk-based GemStone system[MSOP86]). The wisdom of any of these approaches to OODB implementation will only become clear as the respective systems mature and are used to support large applications that will stress them.

For our first supported programming language we have chosen Common Lisp with the Flavors object-oriented extension[5]. Our current platform is the Texas Instruments Explorer™. In the future, we plan to support one of the object-oriented dialects of C, such as C++.

[5] We plan to move to CLOS as soon as it becomes available.

To support seamlessness, programs must be able to interact with the database either by sending messages to objects held by the database (using the same syntax as they would for non-persistent objects) or by explicitly retrieving data structures and acting on them directly. We refer to these two models as the *active* and *passive* object models respectively; the active object model corresponding to the use of encapsulated objects, and the passive object model corresponding to the use of unencapsulated data structures. Since object-oriented programming languages such as CLOS and C++ are free to mix the two approaches (and frequently do), both models must be supported. These two ways of accessing the database are essentially navigational in flavor since they tend to make use of embedded inter-object references. While our customers say that navigational access is most important to them, we are convinced that an associative query facility must also be provided for abstract data types (ADTs). This facility should allow set-oriented queries to be framed using the results of arbitrary methods as predicates.

A less controversial goal, but one that we consider very important as a result of our desire to support a programming environment, is that the OODB must allow orderly and efficient evolution of object definitions as well as data values. While reorganizing the database to change a schema is a concern in conventional databases used in business data processing environments, we believe reorganization and controlled evolution will be critical in object-oriented databases. Since the implementation of an object is independent of its interface, changing a persistent object's implementation should be a low cost operation. This implies that to change the implementation of future objects of a class should not require changing all implementations of past objects of that class; to do so could be very expensive. Thus the database must cope with having multiple implementations of the same object class available at the same time. Further, since we anticipate our system will support the entire life cycle of an application, we must allow programs to evolve by supporting changes to the definitions of object classes. A final issue in managing change is that changes to object state should require minimal data movement that is, the database should support some minimal object versioning at a low architectural level.

3 Zeitgeist Architecture

The Zeitgeist architecture builds the capabilities of persistent objects in the same way the capabilities of objects are built in the programming language world, specifically that of Lisp. The architecture, shown in Figure 1, is composed from three components: The Persistent Object Store (POS), the Object Management System (OMS), and the Set Oriented Interface. Each of these major interfaces is directly available to applications.

Set Oriented Interface
Object Management System
Persistent Object Store

Figure 1: Zeitgeist Architecture

Object Management
Relational Manager
Storage Manager

Figure 2: Alternate Architecture

At the lowest level of Zeitgeist, the Persistent Object Store, we support the passive object paradigm discussed in Section 2. All unencapsulated Lisp data types are supported within the POS, as are class definitions, object instances, methods, and functions, which are passive at this level. The

POS provides persistent storage for objects, concurrency control primitives and atomic transactions, nter-process and inter-machine communications (similar to a remote procedure call), translation of bjects between computational and stored forms, and a transparent on-demand retrieval mechanism alled *object faulting.* The POS currently exists, and is discussed in more detail in Section 4.

The next architectural layer, the Object Management System, implements the active object aradigm. In OMS, messages are sent to surrogates for encapsulated persistent objects. The corresponding objects are materialized by the OMS using POS capabilities, the message is delivered to he materialized object, and the result is returned. The OMS is the layer at which evolution of object lefinitions and implementations is managed. The OMS also feeds information back to the POS to elp identify which pieces of an objects have been modified. This reduces the amount of translation ime and storage when objects are saved. By using its knowledge about object modifications, the)MS provides a finer grain concurrency control mechanism (using POS level locks) than is possible sing the POS alone. We plan to support nested transactions at this level, but the exact mechanism as not yet been designed. The rest of the OMS has been designed, and critical parts have been rototyped. OMS design and implementation will be discussed in detail in a future paper.

The Set Oriented Interface provides set oriented capabilities with respect to encapsulated objects. A major requirement of this interface is that it allow querying based on the results of arbitrary nethods rather than just on state. Further, we wish to allow methods to return the results of queries nd to make no distinction between extensional and intentional sets. In keeping with the concept hat Zeitgeist is primarily an extension of an object-oriented programming environment, we plan to rovide the capability to send messages to the result sets of set oriented queries. When combined with he ability to remotely execute methods, this should provide an elegant way for some applications to chieve a high degree of parallelism. An example of such an interface based on Texas Instruments' Relational Table Management System product has been built directly on the POS.

Supporting the passive object paradigm in a base POS layer is done for a number of reasons. 'irst, the active object paradigm must be able to materialize objects when needed and save an bject's state to a persistent storage medium. Second, programs that use encapsulated objects often se unencapsulated structures as well, and this interface must be available to them. Third, existing rograms that do not use the object-oriented model are more likely to use Zeitgeist if they need not e heavily modified or rewritten to do so. Finally, the operations required to support the passive bject paradigm are sufficiently complex that it makes sense from a development perspective to solate them.

Allowing direct access to active objects through the OMS allows applications to navigate their wn data structures rather than forcing them to access the database by means of set-oriented queries. 'his is one reason we chose the architecture shown in Figure 1 over that of Figure 2. Another reason s that we want to be able to ask relational queries about collections of active objects, using in redicates the results of arbitrary methods. It is not clear to us how this can be done without uplicating functionality if the query processor does not have an understanding of encapsulated bjects.

4 Persistent Object Store

The Persistent Object Store (POS) layer of Zeitgeist is functional, and is being used internally at Texas Instruments by a suite of VLSI CAD tools, an experimental hypermedia system, and a navigation application for the storage of digital maps.

In this section, we present the interface by which an application interacts with the POS, outline the computational model underlying this interface, and give an example of how the interface and the model interact. We then discuss the current POS implementation. The section concludes with a set of lessons we learned about object semantics and data modeling, architectures, and implementation details.

4.1 Computational Model and Application Interface

Applications save objects that they have constructed by first telling the POS that the object is persistent using the function `(make-persistent POS-string-name object-pointer)`. This establishes that the object being pointed to will hereafter be known to the POS by `POS-string-name`. After an object has a name known to POS, it can be saved by the function `(save-object POS-string-name)`. Objects are retrieved by the function `(restore-object POS-string-name &optional time-stamp)`, which returns the value of the object associated with the given `POS-string-name`. If the optional timestamp is present, the value of the object at that point in time is returned. In the absence of an explicit timestamp, a default timestamp is used. A *User Name Server* allows applications to browse the collection of POS-string-names and to organize these names into a directory-like structure.

Typically, the data structures created by Lisp programs are heavily interconnected by pointers. As a result, any object pointer is likely to lead to a graph whose closure may be very large. In fact, the graph is often everything in the environment, including system code. Because programs only traverse the portion of this graph of interest to them, the size of the graph is of no consequence. However, this does create two problems for the POS:

1. translating the entire closure of an object pointer is very costly, and
2. if an application (or applications) save a pair of objects whose closures intersect, simply saving the two closures introduces a dangerous, hidden redundancy for data in the intersection of the two graphs.

For these reasons, the POS data model makes a distinction between *client objects* and *storage objects*. Each storage object is identified by a unique *symbolic name*. Over time, a storage object may assume many values; these *incarnations* are differentiated by timestamps. Storage objects may contain code, data values, internal references, and the names of other storage objects. The values of storage objects are by definition disjoint, i.e., two different storage objects never share state.

The world of persistent objects can be considered to be a directed graph G, whose nodes are the collection of incarnations of storage objects currently in the POS, and whose arcs are the inter-object references between storage object incarnations. When an application saves or restores an object, it is actually saving or restoring a collection of storage objects. Each of these collections is called a *client object*. A client object corresponds to the subgraph of G that is in the closure rooted by some storage object incarnation. The particular storage object incarnation at the root of the client object subgraph is identified by its symbolic name and timestamp. Thus, a symbolic name and timestamp uniquely identify both a storage object incarnation and a version of a client object.

When an application saves or restores a client object, the `POS-string-name` known by the User Name Server is actually mapped by the name server to a symbolic-name/timestamp pair. This pair identifies the subgraph of storage objects that constitutes the client object.

Conceptually, an application is unaware that a single client object is in fact a collection of storage objects; however, there are performance advantages to be gained by understanding what these subobjects are. These advantages are discussed later.

It was noted earlier that each storage object may have many incarnations over time, and that these were differentiated by timestamps. Timestamped incarnations are provided for two reasons. First, a reference from one persistent object to another may have one of three meanings: the value of the referent object at some specified time, the value of the referent object at the time the reference was created, or the most recent value of the referent object. By maintaining a history of object incarnations and delaying resolution of inter-object references until the reference is actually used, Zeitgeist supports all three reference types. A second reason for timestamping concerns managing object evolution. When a client object is saved, it is possible that not all of its constituent storage objects have changed. By making use of timestamps and delayed evaluation, it is possible to write only the subgraph of storage objects that actually changed. The result is a performance gain and a space savings.

To illustrate this idea, consider the following example. Figure 3 shows two client objects: *Joe's House* and *Jane's House*. Each is composed of several storage objects representing general information and the floor plans of different stories. The storage object whose value is the floor plan for the basement is common to both houses. Joe's first floor plan was modified in 6/87, and hence there are two incarnations of that persistent storage object. If a client attempts to see the plans as they were as of 5/87, he would see the 4/87 incarnation of Joe's first floor, and Jane's first floor plan would be undefined.

Note that by representing a client object by a collection of storage objects, we avoid the multicopy inconsistency problems that would have been caused by putting a copy of the basement plan into each house plan. This appears to fill a role similar to the role of normalization in the relational model, i.e., eliminating the problems associated with storing of redundant data.

.2 POS Architecture and Implementation

Figure 4 shows the architecture of the POS.

The *Client Interface* is responsible for providing applications with the impression that the persistent object world is composed of client objects. When an application saves or retrieves a client object, it is the responsibility of the Client Interface to ensure that the required graph of storage objects is present by the time the application touches them. As explained later, this does not mean that the entire client object graph is immediately instantiated.

The *Object Translation* mechanism is responsible for mapping storage objects among the representations that they assume in computational memory, long term storage, and when being passed from machine to machine. Object Translation is responsible for detecting the boundaries of storage objects, but has no concept of client objects. Above the level of Object Translation, all objects are

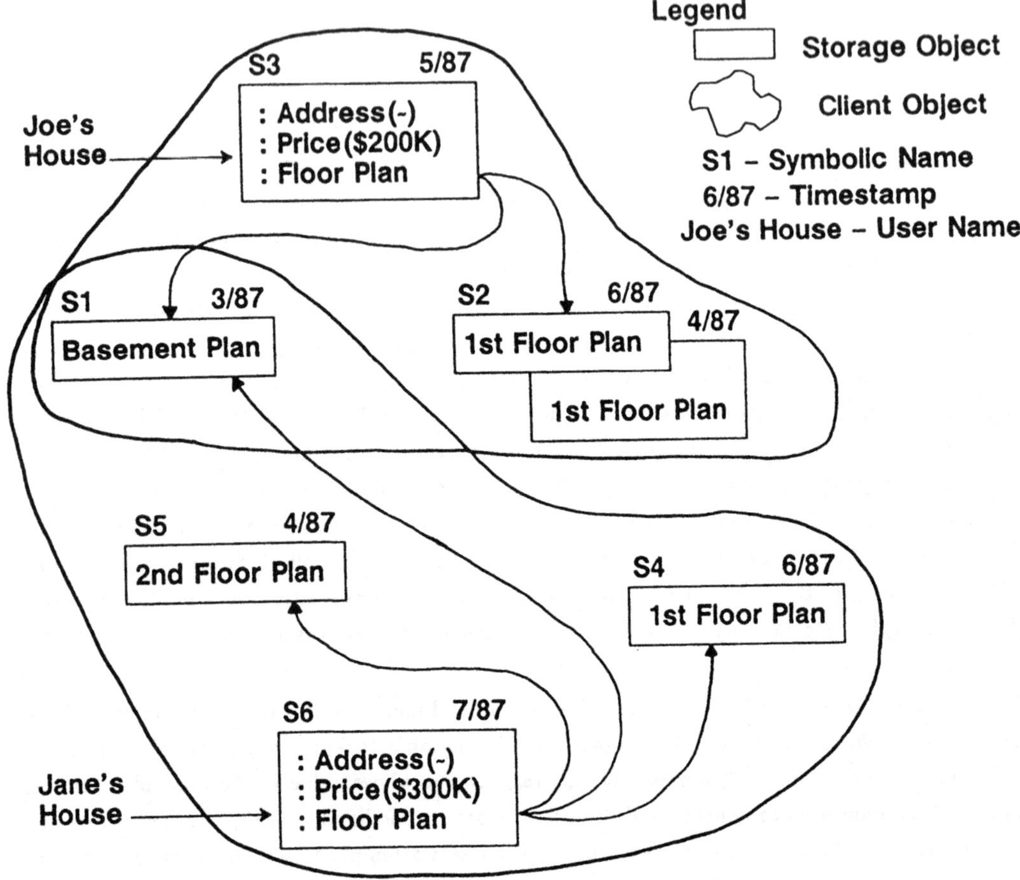

Figure 3: Persistent client and storage objects

Client Interface
Object Translation
Object Transport
Transaction Management
Storage Server(s)

Figure 4: POS Architecture

n a client's computational representation. Below this level, objects are treated as opaque containers with an associated envelope, or *encapsulation*, containing object management information (e.g. object name, type, size, etc.) used by the various subsystems of the POS.

The *Object Transport* subsystem allows inter-process and inter-machine communication by means of a message passing system modeled on a post office. This layer uses Object Translation routines to convert messages to a form acceptable to the underlying communications protocol when crossing machine boundaries.

The *Transaction Management* subsystem provides an atomic commit capability for sets of storage objects and enforces concurrency control by locking collections of storage objects.

Persistent storage of objects is provided by one or more *Storage Servers*. The storage servers maintain a complete history of object incarnations in order to support the timestamp mechanism. Thus there is little distinction between the database and the database log. In the current POS implementation, only a single storage server is allowed to participate in a commit. We plan to remove this restriction soon.

4.2.1 Client Interface

In the current POS implementation, the Client Interface and User Name Server are tightly integrated. They are being separated as part of an overall redesign. The original implementation was used primarily to test ideas and to provide sample interfaces to applications developers for their evaluation. Section 4.2.6 discusses what we learned from this implementation and how it influenced the current design, which is the design discussed in this Section.

The Client Interface presents applications with the impression that they are directly saving and retrieving client objects, i.e., an operation on a client object affects a graph of storage objects. This is accomplished by ensuring that by the time an application program touches a storage object in the graph of a client object the storage object is present in the client's computational memory, and by saving all relevant storage objects when a client object is saved.

To accomplish its task, the Client Interface maintains a *surrogate* for each of the storage object incarnations currently under its control. These surrogates contain the incarnation's symbolic name and timestamp, lock status, computational representation, and stored representation. References between storage objects are always forwarded through the object's surrogate[6].

When a client object is saved, the Client Interface repeatedly invokes the Object Translation mechanism to translate the various storage objects encountered, beginning with the storage object at the root of the client object. The translation mechanism returns the stored representation of the storage object translated, along with a list of all other storage object incarnations it references. The way in which the translation mechanism detects that it has encountered another storage object is described in detail in the next subsection. The Client Interface repeatedly invokes the translator until all storage objects encountered have been translated. These are then passed to the Transaction Manager to be committed. During this process, the translation mechanism must determine if it has encountered something that either is, or should become, a separate storage object. If the data structure encountered is reached by indirection through a surrogate, it is already persistent, and its

[6]This was not the case in an earlier version of the POS, and this lack of indirection made object translation and control much more difficult.

symbolic name is extracted from the surrogate. Other data structures become separately persistent based on information supplied by the Client Interface when translation begins. If neither criterion is met, the data structure becomes part of the storage object currently being translated. By allowing the Client Interface to provide this information, it becomes possible to tailor translation for specific environments and also allow a hook for applications to have object boundaries placed as desired.

When a client object is retrieved, its entire graph is not necessarily instantiated immediately. Instead, the Client Interface implements on-demand loading of objects, similar to how many operating systems implement virtual memory page faulting. The Client Interface requests the stored representation of the root object from a storage server, and then calls the object translation routine to produce its computational representation. This is then stored in the incarnation's surrogate. Surrogates are also created for incarnations referenced by the root object. These surrogates have their computational value slot filled with either their computational value (in the same way as the root) or with an *object fault*. Thus a reference to a storage object will always resolve to either its computational value or an object fault.

If a reference resolves to a computational value, nothing special happens. However, if the reference encounters an object fault, control is transferred by the Common Lisp error handler to the Client Interface, which then retrieves the referenced storage object, replaces the object fault by the object's computational representation, and then resumes the original instruction. The application is unaware that anything unusual has happened. The object fault mechanism is implemented at a very low level of the system and is platform dependent. There are places where the faulting mechanism will not work because of interference from other parts of the Explorer Lisp run-time environment. The Client Interface maintains a list of these places and immediately instantiates objects referenced in these ways, instead of relying on the object fault mechanism. Our object fault support is discussed in more detail in Section 4.2.6.

To improve performance, we plan to prefetch objects based on inter-object reference patterns. When a storage object is requested by the Client Interface, the Storage Server may retrieve additional storage objects based on clustering performed at the server. The stored representations of these additional objects are placed into the surrogates of the corresponding objects by the Client Interface. If a request for one of these incarnations reaches the Client Interface either from an application or as the result of an object fault, the Client Interface will be able to translate the representation that it already holds rather than accessing a Storage Server.

4.2.2 Object Translation

Object Translation provides two services: translation of objects in the client's computational form (i.e., Common Lisp objects in virtual memory) to the equivalent stored representation, and translation of a storage object into its computational form[7].

Generally speaking, all Lisp data structures within a storage object's boundary are copied to one linear data structure with inter- and intra-object references maintained.

We currently make a single pass over the in-memory graph of the data structures, recursively applying to each data structure encountered a translation routine appropriate to its data type. Because we allow arbitrary data structures to be shared, we must determine where sharing occurs.

[7]The stored representation is also the form used for inter-machine communications.

We use heuristics to decide which data structures should be stored as part of the current storage object, which should be stored as separate storage objects, which have already been stored, and which should not be stored at all. This is part of how we achieve seamlessness, a goal discussed in Section 2.

When a data structure is to be stored separately or has already been stored, its symbolic name is requested from the Client Interface and is embedded in the current storage object. When a symbolic name is encountered during the restoration of a storage object, either a reference to the object or a trap for an object fault is inserted into the appropriate place in the parent object.

The current POS system cannot automatically determine if an object has been modified. As a result, unfetched storage objects are the only objects that we can currently guarantee have not been modified. Obviously, when saving a client object we need not save unfetched storage objects contained in the client object's closure. We can simply save a reference to the previously saved incarnation. We are currently working on several approaches to eliminate writing restored but unmodified objects, by detecting modifications as they occur, and by permitting users to declare whether they have modified objects.

Some data structures contain references to objects that are considered part of the runtime environment. These *environmental objects* need not be stored because they are guaranteed to exist in the environment in which the object will be restored. Only the information necessary to correctly splice the restored object into its new environment is saved. System functions and variables are examples of this kind of object.

Because we benefit performance-wise from manipulating large storage objects, and because we have no mechanism for externally referencing sub-objects embedded in storage objects, most of our heuristics are aimed at detecting known shared objects, and making reasonable guesses about potentially shared objects. It is reasonable to guess, for instance, that immediate objects such as fixnums or characters are not shared, and that symbols are, so the former are embedded in their parent's storage object and the latter are saved separately. Because the heuristics are not perfect prophets, the computational model is not 100% faithfully duplicated upon restoration. At present these heuristics are largely embedded within the Object Translation code. To make them manipulable by applications or other parts of Zeitgeist, we are formalizing their structure and providing an interface for their manipulation.

We are currently redesigning Object Translation with one goal being correct preservation of shared state. Since the graph-marking algorithm being considered is expected to degrade performance in the interest of correctness, we will continue to include heuristics that allow the user to declare that certain objects have no shared sub-objects and never will. Even if we can guarantee that in a given situation that all sharing is detected and that all shared data structures are stored separately, we have no guarantee that a previously unshared, unmodified data structure object will not subsequently become shared. To deal with this, we are currently designing a mechanism to support external references to sub-objects embedded in storage objects. Such a facility should also permit the bundling of small logically-related, but shared, objects in one storage object, possibly providing an additional level of clustering and pre-fetching in addition to the benefits of dealing with large storage objects.

Many of the issues that were raised during the implementation and use of the current Object Translation system are discussed as "lessons learned" in Section 4.2.6.

4.2.3 Object Transport

Inter-process and inter-machine communication is provided by a message passing system modeled on a Post Office. When traversing machine boundaries, the Object Translation mechanism is used to convert a complex message created by higher system levels into a byte array for transmission. The use of Object Translation by Object Transport forced a useful modification to Object Translation. Object Translation originally assumed that it was always translating persistent objects for storage and split large objects into a collection of smaller objects. This behavior of the Object Translator had to be changed since our communications protocol expected to see a single byte array. As a result, Object Translation became more modular, and made fewer assumptions about why it was being invoked, instead accepting such information as parameters. Aside from this, the Transport subsystem is uninteresting from a data base perspective.

Changes planned will result in improved robustness, better handling of events such as network or remote server failures, and improved network utilization by packing more than one server command into a single network message.

4.2.4 Transaction Management

The transaction management module is currently very simple, providing atomic commit capability with respect to a single server, conventional read and write locks, and serializable transactions. Applications or the Client Interface may lock single storage objects or groupings, called *storage groups*, to reduce overhead, but at the price of less concurrency. Future implementations will allow multi-server commits, and will provide serializable nested transactions as discussed in [Mos80]. The transaction manager will also support the replication of objects at multiple servers.

Because object incarnations are never deleted, reading need not prevent writing, although this capability will be provided. We also plan to provide notification locks to allow transactions to discover that an object has been modified since it was read. These locks will increase concurrency and enhance Zeitgeist's suitability for certain application categories. Eventually part of the transaction management subsystem will need to migrate to the client interface to allow control of objects that are cached at the client machine.

4.2.5 Storage Servers

The Storage Servers are implemented directly on raw disk partitions to achieve performance and protection improvements compared to what is available from the native Texas Instruments Explorer file system. Each storage server maintains one or more *storage groups*. A storage group is a set of co-located storage objects whose symbolic names all have the same prefix. The intent of storage groups is to partition the name space of symbolic names in order to reduce the overhead in determining which server maintains a given object. Associated with each storage group is an *incarnation name server* for locating the object incarnations in that storage group. In the original implementation of the storage servers, the incarnation name servers were built at boot time from the collection of committed objects. While this saved a small amount of time during commit, it caused boot to take an unacceptably long time. The current version of the storage server maintains an up-to-date incarnation name server.

The incarnation name server is implemented using a tree. Each branch is indexed by bits extracted from the symbolic name. Each leaf is a list of incarnation disk addresses. Because symbolic names are allocated in ascending order from the set of positive integers, and parts of the tree are created only when they are needed, this tree-based index is relatively dense where it exists. The root of the tree is stored in a well known location in the storage group.

We are currently implementing an algorithm, based on [HK88], to cluster storage objects by usage patterns. Clustering will be done during idle periods, and is based on reference statistics collected by the storage server. The clustering will reduce disk and network traffic, and support the prefetching mechanism being implemented in the Client Interface.

In a future implementation, a reliable POS log of incarnation histories will be viewed as the actual database, with the magnetic disk being treated as a cache. When implemented, the log will use write-once optical media for reliable storage of objects.

4.2.6 Lessons Learned

Much of the current architecture, translation policies, and data model evolved from our experience using POS to store and retrieve a small design created by the DROID VLSI design tool set described in Section 5. This section describes those lessons.

There are five major lessons we learned while building our initial implementation. In retrospect, we believe we would not have learned these lessons without the experience of building the initial implementation, using it, discovering where its behavior was either unstable or undesirable from a semantic viewpoint, and trying something better.

We learned

1. What the appropriate level of abstraction for translation and storage is,
2. That the semantics of temporal Lisp objects are undefined,
3. What data model and object boundaries should be,
4. How to implement object faults,
5. What help POS requires from higher levels.

Level of Abstraction: Our original intent had been to gain performance by implementing Zeitgeist at the lowest level of abstraction possible (i.e., very close to the hardware), and to store objects in a representation as close as possible to their computational representation. This caused a number of problems, and we have now decided that Zeitgeist should be implemented at the level of abstraction supported by the language, in our case Common Lisp.

Our original translation routines made extensive use of Explorer Lisp sub-primitives that have access to Explorer tags and addresses. While this appears more efficient than checking types from Lisp and manipulating locatives, sub-primitive use caused serious problems without providing a quantifiable performance benefit.

First, the use of sub-primitives during translation makes the translation code non-portable, since these sub-primitives vary from implementation to implementation, and are not always available. Second, the use of absolute addresses does not work in the presence of garbage collection (something any

Lisp system must worry about), since garbage collection typically runs concurrently with applications and relocates data structures as it runs. Finally, we discovered that attempting to do translation at such a low level was equivalent to writing in assembly language. As a result we became more concerned about individual instructions than algorithm efficiency. Though we have no solid numbers to back us up, we believe that we actually lost performance by being at too low a level of abstraction.

Attempting to use a one-to-one memory to external format mapping for stored objects unexpectedly resulted in increased storage requirements. Many data types, for example a Flavor class definition, are highly redundant in their memory representation in order to improve performance. Since the forms of these object types are known, it is possible to eliminate this redundancy for storage and transmission and recreate it upon materialization. Using a one-to-one mapping also causes problems when coupled with the use of tags. Some Lisp data types, such as packages, are actually implemented using other Lisp data types. For example, on the Explorer, packages are implemented using arrays. Thus translation at too low a level ends up treating the package as an array. This almost works, since the internal structure of the package can be reproduced correctly upon materialization, but other parts of the runtime environment hold references to the package. Since these incoming references are not encountered during translation, they cannot be reconstructed during materialization. Fortunately these references are well defined, and can be reconstructed if the package is typed in external storage as a **package**. To generalize, the internal state of an object does not completely define it. Finally, by focusing on representation rather than logical structure, we lost the ability to port an object to another Common Lisp environment where its representation may be different.

Semantic Issues: Our goal of providing a seamless interface to a programming language (in our case Common Lisp) meant that Common Lisp effectively became our data model. We believe that we have been very careful to preserve Lisp semantics. However, there are several cases in which Common Lisp semantics are not defined in a temporal domain. In these cases, we were required to define what we considered "reasonable" semantics that did not violate existing Lisp semantics. Our clients are apparently satisfied with our decisions, but the full implications might not be fully understood yet. In any event, such decisions are sufficiently important that they should be more widely debated in the context of the language definition.

These semantic problems are typically associated with things that Common Lisp defines as unique, specifically packages and symbols. There can be only one package with a given name, and within a package, symbols are unique. With retrieval of objects having other values, the computational form of the storage object can simply be materialized and bound. However, if the value of the object being retrieved contains one of these unique things, and the environment already contains one of them, a conflict occurs.

For example, if we retrieve an object whose value is a package named `'foo` and such a package already exists, it is not possible to directly materialize the new package since Lisp semantics demand that at the end of the operation there be only one package named `'foo`. Since Common Lisp does not say what to do in such a case, there are several alternate semantics that can be tried. It is possible to delete the existing package, but in that case what happens to references to symbols that do not exist in the new `'foo`? It is also possible to merge the two versions of the packages in some way. However, this just pushes the issue down to the symbol level, since it is not clear what to do f a symbol 'bar exists in both the new and the old versions of 'foo. Should the old version be ıninterned and replaced by the new version? Should the old 'bar assume the value of the 'bar that s being materialized? If there is an attempt to merge symbols, what should be done about functions ınd property lists attached to the symbols? Even in Common Lisp, the scoping rules for these are eft to the discretion of the language implementor.

We have chosen to implement a semantics for symbols and packages that resolves conflicts in avor of the retrieved object, while permitting the user to override this behavior. For example, the ontents of the value cell of a symbol will be saved when the symbol itself is saved unless a certain roperty on the symbol's property list says not to save the value. When the symbol is retrieved, if ts value was saved, the value is restored unless a property on the property list of the in-memory ersion of that symbol says not to restore the value. Saving and restoring are defined as global perations; only dynamic bindings are affected by saves and restores, not local bindings. This may e counter-intuitive to the programmer and may need to be changed.

The relationship of a symbol to the package that contains the symbol also presented some probems. When we save a symbol, we only save enough information about its package to properly intern he symbol upon its restoration. This requires saving some information about the symbol's package, ut does not require that the entire package be saved. Other kinds of references to a package cause he package and all of its symbols to be stored. Saving a package thereby becomes a convenient nechanism for saving and restoring an object with a large number of symbols as entry points.

Lisp's lack of a temporal dimension also impacts the handling of instances of Structures, Flavors, ınd CLOS classes. Currently, instances of different versions of any of these user-defined types cannot egally co-exist in memory simultaneously.

These are all issues which have implications beyond the scope of our database effort.

)bject Boundaries: We had been aware from the beginning that the issue of object boundary was mportant during object translation. Storage objects are bounded by other storage objects (whether xplicitly defined as separate by the client or made into separate objects during translation) and by bjects that are defined to be part of the computational environment that is always available.

The importance of making shared state into a separate storage object was clear from the beginning. Iowever, detecting shared state requires a costly graph marking algorithm. To avoid this cost, we se a collection of heuristics to guess which state is likely to be shared and then splitting that into a eparate storage object. The result was that we sometimes over-split (at a cost of increased overhead), nd sometimes failed to identify all the sharing. Our new mechanism for detecting sharing is not yet ılly developed, but will be based on a combination of graph marking and splitting hints provided y the application. The key to improving performance in the graph marking is that if the client can artition the graph based on application semantics, the effort required to mark all partitions is less han that required for the original graph. Our experience with translation is expected to help us in iving the application developer some hints on how to decompose client objects. This has already een done to some extent by the VLSI CAD tool builders and resulted in a substantial performance nprovement (see Section 5). Allowing only Flavor objects to be persistent would solve the problem, ut at the expense of seamlessness.

The full implications of the "always available" environment with respect to POS translation was not clear initially. We were aware that certain things (`T`, `NIL`, `*standard-io*`, etc) are always present in the environment and need not be translated. We were also aware that objects of interest to applications frequently point into system structures that we did not want to save. Initial attempts to save objects often took hours as a result of over-translating. By watching what was being translated and how the translator was traversing the graph, we were able to gradually reduce over-translation. However, in the initial implementation, this resulted in a massive number of special cases coded into the translation routines, resulting in degraded performance and difficult to maintain code. Our present scheme of allowing the application to define a collection of "packages of interest", and then promising not to put anything into other packages is a response to this experience. At little cost to the application (and in many cases, a better use of the package structure), we are able to have a generalized, low-cost mechanism for defining environmental boundaries.

The current mechanism essentially requires two promises from applications: they will not put anything into packages they have defined as "part of the environment", and they promise that a compatible environment will exist when they try to restore saved objects. Neither has been a problem in practice, since it is customary for applications to expect a stable environment. Something that we consider a research issue is how the environment itself may be allowed to evolve in a way that would still allow the materialization of objects saved in an old environment. Clearly the problem would be solved if the environment itself were saved in the POS, but this is currently beyond our capabilities.

Object Faults: An object faulting mechanism can be implemented in several ways. We initially tried to fault by trapping references to reserved areas of memory. Then we successfully implemented a faulting mechanism entirely in software by modifying the generation of the accessor functions for slots of Flavor and structure instances so that references would ensure that the referenced object had actually been loaded. Finally, our third implementation detects an object fault by using the **`cell-contents-error`** signaled by the microcode when a `NULL` is encountered during instruction or operand decode. We eventually settled on the latter because it required minimal changes to system code and allows faulting on a wider class of object types. However, there are still problems with the mechanism.

The mechanism works by placing an `NULL`-typed pointer to information identifying the object being referenced into a cell in memory. When a reference is made to that cell, an exception occurs that we can trap. At this point we materialize the object and allow the original reference to continue. This works properly except when some other part of the run-time environment corrupts or removes the faulting mechanism. This happens in some situations because in some contexts `NULL` is interpreted as `UNBOUND` and in other contexts `NULL` has some context specific meaning. Essentially, other system code uses `NULL` as a special marker just as we do. To make faulting work properly has been a process of individually identifying the contexts where the traps are being corrupted and immediately instantiating the referenced object without depending on an object fault. The problem would be completely solved if Common Lisp implementations provided some kind of "interrupt" data type that would cause a user-provided function to be invoked if an instance of the data type were encountered.

Help Required by the POS: Because the POS deals exclusively with passive data structures, it cannot detect when a storage object has been modified. As a result, when a client object is saved, modified, and stored, all storage objects that are physically present must be saved[8]. Since the next higher layer in Zeitgeist, the Object Management System, deals with active objects, the OMS will be able to record operations that change client objects and pass this information to the POS. The result will be substantially faster saves, since applications such as the VLSI tool suite estimate that in mature designs a typical interaction will modify less than 1% of a design object.

The ability to detect object modification in the OMS will also help improve concurrency by allowing the correct type of locks to be set in the POS.

5 Application Experience

The POS is currently used by two applications within Texas Instruments: a suite of VLSI design tools, and a hypermedia system. This section contains a description of one of these projects, written by its developers, and a performance analysis based on saving a small design created by the VLSI design tool suite.

5.1 DROID VLSI Tool Suite Developer Experience

The goal of the DROID project (Design Representation in an Object-oriented Integrated Database) is to provide integrated circuit designers a very sophisticated design environment capable of improving their design productivity by a factor of 100, compared with current practice. The approach uses a suite of tightly-coupled, recursively-defined tools which require a fully incremental active data model, and an object-oriented database rather than a traditional relational database. In this integrated tool environment working with very large numbers of objects (estimated to be on the order of 10^7 by the early 1990's), managing change at the object level seems to be a better alternative than a system centered around a file-based database without histories.

Such an ambitious VLSI CAD system places many demands on the database system and the programming paradigm. Zeitgeist is able to respond to most of these demands. First of all, Zeitgeist offers the capability of storing any arbitrary data structures (both active and passive) in the programming paradigm (currently Common Lisp). This is especially important for an application that leverages programming features like macros, on-the-fly compilation, tool generators, daemons, message passing, modularity, etc. Further, this shields the application designer from having to manage and parse the information-structures (not just data-structures, as information is both data and programs). The designer can concentrate on the algorithmic design of the tool, building a system which assists in managing the complexity of the design without the database getting in the way. The use of Zeitgeist led to a considerable reduction in application code size compared to a file based application. These features of Zeitgeist were instrumental in integrating the two systems quickly. Disregarding the time spent to revise the data model, methods, and applications to improve performance (see below), the simulator was moved to Zeitgeist in just a few days. Moving other DROID tools is expected to be accomplished in a similar time frame.

Zeitgeist helps minimize the amount of computational memory used at runtime and will reduce the amount of secondary memory used during the design cycle. By adding a specific Zeitgeist Flavor

[8] As noted previously, storage objects that have never been faulted in cannot have been modified, hence they need not be saved again.

mix-in to object class definitions, the data model designer can direct how client objects are to be split by the translation mechanism, thus determining the stored object granularity. As objects are restored and instantiated in virtual memory, the object faulting mechanism brings in only those objects that are needed by the design tool, reducing the amount of virtual memory used by the tool (DROID only explicitly fetches the root object of the design). Out of all the objects brought into memory, only those that have been modified will be saved back to POS. (Currently, all objects brought in will be saved. This will changed when the OMS layer is completed.) This "incremental update" will lead to a significant reduction in the growth of the database during the complete design cycle compared to systems where creating a new version of a integrated circuit cell creates a file roughly the same size as the previous version. With a slower growth rate of the database size, maintenance of the database will be eased (shuffling cells around the network, deleting unneeded versions, acquiring new disks, etc.).

During the evolution of a design, it is important to experiment with a set of related alternatives before arriving at a final design. From this comes the need to effortlessly manage versions of the design. Zeitgeist assists by providing object persistence throughout the design evolution and also allows the designer to roll back in time to any design stage very easily. The incrementalism offered by Zeitgeist allows new tools/abstractions to be added easily, avoiding tool set obsolescence, and making the system more adaptive to user needs. Further, it provides the "hooks" to include schema evolution and object version management (both coarse and fine grain).

However, there are some words of caution for developers designing an application using Zeitgeist. As with any programming system, there are many things that a developer can do to improve performance. It is very important for the schema designer to cleanly define the transitive closures of data-structures, determine where to use physical versus symbolic pointers for inter-object references, fine tune the size of the objects according to the application requirements, and decide which objects should be saved and which can be recreated or derived from other persistent objects. For example, since cell libraries are not modified as frequently as cells under development, references to them should be made symbolic (effectively defining the object boundary at the library), and things such as the state of a simulation need not be saved since they can be recreated by the application when needed. These decisions are not specific to the use of Zeitgeist; they are related more to the overall system performance and must be considered when building an application. Indeed, Zeitgeist can be used "seamlessly" without making any of these decisions, at the cost of additional (unnecessary) objects being saved and decreased performance.

5.2 Performance Tuning and Analysis

We used the experiences of the DROID designers to determine data model semantics, test the POS, and improve its performance. Our standard test case is storing and retrieving a 3,000 transistor VLSI design. We have successfully saved this design, executed one of the design tools that retrieves the root of the design, faults in a register transfer logic description of the design, simulates the design and synthesizes a layout representation, and saves the augmented design to the POS. Performance statistics were collected using a Texas Instruments Explorer II with 34 megabytes of memory.

Since the initial version seen by the DROID design team (POS-1), the POS has gone through two major revisions. POS-2 had faster object translation. POS-3 obtained faster server initialization by saving certain mapping tables rather than building them at startup time.

During this process, the DROID designers were using their experience to modify their test VLSI design and DROID system to improve its performance with respect to the POS. They also made two major changes to the initial DROID system (DROID-1). DROID-2 partitioned the design and the design environment more appropriately. DROID-3 separated the design libraries from the design and used symbolic object references rather than direct pointers.

DROID Version	POS Release		
	POS-1	POS-2	POS-3
DROID-1	9.4 min. 467KB	3.0 min. 407KB	3.1 min. 409KB
DROID-2	6.8 min. 218KB	2.0 min. 185KB	2.0 min. 188KB
DROID-3	5.3 min. 183KB	1.7 min. 195KB	1.5 min. 173KB

Table 1: Performance Statistics

Table 1 shows the times required to translate and save the design object with each combination of DROID organization and POS version. Also shown is the number of bytes of design information actually saved in each combination. Between DROID and POS improvements, the combination of DROID-3 and POS-3 has performance 6.3X that of the original combination of DROID-1 and POS-1.

Improvements due to DROID changes			
DROID Version	POS Release		
	POS-1	POS-2	POS-3
DROID-1 / DROID-2	1.38X	1.50X	1.55X
DROID-2 / DROID-3	1.28X	1.17X	1.33X
DROID-1 / DROID-3	1.77X	1.76X	2.06X

Improvements due to POS changes	
DROID Version	POS Release POS-1 / POS-3
DROID-1	3.03X
DROID-2	3.40X
DROID-3	3.53X

Table 2: Performance Improvements

Table 2 analyzes the improvement attributable to either POS or DROID changes. In general, POS-2 and POS-3 were 3.3X that of POS-1 for any DROID configuration. POS-3 was essentially the same speed as POS-2, despite the fact that it has a much better initialization time. These improvements are almost all attributable to improvements in the POS translation routines. We hope to achieve another 2X improvement by additional optimization. By properly dividing DROID between design and tools (environment), DROID-2 had performance 1.5X that of DROID-1. By splitting off the design libraries and using more symbolic references, DROID-3 was about 1.25X the performance of DROID-2. The result of all DROID changes is that DROID-3 has about 1.8X the performance of DROID-1.

6 Summary

We have presented a status report on the Zeitgeist Object-Oriented Database project in the Information Technologies Laboratory at Texas Instruments, Inc. The lowest architectural layer of Zeitgeist has been implemented and is being used by two sizable applications. The feedback from the application developers is that our data model is very close to being a seamless interface to Common Lisp, and that putting applications onto Zeitgeist is very easy. It is also claimed that, as with any programming project, a knowledge of the underlying mechanism is essential to obtaining the best performance, as evidenced by the improvements that VLSI designers achieved by a slight reorganization of their data model to make use of what Zeitgeist does well.

Open research and policy issues include how to define Common Lisp and CLOS (and in fact all programming languages) semantics with respect to persistence and time, the need for a generalized user interrupt data type to generically support object faulting, appropriate policies to ensure correct handling of shared state with minimal overhead and application interaction, implementation of the active object paradigm and a mechanism for detecting shared objects, management of CLOS class evolution, and concurrency control for cooperative design and long, nested transactions.

References

[AB87] M. P. Atkinson and O. P. Buneman. Types and Persistence in Database Programming Languages. *ACM Computing Surveys*, 19(2):105–190, June 1987.

[BCG*87] J. Bannerjee, H.T. Chou, J.F. Garza, W. Kim, D. Woelk, N. Ballou, and H.J. Kim. Data Model Issues for Object-Oriented Applications. *ACM Transactions on Office Information Systems*, January 1987.

[FBC*87] D. H. Fishman, D. Beech, H. P. Cate, E. C. Chow, T. Conners, J. W. Davis, N. Derrett, C. G. Hoch, W. Kent, P. Lyngbaek, B. Mahbod, M. A. Neimat, T. A. Ryan, and M. C. Shan. Iris: An Object–Oriented Database Management System. In *Transactions on Office Information Systems*, January 1987.

[HK88] S. Hudson and R. King. Cactis: A Self-Adaptive, Concurrent Implementation of an Object-Oriented Database Management System. *Transactions on Database Systems*, 1988. (to appear).

[Mos80] J. E. B. Moss. *Nested Transactions: An Approach to Reliable Distributed Computing.* PhD thesis, Massachusetts Institute of Technology, Cambridge, Massachusetts, April 1980.

[MSOP86] D. Maier, J. Stein, A. Ottis, and A. Purdy. Development of an object-oriented dbms. In *Proceedings of Object-Oriented Programming Systems, Languages, and Applications Conference (OOPSLA '86)*, pages 472–482, ACM, Portland, OR, Sept 29–Oct 2 1986.

[Ont86] Ontologic. *Vbase Functional Specification.* Ontologic, Inc., Billerica, MA, November 1986.

[RC87] J. E. Richardson and M. J. Carey. Programming Constructs for Database System Implementation in EXODUS. In *Proceedings of SIGMOD*, May 1987.

[SR86] M. Stonebraker and L. Rowe. The Design of Postgres. In *Proceedings of SIGMOD*, pages 340–355, Washington D.C., December 1986.

[Tes86] L. Tesler. Programming Experiences. Interviews with Satisfied Users of Object-Oriented Languages. *Byte*, 11(8), August 1986.

[Ueb87] J. Uebbing. Making Products Using Object–Oriented Programming. In *Panel Discussion at OOPSLA '87*, Orlando, Florida, October 1987.

A Distributed Object Server

Harry H. Porter
Earl F. Ecklund
Denise J. Ecklund
T. Lougenia Anderson
Bruce Schneider

Computer Research Lab, Tektronix Laboratories
Tektronix, Inc.; Beaverton, Oregon 97077; USA

ABSTRACT

One of the major problems in an object-oriented DBMS is supporting interfaces to multiple languages. It is our thesis that this is best done by providing a common, low-level of functionality that can be used to implement various high-level language servers. This paper presents the architecture of such a low-level distributed *object server* with the following features: (1) sharing of persistent objects between sites, (2) resilience of objects in the presence of site crashes, (3) transactions to manage concurrency control, (4) immutable objects to promote efficiency, and (5) historical versions of objects. The objects provided by the server are very simple; basically chunks of storage containing object pointers and raw, uninterpreted data. In particular, there is no notion of message passing or behavior at the level of the server described here. This server is intended to be the lowest layer of a number of different object-oriented database systems in which the higher levels augment the functionality provided by this server to provide a richer object model, including complex object types and message passing behavior. An example of one such system is an extension to the Smalltalk object model [Goldberg and Robson, 1983] to provide a globally shared, resilient object space. This extension is called *Distributed Smalltalk* and is described in a companion paper [Porter, et. al, 1988].

1. Introduction

An Object-Oriented Database Management System (OO-DBMS) represents a marriage between object-oriented programming language technology and database management technology. Most OO-DBMSs to date have selected a particular programming language and implemented persistent storage for the language, thus enforcing a tight coupling between the storage mechanisms and the constructs available in the programming language (PL). However, there is a pressing need to be able to support multiple language interfaces for the same storage mechanisms. For example in our engineering environment at Tektronix, CAD tools are typically written in some variant of C, user interfaces and simulations may be written in Smalltalk, and diagnostic expert systems may be implemented using an object-oriented version of Scheme. All of these applications have DBMS requirements which the application developers want provided in some fairly transparent fashion (i.e., they do not want to import and export their data to/from a relational DBMS, but want to have the PL objects in their applications stored and managed directly by a DBMS).

It is our thesis that multiple language support is best provided by a common, low-level kernel. This kernel should provide functionality that can be used at higher levels to implement various language servers. We call the low-level kernel an *object server*. This paper describes the architecture of such an object server by describing the object model provided by the server to a client system.

The object model seen by a *user* (e.g., a Smalltalk programmer or a C program author of a CAD tool) will be at a more abstract level than the object model provided by the server. This server is intended to form the lowest layer of an *object-oriented (o-o) system* that will completely insulate the user from the primitive model of objects provided by the server. The server provides a shared object space of resilient objects. The upper layer of the o-o system will augment this model to provide such concepts as typing, message passing, inheritance, etc.

One example of an o-o system is a distributed Smalltalk interpreter using this server to implement Smalltalk objects. A second example is the object-oriented DBMS being discussed by the Database Technology Department's Architecture Group at Tektronix. A third example is a suite of CAE/CAD/CASE tools (e.g., written in C) that have their own custom data model. These tools will call the object server directly to provide persistence, resilience, distribution, and concurrency control. In this paper, we refer to the layer implemented on top of this server as the *object-oriented application* layer.

This server is generic, in the sense that it can be used in the implementation of any such o-o system. Although this paper does not discuss or describe any particular o-o system, in order to make our motivations and examples more concrete we will specifically consider the case where the object-oriented application layer is a Smalltalk interpreter, augmented with additional primitives to support the functionality of a distributed object space. Such a *Distributed Smalltalk* system is discussed in more detail in a companion paper [Porter, et. al, 1988].

This paper is organized as follows: Section 2 reviews related work on object servers. Section 3 defines the relevant OO-DBMS concepts and presents the overall design of our object server. Subsections discuss (3.1) the object model, (3.2) the architecture of the system, (3.3) user sessions, (3.4) transactions and commit protocol, (3.5) resiliency, (3.6) multiple processes within sessions, (3.7) semaphores, (3.8) historical versions of objects, (3.9) concurrency control, and (3.10) garbage collection and deletion semantics. Section 4 discusses implementation. Section 5 describes the interface between the o-o application layer and the server. And finally, we summarize in section 6.

2. Related Work

There are two general approaches to implementing a shared object space: send the messages to the objects or move the objects. Servio Logic's Gemstone system chose the former strategy by implementing a centralized object-oriented database [Maier, et. al, 1986; Maier and Stein 1987; Penney, et. al, 1987]. Messages are sent to the central site where they are executed. The goal of our project is to explore the second strategy by implementing a distributed object server in which the global object space is distributed across client workstations and objects migrate to the sites where they are used. This approach may avoid a von Neumann bottleneck at the server and may also improve performance for applications such as CAD/CAE/CASE where a single user's working set will fit in his/her workstation's storage and will be accessed exclusively at one site for long periods of time.

Another closely related project is that of D. Decouchant, who is building a distributed memory manager for Smalltalk [Decouchant 1986]. Like our proposal, they intend to run under Unix and have discovered the necessity of implementing a lightweight process scheduler. They use proxy objects and move an object from one site to another by swapping the object with its proxy. To collect garbage across sites, they use a simple distributed mark-sweep algorithm. The primary difference between their work and ours is that they do not discuss concurrency control or address the issue of resiliency.

Two groups [Bennett 1987; McCullough 1987] have discussed work in distributing objects in the context of Smalltalk. Both groups maintain local proxies for remote objects and forward messages to remote sites. Their implementations are written solely above the virtual machine interface and do not attempt to replace existing, local object management. [Merrow and Laursen 1987] also discuss extensions to the Smalltalk model to support sharing and persistence.

Other groups building distributed and/or persistent object management systems to support object-oriented languages include [Cockshot, et. al, 1984; Caplinger 1987; Wiebe 1986; Weiss 1986; Skarra, et. al, 1986]. These papers include many clever ideas we do not have room to review; it is a hope and goal of this project to synthesize as many of these ideas as possible into a practical object server meeting our specific requirements. However, none of the above work addresses the problem of supporting multiple language nterfaces.

. Functional Concepts and System Design

.1. Objects

The term *object* has several different meanings and there are many proposed object models. Examples include (1) the Smalltalk model of objects, (2) the Abstract Data Type (ADT) model of data objects [see, .g., ADJ 1978], (3) the object abstraction provided by this server to the object-oriented system, and (4) the epresentation of objects used in the implementation of this server. Unless otherwise stated, the term *object* vill mean a server object, i.e., the abstraction provided by this server to the object-oriented system.

A server object is essentially a chunk of storage containing literal data (i.e., raw, uninterpreted byte lata) and pointers (OOPs) to other objects. Each object has a header containing the object's length and an OOP to another object. This distinguished OOP is called the object's *type*, although there is no concept of ype checking at the server level. In fact, there is no notion of operation or message passing at the server's evel of abstraction. (We will discuss the storage layout of objects later in this paper.)

To facilitate sharing, every object is either *local, shared*, or *immutable*. A *local object* resides at one ite and is not accessible from remote sites. (Technically, a local object resides in one session's workspace nd is not accessible from other sessions. We will define *session* below.) Consequently, a local object does ot participate in any concurrency control or sharing. Local objects reside solely in virtual address space, which is expected to reside entirely in RAM. Thus, accesses to local objects will not usually require disk its and will never require network hits. The o-o application layer will use local objects for data which nust be accessible quickly. For example, objects currently being displayed by the user interface will be ocal objects. Local objects are resilient in the sense that they survive hardware crashes with high probability but are not persistent since they do not outlive sessions.

Shared objects are accessible from any site, resilient against hardware failures, and persist between essions. In a port of the Smalltalk-80 image to our server, for example, class objects would be made *hared* while objects related to the window interface (e.g., MVC instances) would be made *local*. For large esign databases, it is expected that there will be a frightening number of shared objects. We expect access o shared objects to be slower than to local objects.

Immutable objects are read-only and might, for example, be used by the o-o application layer to implenent abstract data type (ADT) values or executable code objects*. While immutable objects may be hared, their read-only nature dramatically simplifies concurrency control. Also, supporting the resiliency of mmutable objects is easier since they need to be written to disk only once.

Local objects may contain references to local, shared or immutable objects. Shared objects may only oint to shared or immutable objects. Immutable objects may only point to immutable objects.

.2. Architecture

The o-o application layer and the object server are linked together at system build time into a single xecutable program, called the *complete system*, which is to be executed as a single process on a workstaion. The o-o application layer will make subroutine calls to the object server to retrieve and access shared, ocal, and immutable objects. This interface is at a similar level of abstraction to the Smalltalk *object nemory* interface documented in [Goldberg and Robson 1983]. When an engineer wishes to use the bject-oriented system, he will start the complete system as a user process on his workstation.

The general architecture of the system consists of a network of vanilla-flavored Unix workstations ommunicating across an Ethernet network and is shown in Figure 1. A dedicated workstation process,

* In Smalltalk, *CompiledMethod* objects could be made immutable since methods are never modified. Instead, class objects are modified to point to newer versions of method objects.

called the *Name Server*, will sit on the LAN. The object servers running on the other (client) workstations will communicate with the Name Server to locate shared objects. The name server maintains an object table with an entry for every object and so is required to have disk capacity proportional to the total number of shared objects across all sites.

To improve performance and reduce network communication, the objects themselves are stored at the workstations where they are used. A background daemon process, called the *disk manager*, will run at all times on each workstation. The disk manager will implement a persistent store of shared objects that will be available to remote sites, even when there is not a currently active local session.

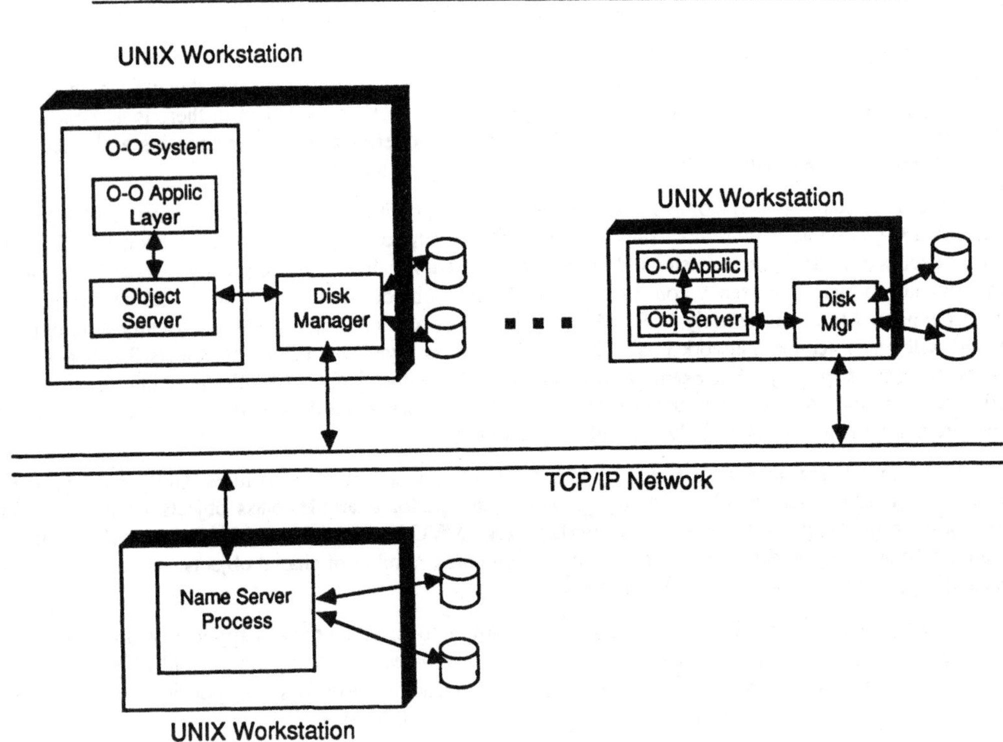

Figure 1: Architectural Overview

3.3. User Sessions

The duration of the user process executing the complete system is called a *session*. A session begins when the user starts the complete system running and ends when the complete system gracefully terminates. The scope of local objects is the session. That is, when the session gracefully terminates, all local objects cease to exist. Any communication between two sessions (whether or not the sessions are running concurrently) must be through shared and immutable objects. Typically, there will be only one session running on a given workstation and the user will interact with all shared data through that session.

.4. Transactions and the Commit Protocol

A user session consists of a sequence of transactions, each terminated when the o-o application layer alls on the object server to perform a *commit* operation. During the transaction, the globally shared object pace appears to be completely owned by the session. The o-o application layer may change local and glo-al objects freely, but the activities of remote sessions are invisible to the local session until a commit is xecuted. The commit operation has the effect of making the current state of all shared objects available to ther sessions and updating the o-o application layer's view of the global object space to reflect changes nade by commits executed in other sessions. Since local objects are only modified within a transaction, ommit has no effect on them.

In the face of potential hardware failures, commits are executed atomically: either to completion or not t all. Thus, the state of the global space of shared objects moves reliably in discrete steps from one state to nother every time a commit is executed. To support the restarting of a session after a hardware failure, a ommit also causes a checkpoint of the current workspace to be made.

.5. Resiliency

Typically, a session lasts many hours or days. A Smalltalk user, for example, would start his o-o sys-em (i.e., the ST interpreter) once and leave it running for days on end. When a workstation crashes, it is ne data of the session that is lost. Thus, the session must be the unit of resilience. After a workstation rash, we must be able to restore the session to a previous state and then restart it. To support the semantics f commit, we must capture the global state of the shared object space during each commit. However, since ne user may elect not to commit a transaction for long periods of time, it is mandatory that he be allowed to apture the state of his session more frequently than at commit times.

There is a tradeoff between capturing the state of the session frequently (incurring a high performance enalty) and capturing the state less frequently with the possibility of losing more work. In engineering pplications, with their high data bandwidths, it seems reasonable to try to keep a working set entirely vithin RAM and capture the system state by taking checkpoints every few minutes. Other techniques, such s write-through logging, can be expected to cause disk arm interference with other processes and to require me for blocking and unblocking disk buffers. Checkpoints can be executed efficiently by copying the ntire RAM image to disk in one transfer.

Consequently, we have chosen the checkpoint model to implement resiliency. We anticipate execut-ng a checkpoint every 10 minutes as well as at commit time. If an engineer's typical working set is around MBytes, the checkpoint operation shouldn't be too irritating. If (or when!) the local workstation crashes, ne checkpoint file can be simply reloaded into memory and the o-o system restarted.

.6. Multiple Processes within a Session

Object-oriented systems generally require light-weight processes while most operating systems pro-ide only heavy-weight processes. Heavy-weight process switching typically takes as much as 1 ms. in Jnix, which is unacceptably high for object-oriented engineering applications. Consequently, the server rovides a simple light-weight process scheduler. The complete system runs as a single user process with he o-o application layer's process scheduling done by the server.

.7. Semaphores

Transaction commit protocol provides some degree of concurrency control and object locking between essions but, alone, is not adequate to support all process synchronization. For example, to lock an object a rocess might simply access that object. The processes of the transaction then have exclusive access to that bject until the transaction commits. However, another process within the transaction may execute a com-nit to achieve sharing for some other unrelated object, thereby releasing the "lock" prematurely.

To support locking and process synchronization independently of transaction commits, the server provides semaphore objects, which the processes of the o-o application may use to achieve their desired degree of concurrency control.

Semaphores may be either local or shared objects. (Obviously, they cannot be immutable.) A *V* operation on a local semaphore object is seen immediately by other processes within the same session. A *V* operation on a global semaphore object is also seen immediately within the session but is not shared between sessions until commits occur. Because of the semantics of shared objects and commits, the remote process is not actually awakened until commits are executed at each site. Note that a single semaphore object may be shared by two o-o applications even though the applications were written in different o-o languages running in different sessions.

Semaphores have a variety of uses. In an e-mail application, for example, global objects might be used to represent the current status about which letters have been sent and which have been read. Each session would contain a notifier process that waits on a shared semaphore. Whenever new mail is sent, the sending process would signal the semaphore, causing the notifier to wake up and display a notification window after the next commit occurs.

We expect that commits will be executed frequently to *enhance* sharing and that applications will use semaphores to *limit* sharing. For example, a librarian or version server object might allow users to check out engineering design objects for days or weeks, although commits occur much more frequently. The version server would use semaphores to ensure that only one user at a time is given permission to access a shared design. Of course the shared design, which may be comprised of thousands of server objects, is not directly protected by semaphores. The server sees no connection between a semaphore object and the other objects representing the design. If the version server wishes to enforce protection of the shared design objects against unwanted access by hostile processes, the server may need to copy objects and/or make them immutable.

3.8. Historical Objects and Versions

There seems to be much debate about the most appropriate versioning model for CAE applications [e.g., Beech and Mahbod 1988; Dittrich and Lorie 1985; Ecklund, et. al, 1987; Katz and Chang 1987; Leblang and Chase 1987; Narayanaswamy and Bapa Rao 1988]. Rather than attempt to satisfy all requirements, the object server supports a simple versioning scheme and relies on the o-o application layer to augment it to provide the functionality ultimately seen by the user.

So far versions have not been mentioned. We implied that only a single version of each object existed and that there were no particular versioning relationships between objects. A primary goal is to provide an object abstraction that can be implemented efficiently for non-versioned applications (e.g., the existing Smalltalk image), as well as supporting the versioning requirements of engineering applications. To simplify the object server, we would prefer an abstraction with no versioning at all, allowing the full modeling power at the o-o application level to be employed in providing a rich versioning abstraction.

However, one common versioning requirement is to maintain enough historical data to reconstruct the complete state of the global object space as of an arbitrary point in the past. Maintaining this amount of data is extremely costly in space and time. We do not feel we can accept the performance degradation of maintaining that data at the o-o application level and that the object server must provide support for capturing object histories directly.

To this end, the object server supports *historical objects*. A historical object is similar to an immutable object. Historical objects may be accessed from any session and may never be modified. Conceptually there is a *time* associated with every historical object, namely the time that the historical object was last committed. Thus, time moves in discrete jumps, with every transaction commit acting as a time quantum. Shared, local or immutable objects may point to historical objects, but a historical object of time t may only point to immutable objects or historical objects whose associated time is less than or equal to t.

To maintain a complete audit trail, we would like to capture the entire state of the database at every commit. There are two reasons why this is impractical: space and time. Our Smalltalk experience suggests that objects will change at a high rate and that commits will occur frequently (perhaps every minute in some applications). We can reduce the amount of disk space consumed by maintaining deltas and compressing everything. Experience [Leblang and Chase 1987] suggests we may be able to store as much as 50-100 versions in the space of 2 uncompressed versions. By maintaining the current version in expanded form and using backward deltas, we can satisfy the goal of not degrading the time to make current references. However, we incur the cost of computing and writing the delta information to disk on every commit.

Instead, we adopt this strategy for capturing historical data. When the o-o application layer wishes to capture the history of an object, thereby creating a historical version for future reference, it does so explicitly by calling a server routine called `makeHistorical`. The o-o application layer passes an OOP to the server, which creates a historical copy for every object reachable from that OOP.

This scheme has two beneficial features. First, if the o-o application layer does not need support for historically versioned objects, it never calls `makeHistorical` and no additional overhead is incurred. Second, if full histories of the entire object space are required at every commit, `makeHistorical` may be called on the root of the object space at each commit.

To access a historical version of an object, the server provides another function (`getVersionOf`) which is passed an OOP to an object, X, and the desired time in the past. An OOP to a historical version of X is returned.

3.9. Concurrency Control

Within the framework of a transaction/commit protocol, we have elected to control concurrent access to shared objects via a variant of two-phase locking. This is in contrast to an optimistic concurrency control scheme in which serializability is realized by aborting transactions that conflict (e.g., Servio Logic's Gemstone database system [Penney, et. al, 1987]). See [Bernstein, et. al, 1987] for a general discussion of transaction-based concurrency control mechanisms. During a transaction, a session must obtain a shared object before it can be accessed. By *obtain*, we mean that the object is migrated from a disk manager into the session's object server's memory. Once obtained, the session does not relinquish the object until the commit is executed. Of course, the acquisition and relinquishing of objects is taken care of by the object server and the o-o application layer need not be aware that it is occurring.

This scheme has the benefit that commit operations do not fail, but the disadvantage that transactions can block waiting to acquire a shared object. The server provides an operation called `testAndLock`, that tests whether an object can be obtained without blocking and, if so, obtains that object. The o-o application layer does not have to use this operation at all, but is free to use it to avoid blocking when global objects are unavailable.

3.10 Garbage Collection and Object Deletion

There is no explicit operation to delete objects; instead all unreachable objects are considered garbage and are periodically collected by the object server. Unreachable shared objects are called *shared garbage* and unreachable local objects are called *local garbage*. Local garbage is generated at a much higher rate than shared garbage and so local garbage must be collected frequently. Since shared garbage collection must involve communication and participation by all sites, shared garbage collection is going to be time consuming. Thus, local garbage and shared garbage must be collected separately.

Within a session, we use a generation scavenging garbage collector [Ungar 1984, 1986] to automatically collect local garbage when the number of local objects in a generation becomes large. The local garbage collector runs independently of other sites and requires no communication, although requests from other sites may be delayed during while the local garbage collector is running.

A second garbage collector, using a distributed variant of the mark-sweep algorithm, is used to collect all unreachable shared objects. Since the number of global objects is expected to be large and since inter-site communication will be required to collect the shared object space, we expect the shared garbage collector to impose large delays on active sessions. Consequently, the shared garbage collector will be invoked explicitly during off-hours.

4. Remarks on Implementation

The background *disk manager* daemon running at every site implements a persistent object store by using several Unix disk files for replicated storage of resilient objects to guard against media failure. Every object is the responsibility of exactly one disk manager at any moment and is resident in that disk manager's persistent store, although an object may move from one disk manager to another disk manager. The name server contains a mapping from OOP to disk manager and can be queried to find out where an object is. The disk manager will communicate with object servers within a session, with disk managers at other sites, and with the name server. Object servers within a session will only communicate with the name server and disk managers. They will not communicate with each other. A disk manager can move an object (securely) to another disk manager or can check an object out to a session.

Conceptually, a session will check out objects from disk managers one after another, read and write the objects, and return them all at commit time. A primary requirement is that commit operations are executed quickly. To achieve this, sessions will actually keep objects across transaction commits, relying on checkpoints for resiliency. When a disk manager needs an object, it will ask the session that currently possesses the object to return it. If the session has not used the object since the last commit, it may check it in immediately. Otherwise, the session will return the object after the next commit operation. A session can keep track of which objects have been accessed since the last commit very quickly, by adding to a list of object references every time a shared object is accessed. If a request for an object arrives, this list can then be searched.

As mentioned above, historical objects are implemented using backward deltas. These deltas are kept in immutable objects that are not directly reachable from the o-o application layer. To implement references to other historical objects, the implementation uses a special flavor of OOP called a *historical reference*, which contains a pointer to an object and an associated time. The o-o application layer is unaware of any difference between normal and historical OOPs. Whenever the o-o application layer makes an access using a historical reference, the server finds the current version of the object and reconstructs the historical image before making the access.

5. The Object Server Interface

Next, we discuss how the o-o application layer creates and accesses objects. In order for the o-o application layer to provide its functionality to the user in an efficient way, there must be a very tight coupling between the o-o application layer and the server. The best way to achieve this tight coupling is to link the o-o application layer and the object server code directly at system-build-time. We describe their interface by describing the subroutine calls that the o-o application layer makes to the server.

The interface is described as subroutine calls for the purpose of abstraction only. Because of our performance requirements [Ecklund and Ecklund 1987], and since true subroutine calls do not have the necessary performance, the integration of o-o application layer and object server must be tighter than we describe here. For example, many of the calls to the server will be expanded inline and optimized accordingly.

5.1. The Storage Layout of a Server Object

Before discussing the protocol through which the o-o application layer and the object server interact we need to specify the format of an object. We will be describing the conceptual presentation of an object by the server to the o-o application layer. The actual representation used by the object server and disk managers is more complex. (For example, there are fields associated with concurrency control, historical ersion information, garbage collection, etc. but these fields are effectively invisible to the o-o application ayer.)

The layout of an object is given in Figure 2. Each object is referenced by an object-oriented pointer OOP). The OOP of an object is assigned by the server and can be considered at the o-o application layer to e an uninterpreted identifier. The o-o application must manage any mappings from string names to OOPs. An object consists of a fixed length header and a variable length body of data. The header contains 3 fields, which we describe next.

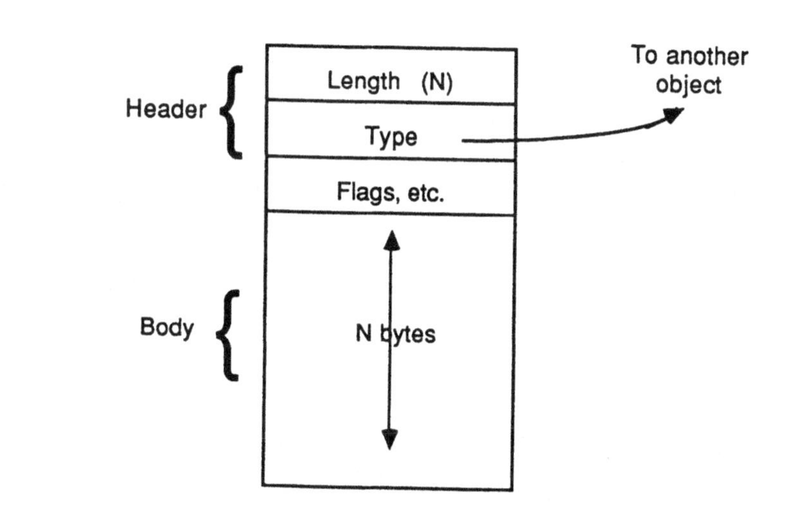

Figure 2: Object Layout

The *length* field is an integer giving the length of the body of the object. We use a 32-bit length field with the corresponding restriction on the maximum size of data in a single object.

The *type* field contains an OOP to another object. For the vast majority of objects, this field is uninterpreted by the object server and may be used as desired by the o-o application layer. A Smalltalk interpreter would, for example, use this field to point to a *class* object.

(There are, however, several cases when the object server communicates with the object-oriented system through objects, so there are several distinguished types (called *server types*) known to both the server and the o-o application layer. Examples of server types include semaphores and processes. The server does not actually read or modify the objects pointed to by the type field of semaphore or process objects. The server only checks (and sets) an object's *type* field when the o-o application layer invokes the relevant operations.)

Similarly to Smalltalk OOPs, our OOP space is partitioned into two formats: references to objects and small, immutable values that are represented literally. In the second format, called a *small integer*, the OOP does not point to an object but contains the object (a 31-bit two's complement integer) literally.

From the o-o application layer's point of view, the first format is a completely unstructured unique object identifier pointing to some object. The size of these pointers is unspecified and unimportant, and the o-o application cannot determine its actual size through calls to the object server interface. In the implementation, the OOPs of shared objects are 64-bits long, in general, but are represented by shorter surrogates within an object server's memory. Additional information (e.g., whether the object is local or shared) may also be included literally in the encoding of OOPs.

Finally, the *flags* field contains information about the object and about the contents of the data portion of the object. The data portion of an object (i.e., the object's body) can have one of two formats: raw or structured.

In the *raw data* format, the object's body consists of uninterpreted bytes. The o-o application layer may use the raw format to represent bitmaps, numerical data, blocks of Smalltalk byte codes (when the o-o application layer is a Smalltalk interpreter), or even blocks of machine-executable code. To support garbage collection and compaction, the server must be able to locate all OOPs. Consequently, raw data objects cannot contain OOPs.

The second format of object, called a *structured object*, contains only OOPs. That is, each field of a structured object either contains a small integer or a pointer to another object.

(If necessary, a third format of objects may be added to the server design later to support hybrid objects containing both raw data and OOPs. For example, Smalltalk *CompiledMethod* objects contain a block of literal OOPs followed by raw byte code data.)

The *flag field* in the object's header also contains information about whether the object is local, shared, or immutable. We do not specify the exact format of the flag field, since the o-o application layer may not directly inspect or modify this field. Instead, the o-o application layer must call on the object server to change the status of an object.

5.2. Object Server Protocol

This section discusses the interaction protocol between the o-o application layer and the object server by describing a number of calls that the o-o application layer makes to the object server. Each subsection discusses a related group of calls and begins with a listing of the subroutine call formats.

Object Creation Protocol

```
OOP := newRaw (length, OOPofType, data)
OOP := newStructured (length, OOPofType)
```

The `newRaw` subroutine is used to create a new object containing raw data. It is passed the length in bytes of the raw data, an OOP pointing to a type object, and the actual data values with which to initialize the object. It creates a new local object of the given size and moves the data into the object. The OOP to the type object is uninterpreted and is placed, as is, in the header of the newly created object. This routine then returns an OOP to the newly created object.

The `newStructured` subroutine is used to create a new object containing OOPs. The object is initialized to contain nil OOPs. Later, the o-o application layer may move other OOPs into this object.

Object Format Protocol

```
boolean := isSmallInteger (OOP)
boolean := isStructured (OOP)
boolean := isRaw (OOP)
boolean := isImmutable (OOP)
boolean := isLocal (OOP)
boolean := isShared (OOP)
integer := length (OOP)
OOP := type (OOP)
```

The first subroutine, `isSmallInteger`, determines whether an OOP is a small integer or a pointer
an object.

The `isStructured` subroutine determines whether an OOP points to a structured object or not.

The `isRaw` subroutine determines whether an OOP points to an object containing raw data or not. ince every OOP is either a small integer, a pointer to a structured object, or a pointer to an object contain- g raw data, every OOP will satisfy exactly one of these 3 subroutines.

There are 3 subroutines that may be used to query the status of an existing object. Every OOP points an object that is either *immutable*, *local*, or *shared*. Thus, exactly one of the subroutines (`isImmut- ble, isLocal, isShared`) will be satisfied. Small integer OOPs are considered to be immutable.

The `length` subroutine is used to determine the size of the body of an object and the `type` subrou- ne is used to fetch the type OOP from an object.

mall Integer Protocol

```
OOP := smallIntegerToOOP (integer)
integer := oopToSmallInteger (OOP)
```

The `smallIntegerToOOP` subroutine is passed an integer and an OOP. It converts the integer to n small integer OOP and returns the result . The `oopToSmallInteger` subroutine does the inverse unction. It is passed an OOP containing a small integer and returns the integer.

rotocol to Manipulate OOP Constants

```
boolean := isNil (OOP)
boolean := isTrue (OOP)
boolean := isFalse (OOP)
boolean := isSemaphoreType (OOP)
boolean := isProcessType (OOP)
boolean := isSmallIntegerType (OOP)
OOP := nil
OOP := true
OOP := false
OOP := semaphoreType
OOP := processType
OOP := smallIntegerType
```

There are several *distinguished* objects, whose OOPs are known to the server. The names of these spe- ial objects are: *nil*, *true*, *false*, *nilType*, *trueType*, *falseType*, *semaphoreType*, *processType*, and *smallIn- gerType*. These objects are part of the initial object space. Their storage is laid out manually at system uild time and is part of the bootstrapping process.

There are several subroutines (e.g., `isNil`) that can be used to test an OOP to determine if it points one of the distinguished objects. There is also a subroutine that returns an OOP pointing to each of the istinguished objects. For example, the routine `nil` returns an OOP pointing to the nil object. The OOP the nil object is called *nil* for short.

ata Manipulation Protocol

```
OOP := getOOP (sourceOOP, sourceOffset)
putOOP (sourceOOP, destOOP, destOffset)
moveData (sourceOOP, sourceOffset, destOOP, destOffset,
                                                   length)
```

```
getRawData (destApplicationLocation, sourceOOP,
                                   sourceOffset, length)
putRawData (sourceApplicationLocation, destOOP,
                                     destOffset, length)
```

The next collection of subroutines is used to move data to and from objects. The routine `getOOP` is passed an OOP to an object and an offset into that object. It returns the OOP at that offset in the object. The source object may be local, shared, or immutable. It must be a structured object. The inverse function, `putOOP`, is used to move an OOP (the source OOP) into a structured object pointed to by the destination OOP. The destination object may be a local or shared object, not an immutable object. It must be a structured object.

The `moveData` routine is used to move large chunks of data from a source object to a destination object. The source object may be local, shared or immutable, while the destination object must be either local or shared (and not immutable). This routine may move either raw data or OOPs, so the source object may be either a raw data object or a structured object. The destination object must match the source object.

The routine `getRawData` is used to move data from the server into the o-o application layer's memory. Consequently, the source OOP must point to an object containing raw data. The source object may be local, shared, or immutable. The inverse function, `putRawData`, is used to move data from the o-o application layer to a raw data object. The destination object may be local or shared, but cannot be immutable.

Moving data from one memory location to another location at the same site is very time consuming. To promote efficiency, we would like to eliminate data movement altogether. The only truly necessary reason to move data from one memory location to another is to change data in a format required by an I/O device into the format used in local memory. Since the object server will manage the disk and communication with remote sites, the only reasons the o-o application layer will need to call `getRawData` and `putRawData` are: (1) moving numerical data to/from numerical processors, (2) moving bitmap data to/from the screen, and (3) other miscellaneous I/O.

Concurrency Control Protocol

```
becomeImmutable (OOP)
becomeShared (OOP)
commit
testAndLock (OOP)
```

The `becomeImmutable` operation is used to transform a local object into an immutable object. Since immutable objects can only point to immutable objects, and since we wish to allow the o-o system to construct cyclic structures of immutable objects, it is necessary that this operation also makes all reachable objects immutable.

The `becomeShared` operation is used to transform a local object into an object that can be shared between sessions. Likewise, since shared objects can only point to shared or immutable objects, this operation needs to visit all reachable objects, making local objects shared. Both the `becomeImmutable` and `becomeShared` operations take effect when the transaction commits.

(If necessary, we may augment the server design to provide a function to transform an immutable object back into a mutable object. Such an operation will necessarily be very costly to execute, but may be necessary in the case of a catastrophe such as making the object root immutable.)

The `commit` operation is called to commit any changes made to shared objects to the global state of the database, making those changes available to other sessions. This operation also makes any changes by other sessions visible to the session executing the `commit` operation. From the point of view of the code alling commit, this operation will always succeed. Note that a session may have a number of processes xecuting. Any one process in the session may execute a commit; all processes in the session will be qually effected by it.

The testAndLock operation may be called to see whether an object is available and accessible. The object server will attempt to locate the object in question and move it into the session's workspace. If he object is in use by another session, the operation will return false. Otherwise, it will return true. This peration need not be called before accessing objects, but can be used to avoid blocking a process that tries o access an object in use elsewhere.

Process Control Protocol

```
fork (codeAddress, OOP)
terminateSelf
p (semaphoreOOP)
v (semaphoreOOP)
```

The fork operation can be called to start a new light-weight process within this session. An argument can be passed to the starting process. The terminateSelf operation can be used to terminate the process executing it.

The p and v operations are each passed an OOP pointing to a semaphore object. The v operation will increment the semaphore and will always execute without suspending the process executing it. The p operation will decrement the semaphore, suspending the process if the decrement would cause the semaphore to go negative.

Timing Control Protocol

```
setAlarm (semaphoreOOP, time)
integer := getTimeNow
```

The setAlarm operation can be used to implement timing delays. The process executing the operation provides a semaphore object and an absolute time. At the desired time, the object server signals the semaphore. This operation could be used, for example, to implement a process that wakes up every 10 minutes, executes a checkpoint operation, and then goes back to sleep.

The getTimeNow operation returns an integer representing the current time.

Historical Version Control Protocol

```
makeHistorical (OOP)
OOP := getVersionOf (OOP, time)
```

The makeHistorical operation is passed an OOP pointing to an object. A version of this object, and every object reachable from it, are created. The time associated with each of the new versions is the time of the next successful commit operation. The getVersionOf operation can be called to retrieve historical objects. It is passed a pointer to an object and a time and returns a pointer to an immutable version of that object as it existed at that time.

Session Control Protocol

```
shutdown
```

The shutdown operation is used to gracefully terminate a session. There is no return from this operation and all remaining processes in the current session are terminated.

Additional Protocol

The above protocol is an outline of the general nature of the interface between the o-o application layer and the object server. It is informal and some details are omitted for the sake of exposition. Also, additional operations may be added to the protocol as a need for them arises. For example, it may be useful to provide operations that return statistics on disk space and OOP usage or operations that accommodate debugging and the bootstrapping process. Nevertheless, we believe that the interface between the o-o application and the object server presented above is generally at the right level of abstraction to partition the problem of implementing a full-functioned o-o system into two reasonably independent and equal sized tasks.

6. Summary

We have described a distributed object server in which the global object space is distributed across client workstations and where objects migrate to the sites where they are used. This object server is intended to form the lowest implementation layer of a complete object-oriented system. The design of the server allows it to potentially be used with several different upper layers. One such upper layer is a Distributed Smalltalk virtual machine interpreter. Other possible systems that might use this server are a distributed, persistent version of another language (e.g., Scheme) or a suite of CAD/CAE/CASE tools written in C. The goal of the server is to create an environment where all such object-oriented applications can share objects.

The objects provided by this server are basically chunks of memory containing OOPs and primitive data. There are two classes of objects, *shared* and *local*. Shared objects may be accessed equally from any site and comprise the state of the global object space. Local objects are optimized for the high performance required of objects involved in the user interface and can only be accessed from a single site. A transaction commit protocol is employed to change the state of the shared object space. Historical versions of objects are also supported by the server for those applications needing to maintain a record of previous states of the shared object space, but the mechanism is designed so that applications that do not require this functionality will not incur any penalty.

References

ADJ 1978

An Initial Algebra Approach to the Specification, Correctness, and Implementation of Abstract Data Types, J.A. Goguen, J.W. Thatcher, and E.G. Wagner, in: *Current Trends in Programming Methodology*, vol. 4, (ed) R. Yeh, Prentice Hall, 1978.

Beech and Mahbod 1988

Generalized Version Control in an Object-Oriented Database, David Beech and Brom Mahbod, Fourth Intl. Conf. on Data Engineering, Los Angeles, p. 14-22, 1988.

Bennett 1987

The Design and Implementation of a Distributed Smalltalk, John K. Bennett, OOPSLA Conference Proceedings, Orlando, FL, p. 318-330, 1987.

ernstein, et. al, 1987

Concurrency Control and Recovery in Database Systems, Philip Bernstein, Vassos Hadzilacos, and Nathan Goodman, Addison-Wesley, 1987.

aplinger 1987

An Information System Based on Distributed Objects, Michael Caplinger, OOPSLA Conference Proceedings, Orlando, FL, p. 126-137, 1987.

ockshot, et. al, 1987

A Persistent Object Management System, W.P. Cockshot, M.P. Atkinson, K.J. Chisholm, P.J. Bailey, R. Morrison, Software-Practice and Experience, vol. 14, p. 49-71, 1984.

ecouchant 1986

The Design of a Distributed Object Manager for the Smalltalk-80 System, D. Decouchant, OOPSLA Conference Proceedings, Portland, OR, p. 444-452, 1986.

ittrich and Lorie 1985

Version Support for Engineering Database Systems, Klaus Dittrich and Raymond Lorie, Technical Report RJ 4769 (50628), IBM Research Laboratory, San Jose, CA, 1985.

cklund and Ecklund 1987

CAD Performance Requirements for Persistent Object Systems, Earl Ecklund and Denise Ecklund, Proceedings of a Workshop on Persistent Object Systems, Appin Scotland, 1987.

cklund, et. al, 1987

DVSS: A Distributed Version Storage Server for CAD Applications, Denise Ecklund, Earl Ecklund, Robert Eifrig, Fred Tonge, Proceedings of the Conference on Very Large Data Base Systems, September, 1987.

oldberg and Robson 1983

Smalltalk 80: The Language and its Implementation, Adele Goldberg and David Robson, Addison-Wesley, 1983.

atz and Chang 1987

Managing Change in a Computer-Aided Design Database, R.H. Katz and E. Chang, Proceedings of the 13th VLDB Conference, Brighton, p. 455-462, 1987.

eblang and Chase 1987

Parallel Software Configuration Management in a Network Environment, David Leblang and Robert Chase, IEEE Software, vol. 4, no. 6, p. 28-35, November, 1987.

Maier, et. al, 1986

Development of an Object-Oriented DBMS, David Maier, Jacob Stein, Allen Otis, Alan Purdy, OOPSLA-86, Portland, OR, p. 472-482, 1986.

Maier and Stein 1987

Development and Implementation of an Object-Oriented DBMS, David Maier and Jacob Stein, in: *Research Directions in Object-Oriented Programming*, (ed) Peter Wegner and Bruce Shriver, MIT Press, 1987.

Merrow and Laursen 1987

A Pragmatic System for Shared, Persistent Objects, Thomas Merrow, Jane Laursen, OOPSLA Conference Proceedings, Orlando, FL, p. 103-110, 1987.

McCullough 1987

Transparent Forwarding: First Steps, Paul McCullough, OOPSLA Conference Proceedings, Orlando, FL, p. 331-330, 1987.

Narayanaswamy and Bapa Rao 1988

An Incremental Mechanism for Schema Evolution in Engineering Domains, K. Narayanaswamy and K.V. Bapa Rao, Fourth Intl. Conf. on Data Engineering, Los Angeles, p. 294-301, 1988.

Penney, et. al, 1987

Is the Disk Half Full or Half Empty?: Combining Optimistic and Pessimistic Concurrency Control Mechanisms in a Shared, Persistent Object Base, Jason Penney, Jacob Stein and David Maier, Proceedings of a Workshop on Persistent Object Systems, Appin Scotland, p. 337-345, 1987.

Porter, et. al, 1988

A Distributed Smalltalk Object Model, Harry Porter, Earl Ecklund, Denise Ecklund, Lougie Anderson, Bruce Schneider, Technical Report, Computer Research Laboratories, Tektronix, Inc., 1988.

Skarra, et. al, 1986

An Object-Server for an Object-Oriented Database System, A. Skarra, S. Zdonik, S. Reiss, Intl. Conf. on Object-Oriented Database Systems, Pacific Grove, CA, 1986.

Ungar 1984

Generation Scavenging: A Non-disruptive High Performance Storage Reclamation Algorithm David Ungar, Proc. of a Software Engineering Symposium on Practical Software Development Environments, p. 157-167, Pittsburgh, PA, 1984.

Ungar 1986

The Design and Evaluation of a High Performance Smalltalk System, David Michael Ungar, Mi Press, 1987.

Weiss, et. al, 1986

DOSS: A Storage System for Design Data, Shlomo Weiss, Katie Rotzell, Tom Rhyne, Arne Goldfein, 2nd Design Automation Conference, June, 1986

Wiebe 1986

A Distributed Repository for Immutable, Persistent Objects, Douglas Wiebe, OOPSLA Conference Proceedings, Portland, OR, p. 453-465, 1986.

Implementation Techniques For Object Oriented Databases

Setrag Khoshafian

Dan Frank

Abstract

In past few years we saw the development of a number of object oriented database systems. However, few papers discussed performance sensitive implementation techniques. In this paper we concentrate on strategies for performing deep equality and duplicate elimination in structurally object oriented databases, which support direct representation and access of complex objects. The three main strategies considered here are: (a) hashing and tagging complex objects; (b) inferencing; (c) implementing complex object operators in the presence of duplicates.

1. Introduction

In the past few years we saw the emergence both in industry [Maier et al 1986] and research [Fishman et al 1987, Bancilhon et al 1987, Hornick and Zdonik 1987, Kim et al 1987 (to name just a few)] of a number of object oriented database languages and systems. Although very rich in representation and functionality, most experts in this field would agree by now that performance is becoming extremely important for the success (and failure) of these object oriented database systems. Efficiency in implementation is becoming critical. In terms of performance, there are at least four areas which need special attention and handling for object oriented databases:

(1) *Complex object storage structures:* this area has received by far the greatest attention and several promising algorithms and strategies have been proposed and implemented [Paul et al 1987, Maier and Stein 1986].

(2) *Query processing and execution strategies:* this area needs a lot of attention. There are very few proposals [Khoshafian et al 1988] and, as observed in the 1987 OOPSLA workshop on object oriented databases, we do not have a technology for query optimization strategies even for the non–first normal form models.

(3) *Special algorithms for concurrency control and recovery:* although some special techniques for compound object locking [Kim et al 1987], as well as workspace shadowing algorithms (optimistic) [Maier et al 1986] have been proposed, it is still unclear what the *best* concurrency control/recovery combination is for object oriented databases, and what novel strategies (if any) needs to be developed.

(4) *Efficient execution strategies for the operators of the language:* this is the main trust of this paper, where we shall outline some techniques for implementing operators in value

based models involving complex objects and specify algorithms for performing deep equality testing.

The algorithms and strategies discussed in this paper apply to models which are at least structurally object oriented [Dittrich 1986]. These techniques could be applied both to object models which support the built–in notion of object identity [Khoshafian and Copeland 1986] like FAD [Bancilhon et al 1987] and OPAL [Maier and Stein 1986], as well as to "value" based models [Ullman 1987] like most of the non–first normal form models [Schek and Scholl 1986]. It applies to the former models when performing "deep" operations (e.g. deep equality, deep duplicate elimination etc.).

As for the significance of this work, besides providing algorithms for performing commonly occurring "deep" operators like *deep–equality* [Khoshafian and Copeland 1986] in object models with identity, we shall be proposing algorithms which will enhance the execution of *all* the operators in value based models. In these models sets are "mathematical" and conceptually should not have any duplicates. The naive approach of running a duplicate eliminator algorithm at the end of each operation is extremely costly, *specially in the presence of complex objects*. Thus we have identified a number of implementation strategies which allow the presence of duplicate in the lower level structures storing the complex objects, while at the same time guaranteeing the correct semantics of the operators.model. We propose three compatible approaches to this attempt:

1) By using cached hash values and a set of hashing based algorithms, we can reduce significantly the number of value comparisons that must be done in equality testing and duplicate elimination. This will be discussed in Section 3.

2) By using marking and inferencing techniques, we can determine which sets, under which operations, cannot possess duplicates. For those sets, we can skip duplicate elimination altogether. This will be discussed in Section 4.

3) By examining the semantics of the operations of the language, we can postpone duplicate elimination, while maintaining correct interpretations of the operations. This will be discussed in Section 5.

As for the rest of the paper, in Section 2 we give an informal presentation of the complex object model. As indicated, in Sections 3–5 we investigate a number of techniques for lowering the cost of duplicate elimination. Finally, Section 6 summarizes our conclusions and future research.

2. A Complex Object Model

In this section we present (somewhat informally) the complex object model. The object space definition is based on [Bancilhon and Khoshafian 1986] and data manipulators are based on FAD [Bancilhon et al. 1987]. It is a "value" based model [Ullman 1987]. By this we mean the uniqueness of an object is determined by its content (value).

The object space is built on top of atomic objects. Integers, floats, booleans, and strings are examples of atomic types. There are two object constructors, "sets" and "tuples".

A set is a collection of objects with no repeating values, and thus corresponds to the usual "mathematical" definition of sets. We shall denote sets by delimiting its elements between "{" and "}". For example {Matthew, Mark, Luke, John} is a set of strings.

Tuples, on the other hand, are collections of <attribute name>:<object> pairs, where each attribute name occurs at most once in a tuple. The object associated with an attribute name is the value of the attribute in the tuple. We shall denote tuples by delimiting the <attribute name>: <object> pairs between "[" and "]". For example [Name: Joe, Age: 30] is a tuple, with attributes "Name" and "Age" whose values are Joe and 30 respectively. If the attribute names are 1, 2, ..., the tuple will be called an *ordered tuple*. The attribute names in an ordered tuple are optional. Thus [Joe, 30] is the same as [1:Joe, 2:30].

The basic operations on sets are *union*, *intersection* and *difference*. The basic operation for tuples is *extract* indicated by a ".". If t is a tuple and a an attribute name, t.a returns the a attribute value of t (e.g., [Name:Joe, Age:30].Name is Joe).

Similar to other persistent programming systems and languages, we need a mechanism for defining the persistent object space. One of the simplest methods is to have a "database" persistent object, and have its value persist between different transaction invocations. This is the approach taken in, for example, PS–Algol [Atkinson et al. 1983] and FAD [Bancilhon et al. 1987]. Therefore we assume the persistent database is a tuple:

db = [R1: ..., R2: ..., Rn: ...]

where each Ri can be a set, a tuple, or an atomic object. With this scheme, **db** is a directory of the persistent objects, with user supplied (attribute) names for the directory entries. For persistent sets we require that sets of tuples have unique *key* attributes. For example if the type of a persistent set is {[a1: t1, ..., an: tn]}, then one (and only one) of the atomic valued attribute ai (with ti as an atomic type) should be specified as its *key*. Updates to the set must not violate this constraint.

To examine duplicate elimination in the context of a language we shall introduce three function constructors which take as arguments function abstractions and set objects.

We shall use the λ abstraction to indicate unnamed functions. For an abstraction:

fun(x1, .., xn) e

e is either (i) a function expression returning an object, (ii) a predicate expression, or (iii) p -> e′ where p is a predicate and e′ is an expression whose value equals e′ if p denotes TRUE (nil otherwise).

The function constructors applying abstractions to set arguments are *filter*, *whiledo*, *group*, and,*pump*.

filter(f, Set1, ..., Setn) where f is an n–ary operator abstraction, and Set1, .., Setn are set objects, applies the abstraction f to every element of the cartesian product of its set arguments. The following example gives the name and salary of employees who make more than 50k. The result is a set whose elements are of type [Ename:string, Esal:integer].

filter(fun(x) (x.salary > 5e4) -> [Ename:x.Ename, Esal:x.Esal], **db**.Employees)

pump(f, g, Set), where f is a unary operator abstraction, g is a binary operator abstraction which is associative, commutative and has an identity element, and Set is a set object, is an object equal to:

nil	if Set = { }
f(x)	if Set = {x}
g(pump(f, g, A),pump(f, g, B))	if Set = A U B and A and B are disjoint

The pump operator's main application is aggregate functions. The following evaluates the number of departments:

pump(fun(x) 1, fun(x,y) x + y, **db**.Departments)

group(f, Set), where f is a unary operator abstraction and Set is a set object, is a set equal to { (f(x), s(x)) | s(x) is a quotient set of s by f(s(x) $\subseteq$ s)}.The following example groups employees by salary: group(fun(x) x.Esal, **db**.Employees)).

3. Comparing Complex Objects

The complex objects in our model are constructed out of set and tuple object constructors. In this section, we discuss algorithms for comparing complex objects through evaluating complex object hash values, and point out the advantages of "tagging" objects with these hash values. The algorithms which evaluate hash values are "well defined" (i.e. equal complex objects have equal hash values).

To demonstrate the cost of complex object compares, Figure 1 we plot the worst case number of comparison for both the tagged and untagged complex objects, consisting of nested tuples of 6 attributes, 3 of which are tuple valued. The x–axis is the object depths. First note the exponential increase in number of comparisons. As expected, the worst case number of comparison of tagged complex objects is always greater than the worst case number of comparisons for untagged complex objects. The tagged scheme incurs an extra comparison per tuple in the complex object

In Figure 2 we plot two ratio curves for complex object comparisons with depths 2, 3, and 5 respectively. First note that in most cases object compares with complex object tags in superior to object comparisons without tags. For "deeper" objects, the difference is quite dramatic. If we assume the corresponding atomic values are picked randomly, then the left hand side of the curves are more significant. Here, comparing complex objects with tags is clearly better though the enhancement increases as a function of the probability. The detailed analysis for the curves of Figure 1 and 2 is given in [Khoshafian and Frank 1987].

We should note that the initial evaluation of the complex object hash values could be more expensive than complex object comparison without hash tags. However, these hash values which are evaluated for the complex object and all its sub–objects, can be maintained and copied with the complex objects and sub–objects. Therefore, the initial extra cost of evaluating the hash values will be worthwhile, especially since the cost of object comparison without hash values can be significantly more than tagged complex object compares, as demonstrated in Figure 2.

3.1 Hashing Techniques

Most of the algorithms discussed here will require one or more hash values to be computed for each object and its sub–objects. In this section, we examine techniques for hashing atomic values, tuples, and sets.

3.1.1 Hashing Atomic Objects

A hash function is a highly type–specific operation. Each atomic type should have an integer–returning hash function. Word sized data is fairly simple to hash with division or multiplication, generally modulo some large prime number [Knuth 1973]. Strings may be hashed via an algorithm which combines repeated addition to and shifting of an accumulator. Complex atomic types such as geometric objects may be dealt with similarly, as may sequences of integers, which are used in computing the hash values of complex objects. Other kinds of atomic types require more subtlety. Large textual data such as documents or images may have 'signatures' computed [Faloustos and Christodoulakis 1987].

Not all types of atomic data can be easily hashed. For example, since we require equal values to yield equal hash values, we have a problem with the *floats.* To satisfy this requirement, we cannot simply generate hash values as functions of the bit representation of floating point numbers. Instead, we should generate the same hash value for floating points within the epsilon which two floating point numbers are considered equal.

3.1.2 Hashing Tuples

Hashing of composite objects like tuples and sets is accomplished by recursively computing hash values for their members (or a subset of their members), then rehashing the resulting sequence of values.

In order to have higher probability of unequal hash values for unequal tuples, it is desirable to distinguish between different orderings of the same values. For example, it is desirable to have for the ordered tuples [1,2,3,4] and [3,2,4,1] different hash values. If the sequence of hash values is rehashed by being added to an accumulator, order dependency may be introduced by shifting before each addition:

```
for each s in sequence
  val = val << 1                /* shift */
  val = val + s                 /* add */
end for
```

We should carefully select the subset of attributes on which we hash in order to obtain two important properties: efficiency and distinguishability. If we can get useful results by only hashing small atomic attributes, we can get most of the benefits of hashing without the costs of a recursive traversal of complex sub-objects. On the other hand, the attributes we pick should (as a composite) hash into a reasonably wide sequence of values. Picking the proper set of attributes can be a difficult problem, especially for transient tuples for which no schema or attribute selectivity information exists, or in which a large number of the attributes are set valued.

In a later section, we will discuss the preservation of keys in transient objects. Briefly, many transient sets of tuples come into being as a projection of some persistent set. As indicated in Section 2, persistent sets are type restricted to contain one key attribute. If this attribute is preserved in the projected transient tuples, then it should be sufficient to use its hash value (or its value) as that of the tuple.

In addition to the presence of keys, persistent sets of tuples may have selectivity information available for them. Even if keys are not preserved in their transient projections, this data may help determine a distinguishable subset of the surviving attributes for hashing.

The only requirement for the ordering of the hashing sequence is that it must be repeatable for tuple objects of the same type. For ordered tuples it can be the numeric order of the attributes. For tuples with attribute names, it can be anything from the order of the attributes in the schema, to a textual ordering of their names, to an integer ordering of their addresses in an attribute name table.

3.1.3 Hashing Sets

Sets are the hardest to hash, since they may vary in cardinality, and their elements do not always possess a natural order. In addition, some transient sets may be stored with duplicates. Having to eliminate duplicates to compute a hash value could have an undesirable effect on efficiency.

We suggest two conceptually similar approaches. Both are based on the distribution of the hash values of set members, rather than a unique sequence of such values, so duplicate elimination is unnecessary. The first algorithm is as follows:

1) Recursively compute the hash values of all members of the set.

2) Sort the resulting sequence of integers.

3) Scan to eliminate duplicates (this can be combined with the next step).

4) Use the remaining, unique sequence of hash values to compute the composite hash value for the set.

If the set contains duplicates, they will give rise to identical hash values, which will be eliminated. Two sets which are identical except for duplicates will be guaranteed to have identical hash values.

A variant on this scheme uses a bitmap to represent the set of possible element hash values. The algorithm:

1) Recursively compute the hash value of every element of the set.

2) As each element hash value is computed, set the bit in the map corresponding to that hash value.

3) When all elements have been processed, treat the bitmap as a sequence of integer values and compute the composite hash function over that sequence.

The cost of this method is the sum of the costs of computing the element hash values, plus a fixed cost linear in the number of possible hash values. The sorting method has a cost which is the sum of the element computation costs, plus a cost O(N log N) logarithmic in the number of elements, plus a cost linear in the number of elements for scanning the hash value sequence. For sets which are large relative to the number of possible hash values, the second method is preferable to the first.

The bitmap approach does have a flaw: for the hash values of sets to be computed in a repeatable way, the bitmap used will have to be the same size for all sets, from the smallest to the largest. If the set is very large, the bitmap may end up almost all '1's, which will yield a poor distribution of hash values and increase the number of set comparisons necessary at some point.

We can eliminate the sorting phase in the first algorithm of the sort/scan algorithm, and use a sequence hashing method insensitive to order (simply adding up all the hash values without the shift operation will accomplish this, since addition commutes). We can also improve on the bitmap approach by evaluating the exclusive of all the bits corresponding to the same hash value.

The presence of non-homogenous elements in sets doesn't present a problem. Items of the same type and value will have the same hash value; those of a different type but the same hash value will be caught by the comparison algorithm.

3.2 Tagging Complex Objects

As indicated earlier, comparing complex objects could be expensive. In the previous sections we introduced several techniques for evaluating hash values for set and tuple objects. We believe we can expect a major performance gain if we tag objects with their hash values, and copy those tags when we copy the object. Because of the nature of our model, it is not possible to change the value of a transient object once it has been created. We will not have to compute an object's hash value more than once, and we will never have to compute the hash values of its copies. In fact, in creating new objects through projecting upon or combining existing complex objects, we can maintain the tags of the sub–objects and easily determine the delta computation which needs to be performed in order to evaluate the hash tag of the new object.

Tagging complex objects and all their complex sub–objects has several advantages:

1) Objects with colliding hash values will be unequal. The likelihood that two unequal complex objects have one–for–one identical sub–object tags is extremely low, and this probability declines even further the deeper we descend in the objects.

2) Even if two complex objects are equal, sub–object tags reduce the cost of making this determination. Most efficient set comparison algorithms use hashing to divide the sets into the smallest possible equivalence classes before using a nested loops approach to compare members of those classes. Having hash values for set elements pre–computed can yield a significant gain in performance.

Not all complex objects need to be tagged. In Section 4, we will describe how we can infer the absence of duplicates in many sets. Some of these are the sets which are *derived* from persistent sets, maintaining the keys. Also, we may never operate on a set in ways which requires elimination of duplicates. In other cases for performance reasons we might be willing to evaluate a hash value per element and consequently a hash value for the set. Thus, tagging should be done only on demand. There should be a flag or reserved tag value which indicates that no tag has yet been computed for an object. When the hash value for an object is first computed, this flag or tag value is removed.

3.3 Equality Testing

We present two variants of an algorithm for equality testing. These two variants differ in how they proceed to determine the equality of sets: the first one, which we will call EQ1, eliminates duplicates before proceeding, which can lead to one important optimization for unsuccessful comparisons. The second, EQ2, relies on a marking strategy to avoid eliminating duplicates, and can also take part in a process of incremental duplicate elimination. The overall strategy of both variants is to limit the depth of the comparison as much as possible, comparing hash tags and atoms high in the complex object tree first, before descending the tree to the more difficult tuples and sets.

We begin by defining algorithm EQ1 recursively, as follows:

1) If the two objects being compared are atomic, use the comparison function for their atomic type to compare them. If they are not equal, the algorithm terminates with "not equal".

- 2) If the two objects being compared are tuples of the same type:

  a) Compare the corresponding hash values of their tagged set or tuple valued attributes terminating with "not equal" when a pair of non–equal hash tags is encountered.

  b) Compare the corresponding atomic attributes, terminating with "not equal" when a pair of non–equal atomic values is encountered.

  c) Compare the corresponding un–tagged set or tuple valued attributes, terminating with "not equal" when a pair of non–equal set or tuple pair is encountered.

  d) Compare the corresponding tagged set or tuple valued attributes, terminating with "not equal" when a non–equal pair is encountered. This is delayed until after (2c) on the assumption that they represent a less promising avenue than attributes whose tags are not known to match.

  e) If the algorithm reaches this point, the two tuples are equal.

- 3) If the two objects are sets (call them S1 and S2):

  a) Eliminate duplicates from the sets (this will have the side effect of computing hash tags for all elements).

  b) Distribute the elements into equivalence classes using the hash values. Keep track of the cardinality of each equivalence class.

  c) For each equivalence class e, do the following:

     Check the cardinality of e in S1 and S2, which was computed in (3b). If it is not the same in both sets, the algorithm terminates with "not equal".

  d) For each equivalence class e, do the following:

     1) For each member M1 of S1e (equivalence class e of S1):

        a) For each member M2 of S2e: perform a value comparison of M1 and M2. If M1 and M2 are equal, remove M1 from S1e and M2 from S2e, and go on to the next member of S1e.

        b) If there are no more members of S2e and no M2 equal to M1 has been found, the algorithm terminates with "not equal".

  e) If the algorithm reaches this point, the two sets are equal.

A few notes about this algorithm:

1) In (2c), we compare un–tagged complex attributes of tuples, rather than first computing and comparing hash values. There are two reasons for this:

   a) The hash values will not be used again in this algorithm.

   b) An unsuccessful value comparison, unlike a hashing pass, is very likely to terminate long before the whole object is traversed.

2) The set equality test is similar in approach to the Grace hash join algorithm [Kitsuregawa et al. 1983], but only in its initial phase. While the Grace algorithm uses sorting within the equivalence classes ("buckets"), we use nested loops. We should be able to extend and enhance our algorithm to sort whenever sorting is more efficient.

Now we present algorithm EQ2. It varies from EQ1 only in step 3, which we replace with the following:

- 3) If the two objects are sets (call them S1 and S2):
  - a) Compute hash values for all un-tagged elements of both sets.
  - b) Distribute the elements into equivalence classes using the hash values.
  - c) For each equivalence class e, do the following:
    - 1) For each member M1 of S1e:
      - a) For each member M2 of S2e: perform a value comparison of M1 and M2. If M1 and M2 are equal:
        - 1) If M1 is marked, remove M2 from S2e and go on to the next element of S2e. This step removes duplicate values from S2.
        - 2) Else if M2 is marked, remove M1 from S1e and go on to the next element of S1e. This step removes duplicate values from S1.
        - 3) Else mark M2 and M1.
      - b) If there are no more members of S2e and no M2 equal to M1 has been found, the algorithm terminates with "not equal".
    - 2) For each member M2 of S2e: if M2 is not marked, then it has a value which is not in S1e, and the algorithm terminates with "not equal".
  - d) If the algorithm reaches this point, the two sets are equal.

Some notes on EQ2:

1) Because of the possibility presence of duplicates, the cardinality of the equivalence classes does not yield any information we could use to terminate the comparison early.
2) In step (3c1a), we remove duplicate elements from S1e and S2e. If we exhaust S1e without algorithm termination, only *this* equivalence class in S1 is then known to be duplicate free. If we reach step (3d), then both S1e and S2e are known to be duplicate free. If we store sets in hash tables, we can thus incrementally eliminate duplicates, flagging those classes that have been "cleaned" to reduce work when a full duplicate elimination pass is called for. Of course, if S1 and S2 are compared and found to be equal, this method will eliminate *all* duplicates in S1 as a side effect.

3.4 Duplicate Elimination

There have been some analytic studies demonstrating the effect of duplicates on the performance of joins [Lu and Carey 1985] and transitive closure [Bancilhon and Ramakrishnan 1986]. The databases in these studies consist of relations with fairly small, homogeneous, and contiguous records. Even in these cases, for some operators such as transitive closure the effect of duplicate elimination could be rather dramatic. In [Khoshafian and Frank 1987] we presented the analysis for comparing the cost of transitive closure.

We believe duplicate elimination is a much more serious problem for complex objects, since efficient comparison of complex objects is expensive. Complex objects are generally defined recursively, with sets inside sets, or sets inside tuples inside sets. Duplicate elimination requires object comparisons. The complex objects are trees, and the cost of traversing them for comparison grows roughly exponentially with their depth. As we see in Figure 1 the number of comparisons for comparing complex objects is an exponentially increasing function of an object's depth.

In general, while executing a program, we will generate sets which could possibly have duplicates. In other words, the storage structures and execution strategies *do not* eliminate duplicates automatically for each set. At the other extreme, we might have objects which are "deep" duplicate free (i.e., all their sub–objects are duplicate free). We might also have sets which are "shallow" duplicate free, (i.e., though the set is duplicate free, it might possibly have sub–objects which are not duplicate free). One naive approach to the problem is to make sure duplicates are eliminated *every time a set is produced.* This solution is rather expensive. For a set with cardinality N, it will require at least O(N) computation (using hashing - O(NlogN) if we sort the set [Friedland and DeWitt 1980]). Interestingly enough in SQL [Date 1987] the default result of queries will contain duplicates and the language provides an explicit operation DISTINCT to eliminate the duplicates.

There are two main reasons for performing duplicate elimination: (1) Semantics and (2) Performance. SQL always maintains the duplicates and lets the user figure out (semantics) when he/she would like to have the duplicates eliminated. However, unlike other models [Dayal et al. 1982, Klausner and Goodman 1985], although SQL is based on relational calculus, it does not provide a semantics of *multisets* (sets with duplicates).

The semantics of sets in our model is "mathematical". Thus to guarantee the correct semantics for our operators we should be aware of the possibility of duplicates and either handle it in the implementation of the operators or perform a duplicate elimination prior to the application of the operators. For some operators the presence of duplicates will not cause any problems and duplicate elimination becomes just a matter of efficiency. Relational algebra operations fall into this category.

In this section we discuss issues relating to the elimination of duplicates in transient sets, and describe an algorithm for duplicate elimination.

3.4.1 Deep and Shallow Duplicate Elimination

There is a distinction between deep duplicate elimination, in which duplicates are eliminated in a set and all its sub–objects recursively, and shallow duplicate elimination, in which duplicates are eliminated only at the top level of a complex set object.

The algorithm that follows makes use of equality testing while eliminating duplicates. Algorithm EQ1 above makes use of duplicate elimination while testing for equality. Since these algorithms are mutually recursive, using EQ1 to test for equality will make all duplicate elimination deep. If we use EQ2 instead, the duplicate elimination performed by the following algorithm will be shallow.

3.4.2 An Algorithm for Duplicate Elimination

Given an algorithm for equality testing, the one for duplicate elimination is simple:

1) Partition the elements of the set into equivalence classes using their hash values (computed for all elements that don't have them).
2) For each equivalence class e:
   a) Pick an element M1 from e. For every other element M2 in e:

      If M2 is value equal to M1, discard M2.
   b) When all other elements in e have been examined, remove M1 from e and put it in the output set.
   c) If elements remain in e, go to 2a. Otherwise go on to the next equivalence class (if any)

4. Inferencing

Having dealt at length with hashing and tagging, we now examine ways to *avoid* duplicate elimination as much as possible. This becomes possible if we can statically infer from the programs the presence or absence of duplicates in sets. There are three mechanisms which enable this static analysis:

4.1 Maintaining Duplicate Freeness

There are some operations whose results will be duplicate free, *if* their arguments are duplicate free. Both *intersection* and *difference* have this property. In fact, with the correct implementation, it is sufficient to have the first argument for *difference* and any one of the arguments for *intersection* be duplicate free. More on this in Section 5.

Also, any operation which selects a subset of the members of a set without operating on them in any other way, preserves duplicate freeness. For example,

filter(fun(x) (x.1 > 12) -> x, S)

will be duplicate free if S is duplicate free.

4.2 Producing Duplicate Free Sets

The **group** operation will always produce a set which is shallow duplicate free. If its argument set is deep duplicate free, it will produce a set which is deep duplicate free. This is because the functional abstraction in group cannot change the set values, but can only affect how they are partitioned.

4.3 Maintaining the Keys

There are two cases where we know sets have keys:

1) In all persistent objects, because of type restrictions.

2) In the result set of the *group* operation.

This last requires some explanation. The group operation partitions a set into equivalence classes based on the result of a user-specified functional abstraction. It produces a set of ordered tuples of the form [<value>, <class set>] where <class set> is a subset of the argument set, and <value> is the result of applying the functional abstraction to any one of those objects. For example, the following expression:

group(fun(x) div(x,5000), {1000,2000,5000,7000,10000,12000})

where div(x,y) indicates the quotient when x is divided by y, will produce the set

{[0,{1000,2000}],[1,{5000,7000}],[2,{10000,12000}]}

which might represent a histogram of salary distributions, for example. The semantics of group make <value> a key of the result set.

Now, given a set of tuples with a key, any function which takes the given set as argument and produces a set of tuples maintaining the key attribute will yield a set with a key. This notion is stronger than duplicate freeness.

For example, consider the expression: filter(fun(x) [x.1, x.3], S). If S is merely duplicate free, we cannot be sure that the result set of this operation is also duplicate free. However, if the first or the third argument is a key, the result will be duplicate free *and* have a key.

We can extend this notion to "composite" keys. If an operation is applied to a cross product of sets with keys, then for the resulting set to have a (composite) key, we must project on each of the keys of the arguments. For example, in

S = filter(fun(x,y,z) e(x,y,z), S1, S2, S3)

e will be applied to each element of S1 x S2 x S3

Assume S1 is of type T1 = [*a11:int*, a12: ...],
S2 is of type T2 = [*a21:int*, a22: ...],
and S3 is of type T3 = [*a31:int*, a32: ...],

and a11, a21, and a31 are respectively keys of S1, S2 and S3. Then S will have a (composite) key if e maintains all these three attributes
(e.g., e(x,y,z) = [b1:x.a11, b2:y.a21, b3:z.a31, ...])

4.4 Inferring Uniqueness and Duplicate Freeness

In this section, we show of how uniqueness and duplicate freeness attributes may be computed statically. These techniques can be used for *filter* and *group*.

There are two, not necessarily exclusive ways that we can gather information about operations statically:

1) Unification [Robinson 1979].

2) Property calculation via attribute grammar techniques [Aho et al. 1986].

In the first approach, we unify an entire expression, or perhaps some part of the expression sub–tree, against an expression known to be duplicate free. An example of such a pattern is: filter(fun(x) p(x) → x, S), where p is any predicate on x. Unification can quickly find common cases based on purely syntactic criteria, but it is in general unable to tell us whether: filter(fun(x) [a1:x.1, a2:x.3], S) has duplicates. To determine this, we need semantic information as well, and for that we can use attribute grammar techniques.

In parsing the operations, assume we associate three attributes with each node of the parse tree:

(i) the type (thus we are also doing type inference.)

(ii) the key (if any) – including composite keys.

(iii) syntactically inferred "duplicate free" flag.

(To show how these (synthesized) attributes can be used, consider a production rule for "filter" of the form filter(fun(x) e, S):

```
FILTER ::= "filter" "(" "fun" "("VAR ")" EXPR1 "," EXPR2")"
```

Then

```
FILTER.type = Set_of (EXPR1.type)
FILTER.key = if (i)   EXPR1.type is tuple
                (ii)  EXPR2.key = Attr ≠ nil
                (iii) Attr is in EXPR1
             then
                      Attr
             else     nil
FILTER.duplicate_flag= if (i)   EXPR2.duplicate_flag
                          (ii)  EXPR1 maintains duplicate freeness
                       then
                                TRUE
```

In this example we were rather vague about the specifics as to how one checks whether, say, Attr is in EXPR1 or how one determines whether an expression maintains duplicate freeness. However, it can easily be seen that one can introduce a number of expression forms to determine these. For example, if the parser is implemented in PROLOG, a predicate which determines one such case is

maintains_duplicate_freeness(EXPR):- EXPR = PRED → X, is_var(X).

where is_var(X) is true iff X is a variable, and PRED -> X represents a predicate abstraction of the form p(x) -> x.

For *group*, the syntax is:

GROUP ::= "group" "(" "fun"("VAR")" EXPR1 "," EXPR2")"

and the semantic rules are:

GROUP.type = Set_of([EXPR1.type, EXPR2.type])
GROUP.key =1
GROUP.duplicate_flag = TRUE

5. Interpreting Operators With Duplicates

In the previous sections we introduced tagging and inferencing techniques for dealing with duplicates. Since transient sets have duplicates, we should be aware of it in the implementation of some of the operations to provide the correct semantics. In fact, we can in some cases postpone the elimination of duplicates to the very last step of generating the answer. Therefore, in this section we concentrate on the implementation of operations in the presence of duplicates.

Union: The simplest implementation of *union(S1, S2)* where S1 and S2 might have duplicates is to maintain the duplicates in S1 and S2 and just "concatenate" their values. Note that eliminating the duplicates prior or after the application of union won't make a difference.

Intersection: Intersection is slightly more interesting. Different implementation strategies will yield different multisets. For example, if we are interested in evaluating the intersection of:

{1,2,2,3} and {2,1,1,3}

(in what follows, we represent multisets in the same way as sets, but with duplicate values) a simple-minded nested loops algorithm would produce the multiset: {1,1,2,2,3}, while one that stopped after it found a match in the inner loop would produce: {1,2,2,3}.

Note, however, that both of these interpretations are "correct" in the sense that if we eliminate the duplicates we get the same result as the intersection of the two sets (with duplicates eliminated).

Difference: Difference requires a bit of care. Given the two sets above, an algorithm which discarded members of the second set as they were matched to members of the first would erroneously produce a result set containing '2' as an element. In general, both intersection and difference, to be implemented efficiently, require something more sophisticated than a simple nested loops algorithm, probably sort/merge or hashing.

Pump: Pump() is an operation which recursively partitions its argument set, terminating when its argument is either empty or singleton. Specifically:

```
pump(f,g,S) =   NULL if S = {}
                f(x) if S = {x}
                g(pump(f,g,A), pump(f,g,B)) where S = A U B and
                A and B are disjoint
```

A slight modification to the f(x) case should make pump() behave appropriately when S = {x,x,...}:

```
pump(f,g,S) =   ...
                f(x) if S = {x}
                f(x) if S = {x,x}
                f(x) if S = {x,x,...}   (* same x repeated *)
```

However, there is a more serious problem. The partitioning of a set S into two sets A and B (to each of which pump() is applied recursively) is non–deterministic (more specifically it is not specified)

Consider the expression:

```
pump(fun(x) 1,  fun(x,y)  x + y,  {a,b,c,c,c,d})
```

which evaluates the cardinality of its set argument. What is its value, presuming f(x) is defined as above? It depends on how the set is partitioned for the recursive invocations of pump(). If the partitioning is {a,b,d} and {c,c,c}, the result will be four. If the partitioning is {a,b,c,d} and {c,c}, the result will be five.

Assuming we want pump() to behave just as it would were duplicates eliminated, *we must ensure that elements with the same value are always in the same partition*, as in the first case above.

Filter: The semantics of filter() is similar to that of the MAP construct in Lisp: an abstraction is applied to every member of a set (or a cross product of set arguments). There is an ambiguity, however: clearly this application is not intended to be performed in any particular order (since sets are not ordered), but does that mean that application is "simultaneous", or "iterative"? For the latter case, is there a deterministic "order" of execution?

If we had a pure functional language, this problem wouldn't arise. The fact is that in abstractions we can update the state of the persistent database. Consider this simple example:

filter(fun(x) <increment P: an element of a persistent set>, S)

If we just iteratively apply the abstraction, the result will differ if we have duplicates in S (for example S = {1, 2} will increment P by 2, whereas if S = {1, 2, 1} the filter will increment it by 3!).

Group: The group() operator produces a set which is free of duplicates. However, given an argument with duplicates, a straightforward implementation could produce a set with sub-objects which are *not* duplicate free. Consider the result of a group() operation on a set with duplicates:

group(fun(x) x, {1,2,2,3,3,4,5})

The result of this operation might be the set:

{(1,{1}), (2,{2,2}), (3,{3,3}), (4,{4}), (5,{5})}

As indicated earlier, not only is this set duplicate free, it is even guaranteed to have a key attribute in its component tuples. Nonetheless, the second element of each tuple is a set which may contain duplicates..

In general, it is sufficient for a set to be shallow duplicate free, as long as care is taken that duplicates are eliminated from its sub-objects if they appear as arguments to duplicate sensitive functions.

6. Conclusion

This paper introduces a number of implementation techniques for structurally object oreineted databases. The emphasis of this paper was the explanation of different execution strategies and equlaity comparison for complex objects in the presence of duplicates.

To complete our work, we need to extend it in two important ways:

(i) evaluation of the strategies to determine those with the highest pay-off/lowest overhead. For example, we need to determine the efficiency of the inferencing techniques. Needless to say, to make these evaluations reasonable, we need to characterize workloads which heavily use complex objects.

(ii) another area which needs further work is the *interaction* of the three strategies with one another. One approach examined here is the possibility of introducing "duplicate free" flags to objects. Another approach being investigated is the introduction of an "eliminate_duplicates" operator, somewhat similar to the SQL approach - assuming the default is sets with duplicates.

Acknowledgement: We would like to thank Haran Boral and Bill Alexander for their input, discussions, and numerous suggestions.

References

[Aho et al. 1986] *Compiler,Principles, Techniques, and Tools,* A. Aho, R. Sethi, and J. Ullman, Addison Wesley, 1986.

[Atkinson et al. 1983] *"An Approach to Persistent Programming"*, M. P. Atkinson, P. J. Bailey, W. P. Cockshott, K. J. Chisholm and R. Morrison, Computer Journal, Vol. 26, November 1983.

[Bancilhon and Khoshafian 1986] *"A Calculus for Complex Objects"*, F. Bancilhon and S. Khoshafian, ACM Int. Symp. on PODS, March 1986.

[Bancilhon et al. 1987] *"FAD, a Simple and Powerful Database Language,"* F. Bancilhon, T. Birggs, S. Khoshafian, and P. Valduriez, proceedings of the 13th International conference on VLDB, Brighton, England, September, 1987.

[Bancilhon and Ramakrishnan 1986] *"An Amateur's Introduction fo Recursive Query Processing Strategies"*, F. Bancilhon and Raghu Ramakrishnan, Proc. 1986 ACM–SIGMOD Conference on Management of Data, May 1986.

[Date 1987] *SQL Standard,* C. J. Date, Addison–Wesley, 1987.

[Dayal et al. 1982] *"An Extended Relational Algebra with Control Over Duplicate Elimination"*, U. Dayal, N. Goodman and R. Katz, Proceedings of PODS, 1982.

[Dittrich 1986] *"Object–Oriented Database Systems: The Notion and the Issues"*, Dittrich K.R., Proceedings of the International Workshop on Object–Oriented Database Systems, Pacific Grove, Ca., September 1986.

[Faloustos and Christodoulakis 1987] *"Description and Performance Analysis of Signature File Methods for Office Filing,"* in ACM Transactions on Office Information Systems, Volume 5, no. 3, July 1987.

[Fishman et al 1987] *"Iris: An Object Oriented Database Management Sytem,"* D. Fishman et al,ACM TOIS, Vol. 5, No. 1, 1987.

[Friedland and DeWitt 1980] *"Duplicate Record Elimination in Large Data Files"*, D. Friedland and D. DeWitt, Technical Report #445, University of Wisconsin, August 1980.

[Hornick and Zdonik 1987] *"A Shared, Segmented Memory System for an Object–Priented database,"* M.F. Hornick and S.B. Zdonik, TOIS, Volume 5, No. 1, January 1987.

[Kim et al 1987] *"Composite Object Support in an Object Oriented database System,"* W. Kim, J. Banerjee, H.T. Chou, J.F.G. Garze, and D. Woelk, Proceedings of OOPSLA 1987.

[Khoshafian and Copeland 1986] *"Object Identity"*, S. Khoshafian and G. Copeland, Proc. of 1st Int. Conf. on OOPSLA, Portland, Oregon, October 1986.

[Khoshafian and Frank 1987] *"Duplicate Elimimination Techniques for Complex Objects,"* S. Khoshafian adn D. Frank, MCC technical Report, 1987.

[Khoshafian et al 1988] *"Parallel Query Processing for Complex Objects,"* S.N. Khoshafian, P. Valduriez, and G.P. Copeland, Proceedings of Fourth Intl. Conference on data Engineering, February 1988.

[Kitsuregawa et al. 1983] *"Application of Hash Data Base Machine and Its Architecture,"* Kitsuregawa et al., New generation Computing, Vol. 1, 1983.

[Klausner and Goodman 1985] *"Multi-relations - Semantics and Languages"*, A. Klausner and N. Goodman, Proc. of the 5th VLDB, Stockholm, 1985.

[Knuth 1973] *The Art of Computer Programming*, Vol. II, Addison-Wesley, 1973.

[Kuper and Vardi 1985] *"On the Expressive Power of The Logical Data Model,"* G. M. Kuper and M. Y. Vardi, Proceedings of SIGMOD 1985.

[Lu and Carey 1985] *"Some Experimental Results on Distributed Join Algorithms in a Local Area Network, "* H. Lu and M. Carey, Proceedings of VLDB 1985.

[Maier et al. 1986] *"Development of an Object-Oriented DBMS"*, Maier D., Stein J., Ottis A., Purdy A., OOPSLA-86, Portland, Oregon, September 1986.

[Maier and Stein 1986] *"Indexing in an Object-Oriented DMBS"*, Maier D., and Stein J., Proceedings of 1986 International Workshop on Object-Oriented Database Systems, Pacific Grove, California, 1986.

[Paul et al 1987] *"Architecture and Implementation of the Darmstadt Database Kernel System,"* H.-B. Paul, H.-J. Schek, M.H. Scholl, G. Weikum, and U. Deppisch, Proceedings of SIGMOD 1987.

[Robinson 1979] *Logic: Form and Function*, J.A. Robinson, North-Holland, 1979.

[Schek and Scholl 1986] *"The relational Model with Relation Valued Attributes,"* H.J. Schek and M.H. Scholl, Information Systems, Volume 11, No. 2, 1986.

[Ullman 1987] *"Database Theory - Past and Future"*, J.D. Ullman, Proceedings of PODS, 1987.

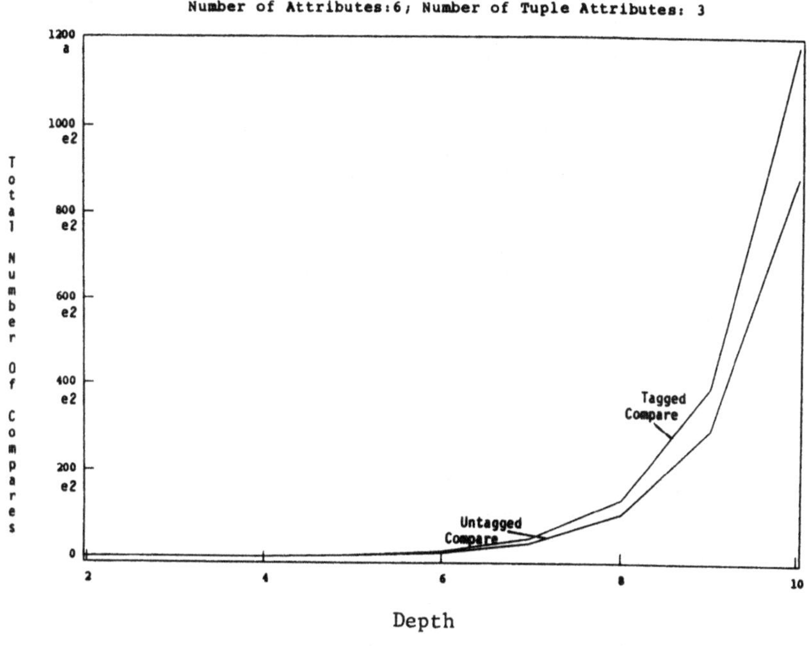

Figure 1

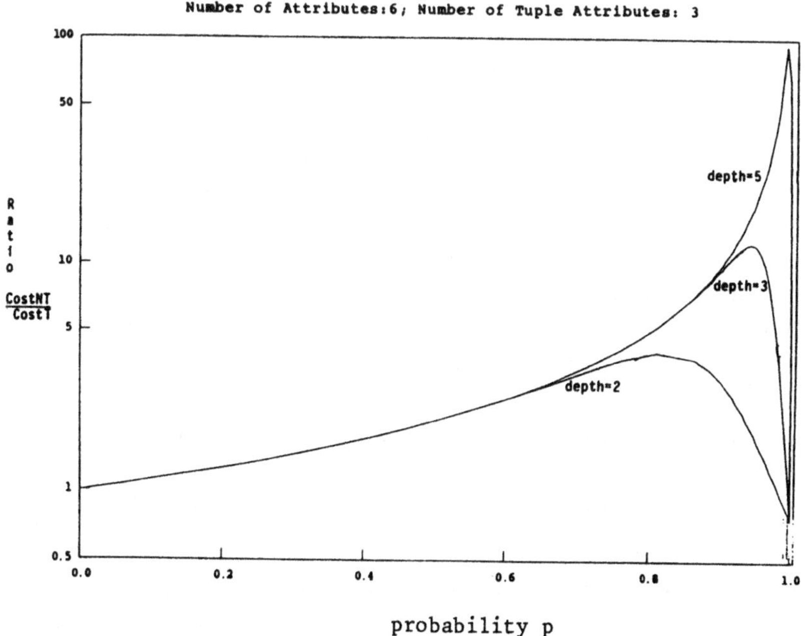

Figure 2

Support for Design Processes in a Structurally Object-Oriented Database System

S. Rehm, T. Raupp, M. Ranft, R. Längle, M. Härtig
W. Gotthard, K. R. Dittrich, K. Abramowicz

Forschungszentrum Informatik,
Haid-und-Neu-Straße 10-14, Germany-7500 Karlsruhe 1

Abstract

Database support for engineering applications requires mechanisms appropriate for managing design processes. The DAMOKLES database system implements a structurally object-oriented data model providing complex objects, general relationships and object versions, and is thus well suited for design environments. In this paper, we describe design transactions in terms of the DAMOKLES data model as a flexible concept to enhance parallelism of design activities and enable controlled exchange of stored design information. Disjoint logical databases assigned to users or user groups are maintained to reflect the hierarchical structure of project organization. During a design transaction, the user may deal with any number of objects by checking them out into her/his private area from any other admissible database. The operational framework of the design transactions supported by the DAMOKLES system is described and a precise definition of the checkout/checkin semantics is given. Subsequently, some implementation aspects are surveyed.

1. Introduction

In the past few years, advanced data base systems have been developed to support a wide variety of engineering applications. Most efforts have been spent on data model issues, and in particular object-oriented data models ([Ditt86], [Banc88]) have attracted great attention. Their importance mainly results from the ability to represent arbitrarily complex objects, without constraints on structure, size and/or behaviour.

The provision of further database features that support integrity, reliability and multiuser cooperation is an absolute necessity to make object-oriented database systems useful for "real" applications. However, the requirements of design applications are different from those of conventional applications, and thus different mechanisms are needed.

In this paper, we focus on requirements derived from the characteristics of engineering design processes and propose concepts for their adequate support by the database system.

The context of our research is the *DAMOKLES* database system prototype whose *Design Object*

Data Model DODM [Ditt87b] is an exponent of a structurally object-oriented data model and which has been developed for supporting software engineering environments. It allows the representation of each object in the design context by exactly one object in terms of the data model. The object may be composed of subobjects that are objects in their own right. Different composite objects may share subobjects. Furthermore, object versions and relationships between objects can be represented explicitly.

1.1 Database Support for Design Processes

A *design process* encompasses a meaningful collection of individual tasks. It starts either from scratch or from predefined designs and proceeds in a goal-oriented sequence ending with the release of a new product. Several members of a project group are typically involved in this process and cooperatively have to manipulate large amounts of data. Requirements of their organizational framework include the following:

- A project may be divided into multiple levels of subprojects which are finally split into tasks. The tasks of a subproject are assigned to individual designers, whereby one designer may be involved in more than one subproject.
- Each task touches a number of design objects. During the (possibly long) duration of a design process the original state of these should be at least readable for other users.
- Parts of the modified design objects need to be made available to other users, even if the design work has not yet finished. Nevertheless, a designer should have the possibility to hide a design object not ready for release.
- A designer may delegate some tasks to another designer for further treatment.

Obviously, this partitioning of design processes suggests an according logical partitioning of the design information managed in an appropriate database system. The distribution of all design data into disjoint private and more or less public logical databases owned by a user or a group enables controlled parallel activities and helps to avoid long-duration inaccessibility of data due to synchronisation. Designers who want to access an object which is not of their own may check it out from the owner's database, which has to be a public one, into their private database. To "checkout" an object means, that the object addressed remains in the public database, whereas an identical copy of it will be brought into the private one. After modifications made in the private database, the updated design will be checked back into the public database. A successful "checkin" operation corresponds to the release of a design object to the next higher level of responsibility and thus has to provide some sort of consistency.

In typical database applications *transactions* are a proper vehicle to preserve consistency. A transaction is a sequence of database operations that transforms a consistent state of a database into another consistent state, without necessarily preserving consistency at all intermediate points. Thus, when a transaction terminates successfully, all its updates are persistent in the database, and when the transaction fails, the effect of its updates must be completely erased from the database. As a consequence, the database system has to prevent concurrently executing transactions from seeing intermediate updates.

When manipulating design objects comprising large amounts of data, transactions become much longer than their counterparts in typical data base applications. It would be unreasonable to force other transactions to wait over this long duration. On the other hand, strict serialization of database accesses is not always required here. Furthermore, in case of a failure a lot of work would have been done for nothing.

The shortcomings of conventional transaction models for design applications gave rise to the development of alternative models. We perceive a ***design transaction*** to comprise a unit of work not limited by the termination of an application program; it encloses an arbitrary series of checkout/checkin operations and maintains the consistency of the databases involved. It enables the designer to manipulate one or more sharable objects in her/his own database without making them completely unaccessable for other designers. However, appropriate synchronisation is provided to coordinate parallel activities. For instance, a designer is prevented from manipulating an object while another designer has checked it out for update. Design transactions are thus the kind of mechanism a database system should provide to support design processes.

1.2 Related Work

Several approaches have been proposed to support design processes in database systems. They agree, at a first glance, in describing the differences between design transactions (or ***conversational transactions*** [Lori83]) and conventional transactions, but they propose different schemes for the underlying partitioning of data and for the various mechanisms for concurrency control and recovery. An exhaustive characterization of design transactions is given in [Katz84] and [Banc85].

[Lori83] and [Katz85] both assume a hierarchical organization providing a collection of private databases subordinated to a public database. [Lori83] decouples conversational transactions, which are used as units of consistency with respect to the public database, from conventional transactions used as the units of recovery with respect to the private databases. The design transactions described in [Katz85] map a consistent version of a design into a new consistent version. In doing so, the old versions persist even after newer versions have been created. Moreover, the system ensures a continuous recovery capability in contrast to [Lorie83] where rollback is performed to the last savepoint taken.

[Klah85] also deals with versions of objects when updating a design. Like [Kim84], he takes into account the teamwork character of design by allowing a designer to check out an object from another designer. [Kim84] introduces the notion of semi-public databases serving as a repository of incomplete design objects which could be checked out further, whereas [Klah85] suggests group and user transactions.

[Banc85], [Kort87] and [Ditt87a] generalize those approaches by permitting a multilevel organization of groups and assigning databases to individual users and groups. Furthermore, [Banc85] and [Kort87] propose different types of transactions. Each project is mapped into a set of cooperating transactions. A cooperating transaction is a hierarchy of client/subcontractor transactions that consists of a set (not a sequence) of short-duration transactions. Further types of transactions above the level of cooperating transactions are also proposed. An associated formal model provides notions for database consistency and for each level of nesting a certain concurrency control mechanism is proposed.

By way of contrast, [Ditt87a] argues not to further enrich already sophisticated concepts like transactions. Instead, two separate but complementary mechanisms are proposed that deal on the one hand with the long-duration aspect of design processes and on the other hand with their specific access control requirements.

1.3 Outline of our Approach

Starting from the above proposals, *DAMOKLES* supports design processes by

- explicitly reflecting a multilevel structure of users and groups within the database system,
- managing multiple databases distributed across a server/workstation architecture which may be "owned" by individual users or groups, and
- providing design transactions which allow to consistently deal with any number of objects checked out from any admissible database.

We claim that our approach simplifies transaction management as it does not require numerous different types of transactions with slightly different semantics. By separating concerns, it should also be easier to understand by users. On the other hand, it is flexible enough to model and support most requirements of typical design processes.

Specific problems arise due to the advanced support of arbitrarily structured objects in the *DAMOKLES* data model. Specifically, object migration between databases (and thus checkin/checkout in design transactions) has to take into account the existence of "overlapping" objects and versions and provide meaningful semantics for those cases (which are not dealt with in other approaches).

In the next chapter, we give a brief overview of the *DAMOKLES* data model underlying our approach. The remainder of the paper focuses on mechanisms for group management and for design transactions, including a precise definition of the set of database instances affected by a checkout or checkin operation. Finally, some implementation details are given.

2. The DAMOKLES design object data model

This chapter outlines the main features of the *DAMOKLES design object data model (DODM)* as far as it is necessary to understand our design transaction concept to be discussed later. For a more detailed description of *DODM*, the reader is referred to [Ditt87b] or [DAMO86].

As mentioned above, the main objective of the design of *DODM* was to make *DAMOKLES structurally object-oriented* [Ditt86]. The DBMS interface thus provides for modeling concepts allowing any object of the universe of discourse to be uniformly and naturally represented by one database object – independent of its internal structure. We have chosen the now classical *Entity-Relationship* approach [Chen76] as the basis of *DODM* and have enriched its concepts essentially by *structured objects* and *object versions*.

Objects represent self-contained units of the universe of discourse. They are described by their properties. Objects with common properties are classified into **object types**. We distinguish two kinds of object properties: *Descriptive properties* are as usual represented by attributes assigning each object elements of some *value sets*. Besides the usual simple value sets, *DAMOKLES* provides for type constructors similar to the typing facilities of popular programming languages to build user-defined composed value sets. Additionally, *DAMOKLES* supports a special value set *LONG_FIELD* for unstructured information of arbitrary length whose internal structure remains unknown to the DBMS. *Structural properties* describe the composition of an object of subobjects and, as will be seen later, subrelationships. Since the *component-of* relationship applies recursively, i.e. subobjects may be structured themselves, object hierarchies may result. *DAMOKLES* makes no restrictions with regard to the composition of object hierarchies:

- objects (and also relationships) may be components of more than one major object, thus allowing the construction of *overlapping* object hierarchies,
- a structured object may have (direct or indirect) component objects of the same type, thus allowing the modeling of *recursive* object structures.

Objects are identified by system-generated unique surrogate keys [Hall76] whose existence is strictly limited to the lifetime of the appropriate instance.

Relationships are N-ary ($N \geq 1$) associations of objects. Relationships of the same kind are classified into **relationship types**. Like objects, relationships may have attributes, may be components of structured objects and are identified by surrogate keys. Objects participate in relationships in *roles*. As usual, the cardinality of relationships in which an object participates in a certain role may be restricted in the schema definition to at least zero or one and at most one or any. Relationships may be established between arbitrary levels of object hierarchies.

Versions represent multiple instances of the (semantically) same object. In our data model, versions generally behave like ordinary objects (i.e. they may have descriptive and structural properties, may participate in relationships and are also identified by surrogate keys). However, versions are always associated with objects. More precisely, a version is always related to exactly one object, called its *generic object*. Consequently, all versions of a certain object have the same kind of structure and attributes. On the type level, each object type may be declared *versioned* by specifying the type of versions within the object type declaration. Among the versions of a generic object, an implicit predecessor-successor relationship is maintained, which may optionally be defined as linear, treelike or acyclic. The generic object may be interpreted as an instantiation of the common properties of all its associated versions.

To illustrate these modeling concepts, let us consider a fairly simplified example from the area of software engineering, namely a module library. The corresponding *DODM* schema is shown in figure 2-1. A module library (object type **LIBRARY**) may contain a number of modules (object type **MODULE**). Each of these modules in a library may exist in several versions representing revisions, alternatives or whatever similar to them of the (semantically) same implementation (generic object of type **MODULE**). Due to the fact that generic objects only represent the factorization of the common properties of the associated versions, we have modeled the module structure as a refinement of the version type **MODULE.VERSION**, whereas properties like e.g. module name, description of module behaviour etc. could have been represented as attributes of type **MODULE**. (For simplicity reasons we have ommitted the attributes in the diagram.) Each module version consists of (exactly) one interface (type **INTERFACE**) and one implementation (type **BODY**), where the "exactly one" restriction can be formulated in DODM as a model inherent consistency constraint. (Note that this modeling supposes that an interface may vary for different module versions. Otherwise, we could have modeled type **INTERFACE** as a component type of the generic type **MODULE**.) The interface description is again refined by component types **P_DECL**, **T_DECL**, etc. expressing that an interface consists of a set of procedure declarations, type declarations and the like. A module implementation may consist of a number of procedure implementations (object type **P_IMPL**) and a set of global type-, constant- and variable declarations. For simplicity reasons, we have not further refined the structure of a procedure implementation. Depending on the needs of the application, the procedure code may be represented either as a long field attribute or by introducing corresponding component types for **P_IMPL**. Additionally, we assume that each implementation has to include the interfaces of other modules that are to be used. This fact is represented by relationships of type **IN-**

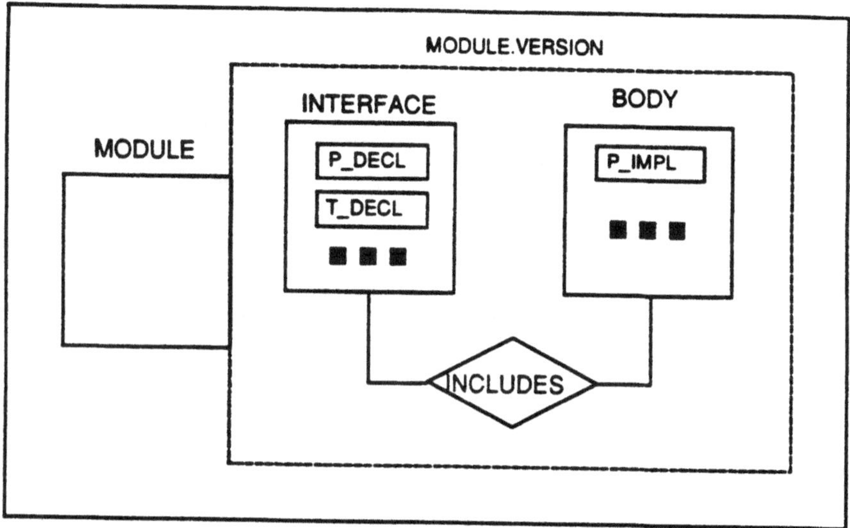

Fig. 2-1: Sample DODM schema

CLUDES, which is also modeled as a component type of **MODULE.VERSION**.

Figure 2-2 presents an excerpt of a sample database adhering to the schema of figure 2-1. Versions are represented by dashed boxes, the predecessor-successor relationships by arrows. Note that in our example the interface **i1**, and thus all its components too, are shared by both versions (**m1.v1** and **m1.v2**) of module **m1** (in the diagram, we have replicated **i1** only for reasons of clarity). Therefore, **m1.v1** and **m1.v2** form overlapping object hierarchies which is useful if we wish to automatically propagate changes of an interface to all versions referring to it.

The *DAMOKLES data manipulation language* (DML) is essentially a procedural "one-instance-at-a-time" interface in our current prototype. It comprises a set of generic operations to store, modify and retrieve data stored in *DAMOKLES* databases. The application accesses the data by ***navigating*** from object to object via the relationships installed between the objects. Not surprisingly, *DAMOKLES* furthermore provides for operations to manipulate entire object hierarchies rather than only the descriptive part of an object. A set-oriented descriptive DML is currently under development.

With respect to data model inherent consistency, *DODM* provides:

- uniqueness of user-defined keys (beyond the system generated surrogates that are per se unique),
- referential integrity for relationships [Date86],
- role cardinalities for both general and 'is component of' relationships.

For further application-specific explicit consistency control, a special event/trigger mechanism like the one proposed in [Kotz88] is included in the system.

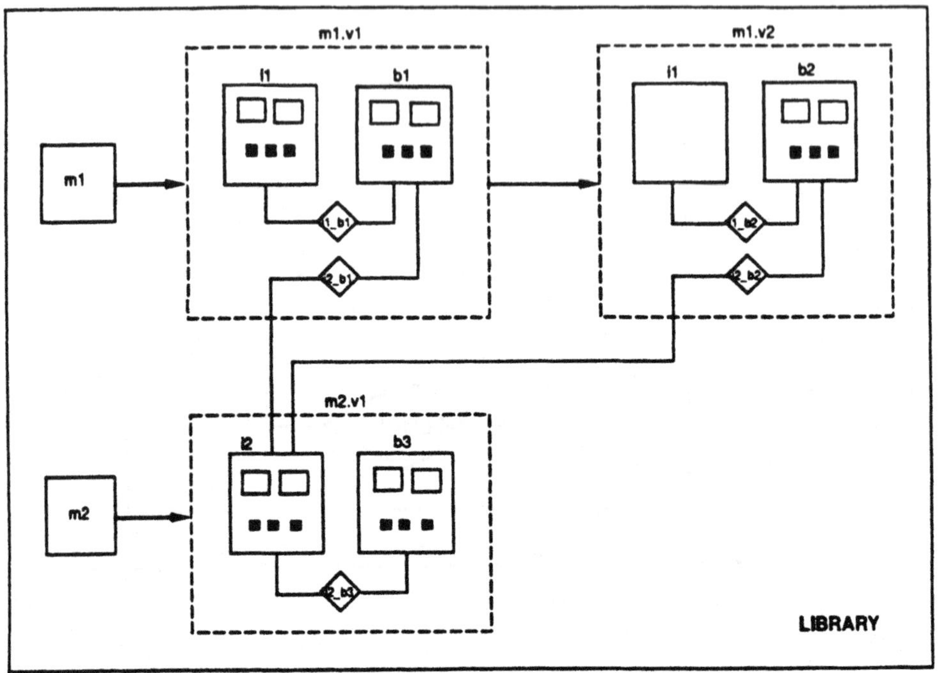

Fig. 2-2: Sample database adhering to the schema of fig. 2-1

3. Supporting controlled cooperation in a multiple database environment

As claimed in chapter 1, support for the controlled cooperation between the individual members of a design project should be offered by powerful design database systems. Therefore, we provide for a framework based on multiple databases and access control closely following the approach proposed in [Ditt87a]. The general idea is to make the desired communication structures known to the system, thus enforcing that data are only accessible along predefined communication paths.

DAMOKLES is capable to deal with multiple databases allowing for a logical partitioning of the data according to the following rules:

- An (atomic or structured) object or relationship is located within exactly one database, i.e. a structured object can not be distributed across different databases.
- A relationship may relate objects from different databases – though the relationship instance itself can obviously exist only within exactly one database.
- Versions may only exist within the database where the associated generic object is located, i.e. the version graph of a generic object is completely stored within one database.

DAMOKLES databases may either exclusively be assigned to an individual user (***private*** databases) or to a defined group of users (***public*** databases). Consequently, besides the common notion of ***user***, *DAMOKLES* is in addition given knowledge about the existence and composition of ***user groups***. Every user group may consist of any number of group members that are either individual users or again other user groups. Also, a user may be a member of more than one user group. Hence, arbitrary hierarchical (not necessarily tree-like) group structures may be installed, reflecting the underlying project organization structure.

An individual user or user group may be the *owner* of one or more *DAMOKLES* databases. For the exchange of data between different databases, the *DAMOKLES* DML provides operations allowing to copy, transfer and, as will be seen later in more detail, to checkout/checkin objects from one database to another. The access and exchange of database objects is controlled by the following ***access rules***:

- every user (or the group administrator, in case of a group) has unrestricted write access to the own databases (in case of a user group, this right is associated with a special role, the ***group administrator***, that need not necessarily be a member of that group),
- direct members of a user group are allowed to ***checkout*** (and in turn to ***checkin***) objects from group databases into their own databases within a design transaction (the semantics of these operations will be precisely defined in the next chapter),
- objects may be ***transferred*** (i.e. removed from the home database and identically reproduced in the target database) between direct members of the same group or from a direct member to its group and vice versa,
- every user has read access to group databases in which she/he is a direct or indirect member. Of course, read access includes the right to copy objects from group databases into member databases.

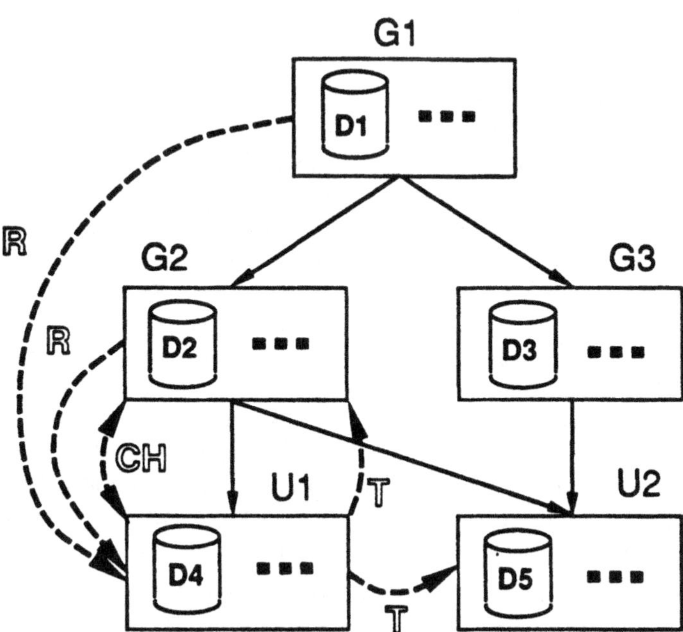

Fig.3-1: User/user group hierarchy with according access rights

Figure 3-1 shows a user/user group hierarchy and the access rights granted to the user **U1**. She/he has write access to the own databases (**D4,...**), may transfer objects from own databases to the databases of group **G2** and of user **U2**, may checkout objects from the databases of group **G2**, where she/he is a direct member, into the private databases (and in turn checkin in the opposite direction) and finally has read access to the databases of groups **G2** and **G1**. Of course, the possession of a certain access right is not necessarily sufficient to access an object; locks and further individual access control regulations must also be considered.

In order to support distributed and parallel design activities as far as possible, *DAMOKLES* has been designed to run in a server/workstation hardware architecture. Public databases, i.e. databases that are owned by user groups, are intended to be located at the server, whereas private databases of individual users may be distributed among the affiliated workstations (including the server itself).

4. DAMOKLES Design Transactions

After introducing the *DAMOKLES* framework for supporting controlled cooperation in a multiple database environment, we are now in a position to precisely define what we call a **DAMOKLES design transaction** (DDT). In section 4.1, we briefly introduce the operational framework of DDT's and discuss its fundamental properties with regard to the requirements outlined in chapter 1. Thereafter, we formally define the semantics of checkout operations in terms of structured *DAMOKLES* objects. Finally, we define certain lock granularities allowing meaningful synchronization between concurrent design transactions.

4.1 Operational framework for DDT's

In most approaches known to us ([Lori83], [Katz84], [Kim84]) design transactions are bracketed by a checkout and a corresponding checkin operation that refer to exactly one design object. In our opinion, this approach is too restrictive. The designer often will not and even cannot decide at the beginning of a design process which parts of the design data will be affected by her/his work. Depending on the progress of the design activities, it may become necessary to access further design objects. Suppose, for instance, the correction of a software module; usually, the programmer will first correct the erroneous parts of the module and only then, if necessary, will update the corresponding documentation. If both, the module implementation and the documentation are modeled as different design objects, the design process "error correction" will involve a sequence of two (independent) checkout/checkin operations for these design objects. This has the advantage that the module can be released before the documentation has been updated, and thus it can be used at the earliest possible time. On the other hand, logical database design (i.e. collecting two objects into a new one or leaving them apart) should not be influenced by transaction processing requirements.

In order to enable the designer to check out several design objects from public databases into the private area (and check them in later on) at any point in time during the design process, *DAMOKLES* provides special operations **begin_lta** and **end_lta** marking the logical begin and end of a DDT. The duration of a DDT is completely independent from operating system processes, and thus a DDT may last over days or even weeks. Within a DDT, the user may check out any number of design objects from (possibly more than one) public databases into one of her/his private databases, provided she/he is a direct member of the corresponding user group. Consequently, a DDT can always be associated with the database where the design work is to be performed. This target database of a DDT is called the ***design database*** of the transaction.

A **checkout** operation may be applied to every *DAMOKLES* object or version. Its effect is to identically replicate an object from a public database in the specified design database and to set locks on that object in the original database. Due to the fact that DDT's are independent from operating system processes, locks have to survive the application process in which the checkout operation has been performed.

After work on a design object has reached a desired state in the design database, the object may be checked back into the original database by performing a corresponding **checkin** operation. At checkintime, all updates that have been performed on the object in the design database are propagated to the original database and the object is removed from the design database. Additionally, the locks held by the transaction on that object in the original database are released, thus allowing access to the object before the transaction has actually finished.

Besides these operations reflecting the "normal" evolution of the design process, *DAMOKLES* provides further operations enabling the user to react on unexpected situations in her/his design activities. If the work on an object in the design database has reached a state that suggests that further work would not be very fruitful, the designer may terminate his work on that object applying an explicit **uncheckout** operation to it. The effect of this operation is to remove the (in the meantime possibly modified) object from the design database and to release all locks held on that object in the original database. Thus, the uncheckout operation allows to recover the object's state before it had been checked out. Beyond that, the designer can **abort** a DDT. In contrast to the usual semantics of aborting a transaction, this operation does not recover the state before the beginning of the DDT – as mentioned in chapter 1 this would neither be meaningful by the designer's viewpoint nor practicable by the systems's viewpoint. Instead, aborting a DDT only causes uncheckout operations to be performed on all objects that are still checked out by the transaction. However, this operation does not undo updates on objects that already have been propagated to the public database(s) by corresponding checkin operations. Therefore, a DDT is not a unit of recovery. For recovery, classical synchronization and (model inherent) consistency control, *DAMOKLES* provides for a fairly conventional transaction mechanism that is largely orthogonal to DDTs. Although the existing interferences between these two distinct transaction mechanisms is an interesting problem in itself, its discussion is beyond the scope of this paper.

In summary, a DDT can be characterized as a series of checkout/checkin operations, allowing the designer to locally operate on identical copies of design objects in her/his private database, thereby preventing other users from undesired access to these objects during her/his design activities. Design processes may thus be reflected by one or more DDTs in *DAMOKLES*. In the next sections, we precisely define the semantics of a checkout operation by formally describing the set of instances ((sub-)objects, versions and relationships) that are affected by applying a checkout operation to a given structured *DAMOKLES* object and define appropriate lock granularities in order to restrict access to checked out objects in the original database in an accurate way.

4.2 Semantics of Checkout

Let us have a closer look at the checkout operation. Assume that a designer wants to checkout an object into her/his private database to manipulate it. Of course she/he is interested in all properties of the object, the descriptive and the structural ones. Consequently, in case of a structured object to be checked out, all of its components should show up in the design database. In addition, if there are versions associated with the object, they should be available too. Thus, the object brought into the design database can be regarded as a set of instances, involving all objects or relationships within reach of the given object, i. e. its subobjects and versions in an arbitrary combination. We want to define this set precisely in the following. For the discussion of this chapter, if we talk of an object we understand its descriptive part only and refer to its versions or components explicitly if needed.

With O the set of all objects belonging to the database at a given time, $V \subseteq O$ the set of all versions in the database, and R the set of relationship instances in the database, we introduce (mathematical) relations to formulate details about

- the structural properties of objects (Sub) and
- the associations of generic objects and versions (Vers).

For each relation r we use the notion $r(x_1,...,x_n)$ to express $(x_1,...,x_n) \in r$.

Sub and Vers are defined as follows:

- $Sub \subseteq O \times (O \cup R)$ and

  $Sub(x,y) \Leftrightarrow$ the instance y is a *direct component* of object x

- $Vers \subseteq O \times V$ und

  $Vers(x,y) \Leftrightarrow$ object y is *version* of object x

Sub^+ is the transitive closure of Sub and describes which objects y are direct or indirect components and $(Sub \cup Vers)^+$ includes versions as well.

The *extent* relation Ext is defined as:

$Ext \subseteq O \times (O \cup R)$ and

$Ext := (Sub \cup Vers)^+$

Thus Ext(x,y) expresses that instance y is *within reach* of an object x. Now the set of instances Ext_x affected by a checkout operation on object x comprises x itself and all instances part of the original database within reach of x. Obviously

$$Ext_x = \{x\} \cup \pi_2 \, \sigma_{1=x} \, Ext$$

with π a projection, σ a selection. The indices denote the columns of the relation.

A checkout operation on an object x causes first of all the determination of Ext_x. Thereafter the section of the original database which covers Ext_x will be replicated in the specified design database with appropriate locking in the original database.

A special treatment is advisable if objects affected by the checkout operation are also within reach of other objects that are not affected at all, so-called *foreign* objects. This situation occurs in two cases, namely

Case 1: $\exists\, z \in Ext_x, \exists\, y \notin Ext_x : Vers(y,z)$

Case 2: $\exists\, z \in Ext_x \setminus \{x\}, \exists\, y \notin Ext_x : Sub(y,z)$

In the first case, versions are affected but not the according generic objects. The second situation arises in case of shared objects where the components of a foreign object may be affected. We handle these cases as follows:

4.2.1 Checkout of Versions

In *DODM*, versions cannot exist without their generic objects. Thus, if a version is part of the extent of an object to be checked out, it must be guaranteed that the generic object is available in the design database, too, even if it is not part of the extent. However, we protect such a generic object from being modified by the designer because there may exist further versions of it in the original database not involved in the design process. Accordingly, it need not be physically brought into the design database at all; but it has to be appropriately locked in the original database. Nevertheless, the designer should be able to navigate to it starting from a version available in the design database.

4.2.2 Checkout of Shared Objects

As mentioned above, *DODM* allows the construction of overlapping objects. Two objects x and y *overlap each other*, if and only if

$$x \notin Ext_y \wedge y \notin Ext_x \wedge \exists\, z \in (Ext_x \cap Ext_y) : Sub^+(x,z) \wedge Sub^+(y,z)$$

Therefore, the situation of case 2 arises if two objects x and y overlap each other or if a generic object exists within reach of x possessing a version that is component of a foreign object y.

There are two possibilities how a designer might want such a situation to be handled. She/he may want to checkout the object completely and thereby cause the locking of parts of a foreign object in the original database and probably the modification of it during a following checkin operation. Otherwise, she/he might want to do it without the instances $Ext'_x \subseteq Ext_x$, that are within reach of a foreign object.

$$Ext'_x = \{\ z \in Ext_x \setminus \{x\} \mid \exists\, y \notin Ext_x : Sub(y,z)\ \}$$

Together with Ext'_x , all instances recursively within reach from there are treated in the same way. We call this set the *cut* of x.

$$Cut_x = \bigcup_{z \in Ext'_x} Ext_z$$

Indeed, the instances of $Cut_x \subseteq Ext_x$ will be brought into the design database, too, but the designer is only allowed to read them, not to modify them. They will be locked appropriately in the original database. The designer selects one of the two possible treatments by a parameter of the checkout operation.

Note that the semantics for checkin, copying and transferring objects have to be defined in a similar way.

4.3 Synchronization of Parallel Work

The proposed checkout/checkin mechanism aims at enhancing the parallelism of activities. Nevertheless, some kind of synchronization is necessary by retaining a checked out object in the original database during a DDT. Thus, objects have to be locked in the original database as long as they are checked out. Consequently, all instances affected by a checkout operation performed on x, i. e. Ext_x, have to be locked.

Database operations are either reading (R) or writing (W). Writing operations affect the descriptive or structural properties of the instance. Assume that the designer wants to manipulate an instance in the design database and propagate these manipulations to the original database later. Of course, nobody should be allowed to write this instance in the original database or concurrently check it out for writing, too, until the checkin operation has been successfully terminated. Reading it in parallel may be admissable in some cases, but not in others. Furthermore, consider that a checked out object is participating in a certain relationship not affected itself by the checkout operation. To remove this relationship or to change the role in the original database is not a writing operation on the object itself, but on its *context*. Operations changing the context of an object (C) should be forbidden, too, since maintaining consistency of the original database requires a fixed context for an object to be manipulated. Summarizing, a designer who wants to checkout an object, beyond specifying whether she/he wants to read or write this object, must also indicate the mode of protection she/he wants to have in the original database during the checkout period: P_W if it should not be concurrently written, P_{W+C} if also the context should remain unchanged, and P_{R+W+C} if it is even required to prohibit parallel reads; *NP* indicates that no protection is needed at all. The checkout operator includes a parameter where the desired combination of protection mode u and access mode v has to be

$$u \in \{ NP, P_W, P_{W+C}, P_{R+W+C} \}, \; v \in \{ R, W \}$$

lock	original database	design database
(NP,R)	R,W,C	R
(P_W,R)	R,C	R
(P_{W+C},R)	R	R
(P_{W+C},W)	R	R,W
(P_{R+W+C},W)	-	R,W

specified. The matrix above shows the meaningful lock modes (combination of protection mode u and access mode v) and the classes of operations permitted in the original and the design database.

A checkout operation itself is regarded either as a reading operation or a writing operation, depending on the kind of work the designer wants to do in the design database. Before a checkout operation can be performed on an instance already checked out into another database ("multiple checkout"), the compatibility of the requested lock with the existing one has to be checked. If they are not compatible the second checkout operation will be rejected. The matrix below shows the compatibility of two locks where the left column indicates the lock already held on an instance, the top row the lock now requested; $+^*$ means intensification of locks. "Serial checkout" across multiple levels of databases is permitted, but only if access and protection mode do not increase.

	(NP,R)	(P_W,R)	(P_{W+C},R)	(P_{W+C},W)	(P_{R+W+C},W)
(NP,R)	+	+*	+*	+*	-
(P_W,R)	+	+	+*	-	-
(P_{W+C},R)	+	+	+	-	-
(P_{W+C},W)	+	-	-	-	-
(P_{R+W+C},W)	-	-	-	-	-

4.4 Example

We refer to the example introduced in chapter 2 to demonstrate the use of design transactions. Bodies b1 and b2 represent two alternative realizations of the same interface i1. Thus in terms of the data model module m1.v1 and m1.v2 share the subobject i1. Procedures p1 and p2 are subobjects of b1, whereas q1, q2 and q3 are subobjects of b2. The subobjects of i1 are denoted with d1 and d2.

Assume that a designer wants to optimize the body b2 by making procedure q3 faster without generating a further version of the module m1. Before we describe a suitable sequence of operations, we describe the computation of *extent* and *cut* with some hypothetical checkouts. A checkout operation performed on object x would lead to the following:

x = q3: Ext_{q3} = { q3 }

x = b2: Ext_{b2} = { b2, q1, q2, q3 }

x = m1.v2: $Ext_{m1.v2}$ = { m1.v2, i1, d1, d2, b2, i1_b2, i2_b2, q1, q2, q3 },

$Cut_{m1.v2}$ = { i1, d1, d2 }

The elements of Ext_x would be replicated in the designer's database, whereas depending on the selected mode, the elements of Cut_x would be prevented from being changed.

To achieve the desired situation, the designer starts a DDT specifying her/his private database as the design database. Since the designer intends not to change interface i1 but to read it for getting type informations, she/he checks out m1.v2 in mode (P_{W+C}, W) and with cut protection. Before modifying q3, the designer also wants to read interface information from i2 and therefore performs a checkout operation on this object, too. Checking out an object for read only instead of reading it directly in the public database, may be useful for the following reason: If the public database is located at the remote server, repeated access to the object is more efficient at the local workstation.

The following sequence of operations shows a possible design process:

1. **begin** DDT "t" in design database "db"

2. **checkout** object m1.v2 from the public database into "db" with lock mode (P_{W+C}, W) and only read access to elements of $Cut_{m1.v2}$

3. **checkout** object i2 with lock mode (P_{W+C}, R)

4. read i1, i2 and modify q3 in "db"

5. **checkin** object m1.v2 from "db" back into the public database
6. **checkin** object i2 from "db" back into the public database
7. **end** DDT "t"

5. Implementation aspects

This chapter gives a brief overview about the realization of the aforementioned DDT concept within the current prototype implementation of the *DAMOKLES* system.

The entire task of DDT management is split into four subtasks that are performed by corresponding system components:

The **design transaction manager (DTM)** records all necessary information about the currently active DDTs. For each DDT, this includes the transaction name, the identification of the user or user group that has started the transaction, the design database where the design activities are to be performed, and the list of objects (referred to by surrogates) that have been checked out (but not yet checked in) within the transaction. Since a DDT is associated with exactly one design database, the information about a DDT can be stored locally in the corresponding design database.

In order to be able to perform a checkout or checkin operation on a given (possibly structured) object, the affected data (i.e. the instances belonging to the extent of the referred object) must be extracted from the local database and transformed to a "compact" representation before sending them out to the target database that may be located on a foreign site of the network. This rather complex task – computing the extent of the requested object, collecting the corresponding data records and building up a buffer containing the linearized representation of the object structure – is done by a special system component, called the **object manager (OM)**. The OM takes advantage of the *DAMOKLES* storage structures that are especially tailored to an efficient access to entire structured objects. Efficient access is achieved by clustering the (direct and indirect) components of a structured object on secondary storage. Note, however, that an optimal clustering can not be achieved in all cases, because *DODM* allows for overlapping object structures. Apart from these clustering conflicts, the set of data records representing the extent even of a large structured object can be extracted from a database by a few page reads only. After an object has been sent to the site of the target database (in case of a checkout operation the design database, in case of a checkin operation the original database), OM has to interpret the linearized object representation: in case of a checkout operation, it has to insert a replication of the object in the design database; in case of a checkin operation, it has to replace the old state of the object in the original database by the new state as received in the object buffer from the design database.

After the OM has extracted an object from a database and built up the buffer with the linearized object representation, the **communication manager (CO)** is responsible for sending the buffer to the site of the requested target database. This is done by formatting a corresponding message on the local computer and sending it to the CO component of the target computer. Over there, the message is decoded and the received object representation is passed to the OM for further processing. However, in our current implementation the communication between server and workstations is somewhat restricted: objects can only be checked out from or checked back into server databases, but not in the opposite direction. This restriction comes due to the fact that in our current implementation the *DAMOKLES* software has to be linked to the application program and hence only single user operation is possible. It will be skipped in ongoing *DAMOKLES* versions when multi-tasking capabilities are provided.

As mentioned above, the system has to maintain locks on checked out objects in order to synchronize access to the objects. Due to the fact that *DODM* instances can not be uniquely related to exactly one root object (as for example in strictly hierarchical data models) and components of a structured object may be accessed independently, locks must explicitly be recorded for each instance being affected by a checkout operation. Therefore, each database is assigned a special lock table containing a correspopding lock entry for each instance that is currently checked out. A lock entry contains information about the lock mode, the transaction that holds the lock and the database where the instance had been checked out. If an object or relationship is to be accessed, the **lock manager (LM)** looks up the lock table in the database concerned and checks possibly existing locks against the required operation. Additionally, if an object is to be checked out more than once, the required locks must be checked against existing locks according to the compatibility matrix defined in chapter 4. Note, that the lock table must be permanent because DDTs, and thus locks too, have to survive application processes. To guarantee fast access to the lock table, we have implemented it as a hash table using the extendible hashing scheme of [Fagi87].

Global information about users, user groups, databases and existing relationships between these are recorded in the system catalogue that is implemented as an ordinary *DAMOKLES* database.

6. Summary

In this paper we have described the *DAMOKLES* approach to support cooperating design processes in a structurally object-oriented database system. The DDT mechanism presented allows for the controlled cooperation between the individual users of one or more design projects in a multiple database environment. As opposed to other approaches, we avoided different types of transactions, thus simplifying transaction management and (hopefully) increasing user acceptance. Though specific problems arise due to the semantic expressiveness of *DODM* – it allows for the construction of recursive and overlapping object structures and the derivation of object versions –, DDTs are an adequate means to model and support most typical design processes.

The DDT concept as presented in this paper has been fully implemented in the *DAMOKLES* prototype 2.0. This prototype, and especially the DDT concept, is currently being used by cooperating software companies that try to implement software tools based on the *DAMOKLES* system. We thus hope to get "real-life" experiences as to how adequate our concepts are in the near future.

7. Literaturverzeichnis

[Banc85] Bancilhon F., Kim W., Korth H.F.:
A Model of CAD Transactions.
Proc. of the VLDB Conference, 1985, pp. 25-33.

[Banc88] Bancilhon F.:
Object-Oriented Database Systems.
Proc. of the Symposium on Principles of Database Systems, March 1988

[Chen76] Chen P. S.:
The Entity-Relationship Model - Toward a Unified View of Data.
ACM Transactions on Database Systems, Vol. 1, No. 1, March 1976, pp. 9-36.

[Date86] Date C.J.:
An Introduction to Database Systems.
Volume 1, Fourth Edition, Addison-Wesley Systems Programming Series, 1986

[DAMO86] Gotthard W. et al.:
DAMOKLES : Database Management System for Design Applications.
Reference Manual, Forschungszentrum Informatik, Karlsruhe, March 1988.

[DeWi84] DeWitt D. J. et al.:
Implementation Techniques for Main Memory Database Systems.
Proc. ACM SIGMOD International Conference on the Management of Data, 1984, pp. 1-8.

[Ditt86] Dittrich K. R.:
Object-Oriented Database Systems: The Notions and the Issues.
Proc. ACM/IEEE International Workshop on Object-oriented Database Systems, 1986, pp. 2-4.

[Ditt87a] Dittrich K. R.:
Controlled Cooperation in Engineering Database Systems.
Proc. of the Conference on Data Engineering, February 1987, pp. 510-515.

[Ditt87b] Dittrich K. R., Gotthard W., Lockemann P.: DAMOKLES - The Database System for the UNIBASE Software Engineering Environment.
Database Engineering, March 1987, pp. 37-47.

[Fagi79] Fagin R., Nievergelt J., Pippenger N., Strong H. R.:
Extendible Hashing - A Fast Access Method for Dynamic Files.
ACM Transactions on Database Systems, Vol 4, No. 3, September 1979, pp. 315-344.

[Hall76] Hall P., Owlett J., Todd S.:
Relations and Entities.
In: Nijssen G.M. (ed.): Modeling in Database Management Systems, North Holland, 1976, pp.201-220.

[Katz85] Katz R. H.:
Information Management for Engineering Design.
Springer Verlag, 1985.

[Katz84] Katz R. H., Weiss S.:
Design Transaction Management.
Proc. of the 21st Design Automation Conference, November 1984, pp. 692-693.

[Kim84] Kim W., Lorie R., McNabb D., Plouffe W.:
A Transaction Mechanism for Engineering Design Databases.
Proc. of the VLDB Conference, August 1984, pp. 355-362.

[Klah85] Klahold P., Schlageter R., Unland R., Wilkes W.:
A Transaction Model Supporting Complex Applications in Integrated Information Systems.
Proc. of the ACM SIGMOD Conference on Management of Data, 1985,
pp. 388-401.

[Kort87] Korth H. F., Kim W., Bancilhon F.:
On Long-Duration CAD Transactions.
Information Science, 1987.

[Kotz88] Kotz A. M., Dittrich K.R., Mülle J.A.:
Supporting Semantic Rules by a Generalized Event/Trigger Mechanism.
Proc. of the International Conference on Extending Database Technology, March 1988,
pp. 76-91.

[Lori83] Lorie R., Plouffe W.:
Complex Objects and Their Use in Design Transactions.
Proc. Engineering Design Applications, Database Week 1983, pp. 115-121.

Object Orientation within the PRIMA-NDBS

C.Hübel, B.Mitschang
University Kaiserslautern
P.O. Box 3049
6750 Kaiserslautern
West-Germany

1. Overview

In the following we wish to highlight the design and implementation concepts of a non-standard database system (NDBS) called PRIMA and its provision for object orientation.

Non-standard database applications such as CAD/CAM, VLSI design, and knowledge-based systems require adequate modeling facilities for their application objects for various reasons [Hä88b]. Data models dedicated to supporting such applications embody some degree of object orientation to the application objects [DD86]. In this context, the notion of complex object has emerged to indicate that such an object holds an internal structure and that access to the entire object as well as to its components (which may again be of a complex type) is provided by means of generic operators - in this sense we speak of *structural object orientation.* To enhance integrity control and semantic as well as operational expressiveness, more object properties (beyond the above introduced structural relationships) have to be specified and preserved - this extended notion of object orientation is also referred to as *behavioral object orientation.* By this means appropriate forms of data abstraction and operational support are provided, thus relieving the application from the burden of

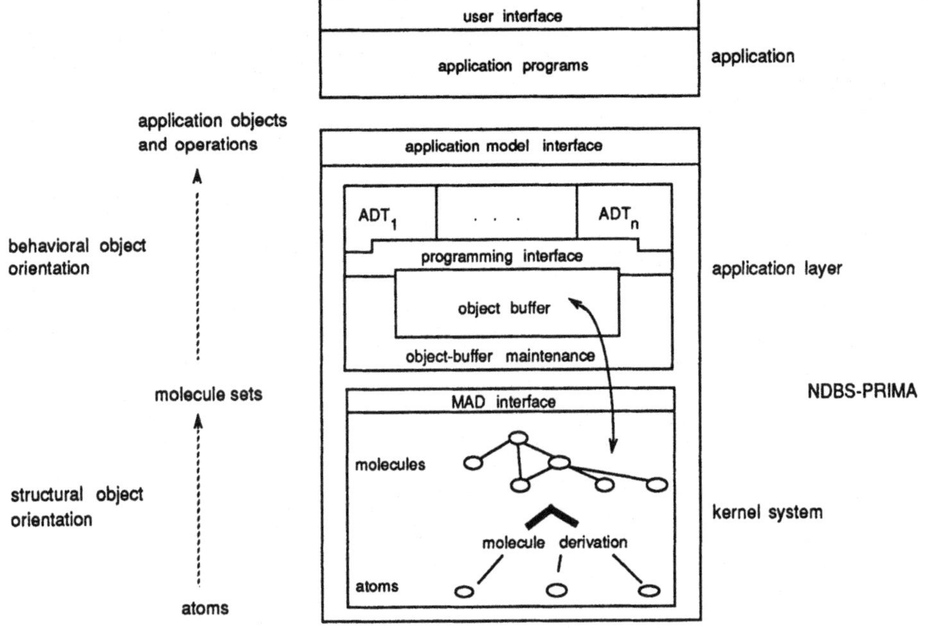

Fig.1: The PRIMA architecture and its provision of object orientation

maintaining and manipulating intricate object representations as well as checking complex integrity constraints.

The Kernel Architecture

The PRIMA-NDBS is a database management system tailored to the support of non-standard applications. As a key idea, its underlying architecture is divided into two parts (Fig. 1):

- The so-called NDBS-kernel offers neutral data management functions embodying structural object orientation. The kernel interface is determined by the MAD model (molecule atom data model) and its language called MQL (molecule query language), which offers composition and decomposition of complex objects, here called molecules [Mi88].
- The application layer provides application-specific support, i.e. behavioral object orientation offered by ADTs. Complex objects offered by the kernel are used and tailored to objects according to the application model of a given application. This mapping is specific for each particular application area. Hence, different application layers exist which offer tailored interfaces in the form of a set of ADT operations for the corresponding application.

In the following, we want to concentrate on the essential characteristics of the MAD model and the most important objectives of the application layer. Both topics are refined with special emphasis on their provision for structural and behavioral object orientation.

2. Structural Object Orientation enabled by the MAD Model

The most important objectives of the MAD model can be characterized as follows:

- complex objects viewed as structured sets of elementary building blocks
- they are dynamically defined and derived
- all relationships among elementary building blocks are represented in a direct and symmetrical way allowing for shared subobjects
- set-oriented processing is offered by the descriptive SQL-like query language MQL.

Atoms and Links as Basic Building Blocks

Atoms are the basic elements of the MAD model used to represent the real world entities. They play a similar role to tuples in the relational model. Each atom is composed of attributes of various types, is uniquely identifiable, and belongs to its corresponding atom type. The attributes' data types can be chosen from a richer selection than in conventional models yielding a more powerful structuring capability at the attribute level. Relationships between atoms (entities) are expressed by so-called links that are defined as link types between atom types. Links are used to efficiently map all types of relationships and recursions. This direct mapping and the consideration of bidirectional yet symmetric links (represented via reference/back-reference pairs) establishes the basis of the MAD model's flexibility. Hence, in the database all atoms connected by links form meshed structures as depicted in Fig. 2a. Based on this atom network, it is feasible to dynamically construct molecules using atoms as elementary building blocks.

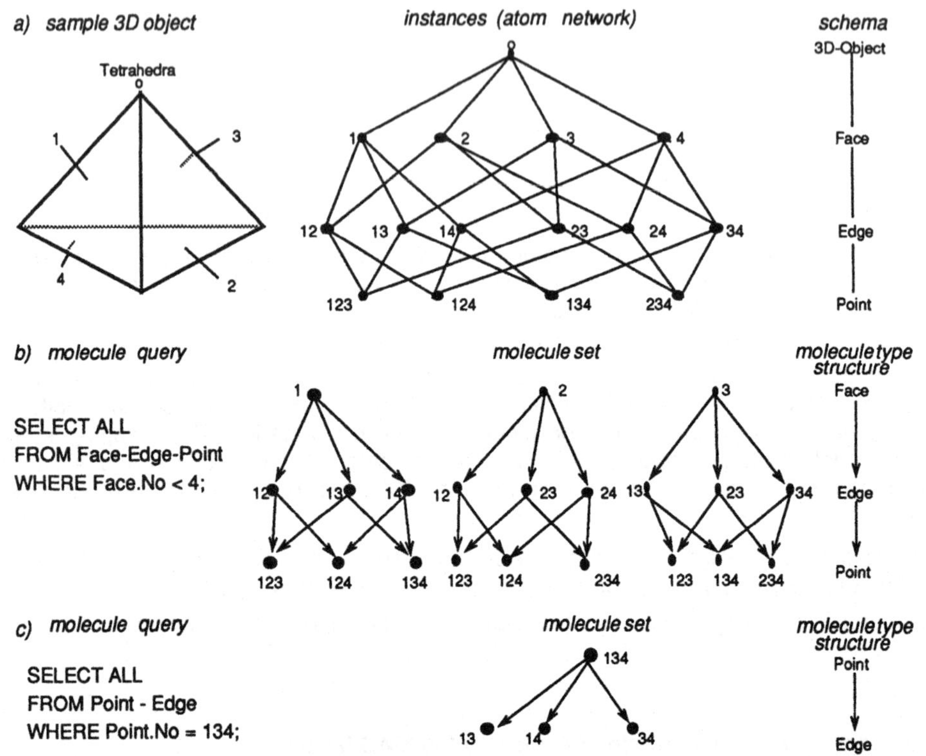

Fig. 2: Dynamic construction of molecules from a sample geometric object

Dynamic Derivation of Molecules

Molecules are defined by MQL statements and have to be derived at run-time (Fig. 2). Each molecule belongs to a molecule type specified in the FROM clause. This type description establishes a connected, directed, and acyclic type graph as subgraph of the database schema. This graph becomes cyclic only when recursive types are involved. Thus, each type description specifies a starting point (i.e. root atom type) and all participating atom and link types (abbreviated by '-'). A simple example depicted in Fig. 2b is the molecule type Face-Edge-Point. Each molecule type determines both the molecule structure as well as the molecule set which groups all molecules with the same structure. At least at the conceptual level, the dynamic derivation of molecules proceeds in a straight-forward way using the type graph as a kind of template: For each atom of the root atom type all children, grandchildren etc. are connected according to the molecule type structure terminating after all leaves have been reached. The derivation of the children atoms means performing the hierarchical join [LK84]. Fig. 2b shows the resulting molecule set for the Face-Edge-Point molecule type, where the set of molecules was restricted by means of the WHERE clause. The SELECT clause defines the final molecule (type) structure and allows a proper molecule projection. The symmetric use of the atom network is shown with the help of the example in Fig. 2c depicting a Point-Edge molecule query and its corresponding result.

In toto, the MAD model offers adequate concepts gaining structural object orientation. The prototype implementation of the MAD model, i.e. the PRIMA kernel [HMMS87], supports efficient molecule processing which is additionally enhanced by a variety of storage structures and tuning mechanisms (e.g. molecule materialization or molecule caching instead of its dynamic derivation). All these performance enhancements are transparent at the data model interface. An in-depth description of the design and implementation concepts of PRIMA can be found in [Hä88a].

3. Issues of the Application Layer

The application layer (AL) constitutes the topmost layer of our NDBS architecture as illustrated in Fig. 1. The main task of the AL lies in the tailoring of the NDBS towards a specific application to achieve the desired behavioral object orientation. Hence, the AL constitutes the linkage between the application-independent NDBS-kernel system and the application at hand. Its interface is also called the application model interface emphazising that the AL is carrying out application-oriented objects and their associated operations. The desired application model is achieved by mapping the application's objects to the molecules offered by the underlying MAD model, and by including special algorithms for the application specific molecule processing. These algorithms describe implicitly the application objects' behavior including their integrity constraints, since they determine the object modification initialized via actions in the application. This encapsulation of data (molecules) and algorithms results in a kind of abstract data type (ADT). Therefore, the AL is organized as a collection of ADTs. AL programs constitute the ADT operations, and ADT instances are represented or defined by references to the molecules.

Embedding of Molecules

First of all, we have to discuss the question of how to embed the molecules (and atoms), which are specified by MQL-queries and delivered by the NDBS-kernel system, into the ADT environment. Hence, embedding means that MAD objects are made directly accessible for AL programs. For this reason, the query's result is stored in a specific part of main memory, the so-called object buffer. This buffer enables the utilization of the access locality of AL programs. To further enhance the processing performance, fast operational access is achieved via a pointer-like reference mechanism. To support the imperative/procedural processing of the complex and network-like data structures stored in the object buffer, we introduce a cursor concept which allows us to define cursors explicitly, to bind them to parts of the atom network, and to move them from one atom to the other in a navigational manner. Since navigational processing of hierarchical molecule components are often required, we allow for the definition of dependent 'flat' cursors yielding a hierarchical cursor concept. Thus, navigation via one 'flat' cursor automatically affects the dependent cursors on subordinate levels.

The object buffer and the cursor concept deliver access to preselected molecule structures. A further question, which concerns the embedding of MAD objects deals with data structure adaptation. That is, how do the AL programs, written in conventional programming languages, 'assimilate' atoms which usually contain attributes of MAD specific data types. This problem is well known as the problem of language binding in the conventional DBMS environment, and multiple solutions are given in the literature. Our own proposal provides the use of a special precompiler, which handles the inclusion of MAD statements, enriches the underlying host language in order to handle MAD specific data types, and additionally integrates particular language constructs to support the navigational and cursor-oriented access concepts mentioned above.

Language Binding Via Precompiler

The use of precompiler statements is sketched in Fig. 3. It depicts the scheme of the sample AL program 'solid_geometry' in a PASCAL-like programming language. We distinguish between the definition of types (query types which contain a MAD statement specification, and cursor types) and the declaration of multiple corresponding instances. These instances are handled like host language variables. The query variable represents the query's result stored in the associated object buffer. The linkage between such a variable and the result of a particular query is done via the built-in function EVAL. EVAL directs actual query parameters to the NDBS-kernel interface and triggers the query evaluation and the result's preparation. The inverse semantics is carried out by the PROPAGATE function. This function propagates all modifications on buffered molecules back to the kernel system. Hence, EVAL and PROPAGATE constitute a kind of check-out/check-in mechanism controlling the contents of the object buffer. Similar to the definition of object buffers (query variables), the ADT programmer can generate cursor instances. The binding of such a cursor variable to an object buffer is provided by the ATTACH function.

The illustrated AL-program gives an example of ADT specification, too. Obviously, it is divided into two parts:

```
ADT  solid_geometry;
QUERY TYPE
      solid_type = 'SELECT ALL
                    FROM 3D-Object-Face-Edge-Point
                    WHERE 3D-Object.No = $no'
                    (no: identifier type);
      ...
CURSOR TYPE
      face_curor_type = Face, Edge, Point -> solid_type;
      edge_cursor_tupe = Edge, (Face, Point) -> solid_type;
      ...
VAR
      solid_buffer : solid_type;
      face_cursor : face_cursor_type;
      edge_cursor : edge_cursor_type;
      ...
      volume : integer;
      ...
```

```
OPERATION
...
activate (number, solid)
      BEGIN EVAL    (solid.solid_buffer, ... number ...);
            ATTACH(solid.face_cursor, solid.solid_buffer);
            ATTACH(solid.edge_cursor, solid.solid_buffer);
            ...
            calculation of the solid's volume
            ...
      END;
      ...
move (solid):
...
union (solid1, solid2, solid);
...
END solid geometry
```

Fig. 3: Data part and operation part of a sample ADT for solid geometry

- the data part determines the type of 'abstract data' (e.g. the ADT-instances) by a collection of type definitions.
- the operation part contains application independent operations, such as 'generate', 'activate', 'deactivate', and 'delete', as well as application-specific operations (e.g. 'move', 'rotate', 'union', 'intersect' and 'difference').

4. Summary and Outlook

At first glance, the PRIMA-NDBS looks like a synopsis of quite different aspects. But in fact these system concepts fortify each other in a very fruitful way resulting in an efficient database support for advanced applications. In the following, the main concepts and their achievements are listed:

- the MAD model at the kernel interface provides structural object orientation
- the object buffer exploits 'near by application' locality,
- the cursor concept allows for efficient pointer-like access capabilities, and
- the ADT concept offers behavioral object orientation.

Furthermore, a number of system design decisions were taken with special emphasis on workstation-oriented environments, which in our opinion are the most realistic and prevailing ones. Workstation-oriented processing could be effectively enhanced by delegating the application layer together with the application programs to the workstation and the NDBS-kernel to the host system. This partitioning is further favored by the set-orientation of the kernel interface minimizing workstation-host communication.

At the moment, we are performing a broad 'in-the-field' validation of these system concepts in the areas of VLSI design and 3D modeling. On the other hand, we are looking for further enhancements achieving intelligent CAD, planning and diagnosis support. Here we consider the integration of ideas known from several knowledge representation methods.

Acknowledgements
The design and implementation of the PRIMA-NDBS was a combined effort of the members of the PRIMA project superintended by T. Härder.

Literature

Di86 Dittrich, K.R.: Object-Oriented Database Systems - A Workshop Report, in: Proc. 5th ER Conf. 1986, North Holland Publ. Group, 1986.

Hä88a Härder, T.: The PRIMA Project - Design and Implementation of a Non-Standard Database System, Research Report No. 26/88 SFB124, University Kaiserslautern, 1988.

Hä88b Härder, T.: Non-Standard DBMS for Support of Emerging Applications - Requirement Analysis and Architectural Concepts, submitted for publication.

HMMS87 Härder, T., Meyer-Wegener, K., Mitschang, B., Sikeler, A.: PRIMA - a DBMS prototype Supporting Engineering Applications, Research Report No. 22/87 SFB124, 1987, in: Proc. VLDB 87, pp. 433-442.

HS88 Hübel, Ch., Sutter, B.: Experiences in Supporting an Engineering Application by PRIMA, in: The PRIMA Project - Design and Implementation of a Non-Standard Database System, Härder, T. (ed.), Research Report No. 26/88 SFB124, University Kaiserslautern, 1988.

LK84 Lorie, R., Kim, W., et. al.: Supporting Complex Objects in a Relational System for Engineering Databases, IBM Research Laboratory San Jose, CA, 1984.

Mi88 Mitschang, B.: Towards a Unified View of Design Data and Knowledge Representation, in: Proc. 2nd. Int. Conf. on Expert Database Systems, Tysons Corner, Virginia, April 1988, pp. 33-49, further publ. by Benjamin/Cummings Publ. Co.

SOOM and Tornado-*
Experience with Database-support for Object-Oriented Applications

Arne J. Berre

Center for Industrial Research
P.O.Box 350, 0314 OSLO 3, NORWAY
uucp: mcvax!si.uninett!berre

Abstract

SOOM, Semantic Object-Oriented Model, and Tornado-* are the datamodel and database-architecture supporting the object-oriented Taskon-Environment. The major component in this environment is a set of structure-oriented editors that manipulate a hypertext-like document-structure. SOOM is a datamodel based on a merge of ideas from structural and behavioral object-oriented datamodels, where relations are added to an object-oriented language, Smalltalk-80. Tornado-* is an architecture based on one or more centralized object-servers and a local workspace on each workstation. The current bottleneck of the initial caching from a centralized server to the local workspace is identified, and a solution based on a distributed object-server is suggested. This paper focus on the multilayer approach used in both the model and the architecture.

1. Introduction

Taskon-Environment is an Engineering Information System which has been developed in the research program "Effectiveness and Quality in Engineering" at Center for Industrial Research, in the period 1983 to 1988. The system is based on an object-oriented architecture in a distributed workstation/server environment, /REEN86/. The main programming language for development of tools and applications has been Smalltalk-80.

The information management in Taskon-Environment is organized around a hypertext-like document-model of interconnected objects. The objects may contain different kinds of information, like text, pictures, drawings, spreadsheets, database-queries etc. The user-interface is managed by a set of structure-oriented editors which uses the structural schema of the document to prevent the user from creating illegal structures. The application-areas for the system have been preparation of bid-proposals in offshore engineering, and information management for software engineering.

The developed datamodel was named SOOM because of its integration of concepts from semantic datamodels and object-oriented programming languages, and the system was named Tornado-* because the Data-Store-part is integrated into our earlier system, Tornado /ULFS82/. Tornado is a network-oriented database with variable-length records, originally developed for CAD/CAM-applications.

2. SOOM - Semantic Object Oriented Model

The datamodel was developed to support complex document-structures, and is a synthesis of ideas from semantic datamodels and object-oriented languages. An object-oriented model like Smalltalk does not support structural abstractions in the same sense as most semantic datamodels. Typical semantic datamodels support relationships to describe 1-to-1, 1-to-many or many-to-many relations between objects, and this is a useful construct for representing complex object-structures.

As has been pointed out in /BERR86/ and /RUMB87/, the notion of relations is a useful semantic construct which is normally missing in object-oriented languages, but should ideally be supported by an object-oriented datamodel.

The following shows how the structural and behavioral aspects of SOOM are integrated in a multi-layered model.

2.1. Different views on the shared data from different applications

Figure 1 shows different mappings for the same object, from storage-object to structural object to behavioral object, and some temporary display-objects which are used to present different views to the user.

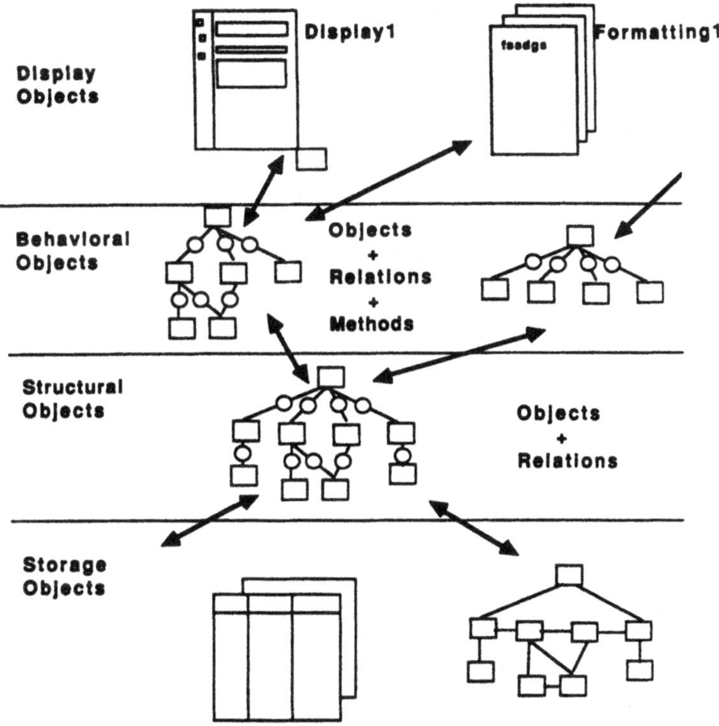

Figure 1 - Multi-layered model

Since different applications might want to present different aspects of a shared structure, there is not a need to share the behavioral part of objects. The structural part represents the information which needs to be persistent. Compared to the ANSI-SPARC 3-schema architecture, the structural schema corresponds to the conceptual schema, the way it is physically stored corresponds to the physical schema, and the aspect of the structural model which is used by an application corresponds to a view on the conceptual model. It is the responsibility of the behavior added in this view to maintain the integrity constraints described by the structural model. This layering gives a freedom to use 1-to-many mappings between conceptual objects and application objects.

The behavioral schema describes the message-interface-protocol for methods applicable to instances of the classes involved in an application. Such an instance is generated based on an instance from the structural model, but can be extended with class-dependent operations, in addition to those inferred from the structural type. The mapping between the structural schema and the behavioral schema is by default one-to-one. An object-type in the structural schema corresponds to a subclass of Model-object in the behavioral schema, and a relation-type corresponds to a subclass of class Relation.

The structural schema can describe 1:1, 1:N and M:N relations between objects. It is important to note that the structural schema describes a structural abstraction which can be realized by different physical data-structures, both in the shared database and in the application-views.

2.2. Structure and Behavior in SOOM

The datamodel-schema has two parts, one part describes the behavioral interface in a normal object-oriented class-hierarchy (A generalization/specialization hierarchy for a behavioral interface), and one part describes the structural model (An aggregation hierarchy for objects and relations between objects). The interface to the structural model is reflected as operations in the behavioral model. The application-programmer sees the structural layer through the behavioral layer which supports operations to manipulate the structure. In addition the programmer can create application-dependent operations or methods, which can make use of the structural operations, and realize operations which are specific for a given application. In the behavioral layer one can also create temporal objects, which are useful for instance for objects created by the user-interface.

The tension between encapsulation of structure in a behavioral object-oriented model, and the revelation of structure in a structural object-oriented model is resolved through making the structural abstraction of relations explicit. Encapsulation of representation is still taken care of, because there are many ways to represent a relation, and the actual representation will be hidden for the users of a class. The application-programmer will directly use relations to traverse and manipulate the object-structure.

The structural schema is also represented as an object-relation structure, and stored in the database in the same way as other structural objects. The same structure-oriented editors can now be used to create both the schema, and the structures which obeys the schema. The description of legal structures is done in the structural schema, which regulates which relations are allowed between pairs of objects. The structure-oriented editors interpret this as a grammar for legal structures.

For easy integration into an existing object-oriented language, Model-object and Relation are subclasses of Persistent-Object. Each object has a list of incoming and outgoing relations and each relation knows its type and object in each direction. Objects can be either Aggregates or Atomic. Atomic objects are used for new basic types like text and drawing.

If the application-programmer defines his own special atomic-classes, he has to write two routines: writeToStream and readFromStream, which encodes and decodes how the content is to be stored. If the substructure contains objects or relations to objects, the identifiers of these objects has to be stored in a special part of the storage objects, which can be interpreted by the structural component of the database. The currently supplied atomic classes are Text, Drawing, BitMap, Spreadsheet-table and Relational query.

The description of legal structures are done in the structural schema, which regulates which relations are allowed between pairs of objects. The structural model will not represent the content of atomic types, but only relations between objects. The content-part will be considered as a sequence of bytes which the behavioral schema knows how to interpret.

Both objects and relations are identified by a surrogate-id which is unique throughout the system. It consists of a database-identifier and a unique identifier within the database. These identifiers are used instead of normal object-oriented pointers, when a message is to be sent to an object. The database-identifier is logical and only used for inter-database references. An object-reference without a special time-stamp is assumed to be the most recent one. If a special time is given, it indicates the object as of a particular time, and the same time is applied to the objects referenced from this object.

3. Tornado-* - An Architecture for realization of SOOM

3.1. An architecture for workstations and servers

The supporting architecture takes advantage of the layer between structural objects and behavioral objects in SOOM. The structural objects according to the structural schema are shared and is stored on a central server, Data Store (DS). Each workstation has a local workspace, Working Store (WS), which maps the structural objects into behavioral objects.

The Data Store is a centralized Object Server that stores structural objects, and makes it possible to check-out different parts of the object-structure to different users.

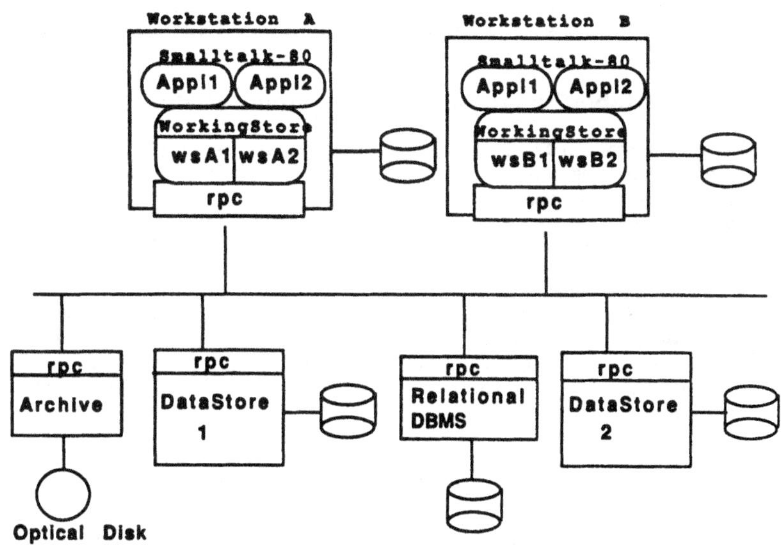

Figure 2 - Application-Working Store-Data Store Interface

The Working Store is a transaction-based private workspace or a local object-manager, and acts as a single-user database. The Data Stores and Working Stores communicates through a remote procedure call (rpc) mechanism. Each Working Store instance is identified by a WS-identifier, used to identify the Working Store in transactions against the Data Store. The Working Store will maintain a history of all changes done locally to an object. When the object is stored back in shared storage, the last version of the object will be stored as default.

The Data Stores represent an interface corresponding to the structural schema. The underlying physical schema, however, stores an object together with its relations in a unit. The interface is based on object-by-object operations to be applied to a single object, or specified to be applied to each object in a set. The underlying storage-system stores objects in variable-length records. Each object is associated with access-attributes and a timestamp.

Since the structure-oriented editors are parameterized by the structural schema, the Data Store is ensured that only legal structures will be inserted, and does not have to verify that at the end of each transaction. It will, however, enforce referential integrity by checking that there are no relations going to objects which are not stored in the database.

3.2. Access to multiple databases

Each Data Store will contain one structural schema, and there might be multiple Working Stores connected to it.

Each Working Store manager can simultaneously operate multiple logical Working Stores and there can be inter-model references between different objects belonging to different Working and Data Stores. An inter-model reference is represented through local proxy-objects which know the identification of the correct Data Store. There is always a one-to-many correspondence between Data Stores and Working Stores.

Access to remote databases of various kinds, like relational databases are handled by viewing them as remote objects with a certain interface e.g. SQL, and sending them messages. A special kind of atomic objects can store SQL-queries and represent the answer of a query.

3.3. Performance suitable for interactive design-applications

The first version of the system fetched objects automatically when they were referenced, hidden from the application-programmer. Since a remote-procedure-call to retrieve an object can be expensive, it was decided that explicit handling of remote operations makes it easier to create good user-applications. In most cases the application can deduce which objects are to be operated on next, or the user is able to decide how deep into the network-structure he wants to go.

The object-relation model lends itself naturally to specification of transitive closures, based on a root-object, a set of object-types to use, and a set of relation-types to follow to a certain depth. This can be used for specifying prefetching of objects. A serial version-history is maintained for each object, and by the use of a timestamp, a Working Store can check if the object it has is the current one.

3.4. Transactions

Normal transactions are considered to be short and to conform to serializability. They are used to ensure that a sequence of operations are atomic. Local transactions are performed on objects already checked out to the workstation, and does not have to involve any remote transaction. A remote transaction has to be started from a local transaction and is supposed to take a short amount of time.

Cooperative Work is supported through a notion of long transactions. To handle long transactions, a checkOut / checkIn - mechanism is used. It is associated with each object in a Data Store if it is checked out, and to which Working Store. The different checkOut modes are: Read, Write, and All. Read will always succeed, while Write and All will only succeed if the object is not checked out in any of these modes already. All gives also update-rights to the access-keys. The users are identified through their WSidentifiers, and the user-names are given each time a new Working Store is created, and kept in the corresponding Data Store.

4. Experiences and future work with SOOM and Tornado-*

Interactive editing-applications require an access-performance which is comparable with access to objects in virtual memory. This means that caching/checking-out to a private workspace is essential. There is currently a significant difference in performance between access-time the first time an object is touched, and has to be brought into the private workspace, and the access-time when it already is cached.

The performance given by a Working Store after objects are checked-out from a Data Store is sufficient for most of our applications, with a retrieval-performance of around 500 objects of 100-1000 bytes per second.

The object-relation structures used in our document-models are fine-grained, and a typical document will contain some thousand objects. The current object-by-object interface between a Working Store and a Data Store is the bottleneck in the system, giving a retrieval-performance of around 5 objects of 100-1000 bytes each per second. This results in an operating mode where users tend to work on local structures in the Working Store, for a day or more.

It seems possible to enhance this performance by shipping larger segments from a server, and to distribute the Data Stores itself out to the workstations and only centralize what is necessary for lock-management and handling of name-tables.

Experience from the use of SOOM suggests that the uniform use of objects and relations in SOOM could be extended to include attribute-properties which belongs directly to an object or a relation. It has also shown that the kind of relations which represents a part-of-hierarchy is extensively used. Both locking and clustering could take advantage of this hierarchy being more explicitly represented.

We are now developing this framework further in two new projects, one is a software engineering environment, and the other an environment for handling medical information.

In order to decide on a future solution for the database-architecture, we have started a performance-evaluation of different approaches. The "Hypermodel Database Benchmark" /BERR88/ is intended to measure performance on operations in a typical design-application model: "A network structure of hierarchical and interrelated objects". We are currently realizing this benchmark for different object-oriented databases and object-management systems.

5. Acknowledgement

The work presented here has been done in the EKI-team at SI, and would not have been possible without the inspiring environment created by professor Trygve Reenskaug, and the other project-members Tor Bothner, Anne Hurlen, Anton Landmark, Odd Arild Lehne, Henrik Lund-Hansen, Else Nordhagen, Eirik Nass-Ulseth, Gro Oftedal, Anne Lise Skaar and Pal Stenslet.

The EKI-program was financed by NTNF (The Royal Norwegian Council for Scientific and Industrial Research).

6. References

/BERR86/ Berre, A.J.
"Sharing of Objects in an Object-oriented language"
Position-statement, OODBMS-I, September 1986, page 209

/BERR88/ Berre, A.J.
"The HyperModel Database Benchmark"
Technical Report, Oregon Graduate Center, forthcoming

/REEN86/ Reenskaug, T.
"The Tender/One Environment"
Technical Report 86-15, Center for Industrial Research
Oslo, Norway

/REEN87/ Reenskaug, T., Skaar A.
"An Environment for Literate Smalltalk Programming"
Technical Report 87-10, Center for Industrial Research
Oslo, Norway

/RUMB87/ Rumbaugh, J.
"Relations as Semantic Constructs in an Object-Oriented Language" OOPSLA-87 Proc, Florida, 466-481

/ULFS82/ Ulfsby, S., Meen, S., Oian J.
"Tornado: A DBMS for Graphics Applications"
IEEE Computer Graphics and Applications, May 1982

Formalizing Objects for Databases using ADABTPL

David Stemple
Adolfo Socorro
Tim Sheard

Department of Computer and Information Science
University of Massachusetts, Amherst, MA 01003

Abstract

Object-oriented concepts appear to facilitate the specification of certain kinds of systems, such as design, control and distributed applications. Addition of object-oriented concepts to a database specification system would therefore add to the modelling power and convenience of the system. In order to accomplish a seamless integration of a formal database specification system with object-oriented constructs, we need to supply formal semantics for the object-oriented constructs. In this paper, we use the existing formalism of a database specification type system to formalize the object-oriented concepts of object identity, class, and shared objects.

1 Introduction

Object-oriented concepts appear to facilitate the specification of certain kinds of systems, such as design, control, and distributed applications. The main benefits accruing to the use of objects in system specification are a natural framework for system modularization, accomodation of the construction of complex entities with shared subcomponents, and flexible module interconnection capabilities beyond the hierarchical structures attainable in most programming languages. Addition of object-oriented concepts to a database specification system would therefore add to the modelling power and convenience of the system.

There are many concepts attached to the term "object-orientation." These include

- the notion of an object as a semi-autonomous agent with a limited set of operations,
- class hierarchies by which objects can acquire properties (including operations) by virtue of being in subclasses of other classes,
- unique identification of each object, allowing for object sharing, and
- a class having a repository for the set of currently existing objects (the extent) of the class.

Though these concepts are present in many object-oriented systems, both in programming language and database systems, they typically lack formal semantics [5]. It is our purpose in this paper to provide formal semantics to the last three of these concepts in the process of adding them to a formal database specification language (which already formalizes encapsulation and inheritance). We will do this by using the type system of the database system specification language ADABTPL [21]. ADABTPL has a formal semantics based on recursive functions and axioms, and supports formal reasoning about systems specified in it [17].

The paper is organized as follows. The next section presents the salient features of the ADABTPL specification system. Following that, we present and discuss object-oriented concepts and their relationship to database issues. We then give the ADABTPL formalization of the concepts of unique object identity, object sharing, object repositories, and object destruction.

2 The ADABTPL System

The ADABTPL system is an environment for specifying and implementing database systems. The ADABTPL language (standing for Abstract DAtaBase Type Programming Language) is a strongly typed language for writing high level specifications of database systems in terms of schemas, transactions and functions. It has a pure recursive function semantics and is formalized by the axioms of four abstract data types – tuples, finite sets, lists, and natural numbers. These abstract data types form the basis for specifying the structures of schemas. The type language includes polymorphic types, encapsulation, discriminated union, and multiple inheritance. Update specifications can be written in an imperative style, but are understood by the system as pure recursive functions. Although ADABTPL contains certain features that are associated with object-orientation, such as encapsulation and inheritance, there is no concept of object. In particular, ADABTPL does not, in its original form, support directly the concept of object identity, sharing subcomponents of complex structures, or automatic maintenance of the set of current instances of a type. Our approach to adding these features to ADABTPL is to add a few lingual constructs to the language for expressing these concepts, and to translate these constructs into the existing ADABTPL features before analysing or compiling a system specification – essentially a macro-expansion approach. This accomplishes two things. First, it keeps the essential formalism to a minimum. Second, it provides an accessible semantics for the user of the concepts. The semantics produced by the translation of the object-oriented concepts is not exactly "operational" since the ADABTPL specifications may be quite different from the mechanisms that are used to implement the concepts, but may provide the same sort of semantic crutch needed by users. In this section, we will present the features of ADABTPL that are needed to understand the object extensions and how they formalize the object concepts added to ADABTPL.

2.1 The system model

An ADABTPL specification consists of a schema, a set of function definitions and a set of transactions. The schema contains type definitions for all the values contained in the database as well as for those used as inputs to the transactions. The schema also consists of a distinguished type for the database object itself. The database object is the only persistent object in the system and is a tacit input, in its entirety, to each transaction. Its components form part of the name space of transactions. There is no input/output specification in transaction definitions. Input parameters form the transactions' view of the external world and the database is directly accessible by component names.

Transactions have a set of typed inputs, a precondition, and a body. The semantics of a transaction is given by a function that takes the database and inputs, and returns a new database [19]. Transaction bodies are sequences of statements that compute values and update the database. Control structures include if-then-else statements and iteration through sets and lists. The **Case** construct is used for making decisions based on the types of values from discriminated union types. The effects of a statement are seen by subsequent statements. However, when a set or list controls a loop, updates to the set or list do not affect the iteration, although intermediate states of the set or list may be passed to a function called from inside the loop. This requirement stems from the fact that the looping semantics is based on terminating recursion through finite sets and lists. Functions can be called by transactions and can be specified in the same imperative style as used for transactions or in recursive expression form as used in functional languages.

```
EmpTuple = [EmpNo: number; EmpName: string; EmpDept: number]
           where EmpNo < 10000;
EmpRel =  Set(EmpTuple) where Key(EmpRel, EmpNo);
DeptRel = Set([DeptNum: Number; DeptName: string; NumOfEmps: number])
          where Key(DeptRel, DeptNum);

Database EmployeeDB : [Emps: EmpRel; Depts: DeptRel]
          where
           Contains(Depts.DeptNum, Emps.EmpDept)
           and
           For all d in Depts:
               d.NumOfEmps =
               Count(All e in Emps where e.EmpDept = d.DeptNum)
```

Figure 1: A relational schema in ADABTPL

2.2 Type construction

Types are constructed using structural specifications for tuple, set, and list types, parameterization for polymorphic types, and inheritance controlling mechanisms for subtyping. By subtyping we mean creating a type (the subtype) whose instances can be used anywhere the instances of another type (the supertype) can be used. Any type definition can contain a predicate that must be satisfied by a prospective instance of the type before the element is a legal value of the type. These predicates are the means of specifying database integrity constraints, though they may also be used to limit the inputs to transactions and functions. We now turn to examples to further illustrate ADABTPL features.

Figure 1 illustrates several ADABTPL type features. The **EmpTuple** type is formed using brackets ("[" and "]") as type constructors. In statements defining tuple types, the component names can be used as variables in **where** clauses to restrict the legal instances of the type – in this case to assure that **EmpNo** values are less than 10000. The predicate in the **where** clause can be any predicate evaluatable on instances of the tuple domain (the cross product of the component domains). The only "free" variables allowed are the component names.

Relation types are formed using the **Set** type constructor and can use **where** clauses having predicates evaluatable on sets of the type being defined. The **Key** predicate is a very useful constraint and has its normal database meaning. The type name itself can be used as a variable standing for an instance of the type. Again we see a component name (**EmpNo**) used in a predicate. In this case, it stands for a component selection function, since the **Key** predicate takes a set and a function as its inputs. **Key** is an example of a higher order (generic) function since it takes a function as an input. Higher order functions are an important feature of database system specification in ADABTPL.

The database itself is the subject of the **Database** statement in an ADABTPL schema. It is the variable declaration that is used implicitly by all transactions and represents the persistent data of the system. The database, named in this case **EmployeeDB**, is typed as a tuple whose components are relations. The relations are typed by the earlier type definitions, and so the database must obey the relational constraints (**where** clauses in those definitions). The **where** clause of the **Database** statement is used to state constraints that are not expressible on single components alone. In this case, we have two such constraints, one for the referential integrity of the **EmpDept** field of **Emps** tuples, expressed by the **Contains** term, and one for the correctness (a redundancy) of the **NumOfEmps** field of **Depts** tuples.

ADABTPL is in no way limited to first normal form relations, nor to relational systems for

```
Task = [ReqDate: Date; TaskDescr: string];
TaskQueue =
  Set([Priority: number;
       TaskList: List(Task)])
  where Key(TaskQueue, Priority)
        and
        Not(TaskList = Nil);
EmpTuple = [EmpNo: number; EmpName: string; Tasks: TaskQueue];
EmpRel = Set(EmpTuple) where Key(EmpRel, EmpNo);

Database EmpTaskDb: [Emps: EmpRel; TotalTasks: number]
         where TotalTasks =
               TaskTotal(EmpRel);

Function TaskTotal(er: EmpRel): number;
 Body
  Initial TaskTotal := 0;
  For each e in er Do
   For each t in Tasks Do
     TaskTotal := TaskTotal + Length(t.TaskList)
 End;
```

Figure 2: Example of a non-relational database specification

that matter. Figure 2 gives a schema for a non-relational database.

In this example, we see tuple domains that are themselves relations, making the database not a first normal form database. And the database has a component, **TotalTasks**, that is not even a relation. This indicates some of the expressiveness of the ADABTPL type system as a schema language.

Abstract data types can be specified in ADABTPL. For example, the **TaskList** component in the last example could be typed as an abstract queue, with only the queue operations valid on it. Figure 3 shows the ADABTPL definition of a queue abstract data type.

In this example, we see that lists have been used to specify the structure and then the behavior of queues. This may seem to be an implementation approach to specification, but is not, since the list structure is defined solely in terms of a set of axioms. Thus, the queue behavior is based on the theory of lists, but may be implemented in any manner that obeys the theory. Lists themselves may have many implementations, each of which must obey the list theory.

There is not too much remarkable about the ADABTPL approach to abstract data types. Note that polymorphism is allowed in abstract types. Polymorphism is an inheritance mechanism, in that all types defined in terms of the polymorphic types, e.g., **Queue(Task)**, are subtypes of the polymorphic type, **Queue(Element)** in this case. Other forms of inheritance are standard features of ADABTPL. In the next section, we outline the ADABTPL approach to inheritance.

2.3 Inheritance mechanisms

As mentioned in the last section, polymorphism permits inheritance of the aspects of a generic type, abstract or not, by types instantiated from the generic type (i.e., by substituting type arguments for the type parameters of the generic type). Two other inheritance mechanisms are supplied by ADABTPL type constructors: discriminated **Union**, in which a new type is constructed that is

```
Queue(Element) =
  Abstract Type
   Structure = List(Element);
   Operations
    Recursive Function Enqueue(E: Element;
                               Q: Queue(Element)
                                 ): Queue(Element);
     Body
      Cons(E, Q)
     End;
    Recursive Function Head(Q: Queue(Element)): Element
               where not EmptyQueue(Q);
     Body
      If EmptyQueue(Cdr(Q))
         Then Car(Q)
         Else Head(Cdr(Q))
     End;
    Recursive Function Tail(Q:Queue(Element)
                              where not EmptyQueue(Q)
                             ): Queue(Element);
     Body
      If EmptyQueue(Cdr(Q))
         Then Nil
         Else Cons(Car(Q), Tail(Q))
     End;
    Recursive Function EmptyQueue(Q:Queue(Element)): boolean;
     Body
      Q= Nil
     End;
   Export Enqueue, Head, Tail, EmptyQueue;
End;
```

Figure 3: Encapsulation of a queue type

a supertype of a set of subtypes, and **Inherits**, which creates a subtype from a set of supertypes (multiple inheritance).

2.3.1 Discriminated union

The following definitions create a new type **CarOrTruck** from the two types, **CarTuple** and **TruckTuple**, using discriminated **Union**.

```
CarTuple =    [NumDoors: 1..8; NumPassengers: 1..26];
TruckTuple = [NumWheels: 4..22; NumAxles: 2..6; Tonnage: number];
CarOrTruck = Union[Car: CarTuple; Truck: TruckTuple];
```

Any new operations defined on values of **CarOrTruck** type, are also defined on **CarTuple** values and on **TruckTuple** values. Anywhere a **CarOrTruck** value can appear, a value of either **CarTuple** or **TruckTuple** type can appear. **CarOrTruck** is thus a supertype of both **CarTuple** and **TruckTuple**.

In order to manipulate values of a **Union** type, the **Case** function must be used. A function returning the number of wheels of a car or truck is given by

```
Recursive Function NumberOfWheels(V: CarOrTruck): number;
 Body
  Case V of
     Car: 4
     Truck: V.NumWheels
 End;
```

2.3.2 Multiple inheritance

Multiple inheritance can be specified in two ways in ADABTPL, a general composition of two types (**Inherits**) and the adding of some tuple components to an arbitrary type (**With**). **With** is a specialization of **Inherits** and is present only because it is such a common form.

The general **Inherits** type constructor takes a set of input types and constructs a new type that is a subtype of all its input types. An instance of an **Inherits** type can be thought of being an instance of all of its input types. All the operations of the input supertypes are applicable to instances of the **Inherits** type. One way of thinking of an instance of an **Inherits** type is as a tuple of unnamed components from the input types. The operations of the supertypes work on an instance of the **Inherits** type by extracting the appropriate part of the instance and using it. The semantics of the supertypes' operations are preserved. This means that if **f** is a function on a supertype **Ti**, **T** is defined by

```
  T = Inherits[Tag1: T1; ...; Tagi: Ti; ...; Tagn: Tn],
```

f takes an instance of **Ti** in some position, and **x** and **y** are instances of type **T** and **Ti**, respectively, then

```
 f(...,x,...) = f(...,y,...)
```

where **y** = **x:Tagi** and all the missing arguments, denoted by the ellipsis, are the same in both calls. The expression **x:Tagi** is to be read as "x as a Tagi" and refers to the part of **x** that is of type **Ti**.

Ambiguities arise whenever functions of the supertypes have the same name. These ambiguities must be removed by specifying the part of the **Inherits** instance to use as input to the function; this causes the appropriate function to be chosen. For example, suppose **f** is a function defined both on inputs of type **T1** and of type **Ti**, and that type **T** is defined as above. If **x** is of type **T**, the expression **f(x)** is ambiguous. If the **f** to be used is the one having as input the **Tagi** part of **x**, for example, then the following must be written:

```
f(x:Tagi)
```

A second opportunity for ambiguity arises whenever two of the input types (to the **Inherits** constructor) have the same type. Though this is a situation that does not seem to have much use, it can arise whenever the input types are type variables that are instantiated in some use of a parametric **Inherits** type (to define a new type). Thus, the case must be detected and handled. The remedy is the same: a tag, e. g., **Tagi** in **T** as defined above, must be used in the same manner as in disambiguating functions, but in this case the disambiguation only serves the purpose of choosing the part of the instance to send to a function.

Equality is an operation of each of the supertypes of any **Inherits** type and is therefore ambiguous. It can be disambiguated in the normal manner. For example, if x and z are both of the type **T** defined above and we want to compare them as **Ti** instances, then we write

```
x:Tagi = z:Tagi
```

This expression is true if and only if the **Tagi** part of x equals the **Tagi** part of z. On the other hand, the expression

```
x = z
```

though ambiguous if = is treated as other functions are treated, is not considered ambiguous, but rather evaluates to true if

```
x:Tagi = z:Tagi
```

is true for each **Tagi** in the definition of **T**'s definition. If any corresponding parts of x and z are not equal, the expression evaluates to false.

The **With** constructor is equivalent to **Inherits**, except that it takes only two input types, the second of which must be a tuple type. The following illustrates its use to keep attributes that are shared by the elements of a set.

```
AugmentedEmps = EmpRel with [InsuranceCompany: string;
                             CurrentTaxRate: 1..100];
```

AugmentedEmps is a type whose instances are both a set and have tuple components, **InsuranceCompany** and **CurrentTaxRate**. This does not add the two components to the types of individual tuples. To do this, we would write

```
AugEmpTuple = EmpTuple with [InsuranceCompany: string;
                             CurrentTaxRate: 1..100];
```

We now show how multiple inheritance and discriminated union can be used to model an ISA hierarchy. Suppose we wanted to maintain a set of vehicles in the database that were either cars or trucks, or we didn't know which. Suppose all vehicles had vehicle identification numbers as well as brands. The following type definition specifies a structure for holding vehicle descriptions.

```
VehicleTuple = Inherits CreateVehicle
               [GenVehicle: [Vid: number;
                             Brand: string;
                             Color: string];
                Specific:   Union[Car: CarTuple;
                                  Truck: TruckTuple;
                                  DontKnow: bottom]];
```

```
VehicleSet = Set(VehicleTuple) where Key(VehicleSet, Vid);

Database CarsAndSuch: [...; Vehicles: VehicleSet; ...]

To add a Ford truck:

Insert CreateVehicle([2743, "Ford", "red"], [16, 3, 3500]: Truck)
        into Vehicles;

To add a generic vehicle:

Insert CreateVehicle([2744, "International", "green"], DontKnow)
        into Vehicles;

To see only the trucks, we use a macro expansion of the identifier
Trucks that acts like a view.

Trucks :== (All v in Vehicles
                where Case v of
                         Truck: true
                         others: false)
```

Figure 4: Using an ISA hierarchy in ADABTPL

Two features of this definition have not been discussed. The first is the introduction of a named constructor function, **CreateVehicle**, into the type definition. This is a feature of both **Inherits** and tuple types. The second is the **bottom** type. This is a type that can be considered a type of distinguished constants that have no other operations other than equality defined on them. Its semantics is similar to enumerated types in Pascal, but it can be combined with other types in **Union** types in order to handle errors or create *bottom* values of recursive types, such as **Nil** for lists. In order to maintain the set of **VehicleTuples** in a database, we need to define a set type and include a component of the set type in the database. This definition along with a method of updating the set and seeing only the **Truck** tuples is shown in Figure 4.

From this discussion, we can see that certain of what are considered by some to be object-oriented concepts are present in ADABTPL. These include, most notably, encapsulation and inheritance. However, there is no concept of uniquely identified objects, nor of the related idea of automatically maintained sets of existing instances of types (or classes).

2.4 Transactions

ADABTPL transactions are written in an imperative style and address the database by using the identifiers of database components. For example, to add a new employee tuple to the database defined in Figure 1, we write

```
Insert [123, "Adrions", 23] into Emps;
```

Of course, this alone is not a good transaction, since it does not update the NumOfEmps field of the proper department tuple. Figure 5 gives a complete transaction specification for adding a new employee to the database.

```
Transaction AddEmp (NewEmpNo: number where number < 10000;
                    Name: string;
                    DNo: number);

Precondition
  NewEmpNo < 10000 and
  Not NewEmpNo in Emps.EmpNo and
  DNo in Depts. DeptNum;
Begin
  Insert [NewEmpNo, Name, DNo] into Emps;
  Update d in Depts where d.DeptNum = DNo
         by [NumOfEmps := NumOfEmps + 1]
End;
```

Figure 5: A transaction in ADABTPL

2.5 The formality of ADABTPL

The formality of ADABTPL is based on recursive functions and a small set of axioms. The axioms are for four abstract data types: tuples (with non-recursive domains), finite sets, simple lists (one non-recursive domain), and natural numbers. The theory of these types, individually and in combination, has been built using mechanical reasoning embodied in theorem provers based on Boyer-Moore computational logic [3]. This theory is quite general and is used to generate the specific theory of the world being modelled by a database described by an ADABTPL schema. The ADABTPL type definitions are translated into axioms and theorems capturing the semantics of the database system being specified. The nature of the resulting theory is very explicit, in that very little implicit knowledge or assumptions are needed to prove properties of systems specified in ADABTPL. The implicit knowledge is in the form of assumptions that transactions are to be executed atomically and that functions are pure functions. No implicit assumptions about the maintenance of sets of instances of types, referential integrity, or any semantic conventions are made. This theory has allowed us to reason effectively about transactions obeying constraints expressed in ADABTPL [17].

The specific theory of an application generated from an ADABTPL schema is divided into three parts. The first part comprises the axioms of particular tuple types, including the database tuple. Each tuple type has a tuple constructor function associated with it. This function takes an element from each of the component types and produces a tuple. Each component name stands for a selector function that takes a tuple of the type and returns the component value. Tuple axioms specify that selector functions return the value used as input for the corresponding component when the tuple was constructed. Finite set and list axioms are much more complex than tuple axioms and are used in their generic form rather than in a specific form for each set or list type, and thus need not be generated for each database. The second part of the specific theory generated from a schema is the set of integrity constraints contained in **where** clauses. The **where** predicates are added to the specific theory of an application by their direct translation into the functional form of the underlying theory.

The most sophisticated theory generation takes place by instantiating lower order forms of higher order theorems about generic functions and predicates that express very general laws of tuple, finite set, list, natural number theory. This third part of a generated specific theory derives from the use of certain ADABTPL primitives, such as **Key** constraints and the **Update** function. These functions are generic functions that have different properties based on the functions supplied to them when they are used to specify a database or transaction. When an ADABTPL schema and its transactions are processed, the particular uses of higher order functions are examined and specific theorems are generated whenever appropriate. This process is somewhat complex and will not be dealt with further in this paper. We refer the interested reader to [17]. The important thing to appreciate is that an ADABTPL specification of a concept formalizes the concept in the strictest sense, axiomatically and semantically (in terms of lambda calculus reduction), and that the formalization serves to facilitate mechanical reasoning. [1]

3 Object-oriented Concepts and Database Issues

Object-oriented database systems try to synthesize the concepts and ideas of object-oriented programming languages and traditional database systems to create a single, uniform system. Why this combination is attractive has been extensively discussed by others [2,4,7,18,8]. Here we will limit ourselves to noting that the main attraction of such a synthesis lies in the observation that databases offer excellent facilities for managing large amounts of data, but are limited in their expression and structuring facilities, while object-oriented programming languages provide excellent facilities for expressing and structuring complex entities (through data abstraction, encapsulation, and inheritance, for example), but are limited in their secondary storage management capabilities. In this section, we review some of the main concepts behind the object-oriented paradigm, mention the primary issues and concerns in the implementation of object-oriented database systems, and briefly discuss the problem of semantic integrity.

3.1 Object-oriented concepts

An object is an encapsulated abstract data type, and as such its properties need not be single values, but can be other entities of arbitrary complexity. This allows us to create a one-to-one mapping between objects and the entities we are trying to model. A single, real-world entity is represented as a single entity: there is no need to break it up and spread it across relations as would be required in a relational database system, for example. Objects are treated as first-class structures, and can thus be embedded in data structures, passed as parameters, and returned as values.

3.1.1 Object identity

Objects are more than just the abstract data types we find in languages such as Ada and Modula/2. The difference lies in that objects provide the entities they capture with a *strong sense* of identity, both in the representational and the temporal dimensions [10]. This is accomplished with the assignment of system-supplied, immutable identifiers to each object. In object-oriented systems,

1. every object has a unique identifier, i.e., an object identifier functionally determines the object's type and value, and

2. for every identifier present in the system there exists an object with this identifier, i.e., no dangling references are allowed.

The strong sense of object identity allows objects to be shared, and associations among entities can be modelled by relating the corresponding objects and not external references, such as user-defined attributes.

[1] We have implemented several reasoners to prove properties and give feedback to database designers [20,17,14].

3.1.2 Messages and methods

Certain object-oriented systems prescribe a style of interaction between objects that is different from the call-return mode of many programming languages. In these systems communication between objects is accomplished through *message passing*. Each message consists of a receiver-object identifier, the particular message name, and the arguments for the message. *Methods* consist of code that manipulates or returns the state of an object. Methods are analogous to procedures and functions, and represent the external interface to objects. For each message understood by an object, there is a corresponding method that executes the message. So, in these systems, messages and their methods completely define the semantics of objects.

3.1.3 Classes

Objects belong to *classes*, which are characterized by a name and the type of its elements. The name of the class denotes the elements of the class currently in existence, while the type gives the structure of its member objects. So we have that objects of the same type belong to the same class, and that each object can only belong to one class (in most systems). Objects are said to be *instances* of their classes. *Class variables* can be associated with each class, and are useful for expressing class-wide information (e.g., all PC ATs use Intel's 80286), or to capture status information (e.g., a count of its members).

Class hierarchies permit the inheritance of properties between the different entities in the system. Object-oriented systems were among the first to incorporate inheritance mechanisms, such mechanisms not being available in traditional database systems. A class hierarchy is usually depicted as a directed acyclic graph whose nodes represent classes and whose edges represent superclass-subclass relationships. An edge from a class A to a class B signifies that A is a superclass of B, meaning that elements of B inherit the properties (e.g. methods and instance variables) of A. This kind of relationship between classes is an ISA relationship, since every element of B is then also an element of A, and is analogous to the supertype-subtype relationship explained in earlier sections. Further, multiple inheritance is generally allowed by having a class be a subclass of more than one class, thus inheriting the properties of all of its parents. The notion of property inheritance along the class hierarchy facilitates top-down design and implementation of large, complex systems.

3.2 Object-oriented database systems

The general approach to building object-oriented database systems has been to take the concepts of object-oriented programming languages and enrich them with persistent features. To that effect, the main concerns have been with providing an efficient secondary storage object manager, and with maintaining the consistency of the system by implementing transactions, both of which require novel techniques due to the complexity of the entities being dealt with. These two issues are not our direct concern in this paper, but the interested reader is referred to [11,18,7,9,16,15,22]. Our concern here is more inclined to the area of integrity constraints. We believe that this area has not received all the attention it deserves, mainly because of the lack of formalism in the different object models [5]. Next, we briefly discuss the issue of specifying and maintaining integrity constraints, and then how it relates to the deletion of entities in a database.

3.2.1 Semantic integrity

One of the major problems of database systems is their inability to allow designers to express the integrity constraints of the world they are trying to model, let alone to enforce such constraints in any reasonable fashion. Systems aspiring to enforce integrity constraints require a formal specification language and a reasoning component, whereas object-oriented systems have mostly taken ad hoc approaches to formality. It has been hinted by some that constraints in an object-oriented database can be captured and maintained in objects' methods [13,6]. This is what is done in the programming language world to deal with integrity requirements, but suffers from undue complexity. We next discuss our view of this issue.

Embedding knowledge (constraints, in our context) in procedural code has been long known to cause more problems than it resolves. AI systems recognized this years ago from the following facts:

1. It is not possible to mechanically analyze this *buried* knowledge (e.g. determine inconsistencies).
2. Knowledge is dispersed throughout the system.
3. It constitutes a *stab in the dark* to add or modify any knowledge, since interactions between the existing and the updated knowledge is impossible to determine.
4. The system is unable to perform the best optimization possible since it cannot be supplied with all the relevant information.

The answer to this problem is to express all such knowledge declaratively. We have adopted this solution in ADABTPL. (A thorough discussion of the integrity maintenance capabilities of ADABTPL can be found in [17].)

3.2.2 Deleting objects

Something must be said about how objects are removed from a database, in regular database systems and in object-oriented systems. The general object-oriented view is that if an object is not being referenced by any other entity then it is *garbage collected*, or deleted. This is an *implicit* delete operation. What if we still want to have the object around even though it is currently not being referred to? We certainly don't want it garbage-collected. In regular database systems, deletes have to be *explicit*: you cannot get rid of something without saying so. We support the view that such *implicitness* is a dangerous thing to have in a database system.

A **DeleteObject** operation seems to be a reasonable operation to have available. There are times when we want to say that a certain entity has ceased to exist, and that any other entity that was assuming its existence is to be notified. Not providing such an operation means that the application program trying to express this fact has to run barefoot through the database searching for all references to the entity that needs to be purged. This seems very inconvenient and error prone.

In our model of an object-oriented system, the **Destroy** operation is an explicit command. If there are references to the object sprinkled throughout the database, then all of those references are nullified if doing so does not conflict with the integrity constraints of the referencing entity (e.g., if there exists an entity with attribute A:list(Cars), where **Cars** is an object type, with the constraint that A $\neq$ nil). We say more about this in section 4.2 where the semantics of **Destroy** are presented.

4 Formalizing Object-orientation Concepts

In this section, we show how we have added the aspects of object-orientation that are missing in ADABTPL, except for the message passing paradigm. This completes the formalization of nearly all of the object-oriented concepts, certain of them, such as inheritance, having already been formalized in the unaugmented ADABTPL. Our purpose is to allow the ADABTPL user to declare certain types to be types of "objects", and to manipulate instances of these types in a special "object-oriented" manner. The salient features of the special treatment of objects have to do with respecting the "identity" of objects. This refers to the ability of an object to appear in many places, i.e., as a part of more than one component of the database, but to have only one identity, guaranteeing that the object's values stay the same even when an update is specified as occurring to it in only one of its incarnations. This allows so-called "sharing" of objects. Our approach to achieving such semantics in ADABTPL is to allow a type to be declared as an object type, using a special type constructor for this purpose. Instances of object types will have certain operations defined on them including creation, updating and destruction operations. Both the object type declarations and the object manipulation expressions will be translated into ADABTPL in a phase prior to compiling. The purpose here is to express all object-oriented semantics in the base ADABTPL primitives, thus giving our version of object-orientation a formal semantics. This approach also has the advantage of giving the users an "operational" semantics of the object concepts.

4.1 User level specification

The user specifies that a type T is to consist of an object constructed from the value of some other type, **alpha**, by writing, in the simplest case,

```
T = Object(alpha) to Define Class ClassOfT
```

The name **ClassOfT** is supplied by the user and is the name that will be used for the set of instances of type **T** maintained as a component of the database. The type can be declared destroyable, and can be given a null object identifier, a **bottom** object, to be used if an object of the type can be destroyed while it is a component of a tuple. Classes can also be given *class variables* in a clause much like the **With** clause. An example containing all three optional parts is

```
T = Destroyable Object(alpha) NullT:bottom
to Define ClassOfT with Class Variables [H:u; W:o];
```

The user can then create an instance of type **T** and name it **x** by writing:

```
CreateT(val) named x;
```

For updating an object that is referred to by expression **x**

```
Update x by  [value-expression of type alpha]
```

or if alpha is a tuple type with components **C1**, ..., **Cn**

```
Update x by [Ci := --; ...]
```

Objects can only be updated using this command, and this command can only appear at the top level of transactions, not inside functions. This rule derives from our desire to keep the underlying semantics expressible by pure functions with limited name scoping.

To destroy an object, the user writes

```
Destroy x
```

Objects of type **object(alpha)** can be passed to functions anywhere a value of a type that is a supertype of **alpha** is required. (Remember that **alpha** is a supertype of **alpha**.) In order to use a function, say **f**, that accepts an **alpha** value and returns an **alpha** (or a subtype of **alpha**) value to update an object **x** of type **object(alpha)** the user writes:

```
Update x by f(x)
```

4.2 Translating from object-oriented forms to basic ADABTPL

We take the approach that all user level references to objects pretend that objects are duplicated when needed and that the integrity of multiple copies is handled by underlying mechanisms. Then, at the user level there is no need for accessing the identifier of an object. Objects themselves are maintained in the ADABTPL specification derived from the object-oriented specification in special "class sets."

Each object type causes a class set to be defined as a part of the database. For each object type **T** defined as above, a class set type and database component is generated as follows:

```
ClassTSet = Set(Inherits[Id:ObjId; Value: alpha])
            where Key(ClassTSet, IdOf);
```

```
(IdOf(x) is defined as x:Id.)
```

```
Database db: [...; ClassOfT: ClassTSet; ..., ObjectId: number]
```

ClassOfT is the identifier supplied in the declaration of the object type. **ObjectId** contains a number that is the least unused object identifier. It is used to get unique identifiers for new objects. All access to **ObjectId** is by generated code; **ObjectId** is not visible to user level ADABTPL.

Class sets are maintained automatically by the ADABTPL code generated from user level object-oriented update specifications. Class sets may also be accessed by user level code, but objects may not be deleted from or inserted into class sets directly, these operations being performed only through the **Create** and **Destroy** operations. At the base ADABTPL level, objects only appear in their class sets and object identifiers (or **bottom** objects) appear everywhere else. This means that only object types are used by users, and that object types are converted to the object id type (augmented by the **bottom** object where specified) everywhere they appear in user specifications. The only appearance of object types in the converted ADABTPL is in access to the object class sets. In order to maintain the consistency of reference of object identifiers to existing objects in the class sets, **Contains** clauses are generated for each appearance of objects in the user level schema. These clauses express the existence of objects in the class set for each object identifier in the database. These integrity constraints are maintained by the ADABTPL translation of the object-oriented extensions, but are included in order to be used in reasoning about the specified systems. The same analysis of an ADABTPL schema used to build these referential integrity clauses can be used to generate ADABTPL code for destroying objects as we will discuss below.

The **Create** operation must get a unique object identifier, pair it with the supplied value, and place the combination in the class set. Unique object identifiers are modelled here as a monotonically increasing integer component, **ObjectId**, of the database. The following translation is applied to **Create** operations.

```
CreateT(val) named x;
-->
Insert [ObjectId, val] into ClassOfT;
ObjectId := ObjectId + 1;
```

Users can express an update to an object "appearing" anywhere in the database and this is converted to an update of the object in its class set. The update operations are translated as follows:

```
Update x by [update expression]    (x typed as an object)
-->
Update z in ClassOfT where z:Id = x by [update expression]
(x typed as an object id)
```

Passive reference to objects, in which the value of the object is to be used in computing some result, must be handled in two ways depending on whether the reference is "direct" or "indirect." Direct reference means that the object is a single object, the result of an expression or for which the transaction has an identifier, such as x after **CreateT(val) named** x. In this case, the reference is translated to a call to a **ValueOf** function that returns the value held in the class set for the object type. Indirect reference is reference to an object by a function that has received a value that contains the objects as components, either as parts of tuples or in lists and sets that form parts of the value. This is a problem since we specifiy that such components are to contain only the object ids, not the values, which are only held in the class sets for the objects' types. Reference to the class set component of the database in order to get an object's value from within a function is only valid if the class set is an input to the function. (ADABTPL is essentially a functional language with limited name scope inside functions.) In order to overcome this difficulty, each type, whether of an object or value, that has object types as components has a function generated that produces an "expanded" value, in which all object ids are replaced by the objects themselves. These expanded values are sent to functions whenever values containing objects are needed. Since all functions are pure functions with *call-by-value* semantics for argument passing, the temporary duplication specificied by this ploy has limited effects, none of which affects the updating of objects. (Remember that object values can only be updated by the **Update** command at the top level of transactions, not inside functions.)

As usual, the equality function needs to be handled in a special manner. There are two important interpretations of equality when objects are to be compared. The first is value equality and the second is object equality or **identity** [10]. These must be differentiated. Our judgement is that value equality is the more useful of the two and so we have used that as the interpretation of the = comparison operator used on objects. In order to specify identity, which is represented by equal object identifiers in our expanded ADABTPL, the user writes **Same(x, y)**. This translates to **x:Id = y:Id**.

Destroy is the most complicated operation to be handled. (There are some who say that it is too ugly to be allowed.) The strongly typed nature of ADABTPL and the precompilation approach to objects makes the problem tractable. The appearance of objects on lists and in sets is fairly simple to deal with. For each value or object, y, which is a list or set of objects of the type being destroyed, a **Destroy** x leads to a

```
Remove o from y where o = x;
```

being generated. (Remember that the x and the o in the generated code are object ids.) The more problematic case arises when an object can be a part of a tuple. In this case every tuple that contains the object must be replaced by the bottom object defined in the object type definition. This is the sole use of this bottom object.

Remember that the ADABTPL code generated from object extensions is only a semantic specification. Many implementations are possible both for expanded values and for destroying objects. Destruction, for example, could be implemented in a *lazy* manner, by deleting the objects but leaving dangling references in lists, sets and tuples until attempts are made to reference the deleted objects and then deleting or replacing the references at that time. Expanded values also admit a lazy approach in which the class set or the actual location of objects is accessed when the objects are needed inside functions by using pointers or other quick reference techniques. The specifications do not in any way preclude such implementations. Implementations need not use pure functions just because the specification does. The specification only states the semantics that must be obeyed by any implementations and allows us to reason about the systems regardless of the sophistication of the implementation techniques.

```
Vehicle = Object(Inherits[
                Generic:  [Vid: IdType;
                           Brand: string;
                           Color: string];
                Specific: Union[Car:  [Numdoors: number;
                                       NumPassengers: number]
                                Truck: [NumWheels: 2..20;
                                        NumAxles: 2..6;
                                        Tonnage: number];
                                DontKnow: bottom]])
        TO DEFINE CLASS VehicleClass where Key(VehicleClass, Vid)
```

Figure 6: Vehicle objects in extended ADABTPL

4.3 An example of object usage

We now turn to an example of object use in extended ADABTPL in order to further elaborate the object concepts we have formalized in the previous section. We revisit the vehicle example of section 2. Figure 6 gives a schema fragment that a user of extended ADABTPL could write to define a Vehicle object and to name its class **VehicleClass**.

The set of all Ford trucks could then be specified by

```
All t in VehicleClass
    where Brand = "Ford"
          and
          Case t of
             Truck: true
             others: false
```

The operation **CreateVehicle** is supplied automatically by the object type expansion and can be used, for example, to add a Ford truck:

```
CreateVehicle([2743, "Ford", "red"], [16, 3, 3500]: Truck) named t;
```

To create a generic vehicle, we write

```
CreateVehicle([2744, "International", "green"], DontKnow) named v;
```

If the database contains a **Fleet** set with type

```
Set([Name:string; Vehicles: Set(Vehicle)])
```

a truck t can be added to Stemple's fleet by

```
For each f in Fleet where f.Name = "Stemple" Do
    Insert t into f.Vehicles;
```

To paint all Ford trucks black:

```
Update t in VehicleClass
       where Case t of
                Truck: true
                others: false
             and
             t.Brand = "Ford"
       by [Color := "black"];
```

This would have the additional effect of painting all the Ford trucks in **Fleet** black, since they must all be in **VehicleClass** as well. If instead, only Stemple's trucks were to be painted black, we would write

```
For each f in Fleet where f.Name = "Stemple" Do
    Update t in f.Vehicles where
       where Case t of
                Truck: true
                others: false
             and
             t.Brand = "Ford"
       by [Color := "black"];
```

This would change Stemple's trucks in **Fleet** as well as in **VehicleClass**. This illustrates the property of identity that allows an object to be updated regardless of the means of access. Note that there is no constraint that requires vehicles to be in only one person's fleet. A vehicle could, in this database, be in two different fleets. An operation that changes one of Stemple's vehicles changes the same vehicle in anyone else's fleet. This is the way in which object sharing is accomplished.

Changing the type of objects can be accomplished in restricted circumstances, namely those involving discrimiated union and multiple inheritance to achieve a class hierarchy as illustrated by the vehicle example. Suppose we have created a **DontKnow** vehicle name **v** as above. Note that this object has types **Vehicle, Generic, Specific** and **DontKnow**. To change the **DontKnow** to **Car** we must supply the Car attributes and use

```
Update v by [v:Specific := [2, 4]:Car];
```

If we wanted to change it again to a Chevy truck for some reason, we would use

```
Update v by [v.Brand := "Chevy"; v:Specific := [16, 6, 20]:Truck];
```

5 Summary

In this paper we have used a formal database specification language, ADABTPL, to formalize certain object-oriented concepts, most notably, object identity and object class as a container for instances of an object type. We noted that the concepts of inheritance and encapsulation were already contained in ADABTPL, and were thus already formalized. The invocation style of some object-oriented systems, namely message passing, was not addressed and is not the ADABTPL style. Questions of mutability were subsumed into the ADABTPL approach to persistence: the database is the sole persistent object, is an implicit input to all transactions, and is the only place objects can appear.

We used the approach of adding a few lingual constructs to ADABTPL in order to capture the missing object-oriented functionality of ADABTPL, and translating these constructs into pure ADABTPL before compilation or analysis of the specifications. This approach produces a formalization of the added features and has two particularly good properties: it keeps the essential concepts needed to a minimum, and it gives the user an "operational" semantics of the added object-oriented features.

6 Acknowledgments

This paper is based on work supported by the National Science Foundation under grants DCR-8503613, IRI-8606424, and a National Science Foundation Graduate Fellowship (for Adolfo Socorro). Support has also been received under the Office of Naval Research University Research Initiative contract, number N00014-86-K-0764.

References

[1] J. Banerjee, H. Chou, J. F. Garza, W. Kim, D. Woelk, N. Ballou, and H. Kim. Data Model Issues for Object-Oriented Applications. *ACM Transactions on Office Information Systems*, 5(1), January 1987.

[2] T. Bloom and S. B. Zdonik. Issues in the Design of Object-Oriented Database Programming Languages. In *Proceedings of OOPSLA '87, Orlando, Florida*, 1987.

[3] R. S. Boyer and J. S. Moore. *A Computational Logic*. Academic Press, New York, 1979.

[4] R. G. G. Cattell and T. R. Rogers. Combining Object-Oriented and Relational Models of Data. In *Proceedings of the First International Workshop on Object-Oriented Database Systems, Pacific Grove, California*, 1986. A position paper.

[5] S. Danforth and C. Tomlinson. Type Theories and Object-Oriented Programming. To appear in ACM Computing Surveys.

[6] N. P. Derrett, D. H. Fishman, W. Kent, P. Lyngbaek, and T. A. Ryan. *An Object-Oriented Approach to Data Management*. Technical Report, Hewlett-Packard Laboratories, January 1986. STL-86-01.

[7] A. M. Keller. Unifying Database and Programming Language Concepts Using the Object Model. In *Proceedings of the First International Workshop on Object-Oriented Database Systems, Pacific Grove, California*, 1986. A position paper.

[8] M. L. Kersten and F. H. Schippers. Towards an Object-centered Database Language. In *Proceedings of the First International Workshop on Object-Oriented Database Systems, Pacific Grove, California*, 1986.

[9] S. Khoshafian and P. Valduriez. Sharing, Persistence, and Object Orientation: A Database Perspective. In *Proceedings of the Workshop on Database Programming Languages, Roscoff, France*, 1987.

[10] S. N. Khoshafian and G. P. Copeland. Object Identity. In *Proceedings of OOPSLA '86, Portland, Oregon*, 1986.

[11] D. Maier. Why Object-Oriented Databases Can Succeed Where Others Have Failed. In *Proceedings of the First International Workshop on Object-Oriented Database Systems, Pacific Grove, California*, 1986. A position paper.

[12] D. Maier, J. Stein, A. Otis, and A. Purdy. Development of an Object-Oriented DBMS. In *Proceedings of OOPSLA '86, Portland, Oregon*, 1986.

[13] F. Manola and U. Dayal. PDM: An Object-Oriented Data Model. In *Proceedings of the First International Workshop on Object-Oriented Database Systems, Pacific Grove, California*, 1986.

[14] S. Mazumdar, D. Stemple, and T. Sheard. Resolving the Tension between Integrity and Security using a Theorem Prover. In *Proceedings of the ACM-SIGMOD International Conference on Management of Data, Chicago, Illinois*, 1988.

[15] J. E. B. Moss. *Nested Transactions: An Approach to Reliable Computing*. Technical Report, M.I.T. Laboratory of Computer Science, December 1981. M.I.T. Report MIT-LCS-TR-260.

[16] P. O'Brien, B. Bullis, and C. Schaffert. Persistent and Shared Objects in Trellis/Owl. In *Proceedings of the First International Workshop on Object-Oriented Database Systems, Pacific Grove, California*, 1986.

[17] T. Sheard and D. Stemple. Automatic Verification of Database Transaction Safety. To appear in ACM Transactions on Database Systems.

[18] K. E. Smith and S. B. Zdonik. Intermedia: A Case Study of the Differences Between Relational and Object-Oriented Database Systems. In *Proceedings of OOPSLA '87, Orlando, Florida*, 1987.

[19] D. Stemple and T. Sheard. Specification and Verification of Abstract Database Types. In *Proc. of the Third ACM SIGACT-SIGMOD Symposium on Principles of Database Sytems, Waterloo, Ontario*, 1984.

[20] D. Stemple, S. Mazumdar, and T. Sheard. On the Modes and Meaning of Feedback to Transaction Designers. In *Proceedings of the ACM-SIGMOD International Conference on Management of Data, San Francisco, California*, 1987.

[21] D. Stemple and T. Sheard. Construction and Calculus of Types for Database Systems. In *Proceedings of the Workshop on Database Programming Languages, Roscoff, France*, 1987.

[22] D. J. Taylor. How Big Can Atomic Actions Be? In *Fifth International Symposium On Distributed Software and Database Systems, Los Angeles, California*, 1986.

[23] P. Wegner. Workshop on Object-Oriented Programming ECOOP 1987, Paris, June 18, 1987. *SIGPLAN Notices*, 23(1), January 1988. A report of the discussion sessions.

Rules Are Objects Too:
A Knowledge Model For An Active, Object-Oriented Database System*

Umeshwar Dayal, Alejandro P. Buchmann, Dennis R. McCarthy

Computer Corporation of America
4 Cambridge Centre
Cambridge, MA 02142
ARPANET: <lastname>@cca.cca.com

Abstract

Event-Condition-Action (ECA) Rules are proposed as a general mechanism for providing active database capabilities in support of applications that require timely response to critical situations. These rules generalize mechanisms such as assertions, triggers, alerters, database procedures, and production rules that have previously been proposed for supporting such DBMS functions as integrity control, access control, derived data management, and inferencing. This paper argues that ECA rules should be thought of as first class objects in an object-oriented data model. It identifies concepts for modelling the components and properties of rule objects: events (database operations, temporal events, abstract signals from arbitrary user processes, and complex events constructed from these primitive ones); conditions (queries over the database); actions (programs in the query language or some programming language); and coupling modes (which describe whether the event, condition, and action components of a rule should be executed in a single transaction or in separate transactions). The paper discusses the association of timing constraints and contingency plans with rules. Finally, it describes operations on rule objects. The emphasis of the paper is on modelling concepts, rather than on specific syntax.

1. Introduction

Many applications (e.g., computer-integrated manufacturing, program trading, battle management, situation assessment, intelligence analysis, network management, office workflow control, and knowledge-based simulation) require access to large, shared data and knowledge repositories, and require timely response to critical situations. For these applications, it is important to monitor conditions defined on states of the database, and then, once these conditions occur, to invoke specified actions, subject to some timing constraints. For example, inventory control in an automated factory requires that the quantity on hand of each item be monitored; if the quantity on hand falls below a threshold for some item, then a reorder procedure may have to be initiated before the end of the working day. A situation assessment application requires that various targets be tracked; if one is discovered to be within a critical distance, then an alert code may have to be displayed on the commander's screen with the highest possible priority.

This work was supported by the Defense Advanced Research Projects Agency and by the Rome Air Development Center under Contract No. F30602-87-C-0029. The views and conclusions contained in this report are those of the authors and do not necessarily represent the official policies of the Defense Advanced Research Projects Agency, the Rome Air Development Center, or the U.S. Government.

Such *time-constrained* applications are not well served by conventional database management systems (DBMSs), because these DBMSs are *passive*: they execute queries or transactions only when explicitly requested to do so by a user or application program. With a passive DBMS, the onus is on the application programs to poll (periodically query) the database to determine if the situations being monitored have occurred. To ensure timely detection of and response to situations, the application program must poll frequently; but then it runs the risk of flooding the system with queries that usually return an empty answer. An alternative to polling is for each program that updates the database to check the situations being monitored after each update, and to invoke the appropriate actions if any situations turn out to be true. Unfortunately, this *procedural embedding* of operational knowledge compromises software modularity: any modification to the situations being monitored or to the corresponding actions will require modifying every application program that updates the database.

Active database management systems attempt to provide both modularity and timely response. Situations, actions, and timing requirements are all specified declaratively to the system. The system now monitors the situations, triggers the corresponding actions when the situations become true, and schedules tasks to meet both timing requirements and consistency constraints over the shared database, without user or application intervention.

Besides supporting external applications, the active database paradigm is useful for implementing several functions of the DBMS itself, -- often in a more general and flexible way than provided by current implementations -- or for extending these functions. Some examples are:

- *Integrity control:* specifying the events that trigger constraint checking, the constraint to be checked, and the action to be taken when a constraint is violated;
- *Access control:* monitoring access to specified data objects, detecting unauthorized access to protected data, and initiating appropriate action when security violations are discovered; support for multilevel security and privacy can also be provided;
- *Derived data handling:* automatically propagating updates on base data to derived data (materialized views, extracts, snapshots [ADIB81], quasicopies [ALON88], derived fields [CODA73]) immediately, on demand, or at some other specified event (e.g., periodically); also, the converse problem of translating updates on a view down to base data using translation procedures supplied by the view definer;
- *Definition and application of inheritance mechanisms in object-oriented data models:* tailoring inheritance mechanisms and their semantics (whereas single inheritance along a class-subclass hierarchy has generally accepted semantics, the semantics of other types of inheritance such as multiple inheritance and inheritance along complex object-component hierarchies are not universally accepted, and indeed, appear to be context dependent);
- *Alerting:* monitoring -- possibly complex -- conditions over the states of the database (or on transitions between states, trends, and historical data), and notifying an application whenever a condition of interest is met;
- *Performance measurement:* monitoring or tracing various database events, or system events in general (e.g., maintaining statistics to assist query optimization, load balancing, or physical database reorganization);
- *Support for inferencing:* providing modelling, storage, retrieval, optimization, concurrency control, and recovery facilities for the large numbers of rules and facts needed by large-scale expert systems;
- *Enforcement of data interchange and configuration management policies:* providing for the integration of heterogeneous CAD systems for which data interchange rules and configuration management policies cannot be hard-coded into the system.

Most previous work on providing active capabilities in DBMSs focused on one or another of the above applications. The earliest examples of active capabilities in DBMSs were the ON conditions of CODASYL [CODA73]. Triggers and assertions were proposed for System R [ESWA75, ESWA76] as mechanisms for enforcing integrity constraints. In [DATE83], these mechanisms were generalized somewhat to integrity rules and triggered procedures. The use of triggers for maintaining materialized views, snapshots, and derived attribute values, and some algorithms for implementing them have been described in [BUNE79, KOEN81, ROUS82, MORG83, BLAK86, HUDS86, LIND86, HANS87]. The term "active database" was used in [MORG83] to describe a system that supports automatic update of views and derived data as base data are updated. Simple triggers (where the conditions involve only a single relation) are supported by some current commercial relational database systems (e.g., Sybase [DARN87]). Time triggers, where the triggering condition is a point in time (e.g., at 2:00:00 on 5/1/1988), have been described for office system applications in [ZLOO82, BARB85].

In [STON82, STON85], Stonebraker pointed out the utility of production (i.e., situation-action) rules as a unifying mechanism for integrity control, access control, and view processing, and for supporting inference via forward and backward chaining.

AI systems have long used production rules [FORG77], actors [HEWI75], daemons, active objects [BOBR83], and procedural attachment to slots of frames [MINS75, BOBR77, KEE85] as "active" knowledge representation and inference mechanisms. However, these representations and their implementations assume small numbers of objects (rules, facts) stored in main (or virtual) memory, not in large databases on secondary storage. Also, they typically assume a single thread of execution, and hence do not provide any concurrency control over shared objects. By providing capabilities for structuring and efficiently retrieving rules and facts, by permitting asynchronous update (not just at the end of an inference cycle), and by controlling concurrent and serializable execution of rules, active DBMSs support a more powerful problem solving paradigm than these AI systems.

Recent work on active database systems is aimed at embedding production rules in a database system [STON85, RASC88, SELL88, DAYA88a,b, KOTZ88]. This requires extensions both to conventional data models in order to represent rules and their associated requirements in a database, and to conventional execution models in order to accomodate the correct execution of system-triggered actions in addition to user- or application-initiated transactions.

This paper describes work in progress on the knowledge model (an extended data model that includes constructs for representing rules) of HiPAC, an active, object-oriented DBMS under investigation at CCA [DAYA88a,b]. A companion paper [HSU88] describes HiPAC's execution model -- an extension of the nested transaction model.

Central to our knowledge model is the concept of *event-condition-action (ECA) rules*, which generalizes the many different mechanisms introduced previously in the literature to support active DBMS functions. The *event* part of an ECA rule specifies database operations, temporal events, or signals from arbitrary processes; the *condition* part specifies database queries; and the *action* part specifies a program. When the event occurs (is *signalled*), the condition is evaluated; if the condition is *satisfied*, the action is executed.

In Section 2, we derive the modelling requirements for rules from the requirements of time-constrained applciations and the various DBMS functions described above. In Section 3, we argue that rules should be treated as first class objects, and show how rule objects can be added to an object-oriented data model. We emphasize modelling *concepts* in this paper, rather than concrete syntax.

2. Requirements for modelling rules

For alerting functions, a variety of event types have to be modelled. These include database updates (e.g., the position of a target was updated), clock signals (e.g., the output of a sensor may be sampled periodically), or any user- or application-generated signal (e.g., a failure signal from a diagnostic routine on a hardware component).

The conditions to be monitored may be complex, and may be defined not only on single data values or individual database states, but also on sets of data objects (e.g., the total of employees' salaries exceeds the departmental budget), transitions between states (e.g., the new position of the target is closer than the old position), trends and historical data (e.g., the output of the sensor increased monotonically over the last hour).

The execution model requirements may differ from application to application. For some applications, in order to provide timely response to critical events, it may be important to evaluate the condition immediately after the event, and to execute the action part immediately after the condition evaluation. In this *immediate* mode of execution, the processing of the remaining steps of the original transaction (which caused the event to occur) is suspended until the fired rule has been completely processed. Long delays can result in completing the processing of the original transaction, especially if the action part of the rule causes the cascaded firing of other rules. Response times and concurrency can be improved if the condition evaluation or action execution are *detached* from the original transaction (i.e., run in a separate transaction). For example, in a situation assessment application, the transactions that append position reports of ships into the database should be committed independently from any triggered transactions that evaluate distances between the ships and potential targets, and from transactions that cause alerts or countermeasures to be initiated. Similarly, in our inventory control example, it may be desirable to delay the reordering action to the end of the day, just in case a previous order is filled during the day and the quantity on hand goes back above the threshold.

When conditions or actions are detached, parameter bindings from the original transaction may have to be propagated to them. For example, the identifier of the item whose quantity on hand was updated must be passed to avoid checking the condition for *all* items in the inventory. Of course, if the action is detached from the condition evaluation, it may need to re-evaluate the condition for the identified item when it executes, because the state of the database may have changed between the transactions.

Whether the conditions and the actions are immediately coupled or detached, they often have to be executed within tight timing constraints, once the firing event has occurred. For example, a program trading system has to spot price differences in different markets and has to take the corresponding actions (placing buy and sell orders) under timing constraints. Considerable losses can occur if these constraints cannot be declared and the actions are executed arbitrarily late. Instead of hard deadlines (which are very difficult to satisfy in a database system), soft constraints such as value functions and relative task priorities/urgencies may be specified. In cases where the timing constraints cannot be satisfied with existing resources, contingencies may be specified. These may include working on less current or approximate data, producing approximate answers, and dropping some actions altogether.

Finally, a mechanism for activating and deactivating individual rules or sets of rules is often needed. For example, once an item in the inventory has been placed on order, it may be necessary to deactivate the rule that evaluates the threshold condition, until the order is filled (lest the rule keep firing at every update, causing multiple orders to be written). The selective activation and deactivation of rules is also useful in providing a context mechanism to restrict the number of rules that must be searched. For example, once the threshold for an item has been crossed, a different set of rules might be applicable: if the item is critical (i.e., it could cause unacceptable production delays), then requests for it must be filled (until it is depleted), but all managers of projects requiring the item must be notified every day of the current quantity on hand. These rules need not be activated, however, until the threshold has been crossed. Similarly, the set of rules being evaluated while a plane is taxiing must be deactivated the moment it becomes airborne, and a different context activated.

For integrity control, ECA rules provide more flexibility than simple triggers in specifying the events that trigger constraint checking and the actions to be performed if some constraints are violated. Some constraints need to be evaluated immediately after an update event occurs (e.g., value within range). Others need to be deferred to the end of the transaction in which the update event occurs (e.g., customer's accounts should balance after a transfer of funds from one to another). Also, when constraint evaluation is deferred to the end of a transaction, it is usually necessary to fire the integrity checking rule only once, no matter how many times the update event occurred during the transaction. This means that the mechanism for passing bindings between the event and the condition evaluation must aggregate the effects of the multiple occurrences of the update event. These options exist in most proposed constraint mechanisms (e.g., [ESWA75, 76, MORG83, KOTZ88, CASA88]).

More powerful capabilities are often needed when trying to enforce consistency constraints in some "non-traditional" application environments. For example, in a CAD environment, the need has been identified for delayed (detached) evaluation of constraints (e.g., at the end of a design phase instead of after every transaction); for evaluation of constraints on explicit user request; and for specifying context-dependent actions when a constraint is violated (e.g., an update that causes some physical law to be violated must be disallowed, but an update that causes some contractual constraint may require notification to the designer and logging for future negotiations. (A wish-list of rule handling capabilities in design environments can be found in [BUCH88]. We conjecture that most of these requirements can be met by HiPAC's ECA rule mechanism.)

For access control, rules are a convenient mechanism for specifying different security and authorization policies. They can be used for detecting unauthorized access to protected data (even if the attempt was unsuccessful) and can initiate appropriate action. They can be used to safeguard an individual's privacy, for example, by presenting only average data in response to a request for an individual's salary.

Access control adds an interesting twist to the modelling of events: it typically requires that the *beginning* of an event be detected and logged. Thus, a database operation cannot be treated as an instantaneous event, but rather as a sequence of events. Also, the events of interest include read operations, in addition to updates. The action parts of these rules should typically execute in detached mode (i.e., in a separate transaction), and, in fact, should be *causally independent* of the original transaction (i.e., should commit independently of the original transaction), so that the security log is written no matter whether the original transaction commits or aborts.

For the maintenance of derived data, materialized views, and snapshots, ECA rules provide flexibility in specifying when action is to be taken -- immediately when the base data is updated, on demand (i.e., on a user signal), or at some other specified event (e.g., periodically); also, rules allows the tailoring of the action (e.g., propagate the update, or merely notify the user). This, however, imposes no new requirements on modelling rules.

3. Rules as first class objects

Triggers and rules, as proposed in previous work on active DBMS capabiliites, satisfy only a subset of the requirements identified in the previous section. They provide only a very limited set of events (often limited to update of a single relation), frequently don't distinguish between the triggering event and the condition, and have a single coupling mode between event, condition and action (condition evaluation and action are either executed immediately after the triggering event, or always at the end of the transaction before committing).

In POSTGRES, for example, rules are used primarily to propagate updates among related objects. Events are implicit: the system determines whether to perform an action when a base object is updated or when the derived object is requested. However, as pointed out in [STON86], the semantics of these two alternative implementations of a rule are not always identical. Also, the execution model semantics are not clear. Do triggered rules execute in the same transaction or in a different transaction as the update event? Again, the user may see different results depending on whether the rule was executed "eagerly" at update time or "lazily" at read time. Finally, no context mechanism is described.

Because of the above limitations, previous descriptions of rule or trigger systems are less concerned with the propagation of argument bindings from the triggering event to condition evaluation, and thence to action execution; assumptions about the bindings are often hidden in the implementation.

Finally, previous triggering or rule mechanisms do not provide for any definition of timing constraints.

In HiPAC's knowledge model, all of these issues are explicitly treated. HiPAC is an object-oriented DBMS. Rules, like all other forms of data, are treated as objects. There is a rule object class, and every rule is an instance of this class. The difference between the rule object class and other object classes is that HiPAC understands the semantics of rules and invokes a particular operation, *fire*, automatically. Other special operations on rules are *enable* and *disable* for activating and deactivating rules selectively.

There are some advantages to treating rules as first class objects in the model. First, rules can be related to other objects and can also have attributes. This is a convenient mechanism for grouping rules by context (e.g., all rules that have a certain attribute value, or all rules that are related to a certain context object), thus reducing the scope of rule searches. It is also possible to create subclasses of the rule object class and define special attributes or operations on those subclasses.

The second advantage of treating rules as first class objects is that they can be created, modified, or deleted in the same way that other objects are. Also, they are subject to the same transaction semantics as other data objects: a transaction must obtain a read lock on a rule object in order to fire it, and a write lock in order to modify, delete, or deactivate it; hence, a rule that is in the process of being fired by one transaction cannot be modified, deleted, or deactivated by another.

The ECA rules described in this section can be added to any object-oriented data model. However, for concreteness, we will start with the data model that we developed for PROBE [MANO86a]. In the PROBE Data Model, real-world objects are modelled as *entities*. Attributes, relationships and operations on objects are modelled as *functions*. Like entities are grouped into *entity types* (object classes), which may be organized in *generalization (IS_A) hierarchies*: subtypes inherit functions from their supertypes. Although the hierarchy may have convergent paths, inheritance conflicts are not allowed (i.e., if a function is inherited along two convergent paths, then there must be a common ancestor along the paths for which the function is defined).

The rest of this section describes the functions defined over the *rule* entity type. We first describe the functions that define the structure of a rule entity; i.e, its components and attributes. Then, we describe the operations supported on rules.

3.1 Structural definition of rules

The following functions specify the structure of a rule:

Rule identifier Like any other entity, each rule has a unique entity identifier.

Event The event that causes HiPAC to fire the rule. Typed formal arguments may be defined for the event; these are bound to actual arguments when the rule fires.

Condition The coupling mode between the triggering transaction and the condition evaluation, and a collection of queries to be evaluated when the rule is fired.

Action The coupling mode between the condition evaluation and the action execution, and an operation to be executed when the rule is fired and the condition is satisfied.

Timing constraints Deadlines, priorities/urgencies, or value functions.

Contingency plans An alternative action to be executed in case the timing constraints cannot be met.

Attributes Additional properties of rules (may yield scalar values such as strings and integers, or complex entities that may themselves have attributes).

Some properties of rules have to be specified, others may be optional and can take on default values. Essential for every rule is the specification of an event, a condition, and an action. Other properties, such as timing constraints and contingency plans, are optional. If not specified, rule processing just ignores these fields.

When HiPAC detects that the event for a rule has occurred (i.e., has been *signalled*), it *fires* the rule. That is, HiPAC saves the bindings of the formal arguments in the event definition to the actual arguments in the event signal, evaluates the rule's condition, and performs the rule's action if the condition is satisfied, subject to whatever concurrency and timing constraints were defined. For each firing, HiPAC creates a system data structure, a *firing* entity, that records the rule identifier, event signal, bindings, and other relevant system state information (e.g., id of the transaction that signalled the event, user or session id, clock time).

3.1.1 Event

The *Event* function for a rule yields an Event entity. As described in [KOTZ88], an event entity has an identifier and a list of typed formal arguments. One operation, *signal*, is defined for the event entity type. This operation is usually executed by "event detector" components of the system, although it may also be explicitly executed by users or application programs. The signal operation binds the formal arguments specified for the event to actual arguments, as discussed below.

We want to model three kinds of primitive events, associated with the following:

1. Data Manipulation Operations
2. Clock Time
3. External Notification

Since HiPAC is an object-oriented DBMS, all data manipulation is expressed as operations (functions) on objects (entities). For example, Insert_Position (Ship_ID : String, Location : (Lat, Long)) inserts an entity instance of the Position entity type into the database; Update_Inventory (I : Selection_predicate, A : Function_name, S : Update_specification) updates the A attribute-values of the inventory entities selected by I. When an operation is executed, the arguments are bound to actual entities and values in the database: Insert_Position (S1234, (40N, 70W)); or Update_Inventory (Item_No = 987, QOH, QOH = QOH - 10).

Actually, since database operation executions are not instantaneous, but occupy intervals of time (their durations), it is possible to define two events for each operation: the *beginning* of the operation and the *end* of the operation. Access control is typically interested in the beginning event and integrity control in the end event. While the semantics of the end event are clear, the semantics of the beginning event may depend on the operation itself: for the Update_Inventory example above, the Selection_predicate itself is not a useful argument, but rather the set of instances qualified by the Selection_predicate. This means that the beginning event should not be signalled until this set of instances has been determined (but before they are updated).

For system-supplied operations, such as updates and retrievals, we can predefine the points during the execution of the operation when the beginning and end events are signalled, and the arguments that are associated with these events. Such events are detected and signalled by components of the system (the transaction manager or query processor; e.g., in POSTGRES, low-level flags or "persistent locks" are set and detected by the lock manager [STON85]).

For user-defined operations (which, of course, are the hallmark of an object-oriented system), the events and their arguments must be specified by the definer of the function. Typically, the arguments of the beginning event are the input arguments of the operation, and those of the end event are the output arguments. (A formal specification language for events is beyond the scope of this paper.)

The beginning and end of a transaction are also considered events in this model. The arguments passed when these events are signalled include the transaction, user, and session identifiers, and -- implicitly -- the entire database state (since this information is maintained by the system anyway). Obviously, these events can be detected and signalled by the transaction manager.

Temporal events are also supported in this model. These can be absolute points in time, defined by the system clock (e.g., 9:00:00 a.m., April 10, 1988) relative (30 secs after event A occurred), or periodic (every day at midnight). Temporal object classes can be defined in the PROBE Data Model as subtypes of the *pointset* entity type (the reader is referred to [DAYA85, MANO86b] for details). Associated with these temporal types are the units for measuring time (seconds, days, etc.), the nature of time (discrete vs. continuous, linear vs. branching), and predicates (after, before, equal); for relative time, we associate a reference event and a reference interval; and for periodic events, we associate a reference point (i.e., the point of first occurrence) and a period (an interval). We postulate the existence of a temporal event detector component in the system, which reads the system clock and signals temporal events as they occur. Arguments (e.g., event_id, description) may be defined for a temporal event; these are passed to the rule firing when the event is signalled.

The third kind of primitive event supported by HiPAC is the *abstract* event, which is not necessarily associated with a database operation or time, and cannot be directly detected by HiPAC. These events and their arguments are defined in the model, but are detected and signalled by users or other programs. An example is Flight_Airborne (Flight_No, Destination, Takeoff_Time, Aircraft, Wind_Speed, Wind_Direction), which is signalled by a user, perhaps, when a flight takes off.

Operations on derived data (e.g., views) may also be considered abstract events. For such events, an *internal rule* may be defined by the database administrator (or view definer) to specify how and when to signal the event as events on the underlying (stored) data are signalled. For example, consider a view Boston_Emp defined over the stored entity type Emp by selecting those Emp entities where City = Boston. A user or application program may be interested in detecting changes to the derived entity set Boston_Emp if the underlying set Emp is updated. For this, the view definer can write an internal rule that is fired when the event Update_Emp is signalled; the condition part of the internal rule checks if the set of Emp entities where City = Boston has changed as a result of the update; if it has, the action part signals the event Update_Boston_Emp. These internal rules are useful in several ways. First, they allow "new" abstract events to be defined. Second, they insulate users from knowing which entities are "stored" in the database and which are "derived." Third, they insulate users from knowing what a particular event detector outputs -- the database administrator can provide internal rules that take detector output and produce the abstract event signals; thus, the original "weak" detector together with the internal rule (and HiPAC's rule evaluation components) comprise the abstract event detector.

In addition to these three classes of primitive events, the model supports *composite* events. Three event constructors are supported, and a composite event specification is, in general, a regular expression built up using these constructors. For each constructor, we must define when the composite event is signalled, and what the arguments of the composite event are.

The *disjunction* of two events, E1 and E2, is a composite event, E, denoted (E1 | E2), that is signalled when either E1 or E2 is signalled. E's arguments are the "outerunion" of E1's arguments and E2's arguments; i.e., if E1 was signalled, then E's arguments are bound to E1's arguments with E2's set to NULL, and vice versa if E2 was signalled. This constructor is useful because it allows rules to be succinctly defined. For example, if both ships and targets can move, then a single rule fired by the composite event (Update_Position (S : Ship) | Update_Position (T : Target)) can check whether the critical distance between ships and targets has been crossed, instead of writing two rules.

The *sequence* of two events, E1 and E2, is a composite event, denoted (E1 ; E2), that is signalled when E2 is signalled, provided that E1 had been signalled before during this same transaction or rule firing. The arguments of the composite event are the union of the arguments of E1 and E2. The utility of this constructor is that it allows us to pass bindings to deferred or detached conditions and actions. Thus, for example, if the event of a rule is (Update_Inventory(I, A, S) ; EOT), then we can pass the specific items that were updated to the condition evaluation, which occurs at end of the transaction; this will allow the condition to be evaluated only for these specific items and not for the entire set of Inventory instances. Without this constructor, it would be necessary to write two rules, each fired by one of the events, and to save the arguments of the first event explicitly in the database (in the action part of the first rule) in order that they may be used in the second rule.

The motivation for the third constructor is that, often, we want a rule to fire only once per transaction, provided a given event was signalled at least once during the transaction, rather than firing every time the event was signalled. We want the arguments of the signals to be accumulated, so that they can be passed to the condition and action. This is especially useful for integrity checking, because we want to know that an update occurred during a transaction, but we do not need to evaluate the constraint until the end of the transaction, at which point -- for reasons of efficiency -- we need the set of instances that were updated. To model this requirement, we introduce the *closure* constructor. The closure of event E is denoted E*, and is signalled after E has been signalled an arbitrary number of times in a transaction. Note that, for definiteness, we require that the closure be followed by another event, thus: (E* ; E'). How E*'s arguments are "accumulated" from E's depends on the type of each argument and must be specified in E*'s definition. For example, if E is the beginning of an event that updates a set of instances each time it is signalled, then E* may include the union of these sets. If E is an abstract event that passes a list argument each time it is signalled, then the corresponding argument of E* may be the concatenation of these lists.

The expressions for defining composite events are similar to regular expressions. Indeed, composite events can be detected by finite state automata, constructed out of primitive event detectors. These automata can be generated at the time the rule is compiled, and do not need to read the state of the database (only the argument bindings passed in the event signals).

3.1.2 Condition

The condition part of a rule is also an object; its structure is described by two functions:

- a *coupling mode* between the triggering transaction (in which the event that caused the rule to fire was signalled) and the condition evaluation; and
- a *collection of queries*;

The coupling mode function of the rule object indicates when a condition should be evaluated relative to the event occuring in the triggering transaction. Four possibilities exist (see [HSU88] for details):

1. Immediately when the triggering event is signalled, in which case the execution of the triggering transaction is suspended until the condition (and possibly the action) is executed.
2. In a deferred mode, in which case the condition is evaluated at the end of the transaction before the triggering transaction commits.
3. Detached but causally dependent, meaning that the condition is evaluated in a separate transaction but after the triggering transaction has commited; if the triggering transaction aborts, the condition is not evaluated.
4. Detached and causally independent, meaning that the condition is evaluated in a separate transaction and that the scheduler is free to schedule this transaction independently of the triggering transaction.

Deferred evaluations were originally introduced in HiPAC's execution model to distinguish between immediate condition evaluation and evaluation at the end of the transaction. The composite triggers introduced in the previous section now make it possible to eliminate the special treatment of this mode: the deferred coupling mode is equivalent to the immediate mode triggered by the sequence of the initial event and the end of transaction event.

The second component of a condition is a collection of queries (expressed in some query language). The condition is said to be satisfied if *all* the queries return non-empty answers. The main reason for allowing the condition to be a collection of queries, rather than a simple predicate, which returns only true or false, is that we gain the flexibility of passing additional arguments to the action part. If the answers to the queries are non-empty, they are added to the firing entity for the rule, and are passed to the action execution, in addition to the arguments that were bound in the event signal. In effect, the successful evaluation of the condition signals an internal event, whose arguments include the original bindings plus the results of the condition evaluation. The action part then can refer to the bindings at event time, at condition evaluation time, and to the state of the database at the time the action is executed. These bindings persist until the action part of the rule has executed, i.e., as long as the firing entity remains. (To save argument bindings beyond a single rule firing, the action part would have to explicitly save them in the database or signal an abstract event that contains these arguments.)

Example 1
Let E1 be the event Beginning_Update_Position (T : Target, Position(T) : (Lat, Long))
and E2 be the event End_Update_Position (T : Target, Position(T) : (Lat, Long))

Event: (E1 ; E2)(T : Target, Position@E1(T) : (Lat, Long), Position@E2(T) : (Lat, Long))

Condition:
  Coupling: Detached/causally dependent
  Query: { S, Ship_No(S), Position(S) |
    S in Ship AND
    Distance (Position(S), Position@E1(T)) > 10 AND
    Distance (Position(S), Position@E2(T)) < 10 }

In this example, the rule is fired when the position of a target is updated; the signal contains the (identifier of the) target, and the old and new positions (i.e., the positions at the beginning and end of the update). The condition, which we have expressed in a calculus-like variant of DAPLEX (we will not define this language formally in this report), retrieves the set of ships, together with their ship numbers and positions, that were more than 10 units distant from the target before it was updated, but now are less than 10 units distant from the target. If this set is non-empty, then an internal event is signalled by the condition monitor to notify the rest of the system that the condition is satisfied.

3.1.3 Action

The action for a rule is also a complex object, whose structure is defined by two functions:

1. a *coupling mode* between the transaction in which the condition was evaluated and the execution of the action; and
2. an *operation* to be executed in the action.

The coupling mode function describes whether the action should be executed immediately after the condition is signalled; deferred to the end of the transaction in which the condition is signalled (note that if the condition evaluation itself was deferred, then the immediate and deferred modes for the action are equivalent); detached and causally dependent; or detached and independent [HSU88].

The operation can be a program in the data manipulation language, which includes database operations (retrievals, updates, abstract event signals, and other function invocations over arbitrary entity types), or a message to an external program or process. The operation is defined over arguments that are passed in the rule firing entity (including those passed by the condition signal). In addition, of course, the operations can refer to the database state at the "current" time, i.e., at the time the operation is executed.

Example 2
Let E1 be the event Beginning_Update_Position (T : Target, Position(T) : (Lat, Long))
and E2 be the event End_Update_Position (T : Target, Position(T) : (Lat, Long))

Event: (E1 ; E2)(T : Target, Position@E1(T) : (Lat, Long), Position@E2(T) : (Lat, Long))

Condition:

Coupling: Detached/causally dependent
Query: { S, Ship_No(S), Position(S) |
S in Ship AND
Distance (Position(S), Position@E1(T)) > 10 AND
Distance (Position(S), Position@E2(T)) < 10 }

Action:

Coupling: Immediate
Operation: begin
Display_Commander ("code red", Position(S), Position@E2(T));
Signal (Prepare_Countermeasure (S, Position(S), T, Position(T));
end

The action part invokes a function to display some information on the commander's screen, and then signals an abstract event. Presumably, there are rules for preparing countermeasures to the alert condition that has just been detected, which will be fired by this abstract event.

3.1.4 Timing constraints

Timing constraints are not exclusive properties of rules, but can be attached to any task in the HiPAC system. Therefore, they are defined as a separate object class, which is linked to the corresponding rule or its condition or action part. This is a topic of ongoing research.

3.1.5 Contingency plans

Contingency plans are alternate actions that can be invoked whenever the action specified in a rule cannot be realized, particularly when operating under timing constraints. For example, if the triggered action involves the analysis of an image and the resources available do not allow the processing to finish in time, the analysis can be carried out in less time on a less detailed image. This image may be obtained, for example, by eliminating one frequency band. Like timing constraints, contingency plans may have a more global scope than the action part of a single rule. For instance, the plan may be to drop some tasks, transactions, or rules altogether, or to process a different set under overload conditions. The modelling concepts for contingency plans have not yet been worked out. Various mechanisms may be considered: special rules (invisible to the end user), internally generated signals, hardcoded modifications to the scheduler (e.g., drop all transactions below a threshold priority level), etc.

3.1.6 Attributes

In addition to the properties discussed above, rules may also have additional attributes, which may be useful for providing context, as we will see in Example 3 below.

3.2 Operations on Rules

The operations on rule objects are:

Create Create a new rule.

Delete Delete an existing rule.

Enable Activate a rule for some combination of the rule's arguments.

Disable Deactivate a rule for some combination of the rule's arguments.

Fire Create a firing entity for the rule; evaluate the rule's condition; if satisfied, signal the condition event; and execute the rule's action.

The first four of these are operations are performed at the request of applications. The fire operation is performed automatically by the system in response to event signals, as described above.

Since rules are objects, the operations on rules are performed in transactions and are subject to concurrency control. Create, delete, enable, and disable are considered write operations, while fire is considered a read operation. Therefore, concurrent firings of a rule are allowed, but the other operations require exclusive access to the rule object.

A rule entity is an instance of a rule type. A rule is created by invoking the create function on the rule type. Rules must be deleted explicitly. They are not automatically "garbage collected", since there may be no reference to a rule in another object.

A rule fires automatically when its event is signalled. An application can explicitly fire a rule by signalling its event. The enable and disable operations are conceptually assumed to manipulate a persistent *status* entity (invisible to the user) associated with the rule, which records whether the rule is currently enabled or disabled for some combination of arguments. A rule will fire when its event is signalled, provided that its status is enabled for the actual arguments bound in the signal. The utility of the enable and disable operations is that they can simplify the specification of conditions in rules by avoiding explicit reference to "status" objects that are stored in the "user visible" part of the database. The following example illustrates this point. The Code_Red subtype of rules is activated by the firing of this rule, simply by executing the Enable command, rather than by setting a flag whose Boolean value would have to be tested in each of the Code_Red rules.

Example 3

Let E1 be the event Beginning_Update_Position (T : Target, Position(T) : (Lat, Long))
and E2 be the event End_Update_Position (T : Target, Position(T) : (Lat, Long))

Event: (E1 ; E2)(T : Target, Position@E1(T) : (Lat, Long), Position@E2(T) : (Lat, Long))

Condition:

Coupling: Detached/causally dependent
Query: { S, Ship_No(S), Position(S) |
S in Ship AND
Distance (Position(S), Position@E1(T)) > 10 AND
Distance (Position(S), Position@E2(T)) < 10 }

Action:

Coupling: Immediate
Operation: begin
Display_Commander ("code red", Position(S), Position@E2(T));
Enable (R in Code_Red_Rules)
Signal (Prepare_Countermeasure (S, Position(S), T, Position(T));
end

4. Summary and Future Work

HiPAC's knowledge model is based on event-condition-action rules, which are treated as first class objects. We have described modelling requirements and concepts, and illustrated these via examples. Concrete syntax for a rule language in which all components of a rule can be defined remains to be developed. Future work also includes expanding the knowledge model to include specifications of timing constraints and contingency plans.

5. References

ADIB81 M. Adiba, "Derived Relations: A Unified Mechanism for Views, Snapshots, and Distributed Data," *Proceedings 7th International Conference on Very Large Data Bases,*, 1981.

ALON88 R. Alonso, D. Barbara, H. Garcia-Molina, and S. Abad, "Quasi-Copies: Efficient Data Sharing for Information Retrieval Systems," *Advances in Database Technology -- EDBT'88*, (J.W. Schmidt, S. Ceri, M. Missikoff, eds.), Lecture Notes in Computer Science 303, Springer-Verlag (1988).

BANC86 F. Bancilhon and R. Ramakrishnan, "An Amateur's Introduction to Recursive Query Processing Strategies," *Proc. 1986 ACM SIGMOD Conference on Management of Data*, pp. 16-52.

BARB85 F. Barbic and B. Pernici, "Time Modeling in Office Information Systems," *Proc. 1985 ACM SIGMOD Conference on Management of Data*, pp. 51-62.

BLAK86 J. Blakely, P. Larson, and F. Tompa. "Efficiently Updating Materialized Views." *Proc. 1986 ACM SIGMOD Conference on Management of Data*, pp. 61-71.

BOBR77 D. Bobrow and T. Winograd. "An Overview of KRL, A Knowledge Representation Language." *Cognitive Science* **1**(1), 1977, pp. 3-46.

BOBR83 D. Bobrow and M. Stefik. *The Loops Manual*. Intelligent Systems Laboratory, Xerox Corporation, 1983.

BUCH88 A. Buchmann and U. Dayal. "Constraint and Exception Handling for Design, Reliability, and Maintainability." *ASME Symposium "Engineering Database Management: Emerging Issues*, San Francisco, August 1988.

BUNE79 P. Buneman and E. Clemons. "Efficiently Monitoring Relational Databases." *ACM Trans. on Database Systems 4*, 3 (September 1979), pp. 368-382.

CASA88 M.A. Casanova, A.L. Furtado, L. Tuckerman. "Enforcing Inclusion Dependencies and Referential Integrity." *Proceedings 14th International Conference on Very Large Data Bases.*, 1986, pp. 384-391.

CODA73 CODASYL Data Description Language Committee. *CODASYL Data Description Language Journal of Development June 1973*. NBS Handbook 113 (1973).

DARN87 M. Darnovsky, J. Bowman. "TRANSACT-SQL User's Guide," Document 3231-2.1, Sybase Inc., 1987.

DATE83 C.J. Date. *An Introduction to Database Systems, Volume II*. Addison-Wesley, Reading, Massachusetts, 1983.

DAYA85 U. Dayal et al. "PROBE - A Research Project in Knowledge-Oriented Database Systems: Preliminary Analysis." Technical Report CCA-85-03, Computer Corporation of America, July 1985.

DAYA88a U. Dayal et al. "The HiPAC Project: Combining Active Databases and Timing Constraints." *SIGMOD RECORD* **17**, No. 1 (March 1988).

DAYA88b U. Dayal et al "HiPAC: a Research Project in Active, Time-Constrained Database Management, Interim Report." Technical Report CCA-88-02, Computer Corporation of America, June 1988.

ESWA75 K. P. Eswaran and D. D. Chamberlain. "Functional Specifications of a Subsystem for Data Base Integrity." *Proc. 1st International Conference on Very Large Data Bases* (September 1975).

ESWA76 K. P. Eswaran. "Specifications, Implementations, and Interactions of a Trigger Subsystem in an Integrated Data Base System." IBM Research Report RJ1820 (August 1976).

FORG77 C.L. Forgy and J. McDermott. "OPS -- A Domain-Independent Production System Language." *Proc. Fifth International Conf. on Artificial Intelligence*, Cambridge, Massachusetts (1977).

HANS87 E. Hanson. "A Performance Analysis of View Materialization Strategies." *Proceedings of the 1987 ACM SIGMOD Conference on Management of Data*, (May 1987), pp 440-453.

HEWI73 C. Hewitt, P. Bishop, and R. Steiger. "A universal modular ACTOR formalism for artificial intellignece." *Proc. 3rd International Joint Conference on Artificial Intelligence*, 1973, pp235-245. 1975.

HUDS86 S. Hudson and R. King. "CACTIS: A Database System for Specifying Functionally-Defined Data." *Proc. 1st International Workshop on Object-Oriented Database Systems* (September 1986), pp.26-37.

HSU88 M. Hsu, R. Ladin, and D. McCarthy. "An Execution Model for Active Data Base Management Systems." *Proc. 3rd International Conference on Data and Knowledge Bases* (June 1988).

KEE85 Intellicorp. *KEE Software Development System User's Manual* (1985).

KOEN81 S. Koenig and R. Paige. "A Transformational Framework for the Automatic Control of Derived Data." *Proc. 7th International Conference on Very Large Data Bases* (September 1981), pp. 306-318.

KOTZ88 A Kotz, K. Dittrich, and J. Mulle. "Supporting Semantic Rules by a Generalized Event/Trigger Mechanism." *Proc. International Conference on Extending Database Technology* (March 1988).

LIND86 B. Lindsay, L. Haas, and C. Mohan. "A Snapshot Differential Refresh Algorithm." *Proc. 1986 ACM SIGMOD Conference on Management of Data*, pp. 53-60.

MANO86a F. Manola and U. Dayal. "PDM: An Object-Oriented Data Model." *Proc. 1st International Workshop on Object-Oriented Database Systems* (September 1986).

MANO86b F. Manola and J. Orenstein. "Toward a general Spatial Data Model for an Object-Oriented DBMS." *Proc. 12th International Conference on Very Large Data Bases*, Kyoto, Japan, August 1986.

MINS75 M. Minsky. "A Framework for Representing Knowledge." in *The Psychology of Computer Vision* (P. Winston, ed.), McGraw-Hill: New York (1975).

MORG83 M. Morgenstern. "Active Databases as a paradigm for Enhanced Computing Environments." *Proceedings 9th International Conference on Very Large Data Bases*, 1983, pp. 34-42.

RASC88 L. Raschid, S.W. Su. "A Transaction-Oriented Mechanism to Control Processing in a Knowledge Base Management System." *Proceedings 2nd International Conference on Expert Database Systems*, 1988, pp. 163-174.

ROSE88 A. Rosenthal and U. Chakravarthy. "Anatomy of a Modular Multiple Query Optimizer", VLDB88, Los Angeles, Sept. 1988.

ROUS82 N. Roussopoulos. "View Indexing in Relational Databases." *ACM Trans. on Database Systems* **7**, No. 2, pp. 258-290 (June 1982).

SELL88 T. Sellis and N. Roussopoulos. "Deep Compilation of Large Rule Bases." *Proc. 2nd International Conference on Expert Database Systems* (April 1988).

STON75 M. Stonebraker. "Implementation of Integrity Constraints and Views by Query Modification." *Proc. 1975 ACM SIGMOD Conference on Management of Data* (May 1975).

STON82 M Stonebraker et al. "A Rules System for a Relational Data Base Management System." *Proc. 2nd International Conference on Databases*, Jerusalem, June 1982.

STON85 M. Stonebraker. "Triggers and Inference In Database Systems." *On Knowledge Base Management Systems*, Brodie and Mylopoulos (Eds.), Springer-Verlag (1986).

STON86 M. Stronebraker, E. Hanson, and C.-H. Hong. "The Design of the POSTGRES Rules System." in *The POSTGRES Papers* (M. Stonebraker and L.A. Rowe, eds.), Memorandum No. UCB/ERL/ M86/85, Electronics Research Laboratory, University of California, Berkeley, California (November 1986).

ZLOO82 M. Zloof. "Office-by-example: a business language that unifies data and word processing and electronic mail." *IBM Systems Journal* **21**, No. 3, pp. 272-304 (1982).

Abstract Object Types for Databases

H.-D. Ehrich
Informatik/Datenbanken, Technische Universität, Postfach 3329, D-3300 Braunschweig, FR GERMANY

A. Sernadas C. Sernadas
Departamento de Matematica, Instituto Superior Tecnico, 1096 Lisboa, PORTUGAL

Abstract - *There is a need for exploring the theoretical and methodological foundations of database design and development with the intention to achieve provably correct systems and higher levels of reusability. To this end, topics rarely addressed so far in this area must be investigated, among them full incorporation of dynamic aspects, static and dynamic integrity checking, formal methods strongly backed by a sound theory, and design-in-the-large issues like modularization and parameterization. Our approach combines the object-oriented paradigm with experiences in formal methods in software engineering, especially algebraic data type theory, logical approaches to systems specification and design, and process algebra. In analogy to algebraic data type theory, we propose mathematical models for the basic notions of object, object type and abstract object type.*

1. Introduction

What is a *database object* in the sense of object-oriented databases? How are database objects put together into *object types*? What is an *abstract* object type? What is it that makes an object or object type *complex*? How can abstract object types be *specified*? How can they be *implemented*? How can we prove *correctness*, both of specification and of implementation?

These questions - and many more - have to be answered satisfactorily in order to provide a reliable fundament for object-oriented databases. There is a need for exploring the theoretical and methodological foundations of database design and development with the intention to achieve provably correct systems and higher levels of reusability.

Object-oriented databases is a rather new field, and the development seems to be somewhat different from that of object-oriented programming. The latter began as early as 1967 with the simulation language SIMULA (DMN67), but the breakthrough is usually attributed to Smalltalk-80 (GR83). According to this development, objects are highly *dynamic* entities, displaying an active behaviour. In contrast to this, the current emphasis in object-oriented databases is more on structural aspects, especially complex object structures (Lo85, DD86). Object dynamics is largely neglected. In fact, there is some confusion about terms: a system with complex objects is not quite the same as an object-oriented system, although there are some relationships. An interesting development towards a database system modelling the behaviour, not just the structure of entities is GemStone (MSOP86, MS87).

Applying object-oriented programming ideas to databases raises a number of problems, mainly concerned with long-term persistence and large collections of objects (Be87). For instance, the problem of object *identity* becomes increasingly important (KC86). Many of these problems are not well understood, there is a definite lack of theory. To a large extent, this also holds for object-oriented programming (Am86), but matters are changing. There is, for instance, the inspiring work of Goguen and Meseguer (GM87) on unifying functional, relational and object-oriented programming on the basis of logic and algebra. Specific database issues are only marginally addressed there, but the work is relevant for databases, too. An algebraic approach to object identity is given in (Eh86, EDG86, SSE87).

We are working on an object-oriented approach to the design of information systems, incorporating object dynamics, static and dynamic integrity checking, formal methods strongly backed by a sound theory, and design-in-the-large issues like modularization and parameterization (SSE87, SFSE88).

In SSE87, we propose a formal approach to the specification of *societies of interacting objects*. The structure and behaviour of each object is defined using a primitive language that also provides the means for specifying the interactions between objects through *event sharing*. An algebraic semantics for this language is outlined. As a byproduct, the Kripke interpretation structure for the invisaged logic of object behaviour is established. The specifications are organized in two layers: (a) the *universe* of objects, their attributes and data; (b) the space of the global *trajectories* and *traces* of the society of objects. *Constraints* of several kinds can be imposed at both layers. The main issue in the construction of the universe is the *naming* of all possible objects. With respect to (b), the emphasis is on the definition of the joint behaviour of objects in terms of the allowed sequences of events that may happen in their lives.

In SFSE88, we discuss the notion of an *abstract* object type, incorporating in a compact and precise form all aspects of object structure and dynamic behaviour, including concurrency. Fundamentally, objects deal with *states* and *processes*. Concepts, tools and techniques are provided for the abstract definition of objects. Each object is described as a temporal entity that *evolves* because of the events that happen during its life. Both lifeness and safety requirements can be stated and verified.

Our current endeavour is to develop an object-oriented specification language for information systems named OBLOG, combining the object-oriented paradigm with experiences in formal methods in software engineering, especially algebraic data type theory, logical approaches to systems specification and design, and process algebra. We take care to provide a mathematical semantics as well as proof methods consistent with the semantics.

For making progress in object-oriented information systems design, we feel it is essential to base specification languages and methodologies and implemetation methods on a careful study of logic and semantic fundamentals. In this paper, we concentrate on the latter, giving a brief outline of what we think is an adequate and useful model for objects, object types, and abstract object types.

2. Objects

What is an object? A common view seems to be that it is something like a *software module* with an interface of named *operations* and a hidden local *state*, employing principles of data abstraction and encapsulation. But this is not the whole story: objects are organized into *object types* which display a sophisticated *subtyping* structure, together with an appropriate *inheritance* mechanism (CW85). Moreover, there is the whole world of object dynamics: objects may be *created*, *changed* and *destroyed*, and they may have an *internal activity* of their own. And there is some mechanism of *communication* or *interaction* between objects, e.g. by means of *messages* or *event sharing*.

Taking a more abstract view, the principle properties of an object are that it has a *state* which can change as a reaction to certain *events*, and which can be *observed*, for instance by means of *attributes* with varying *values*, displaying an observable *behaviour* in time. There have been two approaches to model this in mathematical terms: (1) objects are *state machine* (GM87) or (2) objects are *processes* (HN87) in the sense of process algebra (Ho85).

Let X be a given set of *events*. Events arise from calling methods (in the sense of object-oriented programming) with actual parameters. Thus, in theory, there might be infinitely many events. Let Y be a set of *observations*. Observations arise from values of attributes: if $A=\{a_1,...,a_r\}$ is a finite set of attributes, each with an associated type *type*(a_i), $1 \le i \le r$, then an *observation* is a set $y \subseteq \{(a_1:d_1),\ldots,(a_r:d_r)\}$ of attribute-value pairs where $d_i \in$ *type*(a_i) for $1 \le i \le r$ (undefined attributes do not appear in an observation). Thus, in theory, there might be infinitely many observations. By *obs*(A) we denote the set of all observations over attributes A.

A *state machine* $M=(S,X,Y,\delta,\beta,s_0)$ consists of (possibly infinite) sets S of states, X of inputs, and Y of outputs, together with a state transition mapping $\delta:S \times X \longrightarrow S$, an output mapping $\beta:S \longrightarrow Y$, and an initial state $s_0 \in S$.

A state machine models an object with events X and observations $Y \subseteq$ *obs*(A). We assume δ to be partial and β to be total: not every event may happen in every state, but there exists always an observation (which might, of course, be empty). The initial state s_0 corresponds to non-existence, all other states are states of existence. So the first event applied to an object should *create* it. The further events applied to the object *update* it in some way while it exists, and the last event, if there is one, *destroys* the object by bringing it out of existence. This way, an object processes *streams* $X^\sigma = X^* \cup X^\omega$, i.e. finite or infinite sequences, of events. A *life cycle* of an object is a stream of events that, when starting the machine in s_0, never encounters an undefined transition and ends in s_0 or goes on forever. Note that finite life cycles can be catenated, giving rise to several incarnations of the same object. The observations along life cycles, however, do not depend on previous incarnations.

A *process* over an alphabet X is a set $\Lambda \subseteq X^\sigma$ of streams over X. Thus, the set of life cycles of an object is a process. Our process model for objects is based on life cycles and observations along life cycles, abstracting from internal states. To be precise, an *object* $ob=(X,A,\Lambda,\alpha)$ consists of a set X of events, a finite set A of attributes, a set $\Lambda \subseteq X^\sigma$ of life cycles, and a total observation mapping $\alpha:X^* \longrightarrow$ *obs*(A) saying which attributes have which values after a finite stream (in particular after a finite initial segment of a life cycle).

Given an object as a state machine, it is obvious how to derive the process model for the same object. Not quite so obvious is perhaps that it also goes the other way round (provided we make a few natural assumptions): given an object $ob=(X,A,\Lambda,\alpha)$ as an observed process, there is a canonical state machine M "implementing" it in the sense that the life cycles and observations of the state machine are exactly those of the observed process. M can be constructed using well-known automata-theoretic techniques.

The process model is more abstract than the machine model, and it does not lose essential information. By not dealing explicitly with states, it is mathematically much simpler. So we adopt it as a semantic basis for our work.

An immediate advantage is that it is easy to express the fundamental and important *is* relationship between (single) objects. For example, a patient *is* a person at the same time, showing all attributes that he/she has as a person and being subject to all events that can happen to him/her as a person. That is, patients *inherit* attributes and events from persons, and patients can have additional attributes and events, for instance those having to do with surgery. In the process model, if $ob_i=(X_i,A_i,\Lambda_i,\alpha_i)$, $i=1,2$, are objects, then ob_2 *is* ob_1 iff $X_1 \subseteq X_2$ and $A_1 \subseteq A_2$, and the following compatibility conditions between life cycles and observations hold: (1) $\Lambda_2 \downarrow X_1 \subseteq \Lambda_1$ and (2) $\alpha_1(\tau \downarrow X_1) = \alpha_2(\tau) \downarrow A_1$ for all $\tau \in X_2^*$. Here, $\downarrow X_1$ corresponds to the hiding (concealment) operator on processes and the restriction operator on traces (Ho85), and $\downarrow A_1$ restricts the observation to the attributes in A_1.

This is just a small example of the simplicity and mathematical elegance the process view provides. We only mention that, among others, also the composition of objects to complex objects as well as object interaction, e.g. by event sharing, can be studied very satisfactorily in this setting.

3. Object Types

So far, we have dealt with *single* objects. An object *type* is a set of objects which "belong together", but in which sense ? An obvious idea might be to type objects by similarity of attribute and event structure, but this is not general enough: when it comes to generalization, we want to put objects with quite different attribute and event structures into one type. So what else ? Our answer is *object identity* and *object instantiation*, i.e. a type is determined by a coherent identification system and by saying which object instance is associated with each identifier.

The importance of object identity is strongly emphasized in KC86. Identity is that property of an object that distinguishes it from all other objects. An identification system should be able to distinguish objects regardless of their content, location or addressability, and it should make it possible to share objects. KC86 advocates identification independent of attribute values and addressability. Identification by attribute values is common in the database field, and identification by addressability is common in the programming language field. There are convincing arguments that both approaches compromise identity. Rather, a surrogate-based identification concept is suggested.

Our approach is to provide identity by means of (abstract and semantically rich) *surrogates* and *naming operations*: an *identification system* or *object universe* U=(U,OP) for an object type consists of a set U of object surrogates for the objects of that type, and a set OP of naming operations by which the surrogates can be named uniquely. A simple example is to take the natural numbers as surrogates and operations like 0, successor, addition, subtraction, etc. as naming operations: each term denotes a natural number. Please note that "aliasing", i.e. different terms denoting the same element, presents no conceptual problem.

If we want semantically meaningful identification systems, they are not always such simple. For complex object types, they can be very sophisticated, reflecting the way the type is composed from other types, maybe even recursively. Very generally speaking, an identification system is a set equipped with operations, and that is exactly what a *data* type is in the sense of algebraic data type theory. This viewpoint is also taken in Eh86, EDG86, showing how database-like identification by keys can be handled in this framework. We adopt the viewpoint that *an identification system is an algebraic data type*.

An *object type* OT=(U,ω) consists of an object universe U and an object instantiation mapping ω, associating an object with each object surrogate in the carrier U of the universe.

Complex object types can be treated conveniently in this model: we can exploit the algebraic machinery of data types for building complex universes, using any parameterized data type like set, list, product, coproduct, etc. We only have to define what happens to instantiation, i.e. how the object instances are put together. For generalization, e.g., this is quite simple: the universe is defined by disjoint union of the surrogate sets with the naming operations provided by algebraic coproducts, and each surrogate keeps the object instance it had before. For aggregation, also incorporating interaction between the components of an aggregation, e.g. by event sharing, things are not much more difficult, but we cannot go into details here.

4. Abstract Object Types

An *abstract* object type is an object type "up to unessential details" like specific choice of names, etc. Mathematically speaking, an abstract object type is a *class* of object types, for instance an isomorphism class or an equivalence class with respect to some reasonable equivalence relation, expressing intuitively that any member of the class is acceptable as a concrete implementation of that type. Like in algebraic data type theory, abstract object types come about as model classes of *specifications* based on some logical calculus. Speaking about abstract object types for databases, thus, means to speak about logic-based database specification with a precise mathematical semantics in terms of model classes.

The problem with object-oriented database specification is that there is no obvious logical calculus with a well-known model theory covering all aspects that have to be specified: data types for providing value domains for attributes as well as object types with their attributes, events and processes. For data types, there is a well established theory of equational specification. For attribute structures, general first-order predicate logic can be employed with its reasonably well understood model theory. Aspects of dynamic behaviour in time can be specified in several ways: axiomatically by using (some variant of) temporal logic or constructively by using process algebra. It is not clear yet how these - or other - approaches, though well-known and successfully applied in isolated areas, can be put together to achieve the goals described here.

5. Concluding Remarks

Object-oriented database specification using formal methods presents many more problems than we can outline in this position paper. Among the semantic issues only very briefly mentioned here are all aspects of *interaction* between objects. We favour *event sharing* as the only means of interaction, specifying which event is "the same" as which other event, modelling synchronous and symmetric communication between objects. On these grounds, the notion of an *object society* as a set of interacting objects can be defined and investigated. The mathematics of objects and object types outlined above allows to treat these problems in a precise and elegant way. We are in a position to confirm experiences made elsewhere with formal methods in software engineering: striving for semantic clarity has a beneficial effect on developing languages and methods.

References

Am86 America,P.: Object-Oriented Programming: A Theoretician's Introduction. EATCS Bulletin 29 (1986), 69-84

Be87 Beech,D.: Groundwork for an Object Database Model. In SW87, 317-354

CW85 Cardelli,L.;Wegner,P.: On Understanding Types, Data Abstraction, and Polymorphism. ACM Computing Surveys 17 (1985), 471-522

DD86 Dayal,U.;Dittrich,K.(eds): Proc. Int. Workshop on Object-Oriented Database Systems. IEEE Computer Society, Los Angeles 1986

DMN67 Dahl,O.-J.;Myhrhaug,B.;Nygaard,K.: SIMULA 67, Common Base Language, Norwegian Computing Center, Oslo 1967

Eh86 Ehrich,H.-D.: Key Extensions of Abstract Data Types, Final Algebras, and Database Semantics. Proc. Workshop on Category Theory and Computer Programming (D. Pitt et al, eds.), LNCS 240, Springer-Verlag, Berlin 1986, 412-433

EDG86 Ehrich,H.-D.;Drosten,K.;Gogolla,M.: Towards an Algebraic Semantics for Database Specification. Proc. IFIP WG2.6 Working Conf. DS-2, Albufeira 1986 (final proceedings to be published by North-Holland)

GM87 Goguen,J.A.;Meseguer,J.: Unifying Functional, Object-Oriented and Relational Programming with Logical Semantics. In SW87, 417-477

GR83 Goldberg,A.;Robson,D.: Smalltalk 80: The Language and its Implementation. Addison-Wesley, Reading, Mass. 1983

HN87 Hailpern,B.;Nguyen,V.: A Model for Object-Based Inheritence. In SW87, 147-164

Ho85 Hoare,C.A.R.: Communicating Sequential Processes. Prentice-Hall, Englewood Cliffs 1985

KC86 Khoshafian,S.N.;Copeland,G.P.: Object Identity. Proc. OOPSLA'86, ACM SIGPLAN Notices 21:11 (1986), 406-416

Lo85 Lochovski,F.(ed.): Special Issue on Object-Oriented Systems. IEEE Database Engineering 8:4 (1985)

MS87 Maier,D.;Stein,J.: Development and Implementation of an Object-Oriented DBMS. In SW87, 355-392

MSOP86 Maier,D.;Stein,J.;Otis,A.;Purdy,A.: Development of an Object-Oriented DBMS. Proc. OOPSLA'86, ACM SIGPLAN Notices 21:11 (1986), 472-482

Pa72 Parnas,D.L.: A Technique for Software Module Specification with Examples. Communications of the ACM 15 (1972),330-336

SFSE88 Sernadas,A.;Fiadeiro,J.;Sernadas,C.;Ehrich,H,-D.: Abstract Object Types: A Temporal Perspective. Proc. Colloquium on Temporal Logic and Specification, A. Pnueli et al (eds.), Springer-Verlag (to be published)

SSE87 Sernadas,A.;Sernadas,C.;Ehrich,H.-D.: Object-Oriented Specification of Databases: An Algebraic Approach. Proc. 13th VLDB, P.M.Stocker, W.Kent (eds.), Morgan-Kaufmann Publ. Inc., Los Altos 1987, 107-116

SW87 Shriver,B.;Wegner,P.(eds.): Research Directions in Object-Oriented Programming. The MIT Press, Cambridge, Mass. 1987

Rule Execution in CPLEX: A Persistent Objectbase

Meichun Hsu Thomas E. Cheatham Jr.

Aiken Computation Laboratory
Harvard University

1. Introduction

There has been much interest in recent years in extending the basic database systems with abilities to handle data constructs of richer semantics and more flexible structures, to embed more powerful data manipulation languages, and to execute *rules*, or *triggers*, in addition to "user transactions". CPLEX [Che88a, Che88b] is one such system currently under implementation at Harvard University. CPLEX is essentially a language for defining and manipulating a *persistent, shared, object base*. The data model and data language is based on the DAPLEX functional data model and language [Shi88]. In addition, CPLEX supports two classes of *rules*.

While the ability to execute (i.e., to *fire*) rules asynchronously is considered a desirable extension for database systems [Esw76, Sto86, Syb87 Coh86], not much work has been done in defining the precise semantics of concurrent execution in a system capable of firing rules asynchronously. It is suspected that such an *execution model* for rules may require an extension to the basic *transaction* model.

In this paper we will focus on the rule model in CPLEX. Rules in CPLEX are classified into *consistency rules* and *automation rules*. The execution semantics of these rules are precisely defined in the language. We will also show that the CPLEX rule execution model maps nicely to a subset of an execution model proposed recently [HLM88] in the context of the *Hipac* system, a High Performance Active Database under development at Computer Corporation of America, although these two models were designed independently. This gives some evidence to the generality of the model proposed in [HLM88]. However, we also observe the need for the Hipac model to be extended and refined. In general, these observations may serve as a reference point for future designs of database systems that are to have rule execution capabilities.

The structure of the paper is as follows. In Section 2 we briefly describe the CPLEX object model and language. In Section 3 we present the rule execution model in CPLEX. Section 4 provides a comparison between the CPLEX rule model and that of the Hipac system, and points out additional issues to be addressed for rule execution.

2. Overview of the CPLEX Objectbase and Atomic Transactions

CPLEX is a prototype persistent objectbase under implementation at Harvard University. In this section we will provide a brief introduction to its object constructs and its query language. The description is not intended to be a complete specification of CPLEX. A complete specification for its syntax (grammar rules), semantics, evaluation environment, and implementation strategy can be found in [Che88a].

2.1. Objects in CPLEX

CPLEX is an extension of the programming language C. Its object model is essentially based on the DAPLEX functional data model.

Primitive built-in objects in CPLEX include integers, strings, atoms (as in Lisp), and *entities*, where *entity* corresponds to the conceptual notion like ''person'' or ''car''. An additional type of built-in objects are *lists* whose leaves are integers, strings, atoms and entities. The type system in CPLEX is extensible.

The object base consists of *relations*, which are conceptually sets of tuples whose components are objects. Unary relations correspond to *classes* and a class may be a subclass of another class.

Example. The following are unary relation declarations:

```
DECLARE Person() => ENTITY
DECLARE Student() => Person
```

A *relation*, R, may be thought of as a set of tuples, $<d_{11},..,d_{1n},r_1>, \cdots, <d_{M1},...,d_{Mn},r_M>$. This same relation may be thought of as a function mapping a set of *domain points*, $<d_{11},..,d_{1n}>, \cdots, <d_{M1},...,d_{Mn}>$ to their respective range values. The mapping can be single-valued (=>) or multi-valued (=>>) and partial or total.

Example. The following are some relation declarations:

```
DECLARE CourseTaken(Student) =>> Course
DECLARE Name(Person) => STRING
DECLARE Grade(Student, CourseTaken(Student)) => INTEGER
```

The "functional form" lets us write constructs like:

```
FOR EACH Course(Student S.T. Name(Dept(Student)) = "Computer Science") ...
```

2.2. Update Transactions in CPLEX

An update conceptually specifies the addition or deletion of tuples for a relation. We first illustrate updates in CPLEX through an example.

Example. The following CPLEX code changes the Address of a department entity, adds a new course to the department, and removes another course from the department:

```
FOR THE department SUCH THAT Name(department) = "Computer Science"
    BEGIN
        LET Address(department) <- "Aiken"
        INCLUDE Course(department) <- Course(S.T. Name(Course)="CS161")
        EXCLUDE Course(department) <- Course(S.T. Name(Course)="CS261")
    END
```

An *update* is in general a list of *update statements* bracketed by BEGIN and END; update statements thus bracketed constitute an *atomic update transaction*. An update statement contains one of the three keywords LET, INCLUDE and EXCLUDE. Following the above example, let d be the department being updated. The LET statement removes all tuples of relation Address for the domain point d and add the tuple with range value "Aiken" for that domain point. Similarly, the INCLUDE statement adds tuples and EXCLUDE deletes tuples for the relation Course for the domain point d. An *update* may have a controlling clause of the form FOR A NEW ENTITY. This construct provides the only way to introduce a new entity. The interpretation of an *update* transaction is as follows:

> All the individual additions and deletions of tuples are determined, providing an initial set of proposed modifications to one or more relations. If the proposed modifications are *valid*, then the affected relations are changed to reflect the modifications. Otherwise, the *update* is aborted with no changes being made.

We define what it means for a set of proposed modification to be *valid* next.

3. Consistency and Automation Rules in CPLEX

In general, there are a number of constraints that we wish to impose on the relations comprising some objectbase. A *consistency rule* in CPLEX consists of a *trigger* -- a predicate that may become TRUE as the result of an update -- and, when that predicate does become TRUE, it is assumed that a constraint that we wish to impose is violated. The trigger then *fires*, enabling an associated *repair* to take place. The purpose of the *repair* is to specify one or more updates whose intended effect is to make the relations satisfy the constraints. One of the motivations for capturing the constraints in rules is to *localize* the specification of such constraints in rules instead of embedding the constraint checking and repair actions in the logic of updates. Embedding these activities in the logic of updates implies that all updates must be revised whenever a new constraint is imposed.

We first illustrate with some examples. Suppose that we have the declaration:

```
DECLARE LoginName(Employee) => STRING
```

constraining LoginName to be, as a function, total and single-valued. Thus, adding a new Employee without also providing a login name for that Employee would result in an invalid atomic transaction. Suppose that we wished to provide, as a default value for the login name, the employee's last name. What we can do is to define a consistency rule that "fires" whenever a new Employee was added without being given a login name so that we can add the default value. The following consistency rule does this:

```
PROHIBITED MissingLoginName
    ADD Employee S.T. NOT EXISTS LoginName(Employee)
REPAIR
    LET LoginName(Employee) <- LastName(Employee)
```

The interpretation of this consistency rule is as follows: Whenever a new Employee is added, we evaluate the predicate "NOT EXISTS LoginName(Employee)" with Employee bound to the new employee at the end of the transaction that inserts Employee. If this predicate is TRUE, then the trigger "fires" and we execute the associated repair, adding the default login name. In the body of that repair, Employee is bound to that new employee without a login name.

In order to specify a repair we must, in general, be able to talk about the state of the objectbase before and/or after any modifications that may be made by the current atomic transaction. As an example, suppose that we wanted to repair the addition of an office for someone who already has an office by removing the old office (Never mind that one can use LET ... to achieve this.) The following repair does this:

```
PROHIBITED MultipleOffices
    ADD O1 IN Office(Employee) S.T. EXISTS O2 IN Office(Employee) AND O1 NE O2
REPAIR
    EXCLUDE Office(Employee) <- THE Office(Employee) S.T. OLD Office
```

This trigger fires whenever we add an office, O1, for an employee, E, who already has an office, O2, different from O1. The repair is to remove the old office. The key construct here is OLD Office that is TRUE if Office is bound to an office that existed before the start of the current atomic transaction.

An alternative repair would be:

```
REPAIR
    LET Office(Employee) <- THE Office(Employee) S.T. NEW Office
```

that says to let the office of *Employee* be the "new" one -- that introduced by the atomic transaction currently being evaluated.

An *automation rule* is similar to a consistency rule but the triggers of automation rules are not considered until some set of proposed modifications has been determined to be *valid* in the sense that they cause none of the triggers of consistency rules to fire. As an example of an automation rule, we might have the following:

```
AUTOMATION ClassifyMessage
    ADD Message
REACTION
    Classify(Message)
```

that says that whenever a new Message is added, a function named Classify is to be run with that Message as argument.

A complete atomic transaction can now be described as follows:

(1) Let S be the set of modifications that are proposed by the updates comprising some atomic transaction. For each σ in S, if there is a consistency rule whose trigger fires because of σ, "run" the repair associated with that consistency rule (that will, in general, add more proposed modifications to S). If there is more than one rule triggered, no particular order of the execution of the repair is imposed.

(2) If at least one proposed modification in step (1) was added to S, return to step 1.

(3) If, in step 2, no consistency rule trigger fired, the proposed set of modifications is valid, then *commit* S (i.e., for each σ in S, make the modifications to the relation specified by σ) and proceed as follows: for each σ in S, if there is an automation rule whose trigger fires because of σ, "run" (in a separate atomic transaction) the reaction associated with that automation rule.

Note that an atomic transaction can cycle indefinitely.

The (partial) grammer rules for defining consistency rules and automation rules are: (here, the italic font is used for non-terminals, square brackets surround optional constructs, and a vertical stroke separates alternatives)

declaration ::= PROHIBITED *identifier trigger* [REPAIR *update*]
declaration ::= AUTOMATION *identifier trigger* REACTION *imperative*
trigger ::= *event-key relation-ref* [S.T. *predicate*]
event-key ::= ADD | REMOVE

A consistency rule commences with PROHIBITED followed by a name for the rule, a *trigger*, and then an optional repair that *must* be an *update*. An automation rule is similar but has a reaction that is an *imperative*, which can include *updates*, statements such as PRINT, and arbitrary CPLEX code fragments.

The *trigger* of a consistency rule or automation rule has the keyword ADD or REMOVE followed by a *relation-ref* and an optional "such that" clause. A *relation-ref* is, in its simplest form, a single identifier specifying a member of the class named by that identifier. (Example: ADD Employee S.T. ...) In general it takes the form $I(I_1,...,I_n)$ where I is an identifier and I_j is a *relation-ref* (Example: ADD LoginName(Person) S.T. ...)

The trigger of a consistency rule fires if its *relation-ref* "matches" a tuple being added or removed in the sense that the variables in $I(I_1,...,I_n)$ can be bound so as to identify an addition or removal, and, given those bindings, the associated *predicate* (if present) is TRUE. If the trigger fires, the associated *update* or *imperative* is to be executed with those bindings being present in the current environment.

The contexts in which the temporal constructs NEW variable and OLD variable may occur are strictly limited to the following:

(1) The *trigger* of a consistency rule or automation rule, and

(2) The *update* of a consistency rule.

In particular, they cannot occur in the context of the *imperative* in the reaction of an automation rule. The reason for this is to avoid the bookeeping that would require the support of a general *temporal* database. In AP5 [Coh86] there is a special mechanism for "collecting" data using the temporal constructs that is, effectively, "passed" to the reactions of automation rules. Some mechanism like this may be desirable in the future.

The consistency rules and automation rules proposed here are similar to those in AP5. They differ in that AP5 provides for a completely general predicate being used as a trigger while we "start" the predicate with ADD *relation-ref* or REMOVE *relation-ref*. The reason that CPLEX does this is for simplicity in the implementation of triggers. A given trigger can fire only when its *relation-ref* part "matches" some proposed addition or deletion and only then is the optional *predicate* tested. Clearly the AP5 scheme is more general. However, in looking at many examples, the scheme proposed in CPLEX seems sufficient without imposing an undue burden on the translator. At some future point, it may be appropriate to extend the trigger mechanism to deal with the more general situation.

4. Mapping CPLEX Rules to the Hipac Rule Execution Model

4.1. The Hipac Rule Execution Model

In [HLM88], a model for rule execution for the Hipac system is proposed. In that model, a rule has three components expressed as follows:

(1) *Event*: The event that triggers the rule; it is essentially the invocation of a database operation (e.g. insertion or deletion of a tuple.)

(2) *Condition*: A predicate that is evaluated whenever the event occurs. If the predicate is true, then the action is executed.

(3) *Action*: A sequence of operations to be performed when the event occurs and the condition is true. The action can include database operations and messages to other programs.

Example.

```
Event      Update Quantity_On_Hand(item)
Condition  Quantity_On_Hand(item) < Threshold(item)
Action     Submit_Order(item)
```

In the Hipac Model, *coupling modes* of rules are explicitly specified by users to control the "placement" of the condition evaluation and action execution relative to the event. When a triggering event E occurs in the context of some transaction T, there are three points at which the condition (C) can be evaluated and at which action (A) can be executed:

(1) "Immediate": immediately when event E occurs and before the next operation in T,

(2) "Deferred": after the last operation in T and before T commits, or

(3) "Decoupled": in a separate transaction.

Furthermore, the action A does not have to be executed at the same point where the condition C is evaluated. For example, the condition can be evaluated immediately after the triggering event, while the action is executed in a separate transaction. With this framework, Hipac Model has identified seven *coupling modes*, in which three modes involve the use of immediate execution (of either condition evaluation or action), and another two involve the use of decoupled condition evaluation.

In addition, for *decoupled* execution of condition evaluation and/or action, the separate transaction T1 in which the execution takes place may be specified to be *causally dependent*, in which case T1 can commit only if the triggering transaction commits, or *causally independent*, in which case T1 can commit independent of commitment of the triggering transaction. Finally, *nested subtransactions* are used to model the concurrent execution of rules that are fired simultaneously within a transaction. This applies to both the firing of immediate rules triggered by the same event, and the execution of deferred rules at the end of the triggering transaction.

4.2. Comparison

In comparing the Hipac model proposed with that used in CPLEX, the following correspondence can be made:

(1) The *event* part of the rule in Hipac corresponds to the *event-key* construct in the *trigger* part of CPLEX rules.

(2) The *condition* part of the rule in Hipac corresponds to the optional *predicate* construct in the *trigger* part of CPLEX rules.

(3) The *action* part of the rule in Hipac corresponds to the REPAIR or REACTION construct in CPLEX rules.

(4) The Consistency Rule in CPLEX corresponds to a rule in Hipac with the *deferred* execution for both condition evaluation and action.

(5) The Automation Rule in CPLEX corresponds to a rule in Hipac with the *deferred* execution for condition evaluation, and *decoupled* execution for action, where the decoupled execution runs in a transaction which is *causally dependent*.

We offer the following additional observations based on the similarities and differences among the two models:

Three-part specification: It's interesting to note that both systems have adopted the "3-part" specification for a rule (event-condition-action as in Hipac and eventkey-predicate-REPAIR/REACTION as in CPLEX).

CPLEX is more restricted in the use of coupling modes: In general, one may conclude that the Hipac model is a more general rule execution model than that used in CPLEX. CPLEX makes use of only two out of the seven coupling modes proposed in Hipac (CPLEX uses only deferred condition evaluation and the five modes excluded are precisely those that make use of the immediate or decoupled condition evaluation.) As such, CPLEX avoids the potential need for a general temporal database to allow rule fragments in Hipac to refer to database states as of the time when certain *event* (in the Hipac sense) occurs within a transaction or when certain transaction commits.

CPLEX is more restricted in its event type: CPLEX has also limited the triggering event-key to be either adding (ADD) or deleting (REMOVE) a tuple, rather than the invocation of an arbitrary function (operation) as assumed by Hipac. As such, it simplifies the task of event monitoring.

Variable binding: The simplicity of the current design of CPLEX also enables a straightforward specification for the *binding* of variables that are to be *passed* between the triggering event (or event-key), condition (or predicate) evaluation, and action (or REPAIR/REACTION). For example, when the triggering event-key is "ADD Employee", the employee entity being added is bound to the variable Employee and can be referenced in the predicate part of the rule (e.g. "S.T. NOT EXISTS LoginName(Employee)"), and in the REPAIR/REACTION part of the rule (e.g., "LET LoginName(Employee) <- LastName(Employee).) This strategy may have to be extended for use in Hipac.

One complication does arise in CPLEX when AUTOMATION rule is used. If a variable is bound to some database object during predicate evaluation and is referenced in the REACTION part of the rule, the object bound to the variable may have gone through changes when REACTION is executed. The present design of CPLEX specifies that the binding would remain *static*, i.e., the image of the database object at the time of predicate evaluation is frozen in the variable to be passed. We clarify this point with the following example. Suppose we have an AUTOMATION rule of the form:

AUTOMATION label
 ADD f(x)
REACTION
 foo(f,x)

Then the *values* of f and x at the time the trigger ("ADD f(x)") occurs is saved and passed to foo when foo is executed. Even if the value of the relation f for x, where x is presumably an entity in some class, may have changed in the database when foo is executed, foo would be using the saved value of f when f is referenced in foo. On the other hand, if foo also references, say, g(x) during its execution, it will be accessing the value of the relation g at the time foo is executed, not when the trigger occurs.

Correctness criterion: There is a need in general to capture more formally the "meaning" of *decoupled* executions. Decoupled executions are considered desirable by both CPLEX and Hipac. However, their relationship to the formal notion of *serializability* is unclear. As such, it poses anomalies such as the one mentioned in the previous paragraph, in which arguments to be passed from the the triggering side to the decoupled execution side may be bound to database objects that are changed (or even removed) in between. Decoupled execution may correspond to some correctness criterion for concurrent execution which is weaker (and therefore probably less expensive) than serializability, but more work is needed to clarify the notion.

Ordering among concurrent subtransactions: While it appears that the Hipac model is more general, it does not seem to be able to express one particular execution semantics in CPLEX: that the condition evaluation of an AUTOMATION rule is to occur after the repair actions of all CONSISTENCY rules have finished, although both use deferred condition evaluation (i.e., defer until the end of the update transaction.) Hipac assumes that all deferred rules are to be executed concurrently (as concurrent subtransactions) at the end of the update transaction without further ordering. The CPLEX experience suggests that some generalization in Hipac along the line of allowing for specific ordering of such executions may be desirable.

4.3. Final Remark

CPLEX is designed with an orientation towards satisfying the need of the software engineering database applications, while Hipac is designed for more general database applications. In comparing the two designs, we have identified some intricate design issues in rule execution systems. In designing the rule execution system, generality must be balanced with a concern for efficiency and complexity. The term complexity here applies to both implementation complexity and semantic complexity (i.e., the user must be able to understand what this all *means*.) In addition to refining concepts and discovering better implementation algorithms, it is expected that experimentation and modification of the prototypes are necessary steps towards resolving some of the design issues that are raised in this paper.

5. References

[Che88a] Cheatham, T.E. *The Design of CPLEX, a Software Development Database System*. Technical Report, Harvard University, Center for Research in Computing Technology, April, 1988.

[Che88b] Cheatham, T.E. *CPLEX Users Manual*. Harvard Univeresity Center for Research in Computing Technology, 1988.

[Coh86] Cohen, D. "Automatic Compilation of logical specifications into efficient programs." In *Proc. 5th national Conference on Artificial Intelligence*, August 1986.

[Esw76] Eswaran, K.P. "Specifications, Implementations, and Interactions of a Trigger Subsystem in an Integrated Data Base System." IBM Research Report RJ1820, August 1976.

[HLM88] Hsu, M., Ladin, R. and McCarthy, D. "An Execution Model for Active Database Management Systems," *Proc. Third International Conference on Data and Knowledge Bases*, June 1988.

[Shi88] Shipman, D.W. The Functional Data Model and teh Data Language DAPLEX. *ACM Transactions on Database Systems*, 6(1):140-173, 1981

[Sto86] Stonebraker M. et al. "A Rule Manager For Relational Database Systems." *The POSTGRES Papers*. Univ. of California, Berkley, Ca. Electronics Research Lab, Memo No. UCB/ERL M86/85 (1986).

[Syb87] Sybase, Inc. *Transact-SQL User's Guide*. (1987).

CONSTRAINT ANALYSIS: A TOOL FOR EXPLAINING THE SEMANTICS OF COMPLEX OBJECTS

Susan Darling Urban †
Lois M. L. Delcambre ‡

† Electrical and Computer Engineering Dept., Univ. of Miami, Coral Gables, FL 33124

‡ The Center For Advanced Computer Studies, Univ. of SW Louisiana, Lafayette, LA 70504

Abstract

Constraint analysis is a design tool for object-oriented database environments that makes use of knowledge about constraints to support the design of user views and the specification of propagation actions. The constraint analysis process is supported by the formal, uniform representation of schema constraints. The formal representation supports the ability to analyze and explain constraints; the uniform representation allows both inherent and explicit constraints to be analyzed in the same manner. Using constraint analysis, the effects of constraints can be made explicit at design time to support the flexible specification of database operations that maintain object integrity. This paper presents the constraint representation that supports the analysis and explanation process.

1 Introduction

An important advantage of object-oriented data modeling is the increased level of semantics that can be directly captured within the data description. Viewing each class in an object-oriented schema as an abstract data type, the operations on each class should protect the semantics of the objects involved [Ditt86]. One problem with object-oriented data modeling, however, is that the increased level of semantics associated with a schema tends to complicate the specification of operations on objects. Furthermore, new applications for object-oriented database systems often emphasize the need for expressing and propagating explicit constraints (e.g., [Du87]), further increasing the complexity of specifying object manipulation operations. As a result, there is a strong need for a constraint management tool to assist in the formation of update operations.

The effect of schema semantics on object operations has previously been addressed in the context of update propagation [Brod84, Hech81, Abit85, Mark86, Brod84]. Previous propagation algorithms, however, perform in a pre-defined manner for all users based on propagation rules for structural schema constraints, ignoring the possibility that different users may require different propagation actions. Furthermore, propagation actions for explicit constraints are rarely addressed [Morg84]. Ideally, an object-oriented design environment should support flexibility in specifying propagation actions for inherent and explicit constraints and should also provide tools to insure that propagation actions are correctly specified.

This paper presents a support tool for an object-oriented design environment known as *constraint analysis* [Urba87]. Constraint analysis is a component of a constraint management facility that provides a way of actively using constraints as a source of knowledge for the support of object-oriented design activities. In [Shep84], Shepherd and Kerschberg identify constraint management as an essential aspect in the development of more intelligent environments for managing both data and knowledge.

There are five primary contributions of constraint analysis to object-oriented design. First of all, constraint analysis relies on a formal, declarative representation of both inherent and explicit schema constraints by transforming all constraints into Horn clause form[1]. Schema constraints are

[1]Constraint analysis is currently applied only to constraints that are expressible in Horn clause form.

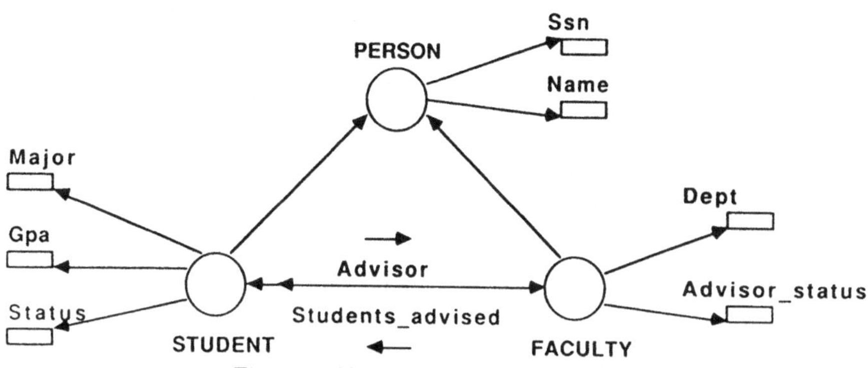

Figure 1: University Subschema

therefore uniformly represented in a knowledge base that supports the ability to automatically reason about constraints. A second contribution of constraint analysis is that related clauses are logically ordered to provide an organized approach to the analysis and explanation of constraints. With all constraints collectively represented in a logical, analyzable manner, a third contribution is that the analysis process helps a designer understand the consequences of stating constraints. As a result, errors in the expression of constraints can be detected early in the design phase.

The fourth contribution of constraint analysis is also a direct result of the ability to explain constraints. Through the explanation process, knowledge about constraints can be used to define the scope and content of user views of abstract objects. The explanation of constraints also enhances the specification of update propagation actions, the fifth contribution of constraint analysis. By making the effects of constraints explicit at design time, constraint analysis supports flexibility in specifying update propagation actions so that different user views can respond to constraint violations in different ways. Flexibility in the design of update operations supports a more creative environment for application design.

This paper concentrates on presenting the uniform representation scheme that supports the correct analysis and explanation of constraints. A detailed presentation of using constraint analysis to form user views and update propagation specifications is beyond the scope of this paper and can be found in [Urba87]. The remainder of the paper is organized as follows. Additional motivation for constraint analysis is presented in Section 2. The general analysis process and the representation of constraints is presented in Section 3, followed by an example of the analysis and explanation of constraints in Section 4. Conclusions and future research are presented in Section 5.

2 Motivation

As an example of the utility of constraint analysis, consider the university subschema in Figure 1 and a view of the STUDENT class that allows modification of the *major*, *gpa*, and *advisor* properties. The following constraint states that a STUDENT object with a *status* of "honor" must have an advisor from the same *dept* as his or her *major* and the *advisor_status* value must also be "honor":

C1: for all S in student (where S.status = 'honor'), there is some F in faculty,
such that: (F is S.advisor and S.major = F.dept and F.advisor_status = 'honor');

If an honor student, S1, previously satisfied C1, a number of different propagation actions can be taken to satisfy the constraint when S1's *major* property is modified. For example, C1 can be satisfied for S1 by also modifying the advisor's *dept* value, or by changing S1's *status* to a value other than "honor". A more likely action is to assign a new *advisor* to S1 having the appropriate *dept* and *advisor_status* values. Considering the same constraint for a view of the FACULTY class, modifying a faculty member's *dept* value implies a modification of the *major* for that faculty member's *students_advised* or an assignment of a new *advisor* to each object in *students_advised.* In this case assigning a new *advisor* value to each object in *students_advised* seems most appropriate. For explicit constraints in general, the specific propagation action depends on the user view.

Constraint analysis as a design tool is directed at helping a designer understand schema constraints so that knowledge about constraints can play a more active role in forming user views and in specifying propagation actions. Although the above example is rather simple, a large schema with a significant number of explicit constraints may *require* a formal, automated approach such as constraint analysis to assist in the specification of update operations.

3 The General Analysis Process and Constraint Graphs

As described in [Nico78], by transforming constraints expressed in first order logic into conjunctive normal form, it is easier to reason about the effects of low-level database operations and to analyze the alternatives that can be taken to satisfy constraints in the case of constraint violations. To illustrate the general analysis process, consider a set of schema constraints where each constraint C_i is denoted as a conjunction of clauses $Cl_{i_1} \& Cl_{i_2} \& \cdots \& Cl_{i_z}$, where all variables are universally quantified. In order for C_i to be satisfied, each clause $Cl_{i_j}, (1 \leq j \leq z)$ in C_i must evaluate to true. Each Cl_{i_j} can be written as an implication $p_{i_{j_1}} \& p_{i_{j_2}} \& \cdots \& p_{i_{j_n}} \rightarrow q_{i_{j_1}} \vee q_{i_{j_2}} \vee \cdots \vee q_{i_{j_m}}$, where $n \geq 1$ and, for the purpose of this research, $0 \leq m \leq 1$. If $m = 0$, Cl_{i_j} is a *negative* clause, written neg(Cl_{i_j}). If $m = 1$, Cl_{i_j} is a *positive* clause, written pos(Cl_{i_j}).

Given an implication such as the inherent ISA constraint stating that a student is a person (i.e., STUDENT(S) $\rightarrow$ PERSON(S)), when S is inserted as a STUDENT, S must already exist as a PERSON or an operation must be invoked to insert S as a PERSON. Otherwise, S cannot be inserted as a STUDENT. Likewise, if S is deleted as a PERSON, the only way to satisfy the clause for S is to also delete S as a STUDENT. The truth value associated with an implication is therefore used to analyze and explain the alternatives for satisfying a clause.

Furthermore, as indicated in [Nico78], clauses in which the predicate of the insert operation appears as a literal on the left-hand side are the clauses to be analyzed in the case of an insert operation; clauses where the predicate of the delete operation appears as a literal on the right-hand side provide the key to the analysis of a delete operation. Viewing schema constraints in the context of Horn logic therefore provides a natural and generalized means of identifying the constraints that affect a given operation, identifying the conditions that must be satisfied for each constraint, and identifying the alternative actions that can be taken to satisfy constraints for different user views.

A problem with the general analysis process, however, is that some constraints translate into a conjunction of two or more clauses which are related due to the scoping of variables in the constraint. As an example, consider the Horn clause form of C1 in Figure 2. To simplify presentation of the constraint, the constraint is represented as a list of Horn clauses with the understanding that the scope of the universally quantified variables is the conjunction of the list of Horn clauses. The advisor object in C1 is an existential object as indicated by the Skolem function fa(S).

Rather than analyzing each clause of the constraint separately, analyzing the clauses as a group allows the constraint to be explained as it was originally stated. Furthermore, important information may be lost if each clause is independently presented. For example, clause 3 by itself does not convey the information that the faculty member involved must be the advisor of the student.

To support the explanation of related clauses, the constraint analysis process depends on organizing the clauses of a constraint into a *constraint graph* [Urba87]. Constraint graphs are formed according to the *dominates* relation that exists among the clauses of a constraint. To understand the dominates relation, it is helpful to view the left-hand side of each Cl_{i_j}, written LHS(Cl_{i_j}), as a set of literals where each literal is either a unary or binary predicate. A unary predicate $p_{i_{j_k}}$ represents a type predicate which defines an object to be an instance of a specific class (e.g., STUDENT(S)). A binary $p_{i_{j_k}}$ represents either a property predicate (e.g., MAJOR(S,M)) or a relational predicate (e.g., EQ(A,honor)). The right hand side of a clause, written RHS(Cl_{i_j}), is either the empty set or

1: STUDENT(S) & STATUS(S,honor) → FACULTY(fa(S)).
2: STUDENT(S) & STATUS(S,honor) → ADVISOR(S,fa(S)).
3: STUDENT(S) & STATUS(S,honor) & MAJOR(S,M) → DEPT(fa(S),M).
4: STUDENT(S) & STATUS(S,honor) & MAJOR(S,M) & DEPT(fa(S),D) → MAJOR(S,D).
5: STUDENT(S) & STATUS(S,honor) & ADVISOR_STATUS(fa(S),B) → EQ(B,honor).

Figure 2: Horn Clause Form of Constraint C1

the set containing one literal. The dominates relation is defined as an ordering of clauses Cl_{i_j} and Cl_{i_k} within one constraint C_i, where Cl_{i_j} dominates Cl_{i_k}, written dom(Cl_{i_j}, Cl_{i_k}), iff LHS(Cl_{i_k}) $\subseteq$ LHS(Cl_{i_j}).

The clauses of C1 in Figure 2 provide an example of the dominates relation. Clause 3 dominates clauses 1 and 2, clause 4 dominates clauses 1, 2, and 3, and clause 5 dominates clauses 1 and 2. Furthermore, clause 1 dominates clause 2 and clause 2 dominates clause 1. In this case, the clauses are said to be *co-dominating*, written co-dom(Cl_{1_1}, Cl_{1_2}) or co-dom(Cl_{1_2},Cl_{1_1}). In a relationship such as the one between clauses 2 and 3, where dom(Cl_{1_3},Cl_{1_2}) but not co-dom(Cl_{1_3},Cl_{1_2}), clause 3 is said to *strictly dominate* clause 2. Clauses 4 and 5 are also referred to as *primary* clauses since they are not strictly dominated by any other clauses in the constraint.

A constraint graph is therefore defined to be a directed graph consisting of the set of nodes, $\{v_{i_1}, \cdots, v_{i_n}\}$, where $n \geq 1$ and each v_{i_k} $(1 \leq k \leq n)$ represents a clause Cl_{i_k}, and the set of edges, $< v_{i_j}, v_{i_k} >$, where each edge represents the dominates relation between v_{i_j} and v_{i_k}, i.e., dom(Cl_{i_j},Cl_{i_k}).

4 The Explanation of Constraint Graphs

To prepare for the constraint analysis process, the inherent constraints of an object-oriented data schema are translated to Horn clause form. The research in [Urba87] presents the general first-order logic description of an object-oriented data model based on the formalization of RML [Gree84]. The self-describing approach [Mark85] is used as a means of generating explicit Horn clauses that describe a specific application schema. The inherent constraints are then combined with the Horn clause form of explicit constraints to create the complete set of constraints to be analyzed. Within the uniformly represented set of schema constraints, each inherent and explicit constraint forms a separate constraint graph.

To analyze an insert or delete operation, all constraint graphs that affect the operation are identified for explanation as described in [Nico78] and as summarized in Section 3. The explanation of each constraint graph is embedded in a recursive analysis process so that when a propagation action is identified, the constraint analysis process recursively analyzes the effects of schema constraints on the operation to be invoked. The depth of recursive constraint analysis depends on the propagation actions selected by the designer.

As an example of explaining a constraint graph for an insert operation, consider an insert operation on the *status* property of a STUDENT object. An important property of constraint graphs is that the left and right hand sides of a clause can only be true if the left and right hand sides of all its dominated clauses are true [Urba87]. Explanation of a constraint graph for an insert operation therefore begins with the nodes containing the predicate of the insert operation that are closest to the leaves of the graph. For example, clauses 1 and 2 are starting points for the explanation of C1. Explanation then recursively continues for each dominating path upward from the starting point, ending with the explanation of a primary clause for each path.

Since clauses 1 and 2 are co-dominating, both clauses can be explained as a unit. The conjunction of clauses 1 and 2 is equivalent to STUDENT(S) & STATUS(S,honor) → (FACULTY(fa(S)) & ADVISOR(S,fa(S))). The constraint analysis process would explain that when a *status* value of "honor" is inserted for STUDENT object S, there must be a FACULTY object that is an *advisor* of S. As alternatives the designer can: 1) assume an *advisor* for S already exists, or 2) select a FACULTY object and insert the FACULTY object as an *advisor* for S, or 3) create a FACULTY object and insert the FACULTY object as an *advisor* for S.

Option 1 indicates that no propagation action is to be taken if a constraint violation occurs. If the designer selects option 2, the insert operation on the *advisor* property will be recursively analyzed (i.e., all clauses where the ADVISOR predicate occurs in the left hand side will be explained as clauses that affect the insert operation on the *advisor* property). If the designer selects option 3, the operations of inserting a new object in the FACULTY class and inserting the object as an *advisor* of S will both be recursively analyzed.

Clauses 3 and 5 are the next candidates for explanation. The order in which these two clauses are examined is immaterial. Suppose then that clause 3 is selected for explanation. Since LHS(Cl_{1_1}) $\subset$ LHS(Cl_{1_3}), the explanation proceeds by explaining the difference between LHS(Cl_{1_3}) and LHS(Cl_{1_1}). For example, the analysis process would explain that if the STUDENT object S having a *status* value of "honor" also has a *major* value of M, the *dept* value of the *advisor* must also be M. The design alternatives are to 1) assume the *advisor* already has the appropriate *dept* value, or 2) modify the *advisor*'s *dept* value. It is most reasonable in this case to assume that the *advisor* will have the appropriate *dept* value. If option 2 is chosen, however, a delete operation on the *dept* of the FACULTY object followed by an insert operation on the *dept* value would be recursively analyzed to explain the effects of constraints on the modify operation.

Clause 5 is explained in a manner similar to clause 3. Since clause 5 is a primary clause, the explanation process for that path in the constraint graph terminates. Explanation continues beyond clause 3, however, to clause 4.

Clauses 3 and 4 together represent an equality constraint between a STUDENT's *major* and a STUDENT's *advisor*'s *dept* value. Since *major* and *dept* are single-valued, explanation of clause 4 is superfluous; clause 4 will always be true if the left and right hand sides of clause 3 are true. Assume, however, that *dept* and *major* are multi-valued. In other words, STUDENT objects can have more than one *major* value and FACULTY objects can be associated with more than one *dept*. Clauses 3 and 4 together state that not only must the advisor be associated with all departments of the student's major but the student must be a major in all departments the advisor is associated with. This condition is probably not what the author of the constraint intended, yet this condition will be enforced at execution time. The explanation of constraints is therefore useful not only for identifying possible propagation actions but also for understanding constraints in general. Using constraint analysis, problems with constraints can be identified early in the design process. In applications with a large number of constraints, the ability to help the designer manage and understand constraints is a major strength of the constraint analysis process.

Analysis of a delete operation proceeds by finding all clauses where the predicate of the delete operation occurs on the right-hand side. Each clause must then be analyzed in the context of the constraint graph in which it appears. For example, clause 3 is the starting point for explaining the effects of C1 on a delete operation for a FACULTY objects *dept* value. The delete analysis of C1 specifically considers the case where the left and right hand sides of clause 3 and its dominated clauses are true for the objects involved at the time the delete operation occurs. Furthermore, the analysis process assumes that all other clauses of the constraint graph have been previously satisfied in some way for the objects involved (i.e., the left hand sides of dominating clauses may have previously evaluated to false). A complete explanation of delete analysis is beyond the scope of the current paper. Analysis of a delete operation is particularly interesting, however, because of the options introduced by existential parameters and because of the need to resatisfy the entire constraint graph. Further details on delete analysis can be found in [Urba87].

5 Summary

This paper has presented an approach known as constraint analysis that forms the basis of a constraint explanation tool for object-oriented database environments. An important strength of constraint analysis is that schema constraints are represented in a formal, uniform manner. The formal representation of constraints supports the analysis and explanation of constraints; the uniform representation of constraints allows both inherent and explicit constraints to be analyzed in the same manner. When a large number of constraints are involved in an application, constraint analysis helps the designer understand the effects of constraints so that operations can be properly specified and so that propagation actions can be handled in a flexible manner. Constraint analysis is also useful simply as an explanation tool so that a designer can verify that constraints will perform as expected.

Constraint graphs are currently being investigated as the basis for constraint enforcement procedures in object-oriented database environments. Future research will also address the development of an object-oriented programming language in which the exception handling facility of the language is closely integrated with the constraint enforcement subsystem of a database system that supports constraint analysis [Bloo87]. Constraint analysis, in general, can be used to form the basis of a design methodology for object-oriented database applications and a prototyping support environment for the design and testing of such applications. All of the above issues are currently being investigated as tools to support the development of intelligent database design environments for object-oriented database systems.

REFERENCES

[Abit85] Abiteboul, S., and Hull, R., "Update Propagation in the IFO Database Model," *Proc. Int. Conf. on Foundations of Data Org.*, Kyoto, May 1985, pp. 243-251.

[Bloo87] Bloom, T. and Zdonik, S. B., "Issues in the Design of Object Oriented Database Programming Languages," *Proc. Object-Oriented Programming Systems, Languages, and Applications Conf.*, Orlando, Oct. 1987, pp. 441-451.

[Brod84] Brodie, M. L. and Ridjanovic, D., *A Strict Database Transaction Design Methodology*, Computer Corp. of America, Tech. Rep., Apr. 1984.

[Ditt86] Dittrich, K. R., and Dayal, U. (eds.) *Proc. of the 1986 Int. Workshop on Object-Oriented Database Systems*, Pacific Grove, California, Sept. 1985.

[Du87] Du, H, C. and Ghanta, S., "A Framework for Efficient IC/VLSI CAD Databases," *Proc. Third Int. Conf. on Data Eng.*, Los Angeles, Feb. 1986.

[Gree84] Greenspan, S. J., *Requirements Modeling: A Knowledge Representation Approach to Software Requirements Definition*, Ph.D. Diss., Univ. of Toronto, Mar. 1984, 124 pp.

[Hech81] Hecht, M. and Kerschberg, L., "Update Semantics for the Functional Data Model," DB Research Rep. No. 4, Bell Laboratories, Jan. 1981.

[Mark85] Mark, L., and Roussopoulos, N., "The New Database Architecture Framework - A Progress Report", *Information Systems: Theoretical and Formal Aspects*, Sernadas, A., Bubenko, J., Olive, A. (eds.), NY, 1985, pp. 3-18.

[Mark86] Mark, L., and Roussopoulos, N., "Metadata Management," *IEEE Computer*, vol. 19, no. 12, Dec. 1986, pp. 26-36.

[Morg84] Morgenstern, M., "Constraint Equations: Declarative Expression of Constraints With Automatic Enforcement," *VLDB*, 1984, pp. 111-125.

[Nico78] Nicolas, J. M., and Yazdanian, K., "Integrity Checking in Deductive Databases," *Logic and Databases*, Gallaire, H., and Minker, J. (eds.), Plenum Press, New York, 1978, pp. 325-344.

[Shep84] Shepherd, A., and Kerschberg, L., "Constraint Management in Expert Database Systems," *Proc. First Int. Conf. on Expert Database Sys.*, Kiawah, Oct. 1984, pp. 309-332.

[Urba87] Urban, S. D., *Constraint Analysis for the Design of Semantic Database Update Operations*, Ph.D. Diss., Univ. of Southwestern La., Sept. 1987.

Providing Uniform Access to Heterogeneous Information Bases

Tim Connors
Peter Lyngbaek

Hewlett-Packard Laboratories
1501 Page Mill Road
Palo Alto, CA 94304

Abstract

We propose the use of object-oriented database management systems (OODBMSs) as tools for providing coordinated access to distributed, heterogeneous, autonomous information bases. The extensible nature of an OODBMS, i.e., the provision for abstract data types and operations, makes it feasible to write interfaces to a wide variety of existing information sources and that way create the illusion of a single integrated database which can be queried in a uniform manner. We illustrate the approach in terms of the Iris OODBMS.

1 Introduction

As organizations evolve and merge, the need for combining information stored in pre-existing information bases grows. In this paper we propose the use of object-oriented database management systems (OODBMSs) as a suitable tool for providing coordinated access to data stored in ***distributed, heterogeneous, autonomous*** information bases.

There are several reasons why the data relevant to a given enterprise is often stored and maintained by systems that are not well integrated. The first is the way in which databases come into being. Typically, a new database is introduced in order to provide persistence and sharing for a very specific class of applications. The choice of a conceptual data model, database management system, and actual schema for the database is therefore strongly influenced by these applications and the state of the current DBMS technology. Thus, over time, an evolving enterprise obtains many heterogeneous databases.

Even given a choice, an enterprise may elect to maintain multiple data systems for performance reasons. The performance of many applications is determined to a large extent by the way data is organized and made available to the applications. Therefore, the performance of some important applications may dictate that data be maintained in separate and differently structured databases, even though other applications require data from both. For example, the structure of a database supporting electronic circuit design is very different from the structure of a parts database containing pricing information. The electronic circuit database must provide fast access to large complex circuit diagrams in order to support applications such as simulators and routers. The parts database, on the other hand, must provide fast access to individual records in order to support billing applications. However, an application computing the cost of circuit boards requires information from both.

Another reason for the existence of multiple data sources is that not all relevant data is controlled or maintained by the enterprise. Examples of such external information sources include airline schedules, weather reports, stock prices, phone directories, parts catalogs, and a rapidly growing number of public databases. Any of this information could be important to an enterprise and all of it is available on-line.

As the number of databases in an enterprise grows, it is likely that new classes of applications emerge which could benefit from the interaction with several databases and/or on-line information services. Since the databases are pre-existing, they may be distributed on various computers, support different data models, and be difficult if not impossible to merge or change. Thus the new applications must be produced without many of the advantages provided by modern DBMSs. As a remedy to this situation, the concept of a *global data manager* or GDM has been introduced [7]. A GDM attempts to provide an application with the illusion of a single data system when, in fact, data is maintained in many databases.

In this paper, we propose to tap the power of object-oriented DBMSs to serve as a GDM by providing uniform access to diverse information bases, some of which may be under foreign control. We will use the general term *information base* to denote any source of information. Typically, an information base contains persistent data. Examples include conventional hierarchical, network, and relational databases; specialized storage subsystems, e.g., for image or textual data; files; and CD-ROMs. However, an information base may also be the source of transient data such as the current time and date or the current value of the Dow Jones Industrial Average.

Object-oriented DBMSs have many features which make their role as a GDM quite natural. In contrast to conventional DBMSs, OODBMSs support the modeling of behavior. New abstract data types and their corresponding operations can be added as an extension to a given OODBMS. The operations, or *functions* as we shall call them (Section 2), may be expressed in a general-purpose programming language and therefore support arbitrary computations. In particular, functions may access data that would otherwise be outside the control of the DBMS. We shall call such functions *information-importing* functions. Even though the information-importing functions obtain their data from external sources, they are part of the schema of the importing database and from the users point of view not considered to be different from any other database operation. That way, it is completely transparent to the user whether a database operation returns data that is stored locally or obtained remotely from a foreign repository.

Previous work on multiple database access can be separated into two categories. The first category includes work on database systems that support the creation and maintenance of distributed, homogeneous databases. R* [19] and Distributed Ingres [18] are examples of such systems. An introduction to distributed DBMSs can be found in [4]. Since the constituent databases are of like kind, a distributed DBMS is not particularly useful as a GDM. Issues of schema integration, heterogeneity, and autonomy of existing databases cannot be addressed.

The advantage of distributed DBMSs is that they offer complete support for transaction processing. However, it is very difficult to guarantee consistency among heterogeneous databases if distributed updates are supported. Without special coordination among the individual transaction managers, it is impossible. The approach proposed in this paper presumes the autonomy of the individual information systems, i.e., they cannot be modified at all. Additionally, the constituent information systems need not even be transaction-based. For these reasons, the current proposal precludes the support of both transaction management and updates. We believe, however, that a solution of "only" the distributed information access problem is of great pragmatic importance.

The second category of multiple database access includes work on database integration [3]. Most existing work concentrates on schema integration, i.e., the construction of a global schema from one or more local schemata that refer to existing databases. This is considered a database design activity which as input takes the local schemata and the local queries and transactions. The outputs of the integration process are a global schema as well as the data and query-mapping specifications. Since a single concept of the distributed application domain can have different representations in the different local schemata, the main concern of the integration activity is to identify possible conflicts, resolve them by conforming the schemata so that they can be merged, and then superimpose the conformed schemata to produce a global schema. Simple examples of schema conflicts include *name conflicts* (i.e., different names for the same fact or one name for several different facts), *scale conflicts* (i.e., different units of measure), and *structural conflicts* (i.e., the same fact modeled by different modeling constructs). Most work deals with the integration of homogeneous databases only. Multibase [9], however, is an example of a system that supports the integration of heterogeneous database schemata.

Existing approaches to schema integration are of a declarative nature. For example, an object class of a global schema may be defined as some composition of the classes of the different local schemas [14,8]. The approach described in this paper has a procedural flavor. By using information-importing functions, it is not necessary to globally conform the local schemas. Rather, the programmer defining an information-importing function explicitly specifies a procedure that implements a mapping from the external information of interest to the importing database. That way, if a fact is represented redundantly in several information bases in possibly different forms, the implementor of an information-importing function is free to choose which form and which specific fact to access. Note also it is not necessary to conform all the different representations to a single common form. External data may be obtained using various local programs such as query processors or special-purpose programs built to support local applications.

Throughout the paper we use the Iris OODBMS [6], a research prototype under development at Hewlett-Packard Laboratories, to illustrate the concepts. The approach could also be supported by other object-oriented database systems supporting operations written in general-purpose programming languages. Such systems include GemStone [13], Vbase [1], and Orion [2]. However, most of those systems lack generalized query processing capabilities and that makes them less qualified as GDMs.

The rest of the paper is organized as follows. Section 2 provides a brief overview of the Iris OODBMS. In Section 3, an example distributed information application for portfolio management is described. Section 4 shows how information-importing functions are implemented in the Iris OODBMS and various tradeoffs and extensions are discussed. Finally, Section 5 provides some conclusions and directions for future research.

2 Overview of the Iris OODBMS

The Iris OODBMS is based on a semantic data model that supports abstract data types. Its roots can be found in previous work on Daplex [17] and the Taxis language [15]. The Iris data model contains three important constructs: *objects*, *types* and *functions*. These are briefly described below. A more complete description of the Iris Data Model and the Iris DBMS can be found in [6,10,12].

2.1 Objects and Types

Objects in Iris represent entities and concepts from the application domain being modeled. Some objects such as the integers and the strings are treated as *literal objects*, being regarded as always available and printable. A non-literal object is represented by a system-generated *object identifier* or *oid*. Examples of non-literal objects include objects representing persons and stocks.

Types have unique names and represent collections of objects that share common properties. For example, all the objects belonging to the Customer type have a Name and a Phone property. Objects serve as arguments to functions and may be returned as results of functions. Objects are constrained by their types to be operands for only those functions defined on the types.

Types are organized in a type structure that supports generalization and specialization. A type may be declared to be the subtype of another type. Functions defined on a supertype are also defined on the subtype.

2.2 Functions

As pointed out earlier, support of extensibility in OODBMSs is provided to a large degree by operations. In Iris, functions are manifestations of operations. Properties of objects, relationships among objects, and computations on objects are expressed in terms of functions. Functions are defined over types and they may be multi-valued and have side-effects. For example, BranchOf is a function defined on customer objects:

```
BranchOf:  Customer → BranchOffice
```

If Smith is assigned to the Dallas office then

```
BranchOf(Smith) = Dallas
```

A type can be characterized by the collection of functions defined on it. The Customer type might have the functions CustomerNumber, Name, BranchOf, and Holdings defined over it:

```
CustomerNumber:  Customer → Integer
Name:  Customer → CharString
BranchOf:  Customer → BranchOffice
Holdings:  Customer → Stock × Integer
```

Note that the Holdings function returns pairs of Stock and Integer objects. The function is also multi-valued. If Smith has 100 Sun Microsystem shares and 50 Digital Equipment Corporation shares then

```
Holdings(Smith) = [(Sun, 100), (Dec, 50)]
```

Functions can also express properties of several objects. For example, the function AssignmentDate defined on customers and branch offices will return the date a customer was assigned to the branch office:

```
AssignmentDate:  Customer × BranchOffice → Date
```

A new function is *declared* by specifying its name together with its argument and result types. For example[1]:

```
create function BranchOf( Customer ) = BranchOffice;
```

Before a function may be used, an *implementation* must be specified. This process is described in Section 2.4.

2.3 Database Updates and Queries

Properties of objects can be modified by changing the values of functions. For example, the operations:

```
set BranchOf(Smith) = Seattle;
add BigCustomers(Dallas) = Smith;
remove BigCustomers(Atlanta) = Jones;
```

[1]Throughout this paper, Iris operations are illustrated by an example syntax. The syntax may differ from the syntax supported by existing Iris interfaces and previously published work on Iris.

will cause the BranchOffice function to return the value Seattle in a future invocation with the parameter Smith, add Smith to the set of important accounts in Dallas, and remove Jones from the set of important accounts in Atlanta.

The database can be queried by specifying a *predicate* on objects and function values. A query specifies a list of results using variables and function applications, a list of existentially quantified variables, and a predicate. The predicate may use variables, constants, nested function applications, and comparison operators. The execution of a query causes the variables to be instantiated. The result of a query is all the instantiated values of the variables and the results of the function applications specified in the result list. The results are returned as a stream. The following query retrieves all the offices to which customers were assigned on 3/1/83:

```
select b
for each Customer c, BranchOffice b
where AssignmentDate( c, b ) = 3/1/83;
```

and the query:

```
select BigCustomer( Dallas );
```

returns all the important customers assigned to Dallas. Additional examples of queries are given in Section 3.

2.4 Function Implementation

So far, we have discussed the declaration of functions and their use in queries and updates. An important additional attribute of a function is the specification of its behavior. Function values may be explicitly stored in the database or they may be computed. The method used is user-specified and is called the function's *implementation.* In general, Iris supports three methods of function implementation: Stored, Derived, and Foreign. The methods are described below and details of how the different kinds of functions are handled in queries are given in Section 4.

Stored Functions

A function may be explicitly stored in a table, i.e., corresponding argument and result values (the graph of the function) are maintained in a single table. Several functions may be stored in the same table in order to improve performance. Stored functions may be updated, that is, the mappings from argument values to result values can be explicitly specified (Section 2.3). The actions of retrieval and updates are implicitly defined in terms of relational operations on the tables. A formal treatment of the mapping of Iris functions to relational tables can be found in [11]. The operations

```
create function Portfolio( Customer, Stock, Integer );
store function Portfolio;
```

declare a boolean valued function which Iris stores as a three column table.

Derived Functions

A function may be derived from other functions that are either stored, derived or foreign. A derived function is defined by an expression which is an Iris query (Section 2.3). It can be thought of as a view. The update semantics of derived functions are not always well-defined. For example, if the derivation expression of a given function requires joining several tables, the function cannot be directly updated. However, the actions of updates are implicitly defined by Iris in those cases where it can solve the "view update" problem. Functions that are defined as inverses of stored functions are examples of updatable derived functions. In other cases, the update semantics may be explicitly specified as part of the function definition. The operations:

```
create function Holdings( Customer ) = ( Stock, Integer );
derive function Holdings( Customer c ) as
   select s, q for each Stock s, Integer q where Portfolio( c,s,q );
```

illustrate the declaration of a function and its derivation.

Foreign Functions

A program written in some general-purpose programming language and compiled outside of Iris may be linked to an Iris function. When the function is invoked, the program is dynamically loaded and executed. Foreign functions cannot be optimized by the Iris system. It is with foreign functions that data may be imported from external information bases. The following is a sample foreign function derivation:

```
create function MarketPrice( Stock ) = Integer;
link function MarketPrice to programfile;
```

The various implementations of functions described above allow functions to represent attributes, relationships, views, and computations. A user invoking a given function does not have to know whether the function returns a stored fact, a derived fact, a computed value, or data retrieved from a foreign database or specialized storage subsystem. Therefore, high levels of data abstraction and data independence are supported.

3 An Example Distributed System

In this section, we present an example of using an OODBMS to access multiple information sources. The example involves managing customer portfolios at a brokerage firm. We use Iris as the specific OODBMS.

A brokerage firm, named McStocks, maintains an Iris database which contains information about its customers and the stocks they own. Additionally, brokers require investment information which is not maintained by the brokerage firm. In our example there are two such external sources of information. The first is a database, called InvestBase, owned and operated by an investment research company. Our brokerage firm subscribes to this service to obtain analyses of companies and historical data on their stock. The second is an on-line quotation service, called TickerTyme, which reports current market prices directly from the floor of the stock exchange. Note that this second service is *not* a database.

To assist its brokers, the firm's database contains a few foreign functions which import information from InvestBase and TickerTyme. This means that questions which would ordinarily involve multiple operations on several information bases might be answered with a single query to the firm's database.

McStocks' database contains four data types of interest: Integer, CharString, Customer and Stock. For convenience, we assume all numerical data to be integer. The database also contains six functions of interest:

```
Holdings:  Customer → Stock × Integer
SymbolOfStock:  Stock → CharString
52WeekLow:  CharString → Integer
Earnings:  CharString → Integer
MarketPrice:  CharString → Integer
Multiply:  Integer i × Integer j → Integer k
```

The function Holdings defines the relationship between customers and the quantity of stocks they own. SymbolOfStock converts a stock into the character string used by the exchanges to denote the stock. These first two functions are maintained locally in McStocks' database. Their values are stored in tables.

The function 52WeekLow takes a stock's symbol as input and returns the lowest closing price over the last year. Similarly, Earnings reports a company's earnings over the latest fiscal year. These two functions are examples of information-importing functions. They provide views of the InvestBase database. When invoked, the programs to which these functions correspond will submit the appropriate query to InvestBase and supply the answers to the Iris query processor. From InvestBase's perspective, the programs are merely applications. Notice that it is not necessary to support the entire InvestBase schema in McStocks' database. This is in contrast to the schema integration approach for distributed information access.

MarketPrice is another information-importing function based on the TickerTyme service. It returns the current price of a given stock. Note that consecutive invocations of MarketPrice may return different results. Since TickerTyme is not a transaction system, it is impossible to completely support transactions in McStocks' database, two-phased commit notwithstanding.

Multiply is a foreign function which does not import any external information. Multiply illustrates that arithmetic in Iris is supported by foreign functions. In general, arithmetic functions are provided by the system. Besides computations, another use of foregin functions is data conversion, e.g., BCD to 2's complement, meters to inches, etc.

The following is a simple scenario which shows how the above functions provide uniform access to the heterogeneous information systems of McStocks', InvestBase and TickerTyme. Suppose Smith calls McStocks worried about his holdings in Sun Microsystems. His broker issues the Iris query

```
select 52WeekLow( 'SUNW' );
```

to assure Smith that his Sun stock was a good buy. Smith is also interested in the earnings of all shares he currently owns. His broker obliges with

```
select c, Earnings(c)
for each CharString c, Stock s, Integer q
where Holdings( Smith ) = ( s, q ) and c = SymbolOfStock( s );
```

If McStocks' brokers find that this query is often asked, it would be advantageous to support it directly in the database schema as a derived function. Now the broker, hoping to leverage the phone call to make a sale, wants to entice Smith with some good deals, i.e., those stocks which are currently selling at their one year low. Note that this operation accesses both InvestBase and TickerTyme in one Iris query.

```
select c
for each CharString c, Stock s
where c = SymbolOfStock( s ) and MarketPrice( c ) <= 52WeekLow( c );
```

Before making a decision, Smith would like to review his portfolio. His broker, disappointed at whetting Smith's appetite for more information instead of purchases, reluctantly requests:

```
select c, v
for each CharString c, Integer v, Stock s, Integer q
where Holdings( Smith ) = ( s, q ) and c = SymbolOfStock( s ) and
    v = Multiply( MarketPrice( c ), q );
```

The above queries illustrate how an OODBMS can be used to provide uniform access to heterogeneous information bases. The possibilities are even greater. For example, the views of InvestBase provided by the functions 52WeekLow and Earnings are obtained with InvestBase queries which are "hard coded" into the functions' programs. One can imagine a "trap door" function whose program takes a character string argument and submits it verbatim to InvestBase as a query in the InvestBase query language. This would give the McStocks database user much more flexibility. One can also imagine a foreign function whose program requests information from several different information bases and merges the results, thus providing *fragmentation transparency*. For example, suppose InvestBase covers only stock listed on the New York Exchange while another database covers Over-the-Counter stocks. The program for earnings might access both databases to find the earnings of a particular stock. Thus McStocks might avoid creating subtypes of the type Stock and thereby keep its schema and queries simpler.

4 Supporting Foreign Functions in Iris

In this section we describe how foreign functions are supported in the Iris prototype and we discuss various tradeoffs in the design of the implementation. Foreign functions differ from stored and derived functions in the way they are implemented and that has certain implications for the query processing system as described below. A thorough description of the Iris query processor and its support for stored and derived functions can be found in [5].

Iris functions and queries are compiled by the system. Internally they are represented by relational algebra trees. The trees that represent functions in their compiled form specify how the values of the functions are obtained from stored and computed data. A stored function, for example, is represented by a single *table node* denoting the table storing the graph of the function. In order to execute that tree, a scan of the table is performed and the values returned.

A derived function is represented by a tree that typically is more complex. The tree is composed in accordance to the query defining the derived function. The compiled representation of a derived function is a composition of the trees representing the functions used in the defining query. These subtrees are combined by *cross-product*, *project*, and *filter* nodes. A derived function may be optimized by transforming its compiled relational algebra tree into a semantically equivalent tree that can be executed more efficiently. The nodes required to support stored and derived Iris functions are similar to the nodes supported by most conventional relational query processors [16].

Five node operations, *Alloc*, *Open*, *Next*, *Close*, and *Dealloc*, are defined on each node type and these operations are applied to the nodes of a given tree in order to execute the tree. The Alloc/Dealloc pair is executed once per execution of the query tree. The operations deal with buffer allocation and deallocation, respectively. In order to execute a query tree, a given subtree may be scanned several times. That is, for example, the case for the inner subtree of a cross-product node. The Open and Close operations are executed once per scan. They are used to initialize counters and buffers. The Next operation obtains the next value of a node in the current scan. It may be called repeatedly until no more values are returned. The type of the node determines how the five node operations are implemented.

The Iris query processor treats foreign functions very much like stored functions. Specifically, a foreign function is represented by a single node, called a *foreign node*, denoting the computation of the function. Unlike table nodes, foreign nodes have input parameters which are used to produce results. From the Iris query engine's point-of-view, a foreign node is treated like other nodes. They are manipulated by the exact same types of node operations, i.e., Alloc, Open, Next, Close, and Dealloc. However, where the Next operation of a table node causes the next tuple of a stored table to be read, the Next operation of a foreign node invokes a program that computes some value.

The implementor of a foreign function is responsible for providing five programs that are to be executed by the five node operations and these programs are treated like black boxes; Iris relies on the computer's instruction engine (CPU) to execute the algorithms encoded by the programs. The query processor need only know how to marshal parameters, how to load, link, and invoke the programs, and interpret their results. Since certain conventions must be adopted by the programs and since the Iris System is vulnerable to bugs in the program code, adding a foreign function is considered to be the task of a DBA or an advanced database designer. This is acceptable for the purpose of a research prototype, but a real production DBMS could benefit from a more user-friendly way of adding foreign functions. Furthermore, stronger protection must be provided for foreign functions, e.g., by executing them in separate processes or memory segments.

The database designer introducing a foreign function must explicitly specify how the function obtains its data and how it is transformed to a format that can be understood and further processed by the importing DBMS. This is done by the programs corresponding to the five node operations. In simple cases, the programs corresponding to the node operations Alloc, Open, Close, and Dealloc are empty. However, if the foreign function is an information-importing function, the program corresponding to the Alloc operation may be responsible for setting up a communication channel, the program corresponding to the Open operations may be responsible for initializing the remote information systems (for example by starting a session if the remote system is a DBMS), and the program corresponding to the Next operation may be responsible for obtaining the remote data (for example by issuing a remote query and managing its cursor), transmitting the result back to the importing database, and returning it in a format that satisfies the interface to the Next operation.

A foreign function cannot be optimized by the system. The implementor of the function is responsible for writing the programs in an optimal way. Note that if a foreign function issues a query to a remote database system, then the request may be optimized locally by that system. A compiled version of the query may even be maintained by the remote system if it supports the compilation approach. The usage of a foreign function can be optimized by the importing database system if certain statistical information is provided. Such information includes the cost of executing the five programs and an estimate of the number of results produced by the foreign function. This information may be used by the query optimizer in the same manner it uses statistical information describing table nodes to determine join orders and join methods.

There is a subtle difference in the way the query optimizer treats table nodes and foreign nodes. A table node corresponding to some stored function is "invertible" or "symmetric" in the sense that given the argument values of the function the corresponding result values can be obtained (from the stored table) or given the result values of the function, the corresponding argument values can be obtained. For example, suppose that CustomerNumber is a stored function. Then the query

```
select c for each Customer c where CustomerNumber( c ) = 1224;
```

specifies that the argument of the function be used to generate returned values based on the constant value 1224 for the function's result. This corresponds to doing a table lookup "backwards." However, a foreign function is "one way only" since the algorithm programmed can usually only calculate in a forward direction. Therefore, a foreign node cannot be executed before its input parameters have been instantiated by the execution of other nodes. This impacts query optimization and query plan generation because the set of possible join orders involving foreign nodes is restricted.

Two other anomalies[2] arise when using foreign functions to access remote information bases. The first is that the notion of transactions across multiple databases is not supported. Of course if an Iris application would like to abort, it may run compensating actions, attempting to undo what has already been done. However, there is no guarantee that even a read-only query involving a remote database (or file for that matter) will return the same answer both times. The second anomaly can occur if two DBMSs are importing from each other. Undetectable deadlocks may result. Because of the lack of support for deadlock detection in the current implementation, it is not recommended to write foreign functions that recursively call Iris.

The parameters passed to foreign functions and the results returned must all have types that are understood by the Iris DBMS as well as the programming languages used to program the foreign functions. The types may have different representations in Iris and the various programming languages. This is no different than the current approach in which Iris and its storage manager use different type representations. A library of conversion routines supports the mappings between the different representations.

The Iris query processor is rule-based. However, the Iris System does not currently support a public interface to the rule system. If such an interface were provided, database designers could add new rules that specify how the usage of foreign functions could be optimized. For example, a rule might specify that two or more foreign functions are equivalent, i.e., they return the same values for the same parameters. That way, the query processor would have more freedom in chosing a query plan involving access to replicated data and *replication transparency* could be supported.

In a distributed database system there is a tradeoff between (1) running a query on a remote database and transmitting the results back to the importing database and (2) transmitting data from the remote database to the importing database for local processing. In a system with a rule-based query translator, such as Iris, the query optimizer could make decisions of the above kind based on user-defined optimization rules.

An important aspect of the implementation of foreign functions has to do with the manner in which the programs of a foreign function are loaded and linked into memory. The time and frequency with which that happens are also essential. If few foreign functions are added over the lifetime of a given schema, it may be acceptable to bring down the DBMS in order to install a new foreign function. However, if new foreign functions are added frequently, it is critical that they be installed without interrupting other users of the system., If a given schema includes foreign functions that have large core images, dynamic loading is a must. In the current Iris implementation, the object code of the foreign functions and that of the query processor are dynamically linked together. Therefore, the programming languages that can be used to implement foreign functions are limited by their parameter passing conventions. Using remote procedure calls and separate processes for foreign functions will alleviate this limitation and also increase protection. However, the implied context switching would significantly degrade performance.

As mentioned previously, information-importing functions are just examples of foreign functions that access remote information bases. As such, the programs that constitute an information-importing function must explicitly provide support for data communication. For example, the address of the remote information system must be encoded in the programs of the foreign functions or be supplied as an input parameter at invocation-time. In either case, the code of the foreign function must implement the required communication protocol. The task of implementing support for data communication can be facilitated by the presence of powerful data communication program libraries. We are also exploring alternative system architectures in which the code supporting the communication aspects of information-importing functions can be cleanly separated from the rest of the code. That way, the communication code can be incorporated into the Iris kernel and shared by many information-importing functions.

[2]Foreign functions also differ from stored and derived functions in that they cannot be directly updated.

5 Conclusions

In this paper we have proposed the use of object-oriented DBMSs as tools for providing uniform access to distributed, diverse, autonomous information sources. An OODBMS allows new operations to be specified in a general-purpose programming language without the need of altering the data model. Such operations can therefore access remote information systems in a user-transparent way. We have demonstrated the approach using the Iris OODBMS. Iris' support for generalized query processing capabilities and operations written in arbitrary programming languages make it a better candidate for a global data manager than many other OODBMSs.

Using an OODBMS as a global data manager supports the integration of heterogeneous data some of which may not be under the control of a transaction manager, preserves the autonomy of the constituent information bases, provides distribution transparency, allows fragmentation and replication transparency, and does not require the introduction of a global schema to which all the local schemata must adhere.

An Iris prototype which supports stored and derived functions has been in use since early 1986. The current prototype supports dynamic linking of foreign functions. In the future, we plan to add more functionality to the Iris DBMS such that no programming is required in order to install information-importing functions that access remote Iris databases.

Acknowledgements

We gratefully acknowledge the contributions of our colleagues in the Iris Extensibility Project, including William Kent, Marie-Anne Neimat, and Kevin Wilkinson. We also thank David Beech and Dan Fishman for their helpful comments on earlier versions of this paper.

References

[1] T. Andrews and C. Harris. Combining language and database advances in an object-oriented development environment. In *Proceedings of ACM Conference on Object-Oriented Programming Systems, Languages, and Applications*, Orlando, Florida, October 1987.

[2] J. Banerjee, H. T. Chou, J. F. Garza, W. Kim, D. Woelk, N. Ballou, and H. J. Kim. Data model issues for object-oriented applications. *ACM Transactions on Office Information Systems*, 5(1), January 1987.

[3] C. Batini, M Lenzerini, and S. B. Navathe. A comparative analysis of methodologies for database schema integration. *ACM Computing Surveys*, 18(4), December 1986.

[4] S. Ceri and G. Pelagatti. *Distributed Databases.* McGraw-Hill, Inc., 1984.

[5] N. Derrett and M. C. Shan. *Rule-Based Query Optimization.* Technical Report STL-87-07, Software Technology Laboratory, HP Laboratories, December 1987.

[6] D. H. Fishman, D. Beech, H. P. Cate, E. C. Chow, T. Connors, J. W. Davis, N. Derrett, C. G. Hoch, W. Kent, P. Lyngbaek, B. Mahbod, M. A. Neimat, T. A. Ryan, and M. C. Shan. Iris: An object-oriented database management system. *ACM Transactions on Office Information Systems*, 5(1), January 1987.

[7] V. D. Gligor and G. L. Luckenbaugh. Interconnecting heterogeneous database management systems. *IEEE Computer*, 17(1), January 1984.

[8] D. Heimbigner. *A Federated Architecture for Database Systems.* PhD thesis, University of Southern California, August 1982.

[9] T. A. Landers and R. L. Rosenberg. An overview of Multibase. In H. J. Schneider, editor, *Distributed Data Bases*, North-Holland Publishing Company, 1982.

[10] P. Lyngbaek and W. Kent. A data modeling methodology for the design and implementation of information systems. In *Proceedings of 1986 International Workshop on Object-Oriented Database Systems*, Pacific Grove, California, September 1986.

[11] P. Lyngbaek and V. Vianu. Mapping a semantic data model to the relational model. In *Proceedings of ACM-SIGMOD International Conference on Management of Data*, San Francisco, California, May 1987.

[12] Peter Lyngbaek. *A Programmatic Interface to the Iris Database System (Version 2.1).* Technical Report STL-TM-87-25, Software Technology Laboratory, HP Laboratories, July 1987.

[13] D. Maier, J. Stein, A. Otis, and A. Purdy. Development of an object-oriented DBMS. In *Proceedings of ACM Conference on Object-Oriented Programming Systems, Languages, and Applications*, Portland, Oregon, September 1986.

[14] A. Motro and P. Buneman. Constructing superviews. In *Proceedings of ACM-SIGMOD International Conference on Management of Data*, Ann Arbor, Michigan, April 1981.

[15] J. Mylopoulos, P. A. Bernstein, and H. K. T. Wong. A language facility for designing database-intensive applications. *ACM Transactions on Database Systems*, 5(2), June 1980.

[16] P. G. Selinger et al. Access path selection in a relational database system. In *Proceedings of ACM-SIGMOD International Conference on Management of Data*, Boston, Massachusetts, May 1979.

[17] D. Shipman. The functional data model and the data language DAPLEX. *ACM Transactions on Database Systems*, 6(1), September 1981.

[18] M. Stonebraker and E. Neuhold. A distributed database version of Ingres. In *Proceedings of Berkeley Workshop on Distributed Data Management Systems*, Berkeley, California, May 1977.

[19] R. Williams, D. Daniels, L. Haass, G. Lapis, B. Lindsay, P. Ng, R. Obermarck, P. Selinger, A. Walker, P. Wilms, and R. Yost. *R*: An Overview of the Architecture.* Technical Report RJ3325, IBM, February 1981.

The Object Shell: An Extensible System to Define an Object-Oriented View of an Existing Database

Rafiul Ahad
Information Systems Group
College of Business and Management
University of Maryland
College Park, Maryland
e-mail: ahad@is1.umd.edu

ABSTRACT

The design of an extensible system, called the object shell, to define and query an object-oriented view of an existing database is described. An object-oriented view is defined by identifying the object types and the functions between them that are present in the existing database. The object shell provides facilities to declaratively define the logical schema, implementation methods for functions, the cost associated with the implementation methods, and the query optimization knowledge. An implementation method is a sequence of *access routine* calls. Access routines are defined by the database administrator (DBA), and each of them encodes the detailed knowledge to access a single physical structure (e.g., a file). The query interface of the object shell allows the user to issue queries against the view. The object shell translates the user query into an efficient program that calls the access routines to retrieve the required data.

1. Introduction

For several reasons such as providing a high-level query interface to an existing database, or to provide an integrated view of heterogeneous databases [Motr81, Daya84, Motr87] an object-oriented view of an existing database is required. In this paper we describe a system, called the object shell, that is designed to support an object-oriented functional view of an existing database with relative ease and efficiency. We do not impose any restrictions on the organization of the physical database, making the object shell useful for all kinds of databases.

Most database management systems (DBMS) are designed for a specific physical storage system (file system). Detailed knowledge about the available organizations and access methods are coded as part of the DBMS. The DBMS or the database administrator (DBA) chooses the organization and access methods of files to represent the logical constructs such as a relation [Codd70]. This mapping information is stored within the DBMS. Thus when a query against the logical database is given, the DBMS knows how to generate code for the file system to evaluate the query. However, if the physical storage model is not fixed, the DBMS may have to keep track of the many possible file organizations and access methods and many variations in the implementations of the file systems. The DBMS will become a very large and complex piece of software that still cannot be used with file systems that it does not know. Therefore we take a different approach in mapping the logical constructs to the physical constructs. We detach the detailed knowledge about the physical storage system from the DBMS. This knowledge is stored in the *access routines*, each of which can access one physical structure (storage or access structure) using one technique (e.g., sequential). In the conventional DBMSs, the mapping between the logical constructs and physical constructs, and query optimization knowledge are coded in the DBMS software. In extensible DBMSs the query optimization knowledge is detached from the DBMS software and the database implementor (DBI) can define the query optimization knowledge to be used by the DBMS. The object shell described in this paper is a DBMS in which both the logical-to-physical mapping knowledge and the query optimization knowledge are detached. The object shell provides facilities for the DBA or DBI to define them in a declarative manner.

In designing the object shell we use many ideas from the work in extensible DBMS [Care86, Daya85, Bato86, Ston86, Schw86, Grae87] and rule-based query optimization [Frey86, Frey87, Rose87]. The distinguishing features of the object shell over the previous extensible systems are:

- It is designed for an object-oriented data model.
- It does not have its own physical database. Any existing physical or logical database can be attached to it.
- It makes no distinction between storage structures and access structures. Both are treated as the same.
- It has no pre-coded methods (e.g., hash join method) for its operators, every method must be coded by the DBA or DBI.

The efficiency of the object shell described in this paper depends on two issues. The first is the object identification scheme. With the existing object-oriented DBMS (e.g., IRIS [Fish87]) where object creation is under the control of the DBMS, system-generated identifiers (or surrogates) can be used to identify them. But with existing databases, such identifiers may not exist. Therefore, we have to use existing symbolic identifiers. Depending on the naming convention used [Kent79] and the length (number of fields) of the symbolic identifiers, the performance of the system varies. We leave this issue for future research and take a simple solution described later in this paper. The second issue is the optimization of query posed in the DML of the model used to define the object-oriented view. In this paper we address this issue.

The architecture of the object shell is shown in figure 1. The user or the DBA uses the data definition interface (DDL interface) to define the schema for an object-oriented view, using a functional data model. The view is queried from the data manipulation interface (DML interface). The DML interface can be made to support both graphic and procedural query languages. A query written in the DML of the data model is first parsed by the *parser*. If the query is valid the parser generates a query graph of it. The query graph is processed by the *query optimizer*. The query optimizer uses the *mapping knowledge base* and the *query optimization knowledge base* to transform the query graph into one which is more efficient to evaluate, called the output query graph. The mapping knowledge base includes specifications of the many-to-many relationships between functions and access routines to materialize them, the characteristics of the access routines, the characteristics of the physical structures, and the cardinality information on the functions. The query optimization rules are similar in spirit to those found in the literature on rule-based query optimization [Frey86, Frey87, Rose87] and they encode the query optimization knowledge. The output query graph is fed to the *code generator* which generates a complete program that, when executed retrieves the response set of the query. The access routine library contains the access routines defined for the physical structures.

The object shell can run on the machine that has the database stored in its secondary memory. However, in practice these machines (or hosts) may not have enough resources to spare for the object shell. To deal with this problem, we are designing a workstation-based architecture whereby a small set of access routines runs on the hosts and a substantial piece of the system, including the program (QEP), resides on the workstation. The program makes remote procedure calls to the hosts to get disk pages.

The remainder of the paper is organized as follows. In section 2 we present the data model. In section 3, we discuss the structure of the query graph. In section 4, we describe how access routines are defined. In section 5 we describe how mapping knowledge is defined. In section 6, we present the query optimization knowledge base. In section 7, we delineate the query optimization process. Section 8 contains concluding remarks.

2. The Data Model

The data model for defining an object-oriented view is a functional data that is a variant of the functional data models found in the literature [Bune79, Ship81]. The basic modeling constructs of this model are objects, object sets, and functions. There are two kinds of objects:

- *descriptor objects* are printable values, e.g., ASCII strings, numbers, etc..
- *abstract objects* are non-printable identifiers that act as surrogates for things or concepts in the real world.

Each set of objects is an ordered or unordered finite subset of an object type. An object type consists of all possible objects sharing common properties, and intuitively corresponds to a type in programming languages. We assume the existence of pre-defined object types from which object sets are defined.

A function maps objects in one object set (called the domain) to objects in another (called the range). Functions are intended to model the relationships among objects. We allow only single-argument functions. A function may be declared as single-valued or set-valued. A single-valued function maps an object in a domain to an object in a range. A set-valued function maps an object in a domain to a subset of the range. For every function f from object set X to object set Y, there exists an inverse function, which if not explicitly named, can be referred to as $\$f$.

A conceptual schema defined with this model consists of definitions of object sets and functions, and can intuitively be described by a directed, labeled, multigraph. Each object set of the schema is represented by a node of the graph; a shaded node for a descriptor object set and a white node for an abstract object set. Each object set must be given a unique name. Each function is represented by a directed edge from the node corresponding to the domain of the function to the node corresponding to the range of the function. The name of the function is represented as the edge label. The name of the function is unique among those having the same domain. To refer to a function whose name is not unique within the schema, it must be appended by the "@" symbol immediately followed by the domain object set name. A single-valued function is distinguished by a single arrowhead drawn on the edge, and a set-valued function by two arrowheads.

As an example, consider a schema to capture the information about students and courses and the enrollment of students in courses. Each student has a social security number, a name, several telephone numbers, and several automobiles. Each automobile has a tag number, year, make and model. Each course has a course number, title, and the number of credits for the course. A course is offered in several semesters. A course may have several other courses as prerequisites. A student enrolls in a course in one of the semesters in which the course is offered and receives a grade for it. The graphical representation of the schema for this database is shown in figure 2.

Several query languages have been proposed for the functional data model [Bune79, Ship81, Ahad86]. Any of these can be used to manipulate the data. In this paper we will use the DML described in [Ahad86] to explain the various functions of OMS.

The main constructs used to manipulate data in the model are *access paths*, set operators and aggregate operators. An access path is a function or a composition of functions; $f_1 \circ \ldots \circ f_n$, is an access path where $f_1, \ldots, f_n$ are functions such that the range of f_i is the same as the domain of f_{i+1} for $1 \leq i < n$; and $\circ$ is the composition operator. An access path corresponds to a directed path in the graphical representation of the schema. For example, some of the access paths of the schema of figure 2 are: *name@STU*, *\$ss#* $\circ$ *tel*, and *ss#* $\circ$ *enr* $\circ$ *cou* $\circ$ *c#*.

Given a set of objects, called the *source*, an access path is traversed to access related objects, called the *destination*. The source of an access path must be a subset of the domain of the first function of the access path. For example, if D is a set containing auto tag numbers, then we can use D as the source of the access path *\$tag#* $\circ$ *\$auto* $\circ$ *name* to access the names of the students who own the automobiles with the given tag numbers. Expressed in conventional notation, the destination set is $\bigcup_{(d \in D)} name(\$auto(\$tag\#(d)))$.

As an example, consider a query to print the ss# and name of the students who took only 4-credit courses and got the grade 'A' in all the courses they took. The query in our DML is shown below.

```
begin
   X = {4} o $cre o $cou;
   Y = {'A'} o $gra;
   Z = X intersect Y;
   for each s in STU do
      E = s o enr;
      if E subsetof Z then print s.ss#, s.name
   end
end
```

Example Query

The meaning of the procedure is as follows. Use $\{4\}$ as the source, and traverse the access path *\$cre* $\circ$ *\$cou*; retrieve the destination into X. Using $\{'A'\}$ as source, traverse the access path *\$gra* and retrieve the destination into Y. Compute Z, the intersection of X and Y. Use each object s of STU in turn as a source, and traverse the access path *enr* and retrieve the destination into E. If E is a subset of Z then print the destination of the access paths *ss#* and *name* using s as source. It should be emphasized that the above is a logical procedure; i.e., the query evaluator may use different access paths when physically evaluating the query.

Although the DML has constructs for database updates, they are not required to support the object-oriented view and are not discussed here. The generalization/specialization abstraction mechanism for the data model is also not discussed since it is not used in the object shell.

3. The Query Graph

When a query is parsed, a structure called the query graph is created for the purpose of optimizing query evaluation and to generate code to evaluate the query. A query graph is constructed from multiple instances of two types of nodes and two types of arcs. The node types are the data node type, and the function node type. The arc types are the data arc type, and the control arc type. The data node type has two subtypes: the object-set subtype and the object subtype. Within each subtype there may be many sub-subtypes corresponding to the data types supported by the Object Shell. The function node type also has two subtypes: the mapping function and the transfer function. Mapping functions are user-defined functions such as *name* in the example in section 2, or system-defined functions such as *union* for set union operation. Transfer functions either convert a set of objects to a stream of objects such as *for-each* function, or convert a stream of objects into a set such as *accumulate-or* function. Transfer functions are described later in this section.

The data nodes have exactly one input port and one output port. Fan-in is not allowed in the input port; i.e., at most one arc may be connected to the input port of a data node. Fan-out is allowed for output ports; i.e., any number of arcs (including zero) may emanate from the output port of a data node. A function node that represents an n-argument function has n input ports that are numbered 1 to n. Function nodes also have one output port but fan-out is not allowed. Each input port of a function node must have exactly one arc connected to it and the output arc must have exactly one arc emanating from it. Both data nodes and function nodes may have control ports that are used for possible generation parallel programs. For sequential program generation, only one of these ports - an input port called *activate* - of function nodes is used. When a Boolean descriptor object 'true' is supplied to the activate port of a function, the function may be evaluated.

There are two rules that govern the creation of a valid graph instance. First, a data arc must either emanate from the output port of a data node and terminate at an input port of a function node or must emanate from the output port of the function node and must terminate at the input port of a data node. Second, A control arc must emanate from a function node and terminate at a different function node. Each data node corresponds to a primary or secondary memory space used to store objects. An arc from the output port of data node to the ith input port of a function node indicates that the object stored in the data node is the ith argument to the function. An arc from the output port of a function to the input port of a data node indicates that the result of the function evaluation is stored in the data node. A transfer node may have several control arcs terminating at it. These arcs control the activation of the transfer node and are used in code generation for proper scoping of loops.

Transfer functions convert sets to streams and vice versa. There are several pre-defined transfer functions. These include the function *for-each* which takes a set of objects as its argument and returns an object of the set each time it is activated. When the set is empty it returns a special descriptor object 'EOS'. There is class of transfer functions called *accumulate* function class whose members convert streams of objects into sets. For example *accumulate-union* inserts an incoming object into the set it is accumulating, if the object is not already a member of the set and the activate port has the Boolean descriptor object 'true'. Otherwise, it discards the object. The functions *accumulate-or* and *accumulate-and* are used to obtain a single Boolean object from the incoming Boolean objects by respectively OR-ing or AND-ing the incoming objects.

For the purpose of exposition, we depict a query graph using the following symbols. A data node is depicted as a square and a function node as circle. A data node that does not have and incoming arc has a label that shows the objects within them (constants) or the name of an object set defined in the schema. For a function node, a number at the place where an incoming arc meets the circle indicates the port number of the function; the number zero indicates the control port. A function node has a label that is the name of the function. Data arcs are shown as solid lines and control arcs are shown as dash lines. Thick solid lines represent sets of objects and thin solid lines represent individual objects.

The query graph for the example query given in section 2 is shown in figure 3.

A query graph is used by the query optimizer to search for an efficient query evaluation plan and by the code generator to generate a target program for the query. When the target program is executed the result of the query is retrieved. Two query graphs are said to be *equivalent* if they retrieve the same answer for all possible states of the database. Clearly, for a given query graph there may be many equivalent query graphs. Although these equivalent query graphs retrieved the same answer, the cost associated with retrieving them may differ. Therefore, to optimize the execution of a given query, one can construct a query graph for it, search for an equivalent query graph whose cost of evaluation is low, and generate the target program from it. This is the essence of our approach. To describe how the cost is computed we need to describe how the maps are defined. Before we describe how the maps are defined, we need to describe how access routines are defined.

4. Access Routines

The access routines are responsible for retrieving desired data items associated with a given data item from the stored data. The stored data is considered to be composed of *structures*. A structure consists of several components some of which are structures (recursive definition) and others are atomic values. Each structure or component has a *reference* and a *value*, both of which are considered to be valid data items. Structures can be referenced with respect to the structure (parent) immediately under which they appear as components. This type of reference is called a local reference. There may be several local references (synonyms) associated with a structure. Structures may also be referenced from a fixed structure (root). This type of reference is called the global reference. The concept of structure is introduced so that file systems and logical data model constructs can be treated in a uniform manner. A structure or a component corresponds to a directory, a subdirectory, a file, a record, or a repeating group in a file system, and to a relation or a tuple in the relational model. The name or address associated with a structure is its reference. For example, a flat file is a structure whose components are the records within it. These components are referenced by their physical addresses, or relative positions, or primary keys. When a record within the file is viewed as a structure, the fields within it are components of the structure. These components are addressed by their relative positions. The components in this case are the atomic values. We make no distinction between storage and access structures; they are both treated identically. For example, an inverted file associated with a data file is considered as a structure just as the data file is considered as a structure.

For each structure, one or more access routines may be defined to access any combination of components of the structure. The routines retrieve a component based on its local reference. If the structure is a file then a procedure must be implemented for each type of local reference (physical address, relative position, or symbolic identifier) to be supported. The component thus retrieved is a structure and its reference is returned by the routine. Another routine can then be used to retrieve components of this structure.

To illustrate this point, we will assume that the host-resident database for the schema shown in figure 2 consists of two non-flat files to represent student and course, a directory to represent automobile information (each tag number is represented as a file), and a flat file to represent enrollment information as shown below.

STUDENT [SS#, NAME, [TEL#], [TAG#], [↑ ENROLL]]
AUTO [TAG# [MAKE, MODEL, YEAR]]
ENROLL [C#, SEM, GRADE]
COURSE [C#, TITLE, [SEM], CREDIT, [↑ COURSE]]

Physical structures for the example database of figure 2.

Here the repeating groups are shown within brackets. ↑ ENROLL denotes a physical pointer to an ENROLL record and ↑ COURSE denotes a physical pointer to COURSE capturing the prerequisites function. Keys are underscored.

We will assume that STUDENT is organized as a hash file and that the disk blocks are linked by physical pointers and that the head of the list is pointed to by a cell called HSTUDENT.

Both the storage and access structures are considered as structures. Thus the components of the structure AUTO are structures each of which represents an automobile and has three components that are values representing the three attributes of an automobile. For example, we could have the routine openstuhash(L) to open the STUDENT structure (file) to access its components (records) using hash technique, and the routine getsturech(L,SS#,R) to get the student component (record) with the given SS# into the structure *R*, the routine getstufld(R,F1,F2,F3,F4,F5) to retrieve any component (field) combination of the structure *R* and the routine closestu(L) to close the structure (file) that was opened as *L*.

The routine getstufld retrieves any combination of the five components (fields) of a STUDENT record. The required components are retrieved in the variable specified in the corresponding parameter position in the routine.

Thus the call sequence openstuhash(L), getsturech(L,123,R), getstufld(R,_,N,_,_,_), close(L) [1] will return the name of the student whose SS# is 123.

We will assume that we also have routines openstuscan(L) that opens the STUDENT structure (file) for scanning and assigns it a logical structure L, closestuscan(L) to close the structure, getnextstu(L,X) that retrieves the next student component (record) from the structure L

[1] This call sequence is not efficient if used to retrieve names of N students since it will open and close the file N times. In section 5, we will show how we can avoid this type of inefficiency.

into structure X; two similar routines on the inverted file INAME: openinamscan(LSTRUCT) and getnextinam(LSTRUCT,X), getinamrec(X,Y) that retrieves the second component of a record of INAME; and getenrpdir(L,P,X) that uses physical addresses to directly access ENROLL, and getenrfld(X,F1,F2,F3) that accesses the fields of ENROLL.

5. Mapping Knowledge Base

The mapping knowledge base contains knowledge about the different ways of evaluating a logical function against the existing database. For each function defined in the database schema the DBA or DBI must specify one or more ***implementation methods*** that retrieve the range objects of the function given a domain object. An implementation method is a sequence of access routine calls. This means that if the range is an abstract object set, say R, the values returned by the implementation method represent abstract objects belonging to R and these values denote the same objects in all the methods that involve the object set R. For example, in the schema shown in figure 1, the values returned by the implementation method for the function *$name* are treated as identifiers of student objects and may be used to retrieve the range objects of all the functions emanating from the set STU. The values returned by an implementation method may be atomic identifiers or tuples representing compound identifiers. A major task for the user is the determination of the scheme to identify abstract objects globally. This requirement implies that sometimes it may be necessary to read many host-resident files to evaluate a function.

A function may have several alternate implementation methods, and an access routine may be used in many implementation methods. Also an access routine may be used to access ranges of several functions having the same domain (e.g., the access routine GETSTUFLD in section 4 is used to retrieve the ranges of the functions *ss#*, *name*, *tel*, *auto* and *enr*) . Allowing several alternate implementations of a function permits the user to model alternate ways of retrieving the range values which increases the scope of optimization. Likewise, allowing an access routine to implement many functions reduces the total number of routines and improves the performance by allowing the possibility of accessing all the range values stored in one I/O unit (e.g., a record).

The mapping knowledge base is used for two purposes: query optimization and code generation. The knowledge needed for code generation is the preamble for each implementation method, the sequence of access routine calls for each implementation method, the parameters for each access routine call, some information about iteration within an implementation method, and the 'postamble' for each implementation method. This knowledge is coded in a language whose syntax, although not described in this paper, is quite intuitive. We will explain how this knowledge is coded using two examples.

Suppose we want to define the implementation method shown in section 4 as implementation method 1 for the function *name*. This knowledge is coded as follows:

```
preamble(name(SSN), 1, [openstuhash(L)]).
method(name(SSN), 1, [getsturech(L,SSN,R); getstufld(R,_,N,_,_,_)]).
postamble(name(SSN), 1, [return(N);close(L)]).
```

Here, *method* is the body of the implementation method. If *name* is to be evaluated for n students, then the body can be iterated n times and the names accumulated in the variable N. A second implementation method for the function *name* can be defined as follows:

preamble(name(SSN), 2, [openstuscan(L)]).
method(name(SSN), 2, loop([getnextstu(L,R); getstufld(R,SSN,N,_,_,_)])).
postamble(name(SSN), 1, [return(N);close(L)]).

Here, the keyword loop indicates that the body has to be iterated until the required record is found. Set-valued functions pose a problem in that the different range values may be scattered among different records, or a multivalued field of the record may use different format from the one object shell uses to represent multiple components within a structure. The first problem is solved by having the keyword 'all' preceding the list of action in the method clause. The second problem is solved by a DBA-written routine for format conversion. For example, consider the function *enr*. If ENR objects are identified by the pair (SS#,C#), one possible implementation method body for the function *enr* is given below.

preamble(enr(SS#), 1, [openstuhash(L); openenrpdir(M)]).
method(enr(SS#), 1, ([getsturech(L,SS#,R);getstufld(S,_,_,_,_,E);
all([next(E,O);getenrpdir(M,O,X); getenrfld(X,C#,_,_)]).
postamble(enr(SS#), 1, [return(SS#,C#); close(L); close(M)]).

In addition to the knowledge about implementation methods, the mapping knowledge base also contains knowledge about the access cost of the implementation methods. This knowledge is defined using the syntax of PROLOG [Cloc86]. The access costs of an implementation method is the cost in number of blocks accessed to execute the implementation method by itself. That is, the cost reduction due to the use of multiple implementation methods that share some of the access routines is not considered. For example, if *name(s)* and *tel(s)* are to be evaluated for the same student object *s*, and if their implementation methods chosen both scan the STUDENT structure, then clearly the total cost is just the cost of one of them. This kind of cost reduction due to factoring of operations is considered by the query optimizer.

For each implementation method for each function, the DBA must provide a fact that resembles (and may be automatically constructed from) the body of the implementation method. The fact is of the form *impl_method(fn, im#, arseq, cseq)* where *fn* is the function name, *im#* is the implementation number, *arseq* is the sequence of access routine names that have non-zero access cost, i.e., those routines that access the structure in the secondary memory, and *cnseq* is the sequence of numbers related to the component number of the structures accessed by the access routines in *arseq*, and is used in cost computation. Some example facts for the implementation methods defined above are given below.

impl_method(name, 1, [getnextstu], [2]).
impl_method(enr, 1, [getsturech, getenrpidr], [5,1]).

In addition to the above facts the following facts are required.

arcost(arname, dcard, cn, Cost).
struct(arname,structname).
relcard(structname, cn, p, q).

Here, *arcost* returns the cost of accessing the structure associated with *dcard* domain objects using the named access routine. *Relcard* says that the number of objects in the cn^{th} component of the given structure related to one object of the domain is q and the number of domain objects related to one object of the cn^{th} component is p. This information is used to compute the number of range objects associated with n domain objects. The details of such estimations is given [Ahad85], and its use in computing the estimated number of objects retrieved for a given number of domain objects is elaborated in [Ahad86].

The fact *arcost* can be defined as a fact or a rule in the mapping knowledge base. For example one way to define the cost of access routine *getnextstu* is as follows.

```
arcost(getnextstu, 1, cn, 100).
arcost(getnextstu, n, cn, 200) :- n > 1.
```

Another way to define the same cost function is to use the following general rule.

```
scanspace(A,S,B) :- struct(A,S), oper(A,scan), space(S,B).
arcost(A,1,Cn,C) :- scanspace(A,S,B), relcard(S,Cn,1,_),C is B/2.
arcost(A,1,Cn,C) :- scanspace(A,S,B), relcard(S,Cn,P,_), P >1, C is B.
arcost(A,D,Cn,C) :- D > 1, scanspace(A,B), C is B.
arcost(A,D,Cn,C) :- oper(A,hash), C is N*1.2.
...
```

In this case the relevant facts should also be in the mapping knowledge base. Some of the facts that are commonly used for cost computation are.

```
struct(a,s).
oper(a,o).
cardinality(s,v1).
length(s,v2).
space(s,v3).
organization(s,v4).
branchFactor(s,v5).
```

where *a* is an access routine name and *o* is any valid file operation such as scan, direct access using physical address, a hash-based search, B-tree search, Binary search, etc., and *s* is the name of a structure. Oper(a,o) states that routine *a* does the operation on the structure *s*. Note that any operation on file can be specified. Cardinality(s,v1) states that the cardinality of the structure *s*, i.e., the number of components in it, is *v*1. Length(s,v2) states that the average length of a component in the structure is *v*2. Space(s,v3) states that the storage space occupied by the structure is *v*3 blocks. Organization(s,v4) shows the file organization; organization(STUDENT, hash) means that the student file is organized as a hash file. And branchFactor(s,v4) states that the branching factor of a node if the organization is a tree.

The cost associated with an implementation method is computed using the following rule.

```
imcost(F,I,D,C) :- impl_method(F,I,M,Cn), C is 0, cost(M,Cn,D,C)
cost([ ],Cn,D, C).
cost([A|M],[B|Cn],D,C) :- arcost(A,D,B,E), C is C + E,
relCard(S,B,P,Q), newD(D,D,P,Q), cost(M,Cn,D,C),!.
```

Here M is the implementation method, C is the cost, and D is the domain size for which the cost is to be computed. The procedure NewD computes the number of objects retrieved by access routine A that will be used as the domain objects in the next access routine. This computation is given in [Ahad86].

6. The Query Optimization Knowledge Base

The query optimization knowledge base contains the ***transformation rules***. Transformation rules specify the semantic-preserving transformations that can be performed on subgraphs of the query graph G. Conceptually, a transformation rule is a triple (E, R, C), where E is a subgraph of the query graph, R is a subgraph that is semantically equivalent to E, and C is a condition that must be true to replace E with R. Transformation rules are divided into three groups: ***equivalence rules***, ***expansion rules*** and ***factoring rules***. Equivalence rules are implementation-independent rules that are used to generate candidate subgraphs for possible replacement with their equivalent subgraphs. If a subgraph E is found in G and condition C of a rule that contains E in its first component is satisfied, then further transformations using the expansion and factoring rules are considered to ascertain the fact that the transformation is indeed beneficial.

The expansion and factoring rules are implementation-dependent rules and are used to assign implementation methods to the function nodes of a query graph. Expansion rules expand the function nodes to capture the implementation method assigned to it. The expanded function node contains nodes corresponding to access routines. Thus expansions rules transform the query graph so that it contains implementation-dependent specifics. Once the implementation methods have been assigned, the factoring rules are used to factor out common access routines so that unnecessary work can be avoided.

A transformation rule T is applied only if Cost(T(G)) < Cost(G), where T(X) is a graph obtained from graph X by applying transformation T, and Cost(X) is the total cost of evaluating the function nodes of graph X. Such a restriction on the application of a rule has a benefit that the application of the transformation rules is somewhat guided and that the cost of the query graph decreases monotonically from the input graph to the output graph. However, to avoid getting 'stuck' in a local minimum, the transformation rules have to be carefully designed. For example, if T1 and T2 are two transformation rules and G is the query graph such that: Cost(T1(G)) > Cost(G) and Cost(T2(T1(G))) < Cost(G), then the transformation rule T3 = T2 ∘ T1 must be in the query optimization knowledge base. Here T(G) denotes the graph obtained from applying the transformation rule T to graph G, and T3 = T2 ∘ T1 means T3(G) = T2(T1(G)).

Knowledge-based query optimization is adopted in the design of object shell so that the DBA can exploit the peculiar properties of the existing database to improve the query evaluation algorithm and/or to shorten the query optimization process. The purpose of knowledge-based query optimization will be defeated if query optimization knowledge cannot be specified in an intuitive manner independent of the existing transformation rules. Therefore, the language to specify the transformation rules becomes a critical factor. We have found that neither OPS5 [Forg85], a production system, nor PROLOG [Cloc86], a logic programming language is suitable for the specification of transformation rules. We wrote the transformation rules in these languages and found the process to be very tedious and long-winded. We are currently designing a production system suitable for graph transformation. In this paper we will use diagrams to explain some of the rules used for the example query. The transformation rules described are special cases of a few of the general transformation rules that encode common query optimization knowledge that is useful for all kinds of databases. We intend to make these rules as bulit-in rules of the object shell.

The first transformation rule (Rule 1) is shown in figure 5. Rule 1 states that O = F(I) for a set I of objects, i.e., $O = \bigcup_{i \in I} F(i)$, is equivalent to

for each object x in Range(F) do
if $F^{-1}(x) \in I$ then $O = O \cup \{x\}$;.

The rule is applicable if F^{-1} is single-valued. If F^{-1} is multi-valued the inclusion test must be replaced by a subset test. If I is a single object and F^{-1} is single-valued the test is object equality (=), and if F^{-1} is multi-valued the the test is inclusion but with ports are switched. Thus rule 1 can be considered as a special case of a more general rule in which a generic test is 'instantiated' with inclusion test to get Rule 1 for the case where I is a set and F^{-1} is single-valued. The general rule itself is a special case of another rule which captures the fact that if for each object x $\in$ X, we evaluate $P(f_1(x), ..., f_n(x))$, where P is a Boolean predicate, and if P if true we evaluate $g_1(x), ..., g_m(x)$ then the inverse functions of a subset of the functions $f_1, ..., f_n$ can be used with appropriate set operators to reduce the cardinality of the set X. In terms of a file system, the rule means that if a file has to be scanned, and for each record several field values are to be tested, and if they satisfy a given predicate the several other fields are to be retrieved, then inverted lists on some of the fields involved in the test can be appropriately manipulated the result used to reduce the number of records accessed.

The remaining rules to be used for our example are shown in figures 6 to 8.

7. The Query Optimizer

The query optimizer takes the input query graph, uses the mapping knowledge base and the query optimization knowledge base to transform the input query graph into an output query graph. The output query graph has the property that its total evaluation cost is no greater than the cost associated with the input query graph. The high-level algorithm used by the query optimizer to transform the input query graph into output query graph is shown below. Here G is the current query graph.

1. For each storage node find the estimated cardinality.
2. Eliminate infinite-cost (i.e., non-existent) functions using equivalence rules.
3. Assign implementation methods using expansion and factoring rules.
4. While there is an 'unused' subgraph S in G do

    if there is a rule R using which S can be replaced by T and the condition for R is satisfied
    then begin

        let G' = G - S ∪ T;

        Assign implementation methods for G' using expansion and factoring rules;

        if Cost(G') < Cost(G) then G := G'

    end

    else mark S as 'used'

The cardinalities of the data nodes that do not have incoming arcs are known at compile time. If X and Y are data nodes and F is a function node, and if the arcs (X,F) and (F,Y) are in the graph, and if the cardinality of X is known then the cardinality of Y can be estimated from the cardinality information associated with F. [Ahad86]

In step 2 of the algorithm, the functions that do not have an implementation method assigned to them are replaced with their inverses using the equivalence rules. In our example, we assume that there is no implementation method defined for *$cre*, *$cou* and *$gra*. Therefore, Rule 1 will be used three times in step 2 to replace these functions with their inverses.

In step 3, implementation methods are assigned to the functions using the expansion and factoring rules. Once the implementation methods have been assigned, their cost could be computed.

In step 4, the two phases of applying equivalence rules and implementation method assignment are iterated until no further rules can be applied. The implementation-independent equivalence rules are used to pick promising candidates. Once a candidate is picked, the implementation-dependent expansion and factoring rules are used to assign the best possible implementation methods to the entire graph that would be obtained if the rule were applied. Then the cost of two graphs are compared to see if the rules should be applied. In our example, the equivalence rules Rule 2, Rule 3, and Rule 4 will be applied in that order to obtain the output query shown in figure 4.

After the query graph has been transformed into an output query graph, it is used to generate a program. This is straightforward an we will not explain the process. The main procedure of the program is a driver that calls other procedures (defined by the user to materialize the functions) as required. The main procedure and the procedures it references are all put together into a program and compiled and linked on the host.

8. Conclusions

We have presented the design of the object shell, an extensible system to support an object oriented view of an existing database. At first it may look like a lot of work is needed to set up the system for a large database. We note that even though we say that an access routine must be provided for each structure using each access method, in reality a single parameterized procedure can be written to access all similarly-organized files. The access routines need only call these procedures with appropriate parameters. This will reduce the amount of work. Furthermore, it is not required to define the object-oriented view of the entire database; this can be done incrementally.

The method described herein is immune to changes in technology. If a new storage structure and access method is discovered, then it can be accessed by the object shell if appropriate access routine and rules are written.

Currently we are implementing the prototype version of the object shell. We have managed to compile queries and produce the query graph. The query graph is currently represented as a set of OPS5 literals. We have coded some rules as OPS5 production rules but found the process to be very tedious primarily due to the trial-and-error nature of subgraph replacement. Also we find that we sometimes need forward-chaining inference engine like OPS5 and sometimes a backward-chaining inference engine like PROLOG. Currently we are trying to design a production system for graph transformation. Although this may have the impact on the syntax of the rules eventually implemented, the spirit of the rules will remain intact.

The objective of this prototype implementation is to identify possible performance bottleneck in the design. We are concerned about two issues: whether the time taken for compilation of queries will be acceptable for ad hoc queries, and whether the object identification scheme that we have adopted will cause excessive amount of work in retrieving data.

In the existing design we have decided to use a single identifier for an object. Although this is sufficient to access all objects related to a given object, it may not necessarily be efficient for all cases. In some cases it may be beneficial to have several identifiers for an object. These synonym identifiers can be kept track in a relation. These are some of the issues that we will study in the prototype implementation.

Finally we note that even though the object shell is designed to be efficient for existing engineering and scientific databases, it can also be used for providing an object-oriented view for any record-based data models. The discussion in this paper has been limited to supporting procedural queries. It can easily be extended to support a graphical interactive query interface with an appropriate interpreter.

7. References

[Ahad85] Ahad, R., Baparao, K., McLeod, D., "On Estimating the Cardinality of the Projection of a Database Relation", to appear in *ACM Transactions on Database Systems.*

[Ahad86] Ahad, R. and McLeod, D., "Performance Optimization Techniques for an Object-Oriented Semantic Data Model", *CRI Technical Report*, USC, 1986.

[Bato86] Batory, D.S. et. al., "GENESIS: A Reconfigurable Database Management System", TR 86-07, Dept. of Computer Sciences, The University of Texas, Austin, 1986.

[Bune79] Buneman, P. and Frankel, R. "FQL–A Functional Query Language", *Proc. ACM-SIGMOD Conference*, May, 1979.

[Care86] Carey, M. et. al., "The architecture of EXODUS Extensible DBMS", *Proc. of the Int. Workshop on Object-Oriented Database Systems*, Asilomar, California, September, 1986.

[Cloc86] Clocksin, W. F. and C. S. Mellish, *Programming in Prolog*, Springer Verlag, 1986.

[Codd70] Codd, E.F.,"A Relational Model of Data for Large Shared Data Banks", *CACM*, 13(6), June 1970.

[Daya84] Dayal, U. and Hwang, H, "View Definition and Generalization for Database Integration in a Multidatabase System", *IEEE Transactions on Software Engineering*, Vol SE-10, November, 1984

[Daya85] Daya, U. and Smith, J., "PROBE: A Knowledge Oriented Database Management System, *Proc. of the Islamorada Workshop on Large Scale Knowledge Base and Reasoning Systems*, February, 1985.

[Fish87] Fishman, D., et. al., "Iris: An Object-Oriented Database Management System",*ACM Transactions on Office Information Systems*, Vol 5, No. 1, January 1987.

[Frey86] Freytag, J.C., and Goodman, N, "Rule-Based Transformation of Relational Queries into Iterative Programs", *Proc. ACM-SIGMOD Conference*, Washington, D.C., May, 1986.

[Frey87] Freytag, J.C., "A Rule-Based View of Query Optimization", *Proc. ACM SIGMOD Conference*, San Francisco, May, 1987.

[Grae87] Graefe, G. and DeWitt, D., "The EXODUS Optimizer Generator", *Proc. ACM SIGMOD Conference* San Francisco, May 1987.

[Kent79] Kent, W., "Limitations of Record-Based Information Models", *ACM Transactions on Database Systems*, 4(1), March, 1979.

[King86] King, R., "A database Management System Based on an Object-Oriented Model", *Proceedings of the First International Workshop on Expert Database Systems*, Kiawah Island, 1986.

[Motr81] Motro, A. and Buneman, P.,"Constructing Superviews", *Proc. SIGMOD 1981.*

[Motr87] Motro, A., "Superviews: Virtual Integration of Multiple Databases", *IEEE Transactions on Software Engineering*, Vol SE-13, No. 7, July 1987.

[Rose87] Rosenthal, A. and Helman, P., "Understanding and Extending Transformation-Based Optimizers", *Database Engineering* 1987.

[Schw86] Schwarz, P. et. al., "Extensibility in the Starbust Database System", *Proc. of the Asilomar Workshop on Object-Oriented Database Systems*, September, 1986.

[Ship81] Shipman, D.W., "The Functional Data Model and the Data Language DAPLEX", *ACM Transactions on Database Systems*, 6(1), March,1981.

[Ston86] Stonebraker, M. and Rowe, L., "The Design of Postgres", *Proc. ACM SIGMOD Conference*, Washington, 1986.

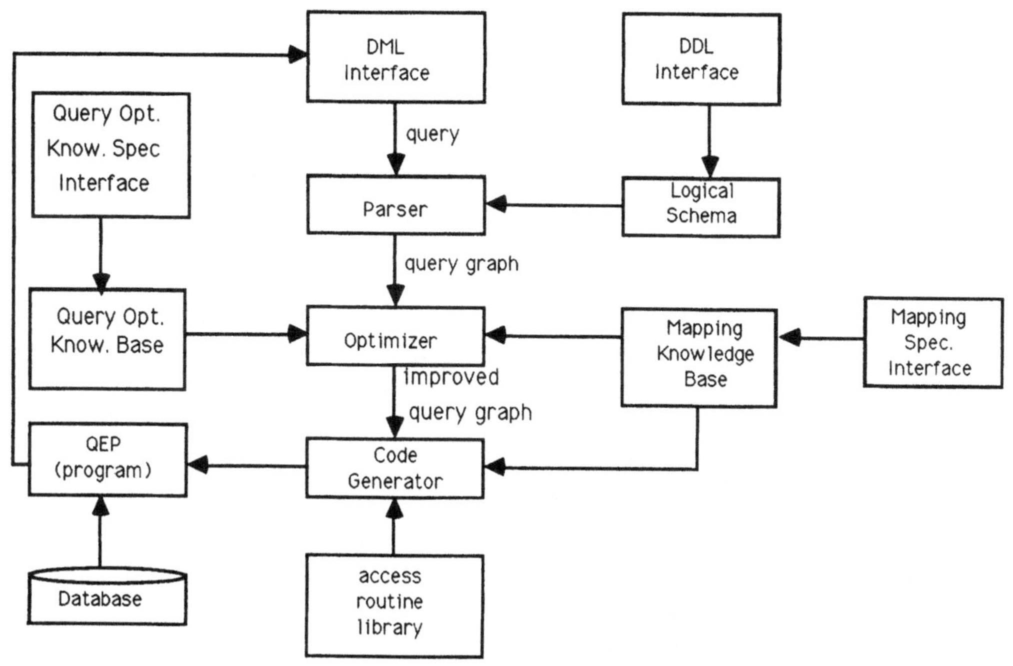

Figure 1. The Architecture of the Object Shell

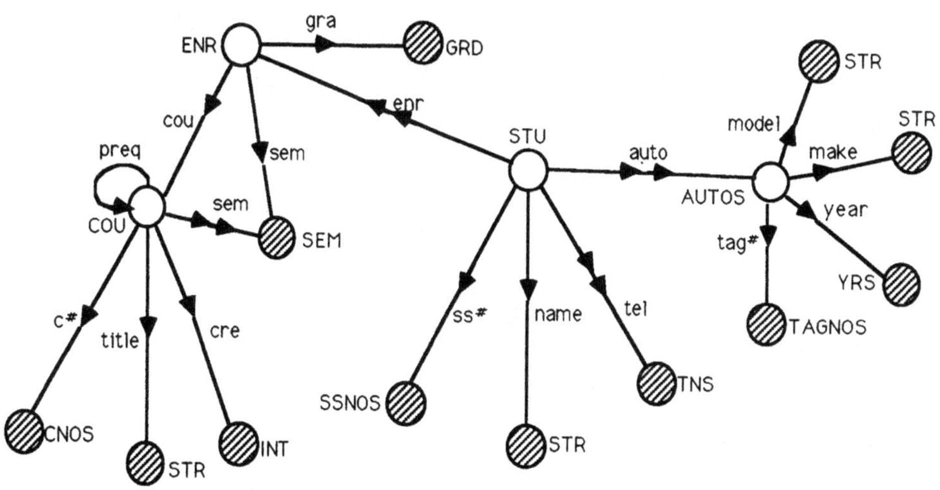

Figure2. Example Schema

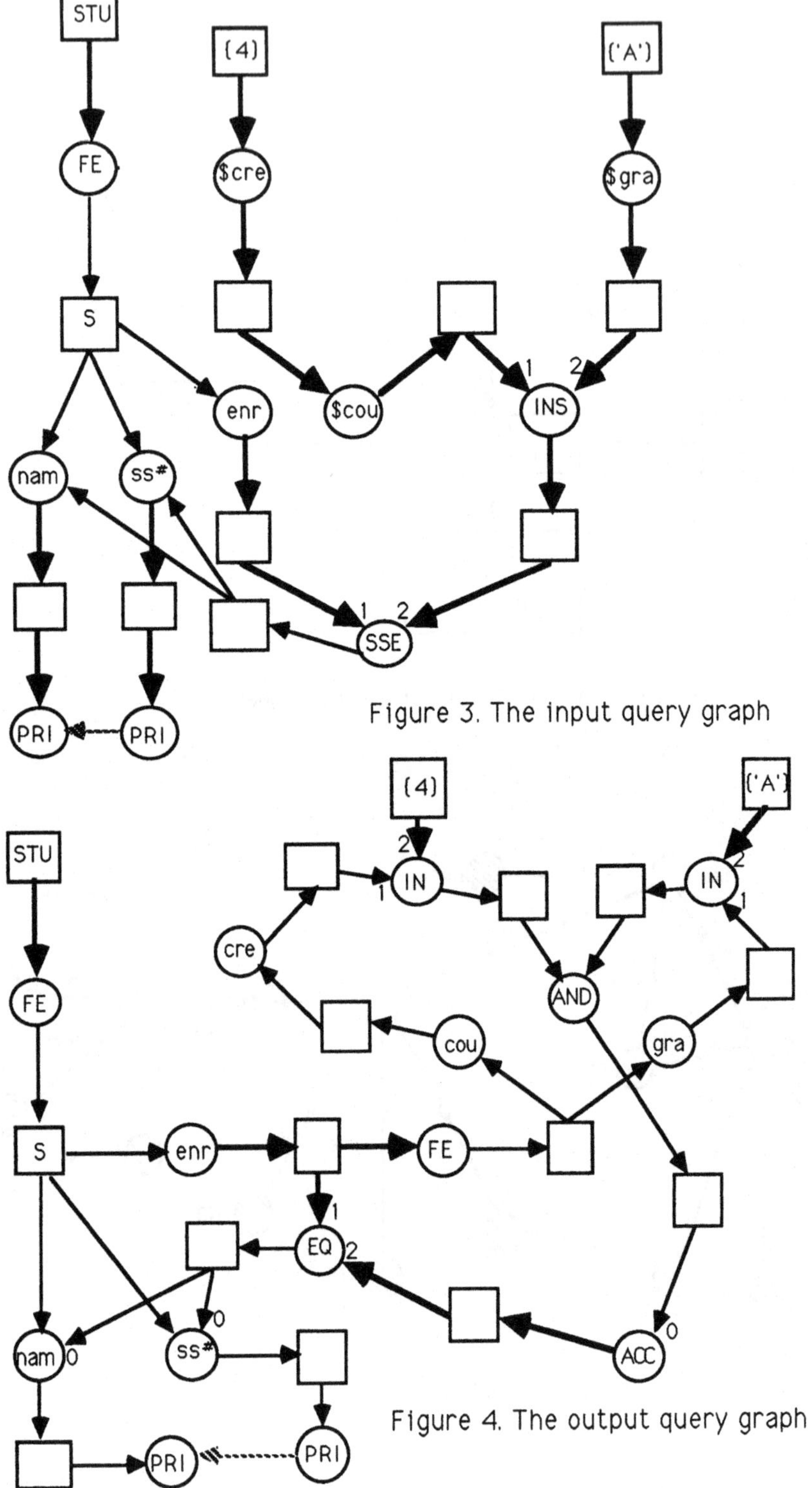

Figure 3. The input query graph

Figure 4. The output query graph

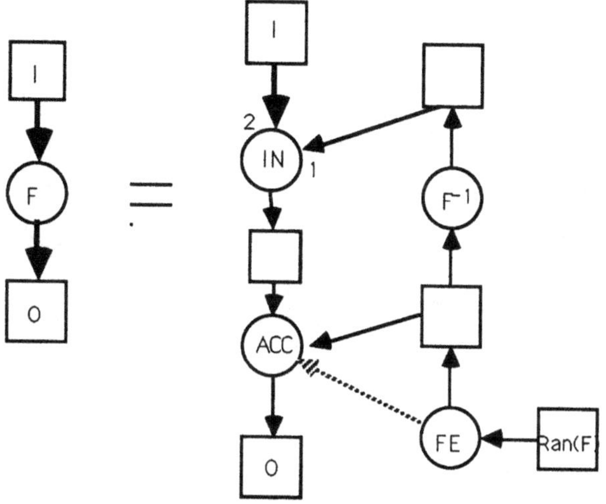

Figure 5. Rule 1

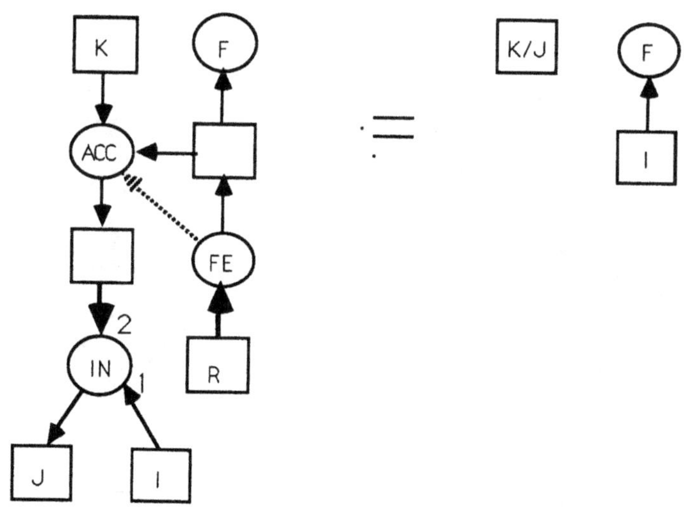

Figure 6. Rule 2.

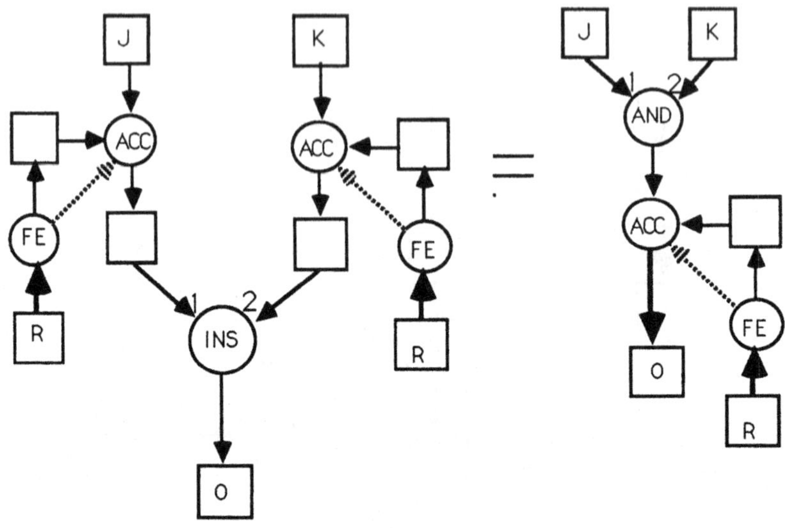

Figure 7. Rule 3.

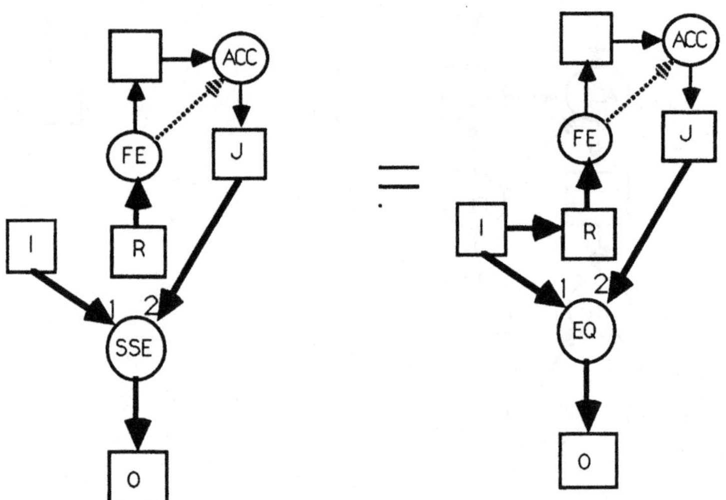

Figure 8. Rule 4.

An Adaptive Derived Data Manager for Distributed Databases

Scott Hudson

University of Arizona
Department of Computer Science
Tucson, Arizona 85721

Roger King

University of Colorado
Department of Computer Science
Boulder, Colorado 80309

Abstract

Cacti is a distributed system designed to support derived data in distributed database environments. A series of novel access and optimization policies are used to reduce I/O costs, support the transparent distribution of data, automatically migrate and replicate data, execute computations in parallel, cluster or reblock data, and perform speculative evaluation of derived data. The behavior of the system is dynamically modified on the basis of heuristics, predictive metrics, and user-supplied hints which form a central theme of self-adaptive optimization. In general, Cacti alters its behavior -- both locally at a single node and globally across the distributed system -- according to the current usage of resources, and typical usage patterns over time.

1. Introduction

A number of database researchers have been focusing recently on developing DBMS tools to support advanced applications such as VLSI and software design environments. One approach to this topic concerns the construction of specialized DBMS's which are tailored to specific applications, such as software environment support [7, 12]. Other researchers are focusing on the development of more general-purpose database systems based on models more expressive than the relational model; examples include object-oriented systems [16] and extended relational systems [22]. Finally, some researchers are developing tailorable toolkits or generators, which are designed to support a wide class of data models and database implementations [1, 3].

This project has been influenced by the first and the third of these approaches. We are developing a system which is at least partially tailorable, but one that is intended to support very specific applications, namely those which manipulate derived data in a distributed environment. Our primary target application is software environment support. Another important distinction is that we are only building one particular layer of a DBMS, namely the part of the physical implementation which maintains computed information. We are not providing low-level I/O routines, indexing methods, storage structures for data objects, or the aspects of a DBMS visible to the user, such as a query language or user interface.

Our approach is to provide an efficient physical data model for maintaining derived or computed data in the distributed environment. In this model, types, objects, and attributes of objects may be represented. Objects may have computed attributes. Our goal is to support many forms of derived data in an efficient, common framework, using a range of optimizations and access methods which use a central theme of self-adaptive behavior. This research is an extension of the Cactis project [9, 10] which developed efficient mechanisms for maintaining derived data in a centralized single processor environment.

This work is being supported by by ONR under contract N00014-86-K-0054, and by Martin-Marietta under contract 19X-CN981V (through DOE contract DE-AC05-840R21400).

1.1. Motivation

Researchers generally agree that traditional database management systems do not provide satisfactory support for engineering design applications, such as software development, and VLSI or printed circuit board (PCB) design. There are a number of limitations of current database systems that have been discussed frequently in recent literature [2, 10, 17]. These include the inability to support long and nested transactions (needed for interactive design sessions), the difficulty in cleanly and efficiently managing large and complex design objects, and the requirement that concurrency control be enforced in a strict fashion (as opposed to the informal, cooperative control needed during team-oriented, interactive design sessions).

In this paper, we concentrate on one specific limitation, one that has very great significance in all phases of engineering design - the inability of hierarchical/network and relational systems to support derived data in a cost-effective fashion. While other researchers have examined the issue of incorporating procedural data into a DBMS (e.g., [22]), we are concerned with finding efficient ways of managing complex derived data at the disk level. We pay special attention to the application of derived data in distributed environments, as current hardware configurations are highly amenable to distributed design systems. Our target hardware is a network of Sun workstations connected via an Ethernet. The system under development is called Cacti (for distributed Cactis).

We rely on software environment technology as being representative of typical engineering applications, and focus our efforts in that direction [7, 18, 21, 23, 26]. A software environment is intended to support the design, construction, testing, use, maintenance, and reuse of software. It is also clear that as workstation technology becomes more prevalent, issues of distribution must be considered. The architecture of the design environment of the future will be a network of workstations. In such an environment, designers will operate from their own desk-top machines. They will check out pieces of designs, work on them locally, and then ship them back to their site of origin.

In every phase of the software life-cycle, we see a need for derived data. In almost all places where there are important relationships between pieces of data, some of the values should depend on or be affected by other related values. Consider the following data relationships that would most likely be found in a software environment: the dependency between a variable declaration and a use of that variable with a program; the dependency between a source module and the corresponding object module; the derivation of a load module from a number of object modules; and finally, the relationship between a set of software modules and the associated documentation, requirements, and project milestones. In all cases, the correct maintenance of one form or another of derived data is essential to the proper operation of the software environment. When declarations change, semantic checks on source code must be performed, object and load modules must be kept consistent with the current versions of source modules, and the various forms of textual information associated with a software project must evolve with the programs they describe. It is easy to see that these requirements are global to many sorts of design environments. VLSI and PCB designers also are concerned with complex objects and relationships, and these relationships imply semantic connections between data items.

With traditional database systems, this sort of derived data must be maintained by application software or directly by end users. This introduces a number of problems. The end user or the database administrator is not likely to write code that is portable from one application to the next. More importantly, application code cannot make use of efficiency measures available to the database management system, causing many forms of derived data to be maintained inefficiently.

In Cacti a series of novel access and optimization policies are used to reduce I/O costs, support the transparent distribution of data, automatically migrate and replicate data, execute computations in parallel, cluster or reblock data, and perform speculative evaluation of derived data. The behavior of these access and optimization policies can be adjusted by the user and operate on the basis of heuristics, predictive metrics, and user-supplied hints. In general, the Cacti system uses self-adaptive techniques to improve its performance. Cacti alters its behavior according to typical usage patterns as well as the wishes of the database system user or implementor.

In the next section, we very briefly describe the existing centralized Cactis system, as the Cacti system is very directly an extension of the Cactis system. Section 2 focuses on the mechanisms used to extend Cactis naturally to a distributed environment. Section 3 describes the sorts of optimizations available in Cacti and how they might be tailored to specific needs. Finally, Section 4 presents concluding remarks.

1.2. The Existing Cactis System

This section very briefly describes the important aspects of the existing centralized Cactis system. A more complete description of the system can be found in [9, 10]. The Cactis system consists of both a logical and a physical data model. The logical model is preserved in the Cacti system, and the physical model is extended to support distributed data.

The Cactis data model supports typed objects which have attributes. As in semantic models [13], these objects can be related by typed and directed relationships which denote important semantic relationships between objects. However, the nature of the relationships found in the Cactis model is fundamentally different from those found in other high-level data models. Unlike other models such as the Entity-Relationship Model [5], the Semantic Data Model [8], and the Functional Data Model [15, 19], Cactis relationships are not defined with types but are defined independently.

In most high level models, an object type definition encompasses the relationships it participates in -- including the range types of the given relationships. In the Cactis model however, the domain and range of a given relationship type is not uniquely defined. Instead each object is said to possess a series of typed *connectors*. A connector indicates that a relationship of a particular type may exist between the object object which possesses the connector and some other object possessing a matching connector. Any two objects possessing properly directed connectors of the same type can be related (one to many relationships are also supported). This relationship is independent of the actual types of the related objects. Knowing the type of one object participating in a relationship does not determine the type of the other object (or objects). This means that objects are more strongly encapsulated than in traditional models. This further implies that objects of a given type may be transparently replaced by objects of an extended type. This ability is crucial for supporting systems like software environments which must be easily extensible.

In addition to its strong encapsulation across relationships, the Cactis data model is also unique in its support for derived or computed data. The attributes of an object may be derived from other data using an equation or *attribute evaluation rule* which tells how to compute its value from other values. The external interface to an object in a Cactis database consists of a set of values imported along relationships and a set of values exported. An attribute evaluation rule describes how a local attribute of an object can be derived in terms of imported values and other local attributes. Attribute evaluation rules must be completely applicative in nature (i.e., have no side effects). Except for this restriction, evaluation rules may perform any computation expressible in C and attributes may use any C data type.

To implement derived data efficiently, the Cactis system uses an incremental update algorithm based on work in incremental evaluation of attribute grammars [12]. This algorithm is lazy in nature and performs very well with respect to the set of attributes that are updated after any change. The basic Cactis incremental update algorithm works using two phases. The first phase identifies which derived values need to be updated after a change. The second phase schedules the evaluation of these attributes in an optimized fashion. To this basic algorithm, the Cactis system adds a number of optimizations designed to improve performance in a disk based setting.

2. Derived Data in the Distributed Environment

In the previous section, we briefly introduced the Cactis model which operates in a single machine, environment. In this section, we discuss new techniques which extend the physical data model to a distributed environment. We will then show how this framework can be used to take advantage of the multiple processors available in the distributed environment to perform parallel derivation and update of data. Of significance is the fact that the Cactis update algorithm is naturally parallel, and therefore can be cleanly transformed into a distributed mechanism.

Before discussing the distributed and parallel implementation of the Cacti system, it is important to reexamine some of properties of the data model in more detail to see how they make this process easier. Of most importance are the strong encapsulation of data and the applicative nature of derivation rules. The strong encapsulation provided by the logical model allows the actual implementation of data items to be changed without affecting the way that data relates to, and interacts with, the rest of the database. As we will see below, this means that we can transparently introduce data objects whose implementation involves access to remote data via a network, while retaining the (logical) appearance of strictly local data.

The property of encapsulation allows us to distribute data across multiple locations. However, adding parallelism to this framework introduces additional difficulties. In a parallel environment, we have much

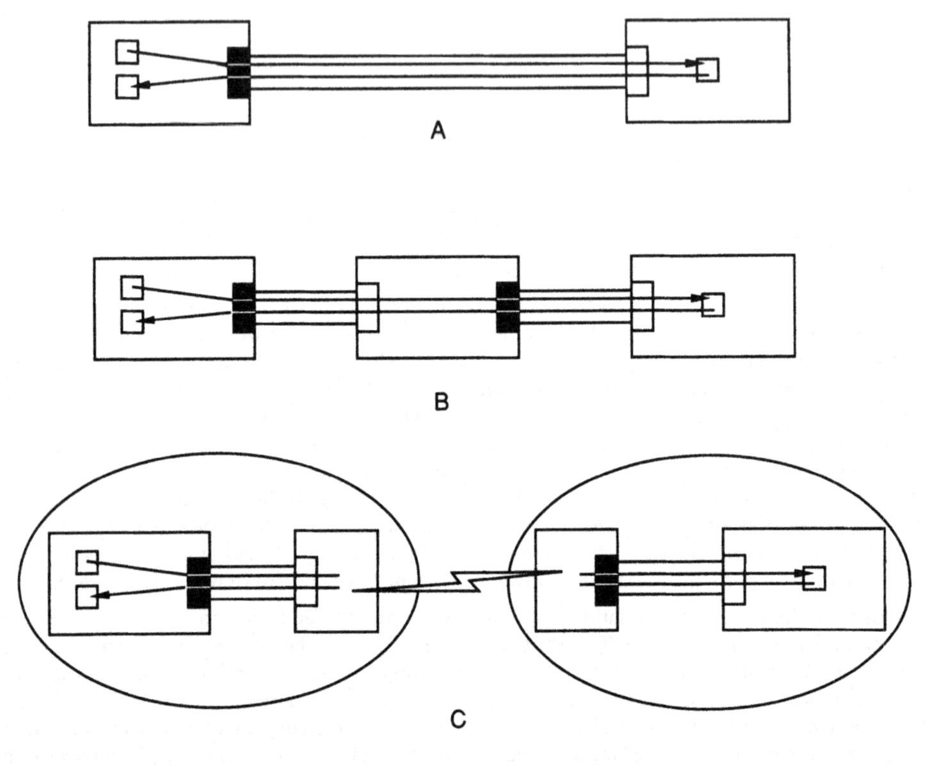

Figure 1. Distributing Data

less control over the timing and ordering of computations. Messages may be delayed, nodes may have different load factors, and different machines may execute at different speeds. Fortunately, because the evaluation rules in a Cactis database are applicative, the system only requires a partial order of computations to be maintained rather than a total order. All values needed to compute an attribute must be up to date before its rule is executed. However, there is no restriction on the order in which these parameter attributes are evaluated. In particular, these values may be computed in parallel, or in any order which the system deems efficient. In all cases the results of the computation will be the same. In the sequential version of the system, this property is the cornerstone of the self-adaptive optimization techniques. As we will see in this section, this property also greatly simplifies the task of distribution.

Applicative rules are convenient for expressing a wide range of computations typical to a design environment. For example, recent work on language dependent environments has largely been based on attribute grammars (which are applicative). Tasks that can be conveniently handled in this framework range from incremental checking and recompilation of programs, to tools for project management and scheduling. For more details on the use of applicative rules in the support of software environments, see [10].

A key feature of the Cactis DBMS is the ability to transparently insert a new object between any two related objects. This is again possible because of the strong encapsulation provided by the logical model. Figure 1 illustrates in a schematic way how we use this property to handle data distributed over multiple workstations. Figures 1a and b show an object being inserted between two existing objects. This new object need only provide the two properly typed connectors and transmit data between the connectors of the existing objects. To support distributed data, we use a similar transformation. At any relationship we may introduce a pair of objects, one on each of two different machines. These objects communicate with each other across a network to simulate the behavior of a single object as shown in Figure 1c.

Because of the strong encapsulation of data within objects, any particular object does not have to know what types of objects it is related to. An object only requires that the proper type and number of values be delivered to it as needed. The fact that these values are transmitted across a network at one or more points is irrelevant. By using the transformation we have outlined above, and providing appropriate network support, we extend the database to a distributed environment without disturbing the logical data model. Of particular importance is the fact that machine boundaries are transparent at the logical level. This means that the physical level is free to place and relocate objects in order to optimize performance (either automatically or based on assistance from the user).

The ability to transparently insert new network objects to implement a distributed system is only one outgrowth of the general property of strong encapsulation provided by the logical data model. This property also allows easy and efficient support for extensible types. An object can always be transparently replaced by an extended object, so long as the new object provides a superset of the external interface provided by the old object. Further, old versions of types can peacefully coexist with new versions. This kind of capability is of primary importance for design environments, and extensible type systems are the focus of a number of major database projects [3, 20, 22]. Previous projects have concentrated largely on storage structures and query processing techniques for supporting new types; our focus will be on the clean encapsulation of new typing information in order to minimize the effects on the algorithms which support derived data.

Because of the flexibility in ordering provided by the logical data model, only two changes from the algorithm outlined in Section 1.2 are needed to support parallelism. First, we must ensure that once an evaluation is started for an attribute, any later requests for that attribute's value will block until the value is computed (instead of starting a new evaluation of the same attribute). Second, we must synchronize the two halves of the evaluation algorithm so that all parts of the first phase finish before any part of the second phase is started.

The first modification is accomplished with a simple semaphore attached to each attribute. When the evaluation of an attribute is first requested, the semaphore is locked. Any later arrivals needing the value will block until the evaluation is complete, at which time they simply read the up to date value. Recall that this is still a single user system and we are not concerned with conflicts between multiple user updates (see below).

The second change requires synchronization of the two halves of the incremental update algorithm. Recall that the algorithm works in two phases, a planning phase and an evaluation phase. The first phase acts by finding all attributes which are directly or indirectly affected by a change and marking these attributes *out-of-date*. The second phase evaluates exactly as many of these out-of-date attributes as needed to make the observable state of the system consistent (a complete analysis of the algorithm can be found in [11]). The system does not guarantee that all attributes will be up to date at all times. When an out-of-date value is required by the user it is recomputed dynamically. It is also possible to designate certain attributes as *important*. The system will guarantee that important attributes, and all other attributes needed to derive them, will be kept up to date at all times. These attributes can be used to check constraints as well as implement conventional notifiers and triggers.

To ensure correct results, the two phases of the algorithm must not overlap -- all parts of the first phase must finish before any part of the second phase is started. This is accomplished by requiring that each independent thread of the first *mark out-of-date* phase report back to its invoker when all its subtraversals have completed. When the complete traversal is finished, the original point of invocation is informed and it broadcasts a message to start the second phase of the computation at each processor. The second phase of the algorithm starts with all attributes which are both important and out-of-date. A list of out-of-date but important attributes is collected by the first phase and retained on each processor. When the second phase is started, each processor starts to work on the second phase concurrently.

In order to support a multi-user environment, the centralized version of Cactis uses a timestamping concurrency control technique which allows serializable updates belonging to different users to proceed concurrently. See [24] for a general discussion of timestamp concurrency control. Because of the possibility of an update involving a long chain of computations which touches many objects, a locking mechanism was judged too costly.

As yet, Cacti is not multi-user. In the multi-user version of Cacti, we hope to implement concurrency control by making use of the efficient undo capability that is naturally supported by Cactis data model. This facility uses the property of the data model that all indirect updates automatically performed by changing one or more attribute values can be just as automatically undone simply by restoring the old values (a similar property holds for structural changes). Consequently, the same mechanism used to derive data, can also "underive" that data with equal ease. At this time, we are working to implement an undo mechanism that may be used in a multi-user environment; the current implementation supports only single user access.

3. Adaptive Policies

The last section outlined the basic mechanisms by which Cacti manages derived data in a distributed environment. In this section we will explore various access policies and optimizations. While these optimizations are diverse, they all revolve around several central principles. First, they are self-adaptive. They measure the performance and usage patterns of the system, use these measurements to predict future behavior, and guide optimization policies on the basis of these predictions. Second, they are opportunistic. They keep track of current resource usage and modify their behavior to make the best use of available time and space. Next, the optimizations are at least partially user controllable. Tradeoffs are involved in utilizing various optimizations. For example, idle processor time may be used for several different optimizations (see Section 3.4 below) and the priority given to each is a tradeoff between them. In general, the direction that is taken with various tradeoffs may be directly controlled by the individual using Cacti as the physical layer of a design system (this individual is best referred to as a database "implementor" [3]). Finally, each of the optimizations is designed to be performed on-line without interrupting the availability of the database or requiring direct intervention of the database administrator.

The adaptive mechanisms supported by Cacti may be broken down into the follow categories: techniques to efficiently migrate data around the network, scheduling policies which reduce disk I/O, adaptive clustering techniques, and strategies which make use of idle time on processor nodes. In addition to being self-adaptive, each of these mechanisms can be adjusted according to various parameters. For example, we allow the database implementor to choose among various heuristics used to drive the scheduling policies discussed in the next section.

3.1. Reducing Disk I/O

In Cacti, as in the sequential Cactis system, past performance is used to predict future performance. Computations are scheduled on a basis of always selecting the one with the least predicted cost. Past performance is measured by one of several metrics. In the Cactis system these metrics use information about what is currently buffered in memory as well as a weighted average of either the total amount of (local) disk I/O to finish a computation or the total number of objects visited. Although versions of these metrics are still reasonable in the distributed environment, a number of other factors involving such things as expected communication delays and system load balancing must also be considered. In Cacti, the database implementor has finer grained control over the application of this scheduling policy, and they way it is balanced with other optimization policies involving distributed data. The implementor may, for example, flag certain computations as high priority and thus override the scheduler, or may change the weight given to purely local metrics as opposed to metrics concerning network behavior and load balancing.

3.2. Migrating Data

In addition to adapting the scheduling policies of Cactis to suit the distributed and extensible needs of Cacti, we also support other novel self-adaptive optimizations. A primary technique is the adaptive migration of data. The proper placement of data in a distributed environment has been examined [4], as has the efficient materialization of data items during the processing of distributed queries [25]. Effective self-adaptive relocation of data improves the execution of updates by placing data on nodes where it is used most frequently.

To see how adaptive migration is performed in the Cacti system, we can note that requests for data values always flow across a relationship. For data items managed by other nodes of the network this relationship will connect to a special *network* object, as illustrated in Figure 1. This object is responsible for working with the network subsystem of the database to arrange communications with other distributed components of the database. Statistics about the past behavior of such requests are associated with the relationship involved, and are maintained automatically by the system. The statistics can measure such things as the average frequency and size of messages sent, and are used along with statistics about expected message delays, system load factors, the size of data objects, and the amount of local access to the objects involved. Together, these metrics are used to determine which optimizations would provide likely improvements under the current usage patterns.

To provide control over the application of data migration mechanisms, we introduce the concept of a *tension* on a data object which may be used to pull it in several directions. The higher the computed metric associated with a relationship, the higher the tension and the more advantageous it would be to move the object in the direction of the tension. When the tension on an object from another node was sufficiently higher than the *local* tension on the object it could be migrated to that node.

To provide good performance in the short run without forcing reorganization of the database in the long run, we support two sorts of metrics: one set for short term temporary movement of data, and another set for determining the long term permanent placement of data. This allows the system to respond to the needs of a particular set of transactions without permanently upsetting the balance of the database. The database implementor may adjust the comparative influence that the long-range and the short-range metrics have over each other. The system also contains hooks so that the database implementor may easily change the functions used to calculate the tensions based on the metrics collected.

Since the locality of data is transparent to the logical data model, the actual migration of data is relatively straightforward. As shown in Figure 2, a data object O can be moved from node A to node B by creating a surrogate network object *net*O to represent it on node B. Existing relationships to object O now relate to *net*O, so that requests for values from O are communicated to node A. In this sense, *net*O acts as a forwarding pointer for the object O. To eliminate the overhead associated with such a forwarding pointer, other nodes are informed of the new location of object O. However, rather than broadcast the new location of O we simply wait until messages bound for O arrive at *net*O. These messages are forwarded to node A

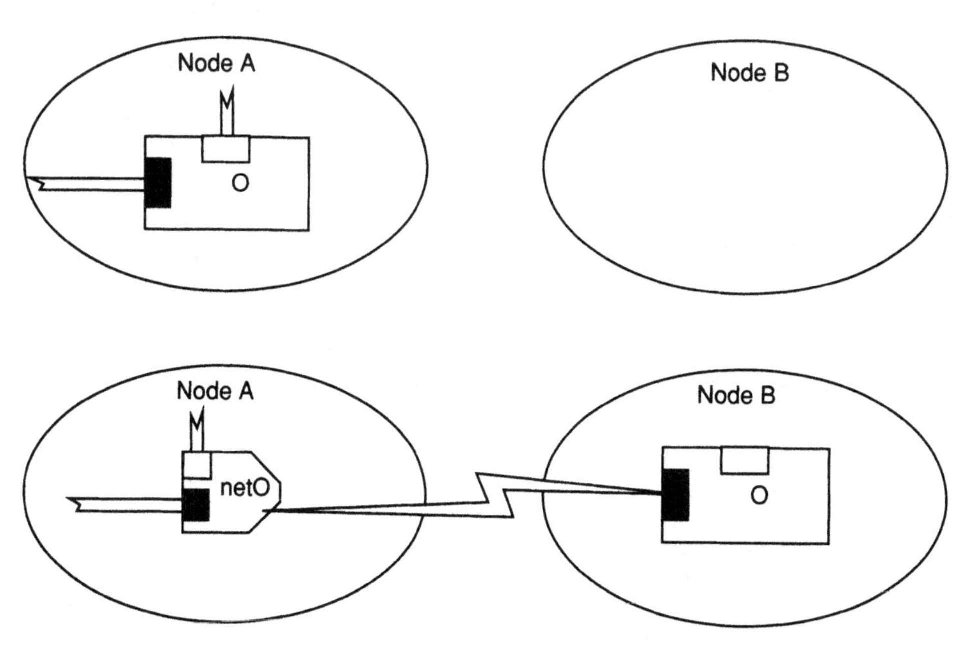

Figure 2. Migrating Data

as usual, but the final response to the message will indicate that the object O is now located at node A. In this way the information about the new location of O is transmitted only as needed. Also, no broadcast is needed and the information is included in (or *piggybacked* on) an existing message. Only the first message from each node to object O will incur the extra cost of the forwarding process.

It is also possible to make direct use of user supplied heuristics. For example the user may know that a group of objects will frequently be used together. Such hints may be used to replace or bias the metrics used to determine when migration should occur. In addition, explicit commands which force particular data objects to reside on a particular node may be used for organizational reasons.

3.3. Replicating Data

Migration of data can greatly enhance performance in a distributed database. However, there will always be instances where data is frequently accessed from two different nodes. Migrating such data to one node will always imply a performance penalty for the other. Further, if data migration is not tuned properly, one might continually move the data from one node to another in response to transient usage increases. To improve this situation Cacti supports replicated data. Maintaining multiple copies of data items has been studied by other researchers [6, 14]; we focus on the uniform treatment of derived and replicated data as a means of cleanly and efficiently maintaining multiple copies of data objects.

In Cactis, when the usage at two or more nodes is high enough, appropriate data items would be replicated and stored at both locations. Control of when to replicate can be done on the basis of user supplied specifications or alternately, can be done automatically. In the former case, the user may dictate which objects are to be replicated. In the automatic case, the tension statistics used for migration are used. When the tension on a node from two different directions becomes too great the node is replicated.

Keeping multiple distributed copies of data consistent is typically quite difficult and is often handled inelegantly. Under the Cactis logical data model we have a unique opportunity to handle redundant or replicated data in a unified and consistent framework with other forms of data. Replicated data is seen as a slight variation or special case of the more general problem of maintaining derived data. In the general case, if data item A is computed from data item B then whenever B changes A must be invalidated and recomputed. Similarly when one copy of a replicated data object changes other copies must be invalidated and updated. If we are willing to designate one copy of the data as the master copy from which the others are derived, then the existing incremental update algorithms will work without change. Whenever the master copy is changed, the slave copies would automatically be marked out-of-date by the normal algorithm. When a slave value was requested it would automatically be derived (copied) from the master.

Unfortunately, establishing a master/slave relationship between replicated copies has a number of drawbacks. Most seriously it implies that the slave copies cannot be directly updated. Instead one must always update the master copy. To overcome this problem, a more equal relationship between replicated copies is needed. Any copy should be modifyable, and when any copy is modified the others should be marked out-of-date. This requires a slight modification to the incremental update algorithm, but does not represent a fundamental change.

The current algorithm uses dependencies between attributes to propagate changes. If attribute A is computed from attribute B then A is said to depend on B. The two phases of the incremental update algorithm traverse the dependency graph formed by this *depends_on* relation. The evaluation phase traverses in the depends_on direction while the mark out-of-date phase traverses in the opposite direction. To support replicated data, we keep two separate graphs for these two directions. In the out-of-date direction, the attributes of all replicated objects are related to the corresponding attributes of all other replicated objects This implies that marking one attribute out-of-date will propagate out-of-date marks to all replicated copies. In the depends_on or evaluation direction, each attribute is computed as normal from other local attributes or from attributes of objects related to the replicated object. With this small modification (to replicated objects only) we support replicated data as easily as we support any other kind of derived data. This represents a significant improvement over the complications that usually arise when dealing with replicated data.

3.4. Using Idle Time

In a distributed environment there are typically times when a particular node is idle. During these times it would be possible to use the otherwise wasted time to perform calculations or optimizations which will improve the future performance of the database. It is also possible to consider optimizations (such as reclustering) that are normally performed off-line, and thus usually conflict with the natural operation of the database. These are examples of opportunistic optimizations that take advantage of currently under used resources -- in this case idle time. Cacti supports two ways of utilizing idle time: performing speculative computations and clustering data on-line. The database implementor may adjust the priority given to each of these optimizations, or rule one or the other out.

First, we discuss *speculative* evaluation. The logical model allows data values which are marked out-of-date to remain out-of-date until they are actually needed. This lazy approach saves calculations whose results are never actually used. However, during times when a processor would otherwise be idle, Cacti may use the otherwise wasted time to calculate some out-of-date values in anticipation of their use. If they are used, the values will not need to be recomputed and response time will improve. If they are not used, that is if the values are later marked out-of-date before the value was actually used, then little is lost since the processor would have been idle anyway. This use of otherwise idle time is what we call speculative evaluation. It is speculative because we speculate or anticipate that the value will be needed. To implement speculative evaluation in Cacti we support evaluations which can be interrupted quickly when "real" work arrives. Such interrupted calculations are restarted when the node becomes idle again.

In addition to speculative evaluations to improve response time, we also plan to support the clustering of data during idle time. The algorithm to perform this has not yet been completed. Clustering involves efficient placement of data objects on disk blocks local to a particular node. In the existing sequential version of the system, off-line clustering is performed periodically to reblock the database on the basis of usage statistics. Performance analysis [12] indicates that this clustering yields substantial savings because it improves the locality of reference in the database. These same techniques can be used in the distributed case. Unfortunately, off-line clustering requires that the database be made inaccessible for a period of time (typically several hours overnight) while reblocking is done. It would be more desirable to cluster on-line while the database remained available. Such an on-line algorithm would be a good use for otherwise idle processor time. When a node became idle, the most frequently used objects at the node could be placed on the same blocks as the related objects which they referenced most often. This greedy block packing approach has worked quite well in the off-line algorithm. As with speculative evaluation we must be prepared to quickly interrupt on-line clustering when "real" work arrives.

4. Conclusions and Directions

In this paper, we have discussed the Cacti system for managing derived data. Cacti is currently under development, with a substantial amount of the code written and running. The goal is to support a number of optimizations which allow computed information to be kept in an efficient fashion. The system currently supports some forms of user-control. However an important future direction is to allow a greater level of tailorability on the part of the database implementor. In particular, we are working on providing alternate, packaged policies, metrics, and heuristics which may be easily "plugged in". This would allow much finer-grained control over system performance. For example, the scheduling policy in use reduces I/O costs based on recent usage statistics, but only supports one exponentially-decaying cost function. As heuristics, policies, and metrics are developed we hope to provide a range of alternatives so that a particular database can be tuned to a particular situation.

Acknowledgements

The authors would like to give special thanks to Chase Turner who has constructed much of the software for the Cacti system.

References

1. D. S. Batory, J. R. Barnett, F. F. Garza, K. P. Smith, K. Tsukauda, B. C. Twichell and T. E. Wise, GENESIS: A Reconfigurable Database Management System, *To appear in IEEE Transactions on Software Engineering*, .

2. P. Bernstein, Database System Support for Software Engineering, *Wang Institute of Graduate Studies Technical Report Tech. Rep.-87-01*, February 1987.

3. M. J. Carey, D. J. DeWitt, D. Frank, G. Graefe, M. Muralikrishna, J. E. Richardson and E. J. Shekita, The Architecture of the EXODUS Extensible DBMS, *Proceedings of the Workshop on Object-Oriented Databases*, Pacific Grove, California, September 23-26, 1986, 52-65.

4. S. Ceri, S. Navathe and G. Wiederhold, Distribution Design of Logical Database Schemas, *IEEE Transactions on Software Engineering SE-9*(July 1983), 487-504.

5. P. P. Chen, The Entity-Relationship Model--Toward a Unified View of Data, *ACM Trans. on Database Systems 1*, 1 (1976), 9-36.

6. E. G. Coffman, E. Gelenbe and B. Plateau, Optimization of the Number of Copies in a Distributed Data Base, *IEEE Transactions on Software Engineering SE-7*(January 1981), 78-84.

7. K. R. Dittrich, W. Gotthard and P. C. Lockemann, DAMOKLES - A Database System for Software Engineering Environments, *Proceedings of the International Workshop on Advanced Programming Enviorments*, Trondheim, Norway, June, 1986, 353-371.

8. M. Hammer and D. McLeod, Database Description with SDM: A Semantic Database Model, *ACM Trans. on Database Systems 6*, 3 (1981), 351-386.

9. S. Hudson and R. King, CACTIS: A Database System for Specifying Functionally-Defined Data, *Proceedings of the Workshop on Object-Oriented Databases*, Pacific Grove, California, September 23-26, 1986, 26-37.

10. S. E. Hudson and R. King, Object-oriented database support for software environments, *Proc. of ACM SIGMOD Intl. Conf. on Management of Data*, San Francisco, California, May, 1987, 491-503.

11. S. E. Hudson, Incremental Attribute Evaluation: An Algorithm for Lazy Evaluation in Graphs, *University of Arizona Technical Report*, Aug. 1987. Tech. Rep. 87-20.

12. S. Hudson and R. King, Cactis: A Self-Adaptive, Concurrent Implementation of an Object-Oriented Database Management System, *ACM Transactions on Database Systems*, to appear.

13. R. Hull and R. King, Semantic Database Modeling: Survey, Applications, and Research Issues, *ACM Computing Surveys*, September 1987, 201-260.

14. R. H. Katz and E. Wong, Resolving Conflicts in Global Storage Design Through Replication, *ACM Trans. on Database Systems 8*, 1 (1983), 110-135.

15. L. Kerschberg and J. E. S. Pacheco, A Functional Data Base Model, Technical Report, Pontificia Universidade Catolica do Rio de Janeiro, Rio de Janeiro, Brazil, February, 1976.

16. D. Maier, J. Stein, A. Otis and A. Purdy, Development of an Object-Oriented DBMS, *Proceedings of the conference on Object-Oriented Programming Systems, Languages, and Applications*, September 29-October 2, 1986, 472-482.

17. J. R. Nestor, Toward a Persistant Object Base, *Proceedings of the International Workshop on Advanced Programming Enviorments*, Trondheim, Norway, June, 1986, 372-394.

18. M. H. Penedo, Prototyping a Project Master Data Base for Software Engineering Environments, *Proceedings of the Second Symposium on Practical Software Environments*, December 1986.

19. D. Shipman, The Functional Data Model and the Data Language DAPLEX, *ACM Trans. on Database Systems 6*, 1 (1981), 140-173.

20. A. H. Skarra and S. B. Zdonik, The Management of Changing Types in an Object-Oriented Database, *Proceedings of the conference on Object-Oriented Programming Systems, Languages, and Applications*, September 29-October 2, 1986, 483-495.

21. H. G. Steubing, A Software Engineering Environment (SEE) for Weapon System Software, *IEEE Transactions on Software Engineering SE-10*(July 1984), 384-397.

22. M. Stonebraker and L. A. Rowe, The Design of Postgres, *Proceedings of International Conference on the Management of Data*, May, 1986, pages 340-355.

23. R. Taylor, Arcadia: A Software Development Environment Research Project, *University of California at Irvine, Dept. of Information and Computer Scinece, Technical Report*, April 1986.

24. J. Ullman, *Principles of Database Systems*, Computer Science Press, Rockville, Maryland, 1982.

25. E. Wong, Dynamic Rematerialization: Processing Distributed Queries Using Redundant Data, *IEEE Transactions on Software Engineering SE-9*(May 1983), 228-233.

26. C. Zaroliagis, P. Soupos, S. Goutas and D. Christodoulakis, The GRASPIN DB - A Syntax Directed, Language Independent Software Engineering Database, *Proceedings of the Workshop on Object-Oriented Databases*, Pacific Grove, California, September 23-26, 1986, 235-236.

Mapping Object-Oriented Concepts into Relational Concepts by Meta-Compilation in a Logic Programming Environment

Johann Christoph Freytag, Rainer Manthey, Mark Wallace

European Computer-Industry Research Centre

Arabellastr. 17

D-8000 München 81, West Germany

Abstract

In this paper we discuss implementation aspects of how to map object-oriented concepts into relational concepts to achieve both, flexibility and efficiency, at the same time. Our past experience shows that such a mapping should not be fixed, but should be flexible for different reasons [Wal86], [B*86b]. On the other hand to ensure an efficient evaluation of requests on the object level, the mapping onto the relational level should not involve any major overhead. We argue that methods of meta-compilation provide an adequate basis for achieving both goals simultaneously [SS86]. In particular, we argue that these techniques are easily implementable in a logic programming environment.

1 Introduction

Over the last years efforts to provide concepts and to implement systems that go beyond relational technology, have focused on two main areas: the extension of relational technology by object-oriented concepts and the combination of logic programming and database technology.

The extension of database technology by object-oriented concepts has been motivated by the need for more expressive data models. Object-oriented data models have been developed e.g. for PROBE [MD86], IRIS [L*86], [LV87], and other systems. The GemStone database system successfully merges database technology into the Smalltalk language [MS86]. More reports on results of the increased (and diverse) research activities to merge object-oriented concepts with database technology can be found in [DD86].

At the same time there has been an increased interest in merging database technology with logic programming concepts. The research work at MCC and at ECRC in particular has focused on combining concepts of both areas. This effort has also recognized the need to provide more powerful data modeling capabilities than what is present in today's logic programming environments. Gallaire emphasized the need to "extend the logic programming paradigm with the object-oriented one" [Gal87]. MCC's languages LDL [TZ86] and FAD [B*86a] include object-oriented concepts. ECRC's KB2 system provides an object-based user language enriched with inheritance and extensive capabilities to manipulate both, data and metadata [Wal86].

Despite all these efforts, little is known about how to map object-oriented concepts into more traditional ones, especially into relational concepts, in a systematical, flexible, and efficient manner. Our own experience with KB2 has made apparent the need for a flexible mapping that can easily be changed depending on various, often conflicting requirements [Wal86]. Lyngbaek and Vianu report on a formal mapping of the IRIS data model into the relational model that serves as the basis for the IRIS implementation [LV87]. However, their work does not discuss the implementation-related aspects of their mapping. In [DKM85], Farmer, King, and Myers describe basic building blocks that help to implement object-oriented "schema" specifications. Valduriez et al. address the mapping problem for complex objects by proposing the N-ary storage model (NSM) and the decomposition storage model (DSM) [V*86].

2 The Approach

Independent of the details of the object-oriented data model, it seems to be generally agreed to represent object-oriented concepts by relational ones and to map operations on objects into operations on relations, respectively. The major advantage of this choice is that one can store data and evaluate queries using existing, well understood relational technology.

However, with this general approach there does not seem to exist **one** agreed, unique mapping from the object to the relational level that satisfies all possible requirements. We therefore argue that a clean separation between the mapping specification and the use of the mapping is necessary and desirable to accommodate different mappings for different object/operation definitions, e.g. NSM and DSM as in [V*86]. This separation leads to two distinct "pieces": the mapping specification and the "interpreter" of this mapping (for objects and operations) from the object level to the relational level (see Figure 1).

Based on this mapping model, we view the interpreter as a function $I_{OR}(MS_{OR}, R_O) \rightarrow R_R$ that produces a request R_R on relations given the initial request R_O on objects, and the mapping specification MS_{OR}. Notice, that the request generated might include operations that are not present in the initial object request. For example, the mapping might generate operations that query "schema information" or check integrity constraints that need to be satisfied for a correct object representation by relational concepts.

Despite the aim of separating the mapping specification from its execution for flexibility reasons, one would prefer a mapping component $M_{OR}(R_O) \rightarrow R_R$ that tightly intertwines the two aspects,

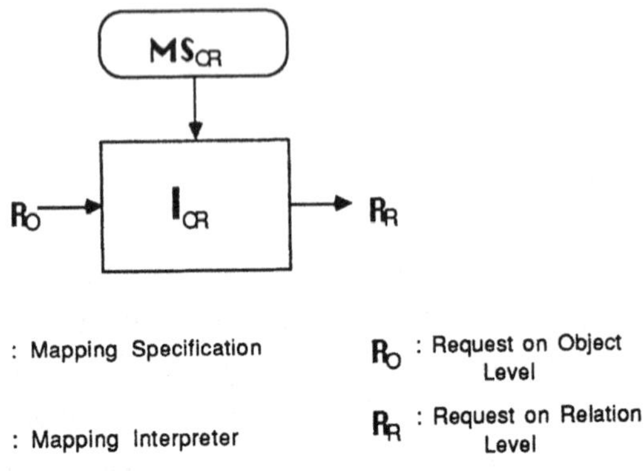

Figure 1: Meta-Interpretation of the Object Mapping

mainly for efficiency reasons. Furthermore, since we can assume that the mapping specification does not change frequently, we would like to reduce the overhead of interpreting the mapping specification each time an object request is translated into a request on relations.

To keep the advantage of a modular approach and to achieve the efficiency of a tight integration, we use a **meta-compiler** $MC_{OR}(I_{OR}, MS_{OR}) \rightarrow M_{OR}$ that generates the desired program M_{OR} based on the mapping interpreter I_{OR} and a specific mapping specification MS_{OR} (see Figure 2). We can view the generated component M_{OR} as a **specialization** of I_{OR}, that is, specialized by

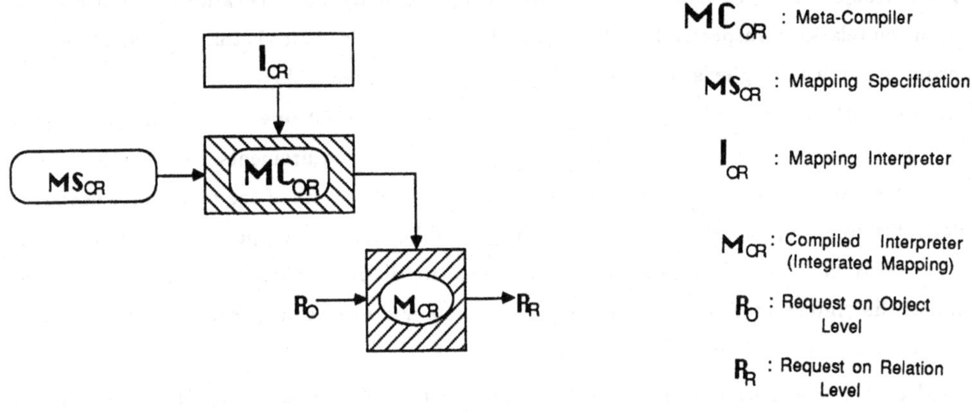

Figure 2: Compilation of the Object-Mapping and the Mapping Interpreter

MS_{OR}. If the meta-compiler is tailored towards the needs of the mapping specification and the mapping interpreter, one can expect that the generated program $MC_{OR}(R_O) \rightarrow R_R$ provides the efficiency as initially required.

3 The Implementation

This section briefly discusses implementation-related aspects. We believe that a logic programming language (i.e. Prolog) provides an excellent basis for implementing the mapping, the mapping interpreter, and the meta-compiler because of its rule-oriented nature and high-level expressiveness. We can implement both the mapping specification and the interpreter in the same language, thus simplifying the task of meta-compilation. For simplicity reasons, one could even use the Prolog interpreter as the mapping interpreter. One could implement the meta-compiler in Prolog too, thus having a uniform implementation of all three components.

Meta-compilation can be based on techniques of program transformation and partial evaluation. Although it still needs to be proved that such an approach works in practice for mapping of object-oriented concepts into relational ones, the results of applying the similar techniques to more traditional database problems, i.e. rule-based query optimization and the transformation of algebraic query specification into iterative programs [LFL86], [FG86], are encouraging signs for a successful implementation.

4 Conclusion

In this position paper we briefly outlined the mapping of object-oriented concepts into relational ones using meta-compilation. In our opinion, this method provides a flexible basis for mapping object-oriented concepts onto relational ones. Furthermore, we also believe that we can later incorporate additional optimizations into the mapping without changing our general approach. The ideas presented in this paper are part of our current effort at ECRC to include objects-oriented concepts into a logic-based language and to develop mapping concepts that take full advantage of a logic programming-based implementation environment.

References

[B*86a] F. Bancilhon et al. FAD, a Powerful and Simple Database Language. In *Proceedings VLDB 1987, Brighton, England*, pages 97–105, August 1986.

[B*86b] J. Bocca et al. Some Steps towards a DBMS based KBMS. In *Proceedings IFIP Congress 86, Dublin, Ireland*, September 1986.

[DD86] K. Dittrich and U. Dayal, editors. *Proceedings International Workshop on Object-Oriented Database Systems*, Sept. 1986.

[DKM85] Farmer D.B., R. King, and D.A. Myers. The Semantic Database Constructor. *IEEE Trans. Software Engineering*, SE-11:583–591, 1985.

[FG86] J.C. Freytag and N. Goodman. Rule-Based Translation of Relational Queries into Iterative Programs. In *Proceedings ACM SIGMOD 1986, Washington, D.C.*, pages 206–214, May 1986.

[Gal87] H. Gallaire. Boosting Logic Programming. In *Proceedings of the Fourth International Conference on Logic Programming, Melbourne, Australia*, pages 962–988, May 1987.

[L*86] P. Lyngbaek et al. *Design and Implementation of the IRIS Object Manager*. Technical Report STL-86-17, Hewlett-Packard Laboratories, Dec. 1986.

[LFL86] M.K Lee, J.C. Freytag, and G. Lohman. Implementing an Interpreter for Functional Rules in a Query Optimizer. In *Proceedings VLDB 1988, Los Angeles, CA*, September 1988.

[LV87] P. Lyngbaek and V. Vianu. Mapping a Semantic Database Model to the Relational Model. In *Proceedings ACM SIGMOD 1987, San Francisco, CA*, pages 132–142, May 1987.

[MD86] F. Manola and U. Dayal. PDM: An Object-Oriented Data Model. In *Proceedings International Workshop on Object-Oriented Database Systems*, pages 18–25, Sept. 1986.

[MS86] D. Maier and J. Stein. Indexing in an Object-Oriented DBMS. In *Proceedings International Workshop on Object-Oriented Database Systems*, pages 171–182, Sept. 1986.

[SS86] S. Safra and E. Shapiro. Meta Interpreters for Real. In *Proceedings IFIP Congress 86, Dublin, Ireland*, pages 271–278, September 1986.

[TZ86] S. Tsur and C. Zaniolo. LDL: A Logic-Based Data-Language. In *Proceedings VLDB 1986, Kyoto, Japan*, pages 33–41, August 1986.

[V*86] P. Valduriez et al. Implementation Techniques of Complex Objects. In *Proceedings VLDB 1986, Kyoto, Japan*, pages 101–110, August 1986.

[Wal86] M. Wallace. *KB2: A Knowledge Base System Embedded In Prolog*. Technical Report KB-12, European Computer-Industry Research Centre, August 1986.

Foundations of Relational Object Management Systems

Andreas Heuer

Institut für Informatik, TU Clausthal
Erzstr. 1, D-3392 Clausthal-Zellerfeld, West Germany

1 Introduction

This paper is dealing with an overview of the foundations for a "relational" object management system to be developed. The object management system is based on relational technology and relational theory in order to use all the advantages of this classical model. Here we describe the ideas for the theoretical basis, especially the *object model*, the *object algebra*, some other possibilities to manipulate objects such as *rules*, *functions* and *complex updates*, the *object access* at the internal level, and the *applications* of the system based on these techniques.

2 Object model

The basis for our object management system is a data model for complex objects called EXTREM (EXTended RElational Model,[Heu]) which is based on the semantic database model IFO ([AH87]), and the NF^2-relational model ([SS86]). The object model concepts such as complex entities, relationships, complex attributes, and is-a-relationships are adequately represented by enhanced NF^2-schemes and additional integrity constraints.

More precisely, the EXTREM model is an integration of four different types of data models: there are four description levels having equivalent power (see Figure 1 for an overview).

- The EXTREM model is defined as a restriction of the **IFO model** [AH87] which consists of *atomic* or *constructed object types*, *functions* between object types, and *is-a-relationships* between object types. EXTREM is restricted to a subset of IFO concepts which are implementable via (flat or nested) relational concepts.

- The conceptual level of the EXTREM model can be seen as an extension of the **Entity-Relationship model** [Che76] by type constructors, is-a-relationships, and a formal semantics. The EXTREM concepts include complex *entity* and *relationship types*, *complex attributes*, *specialization* and *generalization* of entity and relationship types.

- A tabular representation of the EXTREM concepts is given at the nested relational level of EXTREM. *EXTREM relations* are a synthesis of **NF^2-relations** [SS86] and **RM/T-relations** [Cod79] with additional (local and global) dependencies. Especially, nested relations are enhanced by surrogates and "active domains".

- The basis for theoretical investigations and practical implementation is the classical relational level. EXTREM concepts are represented by **flat relations** with keys, inclusion dependencies, and some other dependencies.

	concepts	instances	operations
IFO level	atomic and constructed object types functions is-a-relationships	sets of abstract and concrete symbols connected by functions	function application
EXTREM conceptual level	entities, relationships complex attributes keys is-a-relationships	defined as IFO instances	object algebra
EXTREM nested relational level	nested relation schemes surrogates keys and other dependencies	special nested relations (EXTREM relations)	NF^2-algebra closed under EXTREM relations
classical relational level level	normalized relation schemes keys inclusion dependencies	flat relations	relational algebra

Figure 1: Overview of EXTREM description levels

EXTREM provides mappings of schemes, instances, and operations between these levels. So we can use

- theoretical results of classical relational theory or nested relations concerning dependency implication, database design, relational algebra, and query optimization as a foundation for the object model,
- implementation techniques of flat or nested relational systems (see Section 5)
  - for a prototype implementation of an object management system by means of classical relational methods only,
  - but also as a basis for a more efficient object oriented implementation.

Related research issues are

- mappings and equivalences between different data models (including several semantic models and the classical relational one),
- database design methods for EXTREM-schemes (including physical database design, see Section 5),
- exact characterization of relational concepts, which are an adequate representation of the object model concepts.

The results of these research issues are important for the implementation of efficient manipulation and access methods.

3 Object algebra

The implicit manipulation operations of the object model are algebraic. Since objects can be represented by enhanced NF^2-relations, the object algebra is similar to an NF^2-algebra with complex projection and selection operations (with set comparisons). Further information concerning the object algebra operations is included in [Heu88].

This algebra will mainly be implemented by a flat relational algebra processor with most join operations made implicit by e.g. clustering techniques (see Section 5). The classical relational algebra has to be extended only by

- two types of null-values ("value does not exist", "value not applicable"),
- two types of outer joins introducing these null values,

to represent the object algebra operations. Basis for this implementation is the mapping used in [DW88].

Optimization techniques especially for relational algebra expressions which are mappings of object algebra expressions, are developed; these techniques take into account both algebraic and semantic properties of an expression and object access methods provided at the internal level.

4 Other operations on objects

Besides the object algebra further research issues on manipulation operations are

- *query languages* based on the object algebra for different kinds of users (graphical interfaces for casual users, an embedded version of the object algebra for programmers),
- a query language based on *complex rules* ([San88]); these are mapped formally to an existing relational rule based language, hence we can use evaluating techniques of [Bro86] to implement rules via algebraic operations efficiently,
- providing *functions* on (complex) domains within an algebraic language, and the possibility to define *application-specific operations* (abstract data types as basic attribute domains),
- *update operations* on objects with implicit inheritance mechanisms driven by the object model concepts (e.g., is-a-hierarchies).

5 Object access

At the internal level of our object management system we want to integrate *classical relational methods* like KdB-trees or join indices [Val87] with *object oriented methods* [DPS86] like clustering and object trees. Since our kernel system is relational, we have to materialize joins where possible, and to support joins with adequate access methods where necessary. The development of proper access methods is one subject of our current research; these methods are compared to classical relational access methods and NF^2-methods within a specific cost model.

The mapping of the EXTREM concepts to the relational level includes a preliminary physical database design.

- All the relations belonging to one entity type are stored with object oriented methods.
- Relations that are images of relationship types or shared subtypes are stored using classical relational methods.

This choice avoids storing redundant data but clusters objects as far as possible.

6 Applications

Practical applications for the object management system based on the above concepts are

- management of graphical objects for computer aided design,
- data and metadata management for expert system applications in technical/engineering environments.

Both are current projects at our institute.

References

[AH87] S. Abiteboul und R. Hull. IFO: a formal semantic database model. *ACM Transactions on Database Systems*, 12(4):525–565, 1987.

[Bro86] V. Brosda. *Some problems according to rule based query languages.* Informatik-Bericht 86/4, TU Clausthal, 1986.

[Che76] P.P. Chen. The entity-relationship-model — towards a unified view of data. *ACM Transactions on Database Systems*, 1(1):9–36, 1976.

[Cod79] E.F. Codd. Extending the database relational model to capture more meaning. *ACM Transactions on Database Systems*, 4(4):397–434, 1979.

[DPS86] U. Deppisch, H.-B. Paul, und H.-J. Schek. A storage system for complex objects. *Proceedings of the International Workshop on Object-Oriented Database Systems*, 1:183–195, 1986.

[DW88] M. Dolezyk und U. Wiebking. Flat implementation of a nested relational algebra closed under a subclass of permutable nested relations. In *Informatik-Bericht 88/4, Workshop on Relational Databases and their Extensions*, Institut für Informatik, TU Clausthal, 1988.

[Heu] A. Heuer. A data model for complex objects based on a semantic database model and nested relations. submitted for publication.

[Heu88] A. Heuer. An object algebra and its connection to the NF^2- and flat relational algebra. In *Informatik-Bericht 88/4, Workshop on Relational Databases and their Extensions*, Institut für Informatik, TU Clausthal, 1988.

[San88] P. Sander. Access to complex objects in a rule based query language. In *Informatik-Bericht 88/4, Workshop on Relational Databases and their Extensions*, Institut für Informatik, TU Clausthal, 1988.

[SS86] H.-J. Schek und M.H. Scholl. The relational model with relation-valued attributes. *Information Systems*, 11(2):137–147, 1986.

[Val87] P. Valduriez. Join indices. *ACM Transactions on Database Systems*, 12(2):218–246, 1987.

The COMANDOS Integration System : an Object Oriented Approach to the Interconnection of Heterogeneous Applications

E.Bertino (*), R.Gagliardi (**), M.Negri (+), G.Pelagatti (+o), L.Sbattella (o)

(**) CNUCE, C.N.R., Pisa (Italia)

(+) Dipartimento di Automazione Industriale, Universita' di Brescia (Italia)

(o) Dipartimento di Elettronica, Politecnico di Milano (Italia)

(*) Istituto di Elaborazione della Informazione, C.N.R., Pisa (Italia)

Abstract

This paper describes an approach to the integration of heterogeneous data management applications. The proposed approach is based on techniques derived from the fields of Object Oriented Databases and Object Oriented Programming Languages. The architecture of a system which implements this approach is also briefly described.

1. Introduction

The need of providing support for uniform, integrated access to data stored and managed by different application environments has been widely recognized, especially in the areas of Office Automation and Computer Integrated Manufacturing.

In past years several projects have been developed in order to provide uniform and integrated access to heterogeneous DBMSs [BREI86],[DAYA82], [DEMU87], [FERR83], [BANE87], [DAYA86], [KING86], [LYNG86], [MAIE86]. The limitation of these projects is on the degree of heterogeneity of the systems to be integrated. The main reason of this limitation can be found in the kind of technique which is used for mapping between different systems. In fact, all these projects follow a common approach based on the technique of defining structural mappings between the elements of the various local Schemata. This approach, called **Schema Mapping**, requires from the designer of the distributed application to define these correspondences. Once the mapping is defined, the distributed DBMS supports the translation of operations issued by the distributed applications in terms of operations on the local database. In fact, the mapping is defined only once and all distributed applications use this definition.

The Schema Mapping technique is very powerful from the user point of view. However, it has a limited applicability (low degree of heterogeneity) because there are many situations in which this technique cannot be applied. In particular, this happens when very "navigational" DBMSs are used by the local applications, because the semantics of the data is deeply dependent on the way in which applications manipulate it and is only partially expressed by the Schema. An extreme case of this situation is when local applications are built directly on a File System, without a DBMS and therefore without a Schema at all. In this case the semantics of data is completely embedded in the application logic. Notice that many recent applications in areas where traditional DBMS are not usable fall in this situation (Multimedia applications, involving Text and Graphics, are a typical example).

In this paper we describe the main features of a system which uses a different technique for implementing the mapping in order to overcome the above limitations. This system is called COMANDOS Integration System (CIS) and is part of the project COMANDOS (COnstruction and MANagement of Distributed Office Systems) which is part of the European Strategic Programme for Research in Information Technology (ESPRIT) (1).

The integration technique proposed in CIS consists in implementing on top of each application environment to be integrated an Object-Oriented Abstract View: since the Abstract View is object-oriented, its implementation requires to write a set of procedures (methods), which implement the abstract operations of the view. In this way, it is not necessary that there exists a mapping between the data element manipulated by the local data management system and some "global model". Abstract Views are defined using the **Abstract Data Model** (see next Section) defined as part of CIS.

The approach proposed in CIS exploits the idea of separating the definition of abstract operations from their implementation through the notion of **abstract** and **implementation classes**. Basically, an abstract class describes the behaviour of an objects i.e. all the operations that the object can respond to and all the properties of the object that may be accessed by another object. An implementation class implements an abstract class by providing data structures and procedures to realize the abstract class. Implementation classes provide a mechanism that allows to define more powerful mappings. In fact, it is possible not only to implement the traditional Schema Mapping, but also it is possible to provide Operation Oriented Mappings, when the schema mapping cannot be completely applied (or cannot be applied at all). The Operation Oriented mapping consists in writing explicitely the implementation of the operations associated to the corresponding abstract class as programs local to the data management system to which the implementation class is associated. Since abstract classes can be accessed only through the operations associated to them, the users of abstract classes have no access to the "representation" of the implementation classes. This provides a complete "encapsulation" of the peculiarities of the data structures used by the local applications.

The possibility of having multiple implementation classes corresponding to the same abstract class is a second important point since it provides support for heterogeneity (both at hardware and software levels). Therefore given an abstract class, there may be several implementation classes, one for each system storing data that must be accessed through the abstract class. In this way a uniform interface in terms of abstract classes is provided for implementation of integrated distributed applications.

Another aspect where the CIS approach appears relevant with respect to the problem of integration concerns the issue of software reusability. As we mentioned before it is important to make available at distributed level those operations, implemented by local preexisting applications, that may be of interest in the implementation of distributed applications. In CIS this is achieved by associating at the abstract class level the abstract specifications of the operations implemented by local applications. This specification consists of the operation name, and of the definition of input/output parameters. Therefore local applications are made visible and accessible at distributed level through a standard interface, allowing a most cost effective development of distributed applications.

Furthermore in CIS two levels of operations for manipulating data objects are provided for the integrated applications: **abstract object-at-a-time primitives**, which are based on viewing a class of data objects as a kind of list of objects, and an **associative query language.** When needed, the applications may use the low level primitives and access one object at the time, rather than using the query language. Thereby increased flexibility is provided.

The relationships among abstract classes, implementation classes, query language, and applications are summarized in Figure 1. It should be noted that abstract operations

---

(1) This work has been funded in part by the Commission of the European Communities under ESPRIT Contract n.834. The CIS subsystem described in this paper has been implemented by ARG (I) and IEI-CNR (I).

invoked by a program are executed by calling the corresponding implementation operations. A query is processed by being transformed into an access plan, which is a program using abstract operations. An important point is that parameters concerning implementation classes must be provided to the query processor for optimization as part of the integration process.

Detailed description and specifications of CIS can be found in [COMA87] and [CIS88].

2. Abstract Data Model and Query Language

The Abstract Model used in CIS is the result of merging the concepts of O-O Databases with O-O programming languages. Infact our notion of class is both intensional and extensional, as in Databases [MYLO80], while in programming languages the class notion is intensional (as in Smalltalk [GOLD83]). However the operations defined for abstract classes are derived from the operations on classes (for example, the "new" operation for creating an object) and "collections" of O-O programming languages. As result we have an Abstract Model which is suitable for defining Database Applications (and, in particular, a query language) but which has also the most relevant features of O-O Programming Languages.

Abstract Class Definition and Operations An abstract class (or simply a class where no ambiguity arises) has a **name** (class name) and a set of **properties** (definitional properties). Each definitional property consists of a name (property name) followed by the name of its domain. Definitional properties are called **attributes** if their domain is a basic type (for example integer, boolean, string) or **components** if their domain is an abstract class. Furthermore components are categorized into **independent components** and **dependent components**.

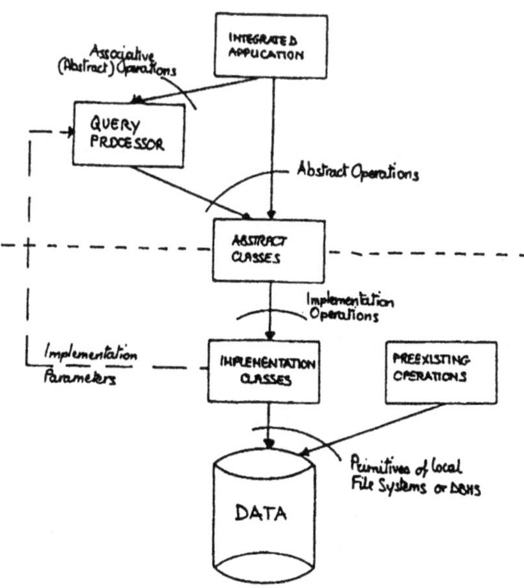

Figure 1: The architecture of CIS

The object value of the latter is dependent on the existence on the object of which it is part, while this is not true for independent components [BANE87]. An object which is a value of a dependent component of a given object cannot be a dependent component of another object.

Any object of the database must be member of an abstract class: as such, an object has a property for each definitional property of its class. An object property has a name (which is the same name of the corresponding definitional property), and a value (property value), which must be a member of the property domain of the corresponding definitional property. This handles the case of single-valued properties; however, in modelling the real world, the need of multi-valued components often arises: to capture this aspect, multi-valued components are included in the model.

Another important feature of the model is the possibility to have components with several different domains in alternative. This is handled with **variant components** of the following kinds (2)

a) **single-valued variant component**: in this case the component can assume as value an object from one of the specified classes;
b) **variant multi-valued component**: in this case all the component values for a specific object must be objects of the same class, among those specified as domains for the component;
c) **multi-valued variant component**: in this case the component values of a specific object must be objects of classes specified as domains for the components. However, values of the same component do not have to belong to the same class (as in the previous case).

The model provides two kinds of operations for handling classes and objects: **Generic Operations** and **User Defined Operations.**

Generic Operations are classified as:

- Operations on classes; these include: insertion of an object in a class, removal of an object from a class, inspection of instances of a class.
- Operations on objects that deal with object property manipulation. They have been further categorized into:
  - ◇ operations on single-valued attributes;
  - ◇ operations on single-valued components;
  - ◇ operations on multi-valued components.

In particular the operations for property manipulation include among the others reading and writing of object properties, adding and removal of values for multi-valued components. The operations, their formats and semantics are described in detail in [CIS88].

The model allows the possibility of **dropping** some of the generic operations on classes and objects. The effect of applying the drop to a given class is to modify the standard set of operations of the class. This option, used in combination with the User Defined Operations, allows restricting access to objects through specific operations, therefore providing abstract data type capabilities.

User Defined Operations can be used in a query as a function or a predicate provided that the operation has no-side effects on the objects stored into the classes.

Query Language The design of the query language, which is logic based, has been influenced by a number of requirements.

A first requirement is the capability of navigating through the object structures. The *dot function* has been introduced. Given a variable x denoting an object and a property name p, $x.p$ returns the object wich is value of property p of x. Dot functions can be nested.

A second requirement arises from the fact that components can be multivalued. From the query language point of view this implies that queries must allow to restrict objects by a quantified predicate.

A third requirement concerns properties having alternative domains (variant compo-

(2) Both components and dependent components can be variant; for simplicity here we use component to denote both.

nents). The query language provides the possibility of restricting objects by specifying predicates for properties with alternative domains of the form:

if domain(prop) is C1 then P1;
if domain(prop) is C2 then P2;
if domain(prop) is Cn then Pn;

where prop is a property name of the class to which the query is addressed; C1 ,..., Cn are classes that are alternative domains for the property prop; and P1 ,..., Pn are predicates expressed in terms of properties/and components of classes C1 ,..., Cn respectively.

To handle this situation, the notion of **composite predicate** has been introduced, that allows, given an object with a variant component, the specification of alternative predicates for each class, domain of the component.

3. CIS Architecture

CIS supports the creation of integrated applications accessing data managed by heterogenous and independent application environments residing on different sites of a computer network. These applications may run on different Hardware and different Operating Systems and DBMS, each one with its own conventions on data representation and storage. CIS models this situation with the notion of (logical) nodes, classified into **Client nodes** and **Server nodes**, and of a (logical) communication network between them.

The notion of logical node (client or server) in CIS bears no relationship to the notion of physical node as used in communication networks.

A Server is the abstraction of (part of) a preexisting application environment. The role of CIS, inside of a server, is to make available to the clients a uniform Object-Oriented interface on top of the local environment. The CIS component that resides on the server is called **Cis_Server**.

A Client is the abstraction of an application based on CIS, accessing the services provided by one or more servers. A client performs an integrated application function using data of different preexisting environments and therefore implements the integration goal of CIS. The CIS component that resides on the client is called **Cis_Client**.

Servers cannot communicate with each other; moreover, each object of the O-O interface must be completely contained in a single server. As a consequence, for CIS there are no relationships between servers except those implemented by clients. A server is therefore an autonomous and independent environment, which groups together a set of objects under a common application semantics. This structure reflects the requirements for loose connection and site autonomy that are relevant for the applications we intend to support. CIS Servers have been designed in order to provide an Object Oriented Programming Environment for the implementation of the Abstract Classes. The main tasks supported by the environment are:

a) receiving and dispatching of messages to objects (Message Manager)
b) creating objects, supporting object identification and garbage collection (Object Data Manager)
c) defining classes (Dictionary Manager)
d) generating an access plan for queries on terms of object operations (Query Processor).

In CIS implementation classes have been designed taking into account the following facts:

(i) There may exist several implementation classes associated to a given class. This allows providing a uniform interface toward the applications of data that may have different implementations because of the distributed and heterogeneous nature of the environment.
(ii) Implementation classes must be designed as independent as possible from each other. Information sharing among different implementation classes is avoided in order to obtain implementation classes as a set of "black boxes" communicating only through message exchanges.

An implementation class consists of a set of procedures and some data structures. The data structure used by implementation classes are internal representations which cannot be manipulated in any way by a program operating at abstract level (i.e. using the operations seen in the previous section) or by procedures belonging to another implementation class. The procedures represent the handles to interact with an implementation class (this concept is quite similar to the programming language concept of abstract data type).

4. Conclusions

In this paper we have presented an object-oriented approach to the problem of interconnecting heterogenous data management systems and applications.

A first CIS prototype is now under development as part of the COMANDOS ESPRIT Project and it is expected to be completed by the end of this year. A Cis_Client will be implemented on Unix using the C programming language and interfaces will be provided from the Cis_Client toward different programming environments. Several Server environments are being evaluated to be used as testbed for the integration. These environemnts include: an application using the UNIX file system; a Databank access application; a relational DBMS application; a CAD application.

References

[**BANE87**] Banerjee J., Chou H.T., Garza J.F., Kim W., Woelk D., Ballou N., Kim H.J., *Data Model Issues for Object-Oriented Applications* ACM Trans. on Office Information Systems, Vol.5, N.1, 1987, pp.3-26.

[**BREI86**] Breibart Y.J., Olson P.L. Thompson G.R., *Database Integration in a Distributed Heterogeneous Database System*, Proc. Second Int. IEEE Conference on Data Engineering, Los Angeles, 1986.

[**CIS88**] COMANDOS Integration System (CIS), *Unified Documentation*, ESPRIT Project 834, (Technical Deliverable), February 1988.

[**COMA87**] COMANDOS *Global Architecture*, ESPRIT Project 834, Report T2.1/D2 (Technical Deliverable), September 1987.

[**DAYA86**] Dayal U., and Manola F., *PDM: An Object-Oriented Data Model*, Proc. IEEE Workshop on Object Oriented DBMS, Asilomar (Calif.), September 1986.

[**FERR83**] Ferrier A., and Stangret C., *Heterogeneity in the Distributed Database Management System SIRIUS-DELTA*, Proc. Eighth Int. VLDB Conference, Mexico City, 1983.

[**GOLD83**] Goldberg A., Robson D., *SMALLTALK-80: the Language and its Implementation*, Addison-Wesley, 1983.

[**HORN87**] Horn C., Krakowiak S., *Object-Oriented Architecture for Distributed Office Systems*, in Proc. fourth ESPRIT Technical Week, Brussels, September, 1987.

[**KING86**] King R., and Hudson S., *CACTIS: A Database System for Specifying Functionally-Defined Data*, Proc. IEEE Workshop on Object Oriented DBMS, Asilomar (Calif.), September 1986.

[**LOHM87**] Lohman G., *Grammar-like Functional Rules for Representing Query Optimization Alternatives*, RJ 5992, IBM Almaden Research Center, San Jose, CA 95120, December 1987.

[**LYNG86**] Lyngbaek P., Kent W., "*A Data Modeling Methodology for the Design and Implementation of Information Systems*, Proc. IEEE Workshop on Object Oriented DBMS, Asilomar (Calif.), September 1986.

[**MAIE86**] Maier D., Stein J., *Indexing in an Object-Oriented DBMS* Proc. IEEE Workshop on Object Oriented DBMS, Asilomar (Calif.), September 1986.

[**MYLO80**] Mylopoulos, J., Bernstein P., Wong, H., *A Language Facility for Designing Database-Intensive Applications*, ACM Trans. on Database Systems, Vol.5, No.2, June 1980, pp.185-207.

A Learning-Based Approach to Meta-Data Evolution in an Object-Oriented Database

Dennis McLeod

Computer Science Department
University of Southern California
Los Angeles CA, USA 90089-0782

1. Introduction

Changes to the conceptual structure (meta-data) of a database are common in many application environments, and are in general inadequately supported by existing database systems. The need for high-level knowledge change is particularly pronounced for design engineering databases, artificial intelligence systems, office information systems, and personal databases. Such change may be required when the real world that the database models evolves, when users' views thereof evolve, and when new patterns of usage are encountered.

Object-oriented databases provide a particularly appropriate forum for the analysis and accommodation of meta-data evolution. The term "object-oriented" has been used to refer to many characteristics and capabilities when applied to database systems. Here, we attempt to characterize an object-oriented database somewhat precisely, by placing it in contradistinction to a record-oriented database. Specifically, an object-oriented database system is one which supports the following:

1. *Individual object identity*:
   Abstract objects can be directly represented and manipulated in a database, independent of symbolic surrogates for them [8,11]. Objects at various levels of abstraction and of various modalities (different media) can be accommodated.

2. *Explicit semantic primitives*:
   Primitives are provided to support object classification, structuring, and integrity. These primitive abstraction mechanisms, supporting such features as aggregation, classification, instantiation, and inheritance, have their roots in "semantic" data models [7,8,10] and artificial intelligence knowledge representation techniques [6].

3. *Active objects*:
   Database objects can be active as well as passive, in the sense that they can exhibit behavior. Various specific approaches to the modeling of object behavior can be adopted, such as an inter-object message passing paridgm (e.g., as described in [21,24]), or abstract datatype encapsulation (e.g., [2]). The important point is that procedures to manipulate data are represented in the database itself.

4. *Object uniformity*:
   All information (or nearly all) in a database is described using the same object model [1,4]. Thus, descriptive information about objects, referred to here as meta-data, is conceptually represented in the same way as specific "fact" objects.

The use of explicit semantic primitives in the conceptual structure of an object-oriented database makes it possible to handle such kinds of evolution as alterations of the object classification scheme (class/type structure) as well as changes to the definitions of inter-object attributes/relationships [3,5,13,20]. The need for multiple versions of structural database objects (e.g., classes, types) and an analysis of the effects of evolution on database behavioral objects has also been recognized [12,18,22]. The intermixing of meta-data and more specific data (traditionally "schema" and "database") also facilitates techniques to allow the evolution of fine-grained facts into more general facts and vice-versa.

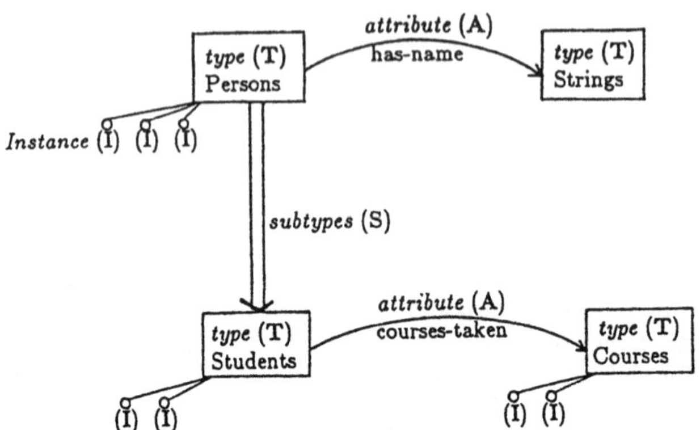

Figure 1: An Example PKM Database

2. A Learning-Based Approach to Evolution

Our approach to evolution in an object-oriented database involves actively supporting change at various levels of granularity and abstraction. The framework for our work is a simple, extensible, object-oriented database model, consisting of two levels: a kernel model and a high level model. This model is supported by an experimental object-oriented database system called *PKM*. Within this framework, the spectrum of kinds of meta-data evolution is considered, and heuristics are provided for important specific kinds of change.

For the kernel model, an important kind of change termed "object flavor evolution" [13] has been studied. This kind of evolution involves changes to the fundamental semantics of objects, vis-a-vis their nature as symbolic, abstract, type (set), relationship (mapping), or behavioral (procedure). For example, a real-world concept modeled in a database as a symbolic object (e.g., a string denoting the name of a person) may later evolve to or be alternatively viewed as an abstract object (e.g., a person entity). For the high level model, kinds of important change include modifications of the database structure, semantic constraints, and derived data (deduction) rules. Examples include the evolution of a binary relationship to a ternary relationship, and the transformation of an semantic integrity rule into a derived fact specification.

In [14], we proposed an active approach to supporting evolution in an object-oriented based in part on applied techniques from machine learning [16,17]. In particular, combinations of *learning from instruction (LFI)*, *learning from exception (LFE)*, and *learning from observation (LFO)* are employed in the PKM system. By applying learning techniques to the problem of database evolution we want to achieve two goals. The first goal is to partially automate certain kinds of evolution. The second goal is to have the system learn more knowledge about the objects from various evolution cases. In this approach, end-users interact with a high level interface, which utilizes an *intelligent concept evolver (ICE)* to support individual evolution cases, based upon three fundamental learning techniques and a set of learning heuristics. ICE also serves as an *interpretor* that translates high level user interactions into the low level kernel database operations.

3. Example High Level Evolution Cases

Here, we study several important example evolution cases for the high level PKM database model, and show how learning can ease evolution tasks for the user; we also examine what the system can learn from various evolution cases. For simplicity here, we focus on illustrative aspects of the high level PKM model; these are the constructs type (**T**), sub/supertype (**S**), attribute (**A**), and instance (**I**). Figure 1 shows a portion of an example **Student Affairs Office** database of a university, defined using this data model.

In this figure, there are four type **T** objects: **Persons, Students, Courses,** and **Strings.** Type **Persons** has an attribute (**A**) **has-name** whose value range is the type **Strings.** Type **Students** is a subtype (**S**) of **Persons.** In addition to the attribute **has-name** inherited from its supertype **Persons, Students** has the attribute **courses-taken** whose value range is the type **Courses.** Each type object has certain instances (**I**), and the instances of a supertype include all the instances of its subtypes.

The example evolution cases described below are based upon the four basic modelling constructs described above, and involve relationships among these modelling constructs. In the following description of evolution cases, we specify:

- the informal semantics of each evolution case,
- a sample situation for the evolution case,
- the learning techniques applied in the course of evolution,
- the learning heuristics used.

(1) **Type** $\Rightarrow_{\textbf{specialize}}$ **Subtypes:**

- Semantics: Specialize a type object O_i into several subtypes. This kind of evolution is needed when the user wants to consider certain groups of instances of O_i as a whole (e.g., to define attributes exclusive to those instances, when certain transactions or constraints apply only to certain instances of O_i, etc.).
- Sample Situation: Suppose there exists a type object **Students** in the database that has three attributes: **has-id#, courses-taken,** and **marriage-status.** Suppose further that the user decides to add a new attribute **has-spouse** to **Students.** Observing that all instances of **Students** whose **marriage-status** = "single" have null values on the newly added attribute **has-spouse,** learning from observation (LFO) suggests specializing the type **Students** into two subtypes: one with **marriage-status** = "single" and one with **marriage-status** = "married"; the attribute **has-spouse** is associated with the second subtype (i.e., married students) only.
- Learning Techniques Applied: LFO
- Learning Heuristics Used: For a type object O_i, if some of its instances have null value for a given attribute A, then suggest specializing that type into subtypes O_j and O_k, with one of them (O_j) containing the instances of O_i that have null value for A; migrate A from O_i to subtype O_k.

(2) **Types** $\Rightarrow_{\textbf{generalize}}$ **Supertype:**

- Semantics: Generalize two type objects O_i and O_j that have certain common attributes into a newly introduced supertype. This is useful when we want to abstract a new type from two closely related types.
- Sample Situation: Suppose there are type objects **Faculty** and **Staff** in the database. Discovering that these two types have certain common attributes (e.g., **employee#, salary,** etc.), LFO suggests generalizing them to a new supertype. With the user's approval, LFI is used to acquire the name (e.g., **Employee**) and the attributes of this new type.
- Learning Techniques Applied: LFO, LFI
- Learning Heuristics Used: For any two type objects O_i and O_j that have no sub/supertype relationship, if they have certain common attributes, then suggest generalizing them into a new supertype O_k whose attributes are those common attributes of O_i and O_j (by default).

(3) **Attribute $\Rightarrow_{\text{objectify}}$ Type:**

- Semantics: Evolve an attribute A to a type object. This often implies that a binary relationship is evolved to a ternary (or higher order) relationship. It is useful if the user wants to view an attribute as a type object, and is necessary when the user wants to associate an attribute with an attribute (or equivalently, with a binary relationship).

- Sample Situation: Suppose at first the type **Students** has an attribute **courses-taken** whose value range is the type object **Courses**. Now the user wants to associate an attribute **has-grade** to the attribute **courses-taken** to record the grades students received in the courses they took. This transaction, however, violates the definition of an attribute; LFE (learning from exception) is used to handle this problem. Specifically, LFE is used to evolve the attribute **courses-taken** to a type object (possibly with a name change, e.g., to **Enrollments**); instances of **Enrollments** are created for each attribute mapping occurence from **Students** to **Courses**. The attributes of the new type object **Enrollments** include: **has-student** and **has-course**.

- Learning Techniques Applied: LFE

- Learning Heuristics Used: If an attribute A (of a type object O_i, with the value range O_j) is to be considered as a type, objectify A by creating a new type O_k with attributes **has-O_i** and **has-O_j**. Create instances of O_k for each attribute mapping occurence defined by A; A is then deleted (alternatively, A could be retained redundantly, with an appropriate integrity constraint specified).

(4) **Instance $\Rightarrow_{\text{promote}}$ Type**

- Semantics: Promote an instance object O_i to be a type object (so instances of O_i can exist).

- Sample Situation: There is a type object **CS-Courses** which contains all the courses offered by computer science (CS) department (e.g., **CS101**, **CS201**, etc.). The course **CS557** was initially offered with one section. Noticing that the course has too many students for one section, the CS department decides to partition this course into two sections: **CS557a** and **CS557b**. The user wishes to create two objects, and desires them as instances of the object **CS557**. LFE is used to help the user to accomplish his/her goal, which results in the instance object **CS557** being evolved to a type object, with the objects **CS557a** and **CS557b** as its instances; the default attribute values of **CS557a** and **CS557b** will be the attribute values of **CS577**.

- Learning Techniques Applied: LFE

- Learning Heuristics Used: If some instance objects O_1,...,O_k are to be made instances of a non-type object O_n, evolve O_n to a type object and add O_1,...,O_k to it, with their default attribute values to be the attribute values of O_n.

(5) **Type $\Rightarrow_{\text{expand}}$ Subtypes:**

- Semantics: Expand a type object O_k by adding new instances that do not conform the definition of O_k, resulting in O_k to have a new subtype that contains all the new instances. This kind of evolution is useful when the user wants to expand the definition of a type.

- Sample Situation: Suppose the type object **Applicants** has three attributes: **has-name, has-GPA,** and **has-address**, having value ranges **Names, GPA,** and **Addresses** (respectively). Assume that the user wants make the object **Robert Chen** an instance of **Applicants** with "Chen, Robert" as his name, "85.00" as his GPA, and "1210 Adams St." as his address. This transaction however, cannot be accomplished because the GPA "85.00" is not compatible with the definition of the type **GPA** (which is 4-scaled, rather than 100-scaled). LFE handles this problem, which obtains from the user the information that GPA can be either 4-scaled or 100-scaled. So it introduces two new type objects **4-Scaled** and **100-Scaled**, making them subtypes of the type object **GPA**.

- Learning Techniques Applied: LFE

- Learning Heuristics Used: For a type object O_i, if new instances that violate its definition need to be added into it, then expand the definition of O_i by introducing subtypes of O_i.

4. Conclusions

In this research, we examine the problem of supporting meta-data evolution in manner that is both active and which requires a minimum amount of database design expertise. A collection of evolution heuristics and an associated evolution methodology have been devised, employing machine learning techniques to actively support evolution. An experimental database evolution tool for end-users who are not database experts is being designed and implemented. This prototype embodies the two-level data model architecture, the evolution heuristics, and an end-user interface. The prototype is being constructed on a network of SUN/3 workstations at USC, using the V-Base object-oriented software system [2], and is being written in a mixture of "C" and LISP. Several example database applications are being utilized to test, evaluate, and refine the prototype, as well as the principles and techniques underlying it. The evolution techniques and methodology can be applied to support meta-data evolution for a single database, the identification and specification of similar/related facts in multiple databases, and the partial integration of autonomous databases [9,15].

References

[1] H. Afsarmanesh, D. Knapp, D. McLeod, and A. Parker. An extensible, object-oriented approach to databases for vlsi/cad. In *Proceedings of the International Conference on Very Large Databases*, VLDB Endowment, August 1985.

[2] T. Andrews and C. Harris. Combining language and database advances in an object-oriented development environment. In *Proceedings of the Conference on Object-Oriented Programming Systems, Langusges, and Applications*, pages 430–440, ACM, 1987.

[3] R. Balzer. Automated enhancement of knowledge representations. In *Proceedings of the International Joint Conference on Artificial Intelligence*, pages 203–207, August 1985.

[4] J. Banerjee, H. Chou, J. Garza, W. Kim, D. Woelk, N. Ballou, and H. Kim. Data model issues for object-oriented applications. *ACM Transactions on Office Information Systems*, 5(1):3–26, January 1987.

[5] J. Banerjee and W. Kim. Semantics and implementation of schema envolution in object-oriented databases. In *Proceedings of the ACM SIGMOD International Conference on Management of Data*, pages 311–322, ACM SIGMOD, May 1987.

[6] M. Brodie and J. Mylopoulos (Editors). *On Knowledge Base Management Systems*. Springer-Verlag, 1986.

[7] E. F. Codd. Extending the database relational model to capture more meaning. *ACM Transactions on Database Systems*, 4(4):397–434, 1979.

[8] M. Hammer and D. McLeod. Database description with sdm: a semantic database model. *ACM Transactions on Database Systems*, 6(3):351–386, September 1981.

[9] D. Heimbigner and D. McLeod. A federated architecture for information systems. *ACM Transactions on Office Information Systems*, 3(3):253–278, July 1985.

[10] R. Hull and R. King. Semantic database modeling: survey, applications, and research issues. *ACM Computing Surveys*, 19(3):201–260, September 1987.

[11] W. Kent. Limitations of record-oriented information models. *ACM Transactions on Database Systems*, 4:107–131, March 1979.

[12] W. Kim and H. Chou. Versions of schema for object-oriented databases. In *Proceedings of the International Conference on Very Large Databases*, VLDB Endowment, IEEE, ACM SIGMOD, September 1988.

[13] Q. Li and D. McLeod. Object flavor evolution in an object-oriented database system. In *Proceedings of the Conference on Office Information System*, ACM, March 1988.

[14] Q. Li and D. McLeod. Supporting object flavor evolution through learning in an object-oriented database system. In *Proceedings of the International Conference on Expert Database Systems*, April 1988.

[15] P. Lyngbaek and D. McLeod. Object sharing in distributed information systems. *ACM Transactions on Office Information Systems*, 2(2):96–122, April 1984.

[16] R. Michalski, J. Carbonell, and T. Mitchell (Editors). *Machine Learning: An Artificial Intelligence Approach (Volume 1).* Tioga Publishing Company, 1983.

[17] R. Michalski, J. Carbonell, and T. Mitchell (Editors). *Machine Learning: An Artificial Intelligence Approach (Volume 2).* Morgan Kaufmann, 1986.

[18] K. Narayanaswamy and K. V. Bapa Rao. An incremental mechanism for schema evolution in engineering domains. In *Proceedings of the International Conference on Data Engineering*, pages 294–301, IEEE, January 1988.

[19] *Vbase Reference Manual - Vbase Release 1.0.* Ontologic, Inc., 47 Manning Road, Billerica MA, 1987.

[20] D. J. Penney and J. Stein. Class modification in the gemstone object-oriented dbms. In *Proceedings of the Conference on Object-Oriented Programming Systems, Langusges, and Applications*, pages 111–117, 1987.

[21] A. Purdy, B. Schuchardt, and D. Maier. Integrating an object server with other worlds. *ACM Transactions on Office Information Systems*, 5(1):27–47, January 1987.

[22] A. H. Skarra and S. B. Zdonik. The management of changing types in an object-oriented database. In *Proceedings of the Conference on Object-Oriented Programming Systems, Langusges, and Applications*, pages 483–495, 1986.

[23] K. Smith and S. Zdonik. Intermedia: a case study of the differences between relational and object-oriented database systems. In *Proceedings of the Conference on Object-Oriented Programming Systems, Langusges, and Applications*, pages 452–465, ACM, 1987.

[24] M. Stefik and D. Bobrow. Object-oriented programming: themes and variations. *AI Magazine*, 6(4):40–62, 1986.

Views, Data Abstraction, and Inheritance in the FUGUE Data Model

Sandra Heiler
Computer Corporation of America

Stanley Zdonik
Brown University

Abstract

This paper defines a view mechanism analogous to relational views that simply and naturally extends the FUGUE[1] object model [HZ88]. The paper then addresses the problems of providing data abstraction and inheritance in FUGUE. The proposed view mechanism is powerful enough to be used to capture the essential features of data abstraction and inheritance, while allowing us also to define application-specific views as is typically done in database systems. We also show how this mechanism can be used to model user-level views as well as system-level views of functions.

1. Introduction

There is often a need in a program development environment to limit the visibility of named entities. Object-oriented type systems typically adopt some flavor of data abstraction and thereby hide the internal representation of an object (e.g., instance variables in Smalltalk [GR83]) from the users of that object. These same systems typically incorporate some notion of type similarity that is expressed by means of an inheritance mechanism. Through type inheritance, one can define a type such as Car with a subtype such as Toyota such that Toyota inherits the behavior defined for Car. Another way of looking at this is that when dealing with an object from the point of view of Car (even if this car is a Toyota), a program can only use the behavior that Car defines. Therefore, some of the behavior of the object is hidden from that program.

Similarly, hiding of named resources happens in relational database systems as well. The traditional database mechanism for accomplishing this is through a view mechanism. Views are usually computed as a function (i.e., a query) on some base set of definitions [Wi86]. The query returns a relation or set of relations through which the user of the view can access the database. Here, again, there is typically much from the underlying definitions that is hidden. This hiding can be manifested by simply blocking named components or by defining new components that are derived from the old hidden components.

In an object-oriented model, one needs the ability to hide methods, as well as data. In this paper, we show how a carefully constructed view mechanism can be used to achieve several desirable types of data and method hiding. In addition, we show how the notions of data abstraction and

---

This work was sponsored by a tri-service DoD program under USAF Contract F33615-87-C-1401.

1 FUnction Generalization in a Uniform Environment

inheritance can be simulated using this mechanism. We will present this discussion in terms of the FUGUE data model [HZ88], a functional, object-oriented model that has been designed to address the requirements of a framework for integrating heterogeneous systems and databases for Engineering Information Systems [LW86].

2. Summary of FUGUE: Objects, Functions, and Types

FUGUE is an object-oriented model built on three basic concepts: *objects*, *functions*, and *types*. The basic paradigm for performing work, i.e., for executing programs, in the model is function application. "Objects" are the things that functions are applied to; they are the inputs and outputs of functions. "Types" organize objects by structure and behavior; a given type specifies which functions can be applied to its instances or produce its instances. FUGUE is based on DAPLEX [Sh81] and the Probe Data Model (PDM) [Ma87], from which it derives many of its fundamental concepts.

Objects

Objects correspond to the entities in the application domain, e.g., designs, tools, gates, and schedules, as well as to entities in the system's model, e.g., relations, tasks, users, and files. There is no built-in granularity for objects; they can be, for example, complete chip designs, integers, engineering methodologies, or bytes.

Objects are defined in terms of functions that can be applied to them or that return them when applied to other objects. A function can be applied to an object to yield a property of the object, to yield related objects, to perform an operation on the object, or to test a constraint on the object. For example, an employee object might have the following functions:

```
Employee e has functions:
        Name(e) -> aString
        Address(e) -> aString
        Department(e) -> aDept#
        Spouse(e) -> aPerson
        Pay(e) ->
        Fire(e) ->
        Overpaid?(e) -> true|false
        Hire(p: Person) -> e
```

One applies an appropriate function to the employee object to yield his name, address, department or spouse or to perform operations on the employee like pay him, fire him, or determine whether he makes more than his manager. One applies the Hire function to a Person object to yield an Employee object.

Objects have "handles" which are used to identify them. Different kinds of objects may be identified by different kinds of handles, as described in [Bl88]. Object handles are passed as the input arguments of functions and functions applied to objects yield the handles of objects, which can be passed as input arguments to still other functions (defined over the resulting objects). The object's handle represents the object itself to the object's functions.

Functions

Functions perform mappings from input arguments (objects) to output arguments (objects). In FUGUE, functions can have multiple input and output arguments. For example, the function Pay could have been defined to take as inputs an employee and an amount or the function Department could have been defined to yield a set of department numbers to which the employee is assigned or even pairs department number, date-assigned for all of the departments in which the employee has worked, as shown below:

```
Pay(emp:Employee, salary:$amt) ->
Department(Employee) -> {(dept:Dept#, assigned:Date)}
```

(In the examples that follow, we show the functions of an object as the set of functions of which it is any (input or output) argument. When a function takes multiple input objects or yields multiple output objects, we assign labels to the specifications of argument types to distinguish them. The function may be shown under any or all of its input or output argument objects.)

FUGUE functions are similar in concept to Lisp functions in that they are "Apply"ed to arguments and yield results. Each has a signature that specifies its selector, domain and range and, possibly, a set of pre- and post-conditions that specify its semantics. Associated with each function is a procedure which may be implemented in a programming language that is outside the model, e.g., Ada or C. This procedure, when invoked with the input arguments, produces the associated output arguments. Because the language in which the procedure is implemented can be outside the model, functions can have side effects that are not described by the function interface.

FUGUE functions are also objects. That is, they have functions of their own. For example, Input_arguments (i.e., domain), Output_arguments (i.e., range), Body (i.e.,procedure), and Apply are all functions of functions. In addition, functions may have other functions (functionals) that can be applied to derive new functions, e.g., one might apply a functional to a pair of functions which yields a new function defined as "Apply the first function to the specified arguments, then Apply the second function to the same arguments and join its results to those of the first by matching argument values." The algebra defined for PDM [Ma87] provides such a set of functionals for deriving new functions from existing functions.

Types

Objects are organized into "types" by the functions that can be applied to them. An object's type specifies its structure and behavior. Specifically, a type defines a set of functions that can be applied to or that yield instances of the type. It may also specify *values* for initializing functions of new instances of the type. The type definition identifies functions in which instances of the type appear in the domain or range. Types are used both for object creation (as templates for the new instance) and for error checking (to determine whether a request to apply a particular function to particular objects is legal).

Because functions can take multiple input arguments and yield multiple output arguments, the function definition must include labels to differentiate them. These same labels appear in type definitions, e.g., one applies the Pay function to an instance of type Employee as the emp argument and an instance of type $amt as the salary argument.

In FUGUE a type is an object with a function that yields a set of **function - argument_label - initial_value** triples. We call this function Instance_fns because it defines the functions of instances of the type. Types may have additional functions, such as a function for creating new instances of the type or a function that yields the extent of the type, as shown below:

```
type t has functions:
        Instance_fns -> {(function, label, value)}
        Create -> t
        Extent -> {all instances of type t}
```

Applying the Create function to t yields a new object whose functions are the members of Instance_fns(t) and whose initial values (for extensionally-defined functions) have been set to the values specified by the type. The semantics of object creation are described in [HZ88]. The implementation of the Create function ensures that the functions specified by all of the types that contribute functions to the new object include the new object in their domains or ranges, as appropriate.

Every object o has a function Types that yields its type objects. That is:

Types(o) -> {types}

where f(o) is defined for each f in Instance_fns(t) for each t in Types(o).

One can think of the "conceptual" type of an object as the type defined as follows:

```
conceptual_type(o)
  Instance_fns => {U Instance_fns(t) for each t in Types(o)}
```

Note that a type object (like type t above) is, itself, an instance of a type called Type (which can be thought of as a "meta-type", i.e., a type whose instances are also types. Other meta-types can be defined, as well.) Type Type has functions as shown below:

```
Instance_fns => {Instance_fns, Create}
Create -> Type
```

3. Type Derivation

New type objects can be derived from existing types by applying functions to the existing types. In the simplest case, one could, for example, define a new type by applying a set operation to the values of Instance_fns of existing types to yield types with the union of those values, e.g.:

```
type Student/Employee
        Instance_fns => {Instance_fns(Student U Instance_fns(Employee)}
```

No conflicts in identifying which functions to include in the union can occur because each element of the Instance_fns sets is uniquely identified by its object handle. If a function appears in both sets, it will have the same handle.

Types can *hide* some of the functions of an object (to support access control) or include *derived* functions, possibly hiding the functions from which they were derived. This may include forming types from subsets of the functions of an existing type, including the "conceptual" types of objects. For example, we might derive a type from Employee that includes only the Name, Address, and Department functions, to ensure that some users cannot apply other functions such as Pay or Fire to employees, even though they can access the employee through the Name, Address, and Department functions.

The type of an object can include any subset of the functions that are defined for that object or that can be derived from those functions. These include subsets of the functions of the object's conceptual type and all functions derivable from them. The functions in these subsets can be taken from the Instance_fns of different types in Types(o) and the subsets that form various types can overlap. As another example, given a type Dept, as described below:

```
Type Dept
        Instance_fns => {     Dept# -> integer,
                              Members -> {Employee},
                              Office_sizes -> {area},
                              Staffing_level -> integer    }
```

One could derive a function Total_space defined as follows:

```
Total_space(d:Dept) := Sum(a in Office_sizes(d))
```

and add it to the Instance_fns of the type Dept.

Type derivation can be far more complicated. In particular, it may require deriving new object s and, of course, their handles, where there is not a straightforward mapping from the Extent of an existing type to that of the new type, e.g., by selection from the existing type.For example, consider the following case in which a new type must be derived. Assume the following type definitions:

```
Part
  Instance_fns => {    Part_no -> integer,
                       Part_name -> string   }
  Create -> Part
  Extent -> {Part}

Supplier
  Instance_fns => {    Supplier_no -> integer,
                       Supplier_name -> string   }
  Create -> Supplier
  Extent -> {Supplier}

  Order
  Instance_fns => {    Order_no -> integer,
                       Quantity_supplied(o: Order, p: Part, s: Supplier) -> integer   }
  Create -> Order
  Extent -> {Order}
```

Notice that Quantity_supplied is a function of all three types, even though it is shown only once under Order. We can derive a new function:

```
Order_items(order:Order) -> {Order_item}
```

using the following type definition and implementation of the Order_items function:

```
Type Order_item
  Instance_fns => {    Item_supplier -> Supplier,
                       Items_supplied -> { (Part, integer) }    }

  Extent => {    all (O, P, S) | O isin Extent(Order) and P isin Extent(Part) and S isin
```

```
Extent(Supplier) and Quantity_supplied(o: O, p: P, s: S) > 0 }

Body(Order_items) => {Select(x in Extent(Order_item) | Order_no(order) = O(x)}
```

Notice that the Body of the Order_items function defines the extent of the type as a set of tuples of Order, Part, Supplier. One could define the representation of instances of types Part, Supplier and Order as tuples, as well, to allow functions implementing relational algebra operations to be applied to them or to the extents of the types. The explicit specification of the internal representation of instances of a type using the Rep function is described in Section 5.

Implementations of all functions of type Order_item, must be provided as well. Notice, however, that type Order_item does not have a Create function. Instances of Order_item are derived from instances from the other types when they are needed as function arguments.

4. Views

In FUGUE, a **view** is a *context* in which functions are applied to objects. A view defines the universe of objects and functions in which the client (human or program) operates. Every request to apply a function to objects occurs within the client's view. The view defines a set of objects and binds each of them to a type that determines the functions that can be applied to them or that yield them in that view.

This concept of view is analogous to the concept of relational views. Relational views make visible the data to which the user operating in that view has access (and hides even the existence of data the user cannot access). FUGUE views make visible *objects* and *functions* to which the view user has access. Unlike relational views, FUGUE views also make visible the particular *operations* (functions) that can be performed on objects in the view, i.e., the methods that apply to objects in the view, by binding each of the objects in the view to a specific type.

A view definition specifies two sets: a set of types and a set of objects that are instances of those types:

```
V defines ({Types}, {Objects})   such that
for each o in {Objects}, Types(o) -> some t in {Types}
```

Each o in {Objects} is bound to exactly one of its types. That is, the view provides a specific abstraction for each object in the view. Although the object is defined by the functions specified by its conceptual type, the object can be bound in the view to a type that hides some of those functions or include derived functions, hiding the functions from which they were derived.

In defining views, one binds specific objects to specific types. One can limit both the objects (to a subset of instances of the specified types) and the types (to a subset of the possible types of the objects). For example, given a type Student with functions:

```
Student
    Instance_fns => {   Name -> string,
                        Level -> string,
                        Gpa -> real          }
```

one could define a view V1 that restricts the objects in the view to graduate students as follows:

```
V1 := {Student}, {s in Extent(Student) | Level(s) = "grad"}
```

Furthermore, we could restrict the functions that can be applied to students by defining a new type Student_restricted_access that includes only the Name and Level functions and a view V2 in which students are bound to the new type as follows:

```
Student_restricted_access
    Instance_fns => { Name -> string,
                      Level -> string        }

    V2 := {Student_restricted_access}, {s in Extent(Student)}
```

to ensure that users of this view cannot apply other functions such as Gpa to students, even though they can access the student through the Name and Level functions.

Notice that each object s in the view is bound to exactly one of its types, Student, even though it may have additional types, e.g., Employee. Furthermore, no other types or objects are visible to the user operating in this view. That is, a user in this view can apply functions to the particular Student objects in the view, but he or she cannot apply functions that are not included in the Student type or to Student instances that are not in the set of objects defined by the view.

Views are, by definition, closed. That is, each of the functions of types to which objects in the view are bound yields objects that are also in the view and that are bound to types in the view. The model primitives are described by a set of basic types and basic objects that are part of every view. They include the primitive types Object, Function and Type. They can be defined to include, as well, other basic types and instances of them, including integer, string, real, etc.

Changing Views

The binding of an object to a particular *type* tells us what functions can be applied to or yield the object. In a sense, the type provides a *view* of individual objects. If we allow an object's type to change, i.e., if we bind the object to another of its types, we are, essentially, allowing that object to be viewed differently. Changing views is, in effect, the process of changing types or binding objects to different types. In what follows, we use the words "type binding" to refer to the type-view of an object.

Each client (human or program) operates in the context of a view, which may include in some of its types functions for switching context to another view. Furthermore, each function (as a client which makes requests for function application) operates in the context of a view. If this view is different from that of the caller (which is likely because the function body may have access to different objects or its input objects may be bound to different types) the function changes views by applying a function to do so. Entering the body of the function automatically makes the needed view change functions available in the function's view.

Human clients may also be able to change views. For example, a user who has V1, i.e., of a set of objects bound to type Student, must change views to one in which the objects are bound to type Employee, in order to apply functions to these objects as employees. To do this the user must have in the type binding for objects in his view a function for changing their type to Employee and must, of course, also have type Employee in his view.

As another example consider the following model of spatial objects that have both a two-dimensional and a three-dimensional type binding and functions for switching between them. Assume that two- and three-dimensional objects are defined by the following types:

```
Type 2D
    Instance_fns => { Height (x: 2D) -> Integer,
                      Width (x: 2D) -> Integer,
                      Area (x: 2D) -> Integer,
                      Convert_to_3D (x: 2D) -> 3D   }

Type 3D
    Instance_fns => { Height (x: 3D) -> Integer,
                      Width (x: 3D) -> Integer,
                      Depth (x: 3D) -> Integer,
                      Volume (x: 3D) -> Integer,
                      Convert_to_2D (x: 3D) -> 2D   }
```

We have defined these two types to allow arbitrary conversion between them. This is accomplished by defining a function on the 2D type called *Convert_to_3D* and a function on the 3D type called *Convert_to_2D* . Applying one of these functions to an object of the specified type binds that object to the other type in the view. If we wanted to restrict the use of one of these objects to be through the 2D type binding only, we would construct another type which contained the functions of the above 2D type without the *Convert_to_3D* function.

In general, we can provide arbitrarily complex conversion paths among a set of n views by controlling the type-conversion functions that are embedded in types in each view. For example, it would be possible in the above case to have a 2D view in which objects could be converted to type 3D that could not be converted back to type 2D, by simply eliminating the *Convert_to_2D* function from the 3D type definition This technique can be generalized to paths between any of n views.

Notice that if an object has a different handle in its different types, view change functions, which change the binding of that object from one type to another, must provide for mapping of the handle of the object in its old type to its handle in the new type. For example, if an object is identified as a Student by its Name and Date_of_birth and as an Employee by its Social_security#, functions that change from a view of the object as a Student to a view of the object as Employee must convert from Name and Date_of_birth to Social_security#. In some cases the only way to rebind to the original type may be to save and restore the value of the object's handle in the original type.

View Derivation

New views are derived by applying functions to view definitions to derive new view definitions. Views that provide the functionality of database views may be created by user instructions to bind specific objects to types that hide some of their functions or derive new functions or objects.. Some views may be created in response to user-specified type definitions. Still others views may be created automatically by the system to achieve linguistic mechanisms such as data abstraction. Typical use of these views involves multiple views all having the same set of objects, but differing in the set of functions.

Each installation will define a base view from which all other views can be derived. One can think of the base view as the conceptual schema of the installation. View derivation functions are defined over the definition of this base view. View definitions, themselves, are objects with functions to yield their sets of types, objects and object bindings, and functions for deriving other views. However, a user can only apply such functions to view definitions that are visible to him or her (i.e., are bound to types in the user's view). These functions preserve the relationship between the set of types and the set of objects that define a view and establish the binding of specific objects in the view to specific types in the view. Notice though, that changing an object's type by applying a function of its current type does not produce a new view.

Every view definition includes the view(s) from which it was derived. This derivation function is not visible at the interface to users of the view (i.e., clients who operate in its context) or even to all users who have views that include the view definition and functions for deriving new views from it. But it is important to the definition of the view and functions that use it as the source of other views. The installation's base view definition is included as one of the sources of every other view definition.

The following rules apply to the construction of views and the binding of objects in the context of a view:

1. An object can potentially appear in many views, but each request to apply a function to the object occurs in the context of only one view at a time, i.e., the client's view.

2. A function always accesses an object by means of a particular view, i.e., the view of the function's body.

3. The binding of an object to a particular type can change by entering or exiting the body of a function. The function can define how these transformations are to be applied through the invocation of a specific function to change the object's type.

4. The view in which the client operates can be explicitly changed from the current view Vi to a new view Vj by executing a special function that changes the view. This function is part of the view Vi.

5. Applying functions available within the view to change an object's type does not produce a new view. Applying functions to view definitions in a view in which such definitions and functions are available, does produce a new view.

6. It must be possible to place constraints on the legal views in a system in order to achieve desired disciplines (e.g., data abstraction).

5. Data Abstraction via Views

We will now show how this view mechanism can be used to simulate data abstraction as provided by many object-oriented languages. In our example, we will be assuming a definition of data abstraction similar to that in the programming language CLU [LG86]. We use the same view mechanism that we defined to provide the functionality that is needed by a database system to provide application-specific views. If an application uses this view mechanism in the proper way, it can achieve the advantages of both data abstraction and generalized views without any additional system features.

Consider the example of an IntegerStack data type that is implemented by (is internally represented by) an IntegerArray. Further, assume that the IntegerArray is implemented by the primitive type ByteString. We define a function Rep that identifies the type that is used to represent instances of a type. In fact, we are defining a relationship (function) between types, i.e., Rep, that indicates that instances of one type are "represented" by instances of the related type. In this example, the types would look like the following:

```
Type IntegerStack
    Rep => IntegerArray
    Instance_fns => { Push (S: IntegerStack, I: Integer),
                      Pop (S: IntegerStack) -> Integer,
                      Length (S: IntegerStack) -> Integer   }

Type IntegerArray
    Rep => ByteString
    Instance_fns => { PutAtIndex (A: IntegerArray, I: Integer),
                      GetAtIndex (A: IntegerArray, I: Integer) -> Integer.
                      Top (A: IntegerArray) -> Integer    }
Type ByteString
    Rep => Primitive
    Instance_fns => { Concat (B1: ByteString, B2: ByteString) -> ByteString,
                      Search (B: ByteString, C: Byte) -> Integer,
                      Head (B: ByteString, I: Integer) -> ByteString,
                      Tail (B: ByteString, I: Integer) -> ByteString,
                      Cardinality (B: ByteString) -> Integer      }
```

If we create an object s of type IntegerStack, the resulting object s has the functions of types IntegerStack, IntegerArray, and ByteString. That is, s has at least three types (i.e., IntegerStack, IntegerArray, and ByteString) that can be used to manipulate it. The object s represents an IntegerStack to users that are outside of the three modules defined above. Inside these modules the view of s, i.e., the binding to a particular type, will change. The way in which we control this ability for the view of s to change allows us to simulate the behavior of data abstraction.

We must also automatically create two other types and corresponding views in order to achieve the desired behavior. These types are constructed by adding one additional function to the external view of the type. This function (called *down* in CLU) provides the facility for changing views to this new internal view by binding the object to its representation type. We will now describe the way the five views are used in moving from the highest level view, IntegerStack to the lowest level view, ByteString.

Suppose that s is an instance of the IntegerStack type. The stack s will have five potential types as discussed above. From the point of view of a client outside of the IntegerStack module, the view that it uses is precisely the one defined by the type IntegerStack. When s is passed to one of the functions of the IntegerStack type such as Push, entering the function will transform the type binding of s from IntegerStack to a type that we will call InIntegerStack. InIntegerStack will have exactly the functions of the IntegerStack type plus one other called Down . The Down function corresponds to the *down* function defined for all abstract types in CLU. Executing the Down function will change the type of s from InIntegerStack to IntegerArray, thereby making all of the functions of IntegerArray available and hiding the functions in the InIntegerStack type. The Down function is, therefore, an example of an explicit rebinding from one type to another.

Another interesting feature of the Down function is that it must provide a way for the object to be rebound to the type from which it came. This is achieved by including an Up function in the IntegerArray type. This Up function will take an IntegerArray and return an object viewed as the type from which the IntegerArray type was constructed. Since many types can have IntegerArray as a representation, it must be possible to construct IntegerArray types with different Up functions to reflect the different types to which the object might be returned.

In general, an Up function in a type of IntegerArray will have the following form:

```
Up : IntegerArray -> <SourceType>
```

This implies that there are potentially many IntegerArray types, one for each type that uses IntegerArray as a representation. We will adopt the convention of naming these types as the name of the type to which we are changing the binding prefixed with the string "From<SourceType>As." In our example, we would have the type FromIntegerStackAsIntegerArray. Instances of this type would have all of the functions of the IntegerArray type plus an Up function of the following form:

```
Up : IntegerArray -> InIntegerStack
```

While we are in the IntegerStack module where the argument object is bound to the InIntegerStack type, we might execute the Down function to rebind it to the FromIntegerStackAsIntegerArray type. This type would contain the Up function that we described above. We might then call a function like PutAtIndex from the IntegerArray type. Upon entering this function, we rebind the argument object to the InIntegerArray type which includes a Down function to convert to the ByteString type

The type binding functions of these types, i.e., their Up and Down functions are summarized below:

```
IntegerStack
    Down : IntegerStack -> InIntegerStack

InIntegerStack
    Down : InIntegerStack -> FromIntegerStackAsIntegerArray
    Up : FromIntegerStackAsIntegerArray -> IntegerStack

FromInIntegerStackAsIntegerArray        //Corresponds to IntegerArray
    Down : FromInIntegerStackAsIntegerArray -> InIntegerArray
    Up : IntegerArray -> InIntegerStack

InIntegerArray
    Down : InIntegerArray -> FromIntegerArrayAsByteString
    Up : InIntegerArray -> FromIntegerStackAsIntegerArray

FromInIntegerArrayAsByteString          //Corresponds to ByteString
    Up : ByteString -> InIntegerArray
```

The one remaining piece of mechanism that is required is a way to ensure that the proper type of the object is preserved at each level as we return from calls to lower-level abstractions for rebinding of the object. To accomplish this, we have each function when exiting automatically call the Up function for each argument which has been bound to a lower-level abstract type.

Notice that in the previous example, each function must do something special on entry and exit. The argument had to be bound to an extended type on entry, and the object had to be rebound to the higher-level type by executing the Up function on exit. This idea can be generalized by associating with each function a piece of code that is called on entry and one that is called on exit. The entry code would be responsible for effecting the conversion from an external type binding to the appropriate internal type binding, and the exit code would be the place in which the Up function was called.As an example of how this might work, consider the Push operation on IntegerStack. The entry and exit code would do the following.

```
IntegerStack$Push entry procedure
    Change_type (s: Stack, "InIntegerStack")
```

```
IntegerStack$Push exit procedure
   Change_type(s:IntegerArray, "FromIntegerStackAsIntegerArray")
```

Notice that in order to achieve the proper data abstraction discipline, the use of the *Change_type* function must be controlled. We only allow this function to be invoked in an entry procedure. We further restrict the value that is acceptable for the second argument. In the example above, the second argument must be precisely "InIntegerStack". For the most part, the entry and exit procedures can be generated automatically by the system.

Also, if IntegerStack$Push needed to use IntegerStack$Pop within its body, a rebinding of the stack object might be required. The Push function could have bound the stack s to type FromInIntegerStackAsIntegerArray. In order to call the Pop function on s, an explicit conversion back to the IntegerStack type would be required. This would be done explicitly by the code in the function body.

In order to support data abstraction, the following constraints are required:

1. The only way to bind objects to their internal representation types is to enter (i.e., to begin execution of the procedure for) a specific function.

2. Entering any function in a group of functions (i.e., the operations for the data abstraction) will always produce the same type bindings.

3. Entering and leaving a function will always produce the proper lower- and higher-level type bindings.

6. Inheritance via Views

In the last section we described a relationship between types, namely **representation** (Rep) which can be modeled using the FUGUE view mechanism. In this section we show how another relationship among types, namely **Is_a** can be modeled using the same mechanism.

In models that support generalization, the specification

t2 **Is_a** t1

where t1 and t2 are types implies that instances of t2 *are substitutable for* instances of t1. When types form a hierarchy based on the Is_a relationship, then instances of a type t are substitutable for any instances of types in the path to t that are higher in the hierarchy. In functional models, this means that any function that can be applied to instances of t1 can always be applied to instances of t2.

For example, suppose we have the following type definitions:

```
type Vehicle
    Instance_fns => { Max_speed,
                      Medium,
                      Max_load  }
type Car
Is_a Vehicle
    Instance_fns => { Cornering_rating,
                      MPG_city,
                      MPG_highway  }
type Toyota
Is_a Car
    Instance_fns => { Import_fee,
                      Special_seatbelts?  }
```

All Instance_fns of Vehicle can be applied to instances of Car and all Instance_fns of both Vehicle and Car can be applied to instances of Toyota.

In FUGUE, application of the function

```
Create_instance(Toyota)
```

yields an object o whose conceptual type includes

```
{ Instance_fns(Vehicle)  U  Instance_fns(Car)  U  Instance_fns(Toyota) }
```

and o is automatically a member of Extent(Vehicle), Extent(Car), and Extent(Toyota).The object o has at least three additional type views from the types Vehicle, Car, and Toyota. When viewed as a Vehicle, o can have applied to it functions of Vehicle but the functions of Car and Toyota are hidden. Note that each of the views derived from the types of o might include functions for changing among the type views as well. Dealing with the problems of allowing types of objects to change is beyond the scope of this paper. ([Zd87] deals with these problems.) Other views that combine functions from various views can be defined, as well, but these three, as well as the conceptual type, can be generated automatically from the specification of the Is_a relationship among the types.

Consider the following piece of code:

```
function  f(c:car)
function  g(t:Toyota)

t := Create(Toyota);
    g(t);
    f(t);
```

The call to g with argument t passes t to a function via a formal parameter of type Toyota. That is, t is bound to type Toyota in g's view. In contrast, the call to f with argument t passes t to a function via a formal parameter of type Car. Function f, then, has a view of t (which is in fact a Toyota) as a car. Inside the body of f, we can only apply Car functions to the object t.

In typed languages with inheritance, assignment of objects to variables or formal parameters is the same as changing types. Notice that assigning objects of a more specific type to a variable of a less specific view allows for static type-checking. If we wish to allow assignment of objects that are being treated as a less specific type to a variable of a more specific type, we must perform dynamic (run-time) type-checking.

Objects can be defined to be instances of multiple types that are not related by Is_a. In this case, the conceptual type of the objects includes all functions from the immediate types (the types specified when the object was created or to which it was explicitly assigned) of the objects as well as all of the functions in the paths to the immediate types from the Is_a hierarchy. No conflict can arise in inheritance from multiple types because the functions in Instance_fns of a type are uniquely identified by their object handles and the function set of the conceptual type is formed by the set union of Instance_fns from each type. For example, suppose we add to the type definitions above the following definition:

```
type Possession
    Instance_fns => { Value,
    Acquisition_date  }
```

and we apply the following function:

```
Create(Toyota, Possession) -> o1
```

Object o1 automatically has the types of Vehicle, Car, Toyota and Possession, as well as a conceptual view that includes the functions of all of them. From the conceptual type (or any other type) additional types can be defined. For example:

```
type V1
    Instance_fns => { Max_speed,
                      Value          }
```

Function Subtypes

Functions, as objects, have types and can participate in generalization (Is_a) hierarchies, as well. Instances of a type of function "inherit" functions of the supertypes in the same way as other objects do. For example, we might have the following type definitions:

```
type Function
    Instance_fns => {       Input_args,
                            Output_args,
                            Body,
                            ...             }

type Optimizable_fn
    Is_a Function
        Instance_fns => {   Timing_estimate,
                            Algebraic_properties,
                            Recursive?,
                            ...                     }
```

The conceptual type of instances of Optimizable_fn will include Instance_fns of both Function and Optimizable_fn. [Note that the Is_a relationship among function types implies constraints on the domains and ranges of instances of the types that are not discussed here.]

7. Function Views

Since functions are objects in FUGUE, they have types to which they can be bound in various views. Views of functions allow us to hide their implementations except from limited system functions, such as those that support function application, while exposing their interfaces to application programs. For example, for a function f, functions like Apply(f), Domain(f), or

Range(f) may be invokable by application programs, whereas functions like Run_time_estimate(f) might be available only to an optimizer function and Body(f) may be available only to functions that derive new functions from f or only to Apply(f).

In essence, views of functions can provide the needed mechanism to allow for access to functions at arbitrary levels of encapsulation. In addition, they can provide other useful abstractions for defining the semantics of new functions as derived from existing functions.

Three views of functions seem particularly useful: an *external* view, in which the function is bound to a type which (partially) specifies the semantics of the function in terms of its signature and pre- and post-conditions; an *implementation* view, which binds the function to a type that specifies the function semantics in terms of the procedure that is invoked to apply it; and a *relational* view, which binds the function to a type that specifies the function semantics in terms of a table of mappings from input arguments to output arguments that the function expresses. Each is described in more detail below.

External View

This type binding of a function might be to a type that includes, for example, functions:

```
Selector -> string
Input_args -> {label / type}       /*the domain
Output_args -> {label / type}      /*the range
Pre_conditions -> {condition}
Post_conditions -> {condition}
Apply -> {}                        /*possibly yields completion codes
```

This view allows the function to be invoked by other functions (or itself) and to determine, for example, the types of the arguments or conditions it guarantees. In general, this is the type to which functions are bound in the views in which all functions (except system functions that perform compilation and execution and derivie new functions) operate.

Implementation View

This type binding of a function might be to a type that includes, for example, functions:

```
Body -> procedure
Language -> programming_lang
Parameters -> {(label,type)}
Hardware_requirements ->
Entry -> {functions}               /*including Change_type*/
Exit -> {functions}
Create_instance -> process
```

This view is seen by the Apply function, as well as other system functions that actually invoke the procedure that implements the function. It provides information needed for compilation and for creating and tracking processes that execute the body of the function. It also includes functions for changing types (to and from the representation types of objects which the procedure accesses, i.e., Down and Up) at entry and exit from the execution of the procedure.

Relational View

Functions can also be thought of as relations that express mappings from input arguments to output arguments, as they are viewed in the PROBE Data Model (PDM) [Ma86]. That is, every function is describable (at least conceptually) by a table in which each row represents a mapping between corresponding input and output values and the columns represent the specific combinations of input and output argument values for which the function is defined. Note that this is true whether the function is intensionally- or extensionally-defined. Though this relation may not be manifest for all functions (e.g., where the domain is an infinite set like the integers) it is sometimes a useful way to view a function. For example the Addition function for positive integers might be represented by the table:

in	in	out
1	1	2
1	2	3
1	3	4
.	.	.
2	1	3
2	2	4
.	.	.

This is the view of the function as a relation that expresses the function mapping. The relation need not be materializable for the view to exist. It is defined in terms of the types and constraints on the arguments. This type binding of the function might be to a type that includes, for example, the functions:

```
Columns -> {type, constraint}
Select(c:condition)-> function
Project(l:column_list) -> function
Join(f: function) -> function
...
```

This type allows the derivation of new functions from existing functions by specifying the semantics of the new functions in terms of relational and set operators applied to functions as relations. The functions that yield a new function, in essence, generate the information needed to generate the functions of the function's other types from the definitions of the input functions, e.g., they produce an appropriate Signature and Body for the new function

The ability to define views of functions and to assign them to the internal functions of the system helps to make reflexivity in systems for function application feasible. That is, it contributes needed control mechanisms for systems where the support for applying functions is implemented as a set of functions (or functionals) which are, themselves, applied, (e.g., functions that create processes, which are treated as instances of functions. The view mechanism controls function visibility (i.e., provides both abstraction and access control), which makes the self-referencing structure manageable.

8. Conclusions

We have presented a simple view mechanism that fits well with our functional data model. It is extremely uniform in that a view is defined by binding objects to types that define collections of functions. These functions can be applied to manipulate objects in an environment in which everything is characterized by functions.

The paper has discussed several examples that demonstrate how the concepts of data abstraction, inheritance, and standard database views can all be related with this single uniform mechanism. We believe that these examples have illustrated some interesting relationships between all of these concepts. They all have to do with controlling visibility, and can therefore be expressed in terms of views which are designed for precisely that purpose.

We have further shown how all of these ideas could be implemented in a single system with a minimum of underlying support. If the proper view mechanism is constructed first, the other features can be built on top of this layer.

References

[Bl88] Blaustein, B., "On Object Identifiers", EIS project working paper, Computer Corporation of America, 1988.

[GR83] Goldberg,A. and D. Robson, "Smalltalk-80, The Language and Its Implementation," Addison-Wesley, 1983.

[HZ88] Heiler S. and S. Zdonik, "FUGUE: A Model for Engineering Information Systems and Other Baroque Applications," Proceedings of the 3rd International Conference on Data and Knowledge Bases, Jerusalem, June, 1988.

[LG86] Liskov, B. and J. Guttag, **Abstraction and Specification in Program Development**, MIT Press, Cambridge, MA, 1986.

[LW86] Linn, J. and R. Winner, "Department of Defense Requirements for Engineering Information Systems,", Institute for Defense Analyses, Arlington, VA, 1986.

[Ma87] Manola, F., "PDM: An Object-Oriented Data Model ," Proceedings of the International Workshop on Object-Oriented Database Systems, September, 1986.

[Sh81] Shipman, D., "The Functional Model and the Data Language DAPLEX," ACM Transactions on Database Systems, March, 1981.

[Wi86] Wiederhold, G., "Views, Objects, and Databases," IEEE Computer, December, 1986.

[Zd87] Zdonik, S., "Can Objects Change Type? Can Type Objects Change?," Proceedings of the Workshop on Database Programming Languages, Roscoff, France, Sept., 1987.

VODAK KERNEL DATA MODEL

Horst Duchêne

Manfred Kaul

Volker Turau

GMD-IPSI / Institute for Integrated Publication and Information Systems
Dolivostr. 15, D-6100 Darmstadt (FRG)

ABSTRACT

At the GMD-IPSI institute integrated information and publication processing systems are developed. All projects are planned to have a common interface to a kernel data model. Conventional database systems are inadequate for the crucial role planned in this environment. They do not provide sufficient semantic modelling features, knowledge representation capabilities or flexible management tools. The semantics of applications have to be handcoded in application programs. Therefore a new generation database system supporting non standard applications efficiently is developed at our institute within the VODAK-project. The system will be based on a compactly described kernel model, that supports *complex objects*, *abstract data types*, *inheritance*, and *message passing*. Up to now there are only few approaches unifying all these features in a single model.

1. Introduction

At the GMD-IPSI institute integrated information and publication processing systems are developed. All projects are planned to have a common interface to a central kernel data model. Conventional database systems are inadequate for the crucial role planned in this environment. Therefore a *new generation database system* supporting non standard applications efficiently is developed at our institute within the VODAK-project.

The objective of the VODAK-group is to support integrated information management systems, which in turn require artificial intelligence tools, such as natural language processors, intelligent human computer interaction management, advanced information retrieval, user modelling capabilities, CAD, sophisticated knowledge navigation and expert systems. These non-standard applications pose requirements on databases which are not or only poorly supported by traditional databases such as relational databases. The main disadvantages are:

- *limited abstraction capability:* Objects that cannot be modelled directly have to be coded into normal relations, thereby potentially meaningful relationships are lost. In a relational database all relations are at the same level. Second order information about the relations cannot be managed naturally. The semantic modelling features and knowledge representation capabilities are obviously insufficient.
- *no implicit knowledge representation:* It is necessary to model relationships down to the lowest level of detail, similarities between different objects must be modelled explicitly.
- *awkward database access:* The application programming interface to the database system is generally difficult due to mismatches between the operations and objects of the database management system and the programming language.

On the other hand the main advantage of the relational model is its relative simplicity and elegance. These advantages can not be overemphasized. Management of databases includes integrity constraints, view modelling and update, security problems, distribution aspects, and complex transaction management, which all have become standard issues for the relational database approach in recent years. With the dangerous increase of apparently new features in data models all these problems have to be solved again. New problems arise with any new feature. On the other hand all projects at our institute should be served as well as possible. Therefore the we decided

- to build a kernel data model with few but powerful features, that can be handled efficiently;
- to provide any project basing on this kernel model with tools for constructing their own data model shells on top of it.

In this paper a formal model for an object-oriented database system is introduced. This model tries to overcome the above mentioned disadvantages. The characteristic features of this model are:

- *complex objects:* the model supports the creation, manipulation and access of complex objects in their entirety. Complex objects are obtained from simple ones using a set of constructors. These constructors can be nested to any depth.
- *data abstraction:* encapsulation of data and behaviour in order to protect the internal state of objects from erroneous manipulations and minimizing the impact of changes in an application: an object is incarnated as an instance of an abstract data type.
- *inheritance* is a powerful tool for logically clustering objects, centralize common properties of objects and to build reusable code: inheritance allows to apply methods to objects of different types via coercions.
- *message passing:* decentralized selection of the appropriate code by each object receiving a message on his own responsibility.

In our approach we distinguish between the database schema and the database instance in order to provide static tools, such as a type checker. Static tools are without doubt necessary for reliable large scale software management.

The encapsulation paradigm which is regarded by any object oriented approach is incorporated into our data model as follows: First, any application program which operates on the database can access the database only through specific database operations. Second, the manipulation of objects can only be done via the methods in the interface of these objects.

Recently there has been some work on formalizing an object-oriented data model ([Mey86] and[Mey87] , the SIGMOD conferences, [Day87] , [ACM87] , the VLDB conferences, [Sto87] and the conferences about data engineering, [IEE87]). Here we can only refer to the most prominent papers. E.g. in [Ric87] a theoretical formulation of a data model is presented. Our data model goes beyond their model, in that we present a more detailed framework for methods and that we allow multiple inheritance. Earlier models are presented in [Hul84] and [Abi84] and[Ban87] but these models are not truely object-oriented, since they do not incorporate methods.

Preliminaries

Before we present our definitions of types and methods we need some preliminaries. To keep the definitions as transparent as possible we introduce the following sets which serve as a resource for names of types and methods. The following sets are assumed to be disjoint:

TypeId	finite set of symbols	(type identifier)
MethId	finite set of symbols	(method identifiers)
ObjId	infinite countable set of symbols	(object identifiers or DB-keys)
Tokens	infinite countable set of symbols	(serve as labels for components of complex objects)
$\{[,], <, >, \{, \}, \uparrow, \delta\uparrow, \Delta\}$		(symbols for constructing type expressions)

If A is a finite nonempty set of symbols, then A* denotes the set of all strings with characters from A. A* contains the empty string.

2. Complex Objects

There are many application areas where the data structures are so complex that the primitive typing facilities offered by commercial databases are totally inadequate. As a consequence of this a number of database programming languages have emerged which offer general facilities for type definition (e.g. Pascal/R, Modula/R). These facilities include constructors such as set, list, tuple and recursive combination thereof. In this section we introduce and formally define the notation of type in our model.

An important requirement to complex objects is, that it should be possible to create, manipulate and access them in their entirety. Hence they must have a name to identify them uniquely. Furthermore, we must specify their syntax and semantics. The following figure illustrates our approach:

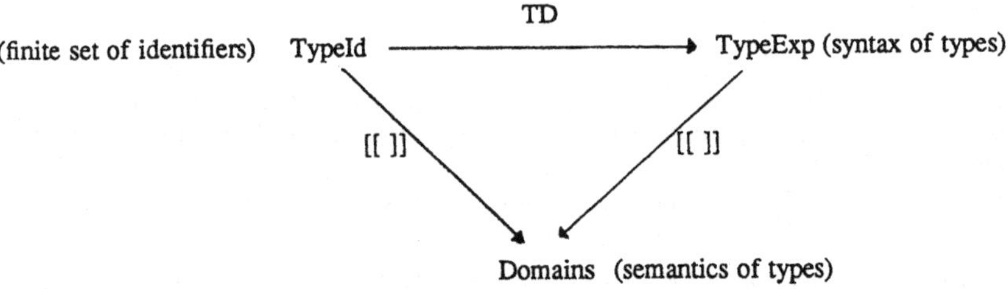

Figure 1.

The map TD assigns to each type identifier a type expression, which represents the syntax of this type. The map [[ ]] from TypeExp to Domains associates with each type expression a domain. An instance of a TypeExp and hence of a type identifier (via TD) will be an element of the associated domain. The definition of TypeExp is inductive. We assume the existence of predefined types (primitive types) and their corresponding methods (primitive methods). These are described in the following section.

2.1. Predefined types and preimplemented methods

To construct more complex types and methods we assume predefined types and preimplemented methods, which can be applied to objects of these types and to components of complex types. We do not develop a new programming language, we rather build a layer on top of a conventional programming language. Thus we assume that our programming language provides some types and the corresponding methods. Examples are:

PrimTypeId	**PrimMethId**
int	+,-,*,<,=
bool	and, or, not
char	≥
string	concat

All primitive methods are in the *interface* of the corresponding primitive types (section 3.4). Let PrimTypeId (PrimMethId) the subset of TypeId (MethId) which denotes the preimplemented types (preimplemented methods). To each primitive TypeId $p \in$ PrimTypeId we assign a predefined domain of values which we denote [[p]]. In addition we assume a distinguished element $\perp$, called *bottom* to element of every primitive domain. For example we have $[[int]] = Z \cup \{\perp\}$, where Z denotes the set of integers.

Every primitive method has a fixed functionality given by the following partial mapping with finite carrier:

PrimMeth: PrimTypeId × PrimMethId → PrimTypeId* × PrimeTypeId
(t,m) → $(t_1 \dots t_s, t')$

Note:

(i) The carrier of PrimMeth is denoted PrimMeths.

(ii) Instead of (t,m) ∈ PrimMeths we also write m_t.

(iii) If PrimMeth (t,m) = $(t_1 \dots t_s, t')$, $s \geq 0$, then dom(t,m) := $t_1 \dots t_s$ and codom(t,m): = t'.

The purpose of the mapping PrimMeth is to group together method symbols to types, allowing one method symbol to be assigned to more than one type (overloading).

Let Pfn(A,B) denote the set of all partial functions from the set A to the set B. Then we have the following predefined interpretation of the primitive methods:

If (t,m) ∈ PrimMeths then [[(t,m)]] ∈ Pfn([[dom(t,m)]],[[codom(t,m)]]). Here $[[t_1 \dots t_s]]$ is defined by $[[t_1]] \times \dots \times [[t_s]]$ which denotes the cartesian product.

2.2. Type Expressions

In the sequel we shall present the syntax of types (type expressions). Complex types can be build from the above defined primitive types via tuple, set and disjoint union constructors. Furthermore, a mechanism for type substitution and reference to a type is provided. In the following type expressions are defined precisely.

Definition 1:

The set TypeExp of type expressions (over Tokens and TypeId) is defined inductively as follows:

(i) p ∈ TypeExp, if p ∈ PrimTypeId (*primitive type*);

(ii) ↑t ∈ TypeExp, if t ∈ TypeId (*independent pointer type*);

(iii) δ↑t ∈ TypeExp, if t ∈ TypeId (*dependent pointer type*);

(iv) Δt ∈ TypeExp, if t ∈ TypeId (*substitution type*);

(v) $[k_1 : \tau_1, \dots, k_n : \tau_n]$ ∈ TypeExp, if $\tau_1, \dots, \tau_n$ ∈ TypeExp, $n \geq 2$ and $k_1, \dots, k_n$ are pairwise different tokens (*tuple type*);

(vi) $\langle k_1 : \tau_1, \dots, k_n : \tau_n \rangle$ ∈ TypeExp, if $\tau_1, \dots, \tau_n$ ∈ TypeExp, $n \geq 2$ and $k_1, \dots, k_n$ are pairwise different tokens (*disjoint union type*);

(vii) {τ} ∈ TypeExp, if τ ∈ TypeExp (*set type*).

Note that we do not exclude recursion in the definition for TypeExp.

Example 1:

In the following examples we demonstrate how our concepts could be applied to the storage and retrieval of large structured documents.

The basic ideas for document representation and management are taken from the office document interchange format ODIF ([Hor85]) which is becoming a standard for office documents. In ODIF the logical structure of an office document, that is the division into chapters and paragraphs can be specified and physical layout is computed from this specification by some typesetting system such as TEX ([Knu86]). In our example parts of both logical and physical structure are represented. We have chosen those parts that illustrate the important features most concisely.

In the following tokens start with lowercase letters and type identifiers with uppercase letters. Comments start in each line with /*.

/* A document consists of a front, body and rear part. From the
/* logical specification the physical pages are computed by the TEX
/* system.

```
TD(Document)     = [   contents :
                       [ front  :      Δ Chapter,
                         body   :      { ↑ Chapter } ,
                         rear   :      Δ Chapter
                       ] ,
                       pages    :      { ↑ Page }          ]

TD(DocPart)      = [   att :
                       <      local :  Δ Attributes ,
                              global:  ↑ Attributes
                       > ,    /* note the difference between Δ and ↑
                       no       :      Integer             ]

TD(Attributes)   = [   font     :      Integer ,
                       style    :      Integer ,
                       statistics :
                       [ no     :      Integer ,
                         average :     Integer ,
                         ...
                                ]                ]


TD(Chapter)      = [   info     :      Δ DocPart ,
                       contents :      { δ ↑ Paragraph } ]

TD(Paragraph)    = [   info     :      Δ DocPart ,
                       contents :      String              ]

TD(Box)          = [   x,y      : Integer ,                /* relative coordinates
                                                           /* within the enclosing box
                                                           /* left lower corner
                       xlength, ylength :  Integer ,  /* width of box
                       <      refinement          :        { δ ↑ Box } , /* inner boxes
                              final                        :        Δ Code /* no inner boxes
                       >                ]

TD(Page)         = [   info     :      Δ Box ,
                       pageno   :      Integer             ]

TD(Figure)       = [   box      :      Δ Box ,
                       docpart  :      Δ DocPart ,
                       figno    :      Integer             ]

TD(Refs)         = {   Δ Ref    }
```

```
TD(Ref)         = [   no         : Integer ,
                      <          figRef    :      Δ FigRef ,
                                 indexRef  :      Δ IndexTerm ,
                                 bibRef    :      Δ BibRef
                      >                                        ]

TD(FigRef)      = [   no         :      Integer ,
                      ref        :      ↑ Figure               ]

TD(FigRefs)     = {   Δ FigRef }

TD(BibRef)      = [   no         :      Integer ,
                      descriptors :
                      [          authors   :      { String } ,
                                 title     :      String ,
                                 publisher :      String ,
                                 year      :      Integer          ]]

TD(BibRefs)     = {   Δ BibRef }

TD(Code)        = <   postscript:       Δ Postscript ,
                      bitmap                   :       Δ BitMap
                  >

TD(Postscript)  =     String

TD(BitMap)      =     String
```

Next, we give a precise definition of the above mentioned mapping TD.

Definition 2:

A *type definition* (for TypeId) is a total mapping

$$TD : TypeId \rightarrow TypeExp$$

such that the below defined directed graph TDG (*Type Definition Graph*) is acyclic.

If $V = TypeId \cup TD(TypeId)$ and $E = \{(t,TD(t)) \mid t \in TypeId\} \cup \{(\tau , t) \mid \tau \in TD(TypeId)$ such that Δt is a terminal symbol of τ $\}$

then TDG is defined as the directed graph with vertices V and edges E. If $\tau = TD(t)$ we also write $t : \tau$.

The definition of TD allows that two different type identifiers can refer to the same type expression. Thus, TD is not necessarily injective. Furthermore, TD is not surjective since there is a infinite number of type expressions. The motivation of the symbols $\delta\uparrow$ and $\uparrow$ is to have a facility to express that a given object of type t points to another object of a possible different type. This allows to model shared objects, inter and intra object relationships and to build recursive data structures. We introduced two different pointer types to allow different update constrains for $\delta\uparrow$ and $\uparrow$ (see chapter 4).

Example 2:

The type definition graph of example 1 is TDG = (V,E) with the following sets V and E: V = {Document, DocPart, Attributes, ...} ∪ PrimTypeId ∪ the set of all type expressions occurring in example 1. E = {(BitMap, String), (Postscript, String), ...} ∪ {([info: Δ DocPart, contents: { δ↑ Paragraph }], DocPart), ([info: Δ DocPart, contents: String], DocPart), ...}.

δ↑ is used in TD(Chapter) to express that all paragraphs of a chapter are deleted if the enclosing chapter is deleted. ↑ Chapter is used in TD(Document) to express that chapters may be stored without assignment to any documents.

With the symbol Δ in a type expression we allow the possibility to build up complex type expressions from already defined ones. The main idea is to substitute Δt by TD(t). This substitution process stops since the TDG is acyclic.

2.3. Domains.

Now we shall define the semantics of the type expressions. We shall associate with each type expression a set, the domain of the type expression. Since type expressions are defined recursively we shall define the domains also recursively.

Definition 3:

Let $\tau \in$ TypeExp, then the domain $[[\tau]]$ of τ is defined as follows:

(i) [[p]], if p ∈ PrimTypeId (see section 2.1);

(ii) [[↑t]] = ObjId, if t ∈ TypeId;

(iii) [[δ↑t]] = ObjId, if t ∈ TypeId;

(iv) [[Δt]] = [[TD(t)]], if t ∈ TypeId;

(v) $[[\ [k_1 : \tau_1, \dots ,k_n : \tau_n]\ ]] = (\{k_1\} \times [[\tau_1]]) \times \dots \times (\{k_n\} \times [[\tau_n]])$, if $\tau_i \in$ TypeExp and $k_i \in$ Tokens;

(vi) $[[\ \langle k_1 : \tau_1, \dots ,k_n : \tau_n\rangle\ ]] = \{k_1\} \times [[\tau_1]] \cup \dots \cup \{k_n\} \times [[\tau_n]]$, if $\tau_i \in$ TypeExp and $k_i \in$ Tokens;

(vii) $[[\{\tau\}]] = P_{fin}([[\tau]])$, if $\tau \in$ TypeExp and k ∈ Tokens.

In addition we assume that every domain of a type expression contains a distinguished element ⊥, called bottom. (In the above definition $P_{fin}([[\tau]])$ denotes the set of all finite subsets of $[[\tau]]$.)

Example 3:

Let [[Integer]] = integer and [[String]] = string be the usual domains of integers and strings. The domain of BibRef in example 1 is:

```
[[BibRef]] = (( {no} × integer )
             × ( {descriptors}
                  × ( {authors} × P_fin(string) )
                  × ( {title}    × string )
                  × ( {publisher} × string )
                  × ( {year}     × integer )
               )
           )
```

2.4. Inheritance.

In this section we shall define an inheritance relationship between types. We shall use this inheritance mechanism to inherit methods. To give precise semantics, we need the following definition.

Definition 4:

(i) Let $\tau = [k_1 : \tau_1, \ldots, k_n : \tau_n]$, $\tau' = [k_{i_1} : \tau_{i_1}, \ldots, k_{i_m} : \tau_{i_m}]$ be type expressions such that $\{i_1, \ldots, i_m\} \subseteq \{1, \ldots, n\}$, $1 \le i_j \le n$. Then $c_{\tau,\tau'}$ denotes the mapping:

$$c_{\tau,\tau'}: \quad [[\tau]] \rightarrow [[\tau']]$$
$$(k_1 : x_1, \ldots, k_n : x_n) \rightarrow (k_{i_1} : x_{i_1}, \ldots, k_{i_m} : x_{i_m})$$

where $x_i \in [[\tau_i]]$. $c_{\tau,\tau'}$ is called a *projection*.

(ii) Let $\tau = \langle k_1 : \tau_1, \ldots, k_n : \tau_n \rangle$, $\tau' = \langle k_{i_1} : \tau_{i_1}, \ldots, k_{i_m} : \tau_{i_m} \rangle$ be type expressions $\{i_1, \ldots, i_m\} \subseteq \{1, \ldots, n\}$, $1 \le i_j \le n$. Then $c_{\tau',\tau}$ denotes the mapping:

$$c_{\tau',\tau}: \quad [[\tau']] \rightarrow [[\tau]]$$
$$k_{i_j} : x_{i_j} \rightarrow k_{i_j} : x_{i_j}$$

where $x_{i_j} \in [[\tau_{i_j}]]$. $c_{\tau',\tau}$ is called an *embedding*.

(iii) Let $\tau = \{ \sigma \}$ and $\tau' = \{ \sigma' \}$ be type expressions and let $c_{\sigma,\sigma'}$ be already defined. Then $c_{\tau,\tau'}$ denotes the mapping:

$$c_{\tau,\tau'}: \quad [[\tau]] \rightarrow [[\tau']]$$
$$\{x_1, \ldots, x_n\} \rightarrow \{c_{\sigma,\sigma'}(x_1), \ldots, c_{\sigma,\sigma'}(x_n)\}$$

where $x_i \in [[\sigma]]$. $c_{\tau,\tau'}$ is called an *extension*.

(iv) Let t,s $\in$ TypeId, then $c_{\uparrow t,\uparrow s}$ denotes the mapping:

$$c_{\uparrow t,\uparrow s}: \quad \text{ObjId} \rightarrow \text{ObjId}$$
$$x \rightarrow x$$

and $c_{\delta\uparrow t,\delta\uparrow s}$ denotes the mapping:

$$c_{\delta\uparrow t,\delta\uparrow s}: \quad \text{ObjId} \rightarrow \text{ObjId}$$
$$x \rightarrow x$$

where $c_{\uparrow t,\uparrow s}$ and $c_{\delta\uparrow t,\delta\uparrow s}$ are both called *identity*.

(v) Let s,t $\in$ TypeId, then $c_{\Delta t,\Delta s} = c_{TD(t),TD(s)}$.

The above defined mappings are called *coercions*.

Example 4:

Some coercions occurring in example 1 are as follows:

(i) *projection*: There is a projection from TD(Page) to TD(Box) $c_{Page,Box}$, that simply deletes the component pageno : Integer.

(ii) *embedding*: There is an embedding from TD(BitMap) to TD(Code) $c_{BitMap,Code}$, that simply keeps the value string unchanged, but changes the type.

(iii) *extension*: $c_{BibRefs,Refs}$ is an extension from TD(BibRefs) = {Δ BibRef} to TD(Refs) = {Δ Ref}.

Now we shall define an ISA-relationship, i.e. a subtyping relation among types. ISA-relationships are defined by the user. Our definition differs from the one originally proposed by L. Cardelli in [Car84] in that we offer several different supertype-subtype relations between two types. To define an ISA-relationship it is necessary to select one of these possibilities. This is done by choosing a coercion from one type to the other.

Definition 5:

ISA is an acyclic graph where the vertices are from the set TypeID and each edge (s,t) is labelled with a map $c_{s,t}$: [[TD(s)]] ---> [[TD(t)]]. The map $c_{s,t}$ must be a combination of coercions as defined in Definition 4. A type s is called a *subtype* of a type t iff there are types $t_1, \dots, t_n$, $n \geq 2$, such that $s = t_1$, $t = t_n$ and $(t_i, t_{i+1}) \in$ ISA for i = 1, ... ,n-1. If n = 2 then s is called *direct subtype* of t. In case s is subtype of t, t is also called *supertype* of s.

Since we defined coercions only between certain types, ISA-relationships cannot exist between arbitrary types.

Example 5:

Consider e.g. the type definitions for type identifiers r,s and t as follows: TD(r) = [a:Boolean, b:Integer], TD(s) = Boolean, TD(t) = < a:Boolean, b:Integer >. The ISA-relationship is given by r ISA s ISA t. Then both coercions c_1 and c_2 defined as follows are possible: c_1 and c_2 map r to t. c_1 maps to the first component a:Boolean and c_2 to the second component b:Integer. Because of this ambiguity it is necessary to select one of both possibilities. The coercion $c_{r,t}$ is demanded to be part of the DB-schema.

In example 1 we can define the following ISA-relationships:

1. by tuple extension

Chapter	ISA	DocPart
Paragraph	ISA	DocPart
Figure	ISA	DocPart
Page	ISA	Box
Figure	ISA	Box

2. by disjoint union

FigRef	ISA	Ref
BibRef	ISA	Ref
Postscript	ISA	Code
BitMap	ISA	Code

3. by set extension

FigRefs	ISA	Refs
BibRefs	ISA	Refs

Note that Figure has two different supertypes (*multiple inheritance*).

3. Methods

A main feature of object-oriented approaches is the encapsulation of type structures together with their methods. Any information about an instance can be retrieved via the interface only, thereby protecting the internal data from illegal access. Private and public data can easily be kept apart. Any manipulation has to be mediated through the interface, thus protecting the internal data from erroneous manipulations and minimizing the impact of changes during database schema evolution.

Two kinds of methods are distinguished: Methods that change the database state and methods that use non persistent storage only. The first kind is discussed in chapter 4. The second kind is discussed within this chapter.

The methods are implemented in some programming language *P*, that we do not want to fix here. We only demand the following features:

- *universal computational power:* any computable function should be programmable; typical control structures such as *if then else, while, for* etc. can be used to build programs;
- *support of the typical primitive types and methods:* integer, boolean, string etc. with typical primitive methods such as addition, comparison, concatenation, coercions between primitive types etc.
- *support of arbitrarily complex user defined types:* from primitive types arbitrarily complex types can be defined and used as function parameter type and function value type; type checking is supported by the compiler for *P*;
- *support of generic methods:* methods for sets with arbitrary element type and methods for tuples with arbitrary component types are available;

No matter which programming language is chosen, the signature (that is the type structure of domain and codomain) of each method is represented within our data model. The formalism for representing signatures is the only interface between the method language and the data model and is given in the next section.

3.1. Signature of methods

Identifiers for types, methods and programs are all related by the following diagram:

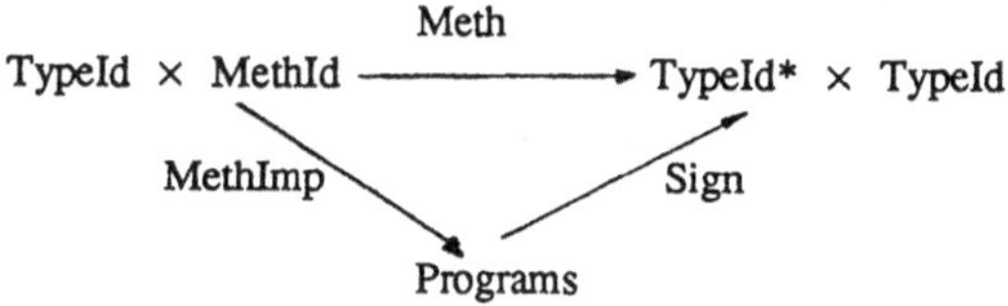

Figure 2. Relating type identifiers, method identifiers and programs

A method is identified by a pair (t,m) $\in$ TypeId × MethId. t is the type identifier and m the method identifier. t is called *type of interest* for m. A method identifier m can have different types of interest, thus yielding some kind of polymorphism concerning method identifiers. Programs denote the set of all programs of the chosen programming language *P*. *Meth* and *MethImp* are partial mappings with finite domain, which are called *Methods* and *ImpMethods* respectively. ImpMethods is a subset of Methods and subsumes all methods implemented directly at the type. A method which is supposed to be implemented at any type t is the method (t,make) which creates a nonpersistent instance of type t . Persistent instances can only be created by DB-methods, cf. section 4.3. A method (t,m) $\in$ ImpMethods is implemented by a program p = MethImp(t,m) and computes a partial mapping with signature Sign(p) = Meth(t,m). The signature is usually written $(t_1 \ldots t_n, t')$ or $t_1 \times \ldots \times t_n \rightarrow t'$, where $t_1, \ldots, t_n$ are the types of the arguments and t' is the type of the function value. Note that TypeId* denotes a string of type identifiers of arbitrary length.

Interface(t) is the subset of *Methods* containing all pairs (t,m) with first component t. The elements of *Interface(t)* can be devided into two different kinds of methods: All pairs (t,m) which are in ImpMethods are implemented directly at the type t. All pairs (t,m) $\in$ *Interface(t)* which are not in ImpMethods inherit their implementation by some supertype of t.

Example 6:

Due to our space limitations we cannot give the interfaces of all types of our example 1. Instead let us consider the types Page and Box for example. The interfaces of Box and Page are given as follows: Interface(Box) = {(Box,make), (Box,move), (Box,stretch)}, Interface(Page) = {(Page,make), (Page,stretch), (Page,PageNo)}. The signature of some of these methods is given in the following. The make-methods are used to create objects of a type Box or Page. The values of all components of Box and Page have to be given as input parameters of the method: (Box,make) : Integer × Integer × Integer × Integer × (P_{fin}(ObjId) + String) → Box, (Page,make) : Integer × Integer × Integer × Integer × (P_{fin}(ObjId) + String) × Integer → Page, where + denotes the disjoint union. Note that Page has a further component pageno. Therefore a further input parameter of type Integer is required for (Page,make). make is a method in the interface of both Box and Page. Therefore (Page,make) is called a reimplemented method.

The stretch-method is used to modify the x-length and/or y-length of a Box or Page. Because the method simply modifies the values of the components xlength, ylength within Box, the same procedure can be used for Box and Page as well. Thus (Page,stretch) is not an implemented method (i.e. it is not in ImpMethods), but an inherited method.

3.2. Inheritance of methods

Let ISA be the acyclic graph introduced in definition 5 and let (t,s) be an edge of ISA. The interpretation of this edge is that s is a *supertype* of t. Synonymeously we can say that t is a refinement of s (structural inheritance), or that the instances of t form a subset of the instances of s (modelling the inclusion dependency), or that instances of t have at least the behavioural possibilities of s (behavioural inheritance). In this chapter we are interested mainly in the latter kind of inheritance.

Definition 6:

If (t,s) ∈ ISA and (s,m) ∈ Interface(s) then we demand (t,m) ∈ Interface(t). If (t,m) ∈ Interface(t) \ ImpMethods then t must have a supertype s such that (s,m) ∈ ImpMethods. (t,m) is called a method *inherited* from s.

The situation that t has several supertypes $s_1,\ldots,s_n$, $n \leq 2$, where m is implemented, is called *multiple inheritance* and discussed in section 3.5 in more detail.

Example 7:

In example 1 the type Figure has two supertypes Box and DocPart, because Figure can simultaneously be considered as a physical Box with some Postscript code and as a logical unit called DocPart.

The inherited methods for Figure are twofold: First, the methods inherited from Box, e.g. stretch, move, concern the physical properties of Figure. Second, the methods inherited from DocPart, e.g. ChangeFont, ChangeStyle concern the logical specification of Figure as a document part.

Note that we do not pose any restriction on the signature of inherited methods. This is because *reimplementation* of inherited methods should be allowed, which is the case when the inherited method (t,m) is element of ImpMethods. Then the mapping MethImp assigns a new program to (t,m), which might have a completely different signature than (s,m).

3.3. Programs implementing Methods

Syntax and semantics are not given completely but only the relevant features are discussed here. Programs are built upon predefined and preimplemented methods, which are

- primitive methods
- generic methods
- coercions

By well-known programming language constructs, such as *if then else, case, while, for,* .. arbitrarily complex programs are supposed to be constructable.

Primitive methods are already discussed in chapter 2.1. Coercions are given in 2.4. A generic methods is e.g. the test for equality $(t,=) : t \times t \rightarrow boolean$, which is assumed to be available for any type t. Furthermore generic methods are needed to handle the types constructed as sets or tuples.

3.3.1. Set Methods

Let $TD(t_1) = \sigma$ and $TD(t_2) = \{ \sigma \}$ be type definitions. Then the following set methods are supposed to be available for t:

isempty: $t_2 \rightarrow$ boolean
iselem : $t_1 \times t_2 \rightarrow$ boolean
before : $t_1 \times t_1 \rightarrow$ boolean
choose : $t_2 \rightarrow t_1$

emptyset: $\rightarrow t_2$
insert : $t_1 \times t_2 \rightarrow t_2$
delete : $t_1 \times t_2 \rightarrow t_2$

Note that ordered sets are used. The linear ordering is given by the predicate *before. choose* is supposed to return the first element. *insert* puts the new element at the end of the linear ordered set.

Example 8:

In example 1 we have TD(Refs) = { Δ Ref } which denotes a set of references. By the help of set methods new references can be inserted into the set and old ones can be deleted.

Note that the ordered set is organized as a queue. The ordering of the set is necessary for clean semantics of the *choose*-function ([Ste86]).

3.3.2. Tuple Methods

Let $TD(t) = [k_1{:}\tau_1, \ldots, k_n{:}\tau_n]$, $n \geq 1$ be a type definition. The following tuple methods are supposed to be available for t:

make : $\tau_1 \times \ldots \times \tau_n \rightarrow t$

$sel_{[k_i]}$: $t \rightarrow \tau_i$, $1 \leq i \leq n$

make constructs a tuple from the components. $sel_{[k_i]}$ selects the component labelled by k_i.

Example 9:

Consider the type definition of Document in example 1. By $sel_{[front]}sel_{[contents]}(d)$, where d is an object of type Document, the chapter constituing the front page may be selected.

3.4. Encapsulation of objects

Information about an object of type t may be retrieved only through the interface of t. An object of type t may be manipulated only by methods from *Interface(t)*.

Encapsulation can be checked statically by inspecting the method definitions only. The check rules are implicitly given by the following definition:

Definition 7:

Let $t_1,...,t_n \in$ TypeId, $n \geq 1$, be all types occurring in the type definition of $t \in$ TypeId. Let $(t,m) \in$ Imp-Methods and p = MethImp(t,m) the program implementing (t,m).

Let $Sign(p) = (s_1...s_{k-1},s_k)$, $k \geq 1$, be the signature of p.

p *regards the encapsulation paradigm* iff all methods used in p are one of the following or from the following sets:

(i) (t,make)

(ii) Interface(t_i) , if $t \neq t_i$, $1 \leq i \leq n$

(iii) Interface(s_j) , if $t \neq s_j$, $1 \leq j \leq k$

(iv) Interface(d) , if d is a supertype of t

(v) Interface(d) , if d is a subtype of t and t is a disjoint union type (*upward inheritance*)

(vi) any coercion $c_{t,d}$, if d is a supertype of t

(vii) generic methods (a) allowing access to any type t' and (b) manipulating any type t' only, that are directly represented in the type definition of t, that is $\Delta t'$ or $\uparrow t'$ is part of the type expression TD(t).

Definition 8:

Let $t_1,...,t_n \in$ TypeId, $n \geq 1$, be all types occurring in the type definition of $t \in$ TypeId.

t_i, $1 \leq i \leq n$ is a *public* component of t, if there is a method (t,m_i) in the interface of t, by which the information about t_i can be retrieved. Otherwise t_i is called *private.*

Example 10:

Consider the type definition TD(t) = [a:Boolean,b:Integer]. Let (t,get_a) $\in$ Interface(t), but (t,get_b) be undefined. Here, get_a provides the actual value of the component a. The only possibility to access a is to use get_a. Then a is called a public component, whereas b is called a private component.

Note that we have already defined the interface of primitive types in chapter 2. Because the type definition graph TDG (see def. 2) is acyclic, the definition above is well defined, that is programs are finitely built from primitive methods only.

3.5. Interpretation of Methods

In this section the relevant features of our way to assign semantics to methods are discussed.

In the literature of denotational semantics ([Sto82]) usually the double bracket [[.]] is used for this purpose. In this paper [[.]] is used uniformly to denote the meaning of types and methods as well. If t is a type then [[t]] denotes the domain represented by t. If (t,m) is a method with signature $(t_1...t_n,t')$, $n \geq 0$, then [[(t,m)]] denotes a partial mapping from $[[t_1]] \times .. \times [[t_n]]$ to [[t']].

Invoking a method (t,m) may be done in two ways: first by calling (t,m), second by calling only m. In the last case the type of the first argument is taken as *type of interest by default.* If no argument exist, the type of interest has to be specified explicitly.

So in general we may assume that the type of interest is known. In order to specify which program is executed when a method (t,m) is called, three different cases have to be considered:

(i) (t,m) is no element of Interface(t). In this case an error message is forwarded.

(ii) (t,m) $\in$ ImpMethods $\cap$ Interface(t). In this case the program MethImp(t,m) is started.

(iii) Otherwise (t,m) $\in$ Interface(t) \ ImpMethods. Then due to definition 6, t must have several supertypes $s_1,...,s_n$, $n \geq 1$, where m is implemented (*multiple inheritance*). If $n = 1$ then MethImp(s_1,m) is invoked. If $n > 1$ then the ambiguity is resolved by some ordering of $s_1,...s_n$ with unique minimum. This ordering is part of the DB-schema. Let s_i be the minimum according to this ordering. Then (t,m) is implemented by the program MethImp(s_i,m).

So in general we may assume that the program p which implements the method (t,m) is known. But we still have to demand that the signature of p and the signature of (t,m) are compatible.

Definition 9:

Let (t,m) be implemented by a program p = MethImp(t,m). Let the signatures be Sign(p) = $(s_1...s_k,s')$, $k \geq 0$, Meth(t,m) = $(t_1...t_n,t')$, $n \geq 0$.

We demand both signatures to be *compatible*, that is

(i) $n = k$; and

(ii) $s_i = t_i$ or t_i is a subtype of s_i, for all $1 \leq i \leq n$.

In order to specify the semantics of the *application* of a method (t,m) with signature $(t_1...t_n,t')$, $n \geq 0$, to arguments $(x_1, ... , x_k)$, $k \geq 0$, of types $s_1,...,s_k$, the following four cases have to be considered:

(i) $k \neq n$. The type checker has to reject this case.

(ii) $s_i = t_i$. Then x_i is passed to the program unchanged, $1 \leq i \leq n$.

(iii) s_i is a subtype of t_i. Then $c_{s_i,t_i}(x_i)$ is passed to the program instead of x_i, $1 \leq i \leq n$, (*coercions from subtypes to supertypes*).

(iv) s_i and t_i are not related via ISA-edges, $1 \leq i \leq n$. The type checker has to reject this case.

Example 11:

Suppose (Refs,Increment) be a method in the interface of Refs, which increments the component *no* of all elements by 1. Then by definition 4 (iii) (see example 4) Increment can be applied to BibRefs with the effect that all references in the set BibRefs are incremented simultaneously.

4. Database

In this section we present a definition of DB-schemas and valid instances of DB-schemas. A central concept in our model is *object-identity*[Kho86] : To each newly created object is assigned an internal object identifier that is independent of its descriptive data (i.e. its value, which is an element of the domain of its type). This identifier is unique to the object during its whole lifetime whereas the descriptive data might change. After its lifetime the identifier is never used again. (When we henceforth use the term "instance of a type" or "object of a type" we mean an object identifier to which is assigned a value of the domain of that type).

A valid DB-schema has to obey several *integrity constraints* which partly depend on our semantics of the ISA-hierarchy of types and the two pointer types:

Inclusion dependencies are modelled with the help of object identifiers. The ISA-dag induces a partial ordering of sets of object identifiers based on set inclusion. One object can belong to more than one type. The collection of all its descriptive data is clustered to one object identifier. In such a situation we demand that the corresponding types are in a subtype-supertype relation and that the corresponding object identifiers are in a subset relationship. In this way we have both structural and behavioural enrichment from supertype to subtype and subset inclusion from subtype to supertype.

Referential integrity: With the help of pointer types we have the ability to relate objects of types that are not in a ISA relationship. A valid DB-instance must insure that there are no dangling pointers.

In addition we can formalize semantic concepts like *abstract types*, *category-spezialisation-of* and *role-spezialisation-of* introduced in [Kla88]

Abstract types must never be instantiated. That means that there must never exist objects of abstract types. Of course we demand that supertypes of abstract types are abstract types as well.

Disjointness constraints: This is a possibility to specify that an object can never simultaneously belong to two subtypes t and s of a type x. In [Kla88] s and t are called *category-spezialisation-of* of x.

Role-inclusion dependency: In general an object can belong to several nonabstract types which may be all subtypes of a single type. We say that this object has several *roles* according to the types it belongs to. It should be possible to specify that if one object has a role t it must always have role s as well (s,t both subtypes of a type x). This is similar to ISA-inclusion dependency but it differs in that the structure and behaviour of an object playing role s and t can be quite different, whereas the case of ISA-inclusion dependency is characterized by the structural and behavioural enrichment from supertyp to subtyp. We call these constrains role-inclusion dependencies.

To express the last three concepts syntactically we introduce a labelling for an ISA-graph.

Definition 10:

ISA*=(ISA, ATypeId, ρ) is a tuple with the following components:

(1) ISA is an acyclic graph as defined in Definition 5.

(2) *Abstract types*: ATypeId $\subseteq$ TypeId is a subset of TypeId (called abstract types) such that if t $\in$ ATypeId and s is a supertype of t then s $\in$ ATypeId as well.

(3) *Role-dependencies*: Let NATypeId = TypeId - ATypeId. t $\in$ NATypeId is called non abstract type. ρ is a map that assigns to each node t $\in$ TypeId with non abstract direct subtypes $t_1,\ldots,t_n$ a matrix $(rd_{ij})_{1\le i,j\le n}$, with $rd_{ij} \in \{d,i,n\}$ (where d,i are symbols for disjoint, role-inclusion-dependency and n for no dependencies).

Example 12:

In Example 1 it is natural to declare the types Code, DocPart and Ref as abstract types, because these are disjoint union types which are mostly declared as abstract types.

To exemplify the notion of role-dependencies suppose you have subtypes PublishedPaper, Draft and SecretPaper of type Document. All of them are declared as non abstract types which can have instances. We here ommit the detailed declaration of the type expressions. Think of all of them as

Documents with some additional attributes expressing the appropriate semantics. We now want to specify that a PublishedPaper has at any time an associated draft (i.e. a PublishedPaper is always an instance of Draft), although they have a different structure (i.e. a PublishedPaper might have the attribute conference whereas a Draft has a structure part which reflects the versions of it). Clearly a PublishedPaper should never be a SecretPaper.

We specify these constraints with the help of the matix rd = ρ(Document):

$rd_{PublishedPaper,Draft} = i$,
$rd_{PublishedPaper,SecretPaper} = d$,

$rd_{i,j} = n$ for all other combinations.

Definition 11:

A *DB-schema* consist of a tuple S = (TypeId, TD, ISA*, MethId, Meth, MethImp). The components in this tuple are defined as in the previous chapters.

To such a DB-schema S we assign a DB-instance at a fixed time T:

Definition 12:

Let S be a DB-schema, then $Instance_{S,T} = \{Value_{t,T} \mid t \in NATypeId\}$ is a valid DB-instance for the DB-schema S at the time T if

(1) "*Object Identity*"
$Value_{t,T}$: ObjId ---> [[t]] is a partial injective mapping with finite carrier called $ObjId_T(t)$.

(2) "*ISA-inclusion dependency*"
If (t,s) ∈ ISA and t,s ∈ NATypeId then $ObjId_T(t) \subseteq ObjId_T(s)$ and the following diagram must commute:

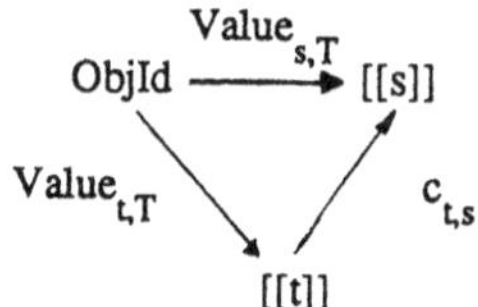

In other words: $Value_{s,T} = c_{t,s} \circ Value_{t,T}$ ("∘" denotes function composition).

(3) "*Referential integrity*"
If s,t ∈ NATypeId and k:↑s (or k:δ↑s) appears in the type expression TD(t) of t then the following condition must be satisfied:
If $x \in Value_{t,T}(ObjId)$ has a value k:oid ($oid \in ObjId_{\uparrow s,T}$) at the leaf k:↑s (or k:δ↑s) then oid ∈ ObjId(s). "All pointers refer to existing objects".

(4) "*Role-dependencies*"
If t ∈ TypeId with non abstract direct subtypes $t_1,...,t_n$ then
$ObjId_T(t_i) \cap ObjId_T(t_j) = \emptyset$, if $\rho(t)_{i,j} = d$ and
$ObjId_T(t_i) \subseteq ObjId_T(t_j)$ if $(\rho(t)_{i,j}) = i$.

Note:

- As mentioned above abstract types do not get instantiated. As a consequence parts of type expressions like k:δ↑s are forbidden if s ∈ ATypeId (abstract types cannot be referenced).
- The condition of the map $Value_{t,T}$ to be injective ensures object identity because we can have no two distinct values (i.e. elements of [[t]]) with the same object identifier.
- The collection $\{Value_{t,T}(oid) \mid t \in NATypeId\}$ represents the state of an object oid ∈ ObjId at a fixed time T. The set of TypeId's t such that $Value_{t,T}(oid) \neq \perp$ represents the roles in which the object oid participates

at the time T. This can change in two different ways: Either the descriptive data might change (i.e. $Value_{t,T}(oid) \neq Value_{t,T'}(oid)$ for $t \in$ NATypeId ,$T \neq T'$) or the object can get a new or loose an old role (membership to a type).

- The commutativity of the diagram in (2) ensures that for an object belonging to two types the data filling the structural part which is common to the type expressions of the two types is the same. That means that we forbid overwriting of attribute values from supertype to subtype but allow a clean storage strategy. Abandoning this rule would make 'attribute overwriting' possible but would complicate update propagation and message passing. Furthermore, a much bigger storage capacity is needed, since 'inherited attribute values' must be stored explicitly.
- Since it is possible to define in a DB-schema a lot of consistency constraints it is likely to create a schema that has no valid DB-instance at all. A type t is called impossible iff $Value_{t,T}$ has always an empty carrier. Two types t, t' are called indistinguishable iff the carriers of $Value_{t,T}$ and $Value_{t',T}$ are always identical. A DB-schema with different indistinguishable types is called redundant. Checking DB-schemas for redundancy and occurrence of impossible types is discussed in[Atz86] But inclusion- and disjoint constraints are only part of the problem of schema checking, which will be addressed in future research. The update propagation for a consistent schema is a difficult problem as well. In a following paragraph we will address this problem.

Example 13:

To give an example of a valid DB-instance of the part of a DB-schema in the previous example we use the abbreviated notation:

(o,t,x) if $o \in$ ObjId, $t \in$ TypeId and $Value_t(o) = x \in [[t]]$

Let o1, o2, o3, o4, o5 $\in$ ObjId. In our Document example we can have the following instances in our DB at fixed time T:

(o1, PublishedPaper, pp1) , where pp1 $\in$ [[PublishedPaper]],
(o2, Draft, df2), where df2 $\in$ [[Draft]],
(o3, Draft, df3), where df3 $\in$ [[Draft]],
(o3, SecretPaper, sp3), where sp3 $\in$ [[SecretPaper]],
(o4, SecretPaper, sp3), where sp4 $\in$ [[SecretPaper]],
(o5, Document, d5), where d5 $\in$ [[Document]].

Note that o3 is both instance of Draft and SecretPaper, that means that it has two roles. The DB-instance above is not yet a valid one because it does not fulfill the condition (2) of Def. 11. We therefor have to add some more tuples to satisfy the inclusion dependencies:

(o1, Document, d1), d1$\in$[[Document]] such that $c_{PublishedPaper,Document}(pp1) = d1$,
(o2, Document, d2), d2$\in$[[Document]] such that $c_{Draft,Document}(df2) = d2$,
(o3, Document, d3), d3$\in$[[Document]] such that $c_{SecretPaper,Document}(sp3) = d3$ and $c_{Draft,Document}(df3) = d3$
(o4, Document, d4), d4$\in$[[Document]] such that $c_{SecretPaper,Document}(sp4) = d4$.

To get a valid DB-instance we must add a last tuple to obey the role inclusion dependency between PublishedPaper and Draft:

(o1, Draft, df1), df1 $\in$ [[Draft]] such that $c_{Draft,Document}(df1) = d1$

(note that there need not exist a coercion between PublishedPaper and Draft).

We now have a valid DB-instance with the following carriers of the Value mappings:

ObjId(PublishedPaper) = {o1},
ObjId(Draft) = {o1,o2,o3},
ObjId(SecretPaper) = {o3,o4},
ObjId(Document) = {o1, o2, o3, o4, o5}.

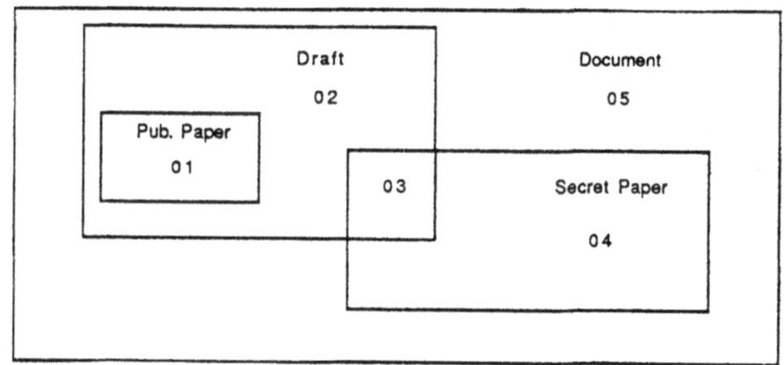

Deletion of the tuple (o3,Draft,df3) would transfer the DB-instance into another valid DB-instance whereas the insertion of a tuple (o3,PublishedPaper,pp3) would contradict the disjointness constraint between PublishedPaper and SecretPaper.

With the help of the previous definition we can easily express deletion constraints: If $Referenced_{t,T}(oid) \neq \emptyset$ for $oid \in ObjId_T(t)$, then the object $Value_{t,T}(oid)$ cannot be deleted from the database at the time T.

So far we did not distinguish the two pointer types $\uparrow$ and $\delta\uparrow$. They differ in their update behaviour and are used to model the concepts "dependent" and "independent component" [Kla88] value of $k : \delta\uparrow s$ in $Value_{r,T}(o)$. Then the deletion of $Value_{r,T}(o)$ has the consequence that $Value_{s,T}(oid)$ is deleted as well, if $Referenced_{s,T}(oid) = \emptyset$. Thus, $Value_{s,T}(oid)$ depends on the existence of $Value_{r,T}(o)$. The following definition is needed to formalize this concept.

Definition 13:

Let $t \in TypeId$ and $oid \in ObjId_T(t)$. Let $Dependent_{t,T}(oid)$ be the set of all pairs (o , s) such that each of the following conditions hold:

(i) $s \in TypeId$ and $o \in ObjId_T(s)$,

(ii) $k : \delta\uparrow s$ appears in the extensional type expression of t,

(iii) the value of $k : \delta\uparrow s$ in $Value_{t,T}(oid)$ is $k : o$.

The atomic DB-methods for a database with a database schema S are described in the following. Let t be always an element of NATypeId. We do not define these DB-methods for abstract types. In this outline we do not consider role-dependencies.

(i) $Value_{t,T}$

$Value_{t,T}$ applied to an object identifier $oid \in ObjId_T(t)$ returns the element of the domain of t which is associated to oid at the time T. Let $Instance_T(t) = Value_{t,T}(ObjId_T(t))$. Then $Instance_T(t)$ is the set of instances of type t at the time T. Note that $Instance_T(t)$ is only defined for nonabstract types.

(ii) $Key_{t,T}$

$Key_{t,T}$ is a partial injective map from [[t]] to $ObjId_T(t)$ and is the inverse of $Value_{t,T}$, i.e.

$Value_{t,T} \circ Key_{t,T} = id_{[[t]]}$ and $Key_{t,T} \circ Value_{t,T} = id_{ObjId}$.

$Key_{t,T}$ applied to an element x of $Instance_T(t)$ returns the object identifier of x at the time T.

(iii) $Insert_{t,T}$

$Insert_{t,T}$ transforms the valid DB-instance at the time T into a valid DB-instance at the time T' and inserts an instance x of type t : $Insert_{t,T}(Instance_{S,T} , x) = Instance_{S,T'}$.

$Instance_{S,T'}$ is defined as follows:

(a) if there is an object identifier oid $\in ObjId_T(t)$, such that $Value_{t,T}(oid) = x$, then $Instance_{S,T} = Instance_{S,T'}$.

(b) if s is a nonabstract supertype of t or s = t then:

$ObjId_{T'}(s) = ObjId_T(s) \cup \{ Key_{t,T'}(x) \}$,
$Key_{s,T'}(c_{t,s}(x)) = Key_{t,T'}(x)$,
$Value_{s,T'}(o) = Value_{s,T}(o)$ for all $o \in ObjId_T(s)$,
$Value_{s,T'}(Key_{s,T'}(x)) = c_{t,s}(x)$.

(c) if s is not a nonabstract supertype of t and $s \neq t$ then:

$Value_{s,T'} = Value_{s,T}$.

(iv) $Delete_{t,T}$

$Delete_{t,T}$ transforms the valid DB-instance at the time T into a valid DB-instance at the time T' and deletes an instance x of type t with object identifier oid.

$Delete_{t,T}(Instance_{S,T} , oid) = Instance_{S,T''}$.

$Instance_{S,T'}$ is defined as follows:

(a) if oid $\in ObjId_T(t)$ or if $Referenced_{s,T}(oid) \neq \emptyset$ for s = t or a subtype s of t then:
$Instance_{S,T} = Instance_{S,T''}$.

(b) if (a) does not apply and s = t or s is a subtype of t then:
$ObjId_{T''}(s) = ObjId_T(s) - \{oid\}$, $Value_{s,T''}(o) = Value_{s,T}(o)$ for all $o \in ObjId_{T''}(s)$ and for all other $r \in TypeId$ we have $Value_{r,T'} = Value_{r,T}$ for a time T'' inbetween T and T'. To get $Instance_{S,T'}$ we have to perform the operations $Delete_{s,T''}(Instance_{S,T''}, o)$ recursively for all $(o,s) \in Dependent_{t,T}(oid)$.

(v) $Update_{t,T}$

$Update_{t,T}$ transforms the valid DB-instance at the time T into a valid DB-instance at the time T' and transforms the object $Value_{t,T}(oid)$ into x:

$Update_{t,T}(Instance_{S,T} , oid , x) = Instance_{S,T''}$. $Instance_{S,T'}$ is defined as follows:

(a) if oid $\in ObjId_T(t)$, or if $x \in [[t]]$ then $Instance_{S,T} = Instance_{S,T''}$.

(b) if (a) does not apply and s = t or s is a nonabstract supertype of t then
$ObjId_{T'}(s) = ObjId_T(s)$, $Value_{s,T'}(o) = Value_{s,T}(o)$ for all $o \in ObjId_T(s) - \{oid\}$,
$Value_{s,T'}(oid) = c_{t,s}(x)$,
if s is a subtype of t such that oid $\in ObjId_T(s)$ then
$ObjId_{T'}(s) = ObjId_T(s)$, $Value_{s,T'}(o) = Value_{s,T}(o)$ for all $o \in ObjId_T(s) - \{oid\}$,
$Value_{s,T'}(oid) = c_{t,s}(x)$,
and for all other $r \in TypeId$ we have: $Value_{r,T'} = Value_{r,T}$

5. Conclusion

We have presented a formalization of an kernel data model that includes the main characteristics of the object-oriented model. These are complex objects as instances of abstract data types, inheritance and message-passing. With the help of five constructors (tuple, set, union, pointer, substitution) we provide the capability to build up arbitrary complex data structures.

To each such type definition we assign a set of methods called the interface of this type. The interface consists of methods which are directly implemented at the type and additionally inherited methods. The inheritance mechanism is defined with a type lattice (allowing multiple inheritance) and coercions that specify the conversion of an object of a subtype to an object of a supertype in order to apply the methods defined at the supertype. Another sort of polymorphism is accomplished with the help of generic tuple and set methods.

Finally we gave a definition of an object-oriented database defining concepts like object identity and referential integrity.

References

[ACM87] ACM, Proc. of the 6th ACM SIGACT SIGMOD SIGART *Symp. on Princ. of DB Systems*, March 23-25, San Diego, CA, ACM, Baltimore USA, 1987.

[Atz86] P. Atzeni and D.S. Parker, "Formal Properties of Net- Based Knowledge Representation Schemes," *Proc. IEEE Conf. on Data Engineering*, pp. 700-706, 1986.

[Ban87] Francois Bancilhon, Ted Briggs, Setrag Khoshafian, and Patrick Valduriez, "FAD, a Powerful and Simple Database Language," *Proc. 13th VLDB Conf. Brighton*, 1987.

[Car84] Luca Cardelli, "A Semantics of Multiple Inheritance," *Semantics of Data Types*, International Symposium, Sophia-Antipolis, France, June 27-29, 1984, Proc., Springer-Verlag, 1984.

[Day87] U. Dayal and I. Traiger, *Proc. of ACM SIG on Management of Data*, SIGMOD, San Francisco, ACM, Baltimore USA, 1987.

[Hor85] W. Horak, "Office document architecture and office document interchange formats," *IEEE Computer 18(10)*, pp. 50-60, 1985.

[Hul84] R. Hull and Chee K. Yap, "The Format Model: A Theory of Database Organisation," *JACM*, vol. 31, pp. 518-537, July 1984.

[IEE87] IEEE, *Proc. 3rd Int. Conf. on Data Eng. Los Angeles*, CA, IEEE Comp. Sci. Press, Mass USA, 1987.

[Kho86] Setrag N. Khoshafian and George P. Copeland, "Object Identity," *OOPSLA Proceedings*, pp. 406-416, 1986.

[Kla88] Wolfgang Klas, Erich J. Neuhold, and Michael Schrefl, "An object oriented datamodel for a knowledge base," *Proceedings of the European Teleinformatics Conference (EUTECO 88), Research into Networks and Distributed Applications*, North Holland, Vienna, April 1988.

[Knu86] D.E. Knuth, in *The TEXbook*, Addison Wesley Publ. Comp., 1986.

[Mey86] Norman Meyrowitz, *Proc. Object-Oriented Programming Systems, Languages and Applications, OOPSLA'86*, ACM, Baltimore USA, 1986.

[Mey87] Norman Meyrowitz, *Proc. Object-Oriented Programming Systems, Languages and Applications, OOPSLA'87*, ACM, Baltimore USA, 1987.

[Ric87] P. Richard and F. Velez, "An Object-Oriented Formal Data Model," *Proc. of the Workshop on Database Progra ming Languages*, pp. 177-192, Sep. 1987.

[Ste86] David Stemple, Tim Sheard, and Ralph Bunker, "Abstract Data Types in databases: Specification, Manipulation and Access," *Data Engineering*, pp. 590-597, 1986.

[Sto82] Joseph Stoy, "Some Mathematical Aspects of Funtional Programming", in *Funtional Programming and its Application*, ed. J.Darlington/P.Henderson/D.A.Turner, Cambridge University Press, 1982.

[Sto87] P. M. Stoker and W. Kent, *Proc. 13th Int. Conf. on Very Large Data Bases VLDB, Brighton, England*, Morgan Kaufmann Publ., Los Altos CA USA, 1987.

A Model for an Object Management System for Software Engineering Environments

Erwin Petry
Nixdorf Computer AG, Abt. EG ST 2
Berliner Str. 95, D-8000 Muenchen 40
e-mail: ...unido!un15.petry.muc

1. Introduction

In Europe big efforts are made to specify, implement and standardize an interface well fit as a basis for the construction of modern software engineering environments. A lot of German companies and research institutes have localized deficiencies in the "european specifications" of such a system ["PCTE": 1, 2] and decided to work together in the German PCTE Initiative (GPI) for a specification [3] that better fits their requirements [4]. Nixdorf is the leading company in this project.

The most important component of the system is the Object Management System (OMS) responsible for managing all data involved in a software engineering environment. This position statement gives an overview of an OMS data model brought into discussion in GPI by Nixdorf [5]. (It is not an agreed GPI model.) The main differences to other models are outlined, lack of space preventing details being presented.

2. Structuring Principles of the Data Model

The OMS model belongs to the class of the entity-relationship models in that it has explicit concepts for objects and relationships. Objects are hierarchically structured with possibly shared components thus building complex objects. Each object can be versionized. N-ary relationships can exist between objects.

On the schema definition level the user specifies a hierarchy (plus recursion) of object type definitions thus describing the allowed structure of complex objects. Only primitive object types (those having no component type) have an explicitly specified data type and only primitive objects have a primitive value of the type specified for the corresponding primitive object type. The value of any other object is determined by looking at its structure and evaluating the values of its component objects. Beside primitive objects all other nodes in a hierarchical complex object structure have no values of their own (apart from system attributes; e.g. access control list). They only represent structural information.

This proposal differs from all other complex object models known to the author in that all these proposals have in each node of a hierarchical (complex object) graph both values and structure where this proposal separates them. To explain this let us look at the following figures.

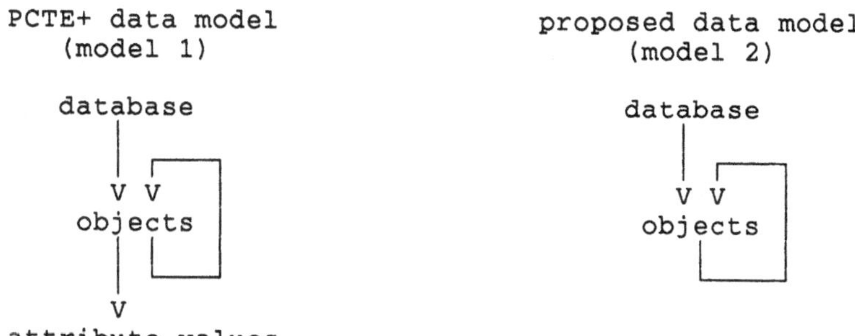

Fig. 1: Structuring Principles of Data Models

Figure 1 reads as follows: Usually (left side of figure 1; model 1; e.g. PCTE+ data model) a database consists of a lot of objects. Each object may have both some component objects and some attribute values. If an object has components we call it a complex object else a primitive object.

According to our proposal (right side of figure 1; model 2) each database consists as well of a lot of objects. But in contrast to model 1 each complex object of this model has only component objects but no attribute values. A primitive object in this model is comparable with an attribute value of model 1. Attribute values of model 1 and primitive objects of model 2 may or may not be structured (not structured in PCTE+).

Figure 2 shows a simple example of some objects and attributes in model 1. Object 1 has three attribute values and two component objects 2 and 3 each having two attribute values.

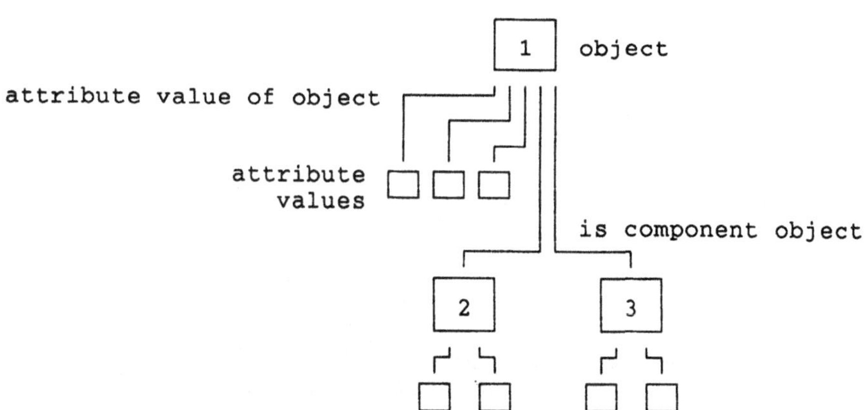

Fig. 2: Objects and Attribute Values in Model 1

How is this database to be interpreted? There are no doubts about objects 2 and 3. But obviously for object 1 there are two possibilities. The three attribute values of object 1 may either be regarded as a "local object" or as belonging to a complex object together with components 2 and 3. Which view is applied depends on the user. He may even have different ways of looking at this database at different times.

The second model clarifies this situation. The user is forced to decide which way of looking he wants to apply. The above two interpretations are expressed as shown in figures 3a and 3b. Notice that values are associated only with primitive objects. Model 2 has the advantage that the database schema and contents reflect the intended semantics. The user should explicitly model what objects he wants to have. He may even want to apply both ways of looking at object 1 of figure 2. This should be expressed in model 2 by introducing a superobject in figure 3a having component objects 1, 2 and 3.

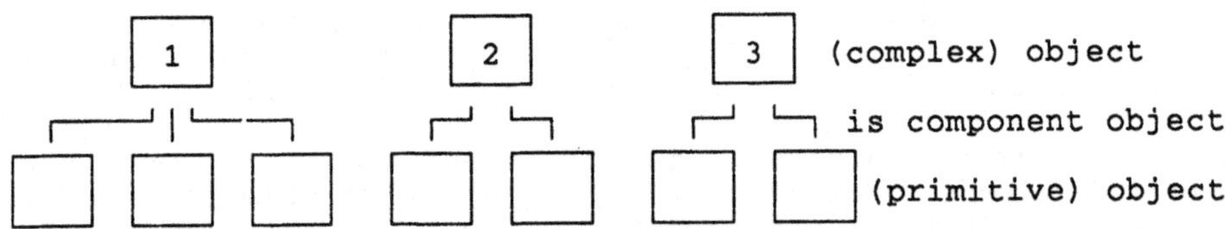

Fig. 3a: Objects Expressed in Model 2
(Object 1 Interpreted as "Local Object")

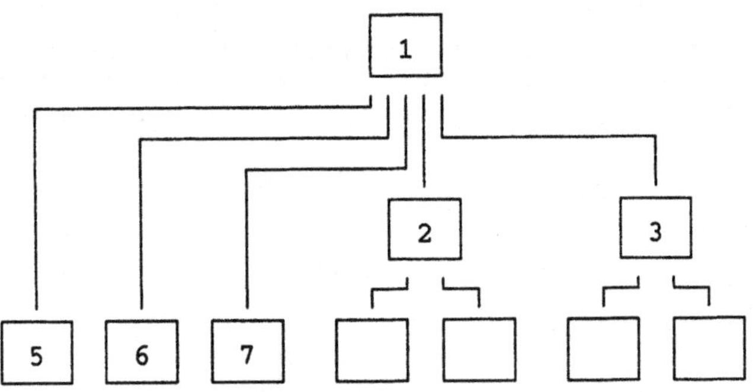

Fig. 3b: Objects Expressed in Model 2
(Object 1 Interpreted as Complex Object)

Model 2 allows to see arbitrary sets of values as components of different objects. The user can also build separate hierarchies of superobjects over the same data values (shared objects) having semantics like "component is part of component", "module imports module" or "module is involved in configuration".

3. Further Aspects of the Data Model

In the object type structure the user has the possibility to specify cardinalities for the number of components and superobjects allowed. He tells the system if components can be versionized (different or same version of a component in every version of the object; e.g. same interface but different implementations) and if a component will be copied or initialized on copying the object.

For data types we consider two alternatives. Either a rich set of predefined types or user defined abstract data types. Each data type has a nullvalue and for each object type each data type involved has a user specified default value.

Objects of all types can be versionized which means that each object can have any number of versions in the OMS database. We can consider an object the aggregate of all its versions (the versionset of the object). This has the advantage that we can name the whole of all versions of an object when we are not interested in a specific version. In each context (superobject) an object is represented by one of its versions. In different contexts this may be different versions. There is the possibility to define a history graph on each versionset and to store the versions by a delta technique.

Besides the complex object structure the user can define n-ary relationship types between object types. We are discussing whether to allow the association of a (complex) object value with each relationship or if to add a n+1st object type to have information with the relationship. Cardinalities control in how many relationships an object must be involved (and (perhaps) how many objects of an object type a relationship must connect).

In combination with relationships our object model offers another advantage. How is a relationship relating object 1 in figure 2 (model 1) with some other object to be interpreted? Does the "local" or the complex object participate in the relationship? Because there are no "local" objects in our model there will be no doubt about the answer.

4. Access Control

In software development it is very important to have a good concept for access control. This is achieved by defining access rights (e.g. read, write, append, navigate, execute and owner) on (the hierarchy of) objects, versions and relationships. To handle these rights is quite easy if we consider only disjoint objects. But our objects build hierarchies allowing for each object many components and superobjects. So we have overlapping data granules.

To guarantee that operations are able to work on a complex object it is important that an access right is valid on the whole object. Therefore our model guarantees that a granted right for an object is also granted for its components. The consequence of this rule is that on components there are in general more rights defined than on superobjects.

Here another advantage of our modelling principle (model 2) becomes obvious. Consider an object (e.g. a library module) being used as component of many complex objects. There are different users designing these complex objects. So they have write-right on all components of their complex objects except on the shared component where all but one only have read-right.

In the above model 1 such a situation is only manageable by either introducing single attribute values as extra granules of access control or by distinguishing two scopes of access control with each object: the "local" and the complex object. The first alternative is nothing else than making attributes to objects concerning access control.

As an example consider figures 2 and 3 with e.g. object 3 being the component with only read-right. Object 1 in figure 3b can not have write-right as a whole while all other objects may have write-right (objects 1 and 2 in fig. 3a and objects 2, 5, 6 and 7 in fig 3b). To have this situation in figure 2 either all attribute values of object 1 or the "local" object 1 must have write-right.

5. Final Remarks

Until now we did not talk about operators retrieving and manipulating complex objects. With our complex objects we have no problem to implement operators for deleting and copying complex objects. We have even defined an operator to generate a complex object together with (direct and indirect) components. But we do not know how to realize an operator to transfer a whole complex object between the database and an application program (retrieve and update a complex object). This is a serious problem especially with our model. For models like model 1 there exist at least exchange operators for primitive and "local" objects. This is anyhow better than to have only exchange operators for our primitive objects (comparable to attribute values in model 1).

It was a requirement for our GPI-project that the OMS to design must know complex objects. Today everybody talks about complex objects but few people deliver an answer to the questions of what the user needs them for and how to use them.

For the moment one OMS-database is a semi-lattice. This means that there is one single root for all objects in the database - a situation comparable to the UNIX file system. So all data of an OMS-database is modelled with the same complex object concepts not regarding whether the data represents a whole project or a procedure declaration in a module. Another possibility would be to have a lot of independent (complex) objects in one OMS-database - comparable to a database (e.g. a relational or a non-standard

DB). This solution must be improved by an extra concept to structure the set of all objects. Isn't it this what we need - separated models to structure small and big data granules? Then the principle question "What is the complex object model?" changes to "What are the models for structuring objects and for structuring databases?".

Acknowledgements:
The author thanks his colleagues H.J. Jeanrond, K. Kuester and M. Simon for their contributions to this paper. The author has learned a lot in the discussions with the GPI-project partners.

References:

[1]: European Strategic Programme for Research and Development in Information Technology (ESPRIT): PCTE - A Basis for a Portable Common Tool Environment, Functional Specifications, Version 1.4.

[2]: Inter European Procuring Group (IEPG) TA-13: PCTE+ Functional Specifications, C Binding, Issue 1. February 1988.

[3]: The German PCTE Initiative (GPI): Sketching the GPI-OMS-datamodel. 1988.

[4]: The German PCTE Initiative: Requirements for the Enhancement of PCTE/OMS, Version 2.0. October 1988.

[5]: E. Petry: Design of an OMS model (in German). Nixdorf Computer AG, Munich, March 1988.

Multiple Inheritance and Genericity for the Integration of a Database Management System in an Object-Oriented Approach

Andrew U. Frank
Computer Science & Surveying Engineering
University of Maine
Orono, ME 04469
FRANK@MECAN1.bitnet

Abstract

Experience in designing and writing application programs using an object-oriented method reveals problems in connecting application programs to Database Management System (DBMS) services. This is due to the difference between the declarative description of data assumed in a DBMS and the behavioral, encapsulated format in an object-oriented language. To overcome this problem, the integration of DBMS services with an object-oriented language must be improved. A method is proposed to achieve seamless integration of DBMS functionality with application code using inheritance. The language must provide 1) **multiple inheritance**, allowing the objects to be stored in the database to inherit the necessary methods, and 2) **genericity**, in order to document what operations each object to be stored in the DBMS must export for use by the DBMS (eg. access operations). Most current object-oriented languages do not provide both features and thus make it difficult to add a DBMS package.

Using multiple inheritance and generic classes, a DBMS package can be written in the same language as the application program, and can be added to an object-oriented programming system. The method is also suitable for integrating other packages than DBMS (geometric data handling, graphics, user interface etc.) in an object-oriented environment.

1. Introduction

We are working on designing and programming Spatial Information Systems (also known as Geographic Information Systems) using an object-oriented software engineering method. The software engineering problems are very similar to the ones encountered in the design of CAD/CAM systems, VLSI, etc. In general, the object-oriented methods of software engineering are beneficial for this class of applications, but the connection of object-oriented application code with the database management system causes a break in the point of view. Since the Pingree Park Conference [SIGMOD 81], attention to the logical integration of DBMS functionality with programming languages and AI has been studied. On a broader base, constructing an object-oriented DBMS requires to bridge the two different concepts of 'global database schema declaration' and the object-oriented modularization.

Object-oriented application code encapsulates module internals (especially the data structure) and makes visible only a behavioral (procedural) interface. The DBMS on the other hand expects a declarative description of the data. The use of layers of modules transforming between the DBMS and object-oriented application modules has been proposed [Härder 1988]. It is in our experience a viable, but not straight forward solution to bridge the conceptual gap. The code in these layers is difficult to write, because it requires understanding of both the DBMS and the application world. At the same time, it is quite schematic. Using such application layers restricts changes in the remainder of the application code.

We propose to use inheritance for the integration of DBMS functionality with the application modules. Using this single language feature, typical for object-oriented programming, overcomes the mismatch between DBMS and object-oriented application programs. We will describe first, how inheritance is used to provide the DBMS operations to the object. Then we will discuss implementation concepts, showing the need for genericity. Objects, which are to be stored in the database (subsequently called DB-objects), inherit the DBMS operations from a superclass 'generic DB-object'. Additionally, each DB-object class must export some operations for the use of the 'generic DB-object' (e.g. operations to access components of the objects). We will then point out, that a language which provides multiple inheritance and supports generic classes, allows writing a DBMS in the same language as the application and adding it as a set of modules to the application. We will conclude with stating that the same concepts and language features can be used to integrate other generic support packages (eg. graphics and user interface support).

The integration of a DBMS as application code is not a trivial problem. Solutions reported use object-based, but not object-oriented languages [Wegner 1987] and a relational data model with a global schema on the level of the application. This contradicts the object-oriented view of data encapsulated in modules. Our own efforts to integrate a DBMS in an object-oriented programming method (based on a Pascal extension) was stifled by problems of understanding how to combine separate object definitions with generic database functions. In this paper, we will argue that these problems can be overcome by using a language that provides multiple inheritance and genericity (eg. EIFEL [Meyer 1986]). The methods reported here are a refined view of the current implementation of the DBMS 'PANDA'.

In order to avoid confusion, the proposal in this paper is not based on a specific data model. The method can be applied with any data model that is compatible with object-oriented programming. If the DBMS code itself is written in an object-oriented language using the proposed mechanism, it will help us to understand the architecture, semantic, design and implementation issues of DBMS in general. This will lead to the DBMS kernel and toolbox [Härder 1985], where specific implementations for DBMS subsystems can be selected to suit the application demand best.

2. Providing DBMS Services to the Application Programmer

An object-oriented language demands the specification of each object type with all pertinent operations in a single module. The only way of accessing data is to use operations defined on the objects. Thus, every class of DB-objects must provide the necessary database operations. The following example out of a geometry application based on a node-edge-face-structure shows, how the class provides also database operations :

```
module node
create (name, x, y) return id
find (id) return node
findByname (name) return node
...
getName (node) return name
getX (node) return coordinate
...
distance (node, node) return real
...
```

Three differences appear in comparing the proposed with the classical approach:

- The data description is encapsulated in a module and not centralized in a DBMS schema.
- Access from the DBMS to the data is through defined interfaces and not directly from the DBMS code to the storage representation.
- Database operations are defined for each object separately and not generally for all DB-objects (and become therefore often simpler, because complex rules for parameter

types and value encoding are not necessary).

In object-oriented languages, the definition of object types can be arranged in a generalization hierarchy, such that properties (eg. operations) of the super classes apply also to all the sub classes[1]. It is thus sufficient to define a 'generic DB-object' with all necessary DBMS operations and have all the classes that should be included in the DBMS inherit its operations.

The module 'generic DB-object' must offer operations to create/store a new object, delete an object and depending on the data model used, find objects based on values using indices, aggregating objects to complex objects, etc. Other DBMS functionality must be provided, for example it must be possible to group changes in transactions, etc.

If 'generic DB-object' is declared with all the DBMS operation, a specification of the form "type node subtype of generic-DB-object" can provide the objects of type node with the required behavior. Application programmers may want to encapsulate this node object in an additional layer and not export the 'raw' database operations. This way even very complex consistency checks can be defined and enforced (without need for an additional formalism beyond the programming language).

To be generally useful, objects like 'node' must be able to inherit the behavior from other super classes than 'generic DB-object' and therefore, multiple inheritance is necessary (in our application, 'node' is also subtype of 'geometric objects', etc). In a language supporting only single inheritance (i.e. in most languages easily available, eg. C++, inheritance is probably used for other aspects of the design and not available to integrate DBMS functions (nor for the same matter, display managers or other packages). Thus multiple inheritance is crucial for this method of integration.

3. Implementation Strategy

Can database operations simply be inherited? In this section we lay out a strategy and list the necessary features of an object-oriented language necessary for its support. The following outline is based on the current structure of 'PANDA', an object-oriented DBMS that we use to build geographic information systems. It does not describe the current structure, which is obscured by, among other things, limitations in the programming language [Egenhofer 1988], but reflects the understanding we gained from building it.
In order to write the code for the 'generalized DB-object', from which DBMS behavior is inherited, we found a need for genericity combined with inheritance. In the next subsection we explain what we understand by genericity (for a more extensive discussion see [Meyer 1986] or [Olthoff 1986], [Cardelli 1985]). The second subsection shows its use for the definition of the 'generic DB-object'.

3.1 Genericity

Generic constructs are very similar to inheritance, but not exactly equivalent. They are, in our opinion, a slightly different formulation of the same concept in two different 'traditions' (specification languages and object-oriented languages). Inheritance in object-oriented languages should be extended to include genericity.

Genericity is theoretically based on the notion of algebraic systems or abstract algebras [Zilles 1984]. For example, a semi group is defined as a structure <S, *>, consisting of the elements in

[1] It has been pointed out [Schaffert 1986], that a type hierarchy can be an implementation hierarchy (eg. Smalltalk-80) or a hierarchy of visible behavior (a specification hierarchy, eg. Trellis/Owl [Schaffert 1986]) - we assume here a specification hierarchy.

the set S with the associative operation '*'. From this definition, different semi groups can be constructed, for example the semi group of positive integers with addition. It is only necessary that the set of objects bound to S has an associative operation which can be bound to '*'. The following example out of [Sutor 1987] shows such a definition of a semi group:

```
semiGroup () : category == set with
    "*" : ($,$) -> $
    associative ("*")
```

Similarly, we can construct sorted lists as algebraic structures over elements which must include an order relation (with the properties reflexive, asymmetric and transitive). Specification languages have modelled this concept by including generic type constructors, allowing the description of abstract types, which are instantiated by bounding the formal type and operation variables to actual types and operations (CLU], ADA , ScratchPad [Sutor 1987], etc). This documents that a new type can only be constructed if the necessary operations are provided. It would be desirable that the language could also test, that the operations have the necessary properties. This is still a topic of ongoing research in programming and specification languages.

Inheritance is very similar to genericity: similarly to the subclasses inheriting all operations from their super class, the instantiations in genericity provide the same operations as their generic type. Inheritance in most object-oriented languages does not allow for type variables, nor formal operation variables required in the subtype, but the same effect is often achieved by using of method selection in the superclass based on 'self', and using the same operation names in all subclasses; however, this latter possibility is more difficult to understand and the class interface does not document the need for operations in the subclasses.

3.2 DBMS Functionality provided as a Generic Class

Providing DBMS functionality by defining the class 'generic DB-object' depends on a number of operations defined for each subclass because a number of DBMS operations need access to certain object components or depend otherwise on values of the objects.

As a simplified example, consider the following definition of a sorted list:
"sortedList of element (with lessOrEqual (a,b: element):boolean)"
operations "initialize", "insert", "find", "getNext" ...
where element is a type variable and the 'with' clause documents, that the implementation depends on an operation 'lessOrEqual' defined for elements. It is possible to write generic code that implements the operations without specific knowledge about the elements of the list, except that a 'lessOrEqual' operation is provided by the element. The following example shows a possible instantiation of the generic sorted list above:
"sortedList of Name (with lessOrEqual mapped to name.before)"
where name.before is an operation that compares two names. Note that this respects encapsulation by using the module interface of 'names' instead of directly accessing the data in 'names'.

We have used the described method extensively for PANDA (without using a language that supports the above shown syntax) to write the functions of 'generic DB-object' for a data model similar to entity relationship [Chen1976] or the molecule concept [Batory 1984] [Härder 1987]. The following operations are typically necessary for each object class:

- comparison of two objects of the same type ('lessOrEqual' and 'equal')
- intersect object-geometry with a given rectangle to maintain a spatial access structure (Field Tree [Frank 1983], similar to Grid File [Nievergelt 1984] or EXHASH [Tamminen 1982])

- computation of an integer for values used for a hashing based index
- conversion to a string for each field (used for a basic output function)

Every DB-object has to provide the necessary operations which are mapped to the formal operations used in the generic definitions of the DBMS operations. We have found that most of these provided operations are very simple to write. Indeed, the code is very regular and can be produced automatically from a higher level description of the objects. In some cases, the programmer needs to write special code, different from the one automatically produced. For example this is the case, when the operation uses a value which is not a component of the object, but must be derived from the components.

4. Integration of DBMS with Object-Oriented Programming System

Following the proposal made, an object-oriented DBMS can be written as an application level package. This is an attractive alternative to the systems that include DBMS functionality within an object-oriented language [Penney 1987]. Most software engineering arguments speak for the former solution:

- The language is not burdened by DBMS functionality, and if DBMS support is not necessary for an application, it need not be included.
- The DBMS is integrated using standard language features. No new constructs need to be learned by the application programmer, and a mismatch between language and DBMS concepts can be avoided.
- The DBMS package can be selected and tailored specifically for an application class without requiring changes in the language.

The latter argument is important for the non-standard applications we work on (engineering databases, spatial information systems, cad/cam, etc.). They pose specific requirements for a DBMS: Depending on the application area, a DBMS must provide special functionality (eg. access based on spatial location), and its implementation must be adapted to yield the performance necessary.

5. Conclusions

We have shown how integration between an object-oriented DBMS and an application program can be achieved using inheritance. A language with multiple inheritance and genericity allows to define the data to be stored as modules which inherit DBMS functionality:

- Multiple inheritance is necessary, in order to allow objects to inherit the DBMS operations as part of their behavior (and still inherit other traits).
- Generic class descriptions with formal operation parameters to document the operations each subclass of the generic DBMS object must provide in order for the DB operations to work.

Data to be stored is defined as subclasses of the 'generic DB-object' that inherit DBMS functions. These subclasses must export a set of operations to be used by the DBMS.

The major advantage of the proposed method is that the interface between the DBMS code and the objects is clearly documented: The DBMS code shows which operations each DB-object must provide. These operations are the only interfaces between DBMS and object internals, thus respecting object-oriented philosophy. No DBMS specific features are necessary in the language and the DBMS can be written as an application level program, without dependency between object-oriented language and DBMS.

We believe, that multiple inheritance and genericity will be generally useful for building large software systems, especially information systems. Similar to DBMS, other functions can also be factored out and one would like to use other pre fabricated packages for presentation graphics and window management, for geometric data processing etc. [Smith 1986] [Sandberg 1986].

References

[Batory 1984] D.S. Batory and A.P. Buchmann. Molecular Objects, Abstract Data Types, and Data Models: A Framework. In: 10th VLDB conference, Singapore, 1984.

[Cardelli 1985] L. Cardelli and P. Wegener. On Understanding Types, Data Abstraction, and Polymorphism. ACM Computing Surveys, 17(4), April 1985.

[Egenhofer 1988] M. Egenhofer and A. Frank. A Precompiler for Modular, Transportable Pascal. SIGPLAN Notices, 23(3), March 1988.

[Frank 1983] A. Frank. Problems of Realizing LIS: Storage Methods for Space Related Data: The Field Tree. Technical Report 71, Swiss Federal Institute of Technology, Zürich (Switzerland), 1983.

[Härder 1985] T. Härder and A. Reuter. Architecture of Database Systems for Non-Standard Applications (in German). In: A. Blaser and P. Pistor, editors, Database Systems in Office, Engineering, and Scientific Environment, Springer Verlag, New York (NY), 1985.

[Härder 1987] T. Härder, K. Meyer-Wegener, B. Mitschang, A. Sikeler. PRIMA - a DBMS Prototype Supporting Engineering Applications. In: 13th VLDB conference, Brighton (England), 1987.

[Härder 1988] T. Härder, B. Mitschang, H. Schöning. Query Processing for Complex Objects. submitted for publication, 1988.

[Meyer 1986] B. Meyer. Genericity versus Inheritance. In: OOPSLA '86, Portland (Oregon), 1986.

[Nievergelt 1984] J. Nievergelt et al. The GRID FILE: An Adaptable, Symmetric Multi-Key File Structure. ACM Transactions on Databases, 9(1), 1984.

[Olthoff 1986] W.G. Olthoff. Augmentation of Object-Oriented Programming by Concepts of Abstract Data Type Theory: The ModPascal Experience. In: OOPSLA '86, Portland (Oregon), 1986.

[Penney 1987] D.J. Penney and J. Stein. Class Modification in the GemStone Object-Oriented DBMS. In: OOPSLA '87, Orlando (Florida), 1987.

[Sandberg 1986] D. Sandberg. An Alternative to Subclassing. In: OOPSLA '86, Portland (Oregon), 1986.

[Schaffert 1986] C. Schaffert, T. Cooper, B. Bullis, M. Kilian and C. Wilpolt. An Intorduction to Trellis/Owl. In: OOPSLA '86, Portland (Oregon), 1986.

[SIGMOD 81] Proceedings of the Workshop on Data Abstraction, Databases and Conceptual Modelling. Pingree Park (Colorado, June 1980), SIGMOD Record, 11(2), February 1981.

[Smith 1986] R.G. Smith, R. Dinitz and P. Barth. Impulse-86: A Substrate for Object-Oriented Interface Design. In: OOPSLA '86, Portland (Oregon), 1986.

[Sutor 1987] R.S. Sutor and R.D. Jenks. The Type Inference and Coercion Facilities in the Scratchpad II Interpreter. In: SIGPLAN '87 Symposium on Interpreters and Interpretive Techniques, St. Paul (Minnesota), 1987.

[Tamminen 1982] M. Tamminen. Efficient Spatial Access to a Data Base. In: ACM-SIGMOD, Orlando (FL), 1982.

[Wegner 1987] P. Wegner. Dimensions of Object-Based Language Design. In: OOPSLA '87, Orlando (Florida), 1987.

[Zilles 1984] S.N. Zilles. Types, Algebras and Modelling. In: M.L. Brodie et al., editors, On conceptual Modelling, Springer Verlag, New York (NY), 1984.

Instance Inheritance Mechanisms for Object Oriented Databases

Wolfgang Wilkes*

FernUniversität Hagen
Postfach 940
D-5800 Hagen
West-Germany

Abstract

Many object-oriented systems and semantic data models offer mechanisms for attribute inheritance based on the concept of generalization. But some applications, for instance from the fields of CAD/CAM or artificial intelligence, need an "instance inheritance relationship" which not only transfers the existence of attributes from one object to another, but also the values of these attributes. This paper discusses several types of instance inheritance and proposes a general inheritance relationship as a framework for the integrated treatment of different types of inheritance.

1. Introduction

One of the key ideas for data modelling in object-oriented systems is the use of generalization to organize object classes in taxonomy hierarchies [MyBW80]. Generalization is an abstraction mechanism which allows to view object classes at several levels of abstraction leaving specific details out of consideration.

The generalization establishes an *IS-A* relationship between a class and its superclasses. Via the IS-A relationship the class inherits the attributes of its superclasses, and every object of the class has the attributes defined in these superclasses. With the projection to these inherited attributes, an object o of class C can be treated as an element of a superclass C_S of C, i.e. there exists a virtual object o_S as instance of C_S which is a view of o (see figure 1).

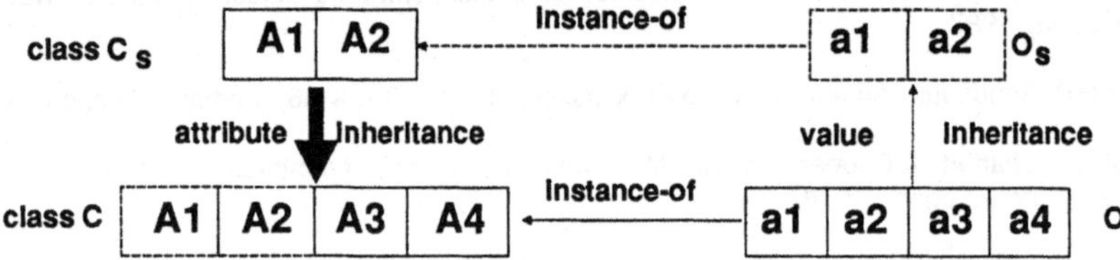

Figure 1: *IS-A* relationship: downward inheritance of attributes, upward inheritance of values

Views depend on their original data. If an object is updated, the abstract views of the object (i.e. the virtual objects which are members of superclasses) are also updated. Thus, the update of inherited attributes not only concerns the object as a member of its original class, but also as a member of its superclasses. If we consider the update propagation from an object to its abstract views as a form of value inheritance, we can state that the direction of value inheritance (bottom-up) is inverse to the direction of attribute inheritance (top-down).

There are some applications where a different form of inheritance is required. In CAD/CAM, for instance, we have design-objects which exist in several versions. The versions have certain common characteristics, often they have a common interface ([BaKi85], [MLNB83]). The interface describes the external phenotype of all versions (and hence of the design object), for example the geometrical and functional description of external pins of a chip. By using the interface it is possible to incorporate design objects into other (more complex) design objects without referring to a specific

* The work presented in this paper was supported by IBM Germany.

version ([WiKS88], [BaKi85]). This leads to the representation of interface data as a seperate interface object.

To ensure that every version of the design object has the same interface, interface data must not be updated within a version. But if updates of the interface are necessary, these updates have to be propagated instantly into all versions. This can be regarded as an inheritance of interface data by versions. But it is not sufficient only to transfer attribute definitions into the versions, since interfaces are described by concrete data (attribute values). Hence, we need an inheritance relationship by which an object not only inherits the existence of attributes, but moreover the attribute values of another object. This relationship has to provide a "value inheritance" (or "instance inheritance") as opposed to the "attribute inheritance" of the *IS-A* relationship.

The specific type of instance inheritance formulated above can be seen as a specification of the *is-a* relationship (mind the small letters). In section 2 the *is-a* relationship (between objects) will be introduced and its correspondence to the *IS-A* relationship (between classes) will be emphazised. There are more application areas requiring an instance inheritance mechanism, and some of them need different kinds of inheritance. In section 3 several types of inheritance will be identified and a framework for their integrated treatment will be proposed. It allows a selective inheritance of parts of objects and the attribute-wise specification of the type of inheritance.

2. *IS-A* and *is-a*: inheritance of attribute definitions and attribute values

The mechanism of generalization connects classes to their superclasses by the *IS-A* relationship. The properties of this relationship are defined in [MyBW80] by the *IS-A relationship postulates*:

1. All classes are organized into the *IS-A* hierarchy built by the binary *IS-A* relationship which is a partial order.
2. Extensional *IS-A* constraint:
   If C' *IS-A* C for classes C' and C then every instance of C' is also an instance of C.
3. Property inheritance rule:
   If A is an attribute of class C with domain D and C' *IS-A* C
   then there exists an attribute A of C' with domain D' and D' *IS-A* D.

Postulate 2 formally states the set inclusion of classes and subclasses, and postulate 3 describes the inheritance mechanism of the *IS-A* relationship. In connection with the inheritance a superclass sometimes will be called "transmitter class" and a subclass will be called "inheritor class".

Our goal is to define a relationship which relates objects and allows the inheritance of attribute values. This relationship will be called *is-a* relationship, and it has to obey the following *is-a value inheritance rule* [Marm87]:

If A is an attribute of object o with value v and o' *is-a* o
then there exists an attribute A of o' with value v', and v' = v.

By this rule *is-a* gets the following semantics: Via the *is-a* relationship an object inherits attribute values from higher level objects. The inherited attribute values of an object must not be changed in order to avoid violating the *is-a value inheritance rule.*

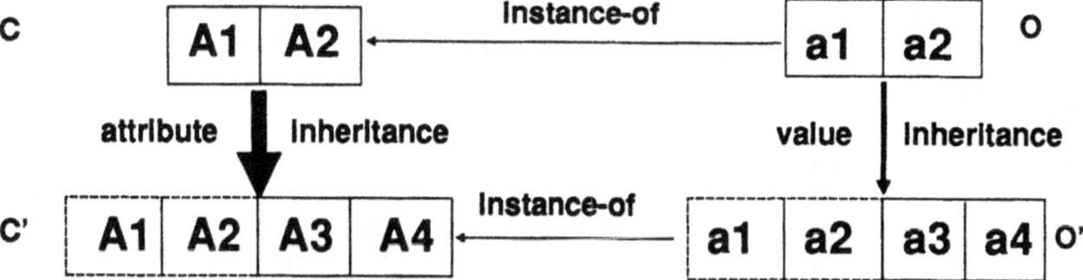

Figure 2: *is-a* relationship: top-down inheritance of attributes and values

If objects o' and o are *is-a* related (o' *is-a* o), then we can not follow that the corresponding classes C' and C, to which o' and o belong, are related by *IS-A*. But if all objects of a class C' are *is-a* related to objects of another class C, it can be shown that C' *IS-A* C.[1] Therefore we extend the *is-a* relationship to all objects of a class:

C' *is-a* C :<==> for every instance o' of C' there exists an instance o of C with o' *is-a* o

To sum up, C' *is-a* C implies (see figure 2):
(1) C' *IS-A* C, i.e. top down inheritance of attribute definitions, and
(2) every object o' of C' inherits attribute values from an object o in C, i.e. top down inheritance of attribute values.

By means of two examples (relationship between objects and versions, import of component's data into composite objects), the next section will illustrate how the *is-a* relationship can be applied.

3. Using the *is-a* relationship

3.1 Modelling of versions

We assume that versions of a gate have a common interface consisting of the name of the gate, the description of its function, its spatial expansion and its pins. This leads to the following definition of the class *GateInterface*:

```
class GateInterface with
      attribute-properties
            GateName:        ObjectNames;
            Function:        TextualDescriptions;
            Length, Width:   Integer;
            Pins:            {[PinId: Integer;   PinClass: (In, Out)]}
end;2
```

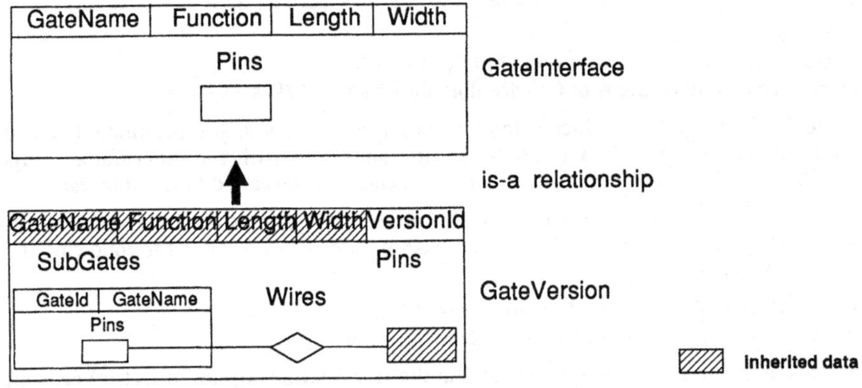

Figure 3: *is-a* relationship between *GateInterface* and *GateVersion*

Versions of gates are characterized by the subgates they use and the connections between them. Every version inherits the interface data of the corresponding *GateInterface* object. This is specified by an *is-a* relationship between *GateVersion* and *GateInterface* (see figure 3):

```
class GateVersion is-a GateInterface with
      attribute-properties
            VersionId:       Integer;
            SubGates:   {[   GateId:                               Integer;
                             GateName:                             ObjectNames;
                             Pins:                                 {PinId: Integer}  ]};
            Wires:      {[   GateId1, PinId1, GateId2, PinId2:     Integer           ]};
end;
```

1 A formal treatment of these subjects can be found in [MaWi88].

2 "[...]" is a record-constructor, "{...}" is a set-constructor.

By this definition every object of class *GateVersion* is *is-a* related to an *GateInterface* object and inherits its attributes and their values. The link to the *GateInterface* object has to be set at creation time of the *GateVersion* object:

```
insert o into GateVersion
    with
        o is-a interface-o;
        o.VersionId = 12; o.SubGates = . . .; o.Wires = . . .
    where
        interface-o.GateName = 'FLIP-FLOP'
```

In the example, the newly created version is linked to an interface object called 'FLIP-FLOP' of class *GateInterface*, thus inheriting its attributes and attribute values.

3.2 Import of component data into composite objects

To assemble gates by previously designed gates, we have to redefine the class *GateVersion*. Since the interface of a design object carries the appropriate information for using it as a component, the component's interface data have to be imported into the composite object. This can be modelled by an inheritance relationship: The composite object inherits the interface data of its components. Therefore, we redefine the attribute *SubGates* of class *GateVersion* in the following way: The new domain of *SubGates* is the class *ComplexSubGates* which is *is-a* related to the class *GateInterface*:

```
class GateVersion is-a GateInterface with
    attribute-properties
        VersionId:      Integer;
        SubGates:       {ComplexSubGate};
        Wires:          {[GateId1, PinId1, GateId2, PinId2]}
end;

class ComplexSubGate is-a GateInterface with
    attribute-properties
        GateId:         Integer;
        GateLocation:   Point;
end;
```

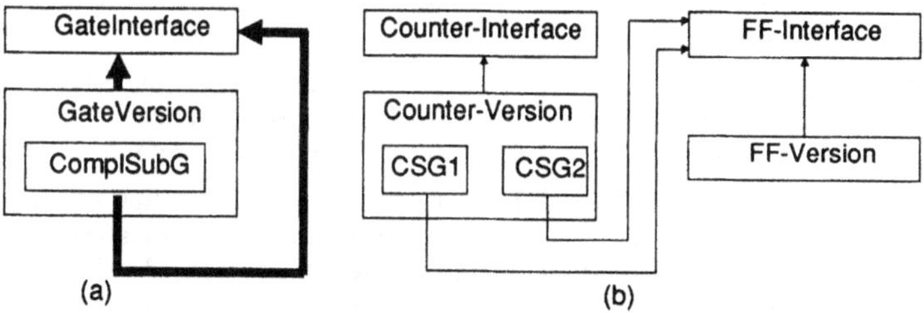

Figure 4: *is-a* relationships at the class level (a) and at the object level (b) to model composite objects

By this definition, every object of class *ComplexSubGate* is related to an object of class *GateInterface* and inherits its data. Thus, via the attribute *SubGates* the component's interface data are visible and can be used, for instance, to connect the pins of components. Figure 4a illustrates the *is-a* relationships between classes *GateInterface*, *GateVersion* and *ComplexSubGate*, and figure 4b shows the corresponding *is-a* relationships at the object level for the assembly of a counter by flip-flops.

4. Defining more specific inheritance relationships

In this section some possibilities to weaken the strict *is-a* relationship will be discussed, and a framework for defining several types of inheritance will be introduced.

Default values

With the *is-a* relationship, the inherited values must not be altered within the inheritor object. But for instance in AI-systems for recognizing given situations, the following mechanism is used: Some objects act as prototypes for "standard situations" and possess properties which are characteristic for these situations. To analyse a given situation the prototype object best fitting the situation is copied, and during the analysis of the given situation prototype properties may be overwritten.

A relationship like that can be regarded as a genuine *IS-A* relationship. But additionally, with the creation of an object of the subclass, an element of the superclass is chosen as prototype, and its attribute values are transmitted to the new object as default values. However, there is no further relationship between the two objects, i.e. updates are not propagated in any direction.

Selective inheritance

Selective inheritance means that not all information of the transmitter object is passed to the inheritor object. Distinction can be made between two cases:

- **Selective value inheritance**
  In this case attribute inheritance takes place, but only some attribute values are inherited by the inheritor object. Thus, the inheritor object is dependent on the transmitter object, but there may be some inherited attributes with values different from the transmitter object.
- **Selective attribute inheritance:**
  In this case the inheritor class does not inherit all attributes (i.e. definitional properties) from its transmitter class, it only inherits part of the attributes. The extensional *IS-A* constraint does not hold any more: Since an instance of the inheritor class not necessarily inherits all attributes of the transmitter class, it is not an instance of this transmitter class. But often it is useful to define some properties only concerning objects at a specific level of the *IS-A* hierarchy and not being inherited by lower level inheritor objects. An example will be given below.

Integrated treatment of different types of inheritance

To model all these cases, the kind of inheritance has to be defined individually for every attribute of the transmitter class. Hence, the definition of an inheritance relationship for a given transmitter class determines for every attribute

- **whether the attribute definition is transmitted (*IS-A* (attribute) inheritance),**
- **whether the value of the attribute is transmitted (*is-a* (value) inheritance),**
- **or whether the value of the attribute is transmitted as default value (*default* inheritance).**

To illustrate this inheritance relationship again we use the example of version management. Besides the representation of common data of versions, the set of versions has to be structured, for instance to keep the derivation history of the versions during the design process. The derivation history can be modelled as a graph of versions, and an edge from v1 to v2 indicates that v2 was derived from v1 ([KSWi86], [Wilk87]). By the following class definition (redefinition of class *GateInterface*), every *GateInterface* object gets an graph attribute for keeping the derivation history of its version set:

```
class GateInterface with
      attribute-properties
            DesignHistory:   Graph of Integer;
            GateName:        ...;          Function:  ...;
            Length, Width:   ...;          Pins:      ...;
end;
```

Since *GateVersion* objects must not inherit the attribute *DesignHistory* of *GateInterface*, we have to tailor the inheritance relationship between an interface and its versions to this situation:

```
inher-rel CommonPropertiesOfVersions with
      transmitter-class:    GateInterface;
      inheriting:           GateName, Function, Length, Width, Pins: is-a;
end;
```

By defining the class *GateVersion* as an inheritor in the relationship *CommonPropertiesOfVersions*, *GateVersion* objects inherit the values of all attributes of their *GateInterface* objects, except the attribute *DesignHistory* which is not transmitted via the *CommonPropertiesOfVersions* relationship:

```
class GateVersion inheritor-in CommonPropertiesOfVersions with
      attribute-properties
            ...
end.
```

5. Conclusion

In this paper several mechanisms of inheritance have been discussed, particularly instance inheritance mechanisms which are required as basic modelling concepts by applications from the field of CAD/CAM and AI. Three basic types of inheritance have been identified: The *IS-A* or attribute inheritance, the *is-a* or value inheritance, and the *default* inheritance. These different types of inheritance can be used in an integrated way by defining specific relationship types which determine for every attribute of the transmitter class the type of inheritance.

The approach to instance inheritance presented in this paper can be characterized as "schema-oriented" since inheritance relationships are defined in the schema (between classes). Two other approaches published in [BKSW88] and [NaBR88] can be regarded as "object-oriented". In [NaBR88] individual objects can evolve into a prototype for similar objects which are linked by an inheritance relationship to it. In our terms its type can be classified as default inheritance. In [BKSW88] objects play also the roles of classes, and the "abstraction relationship" between them covers the properties of *IS-A*, *is-a*, and *instance-of* relationships.

At the University of Hagen the prototype of a version manager is under implementation which offers an *is-a* relationship between objects and their versions. The implementation is based on the NF^2-database AIMP [Dada86], developed at the IBM Scientific Center Heidelberg.

6. References

[BaKi85] D.S.Batory, W.Kim: *Modelling Concepts for VLSI CAD Objects*. ACM TODS, Vol.10, No.3, September 1985

[BKSW88] T.Berkel, P.Klahold, G.Schlageter, W.Wilkes: *Modelling CAD-Objects by Abstraction*. Proc. 3rd Intern. Conf. on Data and Knowledge Bases, Jerusalem, June 27-30, 1988

[Dada86] P.Dadam, et.al.: *A DBMS Prototype to Support Extended NF2-Relations: An Integrated View on Flat Tables and Hierarchies*. Proc. SIGMOD, Washington D.C., May 1986

[KSWi86] P.Klahold, G.Schlageter, W.Wilkes: *A General Model for Version Management in Databases*. Proc. VLDB, Kyoto, August 1986

[MLNB83] D.McLeod, K.Narayanaswamy, K.V.Bapa Rao: *An Approach to Information Management for CAD/VLSI Applications*. Proc. SIGMOD, Engineering Design Applications, San Jose, May 1983

[Marm87] M.Marmann: *Modelling Mechanisms for Database Design and their applicability in the field of CAD/CAM*. Diploma thesis, University of Hagen / University of Dortmund, May 1987 (in German)

[MaWi88] M.Marmann, W.Wilkes: *Instance Inheritance in Databases*. Internal Paper, University of Hagen 1988 (in preparation)

[MyBW80] J.Mylopoulos, P.A.Bernstein, H.K.T.Wong: *A Language Facility for Designing Database-Intensive Applications*. ACM TODS, Vol.5, No.2, June 1980

[NaBR88] K.Narayanaswamy, K.V.Bapa Rao: *An Incremental Mechanism for Schema Evolution in Engineering Domains*. Proc. Data Engineering, Los Angeles, February 1988

[WiKS88] W.Wilkes, P.Klahold, G.Schlageter: *Complex and Composite Objects in CAD/CAM Databases*. Informatik Berichte, FernUniversität Hagen, No. 80, April 1988 (submitted for publication)

[Wilk87] W.Wilkes: *The Notion of Versions and its Modelling in CAD/CAM-Databases*. PhD-thesis, University of Hagen, September 1987 (in German)

IDENTIFICATION OF DATABASE OBJECTS BY KEY

Norman W Paton and Peter M D Gray
Department of Computing Science
University of Aberdeen
Aberdeen
Scotland

ABSTRACT

In relational databases one or more user-supplied scalar values are used to construct an *identifier key* representing the identity of an object. By contrast, object-oriented programming-languages and databases support the notion of *object identity* which is independent of the attribute values of the object. In this paper we compare the two approaches and describe a compromise based upon objects with keys.

1. INTRODUCTION

Since the outset, the relational model [Codd 70] has been associated with user-defined keys which uniquely identify a tuple and *foreign keys* which describe relationships between tuples. While value-based matching is a straightforward and transparent technique for expressing relationships, it provides no implicit support for referential integrity and is a potential source of update anomalies.

Object-oriented and semantic databases have a much stronger notion of object identity [Shipman 81, Khoshafian 86, Bancilhon 87, Beech 88]. Relationships are represented by storing the *object identifier (oid)* of the related object, thereby guaranteeing referential integrity. Updates to the attributes of an object have no effect on its *oid*. When an object is deleted from the database, it is the responsibility of the system to ensure that there are no *dangling references*. In queries, relational joins can be replaced by the more natural concept of path following, and a strong notion of object-identity greatly increases the ease with which semantically meaningful updates can be performed.

Object identity as implemented in most systems does not provide any one-to-one mapping from scalar key to object. We believe that a function on a scalar value which permits unambiguous identification of an object is useful when populating and updating a database which otherwise supports object identity. In this paper we describe an approach to the introduction of keys into Functional Data Model databases.

2. POPULATING OBJECT-CENTRED DATABASES

In this section we outline the syntax and semantics for insertion of data in three object-centred database systems - OSQL [Beech 88], EFDM [Kulkarni 86] and P/FDM [Gray 88]. The P/FDM schema of the database used in the examples is given in *figure 1*.

2.1. OSQL

OSQL is a proposed language for object-oriented databases, the syntax of which is based upon the relational query language SQL. To create an instance of type *company* the command **Create** is used.

```
Create company(country, coname)
instance c1 ('Britain', 'BL');
```

The variable *c1* has been assigned the *oid* of the instance of *company BL* from *Britain*. This variable can later be used in the creation of a *car* which is made by *company c1*.

```
Create car(model, category, is_made_by)
instance c2 ('Metro', 'small', c1);
```

This use of global variables (see also [Poul 88]) is convenient for ad-hoc updates within a session, but is not suitable for use across sessions and has probably been introduced because there is no mechanism in OSQL to permit reference to a particular entity instance given a scalar key.

2.2. EFDM

The EFDM is an implementation of the Functional Data Model of [Shipman 81]. To create an instance of an entity class, the command **new** is used.

```
for a new c in company
let country(c) = 'Britain'
let coname(c) = 'BL';
```

In the EFDM the scope of the variable *c* is local to the expression. To create an instance of class *car* made by *BL*, the command **let** is able to use an instance of *company* retrieved from the database.

```
for a new c in car
let model(c) = 'Metro'
let category(c) = 'small'
let is_made_by(c) =
        the co in company such that country(co) = 'Britain' and coname(co) = 'BL';
```

In the EFDM it is possible to express a constraint upon the instances of an entity class which will guarantee a one-to-one mapping from function values to entity instance.

```
constraint c1 on country(company), coname(company) -> unique;
```

The user of the EFDM can therefore be certain that an expression such as that used to populate *is_made_by* will return only one value.

```
declare company ->> entity
declare coname(company) -> string
declare country(company) -> string

declare car ->> entity
declare modname(car) -> string
declare category(car) -> string

declare co_link ->> entity
declare time(co_link) -> integer

declare owner ->> entity
declare cname(owner) -> string
declare sname(owner) -> string
declare first_saw(owner,car) -> integer

declare employees(company) ->> owner
declare is_made_by(car) -> company
declare has_owner(co_link) -> owner
declare has_car(co_link) -> car

key_of owner is cname, sname
key_of company is coname, country
key_of car is key_of(is_made_by), modname
key_of co_link is key_of(has_owner), key_of(has_car)
```

Figure 1: Example P/FDM schema with key definitions.

2.3. P/FDM

P/FDM is an interface from the logic programming language Prolog to a Functional Data Model Database. The Prolog programmer is given access to a number of predicates for creating and updating the database. In P/FDM, unlike the original DAPLEX [Shipman 81], a key is declared explicitly for each entity class. The command **key_of** is used to describe the components of the key. The syntax of **key_of** in extended BNF notation is

<key_of> ::= key_of <class> is <fields>

<fields> ::= <foreign> , <local> | <foreign> | <local>

<foreign> ::= key_of(<efun>) { , key_of(<efun>) }
<local> ::= <sfun> {, <sfun> }

where <efun> is a single valued function on <class> returning an entity and <sfun> is a single valued function on <class> returning a scalar.

The statement *key_of x is key_of(f), g* can be read as "the key of an entity y of class x is obtained by concatenating the key of the entity returned by f(y) onto the scalar returned by g(y)". Thus keys can be constructed from scalar attributes not only of the actual instance, but also from other related entity instances, which distinguishes P/FDM from other systems.

Definition: Entity class *c1* is *key dependent* upon entity class *c2* if the key of *c1* includes the key of *c2*.

To create an instance of class *company* the predicate **newentity** is used.

```
newentity(company,['BL','Britain'],Oid).
```

The predicate **newentity/3** takes as arguments the name of the entity class along with the key of the instance to be created, and returns the *oid* of the new instance. The functions *country* and *coname* are populated automatically. To create an instance of type car the syntax is similar.

```
newentity(car,['BL','Britain','Metro'],C),
addfnval(category,C,small).
```

In this case, the call to **newentity** populates the functions *is_made_by* and *model* while **addfnval** populates the function *category*. It is not possible to delete the value of any function used in the construction of a key. Since these functions are populated by the same operation as creates the instance, functions used in keys are guaranteed to return a value.

The predicate **getentity/3**, given an entity class and a key, uses an index to obtain the instance of the class with the given key. For example, to add the person *Jim Jones* to the employees of *BL* the following commands are issued.

```
getentity(company,['BL','Britain'],BL),
getentity(owner,['Jones','Jim'],Jim),
addfnval(employees,BL,Jim).
```

2.4. Bulk Loading Of Data

It is clearly very useful to be able to bulk-load data from a text file into the database, and both the EFDM [Kulkarni 83] and P/FDM provide load utilities. Loading data into relational databases is straightforward as relations are tables of data which can be printed. The load utility of an object-oriented database must however describe a network of objects which are subsequently identified by some internal token. Clearly there must be some way of referring to specific entity instances in a load utility.

The EFDM load utility requires that each entity class have associated with it a single-valued scalar function, the result of which uniquely identifies all instances of that class. In many cases it is necessary to invent a function such as *car_number* solely for use with the load utility.

In P/FDM it is the key of an entity class which uniquely identifies its instances and forms the basis for object identification in the load utility. The index which the system creates on the key of each entity class facilitates direct access to all objects referred to in the load file, so load times are independent of the size of the database. A load file for the example database is in *figure 2*.

3. MODIFICATIONS TO OBJECT-CENTRED DATABASES

3.1. Scalar Attributes

Updating scalar values in databases with object identity is straightforward as a clear distinction is made between scalar attributes and relationships. To change the name of a company from *BL* to *Rover* in OSQL the command **Set** is used to replace the old value with the new.

```
Set coname(c) = 'Rover'
for each company c where country(c) = 'Britain' and coname(c) = 'BL';
```

There is no mention in the OSQL proposal of a *for the* construct to guarantee the uniqueness of the

---

```
entity company
coname, country;
*
BL,  Britain;
VW,  Germany
*

entity car
key_of(is_made_by),   modname;   category
*
[BL,Britain],         Metro;     small
[BL,Britain],         Montego;   family
*

entity owner
cname, sname;   key_of(most_likes)
*
Fred, Smith;          [[BL,Britain], Montego]
Jane, Jones;          [[BL,Britain], Montego]
*

entity co_link
key_of(has_owner), key_of(has_car); time
*
[Fred,Smith],[[BL,Britain],Montego];    1
[Fred,Smith],[[BL,Britain],Metro];      2
*

function first_saw
key_of(owner), key_of(car), integer
*
[Fred,Smith], [[BL,Britain],Montego], 2
*

function employees
key_of(company), key_of(owner)
*
[BL,Britain],         [Fred,Smith]
[BL,Britain],         [Jane,Jones]
*
```

Load tables with the heading *entity* are used to create entity instances and populate single valued functions of arity one. In *entity* tables, everything to the left of the semi-colon is concerned with specifying the key. Square brackets are used to indicate levels of indirection between the entity being created and the entity with which the scalar value is directly associated. Load tables with the heading *function* can be used to populate any functions, and are necessary for populating multi-valued functions and functions of arity 2.

Figure 2: Example load file for P/FDM cars database.

result of an expression. When an object class is created it is possible to specify that a particular attribute is *unique,* but it is not clear that a number of attributes taken together can similarly be constrained. In the EFDM it is those features which guarantee the correctness of the update.

In P/FDM there is the complication that *coname* is used in the keys of *company, car* and *co_link.* When the value of a function which is used in the construction of a key is updated, the indexes of all key dependent entity classes are automatically updated. Thus when the *cname* of the *company BL* is changed to *Rover,* the key of the *Metro* is changed to *['Rover','Britain','Metro'].*

In relational databases there is no distinction made between updates to scalar attributes and relationships. When a value which is used as part of a foreign key is updated, it is necessary for the user to propagate the update and ensure the maintenance of referential integrity. As this is not a trivial task in a database with many relations, it is probably wise to forbid updates to the attributes used in the key of a relation [Khoshafian 86].

3.2. Relationships

The syntax for updating a reference from one instance to another is similar to the syntax for updating scalar values. To indicate that *Jane Jones* is no longer an employee of *BL* in the EFDM the command *exclude* is used.

```
for the c in company such that country = 'Britain' and coname = 'BL'
exclude employees(company) =
    { the o in owner such that cname(o) = 'Jane' and sname(o) = 'Jones' };
```

In P/FDM, when a non scalar function which is used in the construction of a key is updated, the indexes of all key dependent instances must be updated. Thus if the *Metro* were to be manufactured by *VW* in place of *BL,* the key of the *Metro* would be changed to *['VW','Germany','Metro'].*

```
getentity(car,['BL','Britain','Metro'],Metro),
getentity(company,['BL','Britain'],BL),
getentity(company,['VW','Germany'],VW),
updatefnval(is_made_by,Metro,BL,VW),
getentity(car,['VW','Germany','Metro'],Metro).
```

3.3. Deleting Objects

Deleting instances of objects is straightforward in all three systems, except for the question of how to identify a particular object in OSQL.

```
Delete each company c
where country(c) = 'Britain' and coname(c) = 'BL';
```

In each system, when an instance is deleted all references to the instance are automatically removed. In P/FDM, all entity instances which are key dependent upon the instance to be deleted are also removed. This often permits a single command to remove all the data associated with a complex object where many might otherwise be required. In a database of protein structures [Paton 88], all the data on a particular protein can be cleanly removed by a single command. As the protein is modelled using many entity instances to represent its primary and secondary structure, hundreds of separate delete operations would be required in the EFDM or OSQL. Automatic deletion of sub-objects will only normally be available using a mechanism such as triggers [Stonebraker 86]. In the example database, deletion of an *owner* results in automatic removal of all associated *co_link* entities and not only the *has_owner* function of *co_link.* This is the desired result, as an instance of *co_link* becomes meaningless when one of the objects it describes is deleted. When an entity instance is deleted all its subinstances are deleted automatically.

4. OBJECT IDENTITY

4.1. Overview

Defintition 1: An object has an existence and an identity which is independent of its value [Bancilhon 88].

Definition 2: Identity is that property of an object which distinguishes each object from all others [Khoshafian 86].

Definition: Two objects are *identical* if they have the same *oid.*

Definition: Two objects are *shallow-equal* if all scalar attributes of the object have the same value and all sub-objects are identical.

Definition: Two objects are *deep-equal* if all scalar attributes have the same value and all sub-objects are deep-equal.

To take account of these different types of equality, object-centred systems often have three equality operators [Bancilhon 87].

4.2. The Effect Of Keys On Object Identity

In P/FDM all objects which are shallow-equal are identical. For example, if the key of a person has been declared to be the concatenation of the christian name and surname of that person there is no way that the system can store data on two different people with the same name. A system which supports objects with unique keys is therefore less expressive than one which supports object identity as defined above. There are certainly applications in which this difference in expressiveness will be noticed. It is our belief that for most applications, the benefits offered by associating objects with a key more than compensate for the corresponding loss of expressiveness.

5. CONCLUSIONS

The introduction of object identity into database systems greatly increases the ease with which databases can be populated and updated. In systems with full object identity there is no consistently reliable way of identifying a particular instance of an entity, which complicates the process of adding data to a database. We have described an approach to introducing keys to Functional Data Model databases which permits direct access to specific entity instances and supports clean deletion of complex objects, while retaining most of the advantages conferred by object identity.

6. REFERENCES

[Bancilhon 87] Bancilhon, F., Briggs, T., Khoshafian, S. & Valduriez P., "FAD, A Powerful and Simple Database Language", Proc 13th VLDB.

[Bancilhon 88] Bancilhon, F.. "Object-oriented Database Systems", Invited lecture, 7th ACM SIGART-SIGMOD-SIGACT Symposium on Principles of Database Systems.

[Beech 88] Beech, D.. "A Foundation for Evolution from Relational to Object Databases", Proc EDBT-88, Springer-Verlag.

[Codd 70] Codd, E. F.. "A Relational Model of Data for Large Shared Data Banks", Comm ACM, Vol 13, No 6.

[Gray 88] Gray, P.M.D., Moffat, D.S. & Paton, N.W.. "A Prolog Interface to a Functional Data Model Database", Proc EDBT-88, Springer-Verlag.

[Khoshafian 86] Khoshafian, S.N. & Copeland, G.. "Object Identity", Proc OOPSLA-86.

[Kulkarni 83] Kulkarni, K.G.. "Extended Functional Data Model - User Manual", Persistent Programming Research Report 7, University of Edinburgh.

[Kulkarni 86] Kulkarni, K.G. & Atkinson, M.P.. "EFDM: Extended Functional Data Model", The Computer Journal, Vol 29, No 1.

[Paton 88] Paton, N.W. & Gray, P.M.D., "An Object-Oriented Database for Storage and Analysis of Protein Structure Data", in "Prolog and Databases: Implementations and Applications", Ellis Horwood.

[Poul 88] Poulovassilis, A.. "FDL: An Integration of the Functional Data Model and the Functional Computational Model", to be published in Proc 6th BNCOD.

[Shipman 81] Shipman, D.W.. "The Functional Data Model and the Data Language DAPLEX", ACM TODS, Vol 6, No 1.

[Stonebraker 86] Stonebraker, M.. "Triggers and Inference In Database Systems", in "On Knowledge Base Management Systems", Springer-Verlag.

The Design of Dynamo: A General-purpose Information Processing Model with a Time Dimension

Kotcherlakota V. Bapa Rao, Anat Gafni, and Georg Raeder

University of Southern California
Advanced Computing Support Center[1]

1 Introduction

Current trends in workstation-based distributed information processing are towards an integration and cross-fertilization of previously disparate information processing disciplines, such as programming languages, database management systems, hypermedia, and document processing. The object-oriented paradigm has played a crucial role in providing a conceptual infrastructure for this movement towards integration.

The research goal of the Dynamo project, underway at the University of Southern California Advanced Computing Support Center, is to gain a deeper understanding of the issues involved in conceptual integration. The Dynamo model attempts to unify the fundamental concepts of the information processing disciplines into a common object-oriented framework. A prototype implementation will be used to apply the model to collaborative document authoring and software construction.

An important and unique feature of the Dynamo model is its treatment of time as a first-class element of the model, in keeping with the central position it occupies in human activities. The concept of time is especially relevant to disciplines that seek to imitate human behavior such as artificial intelligence, and to disciplines that rely heavily on human interaction such as databases, hypertext, office information systems, or software development systems. Time may be considered in an "absolute" sense corresponding to real-world time, or in a "relative" sense that refers to the relative ordering of asynchronous events. The former is difficult to handle in a distributed setting, owing to the asynchronous nature of the environment. Very few information models exist in the literature that take time into account, in either the absolute or the relative sense.

Relative time offers a sound basis for addressing a number of problems that arise in the distributed, multi-user context. At a systems level, relative time provides the means for assigning priorities to requests, for sequencing out-of-order arrivals of messages, and even for achieving better guidelines for space management. Significantly, timestamps provide a way for synchronization of concurrent updates of data objects, as in the management of collaborative work. By "collaborative work" we mean the active interaction and contribution to a common product as well as the passive sharing of information. The main problems in this domain are the synchronization and merging of the efforts of the various collaborators, management of object evolution, maintenance of histories of past actions, and configuration management.

The approach of Dynamo is to associate each object with a *local virtual timestamp* that denotes a measure of the relative recency of that object. Preliminary results of work on the model indicate that an integration of the time dimension into an object-oriented information processing model, in conjunction with the specific strategic decisions taken in the design of the Dynamo model, holds

[1] *Authors' Address:* 3580 Wilshire Blvd. Suite 1910, Los Angeles, CA 90010. *Phone:* (213)743-3752
Electronic Mail: baparao@uscacsc.usc.edu, gafni@uscacsc.usc.edu, raeder@uscacsc.usc.edu

considerable promise in tackling such problems as concurrency control, update synchronization, version control, history tracing, and configuration management.

The aim of this paper is to discuss some of the ideas behind the Dynamo model, as well as some preliminary results of our work. Particular emphasis is placed on the time dimension, as it is an especially novel aspect of our approach.

2 The Approach of Dynamo

The basic information structuring mechanism in our model is the *object*. Information manipulation and retrieval are accomplished by means of *messages* between objects. The model consists of two layers. The *definition layer* provides the essentials of object definition and creation, and views the universe as a collection of objects that communicate via messages. The *interaction layer*, adds the concepts of *nodes* and *links* to those of the definition layer. Nodes and links are refinements of the object concept and are meant to enable the viewing of the universe as a semantic network (or graph) of information nodes with relationships among them.

The Definition Layer

When designing the details of the model, we paid attention to two main features of the Dynamo user environment:

- Dynamo is required to support end-users who are not computer experts. The basic characteristics of the underlying model will be apparent through any user interface. Thus, there is a need for simple, intuitive concepts of object definition and management.
- Dynamo applications will be run on distributed systems and accessed by many individuals over long periods of time. Thus, there is a need for supporting incremental changes without knowing the total application, without having planned the changes when creating the application, and without relying on a central authority like a database administrator.

Thus, we adopted a rather simple object model. An *object* in Dynamo contains a unique object *identifier*, a set of *attributes*, a set of *object constraints*, and a *timestamp*. An attribute consists of a *name*, a write-only *in-value*, a read-only *out-value*, *code* that maps the in-value to the out-value, and an *attribute constraint*.

The in-value or out-value of an attribute can be either an *atomic* data value, or a *reference* to another object. There is in principle no distinction between attributes that act as *properties*, i.e., data values or references, and those that act as *operations*. A property is simply an operation with the code part realizing an identity mapping of the in-value to the out-value (then called the *value*). This extends the information hiding principle to the interpretation of an attribute.

Constraints are predicates that put restrictions on which messages are accepted by an object. There are two kinds of constraints in the model, those attached to individual attributes, and those attached to the whole object. *Attribute constraints* are used for type checking of message parameters. When assigning an in-value to an attribute, the attached constraint must be satisfied for the value being assigned in order for the operation or property assignment to be allowed. Thus, these constraints are *pre-conditions* for the operations. Specifying types in this way amounts to *structural* type equivalence, since any parameter with a structure that satisfies a given constraint can be used as in-value to that attribute. *Object constraints* are attached to the object as a whole and are used for specifying relations that must hold among the object's attributes. Thus, these are integrity constraints on the object's own type. All such constraints are checked whenever an object's state changes. Thus, these constraints are *post-conditions* for messages. It is up to the code parts of the attributes to effect state changes in such a way that the constraints always hold.

Constraint handlers can be placed in the code part of attributes.

The *timestamp* of an object reflects the *virtual time* of the last message received. Whenever an object is modified, it receives a timestamp which is higher than its previous value. A new copy of the object with this new timestamp is made, and the older one is still accessible as an older *version* of the object. By specifying a virtual time value, any version of an object can be retrieved.

Our notion of virtual time was inspired by the work of Jefferson [Jef85]. We employ a modified form of the Time Warp mechanism of Jefferson to synchronize messages. Our scheme works as follows. A read message (any message that does not modify the state is a read message, the others are write messages) with a given time value will yield the version with the highest timestamp less than or equal to the given time. A read with no time will yield the latest version. A write message with no time given will create a new version, whereas a write with a specific time will be rejected if the time is not higher than that of the latest existing version.

Employing virtual time means that there is no global mechanism to synchronize the timestamps of various objects, and thus objects can have widely different timestamps. This is of no concern, however, since synchronization takes place at access time. If an advanced object updates an object that is lagging behind, this will synchronize the latter object. On the other hand, if a lagging object attempts to update an advanced object, its operation will fail, and it will be forced to read the latest version before continuing, thereby updating its own clock. The strength of virtual time is that it extracts the meaningful order relationships in a distributed, asynchronous environment.

There are no object class definitions or schemas in our model. *Cloning* is the basic object creation operation. The *clone* operation creates a copy, or "clone" from an existing *source* object which serves as a prototype. The clone receives copies of all the source's attributes and their contents. It exists independently of the source, and can later be modified in arbitrary ways.

Delegation refers to an information-sharing mechanism whereby references to an attribute of an object (the "child") can be re-routed to another object (the "parent"). The child object can be thought to be "inheriting" the attribute in question from the parent object. The benefits of delegation versus class inheritance are elaborated in [Lie86] and [US87]. We adopted delegation due to its conceptual simplicity and great flexibility, which we believe are crucial qualities that will be reflected in the user interface. The form of inheritance provided in our model can be characterized as *incremental multiple inheritance by delegation*, since we can delegate to multiple sources, and each delegation is specified incrementally by editing the object. Note that data attributes may be delegated as well as code, allowing objects to share data.

The Interaction Layer

The interaction layer partitions objects into *nodes* and *links*, and specifies how messages are sent over links. This layer also provides a few essential operations on nodes and links that are needed for supporting high-level information management functions.

Nodes are objects that represent independent information units meaningful to the application domain. Nodes are the main containers of information, and they provide the granularity of information reuse in different contexts. A *user node* represents the user and his/her actions as part of the information processing model. Its input stream of messages may be viewed as a mailbox. Collaborating users may, thus, correspond as part of the model. Nodes are related to other nodes by *reference attributes* that are references to *link* objects. For a user node they define the locus of interest of the user in an information network.

Links are objects that represent relationships among nodes. Unlike nodes, which have meaning irrespective of the links they are attached to, links have no meaning in the absence of nodes.

Being full-fledged objects, they possess all of the features of objects. Rather than being just a named reference, they may contain extensive information about the relationship, including actions (specified as code) that have to be taken whenever the link is traversed. Links have timestamps that are analogous to those of nodes. When messages from one node to another pass via a link, the link object's attributes are accessed, causing the link's timestamp to be automatically updated in parallel with that of the destination node. This ensures that links are always up-to-date with respect to the nodes they point to, so that they know about the latest versions.

Since links are objects, they can represent complex kinds of relationships between nodes. The ability to specify operations and constraints means that, among other things, n-ary relationships and ordered lists can be easily represented. It also introduces a level of *abstraction*, since a link can map symbolic node names to actual objects (e.g., providing a "next" iterator), and it may specify how components linked to a more abstract node are represented and how they are to be put together.

The interaction layer provides some useful operations on nodes and links. *Compose* and *decompose* help create and manipulate abstractions. The *traverse* operation performs a transitive link formation, essentially moving a node N, with a link to a node A, to another node B, by following a link from A to B and forming a link from N to B.

The *trace* operation allows users to follow and view their past actions and their side effects, starting at a given time in the past. It is useful for purposes of reviewing and debugging. A trace follows all actions in the system rooted at the node initiating the *trace* command, from a given virtual time. This is possible, since the virtual time mechanism keeps message queues that essentially leave footprints of all actions in the system. The values returned to the originator of a trace will be the names of the nodes, the times, and the attributes activated due to all the actions along the trace. The receivers and the timestamps of all messages generated by each traced action serve as input parameters to recursive *trace* calls. This recursive process stops when the originator's *trace* message itself is encountered in the trace. A trace can be parameterized to perform a certain action at all nodes visited.

3 Applications of Virtual Time

In this section we will illustrate how the time-related concepts provided by our model support central functions of an information processing system.

Version Control. We have replaced the conventional version scheme of explicit version creation and symbolic names (as in [Tic85]) by an automatic scheme that relies on *time* as the identifying key to locate a given version. Our time-based scheme has several benefits. It is easier to identify a configuration that existed at a certain time, rather than having to find all the version numbers that make up a given configuration. The scheme solves some of the version update problems identified in the literature [MBK86], such as the *indirect change problem*, that occurs when a new version inherits a link to the previous version, thereby being able to modify it, whereas in our scheme one cannot modify a version with an earlier timestamp. Also the *multiple path problem*, that results from simultaneous creation of a next version by two different nodes, thereby causing ambiguity as to which version should be accessed. With our scheme one of them will get the later timestamp, and only it will be accessed. Our version scheme results in a linear version graph of object *histories*. We can support *alternative* versions (sometimes called *variants*) by cloning. Since the source of a clone is retained, the root of a version tree side branch is maintained.

Configuration Control. Combining components into a bigger construct, or configuration, requires a mechanism for selecting components according to a given criterion, and a component must be allowed to be a part of several different configurations. The composition capability of link objects provides a tool for the definition of a configuration and the linking of the components together, where the selection of components is known in advance. When the selection is done by a user navigating through the system, the *trace* operation described earlier would form a record of those nodes traversed. In this way, the trace concept can be used both to freeze a certain set of versions for a configuration, and to ensure that all components selected have the latest versions. Furthermore, since the time dimension of the model is orthogonal to object network topology, we can set up configurations that will be automatically updated as the components evolve with new versions, by recording the objects that make up a particular configuration.

Synchronization. The rejection of out-of-sync write operations gives us a primitive for *concurrency control* (it is simple to construct a semaphore based on it). If all writes carry the timestamp of the read on which the write operation is based, we can guarantee that several writers do not make updates to the same version. One modification is accepted and the others are notified of their failure. This is the most common concurrency problem in the type of interactive applications we are foreseeing for Dynamo. Note, however, that since we save all versions of all objects, write operations are no longer destructive. This considerably ameliorates concurrency problems like simultaneous writers, in effect transforming them into problems of version management rather than concurrent access. Virtual time also provides sequencing synchronization, for achieving in-order reception of messages in spite of potential out-of-order arrivals. This can serve as a mechanism for solving problems arising in a wide range of application domains, from distributed simulations synchronization problems to sliding window network protocols, and priority systems.

Suggested Versions. Version control allows collaborators to express their different opinions, but it does not support the merging of contributions into a unified work. Dynamo provides the concept of a *suggestion server* for each node, that maintains a "shadow" queue of messages that represent alternative modifications to existing node versions. For example, write operations that failed because of a version mismatch may be queued here. The suggestions can be reviewed and selectively incorporated in the node if appropriate, or a new clone may be established if a suggestion seems to warrant a version side branch. Suggestion messages are identical to regular messages, except for an indication flag. Turning the flag off will cause the message to be forwarded to the node.

4 Further Work

Our immediate further plans for Dynamo call for a prototype implementation, as well as refinement of the model. The prototype will serve as a testbed for our model and our implementation techniques through applications within collaborative document authoring and software construction. These are areas that can benefit greatly from the application integration possible through the conceptual integration of the model.

Although several recent implementation efforts in object-oriented databases [DD86], hypertext systems [Mey86] [GS87], and the Time Warp mechanism [Jef85] can provide guidelines for efficient implementation of the model, Dynamo raises several challenging issues that we intend to investigate. Our constraint scheme requires a new approach to ensuring that only minimal parts of given constraints are recomputed for each message delivery. The incremental nature of the model can be exploited here. Likewise, delegation requires behind-the-scenes administration to ensure that most delegated calls actually will not cause messages through the whole delegation chain.

The notion of time introduces the need for keeping unlimited amounts of data forever. The technology for supporting archival storage is just beginning to emerge today as large-capacity WORM (write once, read many) storage devices [Gai88]. This new technology may play a key role in realizing the model. Note that we can save versions in an incremental fashion, with the write messages constituting the increments. Thus, saving the input queue of messages can serve not only for sequencing and tracing purposes, but also for dynamic version construction.

The time dimension has a bearing on virtual memory replacement policies. The prediction of the "near future" can now not only rely on the recent past access patterns, but also on definite time information. Also, an anticipatory fetch of a working-set of objects, based on the objects connected by links to the currently active objects, will be explored as the basis for execution-time object management.

Our model blurs the distinction between code and data, and thereby between active and passive objects. This forces us to revise the traditional approach to operating system issues. Every object is now viewed as a server whenever it receives a message, and as a client whenever it sends a message to another object. Thus, the difference between the operating system and application layers practically disappears. All software components on a workstation can eventually be recast to be described by this universal client–server model. In particular, we can obtain a unified approach to all system resources: memory, processors, display screens, input devices, database relations, and system programs can all be handled via the same mechanisms and will look the same for all clients. Thus, a few initial objects can contain all the functionality that is traditionally termed the "operating system kernel," and this will be inherited by all other objects in the system. The view of objects as autonomous units also maps immediately onto distributed hardware.

References

[DD86] K. Dittrich and U. Dayal, editors. *Proceedings of the 1986 International Workshop on Object-Oriented Database Systems*. IEEE, 1986.

[Gai88] J. Gait. The Optical File Cabinet: A Random-Access File System for Write-Once Optical Disks. *IEEE Computer*, 21(6), June 1988.

[GS87] P.K. Garg and W. Scacchi. Maintaining Software Life Cycle Documents as Hypertext: Issues, Analysis, and Directions. University of Southern California, Computer Science Department Technical Report, 1987.

[Jef85] D.R. Jefferson. Virtual Time. *ACM Transactions on Programming Languages and Systems*, 7(3), July 1985.

[Lie86] H. Lieberman. Using Prototypical Objects to Implement Shared Behavior in Object-Oriented Systems. In *Proc. of the OOPSLA '86 Conf. on Object-Oriented Programming Systems, Languages and Applications*, 1986.

[MBK86] S. Mittal, D.G. Bobrow, and K.M. Kahn. Virtual Copies: At the Boundary Between Classes and Instances. In *Proc. of the OOPSLA '86 Conf. on Object-Oriented Programming Systems, Languages and Applications*, 1986.

[Mey86] N. Meyrowitz. Intermedia: The Architecture and Construction of an Object-Oriented Hypermedia System and Applications Framework. In *Proc. of the OOPSLA '86 Conf. on Object-Oriented Programming Systems, Languages and Applications*, 1986.

[Tic85] W.F. Tichy. RCS – A System for Version Control. *Software – Practice and Experience*, 15(7), July 1985.

[US87] D. Ungar and R.B. Smith. Self: The Power of Simplicity. In *Proc. of the OOPSLA '87 Conf. on Object-Oriented Programming Systems, Languages and Applications*, 1987.

A Uniform Concept for Storing and Manipulating Engineering Objects *

Alfons Kemper and Mechtild Wallrath

Fakultät für Informatik
Universität Karlsruhe
D-7500 Karlsruhe
West Germany

1 The Uniform Concept

Object-orientation as a basic concept for engineering database systems has become very popular in the last few years. Object-orientation is typically approached from one of two viewpoints: the *behavioral* or the *structural* emphasis. In most object-oriented database management systems it has been tried to meet the engineering requirements by increasing the structural expressiveness of the underlying data model. Some examples are the extensions of the entity-relationship model [5], extensions of the functional data model [3,4], molecular objects [1,7], complex objects [12], nested relations [17,2], and abstract data types that are embedded in various data models [10,18,13,8,11].

Structural object orientation in the data model, however, is not sufficient. The thesis of this paper is that the two concepts, behavioral and structural object-orientation, can be integrated to form a fruitful symbiosis for an engineering database system. This is achieved by utilizing a *uniform* object concept at all system layers, i.e., the query language, the transaction and recovery control component, the programming environment, and even the storage component. The uniform object concept provides for a natural mapping of externally visible application-specific objects to internal database entities. This process can be done without compromising efficiency because the one-to-one correspondence between internal and external representation makes costly transformations oblivious. This homogeneous treatment of objects at all layers allows for further optimizations in the form of function migration. Operations that are used to select objects on the basis of even complex computations can be migrated into the database kernel in order to gain efficiency. Another consequence of the uniform object metaphor is that it facilitates efficient manipulation of persistent database objects within programming environments through caching techniques.

An important characteristic of engineering applications is their need for efficiency, i.e., very often even real time performance. This prohibits to direct each access to a persistent objects over costly DBMS interfaces. Rather, the relevant objects should be cached in a special *object cache* [16,15]. An object cache that resides in main memory allows to selectively cache database objects, manipulate them, and transfer them back into the database. The object

*The work described in this paper was done in the R^2D^2 (Relational Robotics Database System with Extensible Data Types) project. R^2D^2 is a cooperative project among the IBM Scientific Center Heidelberg and the University of Karlsruhe, Fakultät für Informatik.

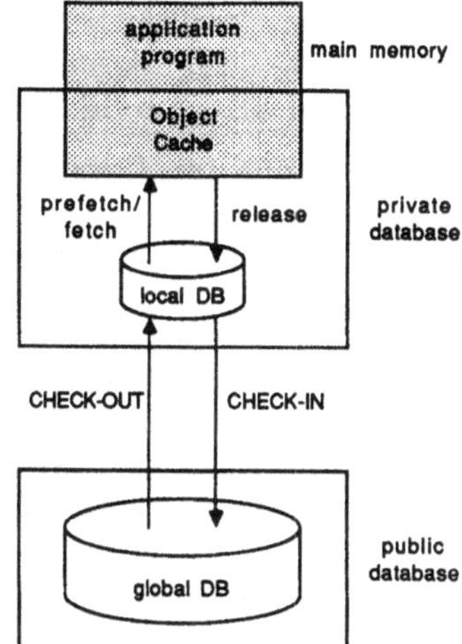

Figure 1: Overall Object Cache Architecture

cache is controlled by an object-oriented transaction mechanism that provides for locking and recovery of database entities.

Typically engineering applications have a server/client architecture with a public database on the database server and a private database on each client. Objects, required for a specific application can then be checked out from the public database into the private database at the beginning of a transaction. Here, they reside on secondary memory (local database) in the same representation as in the public database. The object cache can now be regarded as a buffer between the local database and the application program, i.e., objects transferred into the cache are part of the private database but they do not reside any more on secondary memory but in the main memory, that is, within the address space of the application program. Once the objects are in the object cache, a very efficient access is guaranteed. Thus, the object cache together with the local database form the private database, as shown in Figure 1.

2 The Realization in R^2D^2

Such a homogeneous object concept has been utilized in the R^2D^2 (**R**elational **R**obotics **D**atabase System with Extensible **D**ata Types) system. The structural basis of R^2D^2 is formed by the extended NF^2 data model [14]. The behavioral object-orientation has been achieved by the integration of abstract data types into this data model [8,11]. R^2D^2 supports the definition of user defined data types consisting of an internal (NF^2) representation and a collection of operations to access and manipulate the database objects. The operations are implemented as Pascal subroutines and can be used within the database kernel, i.e., as part of the data manipulation language as well as at the programming interface. Efficient access to database objects at the programming interface is achieved by the object cache [6] which is part of the application program. The transfer of database objects from the local database into the object cache can be initiated by an explicit *prefetch* statement or by an implicit *fetch* statement, i.e., by just referencing them. The *(pre)fetch* statement causes the referenced objects to be transferred into main memory. Thereby they are automatically transformed from database into main memory representation. After the first reference the objects remain in the object cache, where they can be manipulated via the predefined operations, until they are either explicitly or implicitly released from the cache. Thus the object cache and thereby the performance of the application program with respect to transfer of the required objects is optionally under explicit programmer control.

2.1 Interaction Between Global and Local Database

An engineering transaction may request objects from the public (global) database. Objects thus specified are *checked-out* of the public database and stored as a physical copy in the local database – provided no conflict with the check-out specification of another transaction occurred. The local database will typically reside on an engineering workstation. Within the local database objects are still represented in the format of the underlying data model. Objects are either checked-out `for read` or `for update`. In both cases they are appropriately locked in order to avoid any uncontrolled concurrency among parallel transactions. In the case of `for update` the objects are *checked* back *in*to the public database at the end of the transaction. [6] provides a more detailed description of the transaction control mechanism used in R^2D^2.

2.2 Interaction Between the Local Database and the Object Cache

From the local database objects are transferred into the object cache. This can occur via an explicit *prefetch* statement in the program or just by referencing a particular object that exists in the local database. In the latter case it is implicitly *fetched* into the object cache, the disadvantage being, that the operation that references an object not resident in the object cache might be rather inefficient because of the additional time required to transform the object. After the first reference the object remains in the main memory representation until it is either explicitly or implicitly released from the object cache. Thus it is – not considering the performance – transparent to the user whether an object is resident in the cache or in the local database. For implicit release the programmer can – depending on the object size – specify the maximum number of objects of a particular type that may reside in the cache. In case this number is reached the run-time system will release the least recently used object(s) into the local database.

2.3 Transformation of Objects from their Database into Main Memory Representation

As a first host programming language of R^2D^2 we have chosen Pascal. In order to provide convenient access from Pascal to the objects resident in the *object cache* Pascal data structures have been chosen as main memory representation of database objects. This requires that the objects have to be transformed from their database structure into a Pascal data structure (T1) and vice versa (T2). Operations on persistent objects are implemented and executed on this Pascal representation. Schematically this looks as shown in Figure 2.

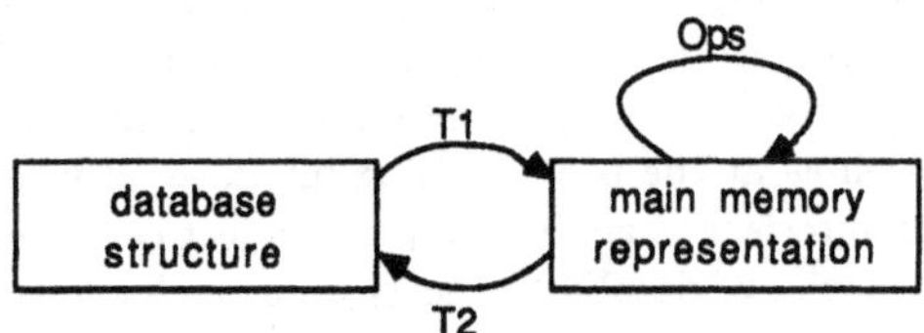

Figure 2: Transformation Steps

The Pascal representation is – under some user control – automatically generated. Steps T1 and T2 of the diagram in Figure 2 are automatically carried out by the system, meaning, in particular, that the program code for the transformations is automatically generated.

3 An Example

In this section we want to illustrate the uniform object concept described in the previous chapters with an example. For this purpose let us model a *cuboid* as an abstract data type. This cuboid can be described by its material and its geometry and by several operations applicable to the cuboid. In R^2D^2 the ADT *cuboid* can be defined as follows:

```
create ADT cuboid is
       [MATERIAL: string(10),                  – [...] denotes a tuple –
       GEOMETRY: ⟨8 FIX [V_ID: string(2),       – ⟨...⟩ denotes a list –
                         LOCATION: vector ]⟩]
with
    operation vertex(i:integer,c:cuboid) returns vector
              ...
    operation in_origin(c:cuboid) returns bool
              ...
    operation volume(c:cuboid) returns real
              ...
    operation rotate(angle:real,c:cuboid) returns cuboid
              ...

end cuboid.
```

Notice, that the attribute LOCATION is not of an atomic type but of type *vector* which is assumed to be a previously defined ADT.

We can now utilize the ADT *cuboid* to define the set *CUBOIDS* as follows:

```
create CUBOIDS { cuboid }
```

In order to transfer objects of type *cuboid* into the private database an object cache variable is declared as:

```
var cuboid_cache : cache of cuboid
```

The preprocessor that translates a program with embedded object cache constructs automatically transforms this declaration into a valid Pascal declaration, e.g.

```
cuboid_cache : array[1..Large_Const] of cuboidptr
```

where *cuboidptr* is a pointer to the Pascal representation of an ADT *cuboid*.

The *check-out* of objects from the global into the local database that is associated to such an object cache is accomplished by an embedded database request statement in the Pascal code. An example would be:

```
select c into cuboid_cache
from  c in CUBOIDS
where volume(c) > 200
for update
```

In this example c is a variable for an instantiation of the abstract data type *cuboid*. The set of *cuboids* retrieved in this statement is now accessible via the cache variable *cuboid_cache* which has been bound to the result set by the "into ..." clause.

Any element of an object cache can be accessed via its position in the pointer array, for example, we could repeatedly apply the functions *display* and *rotate* to the i-th element of the cache `cuboid_cache` as follows:

```
...
for j:= 1  to 36 do
  display(rotate(10 * j, cuboid_cache[i]))
    ...
```

As can be seen from this example the operations defined for the ADT *cuboid*, e.g., *volume* and *rotate*, can be applied within a DML statement, i.e., in the database kernel as well as in the application program.

When elements of an object cache are accessed, two cases can arise:

1. the i-th element of the cache is already resident in main memory as a Pascal structure due to a previous access or a prefetch operation. In this case no additional action is needed.
2. the i-th element is not resident in Pascal representation which is determined by the runtime system from an index table. In this case the referenced object is transferred from the local database into Pascal representation before the first *rotate* is performed.

The *check-in* of objects which have been manipulated in the object cache is initiated via the statement

propagate cuboid_cache

This causes the cache objects to be transferred to the local database and, subsequently, to be propagated to the global database.

4 Conclusions and Future Work

In this paper we have shown how to provide a uniform concept for storing and manipulating engineering objects. The homogeneous treatment of objects, is achieved in R^2D^2 by maintaining a correspondence between objects in the programming environment, i.e., in the object cache, and in the database kernel. Therefore, objects exhibit the same behavior at both system levels. In addition the efficiency required for engineering applications is achieved by the object cache architecture that allows to prefetch objects that are relevant to an application and cache them in main memory representation. Thus, once an application has started, the relevant objects are local within the program's address space and can therefore be manipulated efficiently.

The current implementation status of R^2D^2 is as follows. The integration of ADTs has been implemented for some time. The automatic generation of Pascal structures and the transformation of objects from their NF^2 database structure into Pascal representation and vice versa is fully operational. The object cache is operational for local copy update, that is, objects may be checked out of the global database `for read`. The update propagation mechanism, i.e., *check-in*, is currently being implemented.

A first large application, a robot simulation system called ROSI has just been implemented based on the R^2D^2 system. This implementation has proven that using the object cache interface it is possible to achieve even real time efficiency which is often required in engineering applications. To tune the system for efficiency requires to prefetch – in a loading phase – all relevant objects into the object cache before the execution starts.

References

[1] D. S. Batory and W. Kim. Modeling concepts for VLSI CAD objects. *ACM Trans. Database Syst.*, 10:322–346, 1985.

[2] P. Dadam et al. A DBMS prototype to support extended NF^2 relations: an integrated view on flat tables and hierarchies. In *Proc. ACM SIGMOD Conf. on Management of Data*, pages 376–387, 1986.

[3] U. Dayal et al. Simplifying complex objects: the PROBE approach to modeling and querying them. In H. Schek and G. Schlageter, editors, *Informatik Fachberichte No. 136*, pages 17–38, Springer, Berlin, 1987.

[4] N. P. Derret, D. H. Fishman, W. Kent, P. Lyngbaek, and T. A. Ryan. An object-oriented approach to data management. In *Proc. COMPCON*, pages 330–335, 1986.

[5] K. R. Dittrich, W. Gotthard, and P. C. Lockemann. Complex entities for engineering applications. In Spaccapietra, editor, *Proc. 5th Entity-Relationship Conference*, pages 421–440, North Holland, 1987.

[6] M. Dürr and A. Kemper. Transaction control mechanism for the object cache interface of R^2D^2. In *Proc. of the Third Intl. Conf. on Data and Knowledge Bases: Improving Usability and Responsiveness*, Morgan-Kaufman, Jerusalem, Israel, Jun 1988.

[7] T. Härder, K. Meyer-Wegener, B. Mitschang, and A. Sikeler. PRIMA – a DBMS prototype supporting engineering applications. In *Proc. of the VLDB Conf.*, pages 433–442, Brighton, UK, Sep 1987.

[8] A. Kemper, P. C. Lockemann, and M. Wallrath. An object-oriented database system for engineering applications. In *Proc. ACM SIGMOD Conference on Management of Data, San Francisco*, pages 299–311, May 1987.

[9] A. Kemper and M. Wallrath. An analysis of geometric modeling in database systems. *ACM Computing Surveys*, 19(1):47–91, Mar 1987.

[10] B. Lindsay, J. McPherson, and H. Pirahesh. A data management extension architecture. In *Proc. of the ACM SIGMOD Conf. on Management of Data*, pages 222–227, San Francisco, May 1987.

[11] V. Linnemann et al. Design and implementation of an extensible data base management system supporting user defined data types and functions. In *Proc. of the VLDB Conf.*, Long Beach, Ca., Sep 1988.

[12] R. A. Lorie and W. Plouffe. Complex objects and their use in design transactions. In *Proceedings of Database Week*, pages 115–121, San Jose, May 1983.

[13] S. L. Osborne and T. E. Heaven. The design of a relational database system with abstract data types for domains. *ACM Trans. Database Syst.*, 11(3):357–373, Sep 1986.

[14] P. Pistor and F. Andersen. Designing a generalized NF^2 data model with an SQL-type language interface. In *Proc. Twelfth VLDB Conf.*, pages 278–285, 1986.

[15] A. Purdy, B. Schuchardt, and D. Maier. Integrating an object server with other worlds. *ACM Trans. Office Information Syst.*, 5(1):27–47, Jan 1987.

[16] L. Rowe. A shared object hierarchy. In K. Dittrich and U. Dayal, editors, *Proc. Intl. Conf. on Object-Oriented Database Systems*, IEEE Computer Society Press, Pacific Grove, Ca., Sep 1986.

[17] H. J. Schek and P. Pistor. Data structures for an integrated database management and information retrieval system. In *Proc. VLDB Conf.*, pages 197–207, Mexico City, 1982.

[18] M. Stonebraker and L. Rowe. The design of POSTGRES. In *Proc. ACM SIGMOD Conf. on Management of Data*, Washington, D.C., 1986.

Managing Persistent Data with Mneme: Designing a Reliable, Shared Object Interface*

J. Eliot B. Moss *Steven Sinofsky*†

Department of Computer and Information Science
University of Massachusetts, Amherst

Abstract

We investigate issues that arise when attempting to integrate object-oriented languages and database features. We provide criteria for database/language support in the context of design applications, and consider the advantages of integration over more traditional database systems. We then discuss the design of Mneme, a system that narrows the gap between object-oriented databases and programming languages, both traditional and object-oriented. Mneme includes facilities for sharing, reliability, and clustering of objects, as well as a high degree of flexibility. We compare Mneme with other current and recent research efforts, and describe Mneme's particular contributions.

1 Introduction

In this paper we investigate some of the issues that arise when attempting to integrate object-oriented languages and database features. We consider the advantages over more traditional database systems of such integration in the context of design applications such as software development environments. We describe the design of a system, *Mneme* (NEE-mee, the Greek word for memory), that will narrow the gap between programming language data structures and databases. We further describe the advantages and contributions of Mneme, and compare it with related systems.

The presentation is organized as follows. This introduction describes our motivation, the general issues with which we are concerned, and the specific goals we have for the Mneme system. The next section gives an overview of the concepts Mneme provides to clients. This is followed by a discussion of the internal design for the initial Mneme prototype. We then compare Mneme (as conceived more than as currently implemented) with some other well known current and recent efforts, and conclude, summarizing Mneme's advantages and indicating directions we intend to pursue in the future.

---

*This project is supported by National Science Foundation Grants CCR-8658074 and DCR-8500332, and by Digital Equipment Corporation, Apple Computer, Inc., GTE Laboratories, and the Eastman Kodak Company.

†Authors' present address: Department of Computer and Information Science, Lederle Graduate Research Center, University of Massachusetts, Amherst, MA, 01003; telephone (413) 545-4206; Internet addresses Moss@cs.umass.edu and Sinofsky@cs.umass.edu.

1.1 Motivation

We wish to address the needs of the programmer working on large, complex design applications. Such applications require the cooperative use of shared, distributed, persistent data in a production setting. Applications that would benefit from improved integration include computer aided design (CAD), office automation (OA), and document production, in addition to software development environments (SDEs). An important aspect of these applications is that they demand high functionality and high performance simultaneously.

We believe that integrating programming languages and databases has the promise of meeting the challenge of high functionality and high performance, while also better addressing issues of construction and evolution of application programs by making those programs easier to write. There has been a great deal of work describing and addressing the problems of integrating programming language and database technologies [Buneman, 1984; Atkinson *et al.*, 1984]. Primarily we are concerned with providing truly seamless integration, with database operations as transparent as possible. Traditionally the user of database systems is confronted with the problem of translating ideas first to a programming language model and then to a database language model. If the programming language and database language are tightly integrated, then the user need only be concerned with translating ideas into a single language model. We are also concerned with providing persistent data as described in [Atkinson *et al.*, 1981] and [Atkinson *et al.*, 1984]. Persistence should be an orthogonal property of all existing data structures. In addition, the resulting language should be data type complete: all types must have the same rights and privileges.

Object-oriented languages (OOLs) provide a natural starting point for adding database features to programming languages [Bloom and Zdonik, 1987]. OOLs focus on the structure of data and the operations permitted on data, in other words, the behavior of data. In contrast, object-oriented databases (OODBs) focus on persistent data. Together object-oriented languages and object-oriented databases provide superior support for a wide range of applications. OOLs and OODBs complement each other well, and tight integration of the two will provide the advantages of the object-oriented approach along with persistence. This will considerably simplify programming complex design applications.

While an object-oriented persistent programming language exhibits most of the desired features, there are a number of problems that persistence and object-orientation do not address. As will be discussed, Mneme additionally tackles issues of very large collections of objects, sharing and cooperation, reliability, distributed systems, support for more than one programming language, and support for multiple, heterogeneous data storage servers.

1.2 General Issues

When attempting to integrate traditional database functionality with programming languages for use in design applications, a number of issues must be addressed by any system. Here we indicate our position with respect to some of the most important issues.

Small Objects. In an OOL, we are concerned primarily with a large number of relatively small objects. As an example, we consider individual nodes of an abstract syntax tree to be objects, and the entire tree to be a collection of objects. In contrast, traditional database systems are concerned with a smaller number of relatively larger objects in the form of records, relations, or even files. Traditional databases perform best on records somewhat larger than objects in a typical OOL, and even better on "batch" processing of considerable numbers of records in similar ways. Attempts to use existing databases for object-sized data have proved less than satisfactory. A combined OOL/OODB must be able to fetch a large number of these smaller objects rapidly. Still, the system must cope with large objects, such as unstructured source code strings or image data, in a reasonable manner [Bernstein, 1987].

Pointer Chasing. In an OOL a great deal of emphasis is placed on the relationship between objects. As a result, the traversal of relationships between individual objects – *pointer chasing* – is a common operation in an OOL. When implemented in a relational database, one might call this "relationship traversal". The point is that one is frequently inspecting particular relationships starting from a particular object. Traditional databases are generally not very well tuned to this style of access, and do better on bulk operations, such as relational joins, rather than on selecting one record or field at a time. Not only is pointer chasing significant in OOLs, but it is important in design applications, which typically use structures designed for efficient use within main memory. The generality of the relational model, which is good for ad hoc queries not anticipated in advance, is traded for efficiency on a heavily used data structure. A challenge facing OODB system designers is to provide support for ad hoc queries in addition to efficient pointer chasing. Further, one generally wants to be able to trace relationships in both directions, so OOLs should support relationships in addition to simple pointers or names, as discussed in [Rumbaugh, 1987].

Query Optimization. In order to search a large database efficiently, traditional database systems rely on sophisticated query optimization. Query optimization depends on the fact that the operations defined over a database are simple, few in number, and well-defined. This assumption is not valid under the object-oriented model, since the operations available on a given object depend on the type of that object. In general, design applications depend more on the relationships between types and individual objects than on the relationships between large amounts of data. Queries in a design application are not needed as much as efficient object retrieval, as previously argued. This is good, since query optimization for OODBs is not very well understood yet. Still, the object-oriented model can take advantage of direct links between objects, and is well suited to performing type-specific optimizations, implemented within the code for the type [Bloom and Zdonik, 1987]. Refer to [Banerjee *et al.*, 1987b] for further discussion of queries in object-oriented databases. We believe that querying should be supported, but that it can be layered on top of the basic object-oriented storage manager.

Sharing, Reliability, Cooperation, and Distribution. Since typical database transactions offer concurrency control (concurrency must be considered in any shared system) and reliability features (of obvious value in a design environment), transactions are a good starting point for a framework that includes sharing and reliability. Design applications demand more than traditional databases, though: support for cooperation. It becomes an interesting challenge to provide appropriate primitives for programmers so that they can build a wide variety of design tools that simultaneously prevent unwanted interference, protect application data from the effects of failures, support cooperation, and perform acceptably.

In a design environment, transactions will be both short-term and long-term. Short-term transactions, which typically fetch and update only a few objects, are the most common. These transactions will usually involve a small amount of data. Long-term transactions, typically associated with file check-in/check-out, are also very important, and are related to cooperation in the sense that controlled sharing of intermediate results of long transactions is one of the fundamental means of cooperation.

We model long transactions as a series of short transactions. Short transactions are patterned after those of traditional database systems, and are not designed to support cooperation. For cooperation, the programmer should design a modest number of application-specific atomic data types. An atomic data type is one that provides transaction oriented concurrency control and recovery. The application-specific atomic data types would embody the modes of cooperation desired for that application. A facility for building application-specific atomic data types such that they are integrated with the short-term transaction mechanism will allow virtually any pattern of cooperation while providing concurrency control and recovery as desired. We describe this idea further in Section 3.7.

Since we are concerned with multiple cooperating users, collections of workstations and servers are one of the important hardware environments that must be supported. This is what makes distribution an issue.

Data Modularity. It is important in design systems to be able to isolate and manipulate significant subcollections of the data maintained by the system. This is important for reasons of resiliency, performance (e.g., local copies in workstations), sharing, access control, archival reference, use with other systems and tools, etc. For example, one might wish to retrieve a copy of the source code for a single module and export it to another machine, perhaps by mailing a floppy disk to another user. Traditional databases are not especially good at this; in fact, file systems provided the best examples. We need to provide similar functionality, but at a level that includes object semantics as opposed to simple bags of bytes.

Transparency. The transparency of language integration is important because it simplifies programming. Thus, it is best that the extension of a language to support a reliable, shared collection of objects be as transparent as possible. It is this desire that guides us towards heap-based languages, such as Smalltalk [Goldberg and Robson, 1983] and Trellis/Owl [Schaffert *et al.*, 1986]. A persistent shared heap offers a very high level of transparency, allowing the user to ignore many details of access to persistent data. Some significant aspects of database functionality cannot be totally transparent to the user, however. For example, in order to access shared data or to recover from crashes, the user is required to understand transaction concepts to some degree.

Garbage Collection. A final issue that we must deal with is that of garbage collection. This issue arises primarily because of our preference for arbitrary pointer structure and automatic storage management. Garbage collection of the transient (non-persistent) heap is an issue that has been given a great deal of attention in the past. Garbage collecting a persistent heap is a difficult task, but solutions for large heaps have been proposed [Bishop, 1977]. We intend to adapt these approaches to the integrated persistent environment.

To summarize, in integrating an OOL and OODB in support of design applications, we believe it is important to address these issues: large numbers of small objects; pointer chasing; query processing; sharing, reliability, cooperation, and distribution; data modularity; transparency; and garbage collection. This list is not exhaustive; it is easy to think of many other issues, some of which are being explored in various other OODB projects, including exception handling, schema evolution, versioning mechanisms, design history, access control and protection, etc. The issues we discussed are simply the ones that we most desire to address in our research.

1.3 Specific Goals of the Mneme Project

Above we discussed issues of relevance to our overall research program. We turn now to our goals in the Mneme project. Mneme is a persistent store, rather than an integrated OOL/OODB. The idea is to use Mneme as a basis for exploring some (but not all) of the issues we are addressing in our longer term research program. We desired a tool that could be used with more than one language, that would take advantage of existing storage managers or network servers, that would enable us to wrestle with the critical low level performance problems related to accessing and manipulating small objects on demand, and that would provide maximum functionality consistent with the other goals. We now consider each of these goals in more detail.

Language Independence. Because of the effort involved in building a prototype, we wanted it to apply to more than one language. We also wanted to avoid undertaking very much language design, or compiler writing or modification at this stage in the research. We believe that we can learn many very useful things without getting involved in the linguistic aspects of OOL/OODB integration. As we will describe in more detail later, we decided that Mneme should provide untyped objects, but it does distinguish between object references and other sort of data within each object. That Mneme objects are untyped is a direct result of our desire for language independence. Since Mneme provides in essence a (persistent, distributed, reliable, shared) heap of objects, it meshes best with heap-based languages such as Smalltalk, Trellis/Owl, or even CLU [Liskov *et al.*, 1977; Liskov *et al.*, 1981]. Mneme can be used with more traditional languages such as C [Kernighan and Ritchie, 1978], C++ [Stroustrup, 1986], Pascal [Jensen and Wirth, 1974; ANSI, 1983], or Ada[1][Ichbiah *et al.*, 1979], though, with the degree of transparency determined by the extent to which one is willing to modify the language (a little) and the compiler and run-time system (a lot).

Being language independent in the way we chose (a heap memory model) automatically ruled out query processing. Hence, Mneme does not deal with that issue at all. See our discussion of future plans at the end of the paper for more on this point.

Use Existing Software. We wanted to be able to use, evaluate, and compare a variety of existing and planned storage/object managers/servers, including the Exodus storage manager [Carey *et al.*, 1986], ObServer [Skarra *et al.*, 1987], Camelot [Spector *et al.*, 1986], and the Genesis tool kit [Batory *et al.*, 1986]. This would also save effort in building a fully functional prototype, and prevent "reinventing the wheel".

Explore Performance Problems. The primary performance problems we wished to explore are clustering of objects, caching, concurrency control and recovery algorithms, and object addressing and format conversion techniques. Our intuition was that per-object overheads would destroy performance and must be carefully controlled. The generic nature of Mneme (in that it should support multiple languages) somewhat interferes with achieving the best possible performance. This is because Mneme imposes a format on objects which may not directly correspond to that used by the programming language, thus causing extra copying or conversion of data. For the moment we have decided to live with this and study ways of eliminating all or most of the conversion effort for incorporation at a later stage of our work. This is described in more detail in the discussion of future plans.

Since Mneme is intended to be used with a variety of languages and in a variety of applications, we felt it very important that Mneme provide means to specify and change policy decisions and algorithms, in order to tune performance. This desire led us to determine a policy interface in the architecture, and to require that more than one policy be possible at the same time (but applying to different sets of objects). These ideas will be explained in more detail later.

For reference and comparison, we have used the following as our specific performance goals:

- Object fetching: Assuming average object size to be 30 to 40 bytes, as is our experience with CLU, Smalltalk, and Trellis/Owl heaps, we would like to be able to fetch about 10,000 objects per second. Clearly this will require good object clustering, good physical clustering on secondary storage media, and low system overhead in performing any necessary I/Os.

- Object access: Given that all the relevant objects are resident, we would like to be able to perform at least 100,000 object field/slot accesses per second. This is necessary to support activities such as dragging objects on a workstation screen.

[1]Ada is a registered trademark of the Department of Defense.

- Transaction commit rate: We have not devised either a good measure or a performance target, but we mention this we feel it necessary to obtain a moderate to high rate of commits for short transactions between a single client and a single server.

Maximum Functionality. We wanted Mneme to provide the maximum OOL/OODB functionality consistent with its being a persistent object store, independent of any particular programming language. That is, we wanted to address as many of the OOL/OODB integration issues as possible. The requirements we settled on are:

- Sharing, Reliability, Distribution: Mneme would support short transactions within a distributed system.
- Cooperation: We would provide facilities for building application-specific concurrency control and recovery.
- Object Size: Mneme would support objects of virtually any size, transparently to the client.
- Object References: The object references would normally be the size of a pointer in the programming language, for ease of integration with languages, as well as to conserve storage. At the same time, the total number of objects that can be stored must be limited only by available resources, not by a lack of address bits.
- Garbage Collection: Automatic storage reclamation must be possible, but was not required. This demands the ability to locate and examine object references within objects.
- Data Modularity: A natural and easy to use data modularity facility was required.

Let us briefly mention some of the advantages that accrue to Mneme if these goals are met. Language independence is mainly a labor saving device: it will encourage Mneme to be used more broadly and give us more information with which to evaluate it. Using the same subsystem across languages will also allow more meaningful comparisons to be made, since fewer factors will be different in the comparisons. We will also see just how important query processing really is by trying to get along without it. Getting a handle on the basic performance issues of dealing with large numbers of small objects is clearly important, no matter how seamless the integration of language and database, though some very sophisticated optimizations are ruled out since we have no linguistic notation to analyze and optimize. Exploring policies, and supporting multiple policies, are both likely to be quite important. The functionality required (sharing, reliability, distribution, cooperation, etc.) will make Mneme a very desirable vehicle for a number of applications, and Mneme's policy, language, and storage manager flexibility will serve to increase its range of applicability. In sum, the underlying advantage of our goals is that they are directed towards maximum flexibility and learning in research, while simultaneously providing a really useful tool to the widest variety of potential clients.

2 Overview of Mneme

We now consider the interfaces provided by Mneme. Figure 1 details the system architectural view of Mneme, which is useful in understanding the interfaces and the relationships Mneme has with other system components.

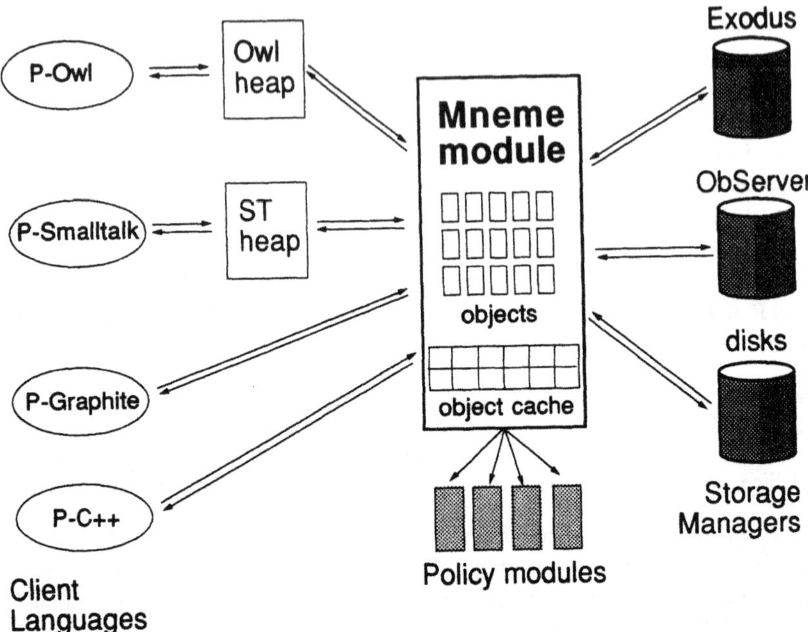

Figure 1: How Mneme fits into overall systems.

2.1 The Client Interface

The client interface consists of a number of routines that may be called to access Mneme facilities. Depending on the language being supported, calls might be avoided or reduced via inline expansion, a possibility with Ada, or via macros, as in C and systems built using C such as our Smalltalk system [Moss *et al.*, 1988] and Trellis/Owl.

Via the client interface, Mneme offers a simple and efficient abstraction of objects. These objects are similar to objects found in traditional OOLs, such as Smalltalk and Trellis/Owl. The objects of Mneme, however, are not biased towards any particular OOL. Mneme objects are intended to be used as the basis for an automatically managed persistent store interfacing to the heap of the OOL. The objects provided by Mneme also can be used from more traditional languages, such as C++ and Ada, as an additional pre-programmed abstract data type. Mneme will also interface with language based tools such as Graphite [Clarke *et al.*, 1986]. Any given copy of Mneme most likely interacts with a single program or tool; data sharing comes about through the use of shared storage managers.

Mneme is truly object-oriented, in the sense that it is based on objects allocated in heap storage. An object can have a set of references to other objects. These references are called *slots*. In addition, an object can have a *data* area consisting of a number of uninterpreted bytes. The objects provided by Mneme reside in a reliable, shared store of objects.

Mneme avoids pre-empting language decisions by defining a very general kind of object but not defining a type system or code execution model for Mneme objects. This implies that Mneme objects must be brought to the language's execution mechanism, thus inhibiting a large amount of back-end processing. This point is discussed further with our future plans.

The client interface actually deals with several other concepts in addition to objects. These will be introduced in later sections.

2.2 Storage Manager Interface

The storage manager interface is the means by which Mneme actually stores and shares data persistently. Mneme supports multiple storage managers, possibly simultaneously. The basic features required of a storage manager are that it store and retrieve sequences of bytes (we call such sequences *segments*), and that it provide some concurrency control and recovery features.

2.3 Policy Interface

Mneme also offers flexibility in the storage management policy and strategy used by a client language. Sets of related objects can be managed by the strategy that is best suited to those objects. Mneme provides a collection of built-in strategies, as well as a facility for users to define and exploit additional strategies. Objects are grouped into *pools*, where each pool has an associated *policy module*. This is explained in more detail later.

2.4 Buffer Manager

Although the buffer manager is actually part of Mneme, it is built as a separate module and is conceptually distinct from the rest of the system. As of this writing we are still working on the details of its relationship to the other system components.

3 Client Concepts

Mneme presents several abstractions to its clients: objects, object identifiers, files, roots, handles, transactions, and pools.

3.1 Objects

A Mneme object has two primary components: an array of slots and a array of bytes. A byte is simply an uninterpreted 8 bit quantity. The bytes part of an object may not contain references to other objects. A slot is the size of a pointer (32 bits on typical machines), and may hold a reference to an object. A slot may also be empty (represented by 0) or hold an *immediate value*. Immediate values are a concession to heap based languages that allow integers and other non-pointer data within slots; CLU, Smalltalk, and Trellis/Owl operate in that way. The sign bit is used to distinguish references (positive) from immediate values (negative).

In addition to slots and bytes, objects have a few attribute bits, which we use to mark them as read-only or as having other special properties. Mneme provides routines to determine the number of slots and bytes an object has, and to fetch and store slots, bytes, and attribute bits. Objects can grow and shrink in either the number of slots or bytes. This is done by truncating or appending empty slots or zero bytes as necessary.

3.2 Object Identifiers

Every object currently accessible to the client has a short name, the size of a pointer, called a *client identifier*, or CID for short. An application can thus name and manipulate up to about 2^{30} objects at a time. The exact value of a CID is not the same as what is stored within a slot of an object inside Mneme. This is because the overall space of objects is not bounded, hence objects cannot be assigned a short unique identifier. What we actually do is best explained step by step, as we go. We call the reference values stored in slots inside Mneme *persistent identifiers*, or PIDs.

3.3 Files

A *file* contains a collection of objects. Files are the unit of data modularity in Mneme, and correspond roughly with the usual operating system notion of file, even to the extent that operating system files might be a reasonable way of implementing Mneme files. Within a given file, each object has a unique PID value, and objects in that same file can refer to the object simply by using the PID. Thus, individual files can contain up to about 2^{30} objects. Since there is essentially no limit on the number of files, there is no limit on the total number of objects that Mneme can store. Mneme files may have new objects added and removed over time.

For those cases in which an object needs to refer to an object in a different file, we support cross-file references. Cross-file references are implemented by having a reference to a specially marked object in the current file, appropriately called a *forwarder*. The forwarder then contains information detailing the file and object desired. It is possible to have a variety of kinds of forwarders, depending on the nature of the names and whether their interpretation or meaning is static or dynamic. We have not yet completed this aspect of the design, but expect to rely on some kind of external name service mechanism so as to avoid developing our own.

The modularization of the Mneme object base into a collection of files has other advantages beyond avoiding a limit on the total number of objects. Having separate files allows parts of the object base to be separated for processing by particular tools, and files can form a natural unit of transfer between systems and organizations. That is, files provide a natural way of avoiding a monolithic database. Files also allow convenient distribution of data; they map nicely onto existing operating systems and servers; they are a familiar concept; and they enhance reliability by providing storage fault isolation and containment. The partitioning of the object world into files is also important for storage reclamation and garbage collection.

Files can have string named, string valued attributes associated with them. These attributes can be used for correctness checks (e.g., "I am a file made by a Smalltalk system", "I belong to Jane", etc.), for policy parameter storage, and so on.

3.4 Roots

Mneme provides a vast sea of objects, and is designed to allow one to trace paths of object references through this sea. One must, however, have some means for getting started and oriented within the sea of objects. Every Mneme file has a *root object.* To start using Mneme one opens an appropriate file (determined by the application and/or the user) and begins at that file's root. This is similar to the notion of the root directory in a file system. In addition to being able to obtain the CID of the root object of a file, Mneme clients can change which object is the root of the file. Files start without roots, so if the client fails to designate a root, then the root fetching operation will fail.

Note that in the present scheme there is no way to identify or name a Mneme object uniquely from *outside of* Mneme. We are considering adding features for such external persistent identifiers.

3.5 Identifier Conversion

Though it is not a concept visible to the client, there is obviously some conversion going on between CIDs and PIDs. This is handled as follows. First, assume that each file predeclares the maximum PID value it will contain (we will see how to relax this assumption in a moment). A particular incarnation of Mneme within a given client maintains an abstract address of CIDs by assigning each file a contiguous non-overlapping chunk of CID values. Such a chunk can be described by its first CID, which we call the *base*, and the number of CIDs in the chunk, which can be any number greater than the maximum PID value for the file. To convert PID to CID we simply add the base for the file; to convert CID to PID, we determine the file (conceptually by searching a table describing the CID range for each file, but actually implemented more like a virtual memory page table mechanism, as discussed later) and subtract the file's base from the CID to get the PID. Given the file and the PID, we can then locate the object as necessary.

There are several ways to deal with the maximum PID value assumption. One is to stick with a hard limit on the file. Note, though, that we just need a limit assigned as we *open* the file, so we could allow a file to grow without bound, but just limit its growth within one session of use. Finally, if we do not care for a limit even during a session of use, we can assign the file another, larger, chunk of CIDs when it grows too big. Old CIDs that have been handed will still translate to the correct objects, but we now use the new base for all CIDs handed out in the future. In any case, the PID to CID conversion is always a simple addition, and the CID to PID conversion involves relatively inexpensive table indexing (to be described later).

3.6 Handles

A Mneme object is manipulated by obtaining a *handle* on the object. A handle is requested by supplying Mneme with the CID of the desired object. While a handle is held on an object, the holder is guaranteed logically exclusive access to the object. Obtaining a handle generally forces the corresponding object to become resident. Handles also allow us to use a number of internal object formats (e.g., small objects with a contiguous representation, and large objects with a tree representation) without sacrificing efficiency. A handle stores a more time-efficient run-time representation of an object than a CID, though it consumes more space. Basically, handles prevent doing the CID to PID conversion, object presence check, and object location determination more than once for a whole series of operations on the same object.

3.7 Transactions

Mneme provides a basic transaction facility as well as features for supporting more sophisticated transaction management. We first present our transaction *semantics*, followed by our implementation strategies. Within a transaction, concurrency control is on a per-object basis, allowing shared read and exclusive update. In addition to concurrency, transactions are units of recovery, with Mneme supporting atomic, all-or-nothing, transaction commitment.

Since locking individual objects is likely to be prohibitively expensive, in the implementation we can lock objects in groups – probably in terms of segments, the units of transfer with storage managers. This is not visible to the client, since segments are not visible through the client interface. The only possible problem is that coarse granularity locking might lead to unexpected deadlock. There are a number of ways to avoid this problem; one is to allow the client to designate objects that must be independently lockable, and guarantee that the objects are in different segments. Whether locking is actually done on segments or objects is a policy decision, determined by the actions of the relevant policy module. This will be discussed more later.

The implementation has considerable latitude in concurrency control strategies. As mentioned, the granularity can be made more coarse without violating the basic semantic guarantees. A variety of algorithms may also be used, with read/write locking and optimistic concurrency control being two prominent alternatives. Further, since policies may be mixed, any set of mutually consistent concurrency control policies can be used at one time.

To encourage transparency, clients do not lock objects explicitly. Rather, observing properties of or reading slots or bytes from an object are considered reads, and changing the object in any way is considered a write. Whether and when a lock is actually acquired is up to the policy module, except that the basic semantics must be preserved. One policy module might lock objects exclusively as soon as they are referenced (very pessimistic about other clients modifying the object and interfering), while another policy module might use optimistic concurrency control and check consistency only at transaction commit time.

With regard to recovery management, logs, shadows, or combinations may be used, and we will address group commit and related optimizations as well. Mneme's client and server interfaces make no assumptions about distribution or replication of files or objects, so additional variation is permitted in those areas.

Since serializability at the object level is sometimes overly restrictive, especially when implementing protocols for cooperation, Mneme provides some support for more sophisticated serializable, or even non-serializable, interaction. The basic concepts include *volatile objects*, *object logs*, and *event notifications*. A volatile object is accessible to other clients and may be changed whenever the client does not have a handle on it, regardless of transactions. This provides the basic mutual exclusion mechanism necessary for building arbitrary concurrency control. Further, a client's uncommitted changes will be visible to other users, and vice versa. Thus, handles provide mutual exclusion on volatile objects, which is the only concurrency control and recovery that volatile objects naturally enjoy.

To support reasonable use of volatile objects, Mneme also provides object logs, wherein past or intended changes can be recorded, so that when a transaction commits or aborts, it can complete or clean up its manipulations of volatile objects. As an example, consider a directory implemented as a volatile object. It is desirable to increase concurrency by allowing non-conflicting access to the directory rather than locking the whole directory for the duration of entire transactions. When making a change, such as adding a new entry, the directory code acquires a handle on the directory. It then performs the update, marking the change as tentative, and releases the handle. The tentative change is then visible to other clients, though the directory code should hide it, probably by forcing clients to wait until the entry is not tentative. This would provide serializable directories, without holding locks on the whole directory for the duration of entire transactions. As an alternative, the directory code could let the change show through, providing non-serializable behavior similar to a check-in/check-out recording data structure, which, rather than blocking, might reply, "Joe already has that checked out; do you really want to go ahead?" The object log is used to record the tentative change, so that is the transaction fails, the change can be removed, and if the transaction commits, the change can be made permanent rather than tentative.

An event notification mechanism is desirable for efficiency, so that clients waiting for resources can be notified of their availability rather than busy waiting or polling.

In sum, volatile objects, object logs, and an event notification system allow one to build application-specific atomic objects, along the lines of [Weihl and Liskov, 1985] and [Spector and Schwarz, 1984], or even non-atomic or non-serializable objects to support various forms of cooperation.

3.8 Pools

A *pool* is a collection of objects managed according to the same storage allocation and object management strategies. A Mneme file consists of one or more pools, with pools partitioning the objects of the file. The pools of a file may have different strategies, as may the pools of different files. We will provide some built-in strategies, but the sophisticated Mneme user will be able to devise new pool types and add them to the system. Pools avoid imposing any single object management strategy, which is bound to fail for some applications. Another advantage of pools is that different subcollections of objects can be managed in different ways, rather than all objects being managed the same way.

Here is an example showing the utility of multiple strategies. Suppose that an application has a small number of high traffic, frequently updated objects, and a large number of objects that are not changed frequently and are rarely touched by multiple users during the same period of time. Transaction management efficiency might well be maximized in this situation by treating the two sets of objects quite differently. The high traffic objects might be placed in a pool that locks objects exclusively when they are first referenced. The low traffic objects could be in a pool managed using optimistic concurrency control. We need only insure that we get a consistent serialization order across all strategies.

The discussion of possible transaction implementations indicates some of the factors that pool strategies can control: the concurrency policy and granularity, and the details of recovery. Other important policies that pools define include: object clustering, storage allocation, object or segment cache loading and cache replacement strategies, and prefetch techniques. Volatile objects belong to volatile pools. Even within volatile pools, there is considerable latitude in policy: when a handle on a volatile object is released, the object or segment might be returned to the storage manager immediately, or it might be retained until the storage manager requests its return.

The pool concept is crucial to making Mneme useful across a range of design applications, because the ability to extend policies and to use multiple policies simultaneously will be necessary in achieving adequate performance.

4 The Initial Design of Mneme

The main parts of the design of Mneme that are not obvious are the location and faulting in of objects, the storage manager interface, and the policy interface. It is easy to dispense with the storage manager and policy interfaces. The storage manager interface must deal with files, provide segments of reasonable sizes (though their size need not be modifiable), support concurrency control on segments (or ranges of bytes within segments), and offer simple (traditional) transactions. The storage manager interface also requires event notification support and some operations to assist in effective uses of large buffer caches (cache coherence verification). As of this writing the details are not available.

The policy interface is also not yet available in detail, but we have determined its basic style. A policy module will consist of a number of routines, one routine for each of a number of specified events, such as "object to be created", "handle requested", and so forth. A policy routine must carry out the requested action using parameters provided in the call, any data in the buffer cache, storage manager routines, etc. We may also arrange things so that handles point to a vector of routines (determined from the pool for the object corresponding to the handle), and each call on a handle indexes into this vector to find the actual routine to call.

An initial object location and faulting mechanism has been designed, and it works as follows. The space of PIDs for each file is broken into "chunks" of 1024 PID values. Such a "chunk" is called a *logical segment*. Note that a logical segment does not refer to any specific number of *bytes*, only to a particular set of objects that all have PIDs with the same high order bits. The segments transferred between the buffer cache and the storage managers are called ***physical segments*** to distinguish them from the logical segments. Every physical segment has some set of logical segments assigned to it, and a logical segment is associated with exactly one physical segment.

Objects are located by splitting the PID into two pieces; the high order bits indicate the logical segment and the low order bits the specific object within the logical segment. Information about the logical segment is found in a *logical segment table*, which is indexed directly by logical segment number. The logical segment table indicates which *physical segment* contains the logical segment, and, if the physical segment is resident, where the logical segment's information actually resides within the physical segment (probably via a direct pointer to the information, in the middle of the physical segment data in the buffer cache). The logical segment information includes a table of self-relative pointers to the 1024 objects of the logical segment; the low bits of the PID are used to index this object table and find the object data.

In addition to the logical segment table, each file has a physical segment table indicating the storage manager's name for the physical segment, the segment's size, where (if anywhere) the segment is resident, and so forth. A non-resident segment is detected by a null pointer in the logical segment table when trying to find an object from its PID. At that time the physical segment is fetched, the physical and logical segment tables updated, and the reference processing continued.

The actual CID to object conversion does not proceed by building a PID and then looking up the object. In one design we concatenate the logical segment tables of all the open files, and index directly with the high order CID bits. This has the same effect as converting to a PID and then indexing, but is faster and avoids a table lookup to determine the file.

The design we are incorporating first is a bit simpler, but more restrictive: no file is allowed to have more than 2^{20} objects, and we use the bits beyond the 20th bit to mean a file number within the current client session. The lookup algorithm extracts the highest order bits to index a table of file information and locate the logical segment table for that file. The middle bits are then used to locate the specific logical segment, and the low bits determine the object within the logical segment. In sum, one indexes the file table, then the file's logical segment table, then the logical segment's object table. The CID format is shown in Figure 2 and the indexing scheme is illustrated by Figure 3.

F = File #	L = Logical Segment #	I = Object #
10–12 bits	10 bits	10 bits

Figure 2: Format of a Client Identifier

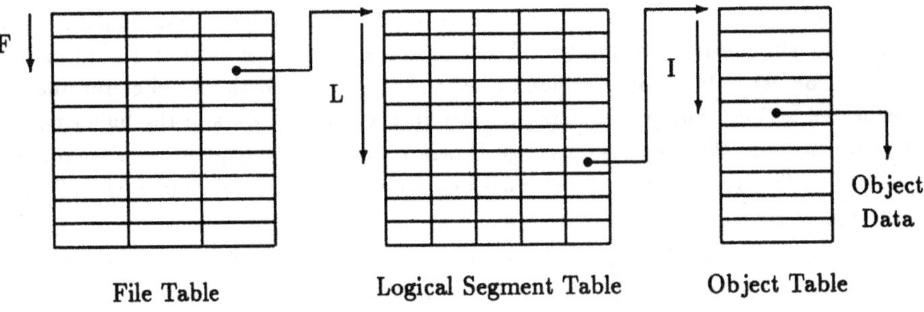

Figure 3: Three Index Object Lookup Scheme

While this three index scheme is a bit slower than the two indexes used in the concatenated logical segment table design, the three index design is much simpler to implement. It may also turn out to be fast enough: initial estimates show that an object can be located from its CID in about 10 instructions, which corresponds well to our 100,000 references per second goal on current hardware.

The resulting object location mechanism is very similar to the virtual address translation mechanism used by many paged virtual memory systems, and is amenable to hardware speedup perhaps, though a translation lookaside buffer is not likely to be as effective.

PIDs are seen to be somewhat location dependent (they always specify a particular logical segment), but the logical segment can be moved anywhere in a file without affecting PID values, and the objects can be moved anywhere within the physical segment containing the logical segment. In particular, the objects in a physical segment can be reorganized and compacted without affecting PIDs. Thus, PIDs have a considerable amount of location independence as well. We believe the scheme represents a good tradeoff between efficiency of locating objects and maintaining location independence.

Object themselves are represented using a header, which contains a format code, size information, and the attribute bits. The header is followed by the slots and then the bytes, padded out to a complete word, as showin in Figure 4. The header is generally one word long; the format code may indicate an object is longer than the limited size field can represent, in which case one or two additional words are used to hold these large sizes.

<table>
<tr><td>Header</td><td>FC</td><td colspan="2">Size Info</td><td>ATTR</td></tr>
<tr><td>Slots</td><td colspan="4">Slot 0</td></tr>
<tr><td></td><td colspan="4">Slot 1</td></tr>
<tr><td></td><td colspan="4">...</td></tr>
<tr><td>Bytes</td><td>Byte 0</td><td>Byte 1</td><td>Byte 2</td><td>Byte 3</td></tr>
<tr><td></td><td>...</td><td colspan="3">PAD</td></tr>
</table>

FC = Format code
ATTR = Attribute bits
PAD = Padding to word boundary

Figure 4: Object Format

A physical segment contains the information pertaining to its logical segments, followed by the object data area. In processing a physical segment upon fetching or storing, a small amount of work must be done for each logical segment, to update the tables, but no per-object work is needed.

5 Comparison With Other Work

We compare Mneme with some representative language and database alternatives, in terms of how they offer support for design tools and environments. Our criteria in evaluating the various approaches are the issues discussed in Section 1.2.

5.1 Integrated Database Languages

An early attempt at integrating programming language and database functionality was the programming language Pascal/R [Schmidt, 1977]. Pascal/R was a major step in the advancement of integrated database languages. The language made use of a consistent type notation, and the program and database had an obvious relationship. Rules of type-checking could be applied to the database, as well as to standard Pascal types. Unfortunately, the database type introduced was not type complete. In fact, a Pascal/R database was permitted to have only the relation type (another type introduced by Pascal/R) as fields, and none of the other standard Pascal types. In addition, the programmer was only allowed to have a single variable of type database. Pascal/R included facilities for taking full advantage of the algebra of relational databases. In general, however, the user of Pascal/R still had to reason with the relationship between two representations of the data: persistence in Pascal/R is neither orthogonal nor type complete. While Pascal/R incorporates some novel concepts in interfacing languages and databases, it does not represent a seamless integration, and its foundation is the traditional relational database. For these reasons it is not a very suitable vehicle for design applications or environments.

A conceptual successor to Pascal/R was PS-Algol [Atkinson *et al.*, 1981; Atkinson *et al.*, 1984]. PS-Algol is in many ways like Pascal/R. A traditional language was extended to include persistence. In PS-Algol, however, the notion of persistence was, for the first time, extended to include type completeness and orthogonality. PS-Algol proved that this view of persistence is feasible. The language, however, did not provide any mechanisms for concurrency or reliability of data, and was therefore ill-suited for cooperative work or design applications.

On the surface LOOM [Kaehler and Krasner, 1983], a large object-oriented virtual memory system, appears to be similar to Mneme in that it extends the Smalltalk heap to include disk storage and does transparent object faulting. In fact, LOOM's goals are substantially different from those of Mneme. In particular LOOM provides a single-user virtual memory or workspace model, and provides no concurrency, reliability, or distribution features. LOOM resembles single user programming environments such as Interlisp [Teitelman and Masinter, 1981] more than it resembles Mneme.

GemStone [Purdy *et al.*, 1987], similar to LOOM, expands the Smalltalk heap to include objects on disk. Unlike LOOM, GemStone does provide considerable database functionality, including queries and an execution model. The GemStone system is distributed, but the database is stored on a single server. In contrast, Mneme will support a multiple server environment, which is desirable for the moderate to large projects typical in design work. GemStone is somewhat specialized to Smalltalk, whereas Mneme is designed to support a variety of languages. In addition, Mneme provides the user the ability to modify and extend object management policies.

5.2 Modern Database Systems

Several modern database systems provide good examples against which we compare Mneme. One is Postgres [Stonebraker and Rowe, 1986], a continuation of the Ingres [Stonebraker *et al.*, 1976] project. Postgres represents an attempt to extend the relational database approach to deal with more kinds of data and to suit a wider range of applications. It is still firmly rooted in relational soil, however. Because Postgres does not provide special support for pointer chasing, and because it is not attempting integration with a programming language, it does not meet the criteria outlined in Section 1.2.

Exodus [Carey *et al.*, 1986] takes an approach different from that of Postgres, providing a core of database functionality and a language, E [Richardson and Carey, 1987], in which to implement revisions or extensions to the system. E does not provide orthogonal or type complete persistence, as is the intent of Mneme. E also does not provide particular support for objects or for control over the storage manager's policies. Further, E is not necessarily intended to be the application programming language, but rather the database implementor's language for databases built using Exodus. While the Exodus storage manager is not suited for use in a distributed system, it does appear useful enough for design applications that we will experiment with it as an underlying storage manager for Mneme.

Genesis [Batory *et al.*, 1986] is a database toolkit, offering a variety of pre-programmed components which may be assembled to devise one's own database system. Again, we will experiment with Genesis components in building disk storage managers for Mneme. ObServer [Skarra *et al.*, 1987] provides objects that are blocks of bytes, with some per-object locking and novel concurrency control, and is intended for use as a server. Neither ObServer nor Genesis provide facilities for language integration.

Finally, Orion [Banerjee *et al.*, 1987a], an object oriented database system, has more ambitions towards integration with a programming language, in this case Common Lisp [Bobrow *et al.*, 1985]. Similar to Pascal/R, Orion's persistence is not orthogonal, and the database type system is rather different from the host language type system.

6 Conclusion

We review Mneme's current status, indicate some questions for further research, and indicate our current thoughts on the next system we would like to build.

6.1 Current Status

We are in the process of implementing the first phase of Mneme. Initially, we will provide for only a single-user, without reliability. This will permit us to experiment with the initial design of most of the client, storage manager, and policy interfaces. We are simultaneously designing and implementing a heap interface for our VAX[2]Smalltalk. Implementation will then proceed with the second and third phases, in which we provide for reliability and then sharing.

6.2 Some Questions for Future Research

The flexibility in the design of Mneme will afford us the opportunity to use Mneme as a testbed for many different solutions to the issues raised by integrating database and programming language functionality. These research problems include both database and language issues:

- In an environment such as Mneme, where persistent objects are both shared and reliable, how can one relocate objects, copy objects, and replace objects, all of which are crucial to design applications?
- How can we expand Mneme's notion of pools to include even more sophisticated object clustering facilities, such as those described in [Hudson and King, 1986]?
- Can persistent semantics be added to a language, while simultaneously providing the ability to modify and expand object management policies?
- What is an appropriate set of primitives for supporting cooperative manipulation of objects in distributed systems?

[2]VAX is a trademark of Digital Equipment Corporation.

6.3 Future Plans

While the above are interesting research questions, some of which we may pursue, we have more specific plans for the future. It is clear that Mneme provides little more than an abstraction of storage: it has little notion of action. This prevents any query processing or optimization, the distribution of execution across system components (e.g., between client and server, or multiple clients), and so forth. The next project in our research will investigate the design of a *virtual machine*, rather than a store. We wish the virtual machine to be somewhat language independent (i.e., be a target for at least several languages) and to support object oriented languages. It should add execution facilities to Mneme, and possibly replace object access (read, write) with operation invocation. This new system would also allow us to address the issue of format conversion, since we would be designing an interpretation/execution engine rather than just a store.

A persistent, distributed, shared, etc., virtual machine will allow the exploration of many more policies alternatives, such as where code is executed, the extent to which and at what time it is compiled, etc. The system should not only be more interesting, in that it offers more functionality, but also present more challenging research problems. It will also move us further along the spectrum towards the consideration of linguistic issues, and certainly involve us in compilation and optimization problems.

References

[ANSI, 1983] ANSI. *IEEE Standard Pascal Computer Programming Language*. IEEE, New York, 1983. Standard ANSI/IEEE770X3.97–1983.

[Atkinson *et al.*, 1981] M. P. Atkinson, K. J. Chisolm, and W. P. Cockshott. PS-Algol: an Algol with a peristent heap. *ACM SIGPLAN Notices 17*, 7 (July 1981).

[Atkinson *et al.*, 1984] M. P. Atkinson, P. Bailey, W. P. Cockshott, K. J. Chisolm, and R. Morrison. Progress with persistent programming. In *Databases—Role and Structure: An Advanced Course*. Cambridge University Press, Cambridge, England, 1984, pp. 245–310.

[Banerjee *et al.*, 1987a] Jay Banerjee, Hong-Tai Chou, Jorge F. Garza, Won Kim, Darrell Woelk, Nat Ballou, and Houng-Joo Kim. Data model issues for object-oriented applications. *ACM Trans. Office Inf. Syst. 5*, 1 (Jan. 1987), 3–26.

[Banerjee *et al.*, 1987b] Jay Banerjee, Won Kim, and Kim Kyng-Chang. Queries in object-oriented databases. MCC Technical Report DB-188-87, Microelectronics and Computer Technology Corporation, Austin, TX, June 1987.

[Batory *et al.*, 1986] D. S. Batory, J. R. Barnett, J. F. Garza, K. P. Smith, K. Tsukuda, B. C. Twichell, and T. E. Wise. Genesis: A reconfigurable database management system. Tech. Rep. TR-86-07, Department of Computer Sciences, University of Texas at Austin, Austin, TX, Mar. 1986.

[Bernstein, 1987] Philip Bernstein. Database system support for software engineering. In *Proceedings of the Ninth International Conference on Software Engineering* (Monterey, CA, Apr. 1987), IEEE.

[Bishop, 1977] Peter B. Bishop. *Computer Systems with a Very Large Address Space and Garbage Collection.* PhD thesis, Massachusetts Institute of Technology, Cambridge, MA, May 1977.

[Bloom and Zdonik, 1987] Toby Bloom and Stanley B. Zdonik. Issues in the design of object-oriented database programming languages. In *Proceedings of the Conference on Object-Oriented Programming Systems, Languages, and Applications* (Orlando, FL, Oct. 1987), ACM, pp. 441–451.

[Bobrow *et al.*, 1985] D. G. Bobrow, K. Kahn, G. Kiczales, L. Masinter, M. Stefik, and F. Zdybel. CommonLoops: Merging Common Lisp and object-oriented programming. Intelligent Systems Laboratory Series ISL-85-8, Xerox Palo Alto Research Center, Palo Alto, CA, 1985.

[Buneman, 1984] Peter Buneman. Can we reconcile programming languages and databases? In *Databases—Role and Structure: An Advanced Course.* Cambridge University Press, Cambridge, England, 1984, pp. 225–243.

[Carey *et al.*, 1986] M. J. Carey, D. J. DeWitt, J. E. Richardson, and E. J. Shekita. Object and file management in the EXODUS extensible database system. In *Proceedings of the 12th International Conference on Very Large Databases* (Kyoto, Japan, Sept. 1986), ACM, pp. 91–100.

[Clarke *et al.*, 1986] Lori A. Clarke, Jack C. Wileden, and Alexander L. Wolf. Graphite: a meta-tool for Ada environment development. In *Proceedings of IEEE Society Second International Conference on Ada Applications and Environments* (Miami Beach, FL, Aug. 1986), IEEE.

[Goldberg and Robson, 1983] Adele Goldberg and David Robson. *Smalltalk-80: The Language and its Implementation.* Addison-Wesley, 1983.

[Hudson and King, 1986] S. Hudson and R. King. CACTIS: A database system for specifying functionally-defined data. In *Proceedings of the Workshop on Object-Oriented Databases* (Pacific Grove, CA, Sept. 1986), ACM, pp. 26–37.

[Ichbiah *et al.*, 1979] J. D. Ichbiah *et al.*. Rationale for the design of the ADA programming language. *ACM SIGPLAN Notices 14*, 6 (June 1979).

[Jensen and Wirth, 1974] Kathleen Jensen and Niklaus Wirth. *Pascal User Manual and Report*, second ed. Springer-Verlag, 1974.

[Kaehler and Krasner, 1983] Ted Kaehler and Glenn Krasner. LOOM–large object-oriented memory for Smalltalk-80 systems. In *Smalltalk-80: Bits of History, Words of Advice*, Glenn Krasner, Ed. Addison-Wesley, 1983, ch. 14, pp. 251–270.

[Kernighan and Ritchie, 1978] Brian W. Kernighan and Dennis M. Ritchie. *The C Programming Language.* Prentice-Hall, 1978.

[Liskov *et al.*, 1977] B. Liskov, A. Snyder, R. Atkinson, and C. Schaffert. Abstraction mechanisms in CLU. *Commun. ACM 20*, 8 (Aug. 1977).

[Liskov *et al.*, 1981] B. Liskov, R. Atkinson, T. Bloom, E. Moss, C. Schaffert, R. Scheifler, and A. Snyder. *CLU Reference Manual.* Springer-Verlag, 1981.

[Moss *et al.*, 1988] J. Eliot B. Moss, Antony L. Hosking, Rajesh Nakhwa, and Steven Sinofsky. Implementing Smalltalk-80 on the VAX. Tech. rep., Department of Computer and Information Science, University of Massachusetts, Amherst, MA, 1988. Work in progress.

[Purdy *et al.*, 1987] Alan Purdy, Bruce Schuchardt, and David Maier. Integrating an object server with other worlds. *ACM Trans. Office Inf. Syst. 5*, 1 (Jan. 1987), 27–47.

[Richardson and Carey, 1987] Joel E. Richardson and Michael J. Carey. Programming constructs for database system implementations in EXODUS. In *Proceedings of the ACM SIGMOD International Conference on the Management of Data* (San Francisco, CA, May 1987), ACM, pp. 208–219.

[Rumbaugh, 1987] James Rumbaugh. Relations as semantic constructs in an object-oriented language. In *Proceedings of the Conference on Object-Oriented Programming Systems, Languages, and Applications* (Orlando, FL, Oct. 1987), ACM, pp. 466–481.

[Schaffert *et al.*, 1986] Craig Schaffert, Topher Cooper, Bruce Bullis, Mike Kilian, and Carrie Wilpolt. An introduction to Trellis/Owl. In *Proceedings of the Conference on Object-Oriented Programming Systems, Languages, and Applications* (Portland, OR, Sept. 1986), ACM, pp. 9–16.

[Schmidt, 1977] J. W. Schmidt. Some high level language constructs for data of type relation. *ACM Trans. Database Syst. 2*, 3 (Sept. 1977), 247–281.

[Skarra *et al.*, 1987] Andrea Skarra, Stanley B. Zdonik, and Stephen P. Reiss. An object server for an object oriented database system. In *Proceedings of International Workshop on Object-Oriented Database Systems* (Pacific Grove, CA, Sept. 1987), ACM, pp. 196–204.

[Spector and Schwarz, 1984] Alfred Z. Spector and Peter M. Schwarz. Synchronizing shared abstract data types. *ACM Trans. Comput. Syst. 2*, 3 (Aug. 1984), 223–250.

[Spector *et al.*, 1986] Alfred Z. Spector, Joshua J. Bloch, Dean S. Daniels, Richard P. Draves, Dan Duchamp, Jeffrey L. Eppinger, Sherri G. Menees, and Dean S. Thompson. The camelot project. Tech. Rep. CMU-CS-86-166, Department of Computer Science, Carnegie-Mellon University, Pittsburgh, PA, 1986.

[Stonebraker and Rowe, 1986] M. Stonebraker and L. A. Rowe. The design of Postgres. In *Proceedings of the ACM SIGMOD International Conference on the Management of Data* (Washington, D.C., May 1986), ACM, pp. 340–355.

[Stonebraker *et al.*, 1976] M. Stonebraker, E. Wong, P. Kreps, and G. Held. The design and implementation of Ingres. *ACM Trans. Database Syst. 1*, 3 (Sept. 1976), 189–222.

[Stroustrup, 1986] B. Stroustrup. *The C++ Programming Language.* Addison-Wesley, 1986.

[Teitelman and Masinter, 1981] W. Teitelman and L. Masinter. The Interlisp programming environment. *Computer 14*, 4 (Apr. 1981), 25–33.

[Weihl and Liskov, 1985] William Weihl and Barbara Liskov. Implementation of resilient, atomic data types. *ACM Trans. Program. Lang. Syst. 7*, 2 (Apr. 1985), 244–269.

Integration of Database Management with an Object-Oriented Programming Language

Steve Riegel, Fred Mellender, and Andrew Straw

Advanced Computing Research Laboratory
Eastman Kodak Company
Rochester, New York 14650

ABSTRACT

Alltalk is an object-oriented programming and database system, based on Smalltalk, being developed at Eastman Kodak Company to support development of advanced information systems. It provides permanence to Smalltalk objects without adding a database sub-language, new language syntax, classes, or methods to Smalltalk. In this paper we describe problems we encountered in integrating Smalltalk with database management and discuss our solutions to these problems. We believe the problems we identify are of a general nature and would arise in augmenting most any object-oriented language with database support.

1. Introduction

Advanced information systems for the office automation and printing/publishing domains require more sophisticated development and delivery environments for cost-effective production than are generally available today. Characteristics of such systems include the need to support sharing of large amounts of of "relationship-rich" data among multiple users in distributed computing environments.[1,2]

It is recognized that object-oriented design techniques enable appropriate modeling of problem domains resulting in good partitioning of functional entities in the final system. An object-oriented programming language reduces the effort involved in translating the resulting application model to that of the implementation language. This fact has been recognized in the emergence of languages and language systems such as C++ [3], Objective-C [4], and Smalltalk-80.[5]

However, such languages and language systems are not adequate in themselves to deal with the size, amount, or distributed nature of the data in advanced information systems. Additional logic must be developed or understood by the programmer to manage the secondary storage requirements and communications needs of the application.

In order to address these problems, we set out to provide these missing "database" services in development and delivery environments by combining an object-oriented language with such services in as "seamless" a manner as possible. The result of our work is known as the Alltalk system.

Alltalk is a Smalltalk-80 implementation designed with secondary storage management and communications needs in mind. The Alltalk bytecodes, interpreter, object manager, and garbage collector differ significantly from traditional Smalltalk-80 implementations in order to provide for these needs. This was done without adding a database sub-language, new language syntax, classes, or methods to Smalltalk. Hence, Alltalk appears to be a normal Smalltalk-80 environment to the Smalltalk programmer, but provides a foundation for recoverability, sharability, and distribution.

The resulting system provides the programmer with a single syntax for accessing objects, be they in memory or on disk. Also, the system deduces the permanent status of objects with no explicit indications required from the programmer. Alltalk eliminates the "impedance mismatch"[6] between the programming language and the database sub-language, (currently an artifact in today's systems).

We chose the Smalltalk-80 language primarily for its "pure" object computation model which provided a context for integrating the "database" services in a particularly transparent and natural way. Also, the existing body of Smalltalk-80 documentation and literature enables us to avoid the definition and maintenance of yet another object-oriented language syntax.

This paper concentrates on particular design problems raised by the Smalltalk-80 language system semantics when combined with "database-like" storage management.

2. Relevant Aspects of Alltalk

The main components of the Alltalk runtime environment are shown in Figure 1. In the discussions of specific problems in Section 3, we will touch on various aspects of these components, particularly the *object manager*, *interpreter* and *garbage collector*. A general overview of these components is presented here. Complete descriptions of these components can be found in references 7 and 8.

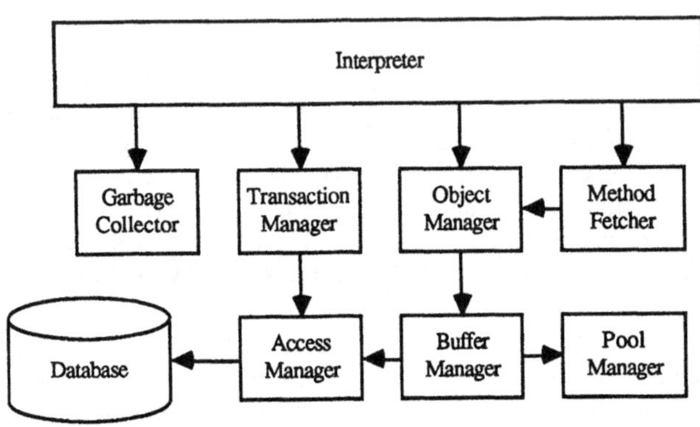

Figure 1 - Architecture of Alltalk

The primary function of the *object manager* is to provide main memory storage management of objects for use by the *interpreter*. This includes capabilities for:

1. Creating a new object of a given class.
2. Obtaining a memory pointer to an object given its id, (fetch).
3. Changing the size of an object.

Because of the design of the *garbage collector* and *transaction manager*, there are well-defined intervals during which memory pointers to objects are guaranteed to be valid for the *interpreter*. This allows the *interpreter* (and its primitive methods) to use this direct pointer to access and/or update an object directly without further calls to the object manager.

Objects are stored in buffers maintained by the *buffer manager* and allocated by the *pool manager*. The *buffer manager* maintains an object table mapping object ids into buffer addresses for in-memory objects. If a request is made for an object which is not already in the buffers, the object is faulted in from the database and an entry is made in the object table.

Note that by using the buffers both as the database staging area and as the area for creation and manipulation of objects by the interpreter, we have essentially combined the functions of the Smalltalk memory heap with those of database buffer management.

In general, an in-memory object is in one of three states in the system:

1. New object - This is an object created at the interpreter's request. Because it is new, the object is not referenced by any other object in the database or in-memory buffers. Hence, the object is eligible for garbage collection ("garbage" object). The object remains eligible for garbage collection unless it is made "reachable" from an object in the database at a commit point. If it is "reachable" at commit time, that is, the object is part of the transitive closure of the database, the object must be written to the database.
2. Non-updated database object - This kind of object was in the database as of the last commit and has not been updated. It is not eligible for garbage collection since other objects in the database may be referencing it. Because the object has not been updated, its transitive closure is guaranteed to be in the database. This implies that garbage collection and commit logic need not examine the object and its references, significantly pruning transitive closure computations for these operations.

3. Updated database object - This object was in the database as of the last commit and, subsequently, had one or more of its instance variables altered. Garbage collection must avoid deleting this object, or any other object in its transitive closure. Commit logic must write this object and any updated or new in-memory objects referenced by the object to the database.

The reader should note that it is never necessary for runtime garbage collection or commit logic to fetch any additional objects from the database to execute their functions.

Runtime garbage collection is highly synchronized with interpreter execution states which are defined by Smalltalk *processes* (threads of control) and *contexts* (activation records). The runtime garbage collector keeps track of objects in groups or *regions* associated with contiguous context activations. Objects in a region can be "adopted" by objects in regions associated with earlier context activations as a result of Smalltalk assignment and return statements. Objects which are still "orphans" in regions whose associated contexts are no longer active can be safely discarded. The database also requires garbage collection to remove unreachable and logically deleted objects (database "garbage"). This is currently handled with an off-line mark/sweep collector.

3. Integration Problems

Problems raised in integrating database management with an object-oriented language stem from several sources. In our minds, the most important problems to be solved were those raised in preserving the Smalltalk language semantics. The next source of problems were in designing proper database management mechanisms in the underlying implementation which would be transparent to the language semantics. Finally, problem areas related to performance considerations had to be addressed. In this section we review some of our more significant problems in these areas.

3.1. Message Send

As in most object-oriented languages, message sending is the core operation in Smalltalk. In the message:

ages at: 'Steve' put: 30

an object in the variable **ages**, known as the *receiver*, is being sent the message **at:put:** with two parameters, the string object **'Steve'** and the integer object **30**. It is likely that the receiver is some sort of associative data structure, probably an instance of class Dictionary. The resulting action is to execute the **at:put:** procedure, (known as a *method*), defined in the class or a superclass of the receiver object. In order to execute the message send, the runtime environment must:

1. Fetch the receiver object.
2. Fetch the class of the receiver object.
3. Look up the id of the method in the "class dictionary".
4. If the method is not found, repeat steps 2 and 3 for each superclass until it is found.
5. Once the method is found, fetch the method code object.
6. Set up a new context and transfer control to the start of the method code.

Fetch operations initiated in steps 1, 2, 4 and 5 require database accesses if the objects are not already in the buffers. These accesses are invisible to the interpreter in our design.

3.2. Assignment Statements

The language semantic used to signal an object update is the assignment statement. When the target of an assignment statement is an instance or class variable, the object is marked as "updated" by the interpreter. This enables commit logic to detect the need to write the object to database, if the object is in the transitive closure of the database at commit.

In addition, garbage collection is simplified by placing the assigned object in the region of the target at the time of assignment. Note that no actual movement or copying of the object takes place, only the region id in the assigned object is updated. When the first context associated with the current region has returned to its calling context, all non-garbage objects are guaranteed to have been moved to lower regions. Garbage collection is reduced to simply releasing the buffer space for the remaining objects in the current, and all higher, regions. Space occupied by updated database objects is not released since it must be preserved until the next commit.

3.3. Chaining of Instances

In a Smalltalk system, all instances of a class appear in a linked list rooted in the class object. Methods are available to the programmer which allow this chain to be traversed.

In a database environment, this presents a problem: commit logic demands that any object reachable from the database (e.g., via the class object) be placed in the database to insure referential integrity. This implies that any new object existing at the time of commit should be written to the database, since it is in the class instance chain anchored in a database object. Except for this chain reference, such an object would be eligible for garbage collection, and we will have wasted expensive database activity during the commit by writing the object to the database. Furthermore, such garbage database objects will have to be deleted by system logic, or worse, explicitly by application programs.

This problem of maintaining an instance chain that includes all objects, yet not needlessly forcing objects to the database has been recognized in reference 9. The Alltalk solution is as follows:

1. On a commit, objects are forced to the database only if they are reachable from a database object in some way other than through the class instance chain.
2. It is ensured that the class instance chain in the database only reflects objects actually in the database. This guarantees the integrity of the chain upon database restart.
3. An in-memory chain is maintained that includes new objects (when they are created) and whose tail links to the chain maintained in the database. This ensures that the programmer can get at *all* objects through the instance chain.
4. The garbage collector removes an object from the in-memory chain when that object is deleted. This keeps the chain up to date for a scan of the instances.

We believe this provides reasonably surprise-free semantics for use of the instance chain.

3.4. Transactions

In keeping with our goal of providing transparent database services, one of our hopes was to find a definition for a transaction (unit of recovery) which would be invisible to the Smalltalk programmer. After attempting a variety of approaches and considering expected applications, a universally appropriate definition did not seem to be discernible from any execution environment cues.

We came to the realization that the primary problem of defining a transaction in an integrated programming language and database management system stems from the fact that the definition of a transaction may be highly application specific. Traditional database systems tend to have a very rigid notion of a transaction around which the application programs are designed. Programs that are not developed in the context of database system range from having no need to save computational state information, to those containing extremely elaborate checkpoint/restart logic, particularly if such programs are long-running.

In order to support this range of application needs, we plan to make the Alltalk transaction manager interfaces for *commit()* and *abort()* operations available at the Smalltalk level. We are currently monitoring experimentation with Alltalk by other groups in Kodak to determine the most useful manner in which to provide access to these functions.

3.5. Buffer Management Issues

As noted earlier, Alltalk combines memory management for new (heap) objects with objects retrieved from the database in a single buffering scheme. This complicates the normal concerns of database buffer management regarding staging and replacement strategies for objects in the buffers. In particular, it is necessary for the interpreter and garbage collector to aid buffer management in determining when objects need no longer be "pinned down" so that the space for objects in the buffers can be reused. Objects required to be "pinned down" include those which are new or have been updated. In addition, for performance reasons, reasonable latitude must be afforded by buffer management to "pin down" objects which will have direct memory pointers to them for specific intervals during execution.

Others have found that reconciling management of the language storage heap and database buffers cannot be made without forcing the applications programmer to distinguish language and database objects.[10] This results in a non-uniform object model in the final system, (i.e., language vs. database objects). Fortunately, Smalltalk does not force us into this situation. In Alltalk, specific cues have been determined from the operation of the interpreter which allow for clean and efficient determination of reference lifetimes for objects in the buffers. These cues enable Alltalk to provide a uniform object model while retaining invisible database support.

A complete description of the Alltalk buffer manager, garbage collector, and interpreter can be found in reference 7. A brief summary is provided here to illustrate how the interpreter and garbage collector help the buffer manager determine when it is safe to release space for "pinned" objects.

Alltalk maintains several buffers, each made up of many fixed-size memory areas known as "slots". Each slot in a buffer can hold exactly one object. Specific buffers are allocated for various sizes of objects. The number and size of the slots in the buffers can be adjusted to fit the distribution of object sizes in database and application runtime needs.

An *in-use* table identifies buffer slots which contain objects that should not be overwritten or moved due to the object being either new, updated, or having a pointer reference which must remain valid for a time. The *reserve_obj()* buffer manager routine causes an entry to be made in this table, returning a pointer to the retrieved object. Entries in the table are tagged with process and garbage collection region ids in effect when the *reserve_obj()* call was made. These ids aid in determining when the entry can be removed and the corresponding buffer slot made available for reuse.

In-use table entries are removed by either the garbage collector or transaction commit logic depending on the state of the object (new, updated db, or non-updated db object). Garbage collection is invoked on method return boundaries which represent transitions between garbage collection regions. As noted earlier, because all non-garbage objects are guaranteed to have been moved to lower regions, each remaining object in regions above the region to which we are returning is either garbage or a database object, (so long as an active region in another process does not reference the object). In-use table entries for the slots holding garbage objects are removed by the collector.

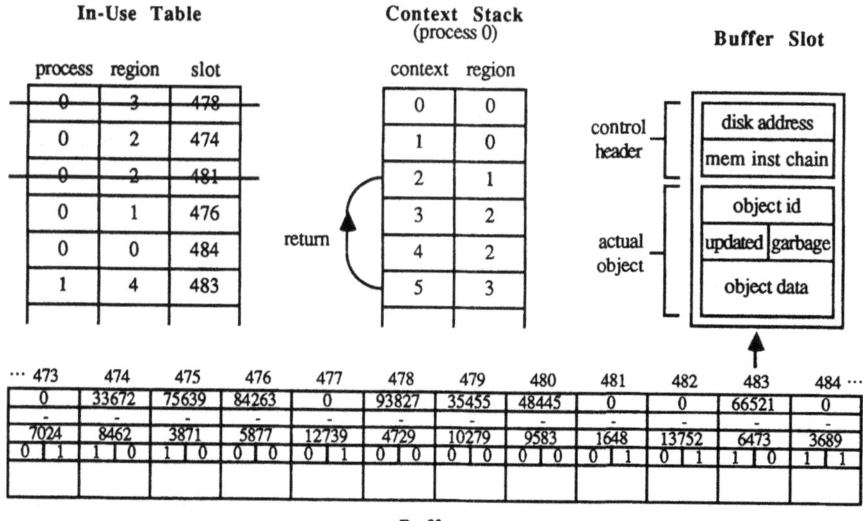

Figure 2 - Removal of In-Use Table Entries

Any entries for slots containing non-updated database objects in these regions are also removed by the collector (copies in the database are valid). Transaction commit logic takes care of removing the remaining entries for slots containing updated database objects (the updated version was flushed to database), but only for those entries with region ids above the current region at the time of the *commit()* call, (lower region entries are still in use).

Figure 2 illustrates removal of in-use table entries. In this example, a return from context 5 to context 2 is occurring in process 0 (Smalltalk contexts do not always exhibit pure stack behavior, returns can "pop" more than one context). This return implies a transition from garbage collection region 3 to region 1, hence all regions greater than 1 can be collected. The garbage collector scans the in-use table looking for entries for process 0 in these regions. In-use table entries for buffer slots 478, 474 and 481 satisfy these criteria. Entries for buffer slots 476 and 484 are not considered since they represent slots in regions <= 1, while entry 483 is for a slot held by process 1. For those in-use table entries which qualify, the collector examines the object in the slot to determine whether it is an updated database object, non-updated database object, or garbage object.

Entries in the in-use table for buffer slots containing garbage objects or non-updated database objects are removed. In the example, the object in buffer slot 481 has its garbage flag set, hence the associated in-use table entry is removed. Buffer slot 478 contains a database object (non-zero disk address) which does not have its updated flag set, therefore its in-use table entry is also removed. The in-use table entry for buffer slot 474 is retained since this slot contains a database object with its updated flag set.

Because our buffer slots are fixed in memory, pointers to objects obtained via the *reserve_obj()* call remain valid as long as the in-use table entry exists. This enables the interpreter to maintain direct pointers to objects such as the current message receiver, method object, and current operation code within the method object (program counter). Furthermore, these direct pointers may be saved and restored as needed to implement subsequent message sends in a similar manner as is done with return address information in stack frames of traditional procedural language implementations.

4. Future Work

Work on recovery, sharability, and distribution are presently underway. For recovery, we are considering the traditional approach of implementing a "redo" log. To address sharability, we expect to augment in-use table entries with a user-id and lock information. Our model of a distributed Alltalk is currently that of a single database system operating on a set of similar workstations in a network in contrast to partioned databases with explicit interfaces for object exchange.

Classes and methods implementing B-trees (in Smalltalk) to support secondary indexes, and our resolution of instance chaining issues provide basic building-blocks for support of queries. We have used Orion[11] as a model of queries in an object-oriented database.

Additions to the Smalltalk software development environment are also being examined. Areas under consideration include support for multiple cooperating developers and improved tools for determining and enhancing reusability (of more than source code alone).

Finally, progress has been made in implementation of a logic programming facility within the object-oriented environment.[12]

References

1. M. Ahlsen, A. Bjornerstedt, S. Gritts, C. Hulten, and L. Soderlund. "An Architecture for Object Management in OIS," *ACM Trans. on Office Information Systems*, Vol. 2, No. 3, July 1984.
2. Woelk, D., and W. Kim. "Multimedia Information Management in an Object-Oriented Database System," in *Proc. Intl. Conf. on Very Large Data Bases*, Brighton, England, Sept. 1987.
3. Stroustrup, B. *The C++ Programming Language*, Addison-Wesley, Reading, MA 1986.
4. *The Objective-C Reference Manual*, The Stepstone Corporation, Sandy Hook, Connecticut 1987. Objective-C is a trademark of The Stepstone Corporation.
5. Goldberg, A. and D. Robson. *Smalltalk-80: The Language and its Implementation*, Addison-Wesley, Reading, MA 1983. Smalltalk-80 is a trademark of Parc Place Systems, Inc.
6. Copeland, G. and D. Maier. "Making Smalltalk a Database System," in *Proc. of ACM-SIGMOD Intl. Conf. on the Management of Data*, ACM, New York, 1984.
7. F. Mellender, S. Riegel, and A. Straw. "Optimizing Smalltalk Message Performance" in *Object-Oriented Concepts, Applications, and Databases*, W. Kim and F. Lochovsky (editors), Addison-Wesley, Reading, MA, to be published.
8. A. Straw, F. Mellender, and S. Riegel. "Object Management in a Persistent Smalltalk System", submitted to Software Practice and Experience.
9. Bloom, T. and Zdonik S. "Issues in the Design of Object-Oriented Database Programming Languages," in *Proc. ACM Conf. on Object Oriented Programming Systems, Languages, and Applications*, Orlando, Florida, October 1987.
10. Richardson, J. and M. Carey. "Programming Constructs for Database System Implementation in EXODUS," in *Proc. of ACM-SIGMOD 1987 Annual Conference*, San Francisco, California, May 1987.
11. J. Banerjee, W. Kim., and K.C. Kim. "Queries in Object-Oriented Databases," in *Proc. 4th Intl. Conf. on Data Engineering*, Los Angeles, California, February 1988.
12. F. Mellender. "An Integration of Logic and Object-Oriented Programming", to appear in ACM SIGPLAN Notices.

On Dynamically Defined Complex Objects and SQL

R. Lorie
H.-J. Schek

IBM Almaden Research Center
San Jose, CA 95120-6099

Current address: Technische Hochshule Darmstadt, F.R. Germany.

Introduction

The initial relational database model is based on tables that are completely independent one from another: a row can be inserted or deleted in a table without consideration of any other table; joins may be expressed on any columns of compatible syntactic types. In other words, the initial model has very little notion of semantics. In the last decade, many authors have emphasized the need for more semantics (see /HK87/ for a survey). The reasons for doing so vary, but the common underlying justification is that, once the system becomes aware of semantic properties, it can make the user's task easier, increase the level of confidence in the data, and even improve performance.

Our main interest in this paper is in extending the semantic contents of the database schema to support a powerful notion of dynamic complex object. Since 1980, several authors have emphasized the importance of the notion of objects in database systems. We are not looking at object databases in the sense of /Di86/, where data are encapsulated with the code used to perform operations on data of a particular type. We are looking at objects in the sense of /HL82/ and /SP82/ which are proposed as extensions to the relational model. Such objects are extremely important in broad classes of applications such as engineering, office, geographical database, and others. A complex object is a collection of tuples that is used to describe a complex real life entity such as a document, a map, a design. The tuples are generally highly interrelated and used as a cluster. Once the system knows the structure of the object, the user's interface, operations, and performance can be improved. In particular, the notion of object enforces referential integrity for the hierarchical relationships; it allows for fetching the whole object from the database in a single call, it supports cascading the delete operation when appropriate, and uses specific internal techniques to implement clustering and access paths.

However, such objects are purely hierarchical and statically defined. As soon as data must be shared, the shared portion must be defined as another object and the initial object, as well as other ones, contain a logical pointer (an identifier) to the shared object. The complex object mechanism per se does not support referential integrity for the non-hierarchical relationships, and does not support global fetch along these non-hierarchical relationships.

What is needed is a way to define an object dynamically. Note that dynamicity does not mean that all object structures should be implemented in the same way; the user could designate a particular structure as a "preferred" one, and the system could then use the same tricks than those used in the implementation of static objects, providing the same performance advantage when that specific object structure is used.

In this short paper we propose an approach to introduce dynamic objects. We start from a semantic data model. Then we show how it can be used to define the structure of an object dynamically, and we discuss how the repetitive use of SQL leads to powerful operations that can be performed on these objects.

Semantic Model

We do not propose a new semantic data model. We rather borrow the basic features from KL-ONE /BS85/, and simplify the terminology. We refer to this simplified model as KLDM and introduce it by example.

Employees work in departments and have history; they are assigned to projects; each employee can work on zero, one or more projects; one project can be covered by zero, one or more employees (see figure).

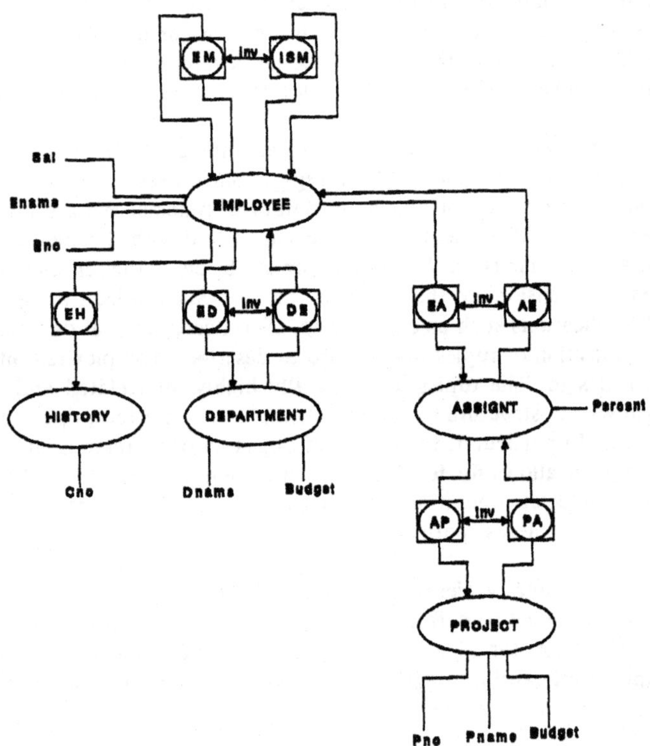

Figure: A KLDM example

Employee records form the EMPLOYEE entity class, called concept in KL-ONE. The arcs leaving an entity class node represent attributes (roles in KL-ONE) and are given a name. Eno, Ename, Sal are attributes; so is EH. An attribute arc points to the domain from which the attribute values are drawn. In fact, for sake of clarity in the figure we omitted the basic primitive classes and the relationships between an attribute and its associated basic class.

The directed connection between two non-primitive entity classes via a role expresses a 1-to-n relationship between a parent entity and a number of child entities. For example, several HISTORY entities can be related to an employee by the relationship EH. One employee can manage other employees, as indicated by the directed arc from EMPLOYEE to EMPLOYEE via EM, the "employee manages" relationship. The inverse relationship can also be given a name: we call it ISM, "is managed".

In general, a 1-to-n relationship and its inverse 1-to-n relationship express an n-to-m relationship. In the example, the relationship EA expresses the fact that an employee is given an assignment. But PA expresses the fact that a project is associated with that assignment. A row is ASSIGNT is actually an instance of an n-to-m relationship between EMPLOYEE and PROJECTS. Some data, such as Percent, can be associated with an entity in ASSIGNT.

Dynamic definition of objects

Consider the simple hierarchy EMPLOYEE - HISTORY. In fact in /HL82/ or /SP82/ we could have implemented an employee and all of his history as a complex object or NF2 record. But here we do not define the structure statically as being an object. Instead, we allow the object to be defined dynamically and we use the semantic net definition as a starting point, ie. as the database schema. Let us first look at how we can just read the information as if it were an object.

```
select object
   A: select Eno, Ename, B  from EMPLOYEE
      where Ename = 'Smith'
   B: select Cno  from EH,HISTORY
end select
```

We clearly select in one operation (select object ... end select are like parentheses delimiting the single operation). We first select the EMPLOYEEs; that resulting set of tuples is called A. Each tuple in A is obtained by projecting out the attributes Eno, Ename and a new set attribute named B; the content of B is defined by the next statement which selects Cno from EH,HISTORY. EH is the relationship name. It specifies that we are interested only in the HISTORY tuples that are associated with the employee via the relationship EH. We may regard the identifier B in the first select clause as a (multivalued) function defined on the EH,HISTORY values. It returns a set of values as defined by the next select-from-where statement.

As another example of a complex object fetch, let us assume we want to retrieve an employee with information about all projects in which he is involved. Again, we look at a path in the semantic network: EMPLOYEE, EA, ASSIGNT, AP, PROJECT. The fetch is as follows:

```
select object
   A: select Ename, Sal, B from EMPLOYEE where...
   B: select Percent, C from EA,ASSIGNT
   C: select Pname, Budget from AP,PROJECT
end select
```

It is clear that we can look at an up-side down view and ask to show the employee information under a project. The query becomes

```
select object
  A: select Pname, Budget, B from PROJECT where...
  B: select Percent, C from PA,ASSIGNT
  C: select Ename, Sal from AE,EMPLOYEE
end select
```

Note that in the first query the path from B to C is along a 1-to-1 relationship; in other words the set C of (Pname, Budget) always contains a single element. Therefore we really do not need three levels in the hierarchy; two levels are sufficient since the information in C can be simply concatenated with the tuple in B. In other words, for every EMPLOYEE tuple returned we will see as many child tuples as the employee has project assignments, but the PROJECT attributes and the ASSIGNT attribute are collapsed into a single tuple.

All examples above retrieve tuples along a linear path in the network. Now, suppose we are interested in tuples along several branches of a tree, such as finding the history and the project assignments of some employees: Then the query will look like

```
select object
  A: select Eno, B, C from EMPLOYEE
  B: select... from EH,HISTORY
  C: select... from EA,ASSIGNMT
end select
```

Predicates

In the above examples of object fetches we did not apply any predicate. In fact predicates can be applied, locally at every level, or across levels. Note that at lower levels, attributes from higher levels act as constants. Let us show a complete example:

Select the employees which make more than 40K together with their projects which have a budget larger than 10 times the salary of the employee.

```
select object
  A: select Ename, B from EMPLOYEE X  where Sal > 40K
  B: select Percent, C from EA,ASSIGNT
  C: select Pname from AP,PROJECT where Budget > X.Sal * 10
end select
```

Note the use of X as in SQL. Note further that there may not exist any project with the desired property in an assignment. In this case C is empty and returned as such to the user. If this is not desirable we may use an aggregate function in the where clause of B as shown in the next section.

Aggregates

It may be interesting to return in an object an aggregate value rather than a complete set of values. For example, assume we want to retrieve information on employees, including the number of projects in which the employee is involved. This can be expressed as

```
select object
  A: select Ename,... count(B) from EMPLOYEE where...
  B: select ... from EA,ASSGNT where...
end select
```

Aggregate values can also be used in a where clause. For example:

```
select object
  A: select Ename, count(B) from EMPLOYEE
       where count(B) > 0
  B: select ... from EA,ASSIGNT where
end select
```

Recursion

First we look at fixed depth "recursion". Suppose we want to fetch an object consisting of an employee and all employees who report to him directly. In the model, there is an arrow from EMPLOYEE to EMPLOYEE via the relationship EM. Actually it does not matter that the target class EMPLOYEE is the same as the origin of the arrow. So we can write, as shown before:

```
select object
  A: select *, B from EMPLOYEE
  B: select Ename from EM,EMPLOYEE
end select
```

Now we can generalize the construct to an arbitrary (and variable) number of levels. The following statement fetches the complete hierarchy under John.

```
select object
  A: select *, B from EMPLOYEE where Ename ="John"
  B: select Ename, B from EM,EMPLOYEE
end select
```

The recursion is indicated by the presence of B in the select list of the second select sub-statement. If John is not a manager, an empty set B is returned since no tuple qualifies in the second select statement. Otherwise the set of names of persons managed by John is returned. For each such person, the set of names of persons he/she manages is returned, and so on, until this set of names is empty. This condition automatically breaks the recursion. In /LS88/ a type definition of the result in a Pascal-like notation is given. It is shown that the result is a recursive nested relation.

Conclusion

Using a semantic data model allows us to specify dynamically the structure of a complex object. We have shown by examples that a sequence of simple SQL statements can be used. It turns out that the object fetch syntax, with its capabilities for projection, selection and aggregates allows to ask complex queries in SQL as an identified group of nicely separated simpler queries. In some cases this may be much easier than forcing the user to rely on a single complex query.

We have shown that our notion of complex objects /HL82, SP82/, often referred to as being too narrow ("no shared subobjects") becomes in fact very general and powerful when dynamic shared objects and recursion are introduced.

A full length paper on this subject /LS88/ discusses more formally what the type of a selected object is, given the types of the KLDM nodes and the select specification itself. It also shows how the notions of view and generalization are supported very naturally. Formal definitions for the interpretation of the select object statement by transforming it into a nested SQL expression appear in /PA86, SS86/. Some interesting points for discussions are: the representation of objects as structures in memory, the insert and update facilities, the impact on the optimizer.

References

BS85: R.J. Brachman, J.G. Schmolze. An Overview of the KL-ONE Knowledge Representation System. Cognitive Science, Vol. 9, 1985.

Da86: P. Dadam et al. A DBMS prototype to support extended NF2 relations: An integrated view on flat tables and hierarchies, ACM SIGMOD, Washington 1986.

Di86: Object-Oriented Database Systems: The Notion and the Issues. Proc. of the Int. Workshop on Object-Oriented Database Systems. Pacific Grove, 1986.

HK87: R. Hull, R. King. Semantic Database Modeling: Survey, Applications, and Research Issues, ACM Computing Surveys, June 1987.

HL82: R. Haskin and R. Lorie. On extending the functions of a relational database system. In Proc. ACM SIGMOD Conf. on Management of Data, ACM, New York, Orlando, 1982.

LS88: R. Lorie and H.-J. Schek. On dynamically Defined complex objects and SQL, to be published.

PA86: P. Pistor, F. Anderson. Designing a Generalized NF2 Data Model with SQL-Type Interface, Proceedings VLDB Kyoto, 1986.

SP82: H.-J. Schek and P. Pistor. Data structures for an integrated database management and information retrieval system. In Int. Conf. on Very Large Databases, pages 197--207, Mexico, 1982.

SS86 H.-J. Schek and M. H. Scholl. The relational model with relation-valued attributes. Information Systems, 11(2):137--147, June 1986.

Common Object-Oriented Repository System

Patrick O'Brien
Digital Equipment Corporation
Object-Based Systems Group
77 Reed Road, HLO2-3/M08
Hudson, MA 01749

The Object-Based Systems Group is building an object-oriented database system. The primary purpose of the database, which we call an *object-repository*, is to provide shared access to persistent objects in a multi-user environment. The repository supports access from multiple languages, including Trellis/Owl, an object-oriented language and programming environment developed at Digital. It also provides the usual database amenities such as concurrency control, recovery, and authorization. The database is intended for applications, such as engineering data management, which have complex data structuring requirements and special data accessing needs.

The Trellis/Owl language [Schaffert *et al* 86] [O'Brien *et al* 87] combines a multiple-inheritance type hierarchy with strict, compile-time type checking. It attempts to integrate the strengths of previous work in object-oriented programming. It uses the power of the "message passing" metaphor and inheritance hierarchies demonstrated by Smalltalk-80[1] [Goldberg 83]. It also builds upon the CLU [Liskov 81] language which demonstrated that an object-oriented language can provide good performance, and, by providing type-abstraction and strict type-checking features, can actively support the programming goals of high reliability and maintainability. Trellis is currently a single-user system that provides automatic storage management and presents a one-level store model to the programmer.

For languages such as Trellis/Owl, we would like to provide shared access to persistent objects in a client/server model. Our objective is to achieve a tight integration of database management concepts within the object-oriented style of Trellis/Owl. This contrasts with traditional language/database interfaces that rely upon a set of function calls or a separate data manipulation language which has little or no interaction with other language features. With the traditional approach, the database complicates the programmer's view by introducing a second level of storage with different data modeling constructs. As well, some objects are temporary, others are persistent and shareable, and decisions must be made about when to update objects in the database. We would like to make the interface between the programming language and the database as transparent as possible (i.e. maintain an illusion of a one level store).

Our database extension to Trellis/Owl (see [O'Brien *et al* 86]) is presented to the programmer as new types added to the library. We use existing facilities for declaration of types and variables, along with existing control structures for iteration and exception handling. This allows programs to access and manipulate database objects in the same manner

[1] Smalltalk-80 is a trademark of Xerox Corporation.

as all other objects. The repository and the Trellis/Owl language support the same data structuring capabilities so there is no impedance mismatch.

As much as possible, we would like to provide this tightly-integrated support for other object-oriented languages as well (see Figure 1). For example, we expect the repository to directly support the C++ type system. Some languages will not be as tightly-integrated, but they will be able to access the repository through a call-level interface, either directly to the repository or through one of the tightly-integrated languages. We are also investigating ways of sharing objects between tightly-integrated languages, while trying to avoid some of the less desirable aspects of a call-level interface.

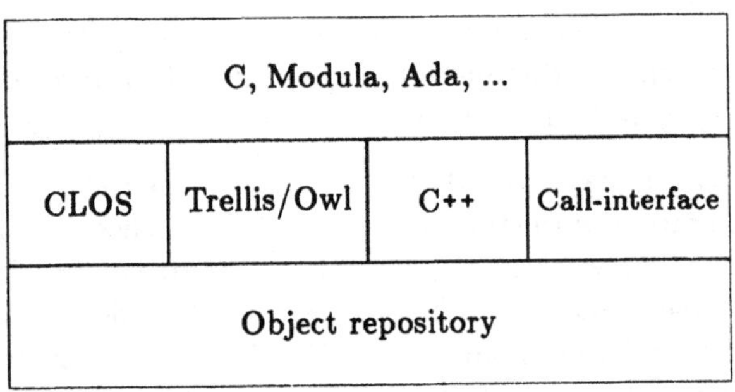

Figure 1: Multi-lingual support

Support for aggregate objects is crucial to provide adequate performance for the applications we are targeting. Support for aggregate objects includes prefetching and clustering. Accessing an object on the repository tends to be expensive, relative to accessing an object in memory. Thus we want to prefetch objects from the repository when it is beneficial to do so. What should get transferred from the database when an object is referenced depends on the particular application's needs. The objects that constitute an aggregate object are also clustered together on disk. This clustering is used to improve the performance of prefetching. We are experimenting with different strategies for clustering and prefetching, as well as different mechanisms for allowing the programmer to describe hints for the system.

Sharing and reliability are also important issues. The repository has to provide a mechanism for coordinating reliable updates to objects which are shared by several programs. The repository provides a recovery scheme for handling failures (either client program failures or the repository itself). We are currently using serializable transactions to allow atomic multi-object updates. But serializable transactions based on locking tend to force a much more serial schedule than is logically necessary, and so they are sometimes too restrictive for the design environments that we want to support. Thus, we are also considering providing user defined atomic types to allow for greater levels of concurrency where needed.

We are also concerned with the granularity of objects that the repository manages. We believe that our performance requirements will not permit us to lock objects or translate external object ids to internal ids at the granularity of a Trellis/Owl or Smalltalk object. Our implementation work includes investigating ways to group objects so the repository can deal with them as a unit for transferring, clustering, and locking. One problem we have encountered is that grouping objects for transferring and locking often produces conflicting requirements.

The repository will provide a flexible scheme for handling program (schema) changes, since we expect that some of the types defined to it may be changing quite frequently. This requires some form of support for versions of objects. For example, the repository will have to support multiple versions of objects of the same type and/or provide the ability to convert an object from an old version of a type to a newer version of that type.

Since user-defined versions (e.g. versions of a document) play an important role in many of the application areas we are targeting, we would like to provide mechanisms that enable applications to provide support for version control. But we believe that it is too early to settle on a single semantics for versions. Instead, we will identify features (such as efficient copying of large objects) that should be present in the repository kernel to support a range of version semantics. In addition, we do not believe that it is the repository's responsibility to provide "long" transactions or CAD style version control. Furthermore, it should not attempt to define histories and provide merging assistance for versions of objects. These facilities and their functionality are defined by our target applications and should be layered on top of the primitives provided by the repository. This does not preclude this functionality from becoming part of the type library and thus reusable by different applications.

Declarative consistency constraints and associative retrieval are important database features. For our target applications database access is dominated by graph walking as opposed to ad hoc querying. Thus, we will provide limited support for associative retrieval in the first version of the system. We believe that this is not as important for our applications as is efficient support for pointer chasing access to objects. Initially, most database style consistency constraints will have to be expressed procedurally. Object-oriented programming makes this much less of a problem since types can ensure that integrity is maintained.

One view of the repository's architecture is shown in Figure 2. The lowest level is the large object layer which provides storage management, concurrency control, and recovery capabilities for the object repository. The large object layer works with large uninterpreted bytes of data which we call segments. The large object layer has no notion of what is inside its segments: it is the responsibility of the higher layers to understand the structure of segments.

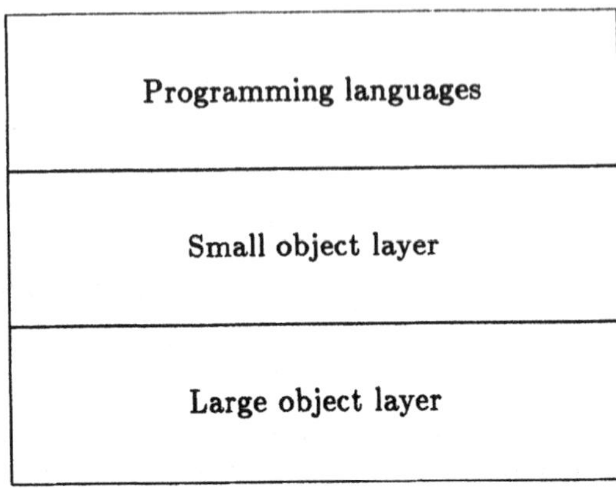

Figure 2: Layers of the object repository

Segments are used for transferring data between clients and servers. In addition, they serve as the primary unit for locking and recovery. Although segments work well for transferring data, we sometimes want to lock objects at a finer level of granularity than a whole segment. We are experimenting with different approaches to achieve finer granularity locking while not impacting performance.

The small object layer resides between the application language and the storage manager. It provides a language-independent abstraction of objects which are similar to objects found in traditional object-oriented languages, such as Smalltalk and Trellis/Owl. These objects are very simple: they contain a set of references (slots) to other objects and a data area consisting of uninterpreted bytes. The small object layer is responsible for bundling objects into and out of the segments provided by the large object layer. The small object layer provides a simple type system but with no type hierarchy and no code execution model.

Through the coupling of the small and large object layers, the object repository provides efficient, reliable, shared storage for multiple programming languages. It relies on the programming languages to provide an execution model and high level abstractions such as type hierarchies and an extensible type system. We are currently implementing the object repository and interfacing the Trellis/Owl language to it. We are also working with internal CAD, CASE, and AI groups to build applications which will test out our design decisions.

References

[Goldberg 83] Adele Goldberg and David Robson. *Smalltalk-80: The Language and its Implementation.* Addison-Wesley, Reading, Massachusetts, 1983.

[Liskov 81] B. Liskov, R. Atkinson, T. Bloom, E. Moss, C. Schaffert, R. Scheifler, and A. Snyder. *CLU Reference Manual.* Springer-Verlag, 1981.

[O'Brien *et al* 86] Patrick O'Brien, Bruce Bullis, and Craig Schaffert. Persistent and Shared Objects in Trellis/Owl. *International Workshop on Object-Oriented Database Systems*, Asilomar Conference Center, Pacific Grove, California, September 1986.

[O'Brien *et al* 87] Patrick D. O'Brien, Daniel C. Halbert, and Michael F. Kilian. "The Trellis Programming Environment." *OOPSLA-87 Proceedings*, Orlando, Florida, October 1987.

[Schaffert *et al* 86] Craig Schaffert, Topher Cooper, Bruce Bullis, Mike Kilian, and Carrie Wilpolt. An Introduction to Trellis/Owl. *OOPSLA86 Proceedings*, Portland, Oregon, September 1986.

On the integration of Object-Oriented and Process-Oriented computation in persistent environments

R.Morrison, A.L.Brown, R.Carrick, R.Connor & A.Dearle

Department of Computational Science, University of St Andrews,
North Haugh, St Andrews, Scotland KY16 9SS

Abstract

Persistent programming is concerned with the construction of large and long lived systems of data [1,2]. Such systems have traditionally required concurrent access for two reasons. The first is that of speed, be it access speed for multiple users or execution speed for parallel activities. The second reason for concurrency is to control the complexity of large systems by decomposing them into parallel activities.

This process-oriented approach to system construction has much in common with the object-oriented approach. We will demonstrate, in this paper, the facilities of the language Napier [17] which allows the integration of the two methodologies along with a persistent environment to provide concurrently accessed object-oriented databases.

1. Introduction

One of the major motivations for concurrent activity, be it user or machine, is execution speed. The need for concurrency increases as machines approach their theoretical speed limit at the same time as the complexity of the applications increases to require even greater power.

There is, however, a second major motivation for concurrency. Many of the activities that we wish to model are inherently parallel and if we wish to capture the essential nature of these real world activities then language primitives powerful enough to model them are required. One of the major breakthroughs in the design and understanding of operating systems was gained by modelling the system as a set of co-operating sequential processes[7]. Since most of the early operating systems modelled in this manner ran on uni-processor machines this modelling was not done to increase speed. It was done to simplify the complexity of the system being built in order to gain greater insight into its operation. This process-oriented method of modelling, first applied to operating systems, has now been applied to database systems, graphics systems and general problems in computer science[12].

The process-oriented methodology yields a new style of program construction and understanding in which the system is decomposed into activities that operate in parallel. Each activity is self contained, communicating with other activities via messages which are synchronised by some protocol. This style of programming is very similar to the object-oriented style except that it does not usually make use of inheritance mechanisms. For this reason we say that it is more akin to a data abstraction methodology than an object-oriented one.

The best known process-oriented methodology is that of actors [11] where there are only two kinds of object in the system's universe of discourse, actors and values. The attractiveness of the actor model is in its simplicity and most of the work on integrating the paradigms has been based on superimposing an actor model on an object-oriented language [10].

Here we will take a different approach and use a strong type system to unify the concepts of process and inheritance. We will allow static data constructors but use process as the main object constructor and integrate this with a persistent environment to yield concurrent object-oriented databases.

2. Processes and Objects

Wegner [18] has defined an object-oriented language to have three essential features. They are

a. the ability to define objects as a set of operations and a state that remembers the effect of the operations.
b. the objects can be categorised by class (type).
c. there is an inheritance mechanism for defining superclasses and subclasses.

In comparison with this, processes traditionally have a state and a method of communicating with each other. By making process a type in the modelling language and ensuring that the type system allows inheritance, then the methodologies can be conveniently integrated. To illustrate this, the table below compares the essential features of both styles.

Object-Oriented	**Process-Oriented**
objects	processes
object state	process state
object type	process type
object operations	process entries
object inheritance	process protocols

We will now demonstrate, by example, the facilities of the language Napier which make this integration possible.

3. Processes and Objects in Napier

In Napier, the type system is similar to one suggested by Cardelli and Wegner [6]. It contains a number of base types such as integer, real, string and boolean and a number of constructors like vectors, structures, first class procedures, abstract data types, environments and processes. The type system is polymorphic and we will introduce the relevent details as we progress through examples. The inheritance method is that of Cardelli [5].

The model of concurrency in Napier is based on CSP [12] and Ada [13]. Process is a type in the language. The type defines the process interface that the process presents to the world. The interface consists of a set of procedures (names) called entries. External to the process the entries act like first class procedures. Inside the process the entries do not act like procedures but are used to establish rendezvous with calling processes. For example, an integer object to which we may read and write could be defined by specifying the following type

```
type shared_int_object is process (write : proc (int ), read : proc ( -> int) )
```

That is, objects (processes) of this type have two entries 'write' and 'read'. 'write' takes as a parameter the integer value to be written and 'read' returns the integer value contained in the process. Within a process the entry name is used to establish a rendezvous. The **receive** clause uses the entry name, its formal parameter list and a clause to be executed during the rendezvous. For example

```
receive write (n : int) do i := n
```

When a rendezvous is established the body of the particular entry is executed. In this case it assigns the parameter value 'n' to the variable 'i'. From the time the call is made until the completion of the rendezvous the caller is suspended. If, however, a **receive** clause is executed before its entry has been called then the callee is suspended until the entry is called. Each **receive** clause defines a body for the entry allowing entry names to have many bodies in a process.

Processes are created and activated by associating a process body (a void clause) with a process type. For example,

```
let int_object = shared_int_object with
        begin
              let i := 0
              while true do
              begin
                    receive write (val : int) do i := val
                    receive read ( -> int) do i
              end
        end   !create a new process running in parallel
```

will create a process of the type 'shared_int_object'. The process once created starts to execute immediately and in parallel with the process which created it. A name may be given to the process by declaring it, as above. In the example, the process 'int_object' will loop servicing requests for writing and reading in strict order. Thus it has the state embodied in its local variable 'i' and its operations are 'read' and 'write'.

To implement the rendezvous there is a separate queue of waiting processes for every entry. These queues are serviced in a first come first served basis. Non-determinism in the system is provided by the **select** clause. For example

```
select
occupancy < 4        : receive enter () do occupancy := occupancy + 1
                     : receive exit () do occupancy := occupancy - 1
selected
```

To execute the **select** clause all the boolean expressions are evaluated in order. An option is open if it does not contain a boolean expression or the boolean expression is **true**. Otherwise it is closed. One of the open options is chosen for execution non-deterministically subject to the constraint that if the clause to be executed is an entry clause it will only be chosen if the entry can be received immediately. If none of the options can be immediately executed, eg if there is no entry pending, the process waits until one can be.

4. Polymorphic Processes

In the following example we demonstrate that by integrating the process concept with the polymorphic type system, we can define polymorphic processes.

```
type shared_object [t] is process (write : proc (t ), read : proc ( -> t) )

let object_generator = proc [t] ( init : t -> shared_object [t])
            shared_object [t] with
            begin
                  let i := init
                  while true do
                        select
                              :   receive write (val : t) do i := val
                              :   receive read ( -> t) do i
                        selected
            end

! create the process objects
let int_object = object_generator [int] (3)
let string_object = object_generator [string] ("Ronald")

!send messages to the processes
int_object (write) (-4213) ; string_object (write) ("Ronald")
```

In this example, a polymorphic procedure 'object_generator' is used to generate processes of a particular type. The procedure is a generic form quantified by the type 't'. It takes as a parameter an object of the type 't' and returns an active process of type 'shared_object' parameterised by 't'. The procedure must be given a particular type and an object of that type to operate correctly. Thus 'int_object' has the type shared_object [int] and 'string_object' the type shared_object [string]. These are not the same type. However, the entry procedures manipulate integers and strings respectively and may be used where procedures of these types are appropriate.

Thus 'int_object' and 'string_object' are handles on processes executing in parallel with the rest of the system. The processes will loop forever receiving requests to 'write' and 'read' in any order. The processes themselves will ensure mutual exclusion of multiple calls.

This example has been deliberately kept simple to illustrate the process mechanism. More generally, the object 'i' represents a generalised database of any type and 'read' and 'write' represent the operations on the database. To be more useful, extra operations on the database would be required. However, the example does illustrate how the object concurrency abstraction mechanism need only be written once and then applied to any type of database. This has benefits in terms of software economics [4].

A second example of a generalised index from any ordered type to any type, modelled as a process is given in Appendix I.

5. Protocols and inheritance

The entry list for a process specifies its type and can be considered as the protocol through which it may be accessed. By utilising the multiple inheritance scheme of Cardelli [5] we can place process types in the type lattice and define a partial ordering of processes. Thus it is possible to define procedures that will operate on processes with at least a given defined protocol. If the process has a more specialised type then that may also be used. For example

```
type shared_int_object is process (write : proc (int ), read : proc ( -> int) )
type write_shared_int_object is process (write : proc (int) )

let Write_object = proc [t ≤ write_shared_int_object] (A : t ; value : int)
                        A (write) (value)

let ron = write_shared_int_object with ...
        ! create a process of type write_shared_int_object

Write_object [write_shared_int_object ] (ron, -42)
        ! pass it to the procedure Write_object andwith the value to be written

let fred = shared_int_object with ... ; Write_object [shared_int_object ] (fred, 55)
```

The procedure 'Write_object' takes as a parameter an object of type 't' which is a process with at least the entry 'write'. In the example, the procedure is called twice with a process parameter. The first 'ron' has exactly the entry 'write' whereas the second 'fred' has more. Inside the procedure, only the entry 'write' may be used. By using this subtype inheritance we can abstract over entry protocols that are common to processes.

Such an inheritance mechanism is important in object-oriented programming. Although the inheritance mechanism is available for all data types in Napier it is particularly important for processes since they are the main system construction type for self contained objects. By structuring the system into co-operating processes and using the other type constructors as data abstraction mechanisms we can impose an object-oriented methodology.

The inheritance mechanism is also important for controlling change in the system. For example, a process may be changed to give more entries in its interface without altering the procedures that work on at least the supertype. This allows dynamic change to the active processes in the system subject to the supertype constraints.

6. Persistence and Object-Oriented Databases

We have defined the persistence of data to be the length of time for which the data exists and is useable[2]. In a persistent system the use of all data is independent of its persistence. Here we extend this notion of persistence to abstract over all the physical attributes of data, for example where data is kept, how long it is kept and in what form it is kept. We have discussed the advantages of persistence elsewhere [3,15,16] and will not labour them here. It is sufficient to say that by ensuring that all data objects are persistent and that the persistence of data is invisible to the programmer, then this level of abstraction yields powerful software engineering gains in the life of large systems. The figure often quoted is 30% of the total cost of a system throughout its life cycle[2].

In Napier, all data is persistent. That is, data is kept for as long as it is useable. This can be determined from the fact that it is reachable by the computation of the transitive closure of objects from the persistence root, PS. When a program terminates all its data objects may be destroyed except those that it has arranged to be reachable from PS.

Processes, and procedures that generate processes, may be stored in the persistent store. Thus when the program that activates a process terminates, the process itself may remain active. As an example we will store the 'object_generator' procedure and the 'int_object' process from previous examples in the persistent store and retrieve them later. We will assume that these objects have already been declared. Storing them in the persistent store may be done by

```
let e = environment ()                  !create a new environment
in e let O_G = object_generator         !store the bindings O_G and
in e let Int_object = int_object        !Int_object in the environment e
in PS let ee = e                        !store the environment e in PS
```

The PS environment contains a binding e : **env** and the ee environment contains the bindings O_G : **proc** [t] (init : t -> shared_object [t]) and Int_object : shared_object [int].

These objects may be retrieved from the persistent store by the following

```
type shared_object [t] is process (write : proc (t ), read : proc ( -> t) )
type shared_int_object is shared_object [int]

use PS with ee : env in
use ee with     O_G : proc [t] (init : t -> shared_object [t]),
```

```
                Int_object : shared_int_object in
begin
        let first = Int_object (read) ()
        let synchronised_int = O_G [int] (first)
        ...
end
```

In this example, the integer that is encapsulated in the 'Int_object' process is used to initialise the database generated by the 'object_generator' procedure, which is called 'O_G' here. It should be obvious that the process 'Int_object' is always active. Getting it out of the persistent store allows the current process to communicate with it.

The example demonstrates that it is possible to store data in the form of a process object in the persistent store. This gives a very primitive form of object-oriented database where the objects are processes that receive and send messages. More traditionally databases are concerned with the stability of data, for integrity, and transaction mechanisms for safe concurrent use.

For stability we provide a low level primitive 'stabilise' that ensures that data is copied onto a stable medium. However, we subscribe to the view that it is premature to build mechanisms for atomic transactions into the low level stable store [1,8,9,14]. The stable store provides a very primitive form of transaction that allows the system to recover from unexpected errors, be they hardware or software. Thus it provides primitive (one level) recovery but not atomicity or general (multi process) reversability. There is little agreement on an appropriate generalised transaction mechanism and for the present we deem it safer to build sophisticated mechanisms for atomic transactions, at a higher level of abstraction, using the concurrency and stability primitives.

Users of the persistent information space access data via concurrency and transaction protocols. This is done by encapsulating the data in concurrency and/or transaction abstractions which may be provided as demonstrated above.

7. Conclusions

The purpose of this paper was to show how the language Napier has integrated the object-oriented and process-oriented design paradigms. This was achieved by illustrating the similarities in the paradigms. By using a type system that allows both inheritance and process as a type in its universe of discourse it was shown how to construct process objects in the object-oriented style.

Furthermore, the Napier system is persistent. That is, it allows all data objects, including processes to persist. Using this persistence, we have demonstrated a method for constructing concurrently accessed object-oriented databases.

8. Acknowledgements

A number of people have help in our understanding of the integration of type, inheritance, concurrency, transactions, stability and persistence. The most prominent of those are Chris Barter, John Hurst, Robin Stanton and Mike Livesey who are all due our thanks. We would also like thank our collaborators in the PISA project and in particular Malcolm Atkinson and Francis Wai who are also working on similar problems. The system is available on request. The work was supported by SERC grants GR/D 4326.6, GR/D 47790 and GR/D 8823.

9. References

1. Atkinson, M.P., Morrison, R. & Pratten, G.D. "Designing a persistent information space architecture". 10th IFIP World Congress, Dublin (September 1986). North-Holland, Amsterdam.
2. Atkinson, M.P., Bailey, P.J., Chisholm, K.J., Cockshott, W.P. & Morrison, R. "An approach to persistent programming". Computer Journal 26,4 (November 1983).
3. Atkinson, M.P. & Morrison, R. "Procedures as persistent data objects". ACM.TOPLAS 7,4 (October 1985).
4. Boehm, B.W. "Understanding and controlling software costs". 10th IFIP World Congress, Dublin (September 1986),. North-Holland, Amsterdam.
5. Cardelli, L. "A semantics of multiple inheritance". In **Lecture Notes in Computer Science**. 173, 51. Springer-Verlag (1984).
6. Cardelli, L. & Wegner, P. "On understanding types, data abstraction and polymorphism". ACM.Computing Surveys 17, 4 (December 1985)
7. Dijkstra, E.W. "The structure of THE multiprogramming system". Comm.ACM 11, 5 (May 1968).
8. Fredrich, M. & Older, W. "HELIX : the architecture of a distributed file system". 4th Conf. on Distributed Computer Systems. (May 1984),.
9. Gammage, N.D., Kamel, R.F. & Casey, L.M. "Remote Rendezvous". Software, Practice & Experience 17, 10 (1987),.

10. Goldberg, A. & Robson, D. **SMALLTALK-80 The language and its implementation**. Addison-Wesley, London. (1983).
11. Hewitt, C.E. "Viewing control structures as patterns of message passing". J. Artificial Intelligence 8, 3 (June 1977),.
12. Hoare, C.A.R. "Communicating sequential processes". Comm.ACM 21, 8 (August 1978),.
13. Ichbiah et al., **The Programming Language Ada Reference Manual.** in **Lecture Notes in Computer Science**. 155. Springer-Verlag (1983).
14. Krablin, G.L. "Building flexible multilevel transactions in a distributed persistent environment". proceedings of Data Types and Persistence Workshop, Appin, August 1985.
15. Morrison, R., Brown, A.L., Dearle, A. & Atkinson, M.P. "An integrated graphics programming environment". 4th UK Eurographics Conference, Glasgow (March 1986). In Computer Graphics Forum 5, 2 (June 1986).
16. Morrison, R., Bailey, P.J., Brown, A.L., Dearle, A. & Atkinson, M.P. "A persistent store as an enabling technology for an integrated project support environment". IEEE 8th International Conference on Software Engineering, London (August 1985).
17. Morrison, R., Brown, A.L., Carrick, R., Connor, R. & Dearle, A. **Napier Reference Manual**. Dept. of Computational Science. University of St Andrews.
18. Wegner, P. "Dimensions of object-based language design". OOPSLA 87 (1987).

Appendix I

```
type general_index [KEY, VALUE] is process (
                                        Enter      : proc (KEY, VALUE),
                                        Lookup     : proc (KEY -> VALUE) )

let generate_general_index = proc [Key, Value] (less_than : proc (Key, Key -> bool) ;
                                    fail_value : Value -> general_index [Key, Value])
general_index [Key, Value] with
begin
      rec type index is variant (node : Node ; tip : null)
      & Node is structure (key : Key ; value : Value ; left, right : index)

      let null_index = index (tip : nil)
              !Compute the empty index by injecting the nil value into the variant

      let i := null_index
              !This is the internal index structure initialisation

      rec let enter = proc (k : Key ; v : Value ; i : index  -> index)
      !Enter the value into the binary tree indexed by key 'k'
      if i is tip then index (node : Node (k, v, null_index, null_index)) else
      case true of
      less_than (k,i'node (key) )  : { i'node (left) := enter (k, v, i'node (left)) ; i }
      k = i'node (key)             : { i'node (value) := v ; i }
      default                      : { i'node (right) := enter (k, v, i'node (right)) ; i }

      let lookup = proc (k : Key ; i : index -> Value)
      !lookup the value in the binary tree
      begin
              let head := i
              while head is node and k ≠ head'node (key)  do
                      head := if less_than (k, head'node (key) )   then head'node (left)
                                                                   else head'node (right)
              if head is node then head'node (value) else fail_value
      end

      while true do
              select
                      : receive Enter (key : Key ; value : Value) do i := enter (key, value, i)
                      : receive Lookup (key : Key -> Value) do lookup (key, i)
              selected
end
```

ROSE: AN OBJECT-ORIENTED DATABASE SYSTEM FOR INTERACTIVE COMPUTER GRAPHICS APPLICATIONS†

Martin Hardwick *David L. Spooner*

Computer Science Department and
Center for Interactive Computer Graphics
Rensselaer Polytechnic Institute
Troy, New York 12180

(518) 276-2712
hardwick@cs.rpi.edu
spoonerd@cs.rpi.edu

1. Motivation

ROSE is an object-oriented database system designed specifically to support interactive computer graphics applications such as engineering design. In ROSE, objects are represented as nested relations, and manipulated using an extended relational algebra that is part of a larger programming environment. To achieve high performance, ROSE clusters data into objects stored as files in secondary storage [Har87]. The typical ROSE application reads these objects into main memory at the start of an engineering design session, *re-organizes them so that they are easier to modify and use*, and then writes them back to secondary storage in their original organization at the end of the session.

Clustering of data into objects is defined in ROSE using an AND/OR tree data model [McL83] that can represent aggregations, associations, and generalizations. The ROSE algebra allows objects defined using this model to be constructed and analyzed in a way that is simple and generic, yet provides great flexibility with a minimum number of concepts. ROSE is operationally object-oriented as defined in Dittrich's classification scheme for object-oriented database systems [Dit86]. To make it behaviorally object-oriented, an Inheritance Manager layer is implemented on top of ROSE. This Inheritance Manager provides an inheritance hierarchy for the objects defined in a ROSE database, and provides a message passing paradigm for invocation of methods defined for the objects in this hierarchy.

One of the advantages of implementing the Inheritance Manager as a layer on top of ROSE is that the inheritance paradigm can be tailored more easily to the requirements of a particular application. A second advantage is that the full power of ROSE is available to implement the Inheritance Manager. The inheritance hierarchy and associated data is stored as a ROSE database and manipulated with the ROSE programming language. A final advantage is a clean separation of object implementation issues in the basic ROSE system from issues of object use in the Inheritance Manager. This leads to a simpler design for both parts of the system, and a more efficient design for the system as a whole.

---

† This work was partially supported by the Industrial Associates Program of the RPI Center for Interactive Computer Graphics; National Science Foundation, Grant Number DMC-8600930; and Air Force, Grant Number FY1175-87-02333. Any opinions expressed or implied are those of the authors.

2. Why ROSE is Different

The "classical" data model of an object-oriented database system divides a database into objects which are aggregates containing "slots" for attributes and methods. The attribute slots contain other objects which may be primitive data values such as numbers and strings, or user-defined objects that contain their own slots. The concepts of dynamic binding, encapsulation, and inheritance supplement this organization to provide a rich environment for modeling the semantics of applications.

An alternate view for this organization is that each "slot" in an object is similar to an attribute in a tuple. Hence, in this sense, a "classical" object-oriented database can be viewed as a relational database in which tuples contain not only primitive data values, but also methods and pointers to other objects. Of course, the superior modeling concepts provided by encapsulation, inheritance, and dynamic binding make the object-oriented data model more powerful than the relational one. However, from the perspective of computer graphics and engineering design applications, the fact that object-oriented data models can be viewed as relational models has some important consequences as indicated below.

The weaknesses of relational database systems for design applications have been documented many times elsewhere [Sid80]. One of these weaknesses is that relational systems force an application programmer to divide the data in a design into many tuples. This causes modeling and performance problems when the design is manipulated because all the tuples must be located and fetched before any operation can be applied to them. An object oriented-database system that models data using "extended" records (tuples) will share these performance problems.

A partial solution to performance and modeling problems that is suited to interactive computer graphics and engineering design applications is to cluster an object with its sub-objects in secondary storage so that they can be retrieved together. Some systems use a *segmentation* approach to accomplish this. If two objects are put into the same segment, they will be placed in the same segment in secondary storage [And87]. Other systems allow the user to declare *"component of"* relationships between objects [Kim87]. Provided an object is a component of only one other object, the database system can store the component with the parent object in secondary storage.

The data model used by the ROSE system is different from the data models in these other systems because it exploits clustering to an even greater degree. ROSE uses AND/OR trees to describe the data structures of objects. From the perspective of segmentation, these AND/OR trees allow segments to be nested into trees so that segments that are needed together can be stored together. From the perspective of declared "component of" relationships, the AND/OR trees allow the user to define different types of "component of" relationships.

3. How ROSE is Different

AND/OR trees in the ROSE data model allow users to create objects that are aggregations, generalizations, and associations of other objects. Four types of nodes are allowed in an AND/OR tree: a *Single AND* node which describes objects that are aggregations of other objects; a *Single OR* node which describes objects that are generalizations of other objects; a *Multiple AND* node which describes objects that are associations (lists) of aggregations of other objects; and a *Multiple OR* node which describes objects that are associations of generalizations of other objects.

Figure 1 describes a simple AND/OR tree for assembly objects. In an AND/OR tree, AND nodes have an arc below their origin and Multiple nodes have a star. Figure 2 contains a sample object with the data structure defined in Figure 1.

AND/OR trees let the programmer describe object data structures similar to those that can be described in common programming languages using record structures, variant records, and arrays. However, by minimizing and regularizing these concepts using AND/OR trees, ROSE describes its data structures in a way that makes the data in a database easier to manipulate with the operators of

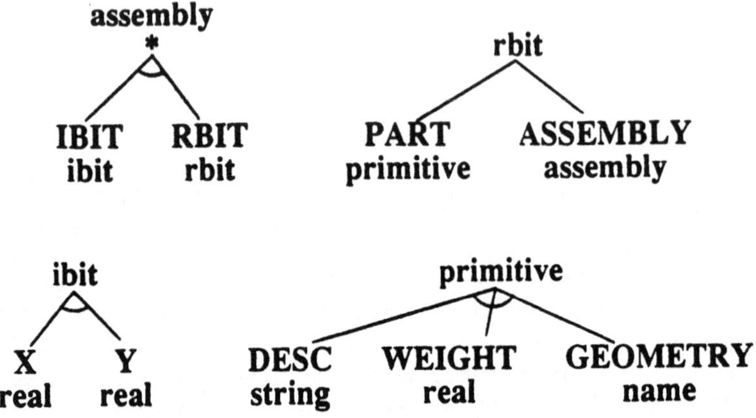

Figure 1: A Data Model for Assembly Objects

```
(ASSEMBLY
    (IBIT (X 10.0) (Y 5.0))
    (RBIT (ASSEMBLY
                (IBIT (X 1.0) (Y 2.0))
                (RBIT (PART (DESC nut)
                            (WEIGHT 1.0)
                            (GEOMETRY nut.dat)))
                (IBIT (X 3.0) (Y 2.0))
                (RBIT (PART (DESC bolt)
                            (WEIGHT 2.0)
                            (GEOMETRY bolt.dat)))))
    (IBIT (X 0.0) (Y 0.0))
    (RBIT (PART (DESC plate)
                (WEIGHT 3.0)
                (GEOMETRY plate.dat))))
```

Figure 2: A Sample Assembly Object

an algebra.

In computer graphics and design applications, AND/OR trees have the advantage of allowing all data in a design to be described with a small number of objects (possibly one). For example, in the trivial structure of Figure 1, all data in an assembly is described by a single assembly object. This clustering defined by AND/OR trees means that an object can be stored and retrieved with a minimum number of I/O operations to secondary memory. It also means that any user wishing to apply an operation to an object does not need to encode an algorithm to find the data in that object. The ROSE algebra using the AND/OR tree data model will do this for him.

With the exception of the clustering features, ROSE is similar to other object-oriented database systems. In particular, using the inheritance manager, ROSE objects can be designed to contain "slots" for attributes and methods like in other systems. The difference in ROSE is that the attribute slots may contain values which are "complex" (clustered) data objects such as the one shown in Figure 2. To avoid confusion these complex data objects are sometimes called entities.

ROSE application programs assemble large objects (entities) from small ones and disassemble large objects into small ones using operators in an algebra. In many applications, a few large objects are read from secondary storage at the start of an application session. These objects are divided into many smaller objects for easier manipulation during the application session using the algebra. Finally, at the end of the session, new versions of the large objects are assembled and written back to secondary storage.

As an example, consider a circuit design system. A circuit might be read into main memory and divided into pins, wires, and sub-circuits; then edited; and written back to secondary storage when finished.

A good circuit design system will divide its data so that each circuit has an interface and one or more implementations [Bat85]. Dividing a circuit into interfaces and implementations allows one user to reference another user's design while the implementation for that design is still being edited. This is important because in most large engineering projects different users must be able to edit different parts of a design concurrently. In ROSE, each of these interfaces and implementations can be represented as a single AND/OR tree object (entity).

In principle, the ROSE data model allows a design to be described by a single large object; but implementing a ROSE database in this way would be impractical. Instead, a design should be divided into pieces rather like a large program is divided into procedures. The result of a database design should be a database with objects defined so that no two designers will need to edit the same design concurrently. (There will always be exceptions to this, however, such as when one designer is teaching another.)

If the result of dividing a database in this way produces a database in which each piece of information can be described by an ordinary record, then ROSE is not an appropriate database system for this application. Instead a relational or "classical" object-oriented system should be used. However, in interactive computer graphics and design applications, we have found that the objects that need to be stored and manipulated are frequently large (and more complex) than records, even after division. For example, all the wires, pins, and sub-circuits (or to be precise, references to other circuit interfaces) in a circuit add up to a substantial unit of data that cannot be described easily by records in a relational database, but can be described as a complex object (entity) using an AND/OR tree data model [Sam86].

4. Results and Experience

The ROSE system is currently being used for a variety of applications in both academic and industrial environments. Some of these applications include solid modeling, user interface management, VLSI design, and control system design. The ROSE system runs under both UNIX and VMS on SUN workstations and MicroVAX II/GPX computers.

Hardwick [Har87] provides performance statistics for the ROSE system. As an example of the performance of the system on an interactive computer graphics application, consider an application in which a wire-frame drawing is modeled as an object composed of sub-objects, each described as a list of polygons composed of points in space. A space shuttle object modeled in this way contains about 3000 points. On a Sun 3/50 workstation, the time required to initialize the ROSE system is approximately 3.8 seconds of real time, 0.7 seconds of application time for the ROSE system, and 0.6 seconds of system time. Once initialized, the time required to load the shuttle object into ROSE's main memory cache is approximately 9.0 seconds of real time, 5.9 seconds of application time for the ROSE system, and 0.2 seconds of system time. Note that these figures include network overhead to reach the file server for the Sun 3/50. Once the object is loaded into the workspace, front and top views of the shuttle can be extracted using the ROSE algebra and drawn using the ROSE graphics system in approximately 12.6 seconds of real time, 8.9 seconds of application time for the ROSE system, and 0.1 seconds of system time.

To date, the largest application of the ROSE system is a user interface management system to define graphical user interfaces for application systems that previously had command line interfaces. This user interface manager uses a ROSE database to store information about the commands supported by an underlying application program, the user, and the current operating environment. This information is used to construct commands for the underlying application from data entered by the user with menus and dialogue boxes. Creation of an interface for a new application requires only defining the ROSE database to describe the application and the control structure (a state tree) that will be used to control the operation of the user interface. This is all done graphically with a set of tools that are part of the user interface manager.

The user interface manager has been used to describe interfaces for UNIX, VMS, an image processing system, a solid modeling system, a stress analysis system, and the user interface manager itself. The interface for the user interface manager is the largest, containing about 700 graphical gadgets such as menus and dialogue boxes. The other applications are more typical, requiring between 50 and 300 graphical gadgets each. The interface manager is divided into two ROSE applications containing a total 12,600 lines of executable code in the ROSE programming language. Each interface is described by 18 objects stored in 18 files. For the VMS user interface (which is one of the smallest), the data in these objects requires 119 blocks at 512 bytes per block on the VMS operating system. Interactive performance of all the interfaces has been acceptable.

One part of the ROSE application used to implement the user interface manager needs to display a tree of nodes representing gadgets in a user interface. For the largest interface this tree contains 700 nodes connected by arcs. In total, at full magnification, the screen contains about 2,000 selectable items. The program that manages the screen is written in the ROSE programming language and contains operations in the ROSE algebra to select, assemble and disassemble ROSE AND/OR objects (entities). In secondary storage the 2,000 objects are stored in one of the 18 objects detailed above.

5. Conclusions

In summary, the ROSE system has been designed to allow efficiency to be combined with flexibility for support of interactive computer graphics applications. The object paradigm is exploited throughout all aspects of the ROSE system because it provides a natural data organization for graphical data, and because it leads to clustering of data in secondary storage to maximize the performance of data retrieval as demanded by high performance interactive computer graphics applications such as engineering design.

References

[And87] T. Andrews and C. Harris, "Combining Language and Database Advances in on Object-Oriented Development Environment", Proc. OOPSLA'87, ACM, Orlando, FL., October, 1987.

[Bat85] D. S. Batory, and W. Kim, "Modeling Concepts for VLSI CAD Objects", ACM Transactions on Database Systems, Vol. 10, No. 3, September, 1985.

[Dit86] K. Dittrich, "Object-Oriented Database Systems: the Notions and the Issues", Proc. Workshop on Object-Oriented Database Systems, IEEE Computer Society Press, 1986.

[Har87] M. Hardwick, "Why ROSE is Fast: Five Optimizations in the Design of an Experimental Database System for CAD/CAM Applications", Proc. ACM SIGMOD Conference, San Francisco, 1987.

[Kim87] W. Kim, et. al., "Composite Object Support in an Object-Oriented Database System", Proc. of OOPSLA'87 Conference, ACM, Orlando, Florida, 1987.

[McL83] D. McLeod, et. al., "An Approach to Information Management for CAD/VLSI Applications", Proc. ACM Database Week, SIGMOD Conference, San Jose, 1983.

[Sam86] G. Samaras, "VLSI Circuit Design Application User Manual", Technical Report, Computer Science Department, 1986.

[Sid80] T. Sidel, "Weaknesses of Commercial Data Base Management Systems in Engineering Applications", Proceedings of the 17th Design Automation Conference, ACM, New York, 1980.

Identity, Equality and Query Optimization

S. L. Osborn
Department of Computer Science
The University of Western Ontario
London, Ontario, Canada N6A-5B7

Abstract

An object-oriented database model is presented, as well as an object algebra. The focus of the paper is on algebraic manipulation of the object algebra for the purpose of query optimization. Various results governing the rearrangement of the algebraic operations in a query are given, and their impact on query optimization for object-oriented databases is discussed.

1 Introduction

In this work, we assume an object-oriented database model which incorporates aggregation hierarchies, generalization hierarchies, and sets, which is class based. Secondly we assume that object identity is important, and that tests for identical objects are possible. We also assume that equality is important, so that users may query objects based on their content as well as their identity. Finally we assume a query language, not just a browser or navigation through objects or sets. In particular, we shall introduce an object algebra, which has various operations for carving up objects and putting them back together again, much as relational algebra does with relations.

The purpose of this paper is to investigate algebraic query optimization on an object algebra, taking into account the difference between identity and equality of the results of two queries. Similar results exist for relational algebra [Ull82,CP84] and non-first normal form relational algebra [Sch86].

2 The Data Model

The model is an object-oriented one, using Wegner's definition [Weg87]; i.e. it is based on objects, classes and inheritance. It contains a number of atomic classes, for example integers, strings, Booleans etc. An arbitrary number of such classes may be defined to suit the application. Just as with relational algebra, the object algebra does not provide operators for carving up atomic objects; however we may look inside, as we would with the comparisons which are part of the Boolean expression in a select operation. We make a distinction between objects being identical and objects being equal [KC86]. Two objects are *identical* if they are the same object. Equality is defined in a different way for each object class. For the atomic classes, objects are *equal* if they are identical.

The second major construct in the data model is strongly typed aggregates in a class hierarchy. Aggregates have named attributes which take on values in a specified class, which could be sets or aggregates, as well as atomic classes. Subclasses inherit the attributes of their superclass. Two aggregate objects are *equal* if they belong to the same class and the values they take on the same attributes are equal.

The third major construct is the set. The model contains both strongly typed sets, i.e. sets whose members all belong to the same class, and sets of arbitrary objects which are not of the same type. Two set objects are *equal* if they belong to the same class and their elements are pairwise equal. All

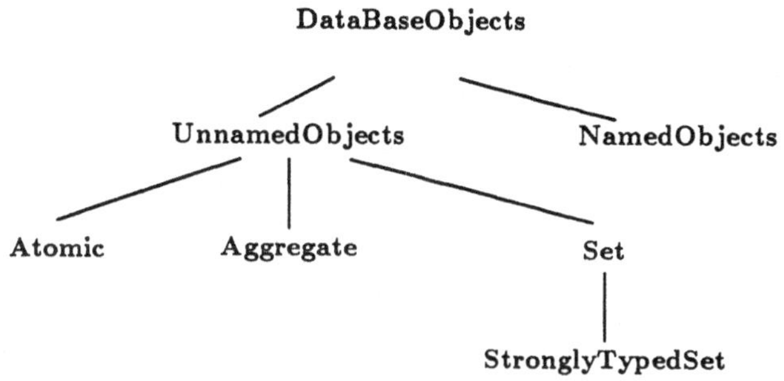

Figure 1: Class Hierarchy of the Model

of the definitions of equality refer to the notion called deep equality in [KC86]. The object algebra allows us to express their shallow-equal if necessary.

Finally, the model contains named objects. Any object can be assigned to a name. Names are treated like atomic objects in that we do not distinguish between identity and equality for names. Named objects are identical if they have the same name and refer to an identical object. Named objects are equal if they have the same name and equal objects.

Figure 1 shows the class hierarchy of the model. We shall discuss where the operations are defined at the end of the next section. When an application is defined, subclasses of the Atomic class will be added as necessary, and many subclasses of Aggregate, with their own subclasses will probably be added. It is less likely that subclasses of Set will be required.

We feel it is important to have both kinds of equality. The object algebra is intended to support various kinds of user interfaces: browsing interfaces, SQL-like interfaces [F*87], or other non-procedural interfaces. In such an interface, the only way a user has of generating a comparison using the identity test is by referring to a named object, or by selecting something through a browser. In an SQL-like interface, objects could be specified by giving their contents, thus instigating an equality comparison. Thus, both kinds of comparisons are important, and neither one should be omitted. Also, the rearrangements of the object algebra expressions sometimes yield identical results, and sometimes equal results. For this, we need both kinds of equality to explain what is happening.

3 The Object Algebra

All operations take one or two objects as operands and return an object as the result. Following the example of relational algebra, we need operations to generate new objects (the way join and Cartesian product do with relations) and operations which carve up objects (the way select and project do). New objects are generated when giving constants in a query. Constants would also be used for insertions and updates, which are not discussed in this paper. Note however that to do updates or deletes, we might want to specify the affected objects by identity or by equality.

Constants: For each atomic object class, some notation must exist for specifying constants. Integer constants are a string of digits, strings are enclosed in quotes, and for Booleans we use T and F. Aggregate constants have the form:

(aggregateClassName | attributeName_1 : object_1, ..., attributeName_n : object_n)

where the attribute names are all unique. The order in which the attribute names appear in the constant is immaterial. The objects may be given as object algebra expressions, constants or by name. Set constants have the form: { setClassName | object_1, ..., object_n }. Objects may be assigned a name by the Name operation: Name_{name}(object), which creates a new NamedObject.

Set Operations: Given two sets belonging to the same class, (either the Set class or one of its subclasses) the following operations in the object algebra create a new object in that class:

Union(object_1, object_2)

$object_1$	$object_2$	class of result	comment
atomic	atomic	not applicable	returns null
atomic	aggregate	not applicable	returns null
atomic	set	not applicable	returns null
aggregate	aggregate	an aggregate class	Result is an aggregate with all the attributes of the operands. All attributes must be unique.
aggregate	set	a set class	Iterates through the set performing Combine of the aggregate and the set member, recursively if necessary.
set	set	a set class	Performs a nested iteration through the two sets, Combining the members pairwise. Note that for strongly typed sets of aggregates, it acts like Cartesian Product.

Table 1: The Combine Operator

Intersect($object_1$, $object_2$)
Subtract($object_1$, $object_2$)

where the last one computes $object_1$ minus $object_2$. Union and Intersection use object identity as their test, so that the Union of two sets may contain equal objects, and objects will be in the intersection only if the identical object is in both operand sets.

Combine: A very general operation, Combine($object_1$, $object_2$), creates new objects from two operands. If the two operands are sets, it acts like Cartesian product. The results for various combinations of operand classes are explained in Table 1. We will see later that Combine is commutative; therefore only one copy of each object class combination is shown in Table 1.

Partition: The other major group of algebra operators are the ones which carve up database objects. As we said above, we do not intend to carve up the atomic objects with object algebra operations. As far as the aggregates are concerned, we need a way to extract one or more attributes. The former is done in relational algebra with dot notation. The latter is done on sets in relational algebra with Projection. To support schema evolution, we have argued elsewhere [Osb88] that it should make no difference whether one is projecting a single aggregate or a set of aggregates; i.e. the operator should also be defined for single aggregates. We will, for convenience, use the same notation for single attribute extraction, although this is not really necessary. Thus, we have the operation: $\text{Partition}_{attr_1,\ldots,attr_n}(\text{object})$. It returns null if the parameter is an atomic object. On an aggregate, it extracts the named attributes and creates a new object with these attributes. Such an object needs to belong to an aggregate class. Since we will never be successful in comparing two such created objects for identity, we only need to make sure that they will be compared for equality when another temporarily created object has the same attribute names and types. Thus, there is a subclass of the general aggregate class which is called CreatedAggregates, which has subclasses for each unique *set* of attribute names and their associated classes thus mentioned.

On a set, Partition iterates through the objects and tries to Partition what it finds. If the object is an aggregate, it will add an object to the result if it contains the named attributes. If the object is a set, nothing is added to the result. If the object is atomic, nothing is added to the result. The set which results when Partition is applied to a set may or may not be strongly typed. If the operand is a strongly typed set of aggregates, then the operation resembles relational algebra projection and produces a strongly typed result. If the operand contains objects of arbitrary classes, the result will not be strongly typed if the values associated with a given attribute name in the set members are of different types. Note that Partition of a set does not remove "duplicates", since each object created has its own object identity, even though it may be equal to another object.

Choose: The final operation in our object algebra is a generalization of the relational algebra select. The syntax for this operation is $\text{Choose}_{BooleanExp}(\text{object})$ where the Boolean expression consists of terms of the form:

object IsNull,
$\text{object}_1 = \text{object}_2$, which is true if the two objects are *equal*,
$\text{object}_1 \equiv \text{object}_2$, which is true if the two objects are *identical*
object InClass C, which is true if the class of the object is C,
object InSubclassOf C, which is true if the class of the object is C or one of its subclasses.

The terms may be enclosed in parentheses, and may be connected by $\vee, \wedge$ and $\neg$ with the usual precedence. In relational algebra, the relation name is used as a tuple variable in the Boolean expression. Here, we will use O, O_1, etc. to refer to the object. When Choose is applied to an atomic object or a single aggregate, the variable then refers to this single object, the result being either the object if the Boolean is true, or null. When it is applied to a set, the variable refers to the set members one at a time as the operator iterates through the set, the answer being that subset of the objects in the set for which the Boolean is true. On strongly typed sets of aggregates, it acts like the relational algebra select. Since we have no guarantee that the object in a Boolean term is atomic, it makes little sense to include comparisons like $<$ since they are not meaningful for sets or aggregates and therefore are not likely defined. In fact, other predicates might be meaningful for non-atomic classes of objects. In this preliminary study we have only included predicates which can be applied to objects of any class.

Naming and Unnaming: The Name operation assigns a name to an object. To strip the name off an object, we merely give its name, which is an operation which returns the object without a name. The other operations of the object algebra operate on objects, not named objects. Thus, nesting a name operation inside another operation is not valid, which means that the Name operation should be the last applied. The transformation rules in the next section support this.

Referring to Figure 1, the Name operation is defined on objects in the NamedObjects class. Union, Intersect, and Subtract are defined on instances of the Set class and inherited by any of its subclasses. Combine, Partition and Choose are operations defined on objects of the UnnamedObjects class and are inherited (and in some cases redefined) by its subclasses.

4 Transformations of Algebraic Expressions

In this section we examine the algebraic properties of the object algebra. In doing this, we will indicate for each transformation whether the two expressions give equal or identical results. O, O_1, etc. refer to objects, names or constants, F_1, F_2, etc. are used to represent Boolean expressions. A_1, $A_2, \ldots, B_1, B_2, \ldots$ refer to attribute names, and N_1, N_2, etc. refer to names.

Lemma 1 *Idempotence of Unary Operators:*

a. $\text{Partition}_{A_1,\ldots,A_n}(O) = \text{Partition}_{A_1,\ldots,A_n}(\text{Partition}_{B_1,\ldots,B_m}(O))$ iff $A_1,\ldots,A_n \subset B_1,\ldots,B_m$,
b. $\text{Choose}_F(O) \equiv \text{Choose}_{F_1}(\text{Choose}_{F_2}(O))$ iff $F = F_1 \wedge F_2$,
c. $\text{Name}_{N_1}(O) \equiv \text{Name}_{N_1}(\text{Name}_{N_2}(O))$

In the following, we need a notion of path expression for an aggregate which may have aggregates as components, which in turn may contain aggregates, etc. With our partition notation, we define a *path expression* to be any valid expression of the form: $\text{Partition}_{A_i}(O)$, $\text{Partition}_{A_i}(\text{Partition}_{B_j}(O))$, etc. Furthermore, we define a *one-level path expression* to be any expression involving a single Partition of a single attribute.

Lemma 2 *Commutativity of Unary Operators:*

a. $\text{Choose}_{F_1}(\text{Choose}_{F_2}(O)) \equiv \text{Choose}_{F_2}(\text{Choose}_{F_1}(O))$
b. $\text{Partition}_{A_1,\ldots,A_n}(\text{Partition}_{B_1,\ldots,B_m}(O)) = \text{Partition}_{B_1,\ldots,B_m}(\text{Partition}_{A_1,\ldots,A_n}(O))$ iff $A_1,\ldots,A_n = B_1,\ldots,B_m$
c. $\text{Name}_{N_1}(\text{Name}_{N_2}(O)) \equiv \text{Name}_{N_2}(\text{Name}_{N_1}(O))$ iff $N_1 = N_2$

d. $\text{Choose}_F(\text{Partition}_{A_1,\ldots,A_n}(\text{O})) = \text{Partition}_{A_1,\ldots,A_n}(\text{Choose}_F(\text{O}))$ iff (i) All one-level path expressions in F refer only to $A_1, \ldots, A_n$, and all deeper path expressions begin with $A_1, \ldots, A_n$, and (ii) All terms in F are of the form: $O_1 = O_2$, $O_1 \equiv O_2$, O_1 IsNull, O_1 InClass C, or O_1 InSubclass C, where O_1 is a path expression on O, and O_2 is either a path expression on O, a constant or a name.

e. $\text{Choose}_F(\text{Name}_{N_1}(\text{O}))$ and $\text{Partition}_{A_1,\ldots,A_n}(\text{Name}_{N_1}(\text{O}))$ are not valid algebra expressions, so Name does not commute with Partition or Choose.

Note that in part (d) of the above lemma, expressions of the form: O inClass C, O inSubclass C, O = constant, O ≡ constant, are valid in F on the right-hand side, but not on the left.

Lemma 3 *Commutativity and Associativity of Binary Operators:*

Union and Intersect are both commutative and associative. Subtract is neither commutative nor associative. Combine is both commutative and associative iff all attribute names are different.

Lemma 4 *Distributivity of Unary Operators over Binary Operators*

a. $\text{Binary}(\text{Name}_{N_1}(O_1), \text{Name}_{N_1}(O_2))$ is not a valid expression for any Binary operation. Therefore Name does not distribute over any Binary operation.

b. $\text{Choose}_F(\text{Combine}(O_1, O_2)) = \text{Combine}(\text{Choose}_{F_1}(O_1), \text{Choose}_{F_2}(O_2))$ iff F is of the form given in Lemma 2(d) and $F = F_1 \wedge F_2$ where F_1 contains only path expressions valid in O_1 and F_2 contains only path expressions valid in O_2.

c. $\text{Partition}_{A_1,\ldots,A_n}(\text{Combine}(O_1, O_2)) = \text{Combine}(\text{Partition}_{Attr(O_1)}(O_1), \text{Partition}_{Attr(O_2)}(O_2))$ where $\text{Attr}(O_1)$ and $\text{Attr}(O_2)$ are disjoint, refer to the attributes within $A_1, \ldots, A_n$ which are attributes of O_1 and O_2 respectively, and where $A_1, \ldots, A_n = \text{Attr}(O_1) \cup \text{Attr}(O_2)$.

d. $\text{Choose}_F(\text{Union}(O_1, O_2)) \equiv \text{Union}(\text{Choose}_F(O_1), \text{Choose}_F(O_2))$.

e. $\text{Choose}_F(\text{Intersect}(O_1, O_2)) \equiv \text{Intersect}(\text{Choose}_F(O_1), \text{Choose}_F(O_2))$.

f. $\text{Choose}_F(\text{Subtract}(O_1, O_2)) \equiv \text{Subtract}(\text{Choose}_F(O_1), \text{Choose}_F(O_2))$.

g. Partition does not distribute over Union, Intersect or Subtract.

5 Discussion

The data model described above is fairly typical of object-oriented data models. The object algebra is unique, incorporating some of the basic operations which should be part of any object-oriented data manipulation language. The algebra could be more powerful; for example in the current version we cannot do the nest and unnest operations of non-first normal form databases, nor transitive closure. Nevertheless, the lemmas of the previous section do allow us to say something about optimizing object algebra expressions.

One observation is that whether sets are strongly typed or not has no effect on the legal manipulations. The result obtained when say Choosing a subset from a strongly typed set is likely to be larger and more predictable, since the Boolean expression will apply more uniformly, but the things one can say about this type of query optimization are not affected. Thus, if this kind of set makes sense for the data model or the application, there is no penalty as far as this aspect of query optimization is concerned. Other ways of supporting efficient queries such as indexes might find non-uniform sets harder to deal with, however.

The major conclusion to draw from the previous section is that not very many algebraic manipulations guarantee *identical* results. Specifically, only those involving Choose and the set operations Union, Intersect and Subtract, and valid combinations of these, give identical results. However, these are the operations which would support a browser, or the query interface of ORION [B*88] which basically uses our Choose and some set operations. With a browser, there is probably some initial query before the user starts moving through the objects, which could be intercepted and optimized.

We have shown quite clearly that including any operations which create new objects means that we cannot have identical responses. We disagree with the approach taken in ORION that one should never be allowed to retrieve objects that are not already in the database. They would not allow projection in relational algebra. It is certainly true that far fewer join-like operations are necessary when complex objects can exist in the database. However, well-understood manipulations which create new objects, such as allowed by our Partition and Combine, are necessary and useful. Databases are for sharing data and integrating applications which use the same data. A good example was given by Stonebraker at the 1988 Data Engineering Conference: someone will want to join the engineering design with the parts data to find out how much the design costs, even if these are in different applications. We do see, however, that the cost of such manipulations in terms of query manipulations is that we will not have identical responses to different versions of the query. In fact, we cannot guarantee identical responses to the same query run on different days, if the query creates new objects.

In relational optimization discussions, the next step is to say which version of the query should be more efficient and then devise an algorithm to transform queries according to these heuristics. With the advent of the rule-based EXODUS optimizer generator [GD87], such an algorithm is now unnecessary. We merely need to translate the positive results from the lemmas into appropriate rules. We do, however, have to specify cost estimates for various versions of a query. These will depend on the implementation of the operators, which is currently underway. One could also, at this point, implement a join-like operation and have a rule which recognizes when it should be used. Nevertheless, the usual heuristic that performing Choose and Partition as soon as possible is still valid, as it reduces the number of bytes one has to deal with. Choose would have to have preference over Partition as it preserves object identity longer.

Extensions to the class hierarchy and to the algebra should also be considered. For example, one might want a sequencing class, which allows us to model sequences of objects ordered by time, space, or a user-defined order. The object algebra operations would have to be defined for objects of this class. Additional Booleans might be defined for specific classes – some specialized ones for atomic classes and others for non-atomic classes. These do not change the lemmas as long as the path expression yields an object over which the Boolean is defined. Algebraic manipulations of extensions to the object algebra should be considered.

References

[B*88] J. Banerjee et al. Queries in object-oriented databases. In *Proceedings of Fourth International Conference on Data Engineering*, pages 31–38, Feb. 1988.

[CP84] S. Ceri and G Pelagatti. *Distributed Databases Principles and Systems.* McGraw-Hill, 1984.

[F*87] D.H. Fishman et al. Iris: an object-oriented database management system. *ACM Trans. Office Information Systems*, 5(1):48–69, Jan. 1987.

[GD87] G. Graefe and D.J. DeWitt. The EXODUS optimizer generator. In *Proceedings 1987 SIGMOD Conference*, pages 160–171, May 1987.

[KC86] S.N. Khoshafian and G.P. Copeland. Object identity. In *OOPSLA '86 Proceedings*, pages 406–416, ACM SIGPLAN Notices, vol. 21, no. 11, Nov. 1986.

[Osb88] S.L. Osborn. Polymorphism in an object-oriented database. June 1988. submitted for publication.

[Sch86] M.H. Scholl. Theoretical foundation of algebraic optimization utilizing unnormalized relations. In *International Conference on Database Theory*, pages 380–396, Springer Verlag, 1986. Lecture Notes 243.

[Ull82] Jefferey D. Ullman. *Principles of Database Systems.* Computer Science Press, second edition, 1982.

[Weg87] P. Wegner. Dimensions of object-based language design. In *OOPSLA '87*, pages 168–182, 1987. SIGPLAN Notices vol 22, no. 12.

Optimization of Object-Retrieval Queries[1]

Henry F. Korth
Department of Computer Sciences
University of Texas at Austin
Austin, TX 78712-1188

1 Introduction

Object-oriented languages are typically based on a message-passing paradigm in which each message causes the execution of a method. Methods are programs written in a computationally complete programming language. This gives the object-oriented model an expressive power that is significantly greater than the relational algebra. This power, though desirable in many applications, places severe restrictions on the potential for the optimization of object-oriented queries: The encapsulation of methods within objects makes it difficult to do global query optimization. The richness of the language used for defining methods causes optimization problems that are decidable for relational algebra expressions to be undecidable for methods. Indeed, critics of the object-oriented approach frequently point to the theoretical limits to optimization as a major drawback to the object-oriented approach as compared with the relational approach.

Although relational optimization techniques cannot be applied to all object-oriented queries, it would be highly advantageous if those queries that are expressible in a relational language could be optimized using standard relational techniques. In particular, we anticipate a substantial number of queries of the form "find the set of objects such that a predicate P holds on its instance variables". Queries of this sort could be expressed as relational algebra queries over relations in which each tuple represents an object. By recasting object queries as relational queries, the power of relational query optimization can be applied to allow efficient query processing in object oriented systems.

In order to represent object queries as relational queries, we must define a canonical relational structure for the storing of objects. Unfortunately, there has been relatively little work done on query processing for nested relational languages. It is, of course, possible simply to translate nested relational expressions into non-nested expressions and then to use standard query processing techniques. However, we shall see that this methodology leads to query processing strategies that are prohibitively costly both in terms of time complexity and in terms of temporary storage required.

The most critical issue in nested relational query processing is the join operator. The definitions of join presented previously in the literature [Roth, Korth and Silberschatz 1988, Schek and Scholl 1986, Deshpande and Larson 1987] are limited in power. We show by example that many natural queries require a more complex notion of join. We introduce a more general form of join that meets this need and present algorithms for computing this join.

2 The Object-Oriented Model

We shall not present a detailed introduction to the object-oriented model here. Such details are available in many references including [Stefik and Bobrow 1986]. Ullman [1987] lists three disadvantages to the object-oriented approach, all of which involve weaknesses in the handling of queries:

1. Difficulty of using a declarative language.
2. Difficulty of using subqueries due to the presense of multiple datatypes.
3. Favoring of "built-in links" in the given set of methods

The relational model, on the other hand, allows declarative queries (relational calculus), a unifying datatype of *relation*, and the ability to choose "links" or access paths internal to the system using a query optimizer.

---

[1]Research partially supported by a grant from the IBM Corporation

The lattermost feature, optimizability, is a critical importance if large object database are to be practical for systems requiring an ad-hoc query capability. Because methods are coded in a general purpose programming language, it is theoretically impossible to achieve the same degree of optimization as is possible in a relational language.

This motivates us to consider an integration of relations and objects that retains the encapsulation features of the object-oriented approach while allowing at least some object-oriented queries to be optimized using relational techniques. Direct representation of object databases using the relational model is inelegant due to the flat (non-hierarchical) nature of relations versus the hierarchical nature of object databases.

3 The Nested Relational Model

One of the main drawbacks of the relational model is the lack of a way to model hierarchical data. This drawback is particularly critical in object databases since we must represent the *class-subclass* hierarchy and the *is-part-of* hierarchy. Although it *is* possible to model any hierarchical database using relations, the resulting model is often awkward and un-intuitive. The need to model hierarchies within the relational framework led to the development of the nested relational model (also called $\neg$1NF or NF^2, for not-first-normal form). The nested relational model allows an attribute to have a set-valued or relation-valued domain, while the traditional (record-oriented) relational model requires that relations be in *first normal form*, that is, the domains of all attributes are scalar-valued. An additional benefit of set-valued domains is the ability to represent repeating fields directly.

We assume, without loss of generality, that all attributes of our relations are contained in a finite universe U of attributes. Each attribute $A \in U$ may assume values drawn from a domain, **DOM**(A). A *relation structure* $\mathcal{R}$ consists of a *relation scheme* R and a *relation* r defined on R, and is denoted $\langle R, r\rangle$. A relation scheme is defined by a *rule* $R = (A_1, A_2, \ldots, A_n)$ where $A_i \in U$, $1 \leq i \leq n$. The set of attributes in a relation scheme rule R are denoted by E_R. An X-value, where $X \subseteq E_R$, is an assignment of values to the attributes in X from their respective domains. Thus, a relation r defined on scheme R is a set of E_R-values, with the elements of this set called *tuples* of r. A *database scheme* is a set of rules each of which has a unique left side.

If an attribute appears on the left side of a rule, it is a *higher-order attribute*, otherwise it is a *zero-order attribute*. In a 1NF scheme, only zero-order attributes appear on the right side of a rule. A nested scheme may have zero or higher order attributes on the right side, provided that the rules are non-recursive. Observe that relations scheme names are simply a special case of attribute names. Names that appear only on the left side of some rule, and nowhere else, are *external* names. Otherwise, they are called *internal* names.

We assume several fundamental concepts and terms from relational database theory, including data dependencies and normal forms. For brevity, we omit these definitions here and refer instead to a database text such as [Korth and Silberschatz 1986].

In addition to the standard relational algebra operators we need to add two operators, nest (ν) and unnest (μ) as in [Fischer and Thomas 1983]. *Nest* takes a relation structure $\mathcal{R} = \langle R, r\rangle$ and aggregates over equal data values in some subset of the attributes in R. *Unnest* takes a relation structure nested on some set of attributes and disaggregates the structure to make it a "flatter" structure.

4 Nested Relational Representation of Objects

It is possible to represent objects in relations in a straightforward manner. A relation is defined for each class, with one attribute for each instance variable. Each object within a class is represented by a tuple in the relation for that class. The value stored in a field of a tuple is either a primitive object (e.g., integers, strings, floats) or the unique identifier of another object. These unique identifiers are, in relational terms, foreign keys. This is essentially the model proposed by Haskin and Lorie [1982], and Lorie and Plouffe [1983].

There are several difficulties with so simple an implementation.

- An instance variable may have a domain for which subclasses exist. For example, if the domain of an instance variable is the class *automobile*, the foreign key may apply to one of several subclasses of *automobile*.
- Retrieval of a complex object (i.e. an object and all objects that are parts of it) requires the combination of tuples from several relations. There is no simple way to treat a complex object as a unit.

As pointed out by Dadam, et al. [1986], a tuple in a nested relation can represent complex objects directly. If the *is-part-of* relationship happens to be a hierarchy, the nested relational model is a perfect fit. However, DAG structured *is-part-of* relationships can arise. For example, a particular bolt-type may be a part of several components of an automobile, and we probably do not want a unique identifier for every bolt. In such cases, we must resort to foreign keys. Empirical observation of examples used in the complex object literature suggests that most real-world *is-part-of* relationships are close to being hierarchies in the sense that deletion of only a small fraction of the edges of the DAG would leave the structure as a hierarchy.

Therefore, we conclude that a nested relational database scheme can come close to capturing a real world *is-part-of* relationship with a nested relational tuple forming a "handle" for access to a complex object. However, we also conclude that on those occasions where the relationship is a DAG, a nested relational join must be computed.

This is not a new observation. We shall see in the next section that existing definitions of nested relational join are not adequate to capture the type of join we need for complex objects. The difficulty arises from the fact that the join attributes may appear at different levels of nesting in the nested relations being joined.

Providing efficient join algorithms for nested relations of complex objects is critical if we are to provide a relational query interface for the object database. Furthermore, the efficiency of these algorithms is the main determining factor in the efficiency of query processing in this environment.

5 Extended Join

The extended natural join ($\bowtie^e$) of Roth, Korth, and Silberschatz [1988] considers only those common attributes that are at the top level of both schemes. Instead of testing equality on common attributes as in $\bowtie$, extended intersection is used. This amounts to requiring equality on zero-order attributes and extended intersection on higher-order attributes. The join ($\bowtie$) of Deshpande and Larson [1987] does not include any special treatment for higher order names. Equality is used for zero order attributes and set equality for higher order attributes.

Neither of these definitions is equivalent to a renested join of fully unnest relations. That is, in general, $\mu^*(r \bowtie^e s) \neq \mu^*(r) \bowtie \mu^*(s)$, where μ^* denotes the complete unnesting of a relation. Consider the database given by the following rules:

$$\begin{aligned}
\mathit{Distributors} &= (\mathit{company},\ \mathit{fee})\\
\mathit{Parts} &= (\mathit{pname},\ \mathit{quantity})\\
\mathit{Composition} &= (\mathit{compname},\ \mathit{compid},\ \mathit{Parts})\\
\mathit{Product} &= (\mathit{prodname},\ \mathit{Composition},\ \mathit{Distributors})\\
\mathit{Source} &= (\mathit{company},\ \mathit{cost})\\
\mathit{Part} &= (\mathit{pname},\ \mathit{weight},\ \mathit{Source})
\end{aligned}$$

The two external names are *Part* and *Product*. The example corresponds to an object database with classes:

- *Product:* An instance of *Product* has a set of components and a set of distributors. These set-valued instance variables are represented by the *Composition* and *Distributors* nested sub-relations.

- *Component:* An instance of *Component* has a name and identification number. It consists of a set of parts (*Parts* sub-relation). Each component is contained in a product, so, for our example, we have no need for a top-level relation for this class.
- *Part:* An instance of *Part* is an atomic component of products. Parts are generic items that may be obtained from one of several companies (perhaps at different costs).

Consider the following example query. We wish to find those companies that are both a distributor and a parts source for some product. (Presumably, this information might be used to negotiate a further discount.) We could express this query as:

$$\Pi_{company}(\mu^*(part) \bowtie \mu^*(product))$$

Although this provides the correct answer, it appears to require the generation of two large intermediate results ($\mu^*(part)$ and $\mu^*(product)$) as temporary relations. This is prohibitively costly in terms of space and a join of such large relations would (even by the best 1NF join algorithms) take a prohibitive amount of time for large databases. Furthermore the extended join ($\bowtie^e$) is of little use since *company and pname* appear at two different nesting levels in *part* and *product*.

Thus it is not sufficient for a theory of query optimization for nested relations to focus solely on join and extended join, despite the central role join plays in processing 1NF relational queries.

We now define $\bowtie^u$, the unnest-join:

$$r \bowtie^u_\Theta s = \mu^*(r) \bowtie_\Theta \mu^*(s)$$

where Θ is a predicate on the zero order attributes. If Θ is omitted then a natural join is performed.

6 Join Algorithms

We have considered two physical file structures for the implementation of nested relations. The first of these represents a clustered file organization as a nested relational scheme. The second is a pointer-based organization designed for efficient processing of general, ad-hoc queries. We consider both of these structures so that we have the flexibility to model a wide variety of physical organizations using nested relational schemes. This flexibility is important to our model since we want our optimization theory to be rich enough to consider as many reasonable low-level implementations as possible.

Next, we consider those places where an index would aid query processing. We must choose between relation-specific indices that refer to only one relation and sub-scheme specific indices that refer to all nested subrelations with a given scheme. The former are the types used typically in 1NF relational databases. The latter offer considerable efficiencies for nested relational databases. Deshpande and Van Gucht [1987] present an exhaustive index technique directed specifically to the needs of nested relational queries.

There are several approaches to computing the unnest-join, including:

- *the naive algorithm:* Computation of the complete unnesting of both relations followed by a standard 1NF natural join.
- *the simple iteration algorithm:* This algorithm consists of an iteration over the tuples in the two relations. It improves over the naive algorithm by requiring relatively little temporary storage beyond the space needed to store the result.
- *the simple iteration algorithm with indices:* The inner loop of the simple iteration algorithm is replaced by a index lookup to identify the tuples of the inner-loop relation that must be scanned. There are many variants of this algorithm, based on the choices for index techniques that we noted above. Depending upon the type of index used, it may be possible only to identify a superset of the tuples needed.
- *the semi-join algorithm:* This algorithm is motivated by semijoin programs used as a distributed join technique. In a distributed system, $r \bowtie s$ may be computed by shipping a

projection of r to the site at which s is stored so that those tuples of s that participate in the join can be identified and shipped to the site at which r is stored. Frequently, such a strategy can reduce communication costs. In computing the unnest-join, we use a similar technique to identify tuples of nested subrelations that do not participate in the join. The final step invokes one of the above join algorithms, but with (in general) smaller argument relations.

In order to define precisely the semijoin algorithm, we must define the notion of a tuple t in either r_1 or a nested subrelation of r_1 *participating* in $r_1 \bowtie^u r_2$. Intuitively, for t to participate, all tuples containing t must participate and for each subrelation of t some tuple must participate as well. Thus "participation in a join" is recursive in both the parent tuple of t and the child tuples of t. It appears at first glance that the definition of this notion may be circular, but this is not the case. We introduce the formal definition by defining first a top-down and a bottom-up notion of participation.

Definition 1: Let the relation structures $< R_1, r_1 >$ and $< R_2, r_2 >$ be given. We say that a tuple $t \in r_1$ *participates top-down* in $r_1 \bowtie^u r_2$ *through* $t' \in r_1 \bowtie^u r_2$ if $t'[X] = t[X]$ where X is the set of zero-order attributes in E_{R_1}. Now let $< R, r >$ be a relation structure nested at some level within r_1. A tuple $t \in r$ *participates top-down* in $r_1 \bowtie^u r_2$ *through* $t' \in r_1 \bowtie^u r_2$ if both of the following hold:

- $t'[X] = t[X]$, where X is the set of zero-order attributes in E_R
- let t'' be the tuple containing r. (That is, $< S, s >$ is a relation structure that is either $< R_1, r_1 >$ or one nested with r_1, such that $t'' \in s$, $R \in E_S$ and $t''[R] = r$.) Then t'' must participate *top-down* in $r_1 \bowtie^u r_2$.

Observe that top-down participation can be computed in a top down manner, and that a symmetric notion of participation can be defined for $< R_2, r_2 >$.

Definition 2: Let the relation structures $< R_1, r_1 >$ and $< R_2, r_2 >$ be given. Let $< R, r >$ be a relation structure nested at a leaf level within r_1. (That is, E_R contains only zero-order attributes). We say that a tuple $t \in r$ *participates bottom-up* in $r_1 \bowtie^u r_2$ *through* $t' \in r_1 \bowtie^u r_2$ if $t = t'[R]$. Now let $< R, r >$ be a relation structure nested at some non-leaf level within r_1. A tuple $t \in r$ *participates bottom-up* in $r_1 \bowtie^u r_2$ *through* $t' \in r_1 \bowtie^u r_2$ if both of the following hold:

- $t'[X] = t[X]$, where X is the set of zero-order attributes in E_R
- for each higher-order attribute $A \in E_R$ there exists a tuple $t'' \in t[A]$ that participates bottom-up through t' in $r_1 \bowtie^u r_2$.

Observe that bottom-up participation can be computed in a bottom-up manner, and that a symmetric notion of participation can be defined for $< R_2, r_2 >$.

Definition 3: Let the relation structures $< R_1, r_1 >$ and $< R_2, r_2 >$ be given. We say that a tuple $t \in r_1$ *participates* in $r_1 \bowtie^u r_2$ *through* $t' \in r_1 \bowtie^u r_2$ if t participates both top-down and bottom-up in $r_1 \bowtie^u r_2$ through t'. Now let $< R, r >$ be a relation structure nested at some level within R_1. A tuple $t \in r$ *participates* in $r_1 \bowtie^u r_2$ *through* t' if both of the following hold:

- t participates both top-down and bottom-up in $r_1 \bowtie^u r_2$ through t'.
- Let t'' be the tuple containing r. (That is, $< S, s >$ is a relation structure that is either $< R_1, r_1 >$ or one nested within r_1 such that $t'' \in s$, $R \in E_s$ and $t''[R] = r$.) Then t'' must participate through t' in $r_1 \bowtie^u r_2$.

The idea behind the semijoin algorithm is to mark those tuples at all levels of nesting that participate in the join. Efficiency is gained by recognizing that as soon as one of the conditions of top-down or bottom-up participation fails, an entire tuple can be eliminated from consideration. Furthermore, a substantial degree of efficiency can be gained by a partial marking, as defined below.

Definition 4: A *marking* of r_1 in $r_1 \bowtie^u r_2$ assigns a marking of 1 to those tuples in r_1 or any nested relation of r_1 that participate in $r_1 \bowtie^u r_2$ and a marking of 0 to those that do not.

Definition 5: A *partial marking* of r_1 in $r_1 \bowtie^u r_2$ assigns a marking of 1 to those tuples in r_1 or any nested relation of r_1 that participate in $r_1 \bowtie^u r_2$ and a marking of 0 or 1 to those that do not.

The partial marking is the more practical notion of marking since it allows maximal advantage to be taken of those indices that exist on the relations being joined, without requiring exhaustive computation of a complete marking.

For 1NF relations, partial or full markings can be obtained by intersecting pointer sets that result from index lookups. In the nested relational model, "pointers" are tuple identifiers that "point" to a tuple at any level of nesting. An intersection algorithm for tuple identifiers must take into account the containment relationship on tuples.

In [Korth 1988], we present a hierarchical definition of tuple identifiers that allows partial markings to be computed without the need to access the relations themselves. Due to space limitations, we present only the intuition of these techniques here. Let T_1 and T_2 be two tuple identifiers referencing tuples in r_1 and r_2, respectively. The longest common prefix T' of T_1 and T_2 represents the most deeply nested tuple containing T_1 and T_2. If T' is not the empty string, then if T_1 and T_2 participate in $r_1 \bowtie^u r_2$, they must do so through the same tuple. Using indices, we can examine the value of the tuples referenced by T_1 and T_2 on at least some of the join attributes, thereby computing a partial marking.

The efficiency of this method depends on the number of zero-order join attributes for which indices exist as well as the efficiency with which we can manipulate tuple identifiers. Details appear in [Korth 1988].

The efficiency of the join processing techniques we have discussed cannot be quantified without a good cost measure for execution of query processing strategies. Unfortunately, no cost model has been developed that includes physical structures implementing nested relations. Current work to define such a model is described in [Korth 1988].

7 References:

Dadam, P., K. et al. [1986], "A DBMS Prototype to Support Extended NF^2 Relations: An Integrated View on Flat Tables and Hierarchies, *Proc. 1986 ACM Sigmod Conference*, 356–367.

Deshpande, V. and P.-Å. Larson [1987], "An Algebra for Nested Relations," Research Report CS-87-65, Computer Science Department, University of Waterloo, 1987.

Deshpande, A. and D. Van Gucht [1987], "A Storage Structure for Nested Relational Databases," *Proc. G. I. Conference on Database Systems for Office Automation, Engineering and Scientific Applications*, Darmstadt, Germany, 481–486.

Fischer, P. and S. Thomas [1983], "Operators for Non-First-Normal-Form Relations," *Proc. 7 Int'l Computer Software Applications Conference*, 464–475.

Haskin, R., and Lorie [1982], "On Extending the Functions of a Relational Database System," *Proc. 1982 ACM Sigmod Conference*, 1982, 207–212.

Korth, H. F. and A. Silberschatz [1986], *Database System Concepts*, McGraw-Hill.

Korth, H. F. [1988], "Query Processing in Nested Relational Databases," manuscript in preparation.

Lorie, R. A., and W. Plouffe [1983], "Complex Objects and Their Use in Design Transactions," *Proc. ACM Sigmod 83 Database Week: Engineering Design Applications*, 115–121.

Roth, M. A., H. F. Korth, and A. Silberschatz [1988], "Extended Algebra and Calculus for ¬1NF Relational Databases," to appear *ACM Transactions on Database Systems*, 1988.

Schek, H-J. and M. H. Scholl [1986], "The Relational Model with Relation-Valued Attributes," *Information Systems*, 11:2, 137–147.

Stefik, M. and D. G. Bobrow [1986], "Object-Oriented Programming: Themes and Variations," *The AI Magazine*, 40–62.

Ullman, J. D. [1987], "Database Theory—Past and Future," *Proc. 6 ACM Symposium on the Principles of Database Systems*, 1–10.

Query Optimization in Object-Oriented Database Systems: A Prospectus

Goetz Graefe
David Maier
Oregon Graduate Center
graefe@cse.ogc.edu, maier@cse.ogc.edu

Abstract

We are exploring a scheme that allows optimizing queries over object-oriented databases with encapsulated behavior. Objects and classes will be able to reveal their behavior in terms of expressions in an algebraic language interpreted by a structural object-oriented database system. An object or class can agree or refuse to reveal its behavior. The structural algebra is richer than relational algebra as it includes operators on complex object collections, and updates and traversals of individual objects. Objects may reveal to the optimizer the structural access paths used by their procedures or cost and other statistics useful for query optimization. The main features of our approach is that the object-oriented user interface language is able to perform general computation and to preserve the encapsulation envelope around classes and types.

1. Introduction

For engineering applications like CASE and CAD systems, none of the currently used file systems, conventional database systems, or custom data managers are totally adequate to the task, because each of them lacks in either modelling power, query optimization, performance on large datasets, or data management services such as authorization, concurrency control, and recovery. File systems put all the burden of mapping complex objects to storage formats on the application programmer, and provide no or only rudimentary support for data abstraction and data management services. Conventional database systems provide concurrency control, recovery, and efficient set-oriented processing, but only for a limited data model and with inadequate performance on complex objects. Custom data managers can give the appropriate data types for an application but usually cannot be modified by the application developer to add new data types as an application evolves, and are often deficient in data management services and in query optimization capabilities. What is needed is a database system with richer data modelling power and the required high performance on both set and object operations.

The goal of the *REVELATION Project*[1] at the Oregon Graduate Center is to combine the advantages of object-oriented and relational technology in an extensible database system. There is, however, a fundamental difference between object-oriented systems on one hand and

---

[1] The reason for the name will be apparent later. Name relationships to the EXODUS project at the University of Wisconsin — Madison and the GENESIS project at the University of Texas at Austin are "purely incidental."

relational and extensible systems currently under development on the other hand. In object-oriented systems, algorithms and processing methods are associated with the individual objects and classes. A query is evaluated by sending a message to an object or group of objects. The actual processing steps performed, i.e., the implementation of the method invoked for the message, are beyond the message sender's control. Encapsulating implementation and control of processing in the class or type is a very powerful abstraction mechanism, and contributes considerably to the success and acceptance of the object-oriented paradigm. In relational and extensible systems, query execution is controlled by a central module, often called *scheduler* or *access plan interpreter*. This module employs a limited, fixed set of algorithms, e.g., algorithms implementing relational algebra operators, in a query specific combination.

In the remaining sections, we lay out our plan to combine previous approaches in a new database management system. In Section 2, we provide an brief overview of related work. Section 3 outlines our approach to query optimization in object-oriented database systems. Sections 4 and 5 describe a preliminary database architecture of a high-performance object-oriented database system, in particular the query optimization component and the query evaluation component. Section 6 contains a summary and our conclusions.

2. Previous Work

Object-oriented database systems are a new and conceptually powerful alternative to existing systems. They support structures and features that are not provided in conventional data models. Among these features are complex objects, object identity, encapsulation of methods and behavior, hierarchies and inheritance of data types, versions of objects, and very large objects [Copeland1984a, Manola1986a, Maier1986a, Maier1986b, Skarra1986a]. These concepts make object-oriented programming and database systems well suited for engineering applications, including CAD, CAM, and CASE. Unfortunately, object-oriented systems do not provide the search performance on large datasets required by these application areas. Engineering data need to be accessible efficiently both in flexible "edit" mode and in large-volume set-oriented "report" mode, as for the relational data model.

Relational systems, on the other hand, place the control solely with an execution module or run-time system, which exists independently of the data. The data in a relational database are purely passive input to algorithms implementing the relational algebra. This view of database management systems, i.e., a general run-time system acting on passive data, is the precondition of query optimization as it is found in existing database systems.

In the last few years, a new direction in database systems research has concentrated on extensibility [Batory1986a, Carey1985a, Carey1986a, Rowe1987a, Schwarz1986a, Stonebraker1986a]. While some of these systems provide extensions and extensibility to basically relational systems, other systems are experimenting with a "toolkit" approach, i.e., software tools and libraries to generate a database system specific to the application domain.

Query optimization has become a wide field of research. Most of the work has focused on relational systems, probably due to the available theoretical framework and to the widespread use of database management systems based on the relational model. A new research direction in database query optimization uses rule-based transformations to determine optimal access plans from algebra expressions. The EXODUS optimizer generator [Graefe1987a] creates a query optimizer from a rule-based description of the algebra to be optimized. The algebra, i.e., the set of operations and the equivalences of algebraic expressions, is independent of the optimizer generator and can be extended by augmenting an algebra description file. Optimization is performed using an expert system search using the equivalence relationships between algebra expressions and cost functions associated with implementation methods for algebra operators.

Other research groups are also using rule-based approaches to query optimization, e.g., Freytag and Lohman are implementing a rule-based query optimizer for the Starburst extensible (relational) database system [Freytag1987a]. Currently, they are defining a rule language and implementing an interpreter for this language with a built-in search engine [Lohman1988a].

3. Revealing Behavior

Our plan for combining the two approaches is as follows. Behavioral abstraction and encapsulation on the logical and application interface level are strictly retained, but the execution model should employ set-at-a-time algorithms and query optimization as much as possible. When a query entered on the interface level is mapped to an appropriate form for the execution level of the database system, the interface determines which message must be sent to which object or class in order to answer the query. Instead of sending this message, however, the objects and classes involved are requested to **reveal** execution information prior to execution. If an object or class refuses to respond to a *reveal* message, the query is evaluated by sending the original message to the object or class. In the sequel, the original message will be called the *evaluate* message. If, however, an object or class does reveal information, it provides an equivalent processing expression and the means to obtain appropriate input for the expression. The processing expression is formed in terms of an algebra designed for a structural object-oriented database system. It is a superset of the relational algebra, with suitable extensions for large and complex objects. The operators of this algebra can be augmented with procedures for arithmetic, predicates, string processing, and formatted I/O. Typically, the revealed expression will not be composed entirely of algebraic operators. Rather, the expression will involve a small number of object-message pairs whose behavior is still encapsulated. Further reveal messages can be sent to these objects in an attempt to transform more of the query into algebraic form. The inputs for the expression are objects or classes and evaluate messages with their parameters to be sent to the objects or classes to obtain the input. These are typically the same messages that the revealing object or class would have used internally to obtain this input.

The revealed expression includes sufficient information about the object's or class's behavior to evaluate the original query. Thus, behavior encapsulated in the class definition is now duplicated, and evaluation of the revealed expression can treat the object as passive, i.e., with no behavior attached to it. Obviously, once information is duplicated, complex problems arise in case of change. For the remainder of this prospectus, we assume that the type definition and behavior do not change until the query has been evaluated, or a suitable notification mechanism is in place. Hence, structural interpretation of a algebraic expression can be substituted for the encapsulated behavior.

If the revelation step is used repeatedly, a number of operations can be revealed, resulting is a complex algebra expression or operator tree. Such trees will be evaluated by a rather conventional query evaluation module. The leaves of this tree represent evaluate messages. Since we expect that the storage manager on which the object system is built will be the same as the one used by the query evaluation module, it is possible that a class reveals that an evaluate message is equivalent to scanning a file or an index. Thus, by using the *reveal* message repeatedly, possibly an entire query can be transformed into an algebra expression.

An algebra expression provides three advantages over the original evaluate message. First, by using set-at-a-time algorithms, we can expect much better performance. If a query is expressed in an algebra expression acting on "passive" data, alternative processing algorithms, possibly distributed and parallel versions, concurrency control, and recovery can be introduced transparently to the query and the database objects. Second, complex object traversal can be pre-planned in order to minimize disk accesses and effort for mapping between object representations on the physical and logical level. Third, this expression can be submitted to a query optimizer.

4. Query Optimization

The optimization paradigm that we have developed in earlier work [Graefe1987a] will be used to optimize revealed algebraic expressions. A program created by the EXODUS optimizer generator optimizes and transforms algebraic expressions (operator trees) and selects implementation methods based on anticipated execution cost. This optimization paradigm is very suitable for the problem at hand. The initial query starts as a single message to a object or class. Looking at it from a different viewpoint, the algebra expression before optimization consists of a single evaluate message. Through several revelation steps a tree is built by expanding leaves. These steps can easily be modelled as tree transformations. When all leaves have been replaced by scan methods or all leaf objects or classes refuse to reveal processing information, the actual optimization phase begins[2]. The operations are reordered according to equivalence rules and heuristics, and algorithms are chosen for the operations. The optimization process and the search strategy employed by optimizers built with the EXODUS optimizer generator is described in more detail in [Graefe1987a, Graefe1987b, Graefe1987c].

5. Query Evaluation

After a query has been optimized, it can be executed by the run-time system. The run-time system will consist of three components, the object processor, the set processor, and the file manager.

The object processor interprets messages to objects and their implementation, for both permanent, disk-based objects and temporary objects. This component is crucial in providing the semantical and computational power expected from an object-oriented system. Since the objects at this level can exhibit behavior by procedures attached to the class or an object itself, the object processor provides the power of a general-purpose programming language, thus allowing for user interaction, screen display, etc.

The set processor interprets algebraic expressions as revealed to and optimized by the optimizer. It consists of an extensible set of processing modules. These modules provide and use a uniform item-at-a-time interface. Items can be either single records, objects, or groups of those. By provinding *send* and *receive* operations using this interface, to be inserted into an algebra expression by the optimizer, the location of storage and processing can be made transparent to all other operations, thus allowing for easy extensibility even in distributed and workstation/server architectures. An object or class that can appear in a leaf of an query evaluation tree provides the same interface using the object processor, allowing for a smooth and efficient interface between object processing and set processing.

The algebra appropriate for query optimization and execution is the initial focus of our research. It has to satisfy several criteria. First, it must be powerful enough to express queries originally expressed in an object-oriented programming or query language. At the least, it must encompass the relational algebra and allow for traversal of complex object structures. Second, it must be simple enough to allow efficient search for alternative expressions by the query optimizer. Third, the operations must allow using efficient algorithms to process large sets of objects. Fourth, the algebra must have a solid theoretical foundation such that extensions can safely be made.

Currently, we plan on using relation algebra operators suitably generalized for complex objects. Furthermore, we will design and use an operator to compose complex objects from

[2] The EXODUS optimizer generator allows segmentation of the rule set and to perform query optimization in several phases.

object id's or object fragments, and operators for object manipulation and transformation.

The same interface is provided by the file manager, which consists of fairly conventional software to efficiently store and retrieve records on disk using file processing and indexing techniques. Due to the uniform interface between the components and modules of the run-time system, it will be quite straightforward to implement extensions to the algebra, the set of processing algorithms, or the storage structures.

6. Summary and Conclusions

In this prospectus, we have outlined a new approach to query optimization in behavioral object-oriented database systems, and have given a preliminary database architecture overview. The principal goal is to build an object-oriented database system with high performance for accessing large volumes of data. The fundamental problem we are addressing is how to utilize set-oriented processing and query optimization techniques without violating the object-oriented programming paradigm. Objects and classes can reveal execution information to the optimizer prior to execution, thus allowing object-at-a-time algorithms to be replaced with more efficient set-at-a-time algorithms. A single message representing a query can be transformed into a an execution tree with messages or file access at the leaves. Such query execution trees can be optimized using an optimizer based on the EXODUS optimizer generator. Query evaluation will be performed by three interacting software components, namely the object processor, the set processor, and the file manager. The set processor consists of an extensible set of algebraic operator implementations. An efficient, standardized interface between these operators allows augmentation of the algebra of object sets if needed.

Using this new database architecture, we hope to be able to provide the power of behavioral object-oriented data models and, by employing a query optimizer, to process queries on large sets of objects efficiently.

Acknowledgements

David DeWitt made the EXODUS optimizer generator possible, and challenged the first author to design a query optimization component for object-oriented database systems.

References

Batory1986a.

D.S. Batory, "GENESIS: A Project to Develop an Extensible Database Management System," *Proceedings of the Int'l Workshop on Object-Oriented Database Systems*, pp. 207-208 (September 1986).

Carey1985a.

M.J. Carey and D.J. DeWitt, "Extensible Database Systems," *Proceedings of the Islamorada Workshop*, (February 1985).

Carey1986a.

M.J. Carey, D.J. DeWitt, D. Frank, G. Graefe, J.E. Richardson, E.J. Shekita, and M. Muralikrishna, "The Architecture of the EXODUS Extensible DBMS: A Preliminary Report," *Proceedings of the Int'l Workshop on Object-Oriented Database Systems*, pp. 52-65 (September 1986).

Copeland1984a.

G. Copeland and D. Maier, "Making Smalltalk a Database System," *Proceedings of the ACM SIGMOD Conference*, pp. 316-325 (June 1984).

Freytag1987a.

J.C. Freytag, "A Rule-Based View of Query Optimization," *Proceedings of the ACM SIGMOD Conference*, pp. 172-180 (May 1987).

Graefe1987a.
G. Graefe, "Rule-Based Query Optimization in Extensible Database Systems," *Ph.D. Thesis*, University of Wisconsin, (August 1987).

Graefe1987b.
G. Graefe and D.J. DeWitt, "The EXODUS Optimizer Generator," *Proceedings of the ACM SIGMOD Conference*, pp. 160-171 (May 1987).

Graefe1987c.
G. Graefe, "Software Modularization with the EXODUS Optimizer Generator," *IEEE Database Engineering*, (December 1987).

Lohman1988a.
G.M. Lohman, "Grammar-Like Functional Rules for Representing Query Optimization Alternatives," *Proceedings of the ACM SIGMOD Conference*, pp. 18-27 (June 1988).

Maier1986a.
D. Maier, J. Stein, A. Otis, and A. Purdy, "Development of an Object-Oriented DBMS," *Proceedings of the ACM Conference on Object-Oriented Programming Systems*, (September-October 1986).

Maier1986b.
D. Maier, "Why Object-Oriented Databases Can Succeed Where Others Have Failed," *Proceedings of the Int'l Workshop on Object-Oriented Database Systems*, p. 227 (September 1986).

Manola1986a.
F. Manola and U. Dayal, "PDM: An Object-Oriented Data Model," *Proceedings of the Int'l Workshop on Object-Oriented Database Systems*, pp. 17-25 (September 1986).

Rowe1987a.
L. Rowe and M. Stonebraker, "The POSTGRES Data Model," *Proceeding of the Conference on Very Large Databases*, pp. 83-96 (August 1987).

Schwarz1986a.
P. Schwarz, W. Chang, J.C. Freytag, G. Lohman, J. McPherson, C. Mohan, and H. Pirahesh, "Extensibility in the Starburst Database System," *Proceedings of the Int'l Workshop on Object-Oriented Database Systems*, pp. 85-92 (September 1986).

Skarra1986a.
A.H. Skarra, Z.B. Zdonik, and S.P. Reiss, "An Object Server for an Object-Oriented Database System," *Proceedings of the Int'l Workshop on Object-Oriented Database Systems*, pp. 196-204 (September 1986).

Stonebraker1986a.
M. Stonebraker and L.A. Rowe, "The Design of POSTGRES," *Proceedings of the ACM SIGMOD Conference*, pp. 340-355 (May 1986).

Object-Oriented DBMS Performance Measurement

R. G. G. Cattell

Information Management Group
Sun Microsystems

Abstract

Performance will be critical to the acceptance of Object-Oriented DBMSs. In the first Workshop on Object-Oriented Database Systems, many claims were made about the performance of differing DBMS architectures. A plea was made for benchmarks to measure the DBMSs, to substantiate competing claims. Last year, we designed such benchmarks (Rubenstein, Kubicar, & Cattell [1987]), and subsequently they have been run on a number of DBMSs, both Relational and Object-Oriented. In this position paper, we discuss what we have learned about performance measurement for database systems, and suggest improvements to our benchmarks for future use.

1. Introduction

Without ten to one hundred times the performance of conventional DBMSs, it doesn't *matter* what additional functionality that Object-Oriented DBMSs provide for engineering applications such as Computer-Aided Software Engineering (CASE) and Computer-Aided Design (CAD) -- they will not be useful for the job. Since engineering customers are very important to us, and Object-Oriented DBMSs are largely targetted at engineering applications, we set out to focus some attention on objective performance measurement in this area.

Measuring performance in a generic way is very difficult, since every application has somewhat different requirements. However, the object-oriented engineering applications we target are quite similar at the lowest levels. Generally, the operations they perform on data cannot be expressed in the abstractions provided by SQL or any other high-level DML we are aware of. Instead, they use a programming language interspersed with operations on individual data objects.

For example, in a CAD application, the components and their interconnections on a circuit board could be stored in a database, and an optimization algorithm might follow connections between components and rearrange them to reduce wire lengths. In a CASE application, program modules and their interdependencies could be stored in a database, and a system-build algorithm might traverse the dependency graph examining version numbers to construct a compilation plan. In both cases, thousands of objects need to be accessed per second, perhaps executing the equivalent of a relational join for each object. Simply adding transitive closure to the query language is inadequate, as the steps performed at each junction can be arbitrarily complex.

2. Approaches

We do not believe that conventional measures of DBMS system performance, the Wisconsin benchmarks [Bitton 85] and TP1 [Anon 85], adequately measure object-oriented engineering performance. The TP1 benchmark is designed to measure transaction throughput with large numbers of users. While some of the Wisconsin measures are relevant to engineering performance, they generally are measures at too course a grain, and focus on the intelligence of the query optimizer on more complex queries that are rare in our applications.

The most accurate measure of performance for engineering applications would be to run an actual application, representing the data in the manner best suited to each potential DBMS. However, we feel it is difficult or impossible to design an application whose performance would be representative of many different engineering applications, and we want a generic measure. Perhaps in the future someone will be successful at this more difficult task [Maier 87].

We decided to measure operations on individual objects, the simple operations out of which all other operations can be composed, and endeavored to measure the times in such a way that performance could be estimated for the more complex operations by adding the individual measures.

3. Benchmarks

The operations we measured are described in detail in [Rubenstein 87]. Briefly, our measurements were:

Name Lookup: This is the simplest database operation, to look up an object given its name. An example would be looking up the record for a particular part given its part number.

Range Lookup: Finding the records with a particular range of values in a particular set of fields. An example would be finding parts built in a particular range of dates.

Reference Lookup: This is a logical pointer-following operation. An example would be following a chain of connections up a hierarchy of departments and sub-departments. In relational systems lacking links or multi-table indices, this measurement is identical to the name lookup measurement.

Group Lookup: This is the *inverse* of reference lookup, going in the one-to-many direction to find all the objects that reference a given one. Where reverse pointers operations are not available in an object-oriented DBMS, it may be necessary to store the reverse connections explicitly and redundantly. Examples would be finding all the author records for a particular document, or all the sub-parts of a particular part.

Record Insert: In some applications, the time to insert new data is critical. There is typically a trade-off between update time and retrieval time, so it is important to include this measure. In general, relational database systems are not very fast for update.

We performed the operations on a large and a small database containing authors and documents. The small database fit entirely in 4 megabytes of main memory, thus demonstrating the speed of the DBMS when there is a working set that an engineer accesses for an extended period of time (typical in many of our applications). We measured the real time required to execute the operations 500 times, thereby including disk overhead but also averaging enough operations to take advantage of main memory caching.

4. Results

Briefly, we found that all of the systems we measured were far from the performance an engineering application would require. At best, they performed about ten operations per second. We experimented with the source code for one relational DBMS to determine what kinds of optimizations resulted in better performance.

We found that over a factor of ten improvement can be had by eliminating overhead associated with initiating a query. Queries must not be parsed, interpreted, or compiled at run-time, or the overhead will swamp the time for the simple operation.

At least another order of magnitude improvement can be had with the ability to lock and cache the entire working database set being accessed in main memory. Note this does not permit the use of database "servers" on a network - the DBMS itself must run on the workstation and perform concurrency control with other workstations at a lower level.

Another order of magnitude improvement is possible on larger databases by utilization of the right access methods. For example, the reference and group benchmark measurements are much faster if physical links or multi-table indices are available.

5. Revised Benchmarks

On the basis of a year's experience and feedback on the benchmarks, we would now make some additions as well as some simplifications of the original benchmarks described above.

First of all, we should have chosen something that "looked" like an engineering database. This is a minor point, but it has been a source of confusion. (We had used a database of authors and documents because we felt everyone would be familiar with it.) We instead propose a database of parts on a circuit board and connections between them. The structure of this database is not very different from the original one. We define the database as two logical records, but the same information can be stored in any way best suitable to the DBMS:

Part: RECORD[id: INT, type: STRING[10], x,y: INT, build: DATE]

Connection: RECORD[from: part-id, to: part-id, type: STRING[10], length: INT]

To be consistent with our original benchmark paper, we would create a database of parts with ids 1 through 20,000, and 60,000 connections, with exactly three connections from each part to other (randomly selected) parts. This small database should fit entirely in main memory (we also specify a larger one scaled up by a factor of 10, see our original paper).

Our second observation from our experiences is that the Name and Range Lookup measurements almost always differ by a constant time, because modern B-tree implementations are used for both in nearly all DBMSs. Thus the Range Lookup could be dropped.

Finally, we had hoped to estimate the time to do complex operations, in particular transitive closure, by composing individual Reference and Group Lookup times. In practice, it was hard to specify these measurements in a way that different implementors got consistent numbers for their DBMS without accidentally including the set-up time, e.g. to fetch the record from which the reference emanated. So, we recommend that the Reference and Group Lookup measurements be replaced by a single Transitive Closure measure composing these lookups, finding all parts connected to a randomly selected part within five or fewer connection "hops".

It has also been suggested that we include update time as well as insert time for completeness. This additional information couldn't hurt, however in our experience update and insert time have always been directly related, so this measure is of lower importance.

In summary, we believe the three most important measures of performance in an object-oriented DBMS are:

(1) *Lookup*. Generate 500 random part ids and fetch the x,y positions for each.

(2) *Traversal*. Find all parts connected to a randomly selected part, or to a part connected to it, and so on, up to 5 hops (approximately 270 parts, with possible duplicates), and fetch their x,y positions.

(3) *Insert*. Time to enter 500 connection records between randomly selected parts. Must include time to update indices or other access structures used in the execution of (1) and (2).

Other measures could optionally be included, and a number of other controls are necessary to insure repeatable and accurate measures... see Rubenstein [1987].

6. Summary

We would like to see more work on performance in Object-Oriented DBMSs. We have designed and used benchmarks to measure performance, and on the basis of our experience with those benchmarks feel that the most important factors are measured by just three numbers. We are now pursuing these further measurements at Sun Microsystems, and hope to be able to report new results later this year. We contend that Object-Oriented DBMSs will not be used in "hard-core" engineering applications unless 1000 random operations can be executed in one second, and we that current implementations do not reach these levels in either the research or product environments.

7. References

[Anon 85]
Anon et al: A Measure of Transaction Processing Power, *Datamation*, Vol. 31, No. 7, April 1, 1985.

[Bitton 83]
Bitton, D., DeWitt, D. J., Turbyfil, C., Benchmarking Database Systems: A Systematic Approach, *Proceedings VLDB Conference*, October, 1983. [Expanded and revised version available as Wisconsin Computer Science TR #526.]

[Maier 87] Maier, David: Making Database Systems Fast Enough for CAD Applications, technical report CS/E-87-016, Oregon Graduate Center, Beaverton, Oregon, 1987.

[Rubenstein 87]
Rubenstein, W. R., Kubicar, M., Cattell, R. G. G.: Benchmarks for Database Response Time, *Proceedings ACM SIGMOD 1987.*

Data Abstraction and Query Optimization

Stanley B. Zdonik
Brown University

Abstract

The use of data abstraction in object-oriented databases places a burden on the ability of the system to perform query optimization. This paper discusses a framework for query specification and optimization that is applicable to object-oriented database systems that take a strict view of data abstraction. It examines techniques that preserve much of the optimization potential of relational languages by limiting the query language. It further examines techniques for query optimization that involve type-specific rewrite rules.

Introduction

Relational database systems have been very successful at providing ad hoc query languages. These languges allow users to write associative retrievals which the query processor is able to optimize. The ability to optimize queries derives largely from the fact that the relational model is very simple and uniform. Studies of relational algebra have led to an understanding of the formal properties of relational operators. For example, it is well-known that the select and join operations commute. This leads to the standard optimization strategy of pushing selections past joins.

In object-oriented databases, we are faced with a data model that allows for extension of the basic types by some form of data abstraction. This is a powerful modeling facility, but it has severe implications regarding how we might do query optimization. No longer is there a single simple model with a limited set of carefully studied operators. Each user-defined type effectively introduces a brand new algebra. How are we to understand the properties of these algebras in order to allow the same degree of optimization that we had in the relational world?

Brief Description of the Model

The ENCORE object-oriented database system [ZW86] provides for type definitions that are based on the notion of abstract types. A type definition T consists of a representation R, a set of operations Op, and a set of properties Pr. R is any other previously defined type. Op is a set of operations that have privileged access to R, and Pr is the definition of the abstract state of the object. A property p that relates an object x to an object y is a pair of the form (x,y) and as such is considered to be an object.

Two types A and B can be related to each other by means of an *is-a* property that requires that they be behaviorly compatible. If B is-a A, then instances of B can be used in any context in which instances of A were expected. Types also induce set objects that we will call *classes*. A type T has a corresponding class Ts that contains all current instances of T. T will be a collection of all objects that have been created as an instance of type T. There may be classes that do not correspond to types. We typically create subtypes to introduce additional operational behavior. A subclass may be created even if members of the subclass have no additional operations than those of the superclass. For example, we might have the type Car and the corresponding class Cars with an additional subclass called Blue_Cars. Blue cars have exactly the same operations as Cars, but can be usefully distinguished for reasons of the application.

It is classes over which we will form queries. A *query* is a function that returns selected members of some class. Classes might have implementations that differ. For example, some classes might be implemented by a B-tree, while others might be a hash table or a heap. The implementations that are chosen for class objects will have a large impact on the efficiency of some searches. Query optimization will select a query processing strategy that will use the different implementaions of classes in the most advantageous way.

Query Language

The type Aggregate (and all its subtypes) define two operations called *Select* and *Image* . *Select* returns those members of a given aggregate that satisfy a given predicate. *Image* takes an Aggregate A and a function f as input and returns an Aggregate that contains the result of applying f to each element of A. A Query is therefore modeled as an application of the Select or Image operations. The language that is used to form queries and query predicates P will be described in this section.

We have chosen to restrict the predicate language to allow only predicates over the abstract state of objects (i.e., its properties). That is, we can build expressions that rely on the values of properties, but we do not allow them to contain calls to arbitrary type-defined operations. As an example, consider the following query expression:

Select [Stacks, lambda (s) pop (s) = 3]

It selects those stacks from the set of all known stacks that if we were to apply the *pop* operation to them would return 3. Although it should be possible to form queries involving user-defined operations, we will not make any attempt to optimize these expressions. This makes query optimization more managable. Adding them is no problem; it simply decreases our ability to do optimization. We will return to this point later.

The query language consists of the following functions:

Select (A: Aggregate, P: Predicate) -> Aggregate
Image (A: Aggregate, F: Function) -> Aggregate
Union (A1: Aggregate, A2: Aggregate) -> Aggregate
Intersection (A1: Aggregate, A2: Aggregate) -> Aggregate
Difference (A1: Aggregate, A2: Aggregate) -> Aggregate

For_all (A: Aggregate, P: Predicate) -> T/F
For_some (A: Aggregate, P: Predicate) -> T/F
Contained_in (A1: Aggregate, A2: Aggregate) -> T/F
Member (x: Object, A: Aggregate) -> T/F

x.p where p is a property defined on objects of the type of x.
=, ≤, ≥, <, > defined on primitive types (i.e., Integer, Real, String)
= defined on identities by each abstract type.
And and **Or** (i.e., Boolean connectives)

Select returns those elements of the given aggregate A that match the given predicate P. That is Select (A, P) = { a | a is in A and P(a) }. *Image* returns an aggregate defined as Image (A, f) = { f(a) | a is in A }. *Union* returns the set union of the two aggregates A1 and A2. The types of the objects that are members of these aggregates must be of a comparable type (i.e., of the same type or of types that are in a type-subtype relationship with each other).

The next four functions are predicate formers. *For_all* returns **true** if every P(x) is true for all x in A. *For_some* returns **true** if there exists an x in A such that P(x) is true. *Contained_in* is **true** if A1 is a subset of S2, and Member is **true** if x is an element of A.

Other operations could be added such as the standard aggregate (not to be confused with Aggregate types) operations of *average*, *count*, *max*, and *min*. We will ignore these for now to simplify the rest of the paper.

Approaches

One way to approach the optimization of queries in an object-oriented database is to perform syntactic query transformations similar to those used in the relational algebra. Although each type provides a new algebra, if we restrict query expressions to use only the abstract state (i.e., properties) of the new types and generic operations over Aggregate types (e.g., the query language defined above), we can write down syntactic rules that are true for any type since the basic semantics of properties and sets are fixed and well-known. The next section gives some examples of this approach.

With the syntactic approach, it is sometimes possible to perform transformations that always produce better results than the original query expression. An example from relational optimization is to always push selection past joins. Another technique requires that we apply transformations selectively to arrive at expressions that make use of underlying access methods. For example, we would like to evaluate expressions early if their computation can take advantage of an index. This later form of optimization requires that the optimizer have knowledge about how things are implemented. We find that this assumption is reasonable in the object-oriented world even though this is a breach of the basic principle of encapsulation. The optimizer is a trusted part of the system and can be allowed to access the implementation as long as other parts of the system and user code cannot.

Another interesting approach involves the use of type-level semantics to transform the query in fundamental ways to a wholly different query that is provably equivalent to the original. Wheres the syntactic methods apply rules that are true in all domains, these techniques apply additional information that is dependent on application-level semantics. This kind of optimization has become known as semantic query optimization [HZ80] and seems well-suited to object-oriented models. Many of the transformations in semantic query optimization rely on inclusion relations between sets. The object hierarchies that appear in object-oriented systems supply exactly the kind of information that is required. A more detailed examination of these methods is beyond the scope of this paper.

Query Transformations

It is possible to discover transformation rules that can generally be applied to query expressions. Like query optimization in relational systems, we can use these transformations to get new query expressions that have lower expected costs. The following five rules are examples:

(1) Select [S1, lambda (s) s.p in S2] =
Image [S2, inverse (p)]

(2) Select [Select [S1, P1], P2] =
Select [Select [S1, P2], P1]

(3) Union [Select [S, P1], Select [S, P2]] =
Union [Select [S, P1 and P2]]

(4) Union [Image [S1, f], Image [S2, f]] =
Image [Union [S1, S2], f]]

(5) Select [S1, lambda (s) s.p1.p2 in S3] =
Select [S1, lambda (s) s.p1 in
Select [S2, lambda (s) s.p2 in S3]]

The following example illustrates the use of the first rule. Consider the following query that retrieves the Employees that work in the shoe department.

Select [Employees, lambda (e) e.dept.dname = "shoe"]

Application of rule (1), will produce the following equivalent query:

Image [Select [Departments, lambda (d) d.dname = "shoe"], inverse (dept)]

This optimization technique relies on the fact that the inverse property exists for the property that was originally used. If the aggregates in the query are being implemented by relations, the computation of the property values and their inverses is all done with a single application of the relational *join* operation. Join is inherently bi-directional. The first rule is analogous to the relational query optimization technique that pushes selections past joins.

Query optimization requires that we also have a mechanism for determining an estimate of the relative costs of two expressions. For the purposes of this paper we will make the simplifying assumption that any set that can be retrieved by using an index is cheaper than one that cannot.

Indices on Abstract Types

We will propose the use of indices as a way to implement efficient access to aggregate types. However, there are a few problems that must first be addressed.

The first involves what can be indexed. An index is really nothing more than a precompiled search. In other words, we store lists of all objects that would be returned if we were to search a set for all occurences of objects that match some criterion. Usually this criterion is that a key value is equal to a given constant. By using the index, we avoid having to do the search. With abstract types, we could potentially index on the result of applying methods. That is, we could keep a list of all objects x that would return a given value v if a method m were to be applied to x. A set of these lists for all possible v would be an index.

$$I_m = \{ (v_i, (x_1, \dots, x_n)) \mid v_i \text{ is a possible value of } m \ \& \ m\ (x_j) = v_i\ (1 \le j \le n) \ \}$$

Notice that m is a function of a single argument. Restricting our attention to methods of one argument that have no side-effects simplifies our approach to query processing. The get_value method that is available for all properties is an example of this type of function. For this reason, we restrict our query expressions to use only properties instead of more general operations.

Our data abstraction facilities allow property values to be computed in arbitrary ways by the get_property_value operation. In many cases, this operation simply looks up the value of the property from a stored piece of the representation. However, it is possible for this operation to compute a complex function based on several pieces of the representation. This conveniently allows a straightforward way to incorporate derived properties into the model. It potentially complicates our ability to analyze query expressions since we cannot always transform them directly onto simple manipulations of the underlying storage.

The existence of an index short-circuits this problem. If we have the value of a property stored in an index, it becomes irrelevant at retrieval time how this value is derived. It is available by doing a lookup on the index.

Another problem is a result of the fact that abstract types can be built on top of other abstract types. An aggregate object type can be built on top of another aggregate type, and so on. It is possible to provide indexes at any of these levels. For example, some level in such an implementaion hierarchy can be impemented by a B-tree which is itself an index. Even though a query expression is written in terms of the highest level interface, we would like to be able to take advantage of indices at deeper levels.

Index Maintenance

An index on property p over a set S captures the current state of the objects in S. An update to p for any object in S would require that the index be changed to reflect this update. When creating an operation Op for an abstract data type T, we would like to avoid having to worry about all of the indices that Op might disturb. We solve this problem by using triggers on the *set_p* operation for the appropriate properties.

The model defines triggers as a triple T=(O, C, P) where O is an operation, C is a condition, and P is a program. The semantics of T is that when operation O is invoked on an object x, if C(x) is true P is executed. This view of triggers is less general than some proposals, but it localizes the decision about whether or not a trigger is applicable to the current operation. It is unnecessary to check the condition C unless the associated operation has been invoked.

The only way that an index I on a property p can be invalidated is if a *set_p* operation is performed on the property p for some instance x. Abstract types can be built on top of other abstract types. This produces multiple levels of abstraction. As an example, a stack type can be built on an array type which in turn can be built on top of a bytestring type.

If an index is provided on a property p at any level in an abstract type, we attach a trigger to the set operation on each piece of state (abstract or stored at the next level) on which the property p depends.

Indexing User-Defined Types

Normally, indices are mappings between primitive values (e.g., integers, strings) and objects that have these values as values of one of their attributes. Our approach treats abstract values as indexable by their surrogates or oid's (i.e., object identifiers). This leads to a data structure that might be pictured as in Figure 1.

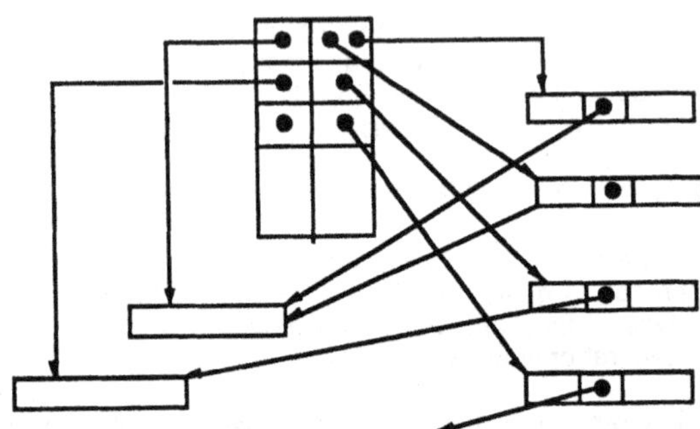

Figure 1 - Index on Structured Objects

The central table in this figure represents an index over a set S for a property p. It contains an entry for each possible value of the property p for each member of the set S. The two rectangles in the lower right represent the values of property p. The rectangles on the right represent the objects in set S. The dark dots represent oid's or pointers to other objects. The entries in the index are all oid values. For a given entry, the left-hand column contains the oid of a property value v (which is a structurted object), and the right-hand column contains a list of the the oids of objects that point to v.

An Example of Index Maintenance

Figure 2 is meant to illustrate a situation in which a type T is represented by a type R. R is a record type that contains fields x and y. T has two properties p and q which are computed as functions of x and y. p is computed as x+y and q is computed as the value of x. The two ovals are instances of the type T showing their R representation inside. The index on the left is computed over the property p for some set containing at least these two instances.

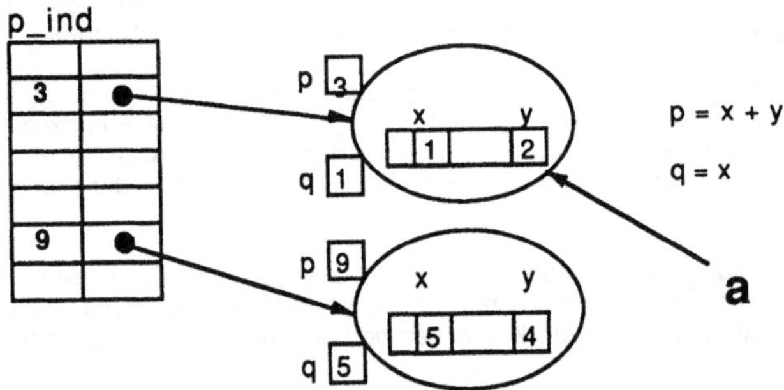

Figure 2 - An Example

Call the top instance a. If we attempt to update the value of the q property of a to the value 3, we must use an operation invocation of the form *set_p (a.q, 3)*. This would of course translate to an update of the x field of the representation of a. Since the p property also depends on the value of the x field, The derived property p will change as well.

The new value of a.p might not be computed until a *get_p* operation is invoked; however, since there is an index on the p property, we must update that structure immediately so that it will be correct next time it is used. It might be possible to store expressions in the index so that evaluation of the derived properties is delayted until the value is requested. This form of lazy evaluation is beyond the scope of this paper.

Our solution involves placing a trigger T on the x field of the representation. When this field is updated, the following code will be executed.

```
set_x (down (a), 3)    // causes T to fire
        T(a) = update_index (p_ind, a, x+y)
```

The set operation on x requires that we convert to the representation type by means of the down operation. The trigger T is attached to this operation. The body of the trigger is given in the second line. It updates the index with the value of x+y.

Conclusions

Although data abstraction presents potential difficulties to the process of query optimization, we feel that it does not preclude it. More study of the kinds of techniques that were sketched in this paper are needed to better understand what the opportunities and tradeoffs are. We have shown how restricting the query language to use known operators with well-behaved signatures (i.e., operations on Type Aggregate and Type Property), leads to a more tractable problem.

Indexing and auxilliary access paths have played an important role in traditional query processing and will continue to be important in object-oriented databases. Techniques to allow for more general forms of indexing on general operations is an important area for further study.

References

[BB84] Batory, D. and A. Buchmann, "Molecular Objects, Abstract Data Types, and Data Models: A Framework," Proceedings of the Conference on Very Large Databases, 1984.

[BKK88] Banerjee, J., W. Kim, and K.C. Kim, "Queries in Object-Oriented Databases",Proceedings of the Fourth International Conference on Data Engineering, Los Angeles, CA, February, 1988.

[GD87] Graefe, G. and D.J. DeWitt, "The EXODUS Optimizer Generator," Proceedings of the ACM SIGMOD Conference, May, 1987.

[HZ80] Hammer, M. and S.B. Zdonik, "Knowledge-Based Query Optimization," Proceedings of the Conference on Very Large Databases, Montreal, Canada, 1980.

[KRB85] Kim, W., D.S. Reiner, and D.S. Batory, "Query Processing in Database Systems," Springer-Verlag, 1985.

[MS86] Maier, D. and J. Stein, "Indexing in an Object-Oriented Database System, " Proceedings of the International Workshop on Object-Oriented Database Systems, Pacific Grove, California, September, 1986.

[MD86] Manola, F. and U. Dayal, "PDM: An Object-Oriented Data Model," Proceedings of the International Workshop on Object-Oriented Database Systems, Pacific Grove, California, September, 1986.

[SBG83] Stonebraker, M., B. Rubenstein, and A. Guttman, "Applications of Abstract Data Types and Abstract Indices to CAD Databases," Engineering Design Applications, Proceedings from SIGMOD Database Week, May, 1983.

[ZW86] Zdonik, S.B. and P. Wegner, "Language and Methodology for Object-Oriented Database Environments," Proceedings of the Nineteenth Annual International Conference on System Sciences, Honolulu, Hawaii, January 1986.

Vol. 296: R. Janßen (Ed.), Trends in Computer Algebra. Proceedings, 1987. V, 197 pages. 1988.

Vol. 297: E.N. Houstis, T.S. Papatheodorou, C.D. Polychronopoulos (Eds.), Supercomputing. Proceedings, 1987. X, 1093 pages. 1988.

Vol. 298: M. Main, A. Melton, M. Mislove, D. Schmidt (Eds.), Mathematical Foundations of Programming Language Semantics. Proceedings, 1987. VIII, 637 pages. 1988.

Vol. 299: M. Dauchet, M. Nivat (Eds.), CAAP '88. Proceedings, 1988. VI, 304 pages. 1988.

Vol. 300: H. Ganzinger (Ed.), ESOP '88. Proceedings, 1988. VI, 381 pages. 1988.

Vol. 301: J. Kittler (Ed.), Pattern Recognition. Proceedings, 1988. VII, 668 pages. 1988.

Vol. 302: D.M. Yellin, Attribute Grammar Inversion and Source-to-source Translation. VIII, 176 pages. 1988.

Vol. 303: J.W. Schmidt, S. Ceri, M. Missikoff (Eds.), Advances in Database Technology – EDBT '88. X, 620 pages. 1988.

Vol. 304: W.L. Price, D. Chaum (Eds.), Advances in Cryptology – EUROCRYPT '87. Proceedings, 1987. VII, 314 pages. 1988.

Vol. 305: J. Biskup, J. Demetrovics, J. Paredaens, B. Thalheim (Eds.), MFDBS 87. Proceedings, 1987. V, 247 pages. 1988.

Vol. 306: M. Boscarol, L. Carlucci Aiello, G. Levi (Eds.), Foundations of Logic and Functional Programming. Proceedings, 1986. V, 218 pages. 1988.

Vol. 307: Th. Beth, M. Clausen (Eds.), Applicable Algebra, Error-Correcting Codes, Combinatorics and Computer Algebra. Proceedings, 1986. VI, 215 pages. 1988.

Vol. 308: S. Kaplan, J.-P. Jouannaud (Eds.), Conditional Term Rewriting Systems. Proceedings, 1987. VI, 278 pages. 1988.

Vol. 309: J. Nehmer (Ed.), Experiences with Distributed Systems. Proceedings, 1987. VI, 292 pages. 1988.

Vol. 310: E. Lusk, R. Overbeek (Eds.), 9th International Conference on Automated Deduction. Proceedings, 1988. X, 775 pages. 1988.

Vol. 311: G. Cohen, P. Godlewski (Eds.), Coding Theory and Applications 1986. Proceedings, 1986. XIV, 196 pages. 1988.

Vol. 312: J. van Leeuwen (Ed.), Distributed Algorithms 1987. Proceedings, 1987. VII, 430 pages. 1988.

Vol. 313: B. Bouchon, L. Saitta, R.R. Yager (Eds.), Uncertainty and Intelligent Systems. IPMU '88. Proceedings, 1988. VIII, 408 pages. 1988.

Vol. 314: H. Göttler, H.J. Schneider (Eds.), Graph-Theoretic Concepts in Computer Science. Proceedings, 1987. VI, 254 pages. 1988.

Vol. 315: K. Furukawa, H. Tanaka, T. Fujisaki (Eds.), Logic Programming '87. Proceedings, 1987. VI, 327 pages. 1988.

Vol. 316: C. Choffrut (Ed.), Automata Networks. Proceedings, 1986. VII, 125 pages. 1988.

Vol. 317: T. Lepistö, A. Salomaa (Eds.), Automata, Languages and Programming. Proceedings, 1988. XI, 741 pages. 1988.

Vol. 318: R. Karlsson, A. Lingas (Eds.), SWAT 88. Proceedings, 1988. VI, 262 pages. 1988.

Vol. 319: J.H. Reif (Ed.), VLSI Algorithms and Architectures – AWOC 88. Proceedings, 1988. X, 476 pages. 1988.

Vol. 320: A. Blaser (Ed.), Natural Language at the Computer. Proceedings, 1988. III, 176 pages. 1988.

Vol. 322: S. Gjessing, K. Nygaard (Eds.), ECOOP '88. European Conference on Object-Oriented Programming. Proceedings, 1988. VI, 410 pages. 1988.

Vol. 323: P. Deransart, M. Jourdan, B. Lorho, Attribute Grammars. IX, 232 pages. 1988.

Vol. 324: M.P. Chytil, L. Janiga, V. Koubek (Eds.), Mathematical Foundations of Computer Science 1988. Proceedings. IX, 562 pages. 1988.

Vol. 325: G. Brassard, Modern Cryptology. VI, 107 pages. 1988.

Vol. 326: M. Gyssens, J. Paredaens, D. Van Gucht (Eds.), ICDT '88. 2nd International Conference on Database Theory. Proceedings, 1988. VI, 409 pages. 1988.

Vol. 327: G.A. Ford (Ed.), Software Engineering Education. Proceedings, 1988. V, 207 pages. 1988.

Vol. 328: R. Bloomfield, L. Marshall, R. Jones (Eds.), VDM '88. VDM – The Way Ahead. Proceedings, 1988. IX, 499 pages. 1988.

Vol. 329: E. Börger, H. Kleine Büning, M.M. Richter (Eds.), CSL '87. 1st Workshop on Computer Science Logic. Proceedings, 1987. VI, 346 pages. 1988.

Vol. 330: C.G. Günther (Ed.), Advances in Cryptology – EUROCRYPT '88. Proceedings, 1988. XI, 473 pages. 1988.

Vol. 331: M. Joseph (Ed.), Formal Techniques in Real-Time and Fault-Tolerant Systems. Proceedings, 1988. VI, 229 pages. 1988.

Vol. 332: D. Sannella, A. Tarlecki (Eds.), Recent Trends in Data Type Specification. V, 259 pages. 1988.

Vol. 333: H. Noltemeier (Ed.), CG'88, Computational Geometry and its Applications. VI, 252 pages. 1988.

Vol. 334: K.R. Dittrich (Ed.), Advances in Object-Oriented Database Systems. Proceedings, 1988. VII, 373 pages. 1988.